Windows Vista

THE MISSING MANUAL

*The book that
should have been
in the box*®

Windows Vista

David Pogue

POGUE PRESS™
O'REILLY®

Beijing • *Cambridge* • *Farnham* • *Köln* • *Paris* • *Sebastopol* • *Taipei* • *Tokyo*

Windows Vista: The Missing Manual
by David Pogue

Published by O'Reilly Media, Inc., 1005 Gravenstein Highway North,
Sebastopol, CA 95472.

O'Reilly Media books may be purchased for educational, business, or sales
promotional use. Online editions are also available for most titles: *safari.oreilly.
com.* For more information, contract our corporate/institutional sales department:
800-998-9938 or *corporate@oreilly.com.*

January 2007:   First Edition.
February 2007:   Second Printing.

 This book uses RepKover™, a durable and flexible lay-flat binding.

ISBN-10: 0-596-52827-2
ISBN-13: 978-0-596-52827-0

Table of Contents

The Missing Credits xi

Introduction 1

Part One: The Vista Desktop

Chapter 1: Welcome Center, Desktop, and the Start Menu 19
The Welcome Center 19
The Vista Desktop—Now with Aero! 22
The Start Menu 24
What's in the Start Menu 28
Start→⏻ (Sleep).. 30
Start→🔒 (Lock)... 32
Start→Log Off, Restart, Hibernate, Shut Down 32
Start→Help and Support 34
Start→Default Programs... 34
Start→Control Panel 35
Start→Connect To.. 35
Start→Network 35
Start→Computer 36
Start→Recent Items... 37
Start→Search 37
Start→Games 38
Start→Music, Pictures 38
Start→Documents 39
Start→[Your Name]: The Personal Folder.. 39
Start→Run 40
Customizing the Start Menu 44

Chapter 2: Explorer, Windows, and the Taskbar............................ 57
Universal Window Controls 57
Explorer Window Controls.. 60
Optional Window Panes.. 63
Tags, Metadata, and Properties.. 69
Icon and List Views.. 71
Sorting, Grouping, Stacking, and Filtering 75
Uni-Window vs. Multi-Window 80
Immortalizing Your Tweaks 81
The "Folder Options" Options... 82

Sizing, Moving, and Closing Windows 86
Windows Flip (Alt+Tab) 89
Windows Flip 3D 90
The Taskbar 92
Taskbar Toolbars 98

Chapter 3: Searching and Organizing Your Files **105**
Meet Vista Search 106
Search from the Start Menu 106
Explorer-Window Searches 119
Saved Searches (Search Folders) 123
The Folders of Windows Vista 126
Life with Icons 130
Selecting Icons 136
Copying and Moving Folders and Files 138
The Recycle Bin 141
Shortcut Icons 145
Compressing Files and Folders 147
Burning CDs and DVDs from the Desktop 151

Chapter 4: Interior Decorating Vista **157**
Aero or Not 157
Dialing Up Your Own Look 160
Desktop Background (Wallpaper) 163
Screen Savers 165
Sounds 167
Mouse Makeover 167
Change Your Theme 170
Monitor Settings 171

Chapter 5: Getting Help **175**
Navigating the Help System 175
Remote Assistance 178
Getting Help from Microsoft 185

Part Two: Vista Software

Chapter 6: Programs, Documents, and Gadgets **189**
Opening Programs 189
Exiting Programs 190
When Programs Die: The Task Manager 192
Saving Documents 194
Closing Documents 198
The Open Dialog Box 198
Moving Data Between Documents 199
Speech Recognition 202
The Sidebar 211

Filename Extensions and File Associations.. 221
Installing Software.. 229
Uninstalling Software.. 233
Running Pre-Vista Programs... 236

Chapter 7: The Freebie Software 239
Default Programs 239
Internet Explorer.. 239
Windows Calendar.. 240
Windows Contacts... 250
Windows Defender... 252
Windows DVD Maker.. 252
Windows Fax and Scan.. 252
Windows Live Messenger Download 252
Windows Mail 252
Windows Media Center.. 253
Windows Media Player... 253
Windows Meeting Space.. 253
Windows Movie Maker... 253
Windows Photo Gallery.. 253
Windows Update.. 253
Accessories.. 253
Extras and Upgrades.. 273
Games... 274
Maintenance 280
Startup 280

Chapter 8: The Control Panel 281
Home View: The Big Vista Change 281
Classic View... 285
The Control Panel, Applet by Applet 286

Part Three: Vista Online

Chapter 9: Hooking Up to the Internet.. 319
Broadband Connections (Cable Modems and DSL)... 319
Wireless Networks 320
Dial-Up Connections.. 321
Connection Management... 325
Details on Dial-Up 327

Chapter 10: Internet Security 333
Security Center 335
Windows Firewall... 336
Windows Defender 340
The Phishing Filter... 346
Privacy and Cookies... 349

History: Erasing Your Tracks.. 352
The Pop-up Blocker.. 353
Internet Security Zones... 357
Hot Spot Security... 359
Protect Your Home Wireless Network... 360
Parental Controls.. 361

Chapter 11: Internet Explorer 7... 367
IE7: The Grand Tour.. 368
Tabbed Browsing... 373
Favorites (Bookmarks) 376
History List... 379
RSS: The Missing Manual.. 380
Tips for Better Surfing.. 382
The Keyboard Shortcut Master List... 387

Chapter 12: Windows Mail 391
Setting Up Windows Mail.. 392
Sending Email.. 393
Reading Email.. 402
Junk Email.. 411
Configuring Windows Mail 414
Newsgroups.. 418

Part Four: Pictures, Movies, and Media Center

Chapter 13: Windows Photo Gallery 423
Photo Gallery: The Application 423
Getting Pictures into Photo Gallery... 424
The Post-Dump Slideshow.. 430
The Digital Shoebox... 432
Tags and Ratings... 442
Editing Your Shots.. 446
Finding Your Audience 455

Chapter 14: Windows Media Player 463
The Lay of the Land.. 464
Online Music Stores... 477
DVD Movies.. 479
Pictures and Videos.. 482

Chapter 15: Movie Maker and DVD Maker 483
Importing Video, Music, and Photos.. 483
Editing Video 487
DVD Maker.. 494

Chapter 16: Media Center 501

Your Gear List.. 501
Setup 502
TV: Your PC as TiVo 509
Music: Your PC as Jukebox.. 517
Photos and Video 523
Advanced Settings... 527

Part Five: Hardware and Peripherals

Chapter 17: Fax, Print, and Scan 533

Installing a Printer 533
Printing.. 538
Controlling Printouts... 542
Fancy Printer Tricks 544
Printer Troubleshooting 549
Fonts.. 550
Faxing 551
Scanning Documents... 557

Chapter 18: Hardware 559

External Gadgets.. 560
Installing Cards in Expansion Slots 563
Troubleshooting Newly Installed Gear 564
Driver Signing 566
The Device Manager 567

Chapter 19: Laptops, Tablets, and Palmtops 571

Laptops.. 571
Tablet PCs 575
Windows Mobile Devices... 586
The Sync Center... 587
Offline Files 589

Part Six: PC Health

Chapter 20: Maintenance and Speed Tweaks 595

Disk Cleanup.. 595
Disk Defragmenter... 596
Hard Drive Checkups 599
Disk Management 601
Task Scheduler... 606
Four Speed Tricks 609
Windows Update.. 614

Chapter 21: The Disk Chapter.. 621
Dynamic Disks 621
Compressing Files and Folders 629
Encrypting Files and Folders.. 633
BitLocker Drive Encryption 637

Chapter 22: Backups and Troubleshooting 641
Automatic Backups 641
Complete PC Backup 647
System Restore 648
Shadow Copies 654
Safe Mode and the Startup Menu.. 656
Problem Reports and Solutions.. 659
Startup Repair (Windows Recovery Environment)...................... 661

Part Seven: The Vista Network

Chapter 23: Accounts (and Logging On)... 665
Introducing User Accounts... 665
Windows Vista: The OS with Two Faces.................................... 667
Local Accounts... 668
Local Accounts on a Domain Computer 679
Local Users and Groups 681
Fast User Switching 686
Logging On.. 688
Profiles 690
NTFS Permissions: Protecting Your Stuff 692

Chapter 24: Setting Up a Workgroup Network 699
Kinds of Networks.. 700
Sharing an Internet Connection 706
The Network and Sharing Center 708

Chapter 25: Network Domains... 717
The Domain... 718
Joining a Domain 720
Four Ways Life Is Different on a Domain.................................. 722

Chapter 26: Network Sharing and Collaboration................................. 729
Sharing Files.. 730
Accessing Shared Files.. 739
Mapping Shares to Drive Letters.. 743
Windows Meeting Space.. 745

Chapter 27: Vista by Remote Control 751

Remote Access Basics 751
Dialing Direct 753
Virtual Private Networking 758
Remote Desktop 760

Part Eight: Appendixes

Appendix A: Installing Windows Vista 769

Before You Begin 769
Upgrade vs. Clean Install 772
Dual Booting 775
Installing Windows Vista 775
Welcome Center 780
Activation 781
Windows Easy Transfer 783

Appendix B: Fun with the Registry 787

Meet Regedit 788
Regedit Examples 791

Appendix C: Where'd It Go? 795

Appendix D: The Master Keyboard Shortcut List 799

The Missing Credits

About the Author

David Pogue is the weekly tech columnist for the *New York Times*, an Emmy-winning correspondent for *CBS News Sunday Morning*, 2006 winner of the Online News Association's award for online commentary, and the creator of the Missing Manual series. He's the author or co-author of 40 books, including 17 in this series and six in the "For Dummies" line (including *Macs, Magic, Opera,* and *Classical Music*). In his other life, David is a former Broadway show conductor, a magician, and a pianist. News, photos, links to his columns and weekly videos await at *www.davidpogue.com*. He welcomes feedback about his books by email at *david@pogueman.com*.

Joli Ballew (Tablet PC and Media Center chapters) is an author, Microsoft columnist, media expert, consultant, teacher, and technical writer. She holds several certifications, including MCSE, A+, and MCDST, and has written almost two dozen books on operating systems, image editing, home organization, and more. Her book *Degunking Windows* won the 2004 Independent Publisher Book Award for best computer book, and was a *Parade Magazine* "Best Bet." Email: *Joli@JoliBallew.com*.

C.A. Callahan (Control Panel chapter) is a ten-year veteran of the IT industry, a Microsoft Certified Trainer, and owner of her own training/technical writing company. She's a frequent presenter at tech conferences and expos, including TechEd Boston, Windows Connections, and LinuxWorld/NetworkWorld Expo, and has co-authored several books, including the best selling technical reference *Mastering Windows Server 2003*. Her new book, due in June 2007, is *Mastering Windows SharePoint Services 3.0*. Email: *callahan@callahantech.com*.

Preston Gralla (security, backup and maintenance chapters) has used every version of Windows since even before Windows 3.1. He's the author of over 35 books, including *Windows Vista in a Nutshell* and the *Windows Vista Pocket Reference*. His articles have appeared in *USA Today, The Los Angeles Times, The Dallas Morning News, PC Magazine, PC World,* and many other newspapers and magazines. Email: *preston@gralla.com*.

Brian Jepson (domain, remote-control, installation chapters; tech editor) is an O'Reilly editor, programmer, and co-author of *Mac OS X Panther for Unix Geeks* and *Learning Unix for Mac OS X Panther*. He's also a volunteer system administrator and all-around geek for AS220, a non-profit arts center in Providence, Rhode Island. AS220 gives Rhode Island artists uncensored and unjuried galleries, performance space, and publications for their work. Brian sees to it that technology, especially free software, supports that mission. Email: *bjepson@oreilly.com*.

About the Creative Team

Teresa Noelle Roberts (copy editor) is a freelance copy editor and proofreader, as well as a published fiction writer and poet. When she can tear herself away from the computer, she may be found gardening, belly dancing, or enjoying the beautiful beaches of New England.

On this edition, she was joined in her editorial duties by Missing Manuals editorial veteran John Cacciatore.

Rose Cassano (cover illustration) has worked as an independent designer and illustrator for 20 years. Assignments have spanned everything from the non-profit sector to corporate clientele. She lives in beautiful southern Oregon, grateful for the miracles of modern technology that make living and working there a reality. Email: *cassano@highstream.net*. Web: *www.rosecassano.com*.

Lesa Snider King (production editor and graphics goddess) assists David Pogue on many projects. As Chief Evangelist for iStockphoto.com and a veteran writer for international graphics publications, Lesa is on a mission to teach the world how to create beautiful graphics. You can see more of her work at *TheGraphicReporter.com*, and catch her live at many conferences. Email: *lesa@graphicreporter.com*.

Shawn King (graphics assistance and beta reader) is the host of a popular Internet broadcast called Your Mac Life, and has been using computers since several years B.D. (Before DOS). Having grabbed a PC mouse and literally followed every single step on every single page of this book to test for accuracy, he can safely say that he now knows more about Windows Vista than he ever hoped to know. Email: *shawn@yourmaclife.com*.

Phil Simpson (design and layout) works out of his office in Southbury, Connecticut, where he has had his graphic design business since 1982. He is experienced in many facets of graphic design, including corporate identity/branding, publication design, and corporate and medical communications. Email: *pmsimpson@earthlink.net*.

Acknowledgments

The Missing Manual series is a joint venture between the dream team introduced on these pages and O'Reilly Media. I'm grateful to all of them, and also to a few people who did massive favors for this book. They include Matt Parretta and Frank Kane, PR guys for Microsoft who devoted themselves to helping me find information; Windows Vista product manager Greg Sullivan, who tolerated being henpecked with my questions; HP and Motion for loaning me testing gear; and proofreaders Sohaila Abdulali, John Cacciatore, Genevieve d'Entremont, Jamie Peppard, Sada Preisch, and Ellen Seebacher.

The book owes its greatest debt, though, to the husband-and-wife team of Shawn King and Lesa Snider King. I'll never forget the 16-hour days of cheerful, professional work they put in during the final three weeks of this book's creation, all in the name of making it the most polished, perfect book it could be. (I doubt they'll forget those days, either.)

Thanks to David Rogelberg for believing in the idea, and above all, to Jennifer, Kelly, Tia, and Jeffrey, who make these books—and everything else—possible.

—David Pogue

The Missing Manual Series

Missing Manual books are superbly written guides to computer products that don't come with printed manuals (which is just about all of them). Each book features a handcrafted index; cross-references to specific page numbers (not just "See Chapter 14"); and RepKover, a detached-spine binding that lets the book lie perfectly flat without the assistance of weights or cinder blocks. Recent and upcoming titles include:

- *Windows XP Home Edition: The Missing Manual,* 2nd Edition by David Pogue
- *Windows XP Pro: The Missing Manual,* 2nd Edition by David Pogue, Craig Zacker, and L.J. Zacker
- *Access 2007: The Missing Manual* by Matthew MacDonald
- *CSS: The Missing Manual* by David Sawyer McFarland
- *Creating Web Sites: The Missing Manual* by Matthew MacDonald
- *Digital Photography: The Missing Manual* by Chris Grover, Barbara Brundage
- *Dreamweaver 8: The Missing Manual* by David Sawyer McFarland
- *Dreamweaver MX 2004: The Missing Manual* by David Sawyer McFarland
- *eBay: The Missing Manual* by Nancy Conner
- *Excel 2007: The Missing Manual* by Matthew MacDonald
- *FileMaker Pro 8: The Missing Manual* by Geoff Coffey and Susan Prosser
- *Flash 8: The Missing Manual* by Emily Moore
- *FrontPage 2003: The Missing Manual* by Jessica Mantaro
- *Google: The Missing Manual,* 2nd Edition by Sarah Milstein and Rael Dornfest
- *Home Networking: The Missing Manual* by Scott Lowe
- *The Internet: The Missing Manual* by David Pogue and J.D. Biersdorfer
- *iPod: The Missing Manual,* 5th Edition by J.D. Biersdorfer

- *PCs: The Missing Manual* by Andy Rathbone
- *Photoshop Elements 5: The Missing Manual* by Barbara Brundage
- *PowerPoint 2007: The Missing Manual* by Emily A. Vander Veer
- *QuickBooks 2006: The Missing Manual* by Bonnie Biafore
- *Word 2007: The Missing Manual* by Chris Grover
- *Switching to the Mac: The Missing Manual,* Tiger Edition by David Pogue
- *Mac OS X: The Missing Manual,* Tiger Edition by David Pogue
- *AppleScript: The Missing Manual* by Adam Goldstein
- *AppleWorks 6: The Missing Manual* by Jim Elferdink and David Reynolds
- *GarageBand 2: The Missing Manual* by David Pogue
- *iLife '05: The Missing Manual* by David Pogue
- *iMovie 6 & iDVD: The Missing Manual* by David Pogue
- *iPhoto 6: The Missing Manual* by David Pogue and Derrick Story
- *iPod & iTunes: The Missing Manual,* 4th Edition by J.D. Biersdorfer
- *iWork '05: The Missing Manual* by Jim Elferdink
- *Office 2004 for Macintosh: The Missing Manual* by Mark H. Walker, Franklin Tessler, and Paul Berkowitz
- *iPhone: The Missing Manual* by David Pogue
- *Photoshop CS3: The Missing Manual* by David Pogue

For Starters

The "For Starters" books contain just the most essential information from their larger counterparts—in larger type, with a more spacious layout, and none of those advanced sidebars. Recent titles include:

- *Windows Vista for Starters: The Missing Manual* by David Pogue
- *Windows XP for Starters: The Missing Manual* by David Pogue
- *Access 2007 for Starters: The Missing Manual* by Matthew MacDonald
- *Excel 2007 for Starters: The Missing Manual* by Matthew MacDonald
- *Quicken 2006 for Starters: The Missing Manual* by Bonnie Biafore
- *Word 2007 for Starters: The Missing Manual* by Chris Grover
- *PowerPoint 2007 for Starters: The Missing Manual* by Emily A. Vander Veer
- *Mac OS X for Starters: The Missing Manual* by David Pogue

Introduction

L et's face it: in the last few years, all the fun went out of using a PC. Viruses, spyware, spam, pop-ups, and other Web nastiness had turned us all into cowering novice system administrators, spending far too much time trying to shore up our computers rather than using them to get things done.

Why on earth didn't Microsoft do something?

Of course, now we know: Microsoft *was* doing something. It just took five years to finish doing it.

That something was Windows Vista, a new version (well, OK, five or seven versions) that came with every porthole sealed, every backdoor nailed shut, and every design flaw reworked by a newly security-conscious squad of Microsofties.

Microsoft won't go as far as saying that Vista is invulnerable; nothing with 50 million lines of code could possibly be bulletproof. The bad guys are certainly going to do their best.

But it's certainly safe to say that Vista is by far the most secure Windows yet, and that the sociopaths of the Internet will have a much, much harder time.

That's not all Microsoft accomplished in writing Vista, though. As you'll notice within the first 5 seconds, the company also gave the operating system a total overhaul, both in its capabilities and its look. Vista is the best-looking version of Windows ever.

What's New in Windows Vista

The real question is, what *isn't* new?

Windows Vista is a *huge* overhaul. Both the guts and the window dressing have been completely renovated. Here's a top-level executive summary.

Security

For five years, through multiple restarts and reshufflings of the Vista project, Microsoft became obsessed with making Windows more secure—and there are few who'd say that its obsession was misplaced.

You could fill several books with nothing but information about the security features—a lot of them are so technical, they'd make your eyes glaze over—but here's a sampling.

- **User Account Control** may look to you like a completely unnecessary annoyance: a dialog box that pops up whenever you try to install a program or adjust a PC-wide setting, requesting that you type your password. Over, and over, and over.

  In fact, UAC is one of Vista's most important new protection features, modeled on something similar in Mac OS X and Unix. It means that *viruses* can no longer make changes to your system without your knowing about it. You'll see one of these dialog boxes, and if *you* aren't the one trying to make the change, you'll click Cancel instead of Continue.

- **The Security Center** offers one-stop shopping for several important security features: the firewall (protects your PC from incoming signals from hackers), Automatic Updates (bug fixes and security patches beamed to you from Microsoft), virus and spyware protection, Internet security settings, and User Account Control.

- **Windows Defender** is a new program that protects your PC from *spyware* (downloads from the Internet that, unbeknownst to you, send information back to their creators or hijack your Web browser).

- **Protected Mode** is a new feature of Internet Explorer that keeps hackers from attacking it.

- **A phishing filter** alerts you when you're about to visit a fake bank or eBay Web page to "update your account settings." In fact, you're probably being scammed. You've been sent a bogus alert email that, in fact, is a trap set by scammers hoping to steal your account and credit-card information.

- **Service Hardening** prevents invisible background programs from tampering with the system files, the Registry, or the network.

- **Corporate features** let network administrators exert a lot more control over what the worker bees are doing. Your company's network geeks, for example, can institute a *group policy* (a corporate network "rule") that bans the use of USB flash drives, to prevent viruses from coming in or important documents from going out. They can also prevent any "unsafe" PC (one whose Microsoft patches and virus program aren't up to date) from even connecting to the network.

- **Parental Controls** lets you, the wise parent, restrict children's use of the PC. You can dictate what Web sites they can visit, which people they correspond with online, and even what times of day they can use the machine.

- **BitLocker Drive Encryption** encrypts your *entire hard drive,* so that even if determined hackers steal your laptop and extract the drive, they'll get no useful information off it.

- **A new backup program** offers two modes: backup by file type (all your photos, music, and Office files, for example) or *complete* PC backup (all your programs, system files, the works).

   And remember System Restore, the life-saving troubleshooting tool that lets you rewind your PC to a time when it was working properly? A sister feature, Shadow Copy, offers the same safety net to individual documents.

- **Address-space randomization** moves system files around in memory randomly. The idea here is to make it extremely difficult to write a virus that will work the same way on every PC.

A Cosmetic Overhaul

As you've probably discovered already, Windows Vista looks much more modern and colorful (and, frankly, Mac-like) than its cosmetically challenged predecessors. Thanks to a new design scheme called Aero, Window edges are translucent; menus and windows fade away when closed; the taskbar shows actual thumbnail images of the open documents, not just their names; all the icons have been redesigned with a clean, 3-D look and greater resolution; and so on.

Note: Not everyone gets to enjoy these features, by the way. Some PCs are too slow to handle all this graphics processing; on those machines, Vista will look shiny and new, but won't have these transparency and taskbar features.

Part of what makes Vista look so much better and more modern stems from a very small tweak: a new system font, called Sergoe UI. New designs for dialog boxes and wizards also give the whole affair a fresher, easier to use personality.

The Start menu is a better-organized, two-column affair; that awful XP business of superimposing the All Programs menu *on top* of the two other columns is long gone.

By the way, if you don't care for the Vista cosmetic changes, you can turn them off selectively, which makes your desktop look and work just as it did in previous versions of Windows. (You'll find instructions throughout this book in special boxes labeled "Nostalgia Corner.") You can also turn off the various animations, drop shadows, and other special effects for a measurable speed boost on slower PCs (see page 612).

Merged OSes

There are no longer separate Windows Media Center and Tablet PC Editions; these features are now built right into certain versions of Vista.

New Programs and Features

Lots of new or upgraded software programs come with Vista (or at least some editions of it). For example;

- **Photo Gallery.** A tidy little digital shoebox, suitable for touching up, organizing, and sharing your digital photos.

- **Instant Search.** With one keystroke (the ⊞ key), you open the Start menu's new Search box. It searches your entire PC for the search phrase you type—even *inside* files that have different names. It's the ultimate efficiency booster—and, by the way, a fantastic way to open programs without ever taking your hands off the keyboard.

- **Windows Calendar.** A very simple calendar for planning your life.

- **Windows Mail.** OK, it's really just Outlook Express with a new name, but it does have a spam filter now.

- **Windows DVD Maker.** Burns video DVDs, complete with a scene menu and background music.

- **Windows Meeting Space.** A Vista-only replacement for NetMeeting. It lets you and your colleagues see each other's screens and pass around notes or documents across the network or the Internet.

- **Snipping Tool** lets you capture rectangular or irregular patches of the screen as graphics, for use in illustrating computer books.

- **Windows Fax and Scan** offers one-stop shopping for scanning, and for sending and receiving faxes.

- **Internet Explorer** 7 has been beefed up. It now has tabbed browsing, RSS news feeds, and about 65,000 new security features.

- **Windows Media Player** 11 has yet another new look. It can share your music and photos across the network with another Vista PC (or an XBox 360), too.

- **Speech Recognition** isn't as accurate as, say, Dragon NaturallySpeaking. But it's light-years better than Windows' old speech-recognition feature. If you have a headset, you should try it out; you can dictate email and documents, and even control Windows itself, all by voice.

- **Laptop goodies** including folder synchronization with another computer, more powerful battery-control settings, and a central Mobility Center that governs all laptop features in one place. The ingenious Presentation Mode prevents dialog boxes, screen savers, alerts, or sounds from going off when you're in the middle of a presentation.

- **SuperFetch** speeds up your PC by analyzing *when* you tend to use certain programs, so they'll be ready and waiting when you are. **ReadyBoost** lets you use the RAM on a flash drive as extra memory for greater speed. (Cool!)

- **The Sidebar.** This feature offers a floating panel filled with tiny, single-purpose programs called gadgets: a stock ticker, weather reporter, address book lookup, and so on.

Note: The Sidebar's resemblance to the Dashboard in Mac OS X is unmistakable. Then again, any number of Vista features can be said to have predecessors on the Mac: Windows Calendar, Photo Gallery, 3-D Chess, instant Search, Personal and Users folders, flippy triangles in folder lists, the Folder List itself, window drop shadows, Flip 3D, rounded window corners, and so on.

Windows fans, though, may well argue, "So what?" You can't copyright an idea—and there's little doubt that these enhancements make Windows better.

New Explorer Window Features

At the desktop, the Explorer windows, where you view the icons of your files and programs, are bristling with new features.

- **New panes.** Explorer windows can now have information panels and controls on *all four* edges, including the new Navigation pane (left); task toolbar (top); Preview pane (right); and Details pane (bottom). You can edit those details (that is, properties) right in the window, even adding tags (keywords) for fast, easy rounding-up later.

- **Stacking, filtering, and grouping.** Every Explorer window offers three new methods of slicing, dicing, finding, and categorizing the files inside.

- **Document preview.** Now you can see what's in a document without having to open it first. Its icon actually *is* the first page of what's inside. That's an especially handy feature when it comes to photos. You can also play movies and music files right at the desktop, without having to fire up a program first.

- **Address bar.** The new Address bar, which displays the path you've taken to burrow into the folder you're now inspecting, is loaded with doodads and clickable spots that make navigation far easier.

Version Hell

You thought Windows XP was bad, with its two different versions (Home and Pro)?

Windows Vista comes in *five* different versions: Home Basic, Home Premium, Business, Enterprise, and Ultimate. And that's not even counting the Starter edition, sold exclusively in poor countries outside North America, or the two "N" versions (like Home Basic N), which are sold in Europe to comply with a different set of antitrust laws.

Microsoft says that each version is perfectly attuned to a different kind of customer, as though each edition had been somehow conceived differently. In fact, though, the main thing that distinguishes the editions is the suite of programs that comes with each one.

Feature	Home Basic	Home Premium	Business	Enterprise	Ultimate
Aero (snazzy new cosmetic design)		•	•	•	•
Attach a second monitor		•	•	•	•
Automated backups		•	•	•	•
Back up to another PC on the network		•	•	•	•
BitLocker drive encryption				•	•
Complete PC backups (disk images)			•	•	•
Domain-network joining			•	•	•
DVD Maker		•			•
Encrypting File System			•	•	•
Fax and Scan program			•	•	•
Group Policy support (system administrators can set company-wide settings)			•	•	•
Media Center		•			•
Mobility Center		•	•	•	•
Movie Maker	•	•			•
Network Access Protection (PCs without virus protection can't join the network)			•	•	•
Network projectors		•	•	•	•
Offline files and folders (auto-sync with network files and folders after being away)			•	•	•
Parental Controls	•	•			•
Remote Desktop	Partial	Partial	•	•	•
Shadow Copy (creates automatic daily backups of files, so you can "rewind" to an earlier version)			•	•	•
Tablet PC features		•	•	•	•
Windows Anytime Upgrade (online upgrade to a higher-priced Vista version)	•	•	•		
Windows Meeting Space (collaboration over networks)	Can view meetings only	•	•	•	•

Tip: Vista Enterprise is not sold in any store. It's sold directly to corporations for mass installation by highly paid network geeks. It's otherwise identical to the Business edition, except that it adds three specialized features: a subsystem for UNIX-based programs, Windows BitLocker Drive Encryption (page 637), and the inclusion of 35 language packs (page 304).

A huge table, showing what's in each version, appears on the facing page. But to save you from having to keep flipping back to this page, each main heading in this book bears a handy cheat sheet, like this:

Home Premium • Business • Enterprise • Ultimate

This lets you know at a glance whether or not that feature discussion applies to you.

UP TO SPEED

32-bit vs. 64-bit Vista

You could say that Windows Vista comes in five editions. You could say that it comes in eight (if you count the overseas versions).

You could also multiply all that, because most Vista versions are *also* available in either 32-bit or 64-bit editions. (Vista Ultimate comes with both versions in the box; the Business or Home versions come with the 32-bit version, with a toll-free number that lets you order the 64-bit version at no charge.)

Which leaves only one question: What does it all mean? Aren't more bits always better?

Not necessarily.

In theory, there are two advantages to a 64-bit computer running a 64-bit operating system. First, you can install a *lot* more memory. The most memory you can install on a 32-bit computer is 4 gigabytes of RAM; on a 64-bit computer, the maximum shoots up to 128 gigabytes. (That's for the Business, Enterprise, and Ultimate editions of Vista; it's 8 GB for Home Basic, and 16 GB for Home Premium.)

Second, certain people in certain rarefied professions—say, Photoshop, digital video, and rocket-science hounds—rely on specialized 64-bit *programs* to get their work done faster. And 64-bit programs require 64-bit computers and operating systems to match.

OK, suppose that you do, in fact, have a computer with a 64-bit *processor*, like an Intel Core 2 Duo or AMD Athlon 64 FX. Even then, you might not want to run the 64-bit version of Vista.

First of all, the 32-bit version runs just great on 64-bit computers; there's no performance penalty.

Second, 64-bit is uncharted territory for most people. 64-bit processors and operating systems have long been used for database servers and other machines that must move large amounts of data quickly. But 64-bit Windows hasn't had much experience running day-to-day productivity programs or video games. If you decide to use 64-bit Vista as your desktop operating system, you're becoming a volunteer tester to give the whole 64-bit Windows notion a shake-down.

Plenty of people say they've gone 64-bit for months with no problems, but an equal number say they have trouble finding stable device drivers for 64-bit Windows. That kind of split is usually a sign that your mileage may vary.

So if you're curious and brave, give the 64-bit version a try. But be prepared to spend some time in the Microsoft Communities Web sites finding answers to issues that come up—and paving the way for the rest of the world to run 64-bit Vista without incident.

Meanwhile, if a description of this or that feature makes you salivate, fear not. Microsoft is only too happy to let you upgrade your copy of Windows Vista to a more expensive edition, essentially "unlocking" features for a fee. See page 273 for details.

About This Book

Despite the many improvements in Windows over the years, one feature hasn't improved a bit: Microsoft's documentation. In fact, Windows Vista comes with no printed user guide at all. To learn about the thousands of pieces of software that make up this operating system, you're expected to read the online help screens.

Unfortunately, as you'll quickly discover, these help screens are tersely written, offer very little technical depth, and lack examples. You can't even mark your place, underline, or read them in the bathroom. Some of the help screens are actually on Microsoft's Web site; you can't see them without an Internet connection. Too bad if you're on a plane somewhere with your laptop.

The purpose of this book, then, is to serve as the manual that should have accompanied Windows Vista. In these pages, you'll find step-by-step instructions for using almost every Windows feature, including those you may not even have understood, let alone mastered.

System Requirements for Your Brain

Windows Vista: The Missing Manual is designed to accommodate readers at every technical level (except system administrators, who will be happier with a very different sort of book).

The primary discussions are written for advanced-beginner or intermediate PC users. But if you're a first-time Windows user, special sidebar articles called "Up To Speed" provide the introductory information you need to understand the topic at hand. If you're an advanced PC user, on the other hand, keep your eye out for similar shaded boxes called "Power Users' Clinic." They offer more technical tips, tricks, and shortcuts for the veteran PC fan.

About the Outline

This book is divided into seven parts, each containing several chapters:

- Part 1, **The Vista Desktop**, covers everything you see on the screen when you turn on a Windows Vista computer: icons, windows, menus, scroll bars, the Recycle Bin, shortcuts, the Start menu, shortcut menus, and so on. It also covers the juicy new system-wide, instantaneous Search feature.

- Part 2, **Vista Software**, is dedicated to the proposition that an operating system is little more than a launch pad for *programs*. Chapter 6 describes how to work with applications and documents in Windows—launch them, switch among them, swap data between them, use them to create and open files, and so on—and how to use the new micro-programs called *gadgets*.

This part also offers an item-by-item discussion of the individual software nuggets that make up this operating system. These include not just the items in your Control Panel, but also the long list of free programs that Microsoft threw in: Windows Media Player, Movie Maker, WordPad, Speech Recognition, and so on.

- Part 3, **Vista Online,** covers all the special Internet-related features of Windows, including setting up your Internet account, Windows Mail (for email), Internet Explorer 7 (for Web browsing), and so on. The massive Chapter 10 also covers Vista's dozens of Internet fortification features: the firewall, anti-spyware software, parental controls, and on and on.

- Part 4, **Pictures, Movies, and Music,** takes you into multimedia land. Here are chapters that cover the new Photo Gallery picture editing and organizing program; Media Player 11 (music playback); Media Center (TV recording and playback); Movie Maker (video editing); and DVD Maker (burn your own video DVDs).

- Part 5, **Hardware and Peripherals,** describes the operating system's relationship with equipment you can attach to your PC—scanners, cameras, disks, printers, and so on. Special chapters describe faxing, fonts, laptops, and Tablet PC touch-screen machines.

- Part 6, **PC Health,** explores Vista's greatly beefed-up backup and troubleshooting tools. It also describes some advanced hard drive formatting tricks and offers tips for making your PC run faster and better.

- Part 7, **The Vista Network,** is for the millions of households and offices that contain more than one PC. If you work at home or in a small office, these chapters show you how to build your own network; if you work in a corporation where some highly paid professional network geek is on hand to do the troubleshooting, these chapters show you how to exploit Vista's considerable networking prowess. File sharing, accounts and passwords, and the new remote-control collaboration program called Windows Meeting Space are here, too.

At the end of the book, three appendixes provide a guide to installing this operating system, an introduction to editing the Registry, and the "Where'd It Go?" Dictionary, which lists every feature Microsoft moved or deleted on the way to Windows Vista.

About→These→Arrows

Throughout this book, and throughout the Missing Manual series, you'll find sentences like this: "Open the Start→Computer→Local Disk (C:)→Windows folder." That's shorthand for a much longer instruction that directs you to open three nested icons in sequence, like this: "Click the Start menu to open it. Click Computer in the Start menu. Inside the Computer window is a disk icon labeled Local Disk (C:); double-click it to open it. Inside *that* window is yet *another* icon called Windows. Double-click to open it, too."

Similarly, this kind of arrow shorthand helps to simplify the business of choosing commands in menus, as shown in Figure I-1.

About MissingManuals.com

You're invited and encouraged to submit corrections and updates to this book's Web page at *www.missingmanuals.com*. (Click the book's name, and then click the Errata link.) In an effort to keep the book as up-to-date and accurate as possible, each time we print more copies of this book, we'll make any corrections you've suggested.

Even if you have nothing to report, you should check that Errata page now and then. That's where we'll post a list of the corrections and updates we've made, so that you can mark important corrections into your own copy of the book, if you like.

In the meantime, we'd love to hear your suggestions for new books in the Missing Manual line. There's a place for that on the Web site, too, as well as a place to sign up for free email notification of new titles in the series.

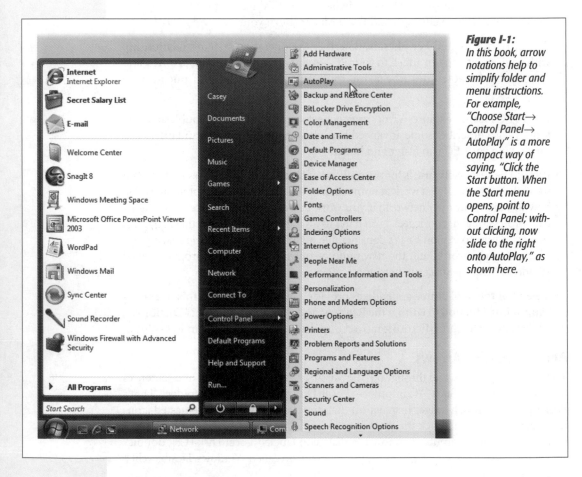

Figure I-1:
In this book, arrow notations help to simplify folder and menu instructions. For example, "Choose Start→ Control Panel→ AutoPlay" is a more compact way of saying, "Click the Start button. When the Start menu opens, point to Control Panel; without clicking, now slide to the right onto AutoPlay," as shown here.

The Very Basics

To get the most out of Windows with the least frustration, it helps to be familiar with the following concepts and terms. If you're new to Windows, be prepared to encounter these words and phrases over and over again—in the built-in Windows help, in computer magazines, and in this book.

Windows Defined

Windows is an *operating system,* the software that controls your computer. It's designed to serve you in several ways:

- **It's a launching bay.** At its heart, Windows is a home base, a remote-control clicker that lets you call up the various software programs (applications) you use to do work or kill time. When you get right down to it, applications are the real reason you bought a PC.

  Windows Vista is a well-stocked software pantry unto itself; for example, it comes with such basic programs as a Web browser, email program, simple word processor, and calculator. Vista comes with a suite of games, too. (Chapter 7 covers all of these freebie programs.)

  If you were stranded on a desert island, the built-in Windows programs could suffice for everyday operations. But if you're like most people, sooner or later, you'll buy and install more software. That's one of the luxuries of using Windows: you can choose from a staggering number of add-on programs. Whether you're a left-handed beekeeper or a German-speaking nun, some company somewhere is selling Windows software designed just for you, its target audience.

- **It's a file cabinet.** Every application on your machine, as well as every document you create, is represented on the screen by an *icon,* a little picture that symbolizes the underlying file or container. You can organize these icons into onscreen file folders. You can make backups (safety copies) by dragging file icons onto a floppy disk or blank CD, or send files to people by email. You can also trash icons you longer need by dragging them onto the Recycle Bin icon.

- **It's your equipment headquarters.** What you can actually see of Windows is only the tip of the iceberg. An enormous chunk of Windows is behind-the-scenes plumbing that controls the various functions of your computer—its modem, screen, keyboard, printer, and so on.

The Right Mouse Button is King

One of the most important features of Windows isn't on the screen—it's under your hand. The standard mouse has two mouse buttons. You use the left one to click buttons, highlight text, and drag things around on the screen.

When you click the right button, however, a *shortcut menu* appears onscreen, like the one shown at left in Figure I-3. Get into the habit of *right-clicking* things—icons, folders, disks, text inside a paragraph, buttons on your menu bar, pictures on a Web page, and so on. The commands that appear on the shortcut menu will make you much more productive and lead you to discover handy functions you never knew existed.

This is a big deal: Microsoft's research suggests that nearly 75 percent of Windows users don't use the right mouse button, and therefore miss hundreds of timesaving shortcuts. Part of the rationale behind Windows Vista's redesign is putting these functions out in the open. Even so, many more shortcuts remain hidden under your right mouse button.

Tip: Microsoft doesn't discriminate against left-handers…much. You can swap the functions of the right and left mouse buttons easily enough.

Choose Start→Control Panel. Click "Classic view." Open the Mouse icon. When the Mouse Properties dialog box opens, click the Buttons tab, and then turn on "Switch primary and secondary buttons." Then click OK. Windows now assumes that you want to use the *left* mouse button as the one that produces shortcut menus.

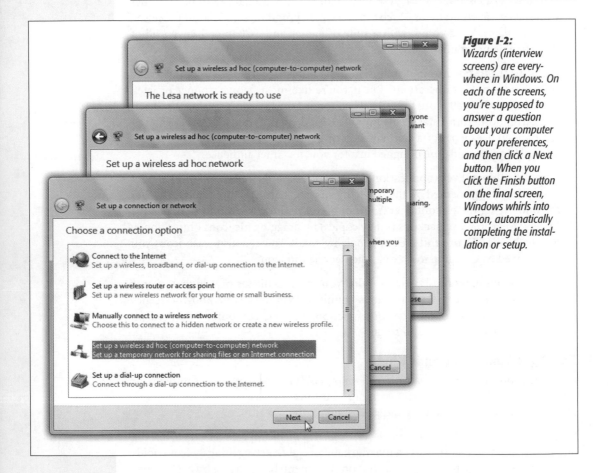

Figure I-2:
Wizards (interview screens) are everywhere in Windows. On each of the screens, you're supposed to answer a question about your computer or your preferences, and then click a Next button. When you click the Finish button on the final screen, Windows whirls into action, automatically completing the installation or setup.

Wizards = Interviews

A *wizard* is a series of screens that walks you through the task you're trying to complete. Wizards make configuration and installation tasks easier by breaking them down into smaller, more easily digested steps. Figure I-2 offers an example.

There's More Than One Way to Do Everything

No matter what setting you want to adjust, no matter what program you want to open, Microsoft has provided five or six different ways to do it. For example, here are the various ways to delete a file: press the Delete key; choose File→Delete; drag the file icon onto the Recycle Bin; or right-click the file name, and then choose Delete from the shortcut menu.

Pessimists grumble that there are too many paths to every destination, making it much more difficult to learn Windows. Optimists point out that this abundance of approaches means that almost everyone will find, and settle on, a satisfying method for each task. Whenever you find a task irksome, remember you have other options.

You Can Use the Keyboard for Everything

In earlier versions of Windows, underlined letters appeared in the names of menus and dialog boxes. These underlines were clues for people who found it faster to do something by pressing keys than by using the mouse.

The underlines are hidden in Windows Vista, at least in disk and folder windows. (They may still appear in your individual software programs.) If you miss them, you can make

---

UP TO SPEED

Scrolling: The Missing Manual

These days, PC monitors are bigger than ever—but so are the Web pages and documents that they display.

Scroll bars, of course, are the strips that may appear at the right side and/or bottom of a window. The scroll bar signals you that the window isn't big enough to reveal all of its contents.

Click the arrows at each end of a scroll bar to move slowly through the window, or drag the rectangular handle (the *thumb*) to move faster. (The position of the thumb in the scroll bar reflects your relative position in the entire window or document.) You can quickly move to a specific part of the window by holding the mouse button down on the scroll bar where you want the thumb to be. The scroll bar rapidly scrolls to the desired location and then stops.

Scrolling is such a frequently needed skill, though, that all kinds of other scrolling gadgets have cropped up.

Your mouse probably has a little wheel on the top. You can scroll in most programs just by turning the wheel with your finger, even if your cursor is nowhere near the scroll bar. You can turbo-scroll by dragging the mouse upward or downward while keeping the wheel pressed down inside the window.

Laptops often have some kind of scrolling gizmo, too. Maybe you have an actual roller, or maybe the trackpad offers drag-here-to-scroll strips on the right side and across the bottom.

Of course, keyboard addicts should note that you can scroll without using the mouse at all. Press the Page Up or Page Down keys to scroll the window by one window-full, or use the up and down arrow keys to scroll one line at a time.

---

them reappear by pressing the Alt key, Tab key, or an arrow key whenever the menu bar is visible. (When you're operating menus, you can release the Alt key immediately after pressing it.) In this book, in help screens, and computer magazines, you'll see key combinations indicated like this: Alt+S (or Alt+ whatever the letter key is).

Note: In some Vista programs, in fact, the entire *menu bar* is gone until you press Alt (or F10). That includes everyday Explorer windows.

Once the underlines are visible, you can open a menu by pressing the underlined letter (F for the File menu, for example). Once the menu is open, press the underlined letter key that corresponds to the menu command you want. Or press Esc to close the menu without doing anything. (In Windows, the Esc key always means *cancel* or *stop*.)

If choosing a menu command opens a dialog box, you can trigger its options by pressing Alt along with the underlined letters. (Within dialog boxes, you can't press and release Alt; you have to hold it down while typing the underlined letter.)

About Shift-Clicking

Here's another bit of shorthand you'll find in this book (and others): instructions to *Shift-click* something. That means you should hold down the Shift key, and then click before releasing the key. If you understand that much, the meaning of instructions like "Ctrl-click" and "Alt-click" should be clear.

You Could Spend a Lifetime Changing Properties

You can't write an operating system that's all things to all people, but Microsoft has certainly tried. You can change almost every aspect of the way Windows looks and works. You can replace the gray backdrop of the screen (the *wallpaper*) with your favorite photograph, change the typeface used for the names of your icons, or set up a particular program to launch automatically every time you turn on the PC.

When you want to change some *general* behavior of your PC, like how it connects to the Internet, how soon the screen goes black to save power, or how quickly a letter repeats when you hold down a key, you use the Control Panel window (described in Chapter 8).

Many other times, however, you may want to adjust the settings of only one particular element of the machine, such as the hard drive, the Recycle Bin, or a particular application. In those cases, simply right-click the corresponding icon. In the resulting shortcut menu, you'll often find a command called Properties. When you click it, a dialog box appears, containing settings or information about that object, as shown in Figure I-3.

Tip: As a shortcut to the Properties command, just highlight an icon and then press Alt+Enter.

It's also worth getting to know how to operate *tabbed dialog boxes*, like the one shown in Figure I-3. These are windows that contain so many options, Microsoft has had to split them up into separate panels, or *tabs*. To reveal a new set of options, just click a different tab (called General, Tools, Hardware, Sharing, Security, and Quota in Figure I-3). These tabs are designed to resemble the tabs at the top of file folders.

Tip: You can switch tabs without using the mouse by pressing Ctrl+Tab (to "click" the next tab to the right) or Ctrl+Shift+Tab (for the previous tab).

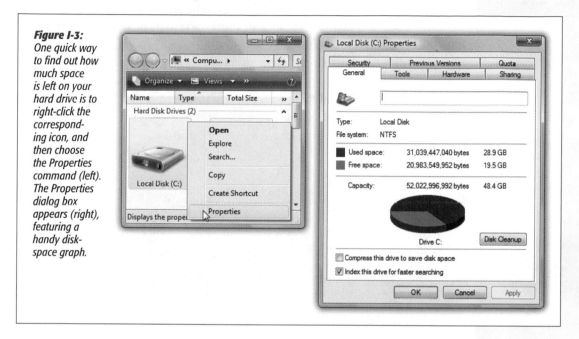

Figure I-3:
One quick way to find out how much space is left on your hard drive is to right-click the corresponding icon, and then choose the Properties command (left). The Properties dialog box appears (right), featuring a handy disk-space graph.

Every Piece of Hardware Requires Software

When computer geeks talk about their *drivers,* they're not talking about their chauffeurs (unless they're Bill Gates); they're talking about the controlling software required by every hardware component of a PC.

The driver is the translator between your PC's brain and the equipment attached to it: mouse, keyboard, screen, DVD drive, scanner, digital camera, palmtop, and so on. Without the correct driver software, the corresponding piece of equipment doesn't work at all.

When you buy one of these gadgets, you receive a CD containing the driver software. If the included driver software works fine, then you're all set. If your gadget acts up, however, remember that equipment manufacturers regularly release improved (read: less buggy) versions of these software chunks. (You generally find such updates on the manufacturers' Web sites.)

Fortunately, Windows Vista comes with drivers for over 12,000 components, saving you the trouble of scavenging for them on a disk or on the Internet. This gigantic library is the heart of Microsoft's Plug and Play feature, which lets you connect a new gadget to your PC without even thinking about the driver software (Chapter 18).

It's Not Meant to Be Overwhelming

Windows has an absolutely staggering array of features. You can burrow six levels down, dialog box through dialog box, and never come to the end of it. There are enough programs, commands, and help screens to keep you studying the rest of your life.

It's crucial to remember that Microsoft's programmers created Windows in modules—the digital-photography team here, the networking team there—with different audiences in mind. The idea, of course, was to make sure that no subset of potential customers would find a feature lacking.

But if *you* don't have a digital camera, a network, or whatever, there's absolutely nothing wrong with ignoring everything you encounter on the screen that isn't relevant to your setup and work routine. Not even Microsoft's CEO uses every single feature of Windows Vista.

Part One:
The Vista Desktop

Chapter 1: Welcome Center, Desktop, and the Start Menu

Chapter 2: Explorer, Windows, and the Taskbar

Chapter 3: Searching and Organizing Your Files

Chapter 4: Interior Decorating Vista

Chapter 5: Getting Help

1

Welcome Center, Desktop, and the Start Menu

Microsoft wants to make one thing perfectly clear: Windows Vista isn't just a whole new ballgame—it's practically a different sport. Compared with Windows XP, Vista is different on the surface, under the hood, and everywhere in between. (It's so different, in fact, that this book includes an appendix called "Where'd It Go?," which lets you look up a familiar Windows landmark and figure out where Microsoft stuck it in Vista.)

But you'll discover all that for yourself, beginning with the very first time you turn on your Vista computer.

It's hard to predict exactly what you'll see at that fateful moment. It may be a big welcome screen bearing the logo of Dell or whomever; it may be the Vista Setup Wizard (Appendix A); or it may be the *login* screen, where you're asked to sign in by clicking your name in a list. (Skip to page 688 for details on logging in.)

Eventually, though, you arrive at something that looks like Figure 1-1: the shining majesty of the new Vista Welcome Center.

The Welcome Center
All Versions

The Welcome Center is supposed to be an antidote to the moment of dizzy disorientation that you'd otherwise feel the first time you fire up Vista. It's basically a window full of links to useful places in the Vista empire. Click a link *once* to read its description in the top part of the window, or *twice* to open up the control panel or program you need to make changes.

Here are a few highlights (you may have to click "Show all 14 items" to see them):

- **View computer details.** Click this icon to read, in the top pane of the Welcome Center, the tech specs of your computer: its name, how much memory it has, what processor chip is inside, which graphics card you have, and so on.

  For even gorier statistical details about your PC's guts, click the "Show more details" link. You're taken directly to the System control panel (page 311). Here's where you can find your Windows Experience Index, a single-digit assessment of your machine's overall horsepower. (See the box below.)

- **Transfer files and settings.** The Vista program called Windows Easy Transfer is a substantially beefed-up version of the old Files & Settings Transfer Wizard. Its purpose is to transfer files and settings from an older PC, and it's described on page 783.

- **Add new users.** If you're the lord of the manor, the sole user of this computer, you can ignore this little item. But if you and other family members, students, or workers *share* this computer, you'll want to consult Chapter 23 about how to set up a separate *account* (name, password, and working environment) for each person.

- **Personalize Windows.** Sure, sure, eventually you'll be plotting rocket trajectories and mapping the genome—but let's not kid ourselves. The first order of

The Windows Experience Index

Quick—which computer is better, an AMD Turion 64 ML-34 processor at 1.80 gigahertz but only 512 megs of RAM, or a Core Duo 2.0 gigahertz with 1 gig of RAM but only a Radon Xpress 200M graphics card?

If you know the answer offhand, you shouldn't be reading a book about Vista; you should be writing your own darned book.

The point is, of course, that Vista is an extremely demanding operating system. It craves horsepower, speed, and memory. But Microsoft didn't really expect the average person, or even the average I.T. manager, to know at a glance whether a particular PC is up to the Vista challenge.

That's why Vista analyzes the guts of your computer and boils the results down to a single numerical rating. To find out yours, choose Start→Control Panel. Click "System and Maintenance," and then click the "Check your computer's Windows Experience Index base score" link.

The final score is the lowest of any of the subscores. For example, if your memory, hard drive, and graphics all get scores over 4, but your processor's score is only 3.1, your overall score is 3.1, which makes it easy to spot the bottleneck.

A score of 5 is the best; it means you'll be able to run all of Vista's features well and fast. (Actually, it's technically possible to get a score *above* 5; if so, all the better.) You need a score of at least 4 to play and edit high-definition video. A 3 is the minimum for running Vista's new Aero look (page 22). A 1 is the worst; Vista will be dog slow unless you turn off some of the eye-candy features, as described on page 612.

True, finding out that the computer you bought last year for $2,800 is now worth only a measly 2 on the Performance scale could deal your ego quite a bruise.

But fortunately, Microsoft also offers the Windows Upgrade Advisor (page 559). This free program reveals your PC's report card *before* you install Vista, so at least you can avoid getting a rude surprise.

business is decorating: choosing your screen saver, replacing the desktop background (wallpaper), choosing a different cursor shape, adjusting your monitor resolution, and so on. Double-click here to open the appropriate control panel.

- **Windows Basics.** Double-click to open the electronic help screen whose articles cover the *very* basics of your PC: how to use the mouse, how to turn off the computer, and so on.

Figure 1-1:
The Welcome Center, new in Windows Vista, offers links to various useful corners of the operating system. Most are designed to help you set up a new PC. (Click once to read a description, and then double-click to open the link.)

Below a horizontal line, you'll find another group of icons called Offers from Microsoft. Needless to say, these are various opportunities for you to spend money on Microsoft software and services, or to download Microsoft add-on programs.

At the *very* bottom of the Welcome Center, you'll find an important checkbox called "Run at startup." This is not some kind of warning that you should evacuate every time the computer boots. Instead, it's the on/off switch for the Welcome Center itself. If you turn off the checkbox, the Welcome Center no longer appears each time you turn on the PC. (You can always bring it back by opening its link in the Control Panel, as described on page 313.)

If you'd rather get rid of the Welcome Center just for now, click its Close box—or press Alt+F4, the universal Windows keystroke for "Close this window."

The Vista Desktop—Now with Aero!

Home Premium • Business • Enterprise • Ultimate

Once you've recovered from the excitement of the Welcome Center, you get your first glimpse of the full Vista desktop.

All of the usual Windows landmarks are here—the Start menu, taskbar, and Recycle Bin—but they've been given a drastic cosmetic overhaul.

If you're into this kind of thing, here's the complete list of what makes Aero Aero:

- The edges of windows are thicker (for easier targeting with your mouse). Parts of the Start menu and window edges are transparent. Windows and dialog boxes cast subtle shadows on the background, as though they're floating.

- A new, bigger, more modern font is used for menus and labels.

- When you point to a window button without clicking, the button "lights up." The Minimize and Maximize buttons glow blue; the Close button glows red.

- The *default* button in a dialog box—the one Microsoft thinks you really want, like Save or Print—pulses gently, using fading color intensity to draw your eye.

NOSTALGIA CORNER

Restoring the Desktop Icons

The Vista desktop, like the XP desktop before it, is a victim of Microsoft's clean-freak tendencies. It's awfully pretty—awfully barren. Windows veterans may miss the handy desktop icons that once provided quick access to important locations on your PC, like My Computer, My Documents, My Network Places, and Internet Explorer.

You can still get to these locations—they're listed in your Start menu—but opening them requires two mouse clicks (including one to open the Start menu)—an egregious expenditure of caloric effort.

However, if you miss the older arrangement, it's easy enough to put these icons back on the

desktop. To do so, right-click a blank spot on the desktop; from the shortcut menu, choose Personalize.

Now the Personalization dialog box appears. In the Tasks pane on the left side, click "Change desktop icons."

As shown here, checkboxes for the common desktop icons await your summons: Computer, Network, Internet Explorer, Control Panel, and User's Files (that is, your Personal folder—see page 38).

Turn on the ones you'd like to install onto the desktop and then click OK. Your old favorite icons are now back where they once belonged.

- Little animations liven up the works, especially when you minimize, maximize, or close a window.

Aero isn't just looks, either—it also includes a couple of features, like Flip 3D and live taskbar icons. You can read about these two useful features in Chapter 2.

Tip: Windows Vista also includes all-new sounds, too—the little blips and bleeps you hear when you wake up or shut down the PC, get an error message, and so on.

Microsoft wishes you to know, in particular, that the new Windows startup sound "has two parallel melodies, played in an intentional 'Win-dows Vis-ta' rhythm; consists of four chords, one for each color in the Windows flag; is 4 seconds long, end to end; and is a collaboration between contributors Robert Fripp (primary melody), Tucker Martine (rhythm), and Steve Ball (harmony and final orchestration)." Any questions?

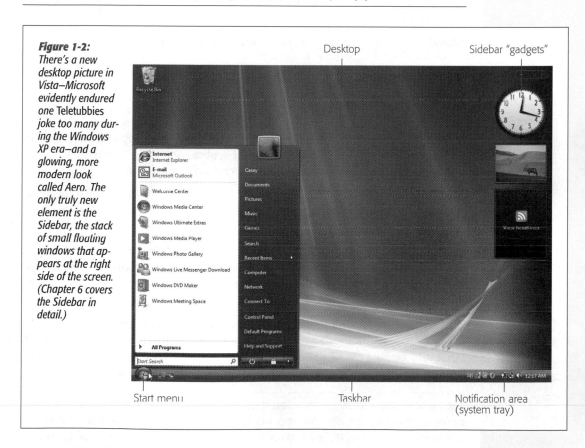

Figure 1-2:
There's a new desktop picture in Vista—Microsoft evidently endured one Teletubbies joke too many during the Windows XP era—and a glowing, more modern look called Aero. The only truly new element is the Sidebar, the stack of small floating windows that appears at the right side of the screen. (Chapter 6 covers the Sidebar in detail.)

Desktop

Sidebar "gadgets"

Start menu

Taskbar

Notification area (system tray)

What you're seeing is the new face of Windows, known to fans as *Aero*. (It supposedly stands for Authentic, Energetic, Reflective, and Open, but you can't help suspecting that somebody at Microsoft retrofitted those words to fit the initials.)

The Aero design may not actually be Authentic or whatever, but it does look clean and modern. You'll see it, however, *only* if you have a fairly fast, modern PC. Basically, you

---

need a Windows Experience Index score of 3 or higher (page 20), meaning a good amount of memory and a recent graphics card with Vista-specific drivers.

Tip: The Windows Upgrade Advisor, described on page 559, can tell you in advance if your PC is capable of showing you the Aero goodies.

Furthermore, the Aero features are available only in the more expensive versions of Vista: Home Premium, Business, Enterprise, and Ultimate.

If you have a slower computer or the Home Basic version, you'll be able to enjoy all of Vista's features—but they just won't look quite as nice. You'll use them without the transparencies, animations, and other eye candy. The pictures in this book will match the buttons and text you'll see on the screen, but without so much decoration around the edges.

Nobody ever said Microsoft's specialty was making things simple.

The Start Menu
All Versions

Windows Vista is composed of 50 million lines of computer code, scattered across your hard drive in thousands of files. The vast majority of them are support files, there for behind-the-scenes use by Windows and your applications—they're not for you. They may as well bear a sticker saying, "No user-serviceable parts inside."

That's why the Start menu is so important. It lists every *useful* piece of software on your computer, including commands, programs, and files. Just about everything you do on your PC begins—or can begin—with your Start menu.

In Vista, as you've probably noticed, the *word* Start no longer appears on the Start menu; now the Start menu is just a round, backlit, glass pebble with a Windows logo behind it. But it's still called the Start menu, and it's still the gateway to everything on the PC.

If you're the type who bills by the hour, you can open the Start menu (Figure 1-3) by clicking it with the mouse. If you're among those who feel that life's too short, however, open it by tapping the ⊞ key on the keyboard instead. (If your antique, kerosene-operated keyboard has no ⊞ key, pressing Ctrl+Esc does the same thing.)

Tip: To find out what something is—something in your Start menu, All Programs menu, or indeed anywhere on your desktop—point to it with your cursor without clicking. A shaded, rectangular Tooltip bar appears, containing a text description. (If the Tooltip doesn't appear, it might be that the window you're pointing to isn't the *active* window on your desktop. Click the window and then try again.)

Anatomy of the Start Menu
The new Start menu is split down the middle into two columns:

- **Left side (white).** At the top, above the thin divider line, is the *pinned items list,* which is yours to modify; it lists programs, folders, documents, and anything else you want to open quickly. This list never changes unless you change it.

  Below that is the standard Windows *most frequently used programs list.* This list is computed automatically by Windows and may change from day to day.

Tip: You can, if you wish, ask Vista *not* to display a list of the programs you've used most recently. You might want to do that if, for example, it would be best if your boss or your spouse didn't know what you've been up to.

If that's your situation (or your boss), right-click the Start button itself; from the shortcut menu, choose Properties. In the resulting dialog box, turn off "Store and display a list of recently opened programs." Click OK.

When you next inspect the Start menu, you'll be surprised—but happy—to see that the lower-left quadrant, where the recently used programs are usually listed, is startlingly blank.

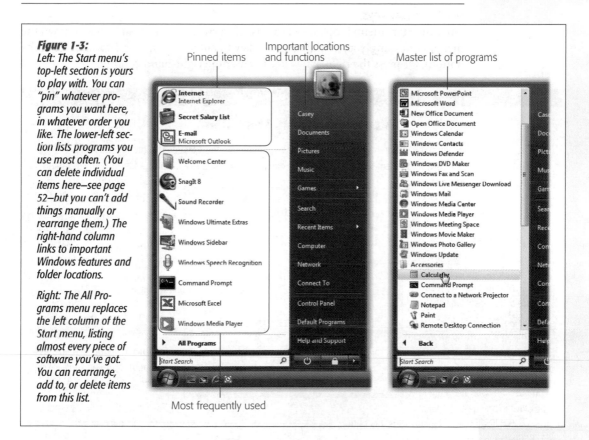

Figure 1-3:
Left: The Start menu's top-left section is yours to play with. You can "pin" whatever programs you want here, in whatever order you like. The lower-left section lists programs you use most often. (You can delete individual items here—see page 52—but you can't add things manually or rearrange them.) The right-hand column links to important Windows features and folder locations.

Right: The All Programs menu replaces the left column of the Start menu, listing almost every piece of software you've got. You can rearrange, add to, or delete items from this list.

Pinned items

Important locations and functions

Master list of programs

Most frequently used

- **Right side (dark).** In general, the right side of the open Start menu is devoted to listing important *places* on the computer: folders like Documents, Pictures, and Music, or special windows like Network, Control Panel, and Computer.

The important new Search command (Chapter 3) appears here, too. And at the bottom, you'll find new buttons that let you turn the PC off or, when you're about to wander away for coffee, lock it so that a password is required to re-enter.

Tip: After 20 years, Microsoft has finally eliminated the prefix My from the important folders of your PC (My Pictures, My Music, My Documents, My Computer, and so on). Maybe it was tired of all the lawsuits from Fisher-Price.

In any case, if you miss that touch of homey personalization, it's easy enough to bring it back; you can rename these special icons just as you would any other icon (page 130). Call it My Computer, call it Your Computer, call it Jar Jar Binks—makes no difference to Vista.

Keyboard Navigation

You can navigate and control the new, improved Start menu in either of two ways:

Use the arrow keys

Once the Start menu is open, you can use the arrow keys to "walk" up and down the menu. For example, press the up arrow key to enter the left-hand column from the bottom. Or press the right arrow key to enter the right-hand column.

NOSTALGIA CORNER

Return to the Old Start Menu

The fancily redesigned Vista Start menu has its charms, not the least of which is its new, translucent look. But it's also confusing to old-time Windows users, and, on slowish PCs, slower to open.

Fortunately, it's easy enough to switch back to the organization and design of the old, single-column Start menu of the pre-Vista, pre-XP days. Just right-click the Start button. Now, from the shortcut menu, choose Properties.

In the dialog box that appears, you'll see the option to return to the old Start menu design—what Microsoft calls Classic Start menu. Click that button, click OK, and enjoy going back to the future.

When you use the Classic Start menu, you'll notice a few differences in the behavior of the Start menu commands. For example, those cascading submenus are back, and everything's listed in one column, not two. (But you knew that, of course, because you're already accustomed to the older Start menu.)

As a convenience, turning on the Classic Start menu also returns the Control Panel icon to your desktop, on the assumption that you *really* liked Windows better the old way.

To restore the new Start menu, repeat the procedure—but this time, in the dialog box shown here, click Start Menu instead.

Either way, once you've highlighted something in either column, you can press the left/right arrow keys to hop to the opposite side of the menu; press the up/down arrow keys to highlight other commands in the column (even the Off and Lock buttons); or type the first initial of something's name to highlight it. (If there's more than one command that starts with, say, W, press W repeatedly to cycle through them.)

Once you've highlighted something, you can press Enter to "click" it (open it), or tap the ⊞ key or Esc key to close the Start menu and forget the whole thing.

Use the Search box

This thing is *awesome*.

The instant you pop open the Start menu, your insertion point blinks in the new Start Search box at the bottom of the menu (Figure 1-4). That's your cue that you can begin typing the name of whatever you want to open.

Figure 1-4:
As you type, Vista winnows down the list of found items, letter by letter. (You don't have to type the search term and then press Enter.) If the list of results is too long to fit the Start menu, click "See all results" below the list. In any case, Vista highlights the first item in the results. If that's what you want to open, press Enter. If not, you can click what you want to open, or use the arrow keys to walk down the list and then press Enter to open something.

The instant you start to type, you trigger Vista's new, very fast, whole-computer search function. This search finds, among other things, anything in the Start menu, making it a very quick way to pull up something without having to click through a bunch of Start menu submenus.

You can read the meaty details about Search in Chapter 3.

What's in the Start Menu
All Versions

The following pages take you on a whirlwind tour of the Start menu itself—from the bottom up, left to right, the way your mouse encounters its contents as it moves up from the Start button.

All Programs

When you click All Programs, you're presented with an important list indeed: the master catalog of every program on your computer. You can jump directly to your word processor, calendar, or favorite game, for example, just by choosing its name from the Start→All Programs menu.

In Vista, as you'll notice very quickly, Microsoft abandoned the superimposed-menus effect of Windows XP. Rather than covering up the regularly scheduled Start menu, the All Programs list *replaces* it (or at least the left-side column of it).

You can restore the original left-side column by clicking Back (at the bottom of the list) or pressing the Esc key.

Tip: When the Start menu is open, you can open the All Programs menu in a number of ways: by clicking the phrase "All Programs," by pointing to it and keeping the mouse still for a moment, or by pressing the up arrow key (to highlight All Programs) and then tapping the Enter key, the right arrow key, or the Space bar.

Keyboard fanatics—once the programs list is open, you can also choose anything in it without involving the mouse. Just type the first few letters of a program's folder's name, or press the up and down arrow keys, to highlight the item you want. Then press Enter to seal the deal.

Folders

As you'll quickly discover, the All Programs list in Vista doesn't just list programs. It also houses a number of *folders*.

Software-company folders

Some of them bear the names of software you've installed; you might see a folder called, for example, Urge (Microsoft's online music-store partner) or Logitech. These generally contain programs, uninstallers, instruction manuals, and other related junk.

Tip: Submenus, also known as cascading menus, have been largely eliminated from the Start menu. Instead, when you open something that contains *other* things—like a folder listed in the Start menu—you see its contents listed beneath, indented slightly, as shown in Figure 1-5. Click the folder name again to collapse the sublisting.

Keyboard freaks should note that you can also open a highlighted folder in the list by pressing the Enter key (or the right arrow key). Close the folder by pressing Enter again (or the left arrow key).

Program-group folders

Another set of folders is designed to trim down the Programs menu by consolidating related programs, like Games, Accessories (little single-purpose programs), and Extras and Upgrades. Everything in these folders is described in Chapter 7.

The Startup folder

This folder contains programs that load automatically every time you start Windows Vista. This can be a very useful feature. For instance, if you check your email every morning, you may as well save yourself a few mouse clicks by putting your email program into the Startup folder. If you spend all day long word processing, you may as well put Microsoft Word in there.

In fact, although few PC users suspect it, what you put into the Startup folder doesn't have to be an application. It can just as well be a *document* you consult every day. It can even be a folder or disk icon whose window you'd like to find open and waiting each time you turn on the PC. (The Documents folder is a natural example.)

Of course, you may be interested in the Startup folder for a different reason: to *stop* some program from launching itself. This is a particularly common syndrome if somebody else set up your PC. Some program seems to launch itself, unbidden, every time you turn the machine on.

Tip: All kinds of programs dump components into this folder. Over time, they can begin to slow down your computer. If you're having trouble determining the purpose of one startup program or another, visit this Web page, which provides a comprehensive list of every startup software nugget known, with instructions for turning off each one: *http://www.sysinfo.org/startupinfo.html.*

Fortunately, it's easy to either add or remove items from the Startup folder:

- **Deleting something.** With the Startup folder's listing visible in the All Programs menu, right-click whatever you want to delete. From the shortcut menu, choose Delete. Click Yes to send the icon to the Recycle Bin.

  Enjoy your newfound freedom from self-launching software.

- **Adding something.** With the All Programs list open, right-click the Startup folder and, from the shortcut menu, choose Open. You've just opened the Startup folder itself.

Once its window is open, navigate to the disk, folder, application, or document icon you want to add. (Navigating your files and folders is described in the following chapters.)

Using the right mouse button, drag the icon directly into the Startup window, as shown in Figure 1-5. When you release the button, a shortcut menu appears; from the shortcut menu, choose Create Shortcuts Here.

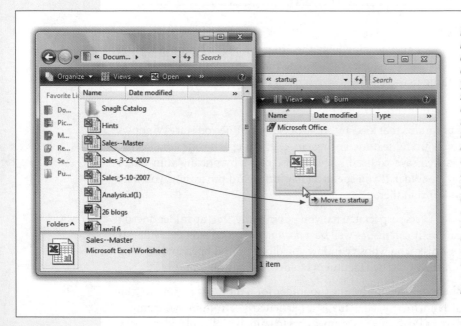

Figure 1-5:
It's easy to add a program or document icon to your Startup folder so that it launches automatically every time you turn on the computer. Here, a document from the Documents folder is being added. You may also want to add a shortcut for the Documents folder itself, which ensures that its window will be ready and open each time the computer starts up.

Close any windows you've opened. From now on, each time you turn on or restart your computer, the program, file, disk, or folder you dragged will open by itself.

Start→⏻ (Sleep)
All Versions

The ⏻ button, at the bottom of the Start menu's right column, is the trigger for one of Vista's most useful new features, Sleep mode. Yes, that's right: one of the best things about Vista is how it behaves when you *turn it off*.

Millions of people shut their PCs off every day, but they shouldn't; it's a huge, colossal waste of time on both ends. When you shut down, you have to wait for all your programs to close—and then the next morning, you have to reopen everything, reposition your windows, and get everything back the way you had it.

Millions of other people, therefore, avoid the whole problem by leaving their computers *on* all the time. That, of course, represents a massive waste of electricity and isn't great for the environment.

A few people knew about Standby mode and used that instead. This special state of PC consciousness reduced the amount of electricity the computer used, putting it in suspended animation until you used the mouse or keyboard to begin working again. Whatever programs or documents you were working on remained in memory.

When using a laptop on battery power, Standby was a real boon. When the flight attendant handed over your microwaved chicken teriyaki, you could take a break without closing all your programs or shutting down the computer.

Unfortunately, there were two big problems with Standby, especially for laptops:

- The PC still drew a trickle of power this way. If you didn't use your laptop for a few days, the battery would silently go dead—and everything you had open and unsaved would be lost forever.

- Drivers or programs sometimes interfered with Standby, so your laptop remained on even though it was closed inside your carrying case. Your plane would land on the opposite coast, you'd pull out the laptop for the big meeting, and you'd discover that (a) the thing was roasting hot, and (b) the battery was dead.

In Windows Vista, Microsoft has fixed Standby. Now it's called Sleep, and now it doesn't present those problems.

First, drivers and applications are no longer allowed to interrupt the Sleep process. No more Hot Laptop Syndrome.

Second, the instant you put the computer to sleep, Vista quietly transfers a copy of everything in memory into an invisible file on the hard drive. But at the same time, it still keeps everything alive in memory—the battery provides a tiny trickle of power—in case you return to the laptop (or desktop) and want to dive back into work.

If you do return soon (within 18 hours, although this period varies by laptop model), the next startup is lightning-fast. Everything reappears on the screen faster than you can say, "Redmond, Washington." After you've enjoyed the speed of a power-up from Sleep mode, the normal startup seems unbearably slow.

But now suppose you *don't* return after 18 hours (or the battery dies while providing the trickle of juice). In that case, Vista cuts power, abandoning what it had memorized in RAM. Now your computer is using no power at all. The laptop battery isn't slowly running down; the desktop isn't contributing to global warming.

Fortunately, Windows still has the hard drive copy of your work environment. So *now* when you tap a key to wake the computer, you might have to wait 30 seconds or so—not as fast as two seconds, but certainly better than the five minutes it would take to start up, reopen all your programs, reposition your document windows, and so on.

So here's the bottom line: when you're done working for the moment—or for the day—put your computer to Sleep instead of shutting it down. You save power, you save time, and you risk no data loss.

You can send a laptop to Sleep just by closing the lid. On any kind of computer, you can trigger Sleep by choosing Start→⏻.

Tip: Keyboard speed freaks should note that on a desktop *or* a laptop, you can trigger Sleep entirely from the keyboard by pressing ⊞, then right arrow, then Enter, in rapid succession.

Start→🔒 (Lock)
All Versions

Also at the bottom of the Start menu's right side, you'll find this little padlock button. Clicking it locks your computer—in essence, it throws a sheet of inch-thick steel over everything you were doing, hiding your screen from view. This is an ideal way to protect your PC from nosy people who happen to wander by your desk while you're away getting coffee or lunch.

All they'll find on your monitor is the standard Logon screen described on page 688. They (and even you) will have to enter your account password to get past it (page 683).

Tip: You can trigger this button, too, entirely from the keyboard. Hit these keys, in sequence: ⊞, right arrow (twice), Enter.

Start→Log Off, Restart, Hibernate, Shut Down
All Versions

To the right off the little 🔒 icon at the bottom of the Start menu is a small arrow button. As shown in Figure 1-6, it offers a more complete listing of ways to end your work session.

Your options include:

FREQUENTLY ASKED QUESTION

Sleep-vs.-Hibernate Smackdown

So if Sleep is so great, why is there still a Hibernate command?

Sleep mode is a two-stage affair (page 30). If you wake up the computer within 18 hours of putting it to Sleep, all your programs and windows pop open instantly, because your PC has been using a thin trickle of power to keep them in memory.

If you wake up the computer after 18 hours, you wait slightly longer (30 seconds), because the PC is retrieving your memorized working environment from the hard drive, which is slower.

Hibernate, in other words, is exactly the same as the *second* phase of Sleep. When you tell the PC to Hibernate, it stores a copy of the open programs on the hard drive and cuts power *immediately*—no 18 hours of standby first.

And now, to the question—why?

First, going straight to Hibernate saves some power, because you eliminate that 18 hours of keeping the RAM alive. Second, you save 18 hours of slight heat buildup in your laptop bag.

Minor differences, to be sure—but at least now you know.

- **Switch User.** This command refers to Vista's *accounts* feature, in which each person who uses this PC gets to see his own desktop picture, email account, files, and so on. (See Chapter 23.)

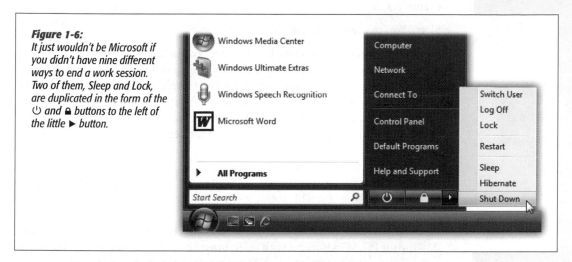

Figure 1-6:
It just wouldn't be Microsoft if you didn't have nine different ways to end a work session. Two of them, Sleep and Lock, are duplicated in the form of the ⏻ and 🔒 buttons to the left of the little ▶ button.

When you choose Switch User, somebody else can log into the computer with her own name and password—to do a quick calendar or email check, for example. But whatever *you* had running remains open behind the scenes. After the interloper is finished, you can log in again to find all of your open programs and documents exactly as you left them.

Note: In Windows XP, the Switch User command was available only if you had turned on something called Fast User Switching. In Vista, there's no Off switch; Fast User Switching is in effect full time.

- **Log Off.** If you click Log Off, Windows closes all of your open programs and documents (giving you an opportunity to save any unsaved documents first). It then presents a new Welcome screen (page 688) so that the next person can sign in.

- **Lock.** When you're going to wander away from your PC for a bit, use this command to protect whatever you were working on, as described above.

FREQUENTLY ASKED QUESTION

Start→Stop

Could someone explain why all the variations of Turn Off Computer are in a menu called Start?

The Name-the-Button committee at Microsoft probably thought that you'd interpret Start to mean, "Start here to get something accomplished."

But you wouldn't be the first person to find it illogical to click Start when you want to stop. Microsoft probably should have named the button "Menu," saving all of us a lot of confusion.

- **Restart.** This command quits all open programs, then quits and restarts Windows again automatically. The computer doesn't actually turn off. (You might do this to "refresh" your computer when you notice that it's responding sluggishly, for example.)

- **Sleep.** You can read about Sleep on page 30.

- **Hibernate.** Hibernate mode is a lot like Sleep, except that it *doesn't* offer a 15-minute period during which the computer will wake up instantly (because it's keeping your open files and programs alive in RAM). Hibernate equals the *second* phase of Sleep mode, in which your working world is saved to the hard drive. Waking the computer from Hibernate takes about 30 seconds—not as fast as waking from the first 18 hours of Sleep, but much faster than starting from Off and having to reopen all your programs.

Tip: You can configure your computer to sleep or hibernate automatically after a period of inactivity, or to require a password to bring it out of hibernation. See page 300 for details.

- **Shut Down.** This is what most people would call "really, really off." When you shut down your PC, Windows quits all open programs, offers you the opportunity to save any unsaved documents, exits Windows, and turns off the computer.

Tip: Once again, it's worth noting that you can trigger any of these commands entirely from the keyboard; save your mouse for Photoshop.

Hit the ⊞ key to open the Start menu. Then hit the right arrow key three times to open the menu shown in Figure 1-6. At this point, you can type the underlined letter of the command you want: L for Log Off, U for Shut Down, and so on.

Start→Help and Support
All Versions

Choosing Start→Help and Support opens the new, improved Windows Help and Support Center window, which is described in Chapter 5.

Tip: Once again, speed fans have an alternative to using the mouse—just press the F1 key to open the Help window. (If that doesn't work, some other program may have Vista's focus. Try it again after clicking the desktop.)

Start→Default Programs
All Versions

This command is just a shortcut to the Default Programs control panel.

It has two functions:

- To let you specify which program (not necessarily Microsoft's) you want to use as your Web browser, email program, instant-messaging program, Java module, and music player—a choice offered by Microsoft to placate the U.S. Justice Department. Details are on page 226.

- To specify which program opens when you double-click a certain kind of document. For example, if you double-click a JPEG graphic, do you want it to open in Photoshop or Windows Photo Gallery? Details on page 223.

Note: Windows veterans may want to note that this file-association function used to be called File Types, and it was in the Folder Options window.

Start→Control Panel
All Versions

This extremely important command opens an extremely important window: the Control Panel, which houses over 50 mini-programs that you'll use to change almost every important setting on your PC. It's so important, in fact, that it gets a chapter of its own (Chapter 8).

Start→Connect To
All Versions

This command opens the "Connect to a network" dialog box, a simple list of all dial-up, VPN (virtual private networking), and wireless networks that your computer can "see" at the moment.

Take special note of this option if you have a laptop or some other mobile PC, because this window offers a simple, clear means of seeing what wireless networks are available (and connecting to a good one). You'll find details on hooking up to a wireless network in Chapter 9.

Start→Network
All Versions

We've come a long way since the My Network Places icon that once graced every Windows desktop.

Now, just choosing Start→Network opens a single, ready-to-use window containing icons of all nearby computers that are on the same network, ready to open and browse for files and folders your comrades have decided to share with you. (It's the equivalent of the View Workgroup Computers command in Windows XP.)

Details on networking in Vista are in Chapters 23, 24, 25, and 26.

Start→Computer

All Versions

The Computer command is the trunk lid, the doorway to every single shred of software on your machine. When you choose this command, a window opens to reveal icons that represent each disk drive (or drive partition) in your machine, as shown in Figure 1-7.

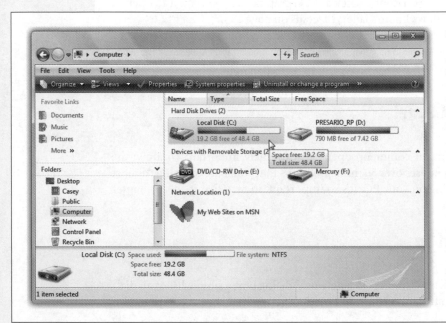

Figure 1-7:
The Computer window lists your PC's drives—hard drives, CD drives, USB flash drives, and so on; you may see networked drives listed here, too. This computer has two hard drives, a USB flash drive, and a CD-ROM drive. (If there's a disk in the CD drive, you see its name, not just its drive letter.) When you select a disk icon, the Details pane (if visible) shows its capacity and amount of free space (bottom).

NOSTALGIA CORNER

Restoring the Traditional Folder Listings

Some of the commands that populated the Start menus of previous Windows versions no longer appear in the Start menu of Vista. Microsoft is trying to make its new operating system look less overwhelming.

But if you miss some of the old folders—Favorites, Printers, and the Run command, for example—it's easy enough to put them back.

Right-click the Start menu. From the shortcut menu, choose Properties. Now the Taskbar and Start Menu Properties dialog box appears; click the Customize button.

In the scrolling list, you'll find checkboxes and buttons that hide or show all kinds of things that can appear in the right column of the Start menu: Computer, Connect To, Control Panel, Default Programs, Documents, Favorites, Games, Help, Music, Network, Pictures, Printers, Run, Search, and System Administrative Tools (a set of utilities described in Chapter 20).

Click OK twice to return to the desktop and try out your changes.

For example, by double-clicking your hard drive icon and then the various folders on it, you can eventually see the icons for every single file and folder on your computer. (The Computer icon no longer appears on the desktop—unless you put it there, as described on page 22.)

Start→Recent Items
All Versions

When you click or highlight this command, a submenu sprouts to the right, listing the last 15 documents you've opened. The point, of course, is that you can *reopen* one just by clicking its name.

This list can save you time when you want to resume work on something you had open recently, but you're not in the mood to burrow through folders to find its icon.

Note, however, that:

- Documents appear on the Recent Items list only if your applications are smart enough to update it. Most modern programs (including all Microsoft programs) perform this administrative task, but not all do.

- The Recent Items list doesn't know when you've deleted a document or moved it to another folder or disk; it continues to list the file even after it's gone. In that event, clicking the document's listing produces only an error message. (At least the message now offers to delete the listing from Recent Items so you don't confuse yourself again the next time.)

- Some people consider Recent Items a privacy risk, since it reveals everything you've been up to recently to whatever spouse or buddy happens to wander by. (You know who you are.)

  In that case, you can remove Recent Items from the Start menu altogether. Right-click the Start button itself; from the shortcut menu, choose Properties. In the resulting dialog box, turn off "Store and display a list of recently opened files." Click OK.

Tip: Of course, there's another easy way to open a document you've recently worked on. To start, simply open the program you used to create it. Many programs maintain a list of recent documents at the bottom of the File menu; choose one of these names to open the corresponding file.

Start→Search
All Versions

This very, very juicy new feature is one of the most compelling reasons to upgrade to Windows Vista. It's the new, superfast, system-wide Search feature, and it's described in depth in Chapter 3.

Note: *This* Search command isn't quite the same thing as the Search *box* at the bottom of the Start menu. This one gives you more control. For example, the window that appears when you use *this* Search lets you confine your search to photos, documents, email messages, and so on.

Start→Games

All Versions

This item is nothing but a shortcut to Vista's Games folder (page 274). Good to know when there's time to kill.

Start→Music, Pictures

All Versions

Microsoft correctly assumes that most people these days use their home computers for managing digital photos and music albums that have been downloaded or copied from CDs. As you can probably guess, the Pictures and Music folders are intended to house your photo and tune collections—and these Start menu commands are quick ways to open them.

FREQUENTLY ASKED QUESTION

Secrets of the Personal Folder

So why did Microsoft bury your files in a folder three levels deep?

Because Vista has been designed from the ground up for *computer sharing.* It's ideal for any situation where different family members, students, or workers share the same PC.

Each person who uses the computer will turn on the machine to find his own separate desktop picture, set of files, Web bookmarks, font collection, and preference settings. (You'll find much more about this feature in Chapter 23.)

Like it or not, Vista considers you one of these people. If you're the only one who uses this PC, fine—simply ignore the sharing features. But in its little software head, Vista still considers you an account holder, and stands ready to accommodate any others who should come along.

In any case, now you should see the importance of the Users folder in the main hard drive window. Inside are folders—the Personal folders—named for the different people who use

this PC. In general, nobody is allowed to touch what's inside anybody else's folder.

If you're the sole proprietor of the machine, of course, there's only one Personal folder in the Users folder—named for you. (You can ignore the Public folder, which is described on page 730.)

This is only the first of many examples in which Vista imposes a fairly rigid folder structure. Still, the approach has its advantages. By keeping such tight control over which files go where, Vista keeps itself pure—and very, very stable. (Other operating systems known for their stability, such as Windows 2000 and Mac OS X, work the same way.)

Furthermore, keeping all of your stuff in a single folder makes it very easy for you to back up your work. It also makes life easier when you try to connect to your machine from elsewhere in the office (over the network) or elsewhere in the world (over the Internet), as described in Chapter 26 and 27.

In fact, you'll probably find that whatever software came with your digital camera or MP3 player automatically dumps your photos into, and sucks your music files out of, these folders. You'll find much more on these topics in Chapters 13 and 14.

Start→Documents
All Versions

This command opens up your Documents folder, a very important folder indeed. It's designed to store just about all the work you do on your PC—everything except Music, Pictures, and Videos, which get folders of their own.

Of course, you're welcome to file your documents *anywhere* on the hard drive, but most programs propose the Documents folder as the target location for newly created documents.

Sticking with that principle makes a lot of sense, because it makes navigation easy. You never have to wonder where you filed something, since all your stuff is sitting right there in Documents.

Note: The Documents folder actually sits in the Computer→Local Disk (C:)→Users→[*Your Name*] folder.)

If you study that path carefully, it should become clear that what's in Documents when *you* log in (page 688) isn't the same thing that other people will see when *they* log in. That is, each account holder (Chapter 23) has a different Documents folder, whose contents switch according to who's logged in.

Start→[Your Name]: The Personal Folder
All Versions

As the box on the facing page makes clear, Windows Vista keeps *all* of your stuff—your files, folders, email, pictures, music, bookmarks, even settings and preferences—in one handy, central location: your *Personal folder*. That's a folder bearing your name (or whatever account name you typed when you installed Vista).

Everyone with an account on your PC has a Personal folder—even if you're the only one with an account.

Note: See Chapter 23 for the full scoop on user accounts.

Technically, your Personal folder lurks inside the C:→Users folder. But that's a lot of burrowing when you just want a view of your entire empire.

That's why your Personal folder is also listed here, at the top of the Start menu's right-side column. Choose this listing to open the folder that you'll eventually fill with new folders, organize, back up, and so on.

Start→Run

All Versions

A clean, new installation of Vista doesn't include the Run command. But power users and über-geeks may well want to put it back in the Start menu, following the instructions in the box on page 46. (Or don't bother. Whenever you want the Run command, you can just press ⊞+R, or type *run* into the Start menu's Search box and then hit Enter.)

After all, the Run command gets you to a *command line,* as shown in Figure 1-8. A command line is a text-based method of performing a task. You type a command, click OK, and something happens as a result.

Note: The command line in the Run dialog box is primarily for *opening* things. Vista also comes with a program called Command Prompt that offers a far more complete environment—not just for opening things, but for controlling and manipulating them. Power users can type long sequences of commands and symbols in Command Prompt.

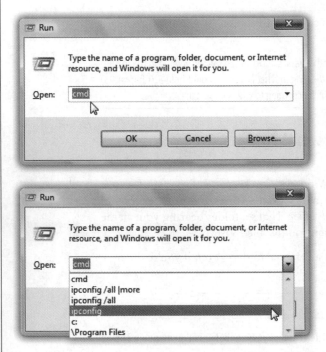

Figure 1-8:
Top: The last Run command you entered appears automatically in the Open text box. You can use the drop-down list to see a list of commands you've previously entered.

Bottom: The Run command knows the names of all of your folders and also remembers the last few commands you typed here. As you go, you're shown the best match for the characters you're typing. When the name of the folder you're trying to open appears in the list, click it to prevent having to type the rest of the entry.

Working at the command line is becoming a lost art in the world of Windows, because most people prefer to issue commands by choosing from menus using the mouse. However, some old-timers still love the command line, and even mouse-lovers encounter situations where a typed command is the *only* way to do something.

If you're a PC veteran, your head probably teems with neat Run commands you've picked up over the years. If you're new to this idea, however, the following are a few of the useful and timesaving functions you can perform with the Run dialog box.

Open a Program

For example, you can use the Run command as a program launcher. Just type any program's *program file name* in the Open text box and then press Enter. That's a useful shortcut for both pros and novices alike, because it's frequently faster to launch a program this way than to click the Start→All Programs menu with the mouse.

Unfortunately, the program file name isn't the same as its plain-English name; it's a cryptic, abbreviated version. For example, if you want to open Microsoft Word, you must type *winword*. That's the actual name of the Word program icon as it sits in your Computer→Local Disk (C:)→Program Files→Microsoft Office→Office folder. Some other common program file names are shown here:

Program's real name	Program's familiar name
iexplore	Internet Explorer
explorer	Windows Explorer
write	WordPad
msworks	Microsoft Works
msimn	Mail
wmplayer	Windows Media Player
palm	Palm Desktop
sol	Solitaire
winmine	Minesweeper
control	Classic Control Panel
regedit	Registry Editor
cleanmgr	Disk Cleanup
defrag	Disk Defragmenter
calc	Calculator

UP TO SPEED

The Path to Enlightenment about Paths

Windows is too busy to think of a particular file as "that family album program in the Program Files folder, which is in the Programs folder on the C drive." Instead, it uses shorthand to specify each icon's location on your hard drive—a series of disk and folder names separated by backslashes, like this: *C:\program files\pbsoftware\beekeeperpro.exe.*

This kind of location code is that icon's *path.* (Capitalization doesn't matter, even though you may see capital letters in Microsoft's examples.)

You'll encounter file paths when using several important Windows features. The Run dialog box described in this section is one. The Address bar at the top of every Explorer window is another, although Microsoft has made addresses easier to read by displaying triangle separators in the Address bar instead of slashes. (That is, you now see Users ▸ Casey instead of Users\Casey.)

To discover the program file name of a favorite program, see "Which One's the Program?" on page 51.

> **Note:** True, the Start Search box at the bottom of Vista's Start menu offers another way to find and open any program without taking your hands off the keyboard. But the Run method is more precise, and may require less effort because you're not typing the *entire* program name.

In fact, keyboard lovers, get this: you can perform this entire application-launching stunt without using the mouse at all. Just follow these steps in rapid succession:

1. **Press ⊞+R.**

   That's the keyboard shortcut for the Run command, whose dialog box now opens.

2. **Type the program file's name in the Open box.**

   If you've typed the name before, just type a couple of letters; Windows Vista fills in the rest of the name automatically.

3. **Press Enter.**

   Windows opens the requested program instantly. Keystrokes: 3; Mouse: 0.

Open Any Program or Document

Using the Run dialog box is handy for launching favorite applications, because it requires so few keystrokes. But you can also use the Run dialog box to open *any* file on the computer.

The trick here is to type in the entire *path* of the program or document you want. (See the box on page 41 if you're new to the idea of file paths.) For example, to open the family budget spreadsheet that's in Harold's Documents folder, you might type *C:\Users\Harold\Documents\familybudget.xls*.

(Of course, you probably wouldn't *actually* have to type all that, since the autocomplete pop-up menu offers to complete each folder name as you start to type it.)

> **Tip:** Typing the path in this way is also useful for opening applications that don't appear in the Start→All Programs menu. (If a program doesn't appear there, you must type its entire pathname—or click Browse to hunt for its icon yourself.)
>
> For example, some advanced Windows Vista utilities (including the *Registry Editor,* an advanced diagnostic program) are accessible only through the command line. You also need to use the Run command to open some older DOS programs that don't come with a listing in the All Programs menu.

Open a Drive Window

When you click Computer in your Start menu, you'll see that Windows assigns a letter of the alphabet to each disk drive attached to your machine—the hard drive, CD-ROM drive, floppy drive, and so on. The floppy drive is A:, the hard drive is usually C:, and so on. (There hasn't been a B: drive since the demise of the two-floppy computer.)

By typing a drive letter followed by a colon (for example, *C:*) into the Run box and pressing Enter, you make a window pop open, showing what's on that drive.

Open a Folder Window

You can also use the Run dialog box to open the window for any folder on your machine. To do so, type a backslash followed by the name of a folder (Figure 1-9, bottom of screen). You might type, for example, *Program Files* to see your complete software collection.

Note: The Run command assumes that you're opening a folder on Drive C. If you want to open a folder on a different drive, add the drive letter and a colon before the name of the folder (for example, *D:\data*).

Figure 1-9:
The Browse dialog box, which makes frequent appearances in Windows, lets you navigate the folders on your PC to find a file. The links at left make it easy to jump to the places where you're most likely to find the document you want. If you enter a drive letter and a colon in the Run dialog box before clicking the Browse button (like C:), the Browse dialog box opens with a display of that drive's contents.

If you're on a network, you can even open a folder that's sitting on another computer on the network. To do so, type *two* backslashes, the computer's name, and then the shared folder's name. For instance, to access a shared folder called Budgets on a computer named Admin, enter *admin\budgets*. (See Chapter 26 for more on sharing folders over the network.)

It might make you feel extra proficient to know that you've just used the *Universal Naming Convention*, or UNC, for the shared folder. The UNC is simply the two-backslash, computer name\folder name format (for example: *ComputerName\foldername*).

Connect to a Web Page

You can jump directly to a specific Web page by typing its Web address (URL)—such as *www.bigcompany.com*—into the Run dialog box, and then pressing Enter. You don't even have to open your Web browser first.

Once again, you may not have to type very much; the drop-down list in the Run dialog box lists every URL you've previously entered. Simply click one (or press the down arrow to highlight the one you want, and then press Enter) to go to that site.

Customizing the Start Menu
All Versions

It's possible to live a long and happy life without ever tampering with the Start menu. In fact, for many people, the idea of making it look or work differently comes dangerously close to nerd territory.

Still, knowing how to manipulate the Start menu listings may come in handy someday, and provides an interesting glimpse into the way Windows works. And tweaking it to reflect your way of doing things can pay off in efficiency down the road.

Note: Thanks to the User Accounts feature described in Chapter 23, any changes you make to the Start menu apply only to *you.* Each person with an account on this PC has an independent, customized Start menu. When you sign onto the machine using your name and password, Windows Vista loads *your* customized Start menu.

Start Menu Settings

Microsoft offers a fascinating set of customization options for the Start menu. It's hard to tell whether these options were selected by a scientific usability study or by a dartboard, but you're likely to find something that suits you.

To view and change the basic options, right-click the Start menu; from the shortcut menu, choose Properties. Now the Taskbar and Start Menu Properties dialog box opens, as seen in Figure 1-10.

When you click the Customize button, you see the dialog box shown at right in Figure 1-10.

In the scrolling list

Here you're offered a random assortment of Start-menu tweaks, neatly listed in alphabetical order; they affect the Start menu in some fairly simple yet profound ways. Here, among other things, is where you'll find the show/hide switches for commands on the *right side* of the Start menu.

- **Computer, Control Panel, Documents, Games, Music, Personal folder.** Beneath each of these headings, you'll find three options. The middle one, "Display as a menu," is extremely useful. It means that instead of simply listing the name of a folder (which is what "Display as a link" means), your Start menu sprouts a submenu listing the *contents* of that folder, as shown at bottom in Figure 1-11.

("Don't display this item," of course, removes the folder in question from your Start menu altogether. That's a good point to remember if you ever sit down at your PC and discover that, for example, the Control Panel appears to have disappeared.)

Figure 1-10:
Top: On this first screen, you can turn off the new, improved Vista two-column Start menu design to return to the single-column Classic Start menu design of Windows versions gone by. Click Customize to get to the good stuff. (The Privacy checkboxes refer to the lower-left section of the Start menu, which lists the programs you use most often, and the Recent Items submenu, which lists documents you've had open. Turn these off if you don't want to risk your supervisor coming by while you're up getting coffee, and noticing that your most recently used programs are Tetris Max, Myst IV, Tomb Raider, and Quake.)

Bottom: Here's the Customize Start Menu dialog box.

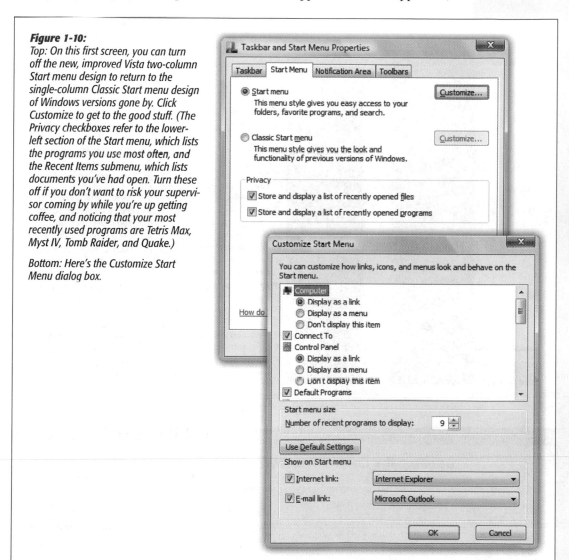

- **Connect To, Default Programs, Favorites menu, Help, Network, Printers, Run command, Search.** All of these items are things that *can* appear in the right-hand column of the Start menu. They're things that you can hide or show, at your whim. Just turn off the checkboxes of the items you consider clutter.

For example, if you've absorbed the fact that pressing the F1 key opens the Windows help program, you may as well reclaim the screen space occupied by this command in the Start menu by turning it off here.

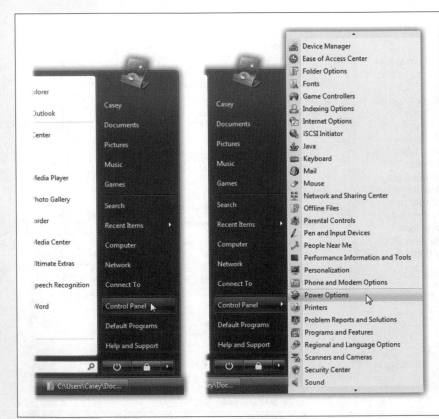

Figure 1-11:
Left: When "Display as a link" is selected for Control Panel, you can't open a particular Control Panel program directly. Instead, you must choose Start→ Control Panel, which opens the Control Panel window; now it's up to you to open the program you want.

Right: Turning on "Display as a menu" saves you a step; you now get a submenu that lists each Control Panel program. By clicking one, you can open it directly. This feature saves you the trouble of opening a folder window (such as Control Panel or Documents), double-clicking an icon inside it, and then closing the window again.

Opening the Control Panel Window When You Can't

OK, I'm with you—I turned on "Display as a menu" for the Control Panel, so now I can open any Control Panel program directly from my Start menu. Trouble is, now I can't open the Control Panel window itself! Nothing happens when I click the Start→Control Panel command. How do I open the Control Panel window?

Ah, there's a troublemaker in every class.

Open the Start menu and then *right-click* Control Panel. Choose Open from the shortcut menu. You're back in business.

Note: The Favorites menu referred to here is a list of your favorite Web sites–the same ones you've book-marked when using Internet Explorer (page 376). Thereafter, you can use the Start menu to launch Internet Explorer and travel directly to the selected site.

- **Enable context menus and dragging and dropping.** Turning on this checkbox has two benefits. First, it lets you customize your Start menu simply by dragging icons onto it, as described in the next section. Second, it lets you right-click Start-menu items, which produces a useful shortcut menu containing commands like Rename and Remove from This List. (If this checkbox is turned off, right-clicking Start menu items has no effect.)

- **Highlight newly installed programs.** Whenever you (or some techie in the building) installs a new program into the Start menu, it shows up with colored highlighting for a few days. The idea, of course, is to grab your attention and make you aware of your expanded software suite. If you could do without this kind of reminder, then just turn off this checkbox.

NOSTALGIA CORNER

Options for the Classic Start Menu

If you've turned on the Classic (single-column) Start menu as described on page 26, clicking the corresponding Customize button shown in Figure 1-10 offers its own dialog box full of options.

The Add, Remove, and Advanced buttons, for example, let you add or remove any icons you like (disks, folders, programs, documents) to the top part of the Start menu for easy access. Sort sorts them, and Clear expunges the list of recent items you've had open (presumably for privacy reasons).

Many checkboxes in the scrolling list match the options described on these pages. The rest either control which commands are listed in the menu (checkboxes beginning with the word Display) or turn certain commands into submenus (checkboxes beginning with the word Expand). This is a very handy feature when applied to the Control Panel, for example.

Finally, note the option called Use Personalized Menus. When this checkbox is turned on, Windows watches you and studies your behavior (that is, even more than usual). If it notices that you haven't been using certain Start menu commands, Windows hides them, making the menu listing shorter.

The >> button at the bottom of the All Programs menu indicates that there's more to the list than you're seeing; click it to see the full menu.

Some people find it disconcerting that Personalized Menus *changes* the Start menu frequently, making it difficult to get used to the positions of familiar items. Other people find that this feature makes the All Programs menu and its submenus easier to use, because it frees them from hunting through commands that they don't use much.

- **Open submenus when I pause on them with the mouse pointer.** When this checkbox is turned on, you don't actually have to click a submenu to view its options.

- **Search communications, Search favorites and history, Search programs.** These checkboxes let you tell Vista which items you want searched whenever you use the new Search command. Turning some of these off means faster searches and, presumably, better results, since you won't be wading through data that you're already sure doesn't contain what you're looking for.

  "Communications" means your email and chat transcripts; "favorites and history" refers to your Web bookmarks and History list in Internet Explorer; and "programs" means the names of your programs. (So what's left? All your documents, for starters.)

- **Sort All Programs menu by name.** Yep, here it is, the new Vista feature that the world's compulsives have been waiting for: a self-alphabetizing All Programs list. (All right, that was uncalled for; truth is, having the list in A-to-Z order can make life easier for just about anyone.)

Note: If you opt to turn off this option, you can always make the All Programs list snap into alphabetical order on your command, as described in the Tip on page 51.

- **Use large icons.** You don't need a book to explain *this* one. It affects the little icon that appears next to each Start menu item's name (in the left column—either the regular Start menu or the All Programs list). Bigger icons are pretty, but of course they limit the number of items the list can hold.

Below the scrolling list

Below the massive list of checkboxes, two additional controls await in the Customize dialog box:

- **Number of recent programs to display.** The number here refers to the lower-left column of the Start menu, the one that lists programs you've used most recently. By increasing this number, you make the Start menu taller—but you ensure that more of your favorite programs are listed and ready to launch. If this item is dimmed, it's because you've turned off "Store and display a list of recently opened items" (page 37).

- **Internet link, E-mail link.** Use these checkboxes and pop-up menus to specify whether or not you want your Web browser and email program listed at the top of the left-hand Start menu column—and if so, which ones.

- **Use Default Settings.** If you've fiddled these checkboxes and buttons to death and made a real mess of your Start menu, one click on this button puts everything back the way it was when it came from the mind of Microsoft.

Adding Icons to the Start Menu

Usually, when you install a new program, its installer automatically inserts the program's name and icon in your Start→All Programs menu. There may be times, however, when you want to add something to the Start menu yourself, such as a folder, document, or even a disk.

The "free" sections of the Start menu

In the following pages, you'll read several references to the "free" portions of the Start menu. These are the two areas that you, the lowly human, are allowed to modify freely—adding, removing, renaming, or sorting as you see fit:

- **The top-left section of the Start menu.** This little area lists what Microsoft calls *pinned* programs and files—things you use often enough that you want a fairly permanent list of them at your fingertips.

- **The All Programs menu.** This, of course, is the master list of programs (and anything else—documents, folders, disks—you want to see listed).

These two legal areas are highlighted back in Figure 1-3.

In other words, most of the following techniques don't work when applied to the listings in the *right* column, nor the lower-*left* quadrant of the Start menu, where Vista lists your most recently used programs.

Method 1: Drag an icon directly

Microsoft wouldn't be Microsoft if it didn't provide at least 437 different ways to do this job. Here are three of the world's favorites:

1. **Locate the icon you want to add to your Start menu.**

   It can be an application (see the box on page 51), a document, a folder you frequently access, one of the programs in your Control Panel's folder, or even your hard drive or CD-drive icon. (Adding disks and folders to the Start menu is especially handy, because it lets you dive directly into their contents without having to drill down through the Computer window.)

Tip: Adding an application name to your All Programs menu requires that you find the program *file*, as described on page 51. To do so, either use the Search command described in Chapter 3, or just dig around for it in any Explorer window. You'll find your program files in the Computer→Local Disk (C:) →Program Files folder.

---

2. **Drag it directly onto the Start button.**

   If you release the mouse now, Windows adds the name of the icon you've just dragged to the bottom of the "pinned items" list (Figure 1-12, right). You're now welcome to drag it up or down within this list.

   Alternatively, if you *keep the mouse button pressed* as you drag onto the Start button, the Start menu itself opens. As long as the button is still pressed, you can drag the new icon wherever you want among the items listed in the top-left section of the menu (Figure 1-12, left).

Note: If this drag-and-dropping business doesn't seem to work, it's because you've turned off "Enable dragging and dropping," as described in the previous section.

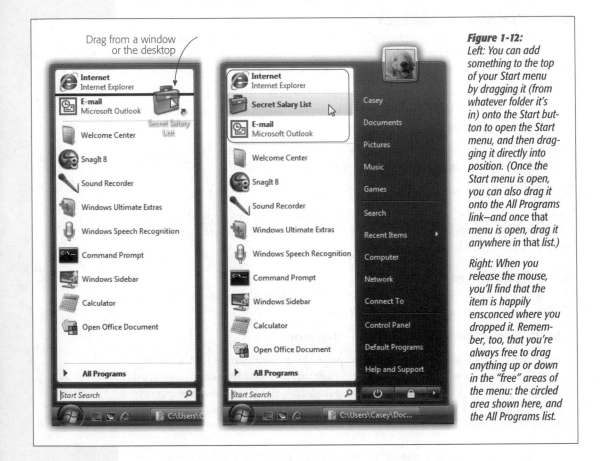

Drag from a window or the desktop

Figure 1-12:
Left: You can add something to the top of your Start menu by dragging it (from whatever folder it's in) onto the Start button to open the Start menu, and then dragging it directly into position. (Once the Start menu is open, you can also drag it onto the All Programs link—and once that menu is open, drag it anywhere in that list.)

Right: When you release the mouse, you'll find that the item is happily ensconced where you dropped it. Remember, too, that you're always free to drag anything up or down in the "free" areas of the menu: the circled area shown here, and the All Programs list.

Similarly, if you drag to the Start button and then onto the All Programs command without releasing the mouse, you can place it exactly where you want in the Start→All Programs menu. (If Vista *doesn't* let you drag it anywhere you like, it's because you've turned on "Sort All Programs menu by name" as described earlier.)

Tip: If "Sort All Programs menu by name" is *not* turned on, your All Programs list may gradually become something of a mess.

If you want to restore some order to it—specifically, alphabetical—just right-click anywhere on the open All Programs menu and choose Sort by Name from the shortcut menu. (This command doesn't appear if "Sort All Programs menu by name" is turned on.)

Method 2: Use the Add Listing wizard

If you've placed your Start menu into the single-column Classic mode, the same drag-and-drop routine works for adding new programs. But you can also use one of Microsoft's wizards for the same purpose. Right-click the Start button; from the shortcut menu, choose Properties; and use the Add, Remove, and Sort buttons.

Method 3: Use the Start Menu folders

Windows Vista builds the All Programs menu by consulting the contents of two critical folders:

- **Local Disk (C:)→ProgramData→Microsoft→Windows→Start Menu→Programs folder.** This folder contains shortcuts for programs that are available to everybody who has an account on your machine (Chapter 23).

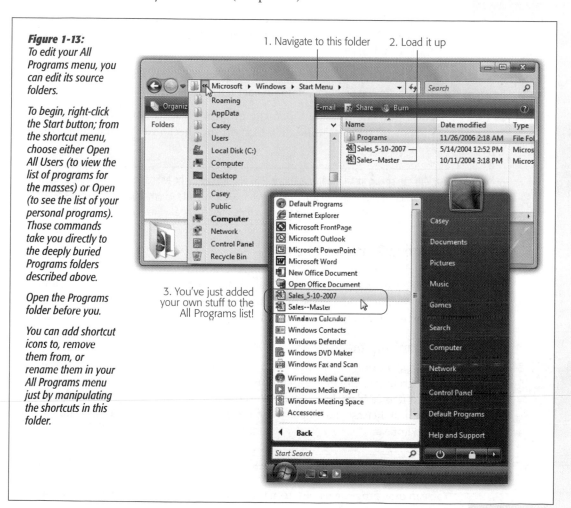

Figure 1-13:
To edit your All Programs menu, you can edit its source folders.

To begin, right-click the Start button; from the shortcut menu, choose either Open All Users (to view the list of programs for the masses) or Open (to see the list of your personal programs). Those commands take you directly to the deeply buried Programs folders described above.

Open the Programs folder before you.

You can add shortcut icons to, remove them from, or rename them in your All Programs menu just by manipulating the shortcuts in this folder.

1. Navigate to this folder   2. Load it up

3. You've just added your own stuff to the All Programs list!

• **Local Disk (C:)→Users→[your name]→AppData→Roaming→Microsoft→
Windows→Start Menu→Programs folder.** This invisible folder stashes shortcuts
for the programs that you have added to the Start menu—and they appear only
when you have logged into the machine.

Therefore, instead of the fancy icon-adding wizards and drag-and-drop schemes
described above, you may prefer to fine-tune your Start menu the low-tech way. Just
open the relevant Start Menu folder—and you don't have to do any burrowing into
invisible folders, either. See Figure 1-13.

Removing Icons from the Start Menu

When it comes time to prune an overgrown Start menu, there are three different sets
of instructions, depending on which section of the Start menu needs purging.

• **The left-side column and All Programs list.** Right-click the item you've targeted
for extinction, and then, from the shortcut menu, choose either "Remove from
this list" or "Delete."

In both cases, you're only deleting the *shortcut* that appears on the menu. Deleting
items from the Start menu doesn't actually uninstall any software.

• **The right-side column.** Open the Properties→Customize dialog box for the
Start menu (page 44), and then turn off the checkboxes for the items you want
expunged.

Tip: You can spawn instant shortcuts (page 145) of anything in the left-hand column of the Start menu by
dragging them off the menu—onto the desktop, for example. That's a handy tactic if you want a desktop icon
for something you use often, so you don't even have to open the Start menu to get at it.

Renaming Start-Menu Items

Although few people realize it, you can rename anything in the Start menu's left side.
Click the Start menu to open it, right-click the command you want to rename, and
choose Rename from the shortcut menu. The name of the command sprouts a little
editing box. Type the new name and then press Enter.

Reorganizing the Start Menu

To change the order of listings in the "free" portions of the Start menu, including the
All Programs list, just drag the commands up and down the lists as you see fit. As you
drag an item, a black line appears to show you the resulting location of your dragging action. Release the mouse when the black line is where you want the relocated
icon to appear.

Tip: If you change your mind while you're dragging, press the Esc key to leave everything as it was.

You can drag program names from the lower-left section of the Start menu, too—but
only into one of the "free" areas.

Tip: A reminder: If you can't seem to drag program names around in the All Programs list, it's probably because you've told Vista to auto-alphabetize this list (page 48).

Add folders to hold submenus

As noted earlier, some of the items in the All Programs list are actually folders. For example, clicking Games reveals a submenu that lists all the games that come with Windows (see Figure 1-14).

In past Windows versions, clicking such folders made them sprout *submenus,* some of which had submenus of their own, and on and on. In Vista, folders no longer expand horizontally that way—they expand vertically, as shown in Figure 1-14.

Figure 1-14:
Some Programs-menu items have submenu folders and sub-submenu folders. As you move through the layers, you're performing an action known as "drilling down." You'll see this phrase often in manuals and computer books—for example, "Drill down to the Calculator to crunch a few quick numbers."

It's worthwhile to know that you can create Programs-menu folders of your own and stock them with whatever icons you like. For instance, you may want to create a folder for CD-ROM–based games, eliminating those long lists from the All Programs menu.

To add a folder to the All Programs menu, follow these steps:

1. **Right-click the Start menu button. From the shortcut menu, choose Explore.**

   The subfolders you are about to create in the All Programs menu will show up only when *you* are logged on. (If you want to make a change that affects *everybody* with an account on this computer, choose Explore All Users from the shortcut menu instead.)

   In any case, the Start Menu Explorer window appears.

2. **Open the Programs folder.**

   Its contents are arrayed before you, as shown in Figure 1-15.

Figure 1-15:
Notice that some of the items in Programs have folder icons; these are the folders that hold submenus. If you click Programs (in the left pane) before creating the new folder, you'll create a folder within the body of the All Programs list. To add a folder whose name will appear above the line in the All Programs menu, click Start Menu (in the left pane) before creating a new folder.

3. **Choose Organize→New Folder.**

Or, if your right mouse button hasn't been getting enough exercise, right-click a blank spot in the right pane, and then choose New→Folder from the shortcut menu.

4. **When the new folder appears, type a folder name and then press Enter.**

Close the window, if you like.

Tip: You can even create folders *within* folders in your Start→All Programs menu. Just double-click to open any of the existing folders in the Programs folder, and then repeat from step 3.

Your new folder appears in the folders list of the Start→All Programs menu, already sorted into alphabetical order.

Now you can put your favorite file, folder, disk, or application icons *into* this new folder. To do so, drag an icon onto the Start→All Programs menu, and then, without releasing the mouse, onto the All Programs link, and then into the new folder/submenu you created.

Explorer, Windows, and the Taskbar

Windows got its name from the rectangles on the screen—the windows—where every computer activity takes place. You look at a Web page in a window, type into a window, read email in a window, and look at lists of files in a window. But as you create more files, stash them in more folders, and open more programs, it's easy to wind up paralyzed before a screen awash with cluttered, overlapping rectangles.

Fortunately, Windows has always offered icons, buttons, and other inventions to help you keep these windows under control—and Windows Vista positively crawls with them.

Universal Window Controls
All Versions

There are two categories of windows in Windows:

- **Explorer windows.** *Windows Explorer* is Microsoft's name for the desktop world of folders and icons. It's the home-base program that greets you when you first turn on the PC. When you double-click a folder or disk icon on your desktop, what opens is an Explorer window. This is where you organize your files and programs.

- **Application windows.** These are the windows where you do your work—in Word or Internet Explorer, for example.

All of these windows have certain parts in common, but as Figure 2-1 shows, a lot has changed since the last version of Windows you probably used. If you're feeling disoriented, firmly grasp a nearby stationary object and read the following breakdown.

Here are the controls that appear on almost every window, whether in an application or Explorer:

- **Title bar.** It's really not much of a title bar anymore, since the window's *title* no longer appears here (Figure 2-1). But this big fat top strip is still a giant handle that you can use to drag a window around.

Tip: If you double-click the title bar area, you *maximize* the window, making it expand to fill your entire screen exactly as though you had clicked the Maximize button described below. Double-click the title bar again to restore the window to its original size.

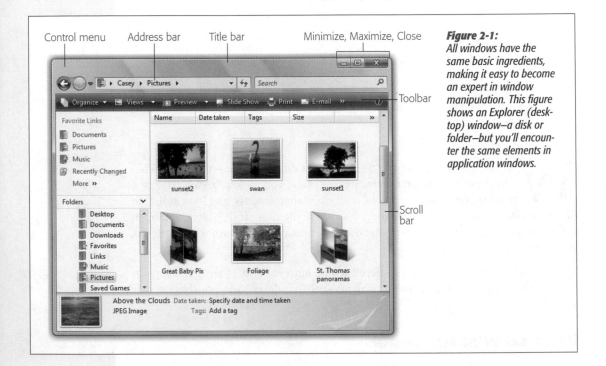

Control menu   Address bar   Title bar   Minimize, Maximize, Close

Toolbar

Scroll bar

Figure 2-1:
All windows have the same basic ingredients, making it easy to become an expert in window manipulation. This figure shows an Explorer (desktop) window—a disk or folder—but you'll encounter the same elements in application windows.

- **Window edges.** Now they're fatter, making them easier to grab with your mouse. And on most computers, window edges are also transparent, revealing a slightly blurry image of what's underneath. (That's the Aero cosmetic overhaul at work; see page 22.)

  Truth to tell, being able to see what's underneath the edges of your window (sort of) doesn't really offer any particular productivity advantage. Sure does look cool, though.

  In any case, you can change the size of a window by dragging any edge except the top. Position your cursor over any border until it turns into a double-headed arrow. Then drag inward or outward to reshape the window. (To resize a full-screen window, click the Restore Down button first.)

Tip: You can resize a window in both dimensions at once just by dragging one of its corners. Sometimes diagonally striped ribs appear at the lower-right corner, sometimes not; in either case, all *four* corners work the same way.

- **Minimize, Maximize, [Restore Down].** These three window-control buttons, which appear at the top of every Windows window, are much bigger in Vista than before, which is supposed to make them easier to click. These buttons cycle a window among its three modes—minimized, maximized, and restored—as described on page 86.

- **Close button.** Click the X button to close the window. *Keyboard shortcut:* Press Alt+F4.

Tip: Isn't it cool how the Minimize, Maximize, and Close buttons "light up" when your cursor passes over them?

Actually, that's not just a gimmick; it's a cue that lets you know when the button is clickable. You might not otherwise realize, for example, that you can close, minimize, or maximize a *background* window without first bringing it forward. But when the background window's Close box beams bright red, you'll know.

- **Scroll bar.** A scroll bar appears on the right side or bottom of the window if the window isn't large enough to show all its contents (as described in the box on page 13).

- **Control menu.** Until Windows Vista came along, there was a tiny icon in the upper-left corner of every Explorer window (Figure 2-1). It was actually a menu containing commands for sizing, moving, and closing the window.

  There are three super-weird nuggets of wisdom to impart about the Control icon in Vista. First, *it's invisible.* There's no icon to let you know it's there. But if you click where it's supposed to be, the menu opens. It's clearly intended for use only by the initiated who pass on the secret from generation to generation.

  Second, one of the Control menu's commands is Move. It turns your cursor into a four-headed arrow; at this point, you can move the window by dragging *any* part of it, even the middle. (And why bother, since you can always just drag the top edge of a window to move it? Because sometimes, windows get dragged *past* the top of your screen. You can hit Alt+Space to open the Control menu, type M to trigger the Move command, and then drag *any* visible part of the window back onto the screen.)

  Finally, it's worth noting that you can open the identical menu by right-clicking *anywhere* on the title bar.

Tip: You can double-click the Control menu to close a window.

Explorer Window Controls

All Versions

When you're working at the desktop—that is, opening Explorer windows—you'll find a few additional controls dotting the edges. Again, they're quite a bit different from the controls of Windows XP and its predecessors.

Address Bar

In a Web browser, the Address bar is where you type the addresses of the Web sites you want to visit. In an Explorer window, the Address bar is more of a "breadcrumbs bar" (a shout out to Hansel and Gretel fans). That is, it now shows the path you've taken—folders you burrowed through—to arrive where you are now (Figure 2-2).

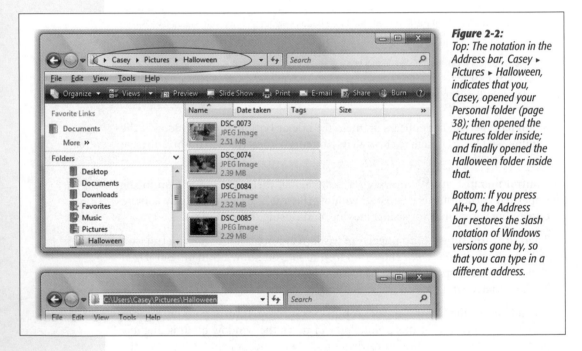

Figure 2-2:
Top: The notation in the Address bar, Casey ▸ Pictures ▸ Halloween, indicates that you, Casey, opened your Personal folder (page 38); then opened the Pictures folder inside; and finally opened the Halloween folder inside that.

Bottom: If you press Alt+D, the Address bar restores the slash notation of Windows versions gone by, so that you can type in a different address.

There are three especially cool things about the new Vista Address bar:

- **It's much easier to read.** Those ▸ little ▸ triangles are clearer separators of folder names than the older\slash\notation. And instead of drive letters like C:, you see the drive *names*.

Tip: If the succession of nested folders' names is too long to fit the window, then a tiny << icon appears at the left end of the address. Click it to reveal a pop-up menu showing, from last to first, the other folders you've had to burrow through to get here.

(The pop-up menu items that are *supposed* to be here—the list of recent places—appears in the same list, below a divider line.)

- **It's clickable.** You can click any breadcrumb to open the corresponding folder. For example, if you're viewing the Casey ▸ Pictures ▸ Halloween, you can click the *word* Pictures to backtrack to the Pictures folder.

- **You can still edit it.** The Address bar of old was still a powerful tool, because you could type in a folder address directly (using the slash notation).

  Actually, you still can. You can "open" the Address bar for editing in any of five different ways. (1) Press Alt+D. (2) Click the tiny icon to the left of the address. (3) Click any blank spot. (4) Right-click anywhere in the address; (5) From the shortcut menu, choose Edit Address.

  In each case, the Address bar changes to reveal the old-style slash notation, ready for editing (Figure 2-2, bottom).

Tip: After you've had a good look, press Esc to restore the ▸ notation.

Components of the Address bar

On top of all that, the Address bar houses a few additional doodads that make it easy for you to jump around on your hard drive (Figure 2-3):

- **Back, Forward.** Just as in a Web browser, the Back button opens whatever window you opened just before this one. Once you've used the Back button, you can then use the Forward button to return to the window where you started. *Keyboard shortcuts:* Alt+left arrow, Alt+right arrow.

- **Recent pages list.** Click the ▾ (to the left of the address box) to see a list of folders you've had open recently; it's like a multilevel Back button.

- **Recent folders list.** Click the ▾ at the *right* end of the address box to see a pop-up menu listing addresses you've recently typed.

- **Contents list.** This one takes some explaining, but for efficiency nuts, it's a gift from the gods.

  It turns out that the little ▸ next to each breadcrumb (folder name) is actually a pop-up menu. Click it to see what's *in* the folder name to its left.

  How is this useful? Suppose you're viewing the contents of the USA ▸ Florida ▸ Miami folder, but you decide that the folder you're looking for is actually in the USA ▸ California folder. Do you have to click the Back button, retracing your steps to the USA folder, only to then walk back down a different branch of the folder tree? No, you don't. You just click the ▸ that's next to the USA folder's name and choose California from the list.

- **Refresh (double swirling arrows button).** If you suspect that the window contents aren't up to date (for example, that maybe somebody has just dropped something new into it from across the network), click this button, or press F5, to make Vista update the display.

• **Search box.** Type a search phrase into this box to find what you're looking for *within this window.* Page 119 has the details.

What to type into the Address bar

When you click the tiny folder icon at the left end of the Address bar (or press Alt+D), the triangle ▸ notation changes to the slash\notation, meaning that you can edit the address. At this point, the Address bar is like the little opening that lets you speak to the driver of a New York City taxi; you tell it where you want to go. Here's what you can type there (press Enter afterward):

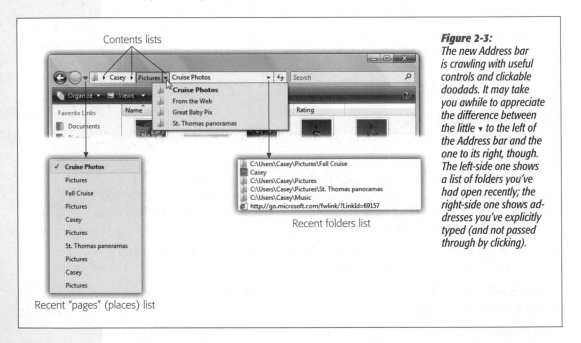

Contents lists

Recent folders list

Recent "pages" (places) list

Figure 2-3:
The new Address bar is crawling with useful controls and clickable doodads. It may take you awhile to appreciate the difference between the little ▾ to the left of the Address bar and the one to its right, though. The left-side one shows a list of folders you've had open recently; the right-side one shows addresses you've explicitly typed (and not passed through by clicking).

• **A Web address.** You can leave off the *http://* portion. Just type the body of the Web address, such as *www.sony.com,* into this strip. When you press Enter (or click the → button, called the Go button), Internet Explorer opens to the Web page you specified.

Tip: If you press Ctrl+Enter instead of just Enter, you can surround whatever you've just typed into the Address bar with *http://www.* and *.com.* See Chapter 11 for even more address shortcuts along these lines.

• **A search phrase.** If you type some text into this strip that isn't obviously a Web address, Windows assumes that you're telling it, "Go online and search for this phrase." From here, it works exactly as though you've used the Internet search feature described on page 371.

• **A folder name.** You can also type one of several important folder names into this strip, such as *Computer, Documents, Music,* and so on. When you press Enter, that particular folder window opens.

Tip: This window has autocomplete. That is, if you type *pi* and then press Tab, the Address bar will complete the word *Pictures* for you. (If it guesses wrong, press Tab again.)

- **A program or path name.** In this regard, the Address bar works just like the Run command described on page 40.

In each case, as soon as you begin to type, a pop-up list of recently visited Web sites, files, or folders appears below the Address bar. Windows Vista is trying to save you some typing. If you see what you're looking for, click it with the mouse, or press the down arrow key to highlight the one you want and then press Enter.

The Task Toolbar

See the colored strip (Organize, Views…) that appears just below the Address bar? That's the new *task toolbar*. It's something like a menu bar, in that some of the words on it (including Organize and Views) are actually menus, yet also something like the task pane of Windows XP, in that its buttons change from window to window. In a folder that contains pictures, you'll see buttons here like Slide Show and E-mail; in a folder that contains music files, the buttons might say Play All and Burn.

Later in this chapter, you'll meet some of the individual commands in the task toolbar.

Note: You can't hide the task toolbar.

Column Headings

Just below the task toolbar, every Explorer window also has another horizontal strip you can't hide: a row of column headings like Name, Date Modified, Size, and so on. These, it turns out, are important tools in sorting and grouping the icons, as described on page 77.

Optional Window Panes

All Versions

Most Explorer windows have some basic informational stuff across the top: the Address bar and the task toolbar, at the very least.

But that's just the beginning. As shown in Figure 2-4, the Organize menu on the task toolbar lets you hide or show as many as four *other* strips of information. Turning them all on at once may make your windows feel a bit claustrophobic, but at least you'll know absolutely everything there is to know about your files and folders.

The trick is to choose a pane name from the Organize→Layout command, as shown in Figure 2-4. Here are the options you'll find there.

Tip: You can adjust the size of any pane by dragging the dividing line that separates it from the main window. (You'll know when you've got the right spot when your cursor turns into a double-headed arrow.)

Search Pane

As shown in Figure 2-1, the Search pane appears across the top of the window, just below the Address bar. Of course, the Search *box* already appears in every Explorer window, next to the Address bar—so why do you need a Search *pane* as well?

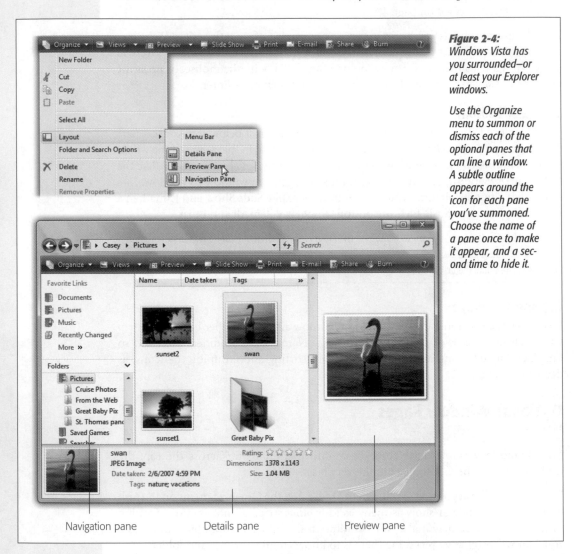

Figure 2-4:
Windows Vista has you surrounded—or at least your Explorer windows.

Use the Organize menu to summon or dismiss each of the optional panes that can line a window. A subtle outline appears around the icon for each pane you've summoned. Choose the name of a pane once to make it appear, and a second time to hide it.

Navigation pane   Details pane   Preview pane

Because the pane gives you a lot more control. It lets you specify more elaborate search criteria, including *where* you want Windows to look. Details are on page 120.

Details Pane

This strip appears at the *bottom* of the window, and it can be extremely useful. It reveals all kinds of information about whatever icon you've clicked in the main part of the window: its size, date, type, and so on.

It's the sort of information that, in previous versions of Windows, you wouldn't be able to see without right-clicking and opening the Properties window.

Some examples:

- For a music file, the Details pane reveals the song's duration, band and album names, genre, the star rating you've provided, and so on.

- For a disk icon, you get statistics about its formatting scheme, capacity, and how much of it is full.

- For a Microsoft Office document, you see when it was created and modified, how many pages it has, who wrote it, and so on.

- If *nothing* is selected, you get information about the open window itself: namely, how many items are in it.

- If you select several icons at once, this pane shows you the sum of their file sizes—a great feature when you're burning a CD, for example, and don't want to exceed the 650 MB limit. You also see the *range* of dates when they were created and modified.

What's especially intriguing is that you can *edit* many of these details, as described on page 70.

Tip: To hide the Details pane, you *could* return to the Organize→Layout command and choose the pane's name a second time. But it's faster to just right-click a blank spot in the pane (usually the lower-right corner works well) and, from the shortcut menu, choose Hide Details Pane.

Preview Pane

The Preview pane appears at the *right* side of the window. That's right: Microsoft has now invented information strips that wrap all four sides of a window.

NOSTALGIA CORNER

Would You Like to See the Menu Bar?

You may have noticed already that in Vista, there's something dramatically different about the menu bar (File, Edit, View and so on): it's gone. Microsoft decided that you'd rather have a little extra space to see your icons.

Fortunately, you can bring it back, in three ways.

Temporarily. Press the Alt key or the F10 key. Presto! The traditional menu bar reappears. You even get to see the classic one-letter underlines that tell you what letter keys you can type to operate the menus without the mouse.

Permanently, all windows. On the Task toolbar, choose Organize→Layout→Menu Bar. The traditional menu bar appears, right above the task toolbar. There it will stay forever, in all Explorer windows, or at least until you turn it off using the same command.

Permanently, all windows (alternate method). Here's another trick that achieves the same thing. Choose Start→Control Panel. Click Classic View, then Folder Options, then the View tab. Turn on "Always show menus," and then click OK.

Anyway, the Preview pane can be handy when you're examining pictures, text files, Office documents, PDF files, sounds, and movies. As you click each icon, you see a magnified thumbnail version of what's actually *in* that document. As Figure 2-5 demonstrates, a controller lets you play sounds and movies right there in the Explorer window, without having to fire up Windows Media Player. (Cool.)

Figure 2-5:
In many windows, the Preview pane can get in the way, because it shrinks the useful window space without giving you much useful information. But when you're browsing movies or sound files, it's awesome; it lets you play the music or the movie right in place, right in the window, without having to open up a playback program.

Navigation Pane

The Navigation pane has two halves: Favorite Links (the top part) and Folders (the bottom part).

Favorite Links list

The primary purpose of this area is to list *places* to which you want quick access. Since this pane will be waiting in every Explorer window you open, listing your favorite folders here can save you a lot of repetitive folder-burrowing. One click on a folder name opens the corresponding window. For example, click the Pictures icon to view the contents of your Pictures folder in the main part of the window (Figure 2-6).

This list also offers icons for Recently Changed and Searches. These links refer to *saved searches.* You can read more about what they are and how they were created on page 123. For now, it's enough to know that Recently Changed summons a quick list of everything on your hard drive that you've modified in the last 30 days, and Searches brings up a window filled with similar canned searches: Recent Documents, Recent E-mail, Shared By Me, and so on.

The beauty of this parking lot for containers is that it's so easy to set up with *your* favorite places. For example:

- **Remove** an icon by dragging it out of the window entirely and onto the Recycle Bin icon; it vanishes from the list. (Of course, you haven't actually removed anything from your *PC*; you've just unhitched its alias from the Navigation pane.)

- **Rearrange** the icons by dragging them up or down in the list. Release the mouse when the thick black horizontal line lies in the desired new location.

Tip: You can also sort this list alphabetically. Right-click anywhere in the list; from the shortcut menu, choose Sort by Name.

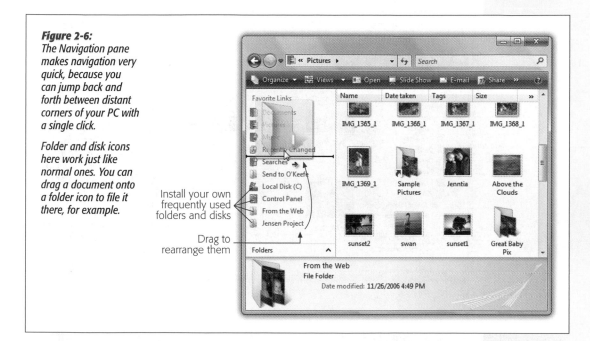

Figure 2-6:
The Navigation pane makes navigation very quick, because you can jump back and forth between distant corners of your PC with a single click.

Folder and disk icons here work just like normal ones. You can drag a document onto a folder icon to file it there, for example.

Install your own frequently used folders and disks

Drag to rearrange them

- **Install a new disk or folder icon** by dragging it off of your desktop (or out of a window) into any spot in the list.

- **Adjust the width** of the pane by dragging the vertical divider bar right or left.

Tip: If you drag carefully, you can position the divider bar *just* to the right of the disk and folder icons, thereby hiding their names. Some people find it a tidier look; you can always identify the folder names by pointing to them without clicking.

Folders list

The bottom of the Navigation pane, if you've chosen to view it (Figure 2-7), is a hierarchical folder "tree" that shows the hierarchy of your entire computer. In essence, this view shows every folder on the machine at once. It lets you burrow very deeply into your hard drive's nest of folders without ever losing your bearings.

Note: In previous editions of Windows, summoning this panel was a special trick used by power users. There were all kinds of shortcuts you could use to open it, like Shift-double-clicking a disk or folder icon, or pressing ⊞+E. All those tricks do in Vista is open up the Navigation pane if you've closed it. Microsoft intends for folder-tree mode to be the standard Windows look.

As you can see, this hierarchical list displays *only* disks and folders; the main window displays the contents (folders *and* files) of whatever disk or folder you click.

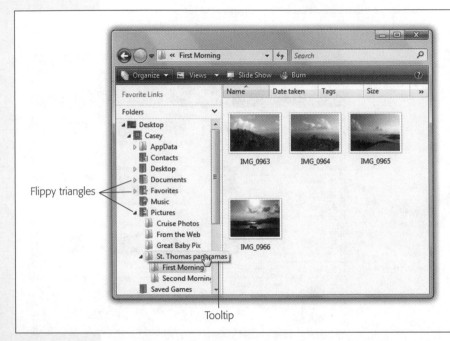

Flippy triangles

Tooltip

Figure 2-7:
When you click a disk or folder in the Folders hierarchy, the main window displays its contents, including files and folders. Double-click to expand a disk or folder, opening a new, indented list of what's inside it; double-click again to collapse the folder list again.

At deeper levels of indentation, you may not be able to read an icon's full name. Point to it without clicking to see an identifying tooltip.

POWER USERS' CLINIC

Folder-List Keyboard Shortcuts

If you arrive home one day to discover that your mouse has been stolen, or if you simply like using the keyboard, you'll enjoy the shortcuts that work in the Explorer window:

F6 or Tab cycles the "focus" (highlighting) among the different parts of the window: Favorite Links, Folders, main window.

Backspace highlights the "parent" disk or folder of whatever is highlighted.

Alt-double-clicking an icon opens the Properties window

for that icon. (It shows the same sort of information you'd find in the Details pane.)

Alt+left arrow key opens the previously viewed window, as though you've clicked the Back button in a browser. (Once you've used Alt+left arrow, you can press Alt+right arrow key to move *forward* through your recent open windows.)

You can also press the letter keys to highlight a folder or file that begins with that letter, or the up and down arrow keys to "walk" up and down the list.

When you double-click a folder or disk name (or single-click the flippy triangle next to it), you turn the list view into an outline; the contents of the folder appear in an indented list, as shown in Figure 2-7. Double-click again, or click the flippy triangle again, to collapse the folder listing.

By selectively expanding folders like this, you can, in effect, peer inside two or more folders simultaneously, all within the single Folders list. You can move files around by dragging them onto the tiny folder icons, too.

If you expand folders within folders to a sufficient level, the indentation may push the folder names so far to the right that you can't read them. You can remedy this problem either by making the pane wider (Figure 2-8), or by pointing to a folder whose name is being chopped off. Vista temporarily displays its entire name.

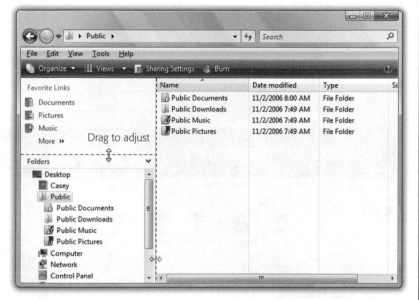

Figure 2-8:
If you don't already see the Folders tree, open it by clicking the ^ button at the bottom of the Navigation pane. You can then adjust its height or width by dragging the top or right edges, as shown here.

Tags, Metadata, and Properties
All Versions

See all that information in the Details pane—Date, Size, Title, and so on? It's known by geeks as *metadata* (Greek for "data about data").

Oddly (and usefully) enough, you can actually edit some of this stuff. (See Figure 2-9.) For a document, for example, you can edit the Authors, Comments, Title, Categories, Status, and others. For an MP3 music file, the Artists, Albums, Genre, and Year can be changed. For a photo, you can edit the Date Taken, Title, and Author.

Some of the metadata is off limits. For example, you can't edit the Date Created or Date Modified info. (Sorry, defense attorneys of the world.) But you *can* edit the star

ratings for music or pictures; in the row of five stars, click the rating star you want.
Click the third star to give a song a 3, for example.

Most usefully of all, you can edit the Tags box for *any* kind of icon. A tag is just a keyword. It can be anything you want: McDuffy Proposal, Old Junk, Back Me Up—anything. Later, you'll be able to round up everything on your computer with a certain
tag, all in a single window, even though they physically reside in different folders.

You'll encounter tags in plenty of other places in Vista—and in this book, especially
when it comes to searching photos, and music.

Note: Weirdly, you can't add tags or ratings to BMP, PNG, AVI, or MPG files.

Many of the boxes here offer autocompletion, meaning Vista proposes (in a pop-up
menu) finishing a name or text tidbit for you if it recognizes what you've started to
type.

Tip: You can tag a bunch of icons at once. Just highlight them all (page 136) and then change the corresponding detail in the Details pane *once.* This is a great trick for applying a tag or star rating to a mass of
files quickly.

Figure 2-9:
*You can edit a lot
of the background
information that
Windows stores
about each icon on
your PC. Click the
information you
want to change; if a
text-editing box ap-
pears, you've hit pay
dirt. Type away, and
then press Enter (or
click the Save button
at the lower-right
corner of the dialog
box).*

Properties

The Details pane shows some of the most important details about a file. But believe
it or not, Windows actually stores even *more* behind-the-scenes metadata about every
icon. If you really want to see the entire dossier for an icon, open its Properties dialog
box using one of these tactics:

- Right-click it. From the shortcut menu, choose Properties.

- Alt-double-click it.

Either way, the Properties dialog box appears. It's a lot like the one in previous versions of Windows, in that it displays the file's name, location, size, and so on. But in Vista, it also bears a scrolling Details tab that's absolutely teeming with metadata details (Figure 2-10).

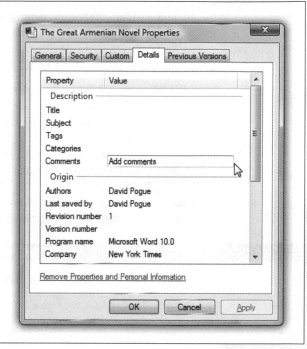

Figure 2-10:
If Windows knows anything about an icon, it's in here. Scroll, scroll, and scroll some more to find the tidbit you want to see—or to edit. As with the Details pane, many of these text morsels are editable.

Icon and List Views
All Versions

Windows' windows look just fine straight from the factory; the edges are straight, and the text is perfectly legible. Still, if you're going to stare at this computer screen for half of your waking hours, you may as well investigate some of the ways these windows can be enhanced for better looks and greater efficiency.

For starters, you can view the files and folders in an Explorer window in either of two ways: as icons (of any size) or as a list (in several formats). Figure 2-11 shows some of your options.

Every window remembers its view settings independently. You might prefer to look over your Documents folder in list view (because it's crammed with files and folders), but you may prefer to view the Pictures folder in icon view, where the icons depict miniatures of the actual photos.

To switch a window from one view to another, you have three options, all of which involve the Views pop-up menu shown in Figure 2-11:

- **Click the Views button.** With each click, the window switches to the next view in this sequence: List, Details, Tiles, Large Icons.

- **Use the Views pop-up menu.** If you click the ▾ triangle next to the word Views, the menu opens, listing Extra Large Icons, Large Icons, Small Icons, List, and so on. Choose the option you want. (They're described below.)

- **Use the slider.** The Views menu, once opened, also contains a strange little slider down the left side. It's designed to let Vista's graphics software show off a little. The slider makes the icons shrink or grow freely, scaling them to sizes that fall *between* the canned Extra Large, Large, Medium, and Small choices.

  What's so strange about the slider is that part way down its track, it stops adjusting icon sizes and turns into a selector switch for the last three options in the menu: List, Details, or Tiles. Try it—you'll see.

Tip: If your mouse has a scroll wheel on top, you've got yourself a handy shortcut for manipulating the icon sizes. Just turn that wheel while pressing your Ctrl key.

- **Icon View.** In an icon view, every file, folder, and disk is represented by a small picture—an *icon*. This humble image, a visual representation of electronic bits

---

GEM IN THE ROUGH

How to Shed Your Metadata's Skin

At the bottom of the Properties dialog box is a peculiarly worded link: "Remove Properties and Personal Information."

This is a privacy feature. What that means is, "Clean away all the metadata I've added myself, like author names, tag keywords, and other insights into my own work routine."

Microsoft's thinking here is that you might not want other people who encounter this document (as an email attachment, for example) to have such a sweeping insight into the minutiae of your own work routine.

When you click this link, the Remove Properties dialog box appears, offering you a scrolling list of checkboxes: Title, Rating, Tags, Com-

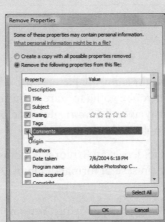

ments, and lots and lots of others.

You can proceed in either of two ways. If you turn on "Create a copy with all possible properties removed," then *all* of the metadata that's possible to erase (everything but things like file type, name, and so on) will be stripped away. When you click OK, Windows instantly creates a duplicate of the file (with the word Copy tacked onto its name), ready for distribution to the masses in its clean form. (The original is left untouched.)

If you choose "Remove the following properties from this file" instead, you can specify exactly *which* file details you want erased from the original. (Turn on the appropriate checkboxes.)

---

and bytes, is the cornerstone of the entire Windows religion. (Maybe that's why it's called an icon.)

What's especially cool is that if you make your icons big enough, *folder* icons appear turned 90 degrees. Now, in real life, setting filing folders onto a desk that way would be idiotic; everything inside would tumble out in a chaotic mess. But in Windows-land, the icons within a folder remain exactly where they are. Better yet, they peek out just enough so that you can see them. In the Music folder, for example, a singer's folder shows the first album cover within; a folder full of PowerPoint presentations shows the first slide or two; and so on. (You can see the effect in Figure 2-11.)

Note: Because you can now view icons at any size you like, Microsoft has done away with the Thumbnails and Filmstrip views.

Figure 2-11:
The Views pop-up menu is a little weird; it actually has two columns. At right, it displays the preset view options for the files and folders in a window. At left, a slider adjusts icon sizes to any incremental degree of scaling–at least until it reaches the bottom part of its track.

In any case, here's a survey of the window views in Vista. From top left: Icon view (small), Icon view (large), List view, Details view, and Tiles view. List and Details views are great for windows with lots of files.

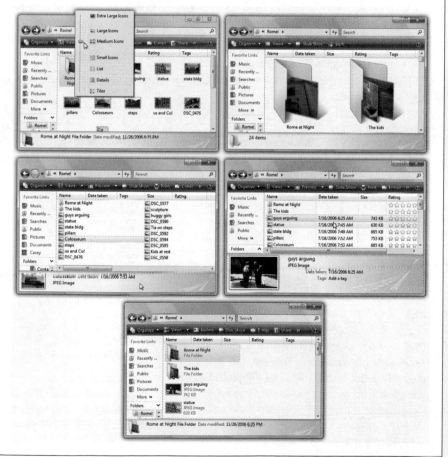

- **Tiles view.** Your icons appear at standard size, with name and file details just to the *right*.

- **List view** packs, by far, the most files into the space of a window; each file has a tiny icon to its left, and the list of files wraps around into as many columns as necessary to maximize the window's available space.

- **Details view** is the same as List view, except that it presents only a single column. It's a table, really; additional columns reveal the size, icon type, modification date, rating, and other information.

POWER USERS' CLINIC

Secrets of the Details-View Columns

In windows that contain a lot of icons, Details view is a powerful weapon in the battle against chaos. Better yet, *you* get to decide how wide the columns should be, which of them should appear, and in what order. Here are the details on Details:

Add or remove columns. Right-click any column heading (like Name or Size). When the shortcut menu opens, you'll see that checkmarks appear next to the visible columns: Name, Date Modified, Size, and so on. Choose a column's name to make it appear or disappear.

But don't think that you're stuck with that handful of common columns. If you click More in the shortcut menu, you open the Choose Details dialog box, which lists *over 200 more* column types, most of which are useful only in certain circumstances: Album Artist (for music files), Copyright, Date Taken, Exposure Time (for photos), Nickname (for people), Video Compression (for movies), and on and on. To make one of these columns appear, turn on its checkbox and then click OK; by the time you're done, your Explorer window can look like a veritable spreadsheet of information.

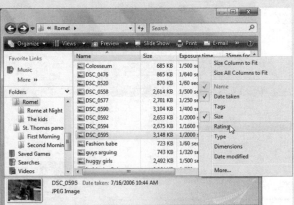

Rearrange the columns. You can rearrange your Details columns just by dragging their gray column headers horizontally. (You can even drag the Name column out of first position.) As you drag, a tiny bold divider line in the column-heading area snaps into place to show where it thinks you intend to drop the column you're dragging.

Change column widths. If some text in a column is too long to fit, Windows displays an ellipsis (...) after the first few letters of each word. In that case, here's a great trick: Carefully position your cursor at the right edge of the column's header (Name, Size, or whatever—even to the right of the ▾ triangle). When the cursor sprouts horizontal arrows from each side, double-click the divider line to make the column adjust *itself,* fitting automatically to accommodate the longest item in the column.

If you'd rather adjust the column width manually, you can do so. Instead of double-clicking the dividing line between two column headings, just drag horizontally. Doing so makes the column to the *left* of your cursor wider or narrower.

Sorting, Grouping, Stacking, and Filtering
All Versions

Until Vista came along, you could sort the files in a window into an alphabetical or chronological list. But that is *so* 2005.

In Windows Vista, sorting is only one way to impose order on your teeming icons. Now there's grouping, stacking, and filtering—new approaches to organizing the stuff in a window.

All of this may get confusing, because every new feature means new controls and new window clutter. But in the end, mastering the stacking-and-grouping bit can pay off in time savings.

As Figure 2-12 shows, the key to sorting, grouping, stacking, and filtering is the pop-up menus hiding within the column headings.

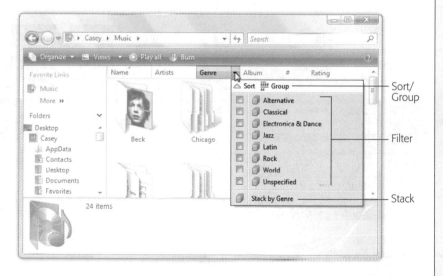

Figure 2-12:
This menu looks simple, but is actually complicated. Or maybe the other way around. In any case, this is the menu that sprouts out of each column heading (Name, Size, and so on). In the following pages, you can read about these controls; the top-to-bottom structure (sort/group at the top, filtering controls in the middle, then the Stack command) is always the same.

Sorting Files

See the column headings at the top of every Explorer window (Name, Date modified, and so on)?

In Details view, they make perfect sense; they're labels for the columns of information. But what the heck are they doing there in Icon view and List view? Your files and folders aren't even lined up beneath those headings!

It turns out that these headings are far more important in Windows Vista than they were before. They're now your controls for sorting the icons—even in icon view. These headings aren't just signposts; they're also buttons. Click Name for alphabetical order, "Date modified" for chronological order, Size to view largest files at the top, and so on (Figure 2-13).

It's especially important to note the tiny, dark triangle in the heading you've most recently clicked. It shows you *which way* the list is being sorted. When the triangle

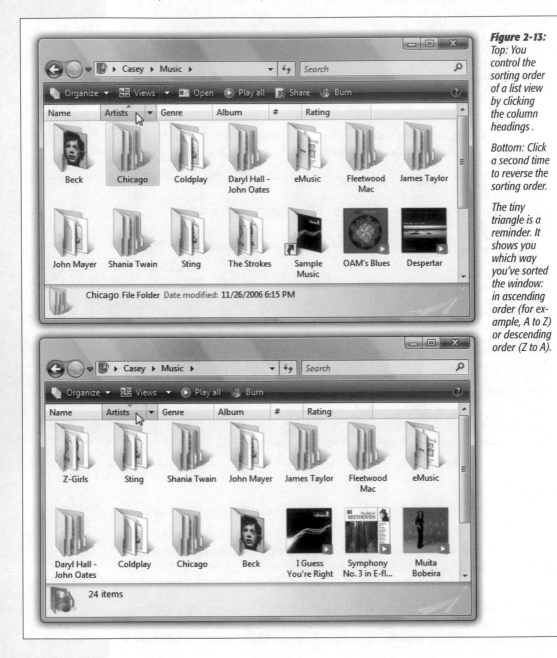

Figure 2-13:
Top: You control the sorting order of a list view by clicking the column headings .

Bottom: Click a second time to reverse the sorting order.

The tiny triangle is a reminder. It shows you which way you've sorted the window: in ascending order (for example, A to Z) or descending order (Z to A).

points upward, oldest files, smallest files, or files whose names begin with numbers (or the letter A) appear at the top of the list, depending on which sorting criterion you have selected.

Tip: It may help you to remember that when the *smallest* portion of the triangle is at the top, the *smallest* files are listed first when viewed in size order.

To reverse the sorting order, just click the column heading a second time. Now newest files, largest files, or files whose names start with the letter Z appear at the top of the list. The tiny triangle turns upside-down.

Note: Within each window, Windows groups *folders* separately from *files.* They get sorted, too, but within their own little folder ghetto.

As you already know, different folders come set up with different columns; the box on page 74 shows you how to specify different column headings. But the point is that you can now sort what's in a window according to all kinds of wild new criteria. You can sort files in your Music folder by Album Title, files in your Pictures folder by Date Taken, and all those Microsoft Office files in your Documents folder by the names of the poor slobs who typed them up.

Grouping

When you *group* the icons in a window, they clump together by type, like kids in a high-school cafeteria. In this case, though, the clumping criteria is up to you. You can view your documents grouped by size, your photos grouped by the date they were taken, your music files grouped by band, and so on. As Figure 2-14 shows, Windows identifies each group with its own headline, making the window look like an index. It's an inspired tool that makes it easier to hunt down specific icons in crowded folders.

To group a window, start by opening the pop-up menu next to the *column heading* that represents the criterion you want: size, date, album, author, whatever (Figure 2-14).

Note: Grouping isn't available in List view—only Icon and Detail views.

Stacking

Stacking's a lot like grouping, actually. The big difference: in stacking, all the members of a particular group are represented by a *single* icon (Figure 2-15). It's designed to look like a crazy stack of icons, all piled on top of each other. Since a single stack icon now represents 10 or 100 or 1,000 icons, you save a *lot* of space in the window.

You create stacks using the "Stack by" command in each column heading's pop-up menu, as shown in Figure 2-15.

When you double-click one of these stacks, a special Explorer window opens, showing the "exploded view" of the icons within. This isn't a real folder window, of course; it's a phantom folder, created just so that you can see the icons that were in its stack. Click the Back button to return to the stacked window.

Tip: What's cool about stacks is that a certain icon may appear in more than one. If you've stacked by author, for example, a document written by collaborators Casey and Robin appears in *both* the Casey stack *and* the Robin stack.

Filtering

Filtering means hiding. When you turn on filtering, a bunch of the icons in a window *disappear*, which can make filtering a sore subject for novices.

Figure 2-14:
Top: This folder might look like chaos. Wouldn't it be nice to see all these icons organized into groups with similar characteristics? Suppose, for example, that you want to see all the songs by each band—no matter what album—grouped together.

So you click ▾ next to the Artists column heading; in the pop-up menu, click Group.

Bottom: Windows adds headlines to separate the different groups and sorts the files alphabetically within each group. At this point, you can group a different way by clicking a different heading. (To return to ordinary sorting, open a column-heading pop-up menu again, but this time click Sort.)

Tip: In case you one day think that you've lost a bunch of important files, look for the checkmark next to a column heading, as shown in Figure 2-16. That's your clue filtering is turned on, that Windows is deliberately hiding something from you.

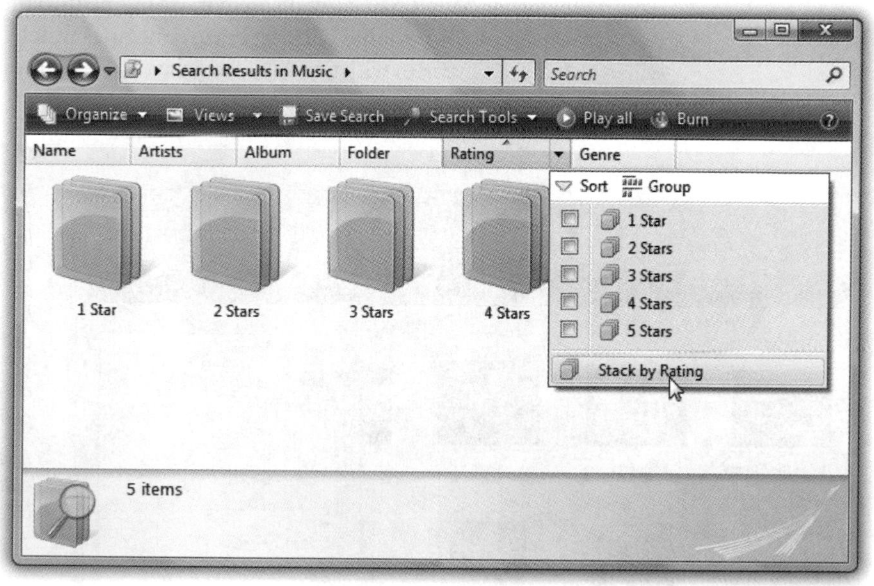

Figure 2-15:
To stack the icons in a window, click the pop-up menu in the appropriate column heading. For example, to stack these photos by star rating, open the Rating pop-up menu and, at the bottom of the pop-up menu, choose "Stack by Rating."

On the positive side, filtering means screening out stuff you don't care about. When you're looking for a document you know you worked on last week, you can tell Windows to show you *only* the documents that were edited last week.

Once again, you turn on filtering by opening the pop-up menu next to the column heading you want. For instance, if you want to see only your five-star photos in the Pictures folder, open the Rating pop-up menu (Figure 2-16).

Sometimes, you'll see a whole long list of checkboxes in one of these pop-up menus (Figure 2-16, bottom). For example, if you want to see only the songs in your Music folder by the Beatles, turn on the Beatles checkmark.

Tip: You can turn on more than one checkbox. To see music by the Beatles *and* U2, turn on both checkboxes.

Filtering, by the way, can be turned on *with* sorting or grouping/stacking.

To stop filtering, open the heading pop-up menu again and turn off the Filter checkbox.

Uni-Window vs. Multi-Window

All Versions

When you double-click a folder, Windows can react in one of two ways:

- **It can open a new window.** Now you've got two windows on the screen, one overlapping the other. Moving or copying an icon from one into the other is a piece of cake. Trouble is, if your double-clicking craze continues much longer, your screen will eventually be overrun with windows, which you must now painstakingly close again.

Figure 2-16:
Top: There are actually hundreds of photos in this folder. So where are they all? They've been filtered out (hidden). You've asked Windows to show you only your five-star photos.

Bottom: The filtering options may be very few or extensive.

- **It can replace the original window with a new one.** This only-one-window-at-all-times behavior keeps your desktop from becoming crowded with windows. If you need to return to the previous window, the Back button takes you there. Of course, you'll have a harder time dragging icons from one window to another using this method.

Whatever you decide, you switch windows between these two behaviors like this: Choose Organize→Folder and Search Options in any Explorer window. In the resulting dialog box, click "Open each folder in the same window" or "Open each folder in its own window," as you like. Then click OK.

Immortalizing Your Tweaks
All Versions

Once you've twiddled and tweaked an Explorer window into a perfectly efficient configuration of columns and views, you needn't go through the same exercises for each folder. Vista can immortalize your changes as the standard setting for *all* your windows.

Choose Organize→Folder and Search Options→View tab. Click the Apply to Folders button, and confirm your decision by clicking Yes.

The Little Filtering Calendar

Some of Explorer's column-heading pop-up menus—Date modified, Date created, Date taken, and so on—display a little calendar, right there in the menu. You're supposed to use it to specify a date or date range. You use it, for example, if you want to see only the photos taken last August, or the Word documents created last week. Here's how the little calendar works:

To change the month, click the ◄ or ► buttons to go one month at a time. Or click the month name to see a list of all 12 months; click the one you want.

To change the year, click the ◄ or ► buttons. Or, to jump farther back or forward, double-click the month's name. You're offered a list of all ten years in this decade. Click a third time (on the decade heading) to see a list of *decades*. At this point, "drill down" to the year you want by clicking what you want. (The calendar goes from

1601 to the year 9999, which should pretty much cover your digital photo collection.)

To see only the photos taken on a certain date, click the appropriate date on the month-view calendar.

To add photos taken on other dates, click additional squares. You can also drag horizontally, vertically, or diagonally to select blocks of consecutive dates.

Unfortunately, there's no easy way to say, "Show me all the photos taken in June and July" or "…in 2004" using this calendar, although you can always create such queries using the Search program described in the next chapter.

The checkboxes below the calendar offer one-click access to photos taken earlier this week, earlier this year, and before the beginning of this year ("a long time ago").

At this point, all of your disk and folder windows open up with the same view, sorting method, and so on. You're still free to override those standard settings on a window-by-window basis, however. (And if you change your mind again, and you want to make all of your maverick folder windows snap back to the standard settings, repeat the process, but click Reset Folders instead.)

The "Folder Options" Options
All Versions

In the battle between flexibility and simplicity, Microsoft comes down on the side of flexibility almost every time. Anywhere that it can provide you with more options, it will; damn the complexity, full speed ahead!

Explorer windows are a case in point, as the following pages of sometimes preposterously tweaky options make clear.

The good news: if Explorer windows already work fine for you the way they are, you can ignore all of this.

If you choose Organize→Folder and Search Options from any Explorer window, and then click the View tab (see Figure 2-17), you see an array of options that affect *all* of the folder windows on your PC. When assessing the impact of these controls,

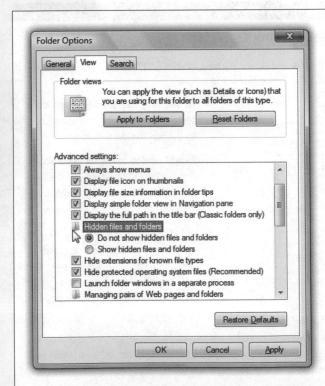

Figure 2-17:
Some of the options in this list are contained within tiny folder icons. A double-click collapses (hides) these folder options or shows them again. For example, you can hide the "Do not show hidden files and folders" option by collapsing the "Hidden files and folders" folder icon.

earth-shattering isn't the adjective that springs to mind. Still, you may find one or two of them useful.

Note: The changes you make in the Folder Options settings are global; they affect *all* Explorer windows.

Here are the functions of the various checkboxes:

- **Always show icons, never thumbnails.** Vista takes great pride in displaying your document icons *as* documents. That is, each icon appears as a miniature, a thumbnail, of the document itself—a feature that's especially useful in folders full of photos.

  On a slowish PC, this feature can really make your processor gasp for breath. If you notice that the icons are taking forever to appear, consider turning this checkbox on.

- **Always show menus.** This checkbox forces the traditional Windows menu bar (File, Edit, View, and so on) to appear in every Explorer window, without your having to tap the Alt key.

- **Display file icon on thumbnails.** Ordinarily, you can identify documents (think Word, Excel, PowerPoint) because their icons display the corresponding logo (a big W for Word, and so on). But in Vista's icon views (Medium size and larger), you see the *actual document* on the icon—the actual image of the document's first page. So does that mean you can no longer tell at a glance what *kind* of document it is?

  Don't be silly. This option superimposes, on each thumbnail icon, a tiny "badge," a sub-icon, that identifies what kind of file it is. (It works on only some kinds of documents, however.)

- **Display file size information in folder tips.** A *folder tip* is a rectangular balloon that appears when you point to a folder—a little yellow box that tells you what's in that folder and how big it is on the disk. (It appears only if you've turned on the "Show pop-up description" checkbox described below.) Talk about tweaky! You turn off *this* checkbox if you want to see only the description, but not the size.

- **Display simple folder view in Navigation pane.** You know how Vista indents each more deeply nested folder in the Folders list, so more buried folders appear farther and farther to the right? Turn off this checkbox if you'd like to see vertical dotted lines to designate each level of folder indenting, as in older versions of Windows.

Note: The lines don't appear or disappear until the *next* time you open a window.

- **Display the full path in the title bar (Classic folders only).** Suppose you've rejected the millions of dollars and years of manpower Microsoft put into Vista's new cosmetic design. You've opted instead for the clunky old Classic theme (page 26). In that case, when this option is on, Windows reveals the exact location of the current window in the title bar of the window—for example, *C:\Users\Chris\ Documents*. See page 41 for more on folder paths. Seeing the path can be useful when you're not sure which disk a folder is on, for example.

- **Hidden files and folders.** Microsoft grew weary of answering tech-support calls from clueless or mischievous customers who had moved or deleted critical system files, rendering their PCs crippled or useless. The company concluded that the simplest preventive measure would be to make them invisible (the files, not the customers).

  This checkbox is responsible for that safety feature. Your Personal and Windows folders, among other places, house several invisible folders and files that the average person isn't meant to fool around with. Yes, Big Brother is watching you, but he means well.

  By selecting "Show hidden files and folders," you, the confident power user in times of troubleshooting or customization, can make the hidden files and folders appear (they show up with dimmed icons, as though to reinforce their delicate nature). But you'll have the smoothest possible computing career if you leave these options untouched.

- **Hide extensions for known file types.** Windows normally hides the three-letter *filename extension* on standard files and documents (.doc, .jpg, and so on), in an effort to make Windows seem less technical and intimidating. Your files wind up named *Groceries* and *Frank* instead of Groceries.doc and Frank.jpg.

  There are some excellent reasons, though, why you should turn *off* this option. See page 222 for more on this topic.

- **Hide protected operating system files.** This option is similar to "Show hidden files and folders," above—except that it refers to even more important files, system files that may not be invisible, but are nonetheless so important that moving or deleting them might turn your PC into a $2,000 paperweight. Turning this checkbox off, in fact, produces a warning message that's meant to frighten away everybody but programmers and power geeks.

- **Launch folder windows in a separate process.** This geekily worded setting opens each folder into a different chunk of memory (RAM). In certain rare situations, this largely obsolete arrangement is more stable—but it slows down your machine slightly and unnecessarily uses memory.

- **Remember each folder's view settings.** Ordinarily, every folder and disk window memorizes its own view setting (List, Details, Tiles, or whatever) independently.

  But if you turn *off* this checkbox, each folder inherits the view setting of the window it's *in*. If you open Documents, for example, and switch it to Large Icons view, all the folders inside it will also open into Large Icons–view windows. Furthermore, if you change one of those inner folders to Details view, for example, it won't stick; instead, it will switch right back to Large Icons the next time you open it.

If you're clever, then, here's how you could set your PC to employ the same view setting all the time (Details view, for example): turn on this option *and* use the Apply to Folders button described on page 81.

- **Restore previous folder windows at logon.** Every time you log off the computer, Windows forgets which windows were open. That's a distinct bummer, especially if you tend to work out of your Documents window, which you must therefore manually reopen every time you fire up the old PC.

  If you turn on this useful checkbox, then each time you log on, Windows will automatically greet you with whichever windows were open when you last logged off.

- **Show drive letters.** Turn off this checkbox to hide the drive letters that identify each of your disk drives in the Computer window (Start→Computer). In other words, "Local Disk (C:)" becomes "Local Disk"—an option that might make newcomers feel less intimidated by Windows.

- **Show encrypted or compressed NTFS files in color.** This option won't make much sense until you've read pages 147 and 663, which explain how Windows can encode and compact your files for better security and disk space use. It turns the names of affected icons green and blue, respectively, so that you can spot them at a glance. On the other hand, encrypted or compressed files and folders operate quite normally, immediately converting back to human form when double-clicked; hence, knowing which ones have been affected isn't particularly valuable. Turn off this box to make them look just like any other files and folders.

- **Show pop-up description for folder and desktop icons.** If you point to an icon, a taskbar button, a found item in Search, or whatever (without clicking), you get a pop-up *tooltip*—a floating colored label that helps identify what you're pointing to. If you find these tooltips distracting, turn off this checkbox.

- **Show preview handlers in preview pane.** This is the on/off switch for one of Vista's best new features: seeing a preview of any selected document icon in the Preview pane. Turn it off only if your PC is grinding to a halt under the strain of all this graphics-intensive goodness.

- **Use check boxes to select items.** Now here's a weird one: this option, new in Vista, makes a *checkbox* appear on every icon you point to with your mouse, for ease in selecting them. Page 136 explains all.

Tip: This option replaces the "Single-click to open an item" option of Windows XP.

- **Use Sharing Wizard.** Sharing files with other computers is one of the great perks of having a network. As Chapter 26 makes clear, this new Vista feature makes it much easier to understand what you're doing. For example, it lets you specify that only certain people are allowed to access your files, and how much access they have. (For example, can they change them or just see them?)

- **When typing into list view.** When you've got an Explorer window, teeming with a list of files, what do you want to happen when you start typing?

  In the olden days, that'd be an easy one: "Highlight an icon, of course!" That is, if you type *piz,* you'll highlight the file called Pizza with Casey.jpg. And indeed, that's what the factory setting means: "Select the typed item within the view."

  But Vista is a whole new ball game, and it has a whole new feature in every window: the Search box (page 119). If you turn on "Automatically type into the Search Box," then each letter you type arrives in that box, performing a real-time, letter-by-letter search of all the icons in the window. Your savings: one mouse click.

Sizing, Moving, and Closing Windows
All Versions

Any Windows window can cycle among three altered states:

- **Maximized** means that the window fills the screen; its edges are glued to the boundaries of your monitor, and you can't see anything behind it. It gets that way when you click its Maximize button (see Figure 2-1)—an ideal arrangement when you're surfing the Web or working on a document for hours at a stretch, since the largest possible window means the least possible scrolling. *Keyboard shortcut:* Press Alt+Space bar, then X.

  At this point, the Maximize button has changed into a Restore Down button (whose icon shows two overlapping squares); click this to return the window to its previous size. *Keyboard shortcut:* Press Alt+Space bar, then R.

Tip: Double-clicking the title bar—the big, fat top edge of a window—alternates a window between its maximized (full-screen) and restored conditions.

- When you click a window's **Minimize** button (Figure 2-1), the window gets out of your way. It shrinks down into the form of a button on your taskbar, at the bottom of the screen. Minimizing a window is a great tactic when you want to see what's in the window behind it.

  You can bring the window back by clicking this taskbar button, which bears the window's name. On Aero machines, this button also displays a handy thumbnail miniature when you point to it without clicking, to remind you of what was in the original window.

  Keyboard shortcut: Press Alt+Space bar, then N.

- A **restored** window is neither maximized nor minimized; it's a loose cannon, floating around on your screen as an independent rectangle. Because its edges aren't attached to the walls of your monitor, you can make it any size you like by dragging its borders.

Moving a Window

Moving a window is easy—just drag the big, fat top edge.

Most of the time, you move a window to get it out of the way when you're trying to see what's *behind* it. However, moving windows around is also handy if you're mov-

Figure 2-18:
Creating two restored (free-floating) windows is a convenient preparation for copying information between them. Make both windows small and put them side-by-side, scroll if necessary, and then drag some highlighted material from one into the other. This works either with icons in Explorer windows (top) or with text in Microsoft Word (bottom). If you press Ctrl as you drag text in this way, you copy the original passage instead of moving it.

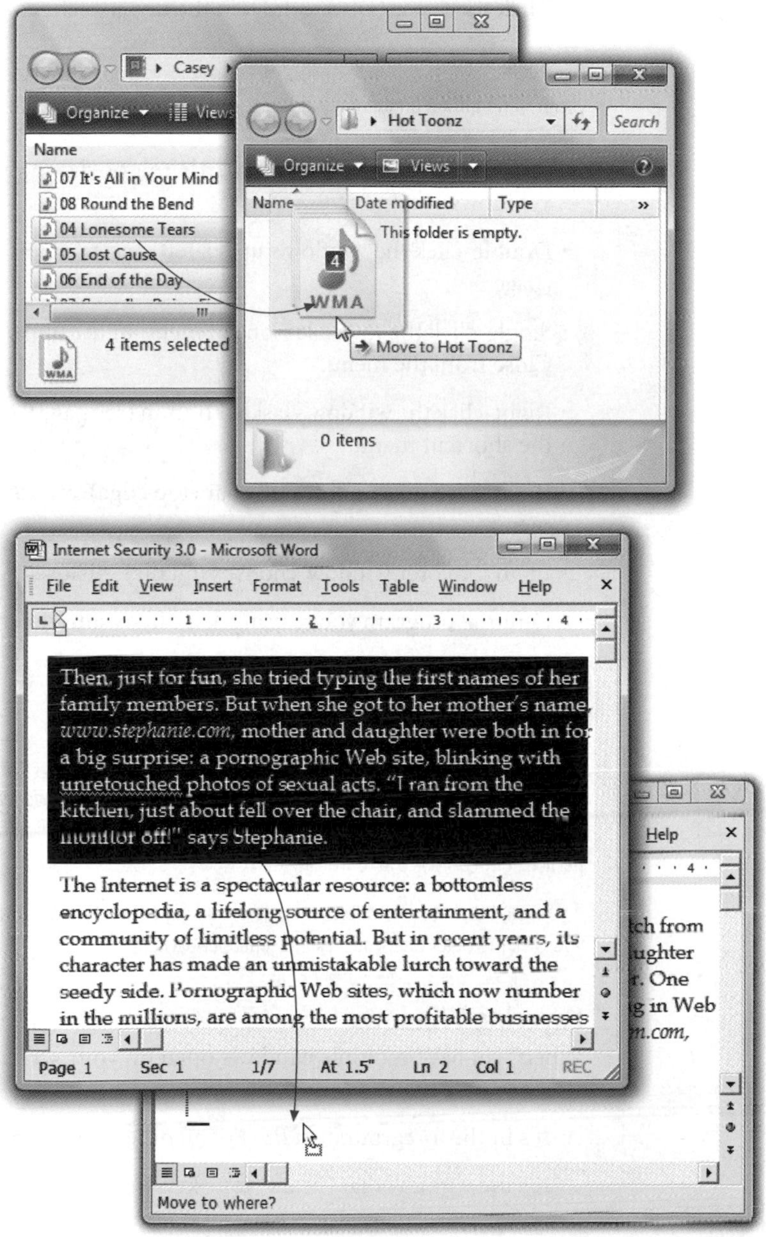

ing or copying data between programs, or moving or copying files between drives or folders, as shown in Figure 2-18.

Closing a Window

Microsoft wants to make absolutely sure that you're never without some method of closing a window. Vista offers at least eight ways to do it:

- Click the Close button (the X in the upper-right corner).

Tip: Shift-click that button to close *all* windows that you opened on the way to the frontmost one (assuming you haven't turned on the uni-window feature described on page 80).

- Press Alt+F4. (This one's worth memorizing. You'll use it everywhere in Windows.)
- Double-click the window's upper-left corner, where the Control menu should be (page 59).
- Single-click the invisible Control menu in the upper-left corner, and then choose Close from the menu.
- Right-click the window's taskbar button (see page 92), and then choose Close from the shortcut menu.
- Right-click the window's title bar (top edge), and choose Close from the shortcut menu.
- In an Explorer window, choose Organize→Close.
- Quit the program you're using, log off, or shut down the PC.

Be careful. In many programs, including Internet Explorer, closing the window also quits the program entirely.

Tip: If you see *two* X buttons in the upper-right corner of your screen, then you're probably using a program like Microsoft Word. It's what Microsoft calls an MDI, or *multiple document interface* program. It gives you a window within a window. The outer window represents the application itself; the inner one represents the particular *document* you're working on.

If you want to close one document before working on another, be careful to click the *inner* Close button. If you click the outer one, you'll exit the entire application.

Layering Windows

When you have multiple windows open on your screen, only one window is *active*, which means that:

- It's in the foreground, *in front* of all other windows.
- It's the window that "hears" your keystrokes and mouse clicks.

- Its Close button glows red. (Background windows' Close buttons are transparent.)

As you would assume, clicking a background window brings it to the front.

Tip: And pressing Alt+Esc sends it to the *back*. Bet you didn't know that one!

And what if it's so far back that you can't even see it? That's where Vista's window-management tools come in; read on.

Tip: For quick access to the desktop, clear the screen by clicking the Desktop button on the Quick Launch toolbar—its icon looks like an old desk blotter—or just press ⊞+D. Pressing that keystroke again brings all the windows back to the screen exactly as they were.

Windows Flip (Alt+Tab)
All Versions

In its day, the concept of overlapping windows on the screen was brilliant, innovative, and extremely effective. In that era before digital cameras, MP3 files, and the Web, managing your windows was easy this way; after all, you had only about three of them.

These days, however, managing all the open windows in all your open programs can be like herding cats. Off you go, burrowing through the microscopic pop-up menus of your taskbar buttons, trying to find the window you want. And heaven help you if you need to duck back to the desktop—to find a newly downloaded file, for example, or eject a disk. You'll have to fight your way through 50,000 other windows on your way to the bottom of the "deck."

In Windows Vista, the same window-shuffling tricks are available that were available in previous editions:

- **Use the Taskbar.** Clicking a button on the taskbar (page 92) makes the corresponding program pop to the front, along with any of its floating toolbars, palettes, and so on.

- **Click the window.** You can also bring any window forward by clicking any visible part of it.

- **Alt+Tab.** For years, this keyboard shortcut has offered a quick way to bring a different window to the front without using the mouse. If you press Tab while holding down the Alt key, a floating palette displays the icons of all running programs, as shown at the top in Figure 2-19. Each time you press Tab again (still keeping the Alt key down), you highlight the next icon; when you release the keys, the highlighted program jumps to the front, as though in a high-tech game of duck-duck-goose.

  This feature has been gorgeous-ized in Windows Vista, as shown in Figure 2-19. It's been renamed, too; it's now called Windows Flip.

Tip: If you just *tap* Alt+Tab without *holding down* the Alt key, you get an effect that's often even more useful: you jump back and forth between the *last two* windows you've had open. It's great when, for example, you're copying sections of a Web page into a Word document.

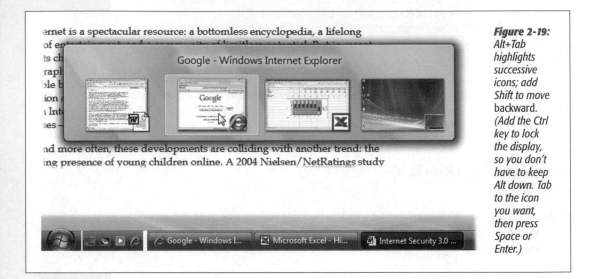

Figure 2-19:
Alt+Tab highlights successive icons; add Shift to move backward. (Add the Ctrl key to lock the display, so you don't have to keep Alt down. Tab to the icon you want, then press Space or Enter.)

Windows Flip 3D
Home Premium • Business • Enterprise • Ultimate

If your PC is capable of running Aero (page 22), Microsoft has something much slicker for this purpose: Flip 3D, a sort of holographic alternative to the Alt+Tab trick.

The concept is delicious. With the press of a keystroke, Vista shrinks *all windows in all programs* so that they all fit on the screen (Figure 2-20), stacked like the exploded view of a deck of cards. You flip through them to find the one you want, and you're there. It's fast, efficient, animated, and a lot of fun.

Tip: You even see, among the other 3D "cards," a picture of the desktop itself. If you choose it, Vista minimizes all open windows and takes you to the desktop for quick access to whatever is there.

Here's how you use it, in slow motion. First, press ▓+Tab. If you keep your thumb on the ▓ key, you see something like Figure 2-20.

Keep your thumb on the ▓ key. At this point, you can shuffle through the "deck" of windows using any of these techniques:

• Tap the Tab key repeatedly. (Add the Shift key to move backward through the stack.)

• Press the down arrow key or the right arrow key. (Use the up or left arrow key to move backward.)

• Turn your mouse's scroll wheel toward you. (Roll it away to move backward.)

When the window you want is in front, release the key. The 3-D stack vanishes, and the lucky window appears before you at full size.

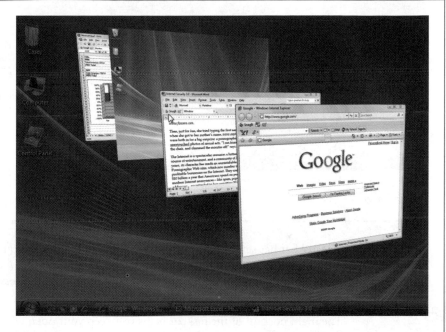

Figure 2-20:
These window miniatures aren't snapshots; they're "live." That is, if anything is changing inside a window (a movie is playing, for example), you'll see it right on the 3D miniature.

By the way: Don't miss the cool slow-mo trick described in Appendix B.

Flip 3D Without Holding Down Keys

That Flip 3D thing is very cool, but do you really want to exhaust yourself by keeping your thumb pressed on that ⊞ key? Surely that's an invitation to getting the painful condition known as Nerd's Thumb.

Fortunately, you can also use Flip 3D without holding down keys. You can trigger it using any of these three methods:

• The Quick Launch toolbar (page 101) comes preinstalled with a tiny icon that, when you point to it, identifies itself as "Switch between windows." Click it.

• Add the Ctrl key to the usual keystroke. That is, press ⊞ +Ctrl+Tab. This time, you don't have to *keep* any keys pressed.

• Press the Flip 3D *key* on your keyboard, if it has one.

Any of these tactics triggers the 3-D floating-windows effect shown in Figure 2-20. At this point, you can use the arrow keys or your mouse's scroll wheel to flip through the open windows *without* having to hold down any keys. When you see the one you want, press the Esc key to choose it and bring it to the front.

The Taskbar

All Versions

The dark, translucent stripe across the bottom of your screen is the *taskbar*, one of the most prominent and important elements of the Windows interface (Figure 2-21).

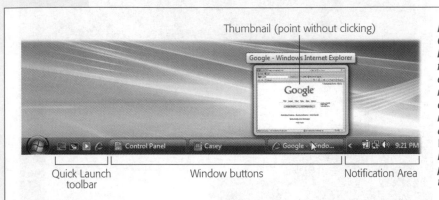

Thumbnail (point without clicking)

Quick Launch toolbar

Window buttons

Notification Area

Figure 2-21:
On the left is the Quick Launch toolbar; drag favorite icons here for easy launching. In the middle are buttons for every program you're running (and every desktop window). When you see nothing but microscopic icons, point without clicking to view a thumbnail.

The taskbar has several segments, each dedicated to an important function. Its right end, the *notification area* (or *system tray,* as old-timers call it), contains tiny status icons. They let you know the time, whether or not you're online, whether or not your laptop's plugged in, and so on.

The main portion of the taskbar helps you keep your open windows and programs under control. You can even dress up your taskbar with additional little segments called toolbars, as described in the following pages.

Tip: You can operate the taskbar entirely from the keyboard. Press ⊞+T to highlight the first button on it. Then tap the left and right arrow keys to "walk" across its buttons.

This section covers each of these features in turn.

The Notification Area (System Tray)

The notification area gives you quick access to little status indicators and pop-up menus that control various functions of your PC. Many a software installer inserts its own little icon into this area: fax software, virus software, palmtop synchronization software, and so on.

Here's your system-tray crash course:

• To figure out what an icon represents, point to it without clicking so that a tooltip balloon appears. To access the controls that accompany it, try both left-clicking and right-clicking the tiny icon. Often, each kind of click produces a different pop-up menu filled with useful controls.

- See the time display at the lower-right corner of your screen? If you point to the time without clicking, a tooltip appears to tell you the day of the week and today's date. If you single-click, you get a handy date-and-time-changing panel. And if you right-click, you get a pop-up menu that lets you visit the Date & Time Control Panel applet.

- If you don't use a tray icon for a couple of weeks, Vista may summarily hide it. See Figure 2-22 for details.

Figure 2-22:
Top: If you see a < button, Windows is telling you that it has hidden some of your notification-area icons.

Bottom: Click this button to expand the notification area, bringing all of the hidden icons into view.

NOSTALGIA CORNER

Turning Off Notification-Area Auto-Hiding

In general, the temporary removal of notification-area icons you haven't used in a while is a noble ambition. Most of the time, you truly won't miss any invisible icons, and their absence will make the icons you *do* use stand out all the more.

Still, you can tell Windows to leave your tray alone—to leave every status icon in full view all the time. To do so, right-click a blank area of the taskbar; from the pop-up menu, choose Properties. At the top of the resulting dialog box, click Notification Area, turn off the "Hide inactive icons" checkbox, and click OK.

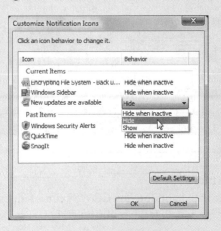

If that seems a little drastic, don't miss the Customize button just to the right of that checkbox. It opens a list of every tray icon that would normally appear, if it weren't for Vista's efforts. Click in the Behavior column to produce a pop-up menu. Choose the status you want for each individual tray icon: "Hide when inactive," "Hide," or "Show."

Before you click OK, though, you might enjoy the four new "System icons" checkboxes that debut in Vista. They offer quick hide/show switches for four important computer-related status icons: Clock, Volume, Network, and Power.

Taskbar Buttons—Now with Thumbnails!

Every time you open a window, whether at the desktop or in one of your programs, the taskbar sprouts a button bearing that window's name and icon. Buttons make it easy to switch between open programs and windows. Just click one to bring its associated window into the foreground, even if it has been minimized.

On PCs that are fast enough to run Aero, in fact, the taskbar does more than display each window's name. If you point to a window button without clicking, you actually see a thumbnail image of *the window itself.* Figure 2-23 shows the effect.

Note: If you don't want these miniature window replicas to appear—maybe because your aging PC is wheezing under the graphical strain, or maybe because you just find the pop-up previews annoying—you can turn them off. Right-click a blank spot on the taskbar. From the shortcut menu, choose Properties. In the resulting window, turn off "Show window previews (thumbnails)" and click OK.

Figure 2-23:
Top: Pointing to a taskbar button without clicking produces these "live" thumbnail previews of the windows themselves, which can be a huge help. After all, you're much more likely to recognize the image of the brochure you're designing than some truncated text button label.

Bottom: If a taskbar button is grouped, then you see only one thumbnail (representing whichever window you opened first in that program). But if you click the button to open its pop-up menu, you can point to each listed window in turn to see its own preview.

Button Groups

The taskbar is the antidote for COWS (cluttered, overlapping window syndrome), thanks in large part to taskbar button *groups.*

In the old days, opening a lot of windows might produce the relatively useless display of truncated buttons, as illustrated in Figure 2-21. Not only were the buttons too narrow to read the names of the windows, but the buttons appeared in chronological order, not software-program order.

Nowadays, though, when conditions become crowded, the taskbar automatically groups the names of open windows into a single menu that sprouts from the corresponding program button, as shown at bottom in Figure 2-23. Click the taskbar button bearing the program's name to produce a pop-up menu of the window names; now you can jump directly to the one you want.

Tip: The visual thumbnails aren't quite so useful when they sprout out of grouped taskbar buttons, because you're shown only *one* window thumbnail (the frontmost one). But once that clustered thumbnail is visible, you can click the taskbar button to view a more traditional list of windows. Best of all, if you now *point* to each name in the list, you get to see its thumbnail. You can move the cursor over the list of window names, admiring each thumbnail as it pops out.

Second, even when there is plenty of room, Windows aligns the buttons into horizontal groups *by program*. All the Word-document buttons appear, followed by all the Excel-document buttons, and so on.

Despite these improvements (which appeared in Windows XP), most of the following time-honored basics still apply:

- To bring a window to the foreground, making it the active window, click its button on the taskbar. (If clicking a button doesn't bring a window forward, it's because Windows has combined several open windows into a single button. Just click the corresponding program's button as though it's a menu, and then choose the specific window you want from the resulting list, as shown in Figure 2-24.)

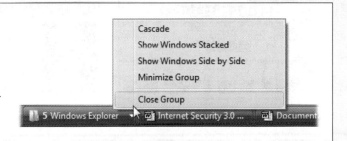

Figure 2-24:
The number on a button indicates that several windows are open in that program; the ▾ is another cue that you must click to see a list of windows.

Right-clicking one of these buttons lets you perform certain tasks on all the hidden windows together, such as closing them all at once.

- To *hide* the frontmost window, click its taskbar button—a great feature that a lot of PC fans miss. (To hide a *background* window, click its taskbar button *twice:* once to bring the window forward, then a pause, then again to hide it.)

- To minimize, maximize, restore, or close a window, even if you can't see it on the screen, right-click its button on the taskbar and choose from the shortcut menu (Figure 2-24, bottom).

- Windows can make all open windows visible at once, either by *cascading* them, *stacking* them, or displaying them in side-by-side vertical slices. (All three options are shown in Figure 2-25.) To create this effect, right-click a blank spot on the taskbar and choose Cascade Windows from the shortcut menu.

Note: Actually, there's a *fourth* way to see all your windows at once: Flip 3D, described in the previous section. The cascading/stacking business is an older method of plucking one window out of a haystack.

Figure 2-25:
Top: Cascading windows are neatly arranged so you can see the title bar for each window. Click any title bar to bring that window to the foreground as the active window.

Bottom: You may prefer to see your windows displayed stacked (left) or side-by-side (right). Either way, if you began by right-clicking the program's name on the taskbar, you arrange only the windows of one program; right-click a blank part of the taskbar if you want to cascade all windows of all programs.

Bringing Back the Old Taskbar

The taskbar's tendency to consolidate the names of document windows into a single program button saves space, for sure.

Even so, it's not inconceivable that you might prefer the old system, in which there's one taskbar button for every single window. For example, once Windows stacks the names of your documents, you no longer can bring a certain application to the front just by clicking its taskbar button. (You must actually choose from its menu, which is a lot more effort.)

To make Windows Vista display the taskbar the way it did in classic versions of Windows, right-click an empty area of the taskbar and choose Properties from the shortcut menu. Turn off the "Group similar taskbar buttons" checkbox and then click OK.

- To minimize all the windows in one fell swoop, right-click a blank spot on the taskbar and choose Show the Desktop from the shortcut menu—or just press ⊞+D.

Tip: When the taskbar is crowded with buttons, it may not be easy to find a blank spot to click. Usually there's a little gap near the right end; you can make it easier to find some blank space by *enlarging* the taskbar, as described on page 98.

- If you change your mind, the taskbar shortcut menu always includes an Undo command for the last taskbar command you invoked. (Its wording changes to reflect your most recent action—"Undo Minimize All," for example.)

The Quick Launch Toolbar

At the left end of the taskbar—that is, just to the right of the Start button—is a handful of tiny, unlabeled icons. This is the Quick Launch toolbar, one of the most useful features in Windows. For details on this toolbar and the others in Windows Vista, see page 98.

Customizing the Taskbar

You're not stuck with the taskbar exactly as it came from Microsoft. You can resize it, move it, or hide it completely. Most people don't bother, but it's always good to know what options you have.

Moving the taskbar

You can move the taskbar to the top of your monitor, or, if you're a true rebel, to either side.

To do so, first ensure that the toolbar isn't *locked* (which means that you can't move or resize the taskbar—or any of its toolbars, for that matter). Right-click a blank spot on the taskbar to produce the shortcut menu. If "Lock the taskbar" is checked, select it to make the checkmark disappear.

Now you can drag the taskbar to any edge of the screen, using any blank spot in the central section as a handle. Release the mouse when the taskbar leaps to the edge you've indicated with the cursor.

When the taskbar is on the left or right edge of the screen, Windows Vista widens it automatically so that you can read the button names, which remain horizontal. In truth, this isn't a bad idea, considering your screen probably has more unused space horizontally than vertically. (Ergonomic studies have indicated that keeping your neck bent at a 90 degree angle to read vertical buttons isn't so hot for your spine.)

Tip: No matter which edge of the screen holds your taskbar, your programs are generally smart enough to adjust their own windows as necessary. In other words, your Word document will shift sideways so that it doesn't overlap the taskbar that you've dragged to the side of the screen.

Resizing the taskbar

Even with the new button-grouping feature, the taskbar can still accumulate a lot of buttons and icons. As a result, you may want to enlarge the taskbar to see what's what.

Begin by making sure that the taskbar isn't locked, as described above. Then position your pointer on the upper edge of the taskbar (or, if you've moved the taskbar, whichever edge is closest to the center of the screen). When the pointer turns into a double-headed arrow, drag to make the taskbar thicker or thinner.

Note: If you're resizing a taskbar that's on the top or bottom of the screen, the taskbar automatically changes its size in full taskbar-height increments. You can't fine-tune the height; you can only double or triple it, for example.

If it's on the left or right edge of your screen, however, you can resize the taskbar freely.

Hiding the taskbar

If you work on a smallish monitor, you may wish that the taskbar would make itself scarce now and then—like when you're working on a word-processing or Web-page document that needs every pixel of space you can get.

Fortunately, it's easy to make the taskbar hide itself until you need it. Start by right-clicking a blank spot on the taskbar, and then choose Properties from the shortcut menu. The dialog box that appears offers these options, among others:

- **Auto-hide the taskbar.** This feature makes the taskbar disappear whenever you're not using it—a clever way to devote your entire screen to application windows and yet have the taskbar at your cursor tip when needed.

  When this feature is turned on, the taskbar disappears whenever you click elsewhere, or whenever your cursor moves away from it. Only a thin blue line at the edge of the screen indicates that you have a taskbar at all. As soon as your pointer moves close to that line, the taskbar joyfully springs back into view.

Tip: Alternatively, you can summon the taskbar just by tapping the ⊞ key. (If your keyboard doesn't have one, Ctrl+Esc works, too.)

- **Keep the taskbar on top of other windows.** This option—the factory setting—permits no other window to cover up the taskbar. Your program windows automatically shrink as necessary to accommodate the taskbar's screen bulk. (If you turn off this option, full-screen application windows overlap the taskbar.)

Taskbar Toolbars
All Versions

Taskbar *toolbars* are separate, recessed-looking areas on the taskbar that offer special-function features. You can even build your own toolbars—for example, one stocked with documents related to a single project. (Somewhere in America, there's a self-help group for people who spend entirely too much time fiddling with this kind of thing.)

To make a toolbar appear or disappear, right-click a blank spot on the taskbar and choose from the Toolbars submenu that appears (Figure 2-26). The ones with checkmarks are the ones you're seeing now; choose one with a checkmark to make the toolbar disappear.

Here's a rundown of the ready-made taskbar toolbars at your disposal.

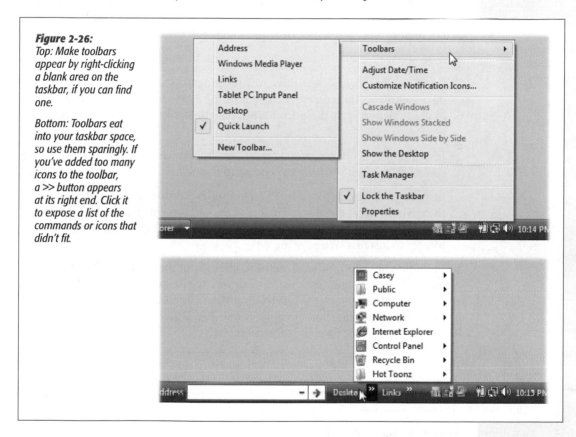

Figure 2-26:
Top: Make toolbars appear by right-clicking a blank area on the taskbar, if you can find one.

Bottom: Toolbars eat into your taskbar space, so use them sparingly. If you've added too many icons to the toolbar, a >> button appears at its right end. Click it to expose a list of the commands or icons that didn't fit.

Address Toolbar

This toolbar offers a duplicate copy of the Address bar that appears in every Explorer window, complete with a Recent Addresses pop-up menu—except that it appears in the taskbar at all times. That way, it's always available, even if no Explorer window happens to be open.

Windows Media Player Toolbar

You may be a bit baffled when you choose this one's name from the Toolbars list—and *nothing happens.*

That's because this toolbar only deigns to make itself visible when (a) you're actually *running* Windows Media Player (Chapter 14), and (b) you've then *minimized* it. Only then do you see the full glory of the Windows Media Player Toolbar.

Links Toolbar

From its name alone, you might assume that the purpose of this toolbar is to provide links to your favorite Web sites. And sure enough, that's one thing it's good for.

But in fact, you can drag *any icon at all* onto the toolbar—files, folders, disks, programs, or whatever—to turn them into one-click buttons. In short, think of the Links toolbar as a miniature Start menu for places and things you use most often.

Here are a few possibilities, just to get your juices flowing:

- Install toolbar icons of the three or four programs you use the most (or a few documents you work on every day). Sure, the Start menu and the Quick Launch toolbar can also serve this purpose, but only the Links toolbar keeps their names in view.

- Install toolbar icons for shared folders on the network. This arrangement saves several steps when you want to connect to them.

- Install toolbar icons of Web sites you visit often, so that you can jump directly to them when you sit down in front of your PC each morning. (In Internet Explorer, you can drag the tiny icon at the left end of the Address bar directly onto the Links toolbar to install a Web page there.)

You can drag these links around on the toolbar to put them into a different order, or remove a link by dragging it away—directly into the Recycle Bin, if you like. (They're only shortcuts; you're not actually deleting anything important.) To rename something here—a good idea, since horizontal space in this location is so precious—right-click it and choose Rename from the shortcut menu.

Tip: Dragging a Web link from the Links toolbar to the desktop or an Explorer window creates an *Internet shortcut file.* When double-clicked, this special document connects to the Internet and opens the specified Web page.

Tablet PC Input Panel

This toolbar is useful only if you're working on a Tablet PC, which has a touch screen and stylus. It provides quick access to Vista's handwriting-recognition software. Chapter 19 has the details.

Desktop Toolbar

The Desktop toolbar (Figure 2-26, bottom) offers quick access to whichever icons are sitting on your desktop—the Recycle Bin, for example, and whatever else you've put there. As a convenience, it also lists a few frequently-used places that *aren't* on the desktop, including Internet Explorer and the Control Panel (complete with a pop-up menu that lists the *individual* Control Panel applets for even faster access).

When it first appears, the Desktop toolbar takes the form of a >> button at the right end of the taskbar. You can widen the Desktop toolbar if you like, making its buttons appear horizontally on the taskbar, although there's not room for more than a couple of items (unless you hide the text labels, as described below). You might as well just use the pop-up menu; it provides a useful way to get at your desktop stuff when your screen is filled with windows.

Quick Launch Toolbar

The Quick Launch toolbar is fantastically useful. In fact, in sheer convenience, it puts the Start menu to shame. Maybe that's why it's the only toolbar that appears on your taskbar automatically. It contains icons for functions that Microsoft assumes you'll use most often. They include:

- **Desktop**, a one-click way to minimize (hide) *all* the windows on your screen to make your desktop visible. Don't forget about this button the next time you need to burrow through some folders, put something in the Recycle Bin, or perform some other activity in your desktop folders. *Keyboard shortcut:* ⊞ +D.

- **Switch between windows**, a one-click trigger for the Flip 3D effect described on page 90. *Keyboard shortcut:* ⊞ +Tab.

- **Launch Internet Explorer Browser**, for one-click access to the Web browser included with Windows.

But what makes this toolbar great is how easy it is to add your *own* icons—particularly those you use frequently. There's no faster or easier way to open them, even when your screen is otherwise filled with clutter.

To add an icon to this toolbar, simply drag it there, as shown in Figure 2-27. To remove an icon, just drag it off the toolbar—directly onto the Recycle Bin, if you like.

Figure 2-27:
You can add any kind of icon to the Quick Launch toolbar by dragging it there (top); a vertical bar shows you where it'll appear.

(You're not actually removing any software from your computer.) If you think you'll somehow survive without using Internet Explorer each day, for example, remove it from the Quick Launch toolbar.

Language Toolbar

Windows has long been able to run software in multiple languages—if you installed the correct fonts, keyboard layouts, and localized software (a French copy of Windows, a French version of Outlook, and so on). In fact, you can even shift from language to language (or keyboard layout to keyboard layout) on the fly, without reinstalling the operating system or even restarting the computer.

POWER USERS' CLINIC

Installing Languages and Keyboard Layouts

Windows can display many different languages, but *typing* in those languages is another matter. The symbols you use when you're typing Swedish aren't the same as when you're typing English. Microsoft solved this problem by creating different *keyboard layouts,* one for each language. Each rearranges the letters that appear when you press the keys. For example, when you use the Swedish layout and press the semicolon key, you don't get a semicolon (;)—you get an ö.

Microsoft even includes a Dvorak layout—a scientific rearrangement of the standard layout that puts the most common letters directly under your fingertips on the home row. Fans of the Dvorak layout claim greater accuracy, better speed, and less fatigue.

To install a new keyboard layout, choose Start→Control Panel. Under "Clock, Language, and Region," click "Change keyboards or other input methods." In the Regional and Language Options dialog box, click "Change keyboards." In the *next* dialog box, click Add. You see an astonishingly long list of keyboard layouts: Afrikaans, Albanian, Alsatian, Amharic, and on and on. Expand the + buttons until you see the layout you want; click the layout name; and click OK.

To install a new language (for dialog boxes, help screens, and so on), you first have to download the appropriate language *kit.* They're available from Microsoft's Web site, and available in two varieties: half-hearted and complete. (The complete ones are available only for the Enterprise and Ultimate editions of Vista.) For details, search Windows Help for "language files."

Once you've installed the language kit, choose Start→ Control Panel. Under "Clock, Language, and Region," click "Change display language." In the Regional and Language Options dialog box, click "Install/uninstall languages"; authenticate yourself (page 191). In the *next* dialog box, click "Install languages"; navigate to the downloaded language kit.

Once either kind of installation is complete, you can switch from layout to layout, or language to language, using the Language bar—or, if you're in no hurry, using the same Regional and Language Options dialog box you encountered in these steps.

Chances are that you don't speak *all* of the world's useful languages, though. So the idea here is to install the software necessary only for the languages and layouts you *do* use (see the box on the facing page). After that, you can use the Language bar to switch among them with a quick click.

Redesigning Your Toolbars

To change the look of a toolbar, right-click any blank spot within it.

Tip: How much horizontal taskbar space a toolbar consumes is up to you. Drag the border at the left edge of a toolbar to make it wider or narrower. That's a good point to remember if, in fact, you can't *find* a blank spot to right-click.

The resulting shortcut menu offers these choices, which appear *above* the usual taskbar shortcut menu choices:

- **View** lets you change the size of the icons on the toolbar.

- **Open Folder** works only with the Quick Launch and Links toolbars.

  It turns out that the icons on these toolbars reflect the contents of corresponding *folders* on your PC. To see one, right-click a blank spot on the toolbar itself; from the shortcut menu, choose Open Folder.

  Why is that useful? Because it means that you can add, rename, or delete icons en masse, by working in the folder instead of on the toolbar itself. Of course, you can also delete or rename any icon on these toolbars by right-clicking it and choosing Delete or Rename from the shortcut menu. But a window isn't nearly as claustrophobic as the toolbar itself.

- **Show Text** identifies each toolbar icon with a text label.

- **Show Title** makes the toolbar's name (such as "Quick Launch" or "Desktop") appear on the toolbar.

- **Close Toolbar** makes the toolbar disappear.

Build Your Own Toolbars

The Quick Launch area of the taskbar is such a delight that you may actually develop a syndrome called Quick Launch Envy—you'll find that having only one isn't enough. You might wish to create several *different* Quick Launch toolbars, each stocked with the icons for a different project or person. One could contain icons for all the chapters of a book you're writing; another could list only your games.

Fortunately, it's easy to create as many different custom toolbars as you like, each of which behaves exactly like the Quick Launch toolbar.

Windows creates toolbars from *folders;* so before creating a toolbar of your own, you must create a folder and fill it with the stuff you want to toolbarize.

Next, right-click a blank spot on the taskbar. From the shortcut menu, choose Toolbars→New Toolbar to open the New Toolbar dialog box, as shown in Figure 2-28. Find and click the folder you want, and then click Select Folder.

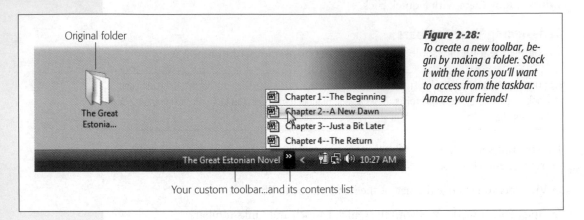

Original folder

Figure 2-28:
To create a new toolbar, begin by making a folder. Stock it with the icons you'll want to access from the taskbar. Amaze your friends!

Your custom toolbar...and its contents list

Now there's a brand-new toolbar on your taskbar, whose buttons list the contents of the folder you selected. Feel free to tailor it as described in the previous discussions—by changing its icon sizes, hiding or showing the icon labels, or installing new icons onto it by dragging them from other Explorer windows.

Searching and Organizing Your Files

Every disk, folder, file, application, printer, and networked computer is represented on your screen by an icon. To avoid spraying your screen with thousands of overlapping icons seething like snakes in a pit, Windows organizes icons into folders, puts those folders into *other* folders, and so on. This folder-in-a-folder-in-a-folder scheme works beautifully at reducing screen clutter, but it means that you've got some hunting to do whenever you want to open a particular icon.

Helping you find, navigate, and manage your files, folders, and disks with less stress and greater speed was one of the primary design goals of Windows Vista—and of this chapter. The following pages cover Vista Search, plus icon-management life skills like selecting them, renaming them, moving them, copying them, making shortcuts of them, assigning them to keystrokes, deleting them, and burning them to CD or DVD.

Tip: To create a new folder to hold your icons, right-click where you want the folder to appear (on the desktop, or in any desktop window except Computer), and choose New→Folder from the shortcut menu. The new folder appears with its temporary "New Folder" name highlighted. Type a new name for the folder and then press Enter.

Directories vs. Folders

Before Windows took over the universe, folders were called directories, and folders inside them were called subdirectories.

Keep that in mind the next time you're reading an old user guide, magazine article, or computer book.

Meet Vista Search
All Versions

Every computer offers a way to find files. And every system offers several different ways to open them. But Search, a star feature of Vista, combines these two functions in a way that's so fast, so efficient, and so spectacular, it reduces much of what you've read in the previous chapters to irrelevance. It works like Google Desktop (or Spotlight on the Macintosh), in that it finds files *as you type* what you're looking for—not like Windows XP, which doesn't start searching until you're finished typing, and takes a very long time to find things at that.

It's important to note, though, that you can search for files on your PC using the superfast Search box in two different places:

- **The Start menu.** The Start Search box at the bottom of the Start menu searches *everywhere* on your computer.

- **Explorer windows.** The Search box at the top of every desktop window searches only *that window* (including folders within it). You can expand it, too, into something called the Search *pane*—a way to limit the scope of your search to certain file types or date ranges, for example.

Search boxes also appear in the Control Panel window, Internet Explorer, Windows Mail, Windows Media Player, and other spots where it's useful to perform small-time, limited searches. The following pages, however, cover the two main Search boxes, the ones that hunt down files and folders.

Search from the Start Menu
All Versions

Start by opening the Start menu, either by using the mouse or by pressing the ⊞ key.

The Start Search text box appears at the bottom of the Start menu; you can immediately begin typing to identify what you want to find and open (Figure 3-1). For example, if you're trying to find a file called "Pokémon Fantasy League.doc," typing just *pok* or *leag* will probably work.

Tip: This one's for you, power users. You can also type command-line prompts into the Search box, like *control date/time* to open your Date & Time control panel or *ping nytimes.com* to see if your machine can reach the outside world. See page 255 for more on the command prompt.

As you type, the familiar Start menu items disappear, and are soon replaced by search results (Figure 3-1, bottom). This is a live, interactive search; that is, Vista modifies the menu of search results as you type—you do *not* have to press Enter after entering your search phrase.

The results menu lists every file, folder, program, email message, address book entry, calendar appointment, picture, movie, PDF document, music file, Web bookmark, and Microsoft Office document (Word, PowerPoint, and Excel) that contains what you typed, regardless of its name or folder location.

Vista isn't just searching icon *names*. It's also searching their contents—the words inside your documents—as well as all your files' *metadata*. (That's descriptive text information about what's in a file, like its height, width, size, creator, copyright holder, title, editor, created date, and last modification date. Page 69 has the details.)

Note: Vista is constantly updating its invisible index (page 112) in real time. You can prove it to yourself like this: Open a text document (in WordPad, for example). Type an unusual word, like *wombat*. Save the document using a different name—say, "Fun Pets." Now *immediately* do a search. Hit the ⊞ key and type *wom*, for example. You'll see that Vista finds "Fun Pets" even though it's only moments old. That's a far cry from, for example, the old Windows Indexing Service, which updated its index only once a day, in the middle of the night!

Figure 3-1:
Press ⊞, or click the Start-menu icon, to see the Search box. As you type, Vista builds the list of every match it can find, neatly arranged in four categories: Programs, Favorites and History, Files, and Communications (which means email and chat transcripts).

You don't have to type an entire word. Typing kumq *will find documents containing the word "kumquat." However, it's worth noting that Vista recognizes only the beginnings of words. Typing* umquat *won't find a document containing—or even named—Kumquat.*

Press the up/down arrow keys to walk through the list one item at a time.

If you see the icon you were hoping to dig up, double-click it to open it. Or use the arrow keys to "walk down" the menu, and then press Enter to open it.

If you choose a program (programs are listed first in the results menu), well, that program pops onto the screen. Selecting an email message opens that message in your email program. And so on.

As you'll soon learn, Vista Search is an enhancement that's so deep, convenient, and powerful, it threatens to make all that folders-in-folders business nearly pointless. Why burrow around in folders when you can open any file or program with a couple of keystrokes?

Limit by Size, Date, Rating, Tag, Author...

Suppose that you're looking for a file called Big Deals.doc. But when you type *big* into the Search box, you wind up wading through hundreds of files that *contain* the word big.

It's at times like these that you'll be grateful for Vista's little-known *criterion* searches. These are little-known syntax tricks that help you create narrower, more targeted searches. All you have to do is prefix your search query with the criterion you want, followed by a colon.

One example is worth a thousand words, so *several* examples should save an awful lot of paper:

- *name: big* finds only documents with "big" in their *names*. Vista will ignore anything with that term *inside* the file.

GEM IN THE ROUGH

Natural Language

OK, so very cool: you can search for *author: (Casey OR Robin NOT Smith) created: <yesterday.*

That's powerful, all right, but also totally intimidating. Ask yourself: would your mother have any idea what that means?

The New Microsoft, the one that created Windows Vista and tried to make it user-friendly and elegant, is way ahead of you on this one. It has given you an alternative way to set up criteria searches: *natural-language searching.* That just means using plain English phrases instead of the usual codes.

To turn on this feature, open Folder Options. (For example, choose Start→Control Panel. Click Classic View, then open Folder Options.) Click the Search tab and turn on "Use natural language search." Click OK.

From now on, you can type in search phrases like these:

documents created last week

music by Beethoven

e-mail from Xavier

e-mail from Robin sent yesterday

pictures of Casey taken January 2007

*classical music rated *****

It may take you some time to experiment to a point where you can trust these searches, but they're certainly easier than using a bunch of colons and parentheses. (Which you can still use, by the way, even when "natural language search" is turned on.)

- *tag: crisis* finds only icons with "crisis" as a tag—not as part of the title or contents.

- *created: 12/25/2006* finds everything something you wrote on December 25, 2006. You can also do *modified: today* or *modified: yesterday,* for that matter. Or don't be that specific. Just use *modified: December* or *modified: 2006.*

  You can use symbols like < and >, too. To find files created since yesterday, you could type *created:>yesterday.*

- *size: >2gb* finds all the big files on your PC.

- *Rating: <**** finds documents to which you've given ratings of three stars or fewer.

- *Camera model: Nikon D80* finds all the pictures you took with that camera.

Tip: You can combine multiple criteria searches, too. For example, if you're pretty sure you had a document called "Naked Mole-Rats" that you worked on yesterday, you could cut directly to it by typing *mole modified: yesterday* or *modified:yesterday mole.* (The order doesn't matter.)

So where's the master list of these available criteria? It turns out that they correspond to the *column headings* at the top of your Explorer windows: name, date modified, type, size, and so on.

Truth is, though, that you can use *any* icon criteria for searches—not just the ones in the Explorer-window headings, but even the ones that *can* be Explorer-window headings. To see them all, right-click any of the existing column headings. From the shortcut menu, choose More. There they are: 115 different criteria, including Size, Rating, Album, Bit rate, Camera model, Date archived, Language, Nickname, and so on. Here's where you learn that, for example, to find all your Ohio address-book friends, you'd search for *home state or province:OH.*

Dude, if you can't find what you're looking for using all of *those* controls, it probably doesn't exist.

Special Search Codes

Shortcuts in Vista's search boxes can give your queries more power. For example:

- **Document types.** You can type *document* to find all text, spreadsheet, and PowerPoint files. You can also type a filename extension—*.MP3* or *.doc* or *.jpg,* for example—to round up all files of a certain file type.

- **Tags, authors.** This is payoff time for applying *tags* or author names to your files, too (page 69). Into a Search box, you can type, or start to type, *Gruber Project* (or any other tag you've assigned), and you'll get an instantaneous list of everything that's relevant to that tag. Or you can type *Mom* or *Casey* or any other author's name to see all the documents that person created.

- **Quotes.** If you type in more than one word, Vista Search works just the way Google does. That is, it finds things that contain both words *somewhere* inside.

If you're searching for a phrase where the words really belong together, though, put quotes around them. For example, searching for *military intelligence* rounds up documents that contain those two words, but not necessarily side-by-side. Searching for *"military intelligence"* finds documents that contain that exact phrase. (Insert your own political joke here.)

- **Boolean searches.** Windows also permits combination-search terms like AND and OR, better known to geeks as Boolean searches.

  That is, you can round up a single list of files that match *two* terms by typing, say, *vacation AND kids.* (That's also how you'd find documents co-authored by two specific people—you and a pal, for example.)

Tip: You can use parentheses instead of AND, if you like. That is, typing *(vacation kids)* finds documents that contain both words, not necessarily together.

If you use OR, you can find icons that match *either* of two search criteria. Typing *jpeg OR mp3* will turn up photos and music files in a single list.

The word NOT works, too. If you did a search for *dolphins,* hoping to turn up sea-mammal documents, but instead find your results contaminated by football-team listings, by all means repeat the search with *dolphins NOT Miami.* Vista will eliminate all documents containing "Miami."

Note: You must type Boolean terms like AND, OR, and NOT in all capitals.

You can even combine Boolean terms with the other special search terms described in this chapter. Find everything created in the last couple of months by searching for *created: September OR October,* for example. Find documents authored by Casey and Robin working together using *author: (Casey AND Robin).*

Results Menu Tips

It should be no surprise that a feature as important as Vista Search comes loaded with options, tips, and tricks. Here it is—the official, unexpurgated Search Tip-O-Rama:

- You can open anything in the results menu by highlighting it and then pressing Enter to open it.

  It's incredibly convenient to open a *program* using this technique, because the whole thing happens very quickly and you never have to take your hands off the keyboard. That is, you might hit 🪟 to open the Start menu, type *cale* (to search for Windows Calendar), and press Enter.

  Why does pressing Enter open Windows Calendar? Because it's the first item in the list of results, and its name is highlighted.

- If Vista doesn't find a *program* whose name matches what you've typed, it doesn't highlight anything in the list. In that case, pressing Enter has a different effect: it opens up the Search Results *window,* which has no length limit and offers a lot more features (page 114).

Alternatively, you can use the mouse or the arrow-key/Enter method described above to open one of the search results.

• Vista's menu shows you only 20 of the most likely suspects. They appear grouped into four categories: **Programs** (including Control Panel applets), **Favorites and History** (that is, Web sites), **Files** (which includes documents, folders, and short-cuts), and **Communications** (email and chat transcripts).

To see the complete list, you have to open the Search results *window* by clicking "See all results" (Figure 3-2). On the other hand, having such a short list means that it's easy to "walk" to the menu item you want to open, using the down arrow key on your keyboard.

Tip: You can eliminate some of the categories (like Communications or Favorites and History) to permit more of the *other* kinds of things to enjoy those 20 seats of honor. Details on page 118.

• The Esc key (top left corner of your keyboard) is a quick "back out of this" keystroke. Tap it to close the results menu and restore the Start menu to its original form.

• To clear the Search box—either to try a different search, or just to get the regularly scheduled Start menu back—click the little x at the right end of the Search box.

• When you need to look up a number in Address Book, don't bother opening Mail to get to its address book; it's faster to use Search. You can type somebody's name or even part of someone's phone number.

• Among a million other things, Vista tracks the *tags* (keywords) you've applied to your pictures. As a result, you can find, open, or insert any photo at any time, no matter what program you're using. This is a fantastic way to insert a photo into

GEM IN THE ROUGH

Beyond Your Own Stuff

Ordinarily, Windows searches only what's in *your* account—your Personal folder (page 38). From the Start menu, you can't search what's inside somebody else's stuff.

Yet you *can* search someone else's account—just not from the Start menu and not without permission.

Start by opening the Start menu→Computer→Users folder. Inside, you'll find folders for all other account holders.

Manually open the one you want to search—and then search using the Search box at the top of the Explorer window.

You won't be given access, though, without first supplying an Administrator's password. (You don't necessarily have to know it; you could just call an administrator over to type it in personally.) After all, the whole point of having different accounts is to ensure privacy for each person's stuff—and only the administrator, or *an* administrator, has full rein to stomp through anyone's stuff.

an outgoing email message, a presentation, or a Web page you're designing. (In a page-layout program, for example, use the Insert command, and then use the Search box that appears at the top of the Open dialog box.)

- If you point to an item in the results menu without clicking, a little tooltip box appears. It tells you the item's actual name and its folder path (that is, where it is on your hard drive).

  You can also jump to a search result's actual icon, sitting there in its actual window, instead of opening it. To do that, right-click its name, and, from the shortcut menu, choose Open File Location.

- At the bottom of the results menu, the "Search the Internet," of course, opens up your Web browser and searches the *Web* for your search term, using Google or whatever search site you've designated as your favorite.

Tip: If, for some inconceivable reason, you don't actually *like* having the mind-blowing ability to find anything on your PC in seconds, right from the Start menu, without ever taking your hands from the keyboard—surely there's *someone* who doesn't—you can get rid of the Start Search box. Right-click the Start menu; from the shortcut menu, choose Properties. Click Customize and, in the resulting dialog box, turn off "Search box." Click OK twice.

What Vista Knows

The beauty of Vista's Search is that it doesn't just find files whose names match what you've typed. That would be *so* 2004!

No, Vista actually looks *inside* the files. It can actually read and search the contents of text files, email, Windows Contacts, Windows Calendar, RTF and PDF documents, and documents from Microsoft Office (Word, Excel, and PowerPoint).

But that's only the beginning. Vista searches files not only for the text inside them, but also over 115 other bits of text—a staggering collection of informational tidbits including the names of the layers in a Photoshop document, the tempo of an MP3 file, the shutter speed of a digital-camera photo, a movie's copyright holder, a document's page size, and on and on.

Technically, this sort of secondary information is called *metadata*. It's usually invisible, although a lot of it shows up in the Details pane described in Chapter 2.

You might think that typing something into the Search box triggers a search. But to be technically correct, Vista has already done its searching. In the first 15 to 30 minutes after you install Vista—or in the minutes after you attach a new hard drive—Vista invisibly collects information about everything on your hard drive. Like a kid cramming for an exam, it reads, takes notes on, and memorizes the contents of all of your files.

It stores all of this information in an invisible, multimegabyte file called, creatively enough, the *index*. (If your primary hard drive is creaking full, you can specify that you want the index stored on some other drive; see page 118.)

Once it has indexed your hard drive in this way, Vista can produce search results in seconds. It doesn't have to search your entire hard drive—only that single card-catalog index file.

After the initial indexing process, Vista continues to monitor what's on your hard drive, indexing new and changed files in the background, in the microseconds between your keystrokes and clicks.

Where Vista Looks

Start-menu searches don't actually scrounge through every last file on your computer. Searching inside Windows's own operating-system files and your software applications, for example, would be pointless to anyone but programmers, so Vista doesn't bother.

What it *does* index is everything in your Personal folder (page 38): email, pictures and music, videos, program names, entries in your address book and calendar, Office documents, and so on. It also searches *offline files* that belong to you, even though they're stored somewhere else on the network (page 589). Finally, it searches the Start menu. You can, if you wish, add other folders to the list of indexed locations (page 117).

In an effort to keep searches fast (and hold down the size of the invisible index file), Vista doesn't index Windows system files and application support files. It indexes all the drives connected to your PC, but not other hard drives on the network.

It does index the Personal folders of everyone else with an account on your machine (Chapter 23), but you're not allowed to search them from the Start menu. So if you were hoping to search your spouse's email for phrases like "meet you at midnight," forget it.

If you try to search anywhere that Windows *hasn't* incorporated into its index—in a Windows system folder, for example, or a hard drive elsewhere on the network—a message appears. It lets you know that because you're working beyond the index's wisdom, the search is going to be slow, and the search will include file names only—not file *contents* or metadata.

Furthermore, this kind of outside-the-index searching does *not* find things as you type. This time, you really do have to press Enter after typing the name (or partial name) of what you want to find.

The Results Window

As you may have noticed, the Vista menu doesn't list *every* match on your hard drive. Unless you own one of those extremely rare 60-inch Skyscraper Displays, there just isn't room.

Instead, Vista uses some fancy behind-the-scenes analysis to calculate and display the 20 *most likely* matches for what you typed. But at the bottom of the menu, a link called "See all results" is a reminder that there may be many other candidates. Click it to open the results *window,* shown in Figure 3-2.

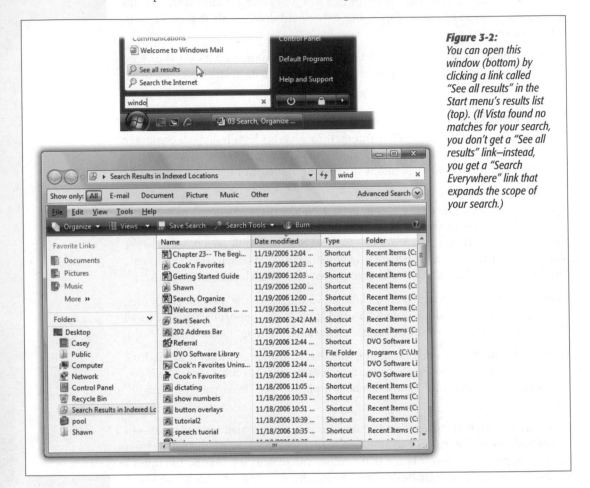

Figure 3-2:
You can open this window (bottom) by clicking a link called "See all results" in the Start menu's results list (top). (If Vista found no matches for your search, you don't get a "See all results" link—instead, you get a "Search Everywhere" link that expands the scope of your search.)

Now you have access to the *complete* list of matches, listed in typical Explorer-window format. You can sort this list, group, stack, or filter it exactly as described in Chapter 2.

The only difference is that the task toolbar (Organize, Views, and so on) offers a few useful buttons that don't usually adorn standard folder windows, like Save Search and Search Tools. Details on these buttons appear later in this chapter.

Note: At the bottom of the search-results list, there's always a "Search the Internet" link. Click it to fire up your Web browser, which plugs your search term into Google or whatever search service you've set up (page 371). It's a handy trick; it means that you can search the Web right from the Start menu.

Customizing Search

You've just read about how Vista Search works fresh out of the box. But you can tailor its behavior, both for security reasons and to customize it to the kinds of work you do.

Unfortunately for you, Microsoft has stashed the various controls that govern searching in three different places. Here they are, one area at a time.

Folder Options

The first source is in the Folder Options→Search dialog box. To open it, use one of these three methods:

- In any Explorer window, choose Organize→Folder and Search Options. In the resulting dialog box, click the Search tab.

- In the Control Panel (Chapter 8), click Classic View, and then open Folder Options. In the resulting dialog box, click the Search tab.

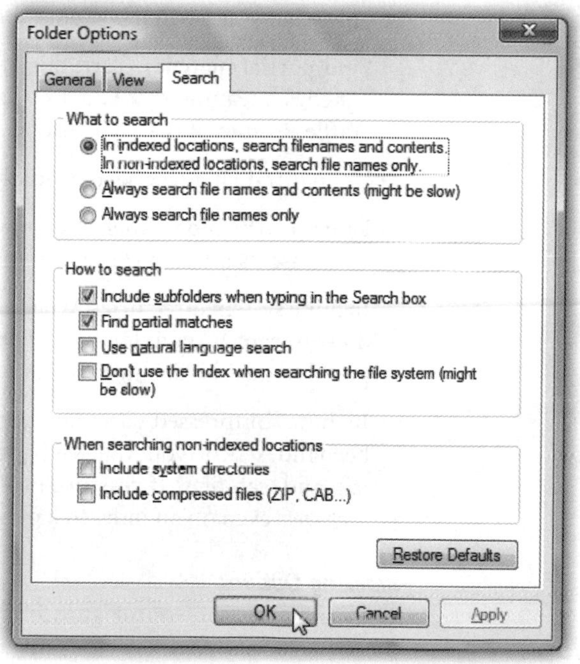

Figure 3-3:
Search actually works beautifully right out of the box. For the benefit of the world's tweakers, however, this dialog box awaits, filled with technical adjustments to the way Search works.

- Following any Explorer-window search, open the Search Tools pop-up menu in the task toolbar at the top. Choose "Search options."

Either way, you wind up at the dialog box shown in Figure 3-3.

- **What to search.** As you know from page 112, Vista's search mechanism relies on an *index*, a single, invisible database file that tracks the location, contents, and metadata of every single file on your computer. If you attach a new hard drive filled with stuff, or attempt to search another computer on the network that hasn't been indexed, Vista ordinarily just searches its files' *names.* After all, it has no index to search for that drive.

    The options here tell Vista that you *want* to search the text inside the other drive's files, even without an index, which can be painfully slow. (Turn on "Always search file names and contents.").

    On the other hand, you may well find that Vista's tendency to round up files based on their contents is actually *annoying,* because it fills the results list with icons that have nothing to do with your query. You might actually prefer the old way, in which Windows searches for files only by name. In that case, turn on "Always search file names only."

- **Include subfolders when typing in the Search box.** When you use the Search box at the top of an Explorer window, Vista ordinarily searches the currently open window *and* the folders inside it. Turn off this option if you want Vista to search only what you see in the window before you.

- **Find partial matches.** Turn this off if you want Vista to find only whole-word matches, meaning that you'll no longer be able to type *waff* to find Mom's Best Waffle Recipes of the Eighties.doc.

- **Use natural language search.** See the box on page 108.

- **Don't use the Index when searching the file system.** If you turn this item on, Vista won't use its internal Dewey Decimal system for searching Windows itself.

- **Include system directories.** When you're searching a disk that hasn't been indexed, do you want Vista to look inside the folders that contain Windows itself (as opposed to just the documents that people have created)? If yes, turn this on.

- **Include compressed files (.zip, .cap...).** When you're searching a disk that hasn't been indexed, do you want Vista to search for files inside compressed archives, like .zip and .cab files? If yes, turn on this checkbox. (Vista doesn't ordinarily search archives, even on an indexed hard drive.)

Indexing Options

The dialog box shown in Figure 3-3 is the master control over Vista's search *index,* the massive, invisible, constantly updated database file that tracks your PC's files and what's in them. The factory settings are perfectly fine, but you may have occasional need to change what's indexed, or where the index is stored.

To open Indexing Options, choose Start→Control Panel. Click Classic View, then double-click Indexing Options.

Here's what you can do in this dialog box:

• **Stop, or start, indexing certain folders.** Ordinarily, Vista doesn't consider any corner of your hard drive off-limits. It looks for matches wherever it can except in other people's Personal folders. (That is, you can't search through other people's stuff. Vista doesn't search your Programs or Windows folders, either.)

But even within your own account's world, you can hide certain folders from searches. Maybe you have privacy concerns—for example, you don't want your spouse searching your stuff while you're away from your desk. Maybe you just want to create more focused searches, removing a lot of old, extraneous junk from Vista's database.

Similarly, you can *add* folders to Vista's index—folders from an external hard drive, for example—so that you'll be able to include them in your speedy searches.

Either way, the steps are simple. Open the Indexing Options control panel, as described above, and click Modify. Click "Show all locations" and authenticate yourself in the User Account Control dialog box (see page 191). See Figure 3-4 for the rest of the procedure.

Figure 3-4:
You can add or remove disks, partitions, or folders to the list of searchable items. Start by expanding the flippy triangles, if necessary, to see the list of folders on your hard drive. Turn a folder's checkbox on (to have Vista index it) or off (to remove it from the index, and therefore from searches). In this example, you've just turned on an external hard drive for indexing.

Tip: In the heart of battle, you can save a little time in getting to the Indexing Options dialog box. Here's the shortcut: Following any Explorer-window search, open the Search Tools pop-up menu in the task toolbar at the top. Choose Modify Index Locations.

Advanced Indexing Options

To find this third area of search options, start in the Indexing Options dialog box (control panel) and click Advanced. Authenticate yourself in the User Account Control dialog box (see page 191). Now you're ready to perform these powerful additional tweaks:

- **Move the index.** Ordinarily, Vista stores its invisible index file (page 112) on your main hard drive. But you might have good reason for wanting to move it. Maybe your main drive is getting full. Or better yet, maybe you've bought a second, faster hard drive; if you store your index there, searching will be even faster.

  In the Advanced Options dialog box, click "Select new." Navigate to the disk or folder where you want the index to go, and then click OK. (The actual transfer of the file takes place the next time you start up Windows.)

- **Teach Vista about new kinds of files.** Vista ordinarily searches for just about every kind of *useful* file: audio files, program files, text and graphics files, and so on. It doesn't bother peering inside things like Windows operating system files and applications, because what's inside them is programming code with little relevance to most people's work. Omitting these files from the index keeps the index smaller and the searches fast.

  But what if you routinely traffic in very rare Venezuelan Beekeeping Interchange Format (VBIF) documents—a file type your copy of Windows has never met before? You won't be able to search for their contents unless you specifically teach Vista about them.

  In the Advanced Options dialog box, click the File Types tab. Type the filename extension (such as VBIF) into the text box at the lower-left. Click "Add new extension" and then OK. From now on, Vista will index this new file type.

- **Turn off categories.** If you find that Vista uses up valuable menu space listing, say, Web bookmarks—stuff you don't need to find very often—you can tell it not to bother. Now the results menu's precious 20 slots will be allotted to icon types you care more about.

  To remove file types from Vista's searching, click the File Types tab of the dialog box shown in Figure 3-5, and then turn the checkboxes on or off to make Vista start or stop indexing them.

- **Index encrypted files.** Some Vista versions (Business, Enterprise, and Ultimate) can *encrypt* files and folders with a quick click, making them unreadable to anyone who receives one by email, say, and doesn't have the password. This checkbox lets Vista index these files (the ones that *you've* encrypted, of course; this isn't a back door to files you can't otherwise access).

- **Handle diacritical marks.** The word "ole," as might appear cutely in a phrase like "the ole swimming pool," is quite a bit different from "Olé," as in, "You missed the matador, you big fat bull!" The difference is a *diacritical mark* (øne öf mâny littlé länguage marks). Ordinarily, Windows ignores diacritical marks; it treats "ole" and "olé" as the same word in searches. That's designed to make it easier for the average person who can't remember which direction a certain marking goes, or even how to type it. But if you turn on this box, Vista will observe these markings and treat marked and unmarked words differently.

- **Troubleshoot Vista searching.** If Vista's Search command ever seems to be acting wacky—for example, it's not finding a document you *know* is there—you can use this function to make it rebuild its own index file on the problem disk. When you click Rebuild (and then OK to confirm, if necessary), Windows *wipes out* the index it's been working with, completely deleting it—and then begins to rebuild it again. You're shown a list of the disks and folders that Vista has been instructed to index; the message at the top of the dialog box lets you know its progress. With luck, this process will wipe out any funkiness you've been experiencing.

Figure 3-5:
Using the "How should this file be indexed" options at the bottom of the box, you can also make Vista stop searching these files' contents—the text within them—for better speed and a smaller index.

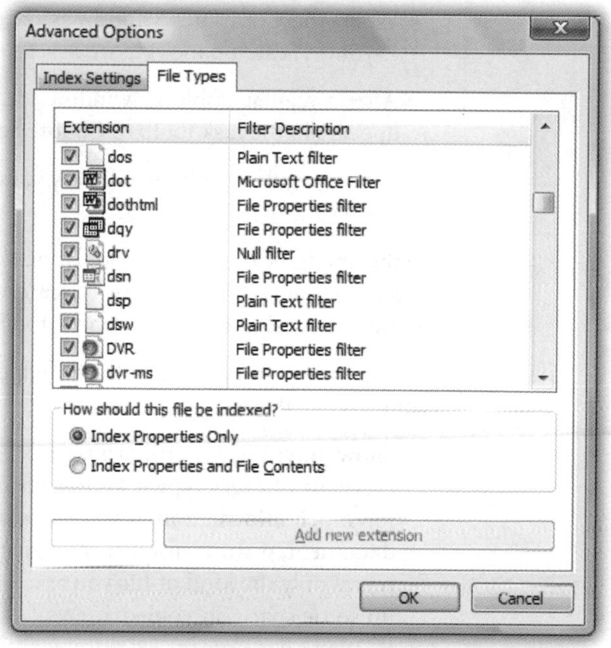

Explorer-Window Searches
All Versions

See the Search text box at the top of every Explorer window? This, too, is a piece of the Vista Search empire. But there's a big difference: The Search box in the Start menu searches *your entire computer.* The Search box in an Explorer window searches *only this window* (and folders within it).

As you type, the window changes to show search results *as* you type into the Search box, much the way the Start menu changes. As described on pages 109–110, a whole range of power tips is available to you, including file-type searches, AND searches, OR searches, and so on.

Once the results appear, you can sort, filter, group, and stack them just like the icons in any other Explorer window.

The Search Pane

As described in Chapter 2, you can adorn every Explorer window with up to four different *panes*—inch-wide strips at the left, right, top, and bottom of a window. One of them is the Search pane.

You can get to it in several ways:

• Press ⊞+F, which is the keyboard shortcut for the Search window (for *find*, get it?).

• When the Computer window is open (Start→Computer), choose Organize→ Layout→Search pane (Figure 3-6, top).

• After a regular Explorer-window search, open the Search Tools menu that now appears in the task toolbar. Choose Search Pane.

• After a regular Explorer-window search, click Advanced Search at the bottom of the results list (Figure 3-6).

In the first three cases, you see only the *top* of the Advanced Search pane—the "Show only:" toolbar described below. To see the full range of options, click Advanced Search at the right end of the "Show only:" toolbar.

As you can see in Figure 3-6, the Search pane lets you fine-tune the search by adding controls like these:

• **Show only:** Vista is ordinarily an extremely passionate little fetcher. It shows you every file of every type it knows when you do a search. Often, though, it displays too much information. If you know what you're looking for is an email message, document, picture, or music file, click the corresponding button. Your search will reveal only the kind of file you asked for. For example, when you're trying to free up some space on your drive, you could round up all your gigantic photo files. ("Other," here, means everything *except* email, documents, pictures, or music.)

• **Location.** The choices in this pop-up menu—Everywhere, Indexed Locations, Computer, Local Hard Drives, and so on—affect the scope of your search. Remember: Ordinarily, searching in an Explorer window finds icons *only* within the open window, including what's in its subfolders. But using this pop-up menu, you can make an Explorer-window search do what a Start-menu search always does: search your *entire* computer. Or only your main hard drive. Or all hard drives. Whatever.

In fact, if you choose "Choose search locations" from this pop-up menu, you get a collapsible, flippy-triangle list of *every* disk and folder associated with your PC (Figure 3-7). Checkboxes give you complete freedom to specify any crazy, mixed-up assortment of random folders you'd like to search at once.

Tip: This option is especially useful when you want to search other hard drives on your network.

At the bottom of this pop-up menu, by the way, is a list of folders you've recently searched, for your déjà vu pleasure.

- **Date modified/created.** When you choose one of these options from the first pop-up menu, the second and third pop-up menus let you isolate files, programs, and folders according to the last time you changed them or when they were created.

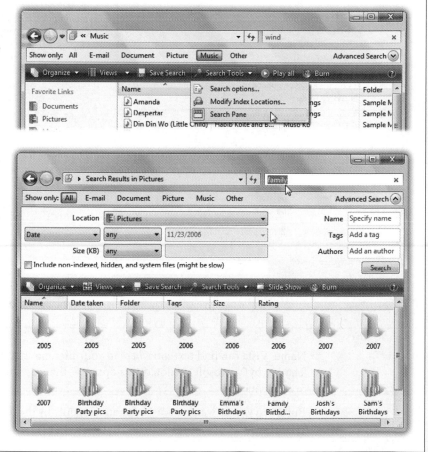

Figure 3-6:
You can gain much more control over the search process using the Search pane.

Top: One way to make it appear is to choose "Search pane" from the Search Tools menu, which appears after you perform a regular Explorer-window search.

Bottom: At that point, you can click Advanced to open a much more powerful, expanded version of the Search strip.

The second pop-up menu offers commands like **Any, is, is before,** and **is after,** and the third offers a little pop-up calendar. The idea is that you can build a phrase out of the three pop-up menus. For example, you can ask Vista to round up items that you last opened or changed before, after, or on a specific day, like 5/27/06.

Tip: You can use the little pop-up menu calendar to specify a *range* of dates, which can be very useful. You might want to see all email from a certain four-day period, for example, or all documents you created last month.

For details on selecting multiple dates on Vista's little date-chooser calendar, see the box on page 81.

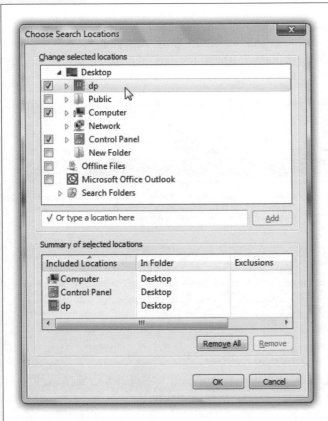

Figure 3-7:
To limit a search by restricting it to a certain disk or folder, choose "Choose search locations" from the Location pop-up menu shown in Figure 3-6. This list box appears. You can turn on the checkboxes of folders you want searched, or you can add a new disk or folder to the list by typing its folder path into the box (below the checkboxes), using folder path notation (page 41)—and then click Add.

- **Name.** Vista can find text *anywhere* in your files, no matter what their *names* are. That's why Microsoft demoted this option—the icon's name—to this Advanced Search pane.

  But when you do want to search for an icon only by the text that's in its name, this is your ticket. Capitalization doesn't matter.

- **Tags.** If you're in the practice of assigning *tags* (keywords) to your documents, as described on page 69, you can use the tag search feature to round up all icons that have a certain tag. They might be all files pertaining to a certain project, for example, or that you wrote during your dry spell of '06.

- **Authors.** Also as described on page 69, you can identify who worked on certain documents by filling in their names in the Authors box of Microsoft Office documents when you save them. You can round them up again later using this field.

- **Include non-indexed, hidden, and system files.** This option makes more sense if you've already read about the little Windows Dewey-Decimal catalog known as the *index* (page 112). Bottom line: to save disk space and time, Vista doesn't usually catalog what's in the operating system itself, or what's inside your program files. You *can* search these items, if you like, by turning on this checkbox. But you'll have to be patient, and you can search for file *names* only.

- **Size.** Using this control, and its "equals/is less than/is greater than" pop-up menu, you can restrict your search to files of a certain size. Use the text box to specify the file's size, in kilobytes. If you want to round up files larger than 5 gigabytes, for example, you'll have to type *5242880*, or, if "close enough" is close enough, *5000000*.

Tip: If you're not handy with kilobyte/megabyte/gigabyte conversions—or even area, weight, mass, volume, or other conversions—Google can help you. Type this right into Google's main search box: *kilobytes in 5 gigabytes* or whatever. When you hit Enter, Google displays the answer.

A key feature of the Advanced Search pane is that it lets you *combine* criteria. Using these controls, you can set up a search for email messages created last week with file sizes over 200 K, for example, or pictures under 500K that are at least two months old and bear the tag *Detroit Coffee-Table Book Project*.

The Search Window

If you've slogged through this chapter up to this point, you're probably under the impression that searching *all* your stuff (not just one window) requires using the Start menu.

Technically, however, that's not quite true. Vista also offers a Search *window,* a sort of hybrid of the Search and Explorer methods. Figure 3-8 explains; for now, just note that you can open the Search window by pressing F3 or ⊞+F.

Saved Searches (Search Folders)
All Versions

Once you've grown comfortable with the layout of the Search pane, you may notice a little button in its task toolbar called Save Search. This button also appears in the search *results* window for Explorer-window searches.

This button generates a *search folder*, a new concept in Windows. It's a self-updating folder that, whenever you click it, performs an instantaneous update of the search you originally set up. (Behind the scenes, it's a special document with the filename extension .search-ms.)

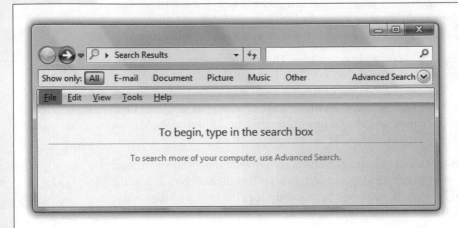

Figure 3-8:
Like the Start menu Search box, the Search window searches your entire PC. But like Explorer searches, file-type filters (and, if you like, the Advanced Search pane) are available at the top. The results list works just like an Explorer-window search.

To create a search folder, open an Explorer window, open its Advanced Search pane (Organize→Layout→Search Pane), and set up the criteria as though you're about to do a search. But instead of clicking Search, click the Save Search button below the pane, in the task toolbar (Figure 3-9, top). You're then asked to name and save your search folder. Windows proposes stashing it in your Searches folder, but keep in mind that you can expand the Save As dialog box (page 194) and choose any location you like—including the desktop.

Here's a common example. Suppose that every week, you want to round up all of the documents authored by either you or your business partner that pertain to the

---

GEM IN THE ROUGH

Keystrokes of the Fast and Furious

As you navigate your folders, double-clicking to open folder after folder, keep in mind the power of the Backspace key. Each time you press it, you jump to the *previous* window. For example, if you open your Personal folder and then Pictures, pressing Backspace returns you to your Personal window.

Likewise, the Alt key, pressed with the right and left arrow keys, serves as a Back and Forward button. Use this powerful shortcut (instead of clicking the corresponding buttons on the toolbar) to "walk" backward or forward through the list of windows most recently opened.

Finally, there's a new keystroke in Vista that's well worth learning: Alt+*up* arrow key. It opens the *parent* folder, the one that *contains* whatever you're now looking at. That's not quite the same thing as hitting the Back button (or Back keystrokes), because sometimes you'll find yourself in a window that you *didn't* get to by burrowing through its parent folders.

Higgins proposal, and burn them onto a CD. A search folder can do the rounding-up part with a single click.

So you open an Explorer window, open its Advanced Search pane, and set up the Authors text box with an OR search (page 110). Type *Higgins* into the Tags box. (Of course, you've been painstakingly tagging your documents with tags and author names, in readiness for this glorious moment.) You click Save Search. You name the search folder something like Our Higgins Files, and save it to your hard drive (Figure 3-9).

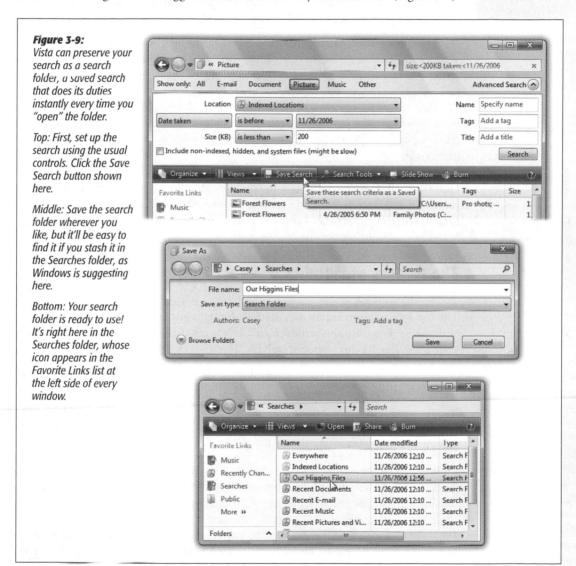

Figure 3-9:
Vista can preserve your search as a search folder, a saved search that does its duties instantly every time you "open" the folder.

Top: First, set up the search using the usual controls. Click the Save Search button shown here.

Middle: Save the search folder wherever you like, but it'll be easy to find it if you stash it in the Searches folder, as Windows is suggesting here.

Bottom: Your search folder is ready to use! It's right here in the Searches folder, whose icon appears in the Favorite Links list at the left side of every window.

From now on, whenever you open that search folder, it opens to reveal all of the files you've worked on that were tagged with Higgins and written by you or your partner.

The great part is that these items' real locations may be all over the map, scattered in folders all over your PC. But through the magic of the search folder, they appear as though they're all in one neat folder.

So how do you *find* a search folder once you've created it?

If you accept Microsoft's suggestion at the moment of creation, and you save it into the Searches folder, then no sweat. The Searches folder itself is technically a folder inside your Personal folder (page 38), which is good to know if you ever want to back it up, distribute your search-folder masterpieces to co-workers, and so on.

But as a convenience, Microsoft has added its icon to the Navigation pane at the left side of every Explorer window (see Figure 3-9). Click Searches, double-click the search folder you saved, and off you go.

Tip: Microsoft starts you off with some useful, ready-made search folders; you'll find them in the Searches folder of your Navigation pane. For example, Recent Documents instantly shows you all the documents you've had open recently, and Recently Changed shows all the files you've recently *edited,* which is not quite the same thing.

Unfortunately, there's no easy way to edit a search folder. If you decide your original search criteria need a little fine-tuning, the simplest procedure is to set up a new search—correctly this time—and save it with the same name as the first one; accept Windows's offer to replace the old one with the new.

The Folders of Windows Vista
All Versions

The top-level, all-encompassing, mother-ship window of your PC is the Computer window. From within this window, you have access to every disk, folder, and file on your computer. Its slogan might well be, "If it's not in here, it's not on your PC."

To see it, choose Start→Computer, or double-click its icon on the desktop, if you've put it there (page 22).

No matter how you open the Computer window (Figure 3-10), you wind up face-to-face with the icons of every storage gizmo connected to your PC: hard drives, CD and DVD drives, USB flash drives, digital cameras, and so on.

Most people, most of the time, are most concerned with the Local Disk (C:), which represents the internal hard drive preinstalled in your computer. (You're welcome to rename this icon, by the way, just as you would any icon.)

Tip: The drive letters, such as C: for your main hard drive, are an ancient convention that doesn't offer much relevance these days. (Back at the dawn of computing, the A: and B: drives were floppy drives, which is why you rarely see them any more.)

Since Windows now displays icons and plain-English names for your drives, you might consider the drive-letter display to be a bit old-fashioned and cluttery. Fortunately, you can hide the drive letter (page 85).

What's in the Local Disk (C:) Window

If you double-click the Local Disk (C:) icon in Computer—that is, your primary hard drive—you'll find these standard folders:

Users

Windows' *accounts* feature is ideal for situations where different family members, students, or workers use the same machine at different times. Each account holder will turn on the machine to find her own separate, secure set of files, folders, desktop pictures, Web bookmarks, font collections, and preference settings. (Much more about this feature in Chapter 23.)

If you're the only one who uses this PC, fine—you can simply ignore the sharing features. But in its little software head, Windows still considers you an account holder, and stands ready to accommodate any others who should come along.

In any case, now you should see the importance of the Users folder. Inside are folders —the *Personal folders*, described in a moment—named for the different people who use this PC. In general, standard account holders (page 669) aren't allowed to open anybody else's folder.

Program Files

This folder contains all of your applications—Word, Excel, Internet Explorer, your games, and so on.

Of course, a Windows program isn't a single, self-contained icon. Instead, it's usually a *folder*, housing both the program and its phalanx of support files and folders. The actual application icon itself generally can't even run if it's separated from its support group.

Windows

Here's a folder that Microsoft hopes its customers will simply ignore. This most hallowed folder contains Windows itself, the thousands of little files that make Windows, well, Windows. Most of these folders and files have cryptic names that appeal to cryptic people.

Note: This folder is almost always called Windows. It might conceivably be called something else, like WINNT, if your computer has been the subject of a series of upgrades reaching back into the Windows NT or Windows 2000 days. Of course, if you're the owner of such a computer, you're perfectly capable of understanding that every time you see "Windows folder" in this book, it means, "the folder called WINNT or whatever it was called when you started upgrading your machine from Windows 2000."

In general, the healthiest PC is one whose Windows folder has been left alone. (One exception: the Fonts folder contains the icons that represent the various typefaces installed on your machine. You're free to add or remove icons from this folder.)

Your Personal Folder

Everything that makes your Vista experience your own sits inside the Local Disk (C:)→Users→[your name] folder. This is your *Personal* folder, where Windows stores your preferences, documents, email, pictures, music, Web favorites and *cookies* (described below), and so on. You can get to it more directly by choosing your name from the top right of the Start menu, or by clicking it in the Folders list (page 67).

Inside your Personal folder, you'll find folders like these:

- **Contacts.** Windows Vista has a new address-book program called Windows Contacts, but it doesn't work like a traditional program. Instead, this folder *is* the address book. Every person in it is represented by an individual, double-clickable icon. You can read more about Windows Contacts on page 250.

- **Desktop.** When you drag an icon out of a folder or disk window and onto your Windows Vista desktop, it may *appear* to show up on the desktop. But that's just an optical illusion—a visual convenience. In truth, nothing in Windows Vista is ever really on the desktop; it's just in this Desktop *folder,* and mirrored on the desktop area.

  Remember that everyone who shares your machine will, upon logging in (page 688), see his own stuff sitting out on the desktop. Now you know how Windows Vista does it; there's a separate Desktop folder in every person's Personal folder.

  You can entertain yourself for hours trying to prove this. If you drag something out of your Desktop folder, it also disappears from the actual desktop. And vice versa.

- **Documents.** Microsoft suggests that you keep your actual work files in this folder. Sure enough, whenever you save a new document (when you're working in Word or Photoshop Elements, for example), the Save As box proposes storing the new file in this folder.

Tip: You can move the Documents folder, if you like. For example, you can move it to a *removable* drive, like a pocket hard drive or USB flash drive, so that you can take it back and forth to work with you and always have your latest files at hand.

To do so, open your Documents folder. Right-click a blank spot in the window; from the shortcut menu, choose Properties. Click the Location tab, click Move, navigate to the new location, and click Select Folder.

What's cool is that the Documents *link* in every Explorer window's Navigation pane still opens your Documents folder. What's more, your programs still propose storing new documents there—even though it's not where Microsoft originally put it.

- **Downloads.** When you download anything from the Web, Internet Explorer suggests storing it on your computer in this Downloads folder. The idea is to save you the frustration of downloading stuff and then not being able to find it later.

  So why doesn't Internet Explorer just download things to the desktop like it used to, where you can't miss them? Microsoft is just trying to help you keep things neat.

Tip: Consider adding the Downloads folder to your Favorite Links list (page 66), so you can find your downloaded goodies with a single click.

- **Favorites.** This folder stores shortcuts of the files, folders, and other items you've designated as *favorites* (that is, Web bookmarks). This can be handy if you want to delete a bunch of your favorites all at once, rename them, and so on.

- **Links.** This folder's shortcut icons (page 145) correspond exactly to the easy-access links in the Favorite Links list at the left side of your Explorer windows (page 66). Knowing this little tidbit can be handy if you want to delete these links, rename them, or add to them. (Yes, you can perform these duties directly in the Favorite Links lists, but only one link at a time.)

- **Music, Pictures, Videos.** You guessed it: these are Microsoft's proposed homes for your multimedia files.

- **Saved Games.** When you save a computer game that's already in progress, it should propose storing it here, so you'll be able to find it again later. (Needless to say, it may take some time before the world's games are updated to know about this folder.)

- **Searches.** This folder stores shortcuts that correspond to any search folders you create, and lists the starter set that Microsoft provides. It's the folder represented by the Searches link in the Favorite Links list (page 129).

Note: Your Personal folder also stores a few hidden items that are reserved for use by Windows itself. One of them is AppData, a very important folder that stores your Media Center recordings, Internet Explorer security certificates, changes you've made to your Start menu, and so on. In general, there's not much reason for you to poke around in them, but in this book, here and there, you'll find tips and tricks that refer you to AppData.

POWER USERS' CLINIC

Long Names and DOS Names

Windows Vista permits long filenames, but DOS—the ancient operating system that used to lurk beneath Windows—doesn't.

PC pros refer to the folder DOS naming system as the "eight dot three" system, because the actual name of the folder or file can't be any longer than eight characters, and it requires a file suffix that's up to three letters long. To accommodate DOS rules, Windows Vista creates an 8.3 version of every long filename. As a result, every file on your computer actually has two *different* names—a long one and a short one.

Every now and then, you'll run up against DOS filename limitations. This quirk explains why the actual name of an application is a cryptic, shortened form of its full name (WINWORD instead of Microsoft Word, for example).

Windows creates the shortened version by inserting the tilde character (~), followed by sequential numbers, after the sixth character of the filename—plus the original extension. For example, if you name a file *letter to mom.doc*, it appears in DOS as *letter~1.doc*. If you then name a file *letter to dad.doc*, it appears in DOS as *letter~2.doc*, and so on.

This naming convention only becomes important if you work in DOS, or you exchange files with someone who uses Windows 3.1 or DOS.

Life with Icons
All Versions

Windows Explorer, the program that runs automatically when you turn on your PC, has only one purpose in life: to help you manage your file, folder, and disk *icons*. You could spend your entire workday just mastering the techniques of naming, copying, moving, and deleting these icons—and plenty of people do.

Here's the crash course.

Renaming Your Icons

To rename a file, folder, printer, or disk icon, you need to open up its "renaming rectangle." You can do so with any of the following methods:

- Highlight the icon and then press the F2 key at the top of your keyboard.

- Click carefully, just once, on a previously highlighted icon's name.

- Right-click the icon and choose Rename from the shortcut menu.

Tip: You can even rename your hard drive, so that you don't go your entire career with a drive named "Local Disk." Just rename its icon (in the Computer window) as you would any other.

In any case, once the renaming rectangle has appeared around the current name, simply type the new name you want, and then press Enter. Feel free to use all the standard text-editing tricks while you're typing: Press Backspace to fix a typo, press the left and right arrow keys to position the insertion point, and so on. When you're finished editing the name, press Enter to make it stick. (If another icon in the folder has the same name, Windows beeps and makes you choose another name.)

Tip: If you highlight a bunch of icons at once and then open the renaming rectangle for any *one* of them, you wind up renaming *all* of them. For example, if you've highlighted folders called Cats, Dogs, and Fish, renaming one of them *Animals* changes the original set of names to Animals (1), Animals (2), and Animals (3).

If that's not what you want, press Ctrl+Z repeatedly (that's the keystroke for Undo) until you've restored all the original names.

A folder or file name can technically be up to 260 characters long. In practice, though, you won't be able to produces filenames that long; that's because that maximum must also include the *file extension* (the three-letter suffix that identifies the file type) and even the file's *folder path* (like C:\Users\Casey\Pictures).

Note, too, that because they're reserved for behind-the-scenes use, Windows doesn't let you use any of these symbols in a Windows file name: \ / : * ? " < > |

You can give more than one file or folder the same name, as long as they're not in the same folder.

Note: Windows Vista comes factory-set not to show you *filename extensions*. That's why you sometimes might *think* you see two different files called, say, Quarterly Sales, both in the same folder.

The explanation is that one file name may end with *.doc* (a Word document), and the other may end with *.xls* (an Excel document). But because these suffixes are hidden (page 222), the files look like they have exactly the same name.

Icon Properties

Properties are a big deal in Windows. Properties are preference settings that you can change independently for every icon on your machine.

To view the properties for an icon, choose from these techniques—the first three open the Properties dialog box:

- Right-click the icon; choose Properties from the shortcut menu.

- While pressing Alt, double-click the icon.

- Highlight the icon; press Alt+Enter.

- Open the Details pane (page 64), and then click an icon.

Tip: You can also see some basic info about any icon (type, size, and so on) by pointing to it without clicking. A little info balloon pops up, saving you the trouble of opening the Properties box or even the Details pane.

These settings aren't the same for every kind of icon, however. Here's what you can expect when opening the Properties dialog boxes of various icons (Figure 3-11).

Computer

There are about 500 different ways to open the Properties dialog box for your Computer icon. The quickest is to right-click Computer *in the Start menu*. Another is to open the System applet in the Control Panel (Chapter 8).

Either way, the System Properties window is packed with useful information about your machine: what kind of processor is inside, how much memory (RAM) your PC has, its overall "Experience Index" (horsepower score), and what version of Windows you've got.

The panel at the left side of the window (shown in Figure 3-11) includes some useful links—Device Manager, Remote settings, System protection, and Advanced system settings—all of which are described in the appropriate chapters of this book.

Note, however, that all of them work by opening the *old* System Properties Control Panel, also shown in Figure 3-11. Its tabs give a terser, but more complete, look at the tech specs and features of your PC. These, too, are described in the relevant parts of this book—all except **Computer Name.** Here, you can type a plain-English name for your computer ("Casey's Laptop," for example). That's how it will appear to other people on the network, if you have one.

Disks

In a disk's Properties dialog box, you can see all kinds of information about the disk itself, like its name (which you can change), its capacity (which you can't change), and how much of it is full.

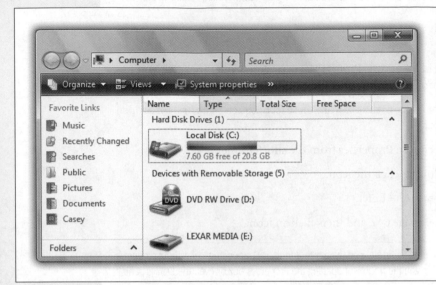

Figure 3-10:
The Computer window is the starting point for any and all folder-digging. It shows the "top-level" folders: the disk drives of your PC. If you double-click the icon of a removable-disk drive (such as your CD or DVD drive), you receive only a "Please insert a disk" message, unless there's actually a disk in the drive.

This dialog box's various tabs are also gateways to a host of maintenance and backup features, including Disk Cleanup, Error-checking, Defrag, Backup, and Quotas; all of these are described in Chapters 20 and 21.

Data files

The Properties for a plain old document depend on what kind of document it is. You always see a General tab, but other tabs may also appear (especially for Microsoft Office files).

- **General.** This screen offers all the obvious information about the document—location, size, modification date, and so on. The *read-only* checkbox locks the document. In the read-only state, you can open the document and read it, but you can't make any changes to it.

Note: If you make a *folder* read-only, it affects only the files that are already inside. If you add additional files later, they remain editable.

Hidden turns the icon invisible. It's a great way to prevent something from being deleted, but because the icon becomes invisible, you may find it a bit difficult to open *yourself*.

The Advanced button offers a few additional options. *File is ready for archiving* means, "Back me up." This message is intended for the Windows Backup program described in Chapter 22, and indicates that this document has been changed since the last time it was backed up (or that it's never been backed up). *Index this file for faster searching* lets you indicate that this file should, or should not, be part of the quick-search index described earlier in this chapter.

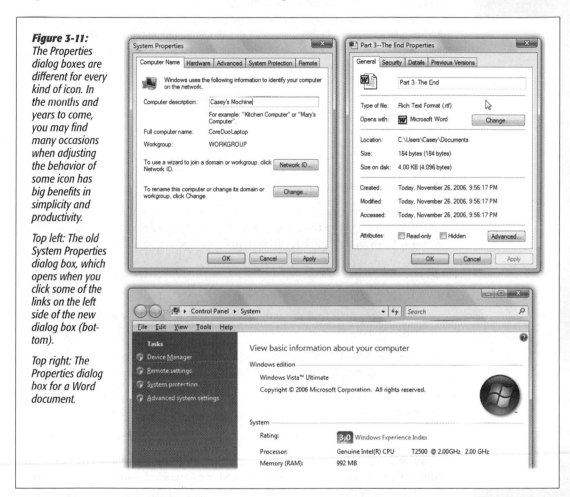

Figure 3-11:
The Properties dialog boxes are different for every kind of icon. In the months and years to come, you may find many occasions when adjusting the behavior of some icon has big benefits in simplicity and productivity.

Top left: The old System Properties dialog box, which opens when you click some of the links on the left side of the new dialog box (bottom).

Top right: The Properties dialog box for a Word document.

Compress contents to save disk space is described later in this chapter. Finally, *Encrypt contents to secure data* is described on page 633.

- **Custom.** As explained below, the Properties window of Office documents includes a Summary tab that lets you look up a document's word count, author, revision number, and many other statistics. But you should by no means feel limited to these 21 properties—nor to Office documents.

Using the Custom tab, you can create properties of your own—Working Title, Panic Level, Privacy Quotient, or whatever you like. Just specify a property type using the Type pop-up menu (Text, Date, Number, Yes/No); type the property name into the Name text box (or choose one of the canned options in its pop-up menu); and then click Add.

You can then fill in the Value text box for the individual file in question (so that its Panic Level is Red Alert, for example).

Note: This is an older form of tagging files—a lot like the tags feature described on page 69, *except* that you can't use Vista's Search to find them. Especially technical people can, however, perform query-language searches for these values.

- The **Summary** tab reveals the sorts of details—tags, categories, authors, and so on—that *are* searchable by Vista's new search command. You can edit these little tidbits right in the dialog box.

  This box also tells you how many words, lines, and paragraphs are in a particular Word document. For a graphics document, the Summary tab indicates the graphic's dimensions, resolution, and color settings.

- The **Previous Versions** tab (Business, Enterprise, and Ultimate editions of Windows only) lets you revert a document or a folder to an earlier version. It's part of the Shadow Copy automatic backup system described on page 654.

Folders

The Properties dialog box for a folder offers five tabs:

- **General.** Here you'll find the same sorts of checkboxes as you do for data files, described above.

- **Sharing** makes the folder susceptible to invasion by other people—either in person, when they log into this PC, or from across your office network (see Chapter 26).

- **Security** has to do with the technical NTFS permissions of a folder, a technical set of on/off switches that governs who can do what to the contents (page 692).

- **Previous Versions** lets you rewind a document to an earlier state; see page 655.

- **Customize.** The first pop-up menu here lets you apply a *folder template* to any folder: Documents, Pictures and Videos, Music Details, or Music Icons. A template is nothing more than a canned layout, with a predesigned set of task toolbar buttons, icon sizes, and column headings.

  You may already have noticed that your Pictures folder displays a nice big thumbnail icon for each of your photos, and your Music folder presents a tidy Details-view list of all your songs, with task toolbar buttons like "Play All," "Sharing Settings," and "Burn." Here's your chance to apply those same expertly designed templates to folders of your own making.

Note: The standard template for the Music folder is the one referred to here as Music Details. If you choose Music Icons instead, then each band is represented as a filing folder standing on edge, with an actual representative album cover peeking out.

Program files

There's not much here that you can change yourself, but you certainly get a lot to look at. For starters, there are the General and Details tabs described above.

But there's also an important Compatibility tab, which may one day come to save your bacon. As described on page 236, it lets you trick a pre-Vista program into running on Microsoft's latest.

Changing Your Icons' Icons

You can change the actual, inch-tall illustrations that Windows uses to represent the little icons replete in your electronic world. You can't, however, pick a single method to do so; Microsoft has divided up the controls among at least two different locations.

Standard Windows icons

First, you can also change the icon for some of the important Windows desktop icons: the Recycle Bin, Documents, and so on. To do so, right-click a blank spot on the desktop. From the shortcut menu, choose Personalize.

In the resulting window, click "Change desktop icons" in the task pane at the left side. You'll see a collection of those important Windows icons. Click one, and then click Change Icon to choose a replacement from a collection Microsoft provides. (You haven't *lived* until you've made your Recycle Bin look like a green, growing tree!)

Folder or shortcut icons

Finally, if you're sneaky, you can replace the icons for individual folder and shortcut icons (but, alas, not document icons). Here's how:

1. **Right-click the folder or shortcut whose icon you want to change. From the shortcut menu, choose Properties.**

   The Properties dialog box appears.

2. **Click the Customize tab (for a folder) or the Shortcut tab (for a shortcut). At the bottom of the dialog box, click the Change Icon button.**

   Yet another dialog box, filled with prefab replacement icons, appears. If you see one that suits your fancy, click it; otherwise, continue.

3. **Click Browse.**

   Windows Vista now lets you hunt for icons on your hard drive. These can be icons that you've downloaded from the Internet, icons embedded inside program files and .dll files, or icons that you've made yourself using a freeware or shareware icon-making program like AX-Icons (available at *www.missingmanuals.com*, among other places).

4. **Click OK twice.**

   You return to the desktop, where you should see your new replacement icon happily in place.

Selecting Icons
All Versions

Before you can delete, rename, move, copy, or otherwise tamper with any icon, you have to be able to *select* it somehow. By highlighting it, you're essentially telling Windows what you want to operate on.

In Windows Vista, this simple act has taken on some startling new dimensions.

Use the Mouse

To select one icon, just click it once. To select *multiple* icons at once—in preparation for moving, copying, renaming, or deleting them en masse, for example—use one of these techniques:

- **Select all.** Highlight all of the icons in a window by choosing Organize→Select All. (Or press Ctrl+A, its keyboard equivalent.)

- **Highlight several consecutive icons.** Start with your cursor above and to one side of the icons, and then drag diagonally. As you drag, you create a temporary dotted-line rectangle. Any icon that falls within this rectangle darkens to indicate that it's been selected.

  Alternatively, click the first icon you want to highlight, and then Shift-click the last file. All the files in between are automatically selected, along with the two icons you clicked. (These techniques work in any folder view: Details, Icon, Thumbnails, or whatever.)

Tip: If you include a particular icon in your diagonally-dragged group by mistake, Ctrl-click it to remove it from the selected cluster.

- **Highlight non-consecutive icons.** Suppose you want to highlight only the first, third, and seventh icons in the list. Start by clicking icon No. 1; then Ctrl-click each of the others. (If you Ctrl-click a selected icon *again*, you *de*select it. A good time to use this trick is when you highlight an icon by accident.)

Tip: The Ctrl key trick is especially handy if you want to select *almost* all the icons in a window. Press Ctrl+A to select everything in the folder, then Ctrl-click any unwanted subfolders to deselect them.

Use the Keyboard

You can also highlight one icon, plucking it out of a sea of pretenders, by typing the first couple letters of its name. Type *nak,* for example, to select an icon called "Naked Chef Broadcast Schedule."

Checkbox Selection

It's great that you can select random icons by holding down a key and clicking—if you can remember *which* key must be pressed.

Turns out novices were befuddled by the requirement to Ctrl-click icons when they wanted to choose more than one. So Microsoft did something in Windows that nobody's ever done before—it created a checkbox mode. In this mode, any icon you point to temporarily sprouts a little checkbox that you can click to select (Figure 3-12).

Figure 3-12:
Each time you point to an icon, a clickable checkbox appears. Once you turn it on, the checkbox remains visible, making it easy to select several icons at once. What's cool about the new checkboxes feature is that it doesn't preclude your using the old click-to-select method; if you click an icon's name, you deselect all checkboxes except that one.

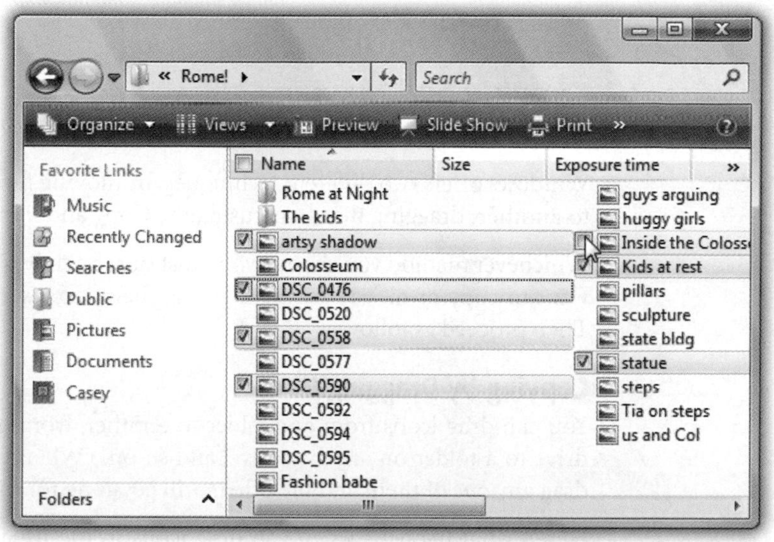

To turn this feature on, open any Explorer window, and then choose Organize→Folder and Search Options. Click the View tab, scroll down in the list of settings, and then turn on "Use check boxes to select items." Click OK.

With the checkboxes visible, no secret keystrokes are necessary; it's painfully obvious how you're supposed to choose only a few icons out of a gaggle.

Eliminating Double-Clicks

In some ways, an Explorer window is just like Internet Explorer, the Web browser. It has a Back button, an Address bar, and so on.

If you enjoy this PC-as-browser effect, you can actually take it one step further. You can set up your PC so that *one* click, not two, opens an icon. It's a strange effect that some people adore, and others turn off as fast as their little fingers will let them.

In any Explorer window, choose Organize→Folder and Search Options.

The Folder Options control panel opens. Turn on "Single-click to open an item (point to select)." Then indicate *when* you want your icon's names turned into underlined links by selecting "Underline icon titles consistent with my browser" (that is, *all* icons' names appear as links) or "Underline icon titles only when I point at them." Click OK. The deed is done.

Now, if a single click opens an icon, you're entitled to wonder how you're supposed to *select* an icon (which you'd normally do with a single click). Take your pick:

- Point to it for about a half-second without clicking. (To make multiple selections, press the Ctrl key as you point to additional icons. And to *drag* an icon, just ignore all this pointing stuff—simply drag as usual.)

- Turn on Checkbox mode described above.

Copying and Moving Folders and Files
All Versions

Windows offers two different techniques for moving files and folders from one place to another: dragging them, and using the Copy and Paste commands.

Whichever method you choose, you must start by showing Windows which icons you want to copy or move—by highlighting them, as described on the previous pages. Then proceed as follows.

Copying by Dragging Icons

You can drag icons from one folder to another, from one drive to another, from a drive to a folder on another drive, and so on. (When you've selected several icons, drag any *one* of them and the others will go along for the ride.)

Here's what happens when you drag icons in the usual way (using the left mouse button):

- Dragging to another folder on the same disk *moves* the folder or file.

- Dragging from one disk to another *copies* the folder or file.

- Holding down the Ctrl key while dragging to another folder on the same disk *copies* the icon. (If you do so within a single window, a duplicate of the file called "[File name] - Copy" is created.)

- Pressing Shift while dragging from one disk to another *moves* the folder or file (without leaving a copy behind).

Tip: You can move or copy icons by dragging them either into an open window or directly onto a disk or folder *icon*.

The right mouse button trick

Think you'll remember all of those possibilities every time you drag an icon? Probably not. Fortunately, you never have to. One of the most important tricks you can learn is to use the *right* mouse button as you drag. When you release the button, the menu shown in Figure 3-13 appears, letting you either copy or move the selected icons.

Tip: Press the Esc key to cancel a dragging operation at any time.

Dragging icons into the Navigation pane

You may find it easier to copy or move icons using the Navigation pane (page 66),
since the two-pane display format makes it easier to see where your files are and
where they're going.

Figure 3-13:
Thanks to this shortcut menu, right-dragging icons is much easier and safer than left-dragging when you want to move or copy something. New in Vista: the handy numeric "badge" on your cursor, which reminds you how many things you're about to move or copy.

Just expand the flippy triangles of the Navigation pane until you can see the destination folder. Then locate the icon you want to move in the right pane and drag it to the
appropriate folder in the left pane (Figure 3-14). Windows copies the icon.

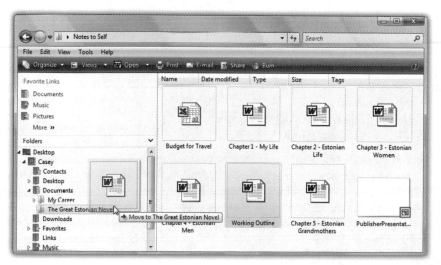

Figure 3-14:
The file Working Outline is being dragged to the folder named The Great Estonian Novel (in the Documents folder). As the cursor passes each folder in the left pane, the folder's name darkens. Release the mouse when it's pointing to the correct folder or disk.

Copying with Copy and Paste

Dragging icons to copy or move them feels good because it's so direct; you actually see your arrow cursor pushing the icons into the new location.

But you also pay a price for this satisfying illusion. That is, you may have to spend a moment or two fiddling with your windows, or clicking in the Explorer folder

---

POWER USERS' CLINIC

Secrets of the Send To Command

If you find yourself copying or moving certain icons to certain folders or disks with regularity, it's time to exploit the Send To command that lurks in the shortcut menu for almost every icon. (If you press the Alt key to make the menu bar appear, the Send To command is also in the File menu of every Explorer window.)

This command offers a quick way to copy and move highlighted icons to popular destinations. For example, you can teleport a copy of a highlighted file directly to your CD burner by choosing Send To→CD-R Drive, or to the desktop background by choosing Send To→Desktop (create shortcut).

Then there's the Send To→Mail Recipient, which bundles the highlighted icon as an email attachment that's ready to send. You can also zip

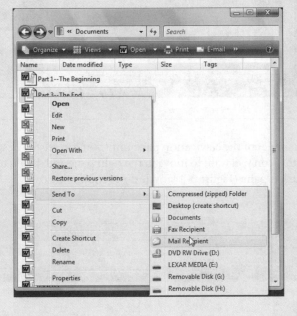

up a folder (see the end of this chapter) by choosing Send To→"Compressed (zipped) Folder."

But the real power of the Send To command is its ability to accommodate your *own* favorite or frequently used folders. Lurking in your Personal folder (page 38) is a folder called SendTo. Any shortcut icon you place here shows up instantly in the Send To menus within your desktop folders and shortcut menus.

Alas, this folder is among those that Microsoft considers inappropriate for inspection by novices. As a result, the SendTo folder is *hidden*.

You can still get to it, though. Right-click your Start menu; from the shortcut menu, choose Explore. In the window that now opens, take a look in your Navigation pane–in the folder list at the left side of the window. Just above the Start Menu listing is a folder called, sure enough, SendTo.

Most people create shortcuts here for folders and disks (such as your favorite backup disk). When you highlight an icon and then choose Send To→Backup Disk, for example, Windows copies the icon to that disk. (Or, if you simultaneously press Shift, you *move* the icon to the other disk or folder.)

You can even add shortcuts of *applications* (program files) to the SendTo folder. By adding WinZip to this Send To menu, for example, you can drop-kick a highlighted icon onto the WinZip icon (for decompressing) just by choosing Send To→WinZip. You can even create shortcuts for your printer or fax modem, so that you can print or fax a document just by highlighting its icon and choosing File→Send To→ [printer or fax modem's name].

---

hierarchy, so that you have a clear "line of drag" between the icon to be moved and the destination folder.

Fortunately, there's a better way. You can use the Cut, Copy, and Paste commands to move icons from one window into another. The routine goes like this:

1. **Highlight the icon or icons you want to move.**

   Use any of the tricks described on page 136.

2. **Right-click one of the icons. From the shortcut menu, choose Cut or Copy.**

   Alternatively, you can choose Organize→Cut or Organize→Copy, using the task toolbar at the top of the window. (Eventually, you may want to learn the keyboard shortcuts for these commands: Ctrl+C for Copy, Ctrl+X for Cut.)

   The Cut command makes the highlighted icons appear dimmed; you've now stashed them on the invisible Windows Clipboard. (They don't actually disappear from their original nesting place until you paste them somewhere else.)

   The Copy command also places copies of the files on the Clipboard, but doesn't disturb the originals.

3. **Right-click the window, folder icon, or disk icon where you want to put the icons. Choose Paste from the shortcut menu.**

   Once again, you may prefer to use the appropriate menu bar option, Organize→Paste. *Keyboard equivalent:* Ctrl+V.

   Either way, you've successfully transferred the icons. If you pasted into an open window, you'll see the icons appear there. If you pasted onto a closed folder or disk icon, you need to open the icon's window to see the results. And if you pasted right back into the same window, you get a duplicate of the file called "[File name] - Copy."

The Recycle Bin
All Versions

The Recycle Bin is your desktop trash basket. This is where files and folders go when they've outlived their usefulness. Basically, the Recycle Bin is a waiting room for data oblivion, in that your files stay here until you *empty* it—or until you rescue the files by dragging them out again.

While you can certainly drag files or folders onto the Recycle Bin icon, it's usually faster to highlight them and then perform one of the following options:

- Press the Delete key.
- Choose File→Delete.
- Right-click a highlighted icon and choose Delete from the shortcut menu.

Windows asks if you're sure you want to send the item to the Recycle Bin. (You don't lose much by clicking Yes, since it's easy enough to change your mind, as noted below.) Now the Recycle Bin icon looks like it's brimming over with paper.

Tip: To turn off the "Are you sure?" message that appears when you send something Bin-ward, right-click the Recycle Bin. From the shortcut menu, choose Properties, and turn off "Display delete confirmation dialog." Turning off the warning isn't much of a safety risk; after all, files aren't really being removed from your drive when you put them in the Recycle Bin.

You can put unwanted files and folders into the Recycle Bin from any folder window or even inside the Open File dialog box of many applications (see Chapter 6).

Note: All of these methods put icons from your *hard drive* into the Recycle Bin. But deleting an icon from a removable drive (floppy or Zip drives, for example) or other computers on the network, does *not* involve the Recycle Bin, giving you no opportunity to retrieve them. (Deleting anything with the DOS *del* or *erase* commands bypasses the Recycle Bin, too.)

Restoring Deleted Files and Folders

If you change your mind about sending something to the software graveyard, simply open the Recycle Bin by double-clicking. A window like the one in Figure 3-15 opens.

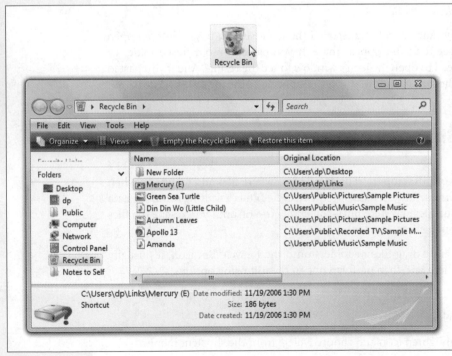

Figure 3-15:
When you double-click the Recycle Bin (top), its window (bottom) displays information about each folder and file that it holds. To sort its contents, making it easier to find a deleted icon, click the gray column heading for the type of sort you need.

To restore a selected file or a folder—or a bunch of them—click the "Restore this item" link on the task toolbar. Or right-click any one of the selected icons and choose Restore from the shortcut menu.

Restored means returned to the folder from whence it came—wherever it was on your hard drive when deleted. If you restore an icon whose original folder has been deleted in the meantime, Windows even recreates that folder to hold the restored file(s).

Tip: You don't have to put icons back into their original folders. By *dragging* them out of the Recycle Bin window, you can put them back into any folder you like.

Emptying the Recycle Bin

While there's an advantage to the Recycle Bin (you get to undo your mistakes), there's also a downside: the files in the Recycle Bin occupy as much disk space as they did when they were stored in folders. Deleting files doesn't gain you additional disk space until you *empty* the Recycle Bin.

That's why most people, sooner or later, follow up an icon's journey to the Recycle Bin with one of these cleanup operations:

- Right-click the Recycle Bin icon, or a blank spot in the Recycle Bin window, and choose Empty Recycle Bin from the shortcut menu.

- Click the "Empty the Recycle Bin" link on the task toolbar in the Recycle Bin window.

- In the Recycle Bin window, highlight only the icons you want to eliminate, and then press the Delete key. (Use this method when you want to nuke only *some* of the Recycle Bin's contents.)

- Wait. When the Recycle Bin accumulates so much stuff that it occupies a significant percentage of your hard drive space, Windows empties it automatically, as described in the next section.

The first three of these procedures produce an "Are you sure?" message.

Customizing the Recycle Bin

You can make two useful changes to the behavior of the Recycle Bin. To investigate these alterations, right-click the Recycle Bin icon and choose Properties from the shortcut menu. The Recycle Bin Properties dialog box appears (see Figure 3-16).

Skip the Recycle Bin

If you, a person of steely nerve and perfect judgment, never delete a file in error, then your files can bypass the Recycle Bin entirely when you delete them. Furthermore, you'll reclaim disk space instantly when you press the Delete key to vaporize a highlighted file or folder.

To set this up, turn on the "Do not move files to the Recycle Bin" checkbox (shown in Figure 3-16). And voilà! Your safety net is gone (especially if you *also* turn off the confirmation dialog box shown in Figure 3-16—then you're *really* living dangerously.)

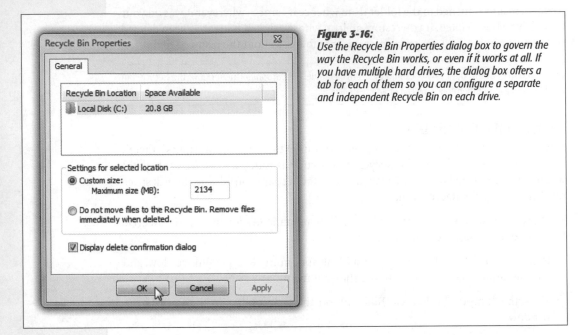

Figure 3-16:
Use the Recycle Bin Properties dialog box to govern the way the Recycle Bin works, or even if it works at all. If you have multiple hard drives, the dialog box offers a tab for each of them so you can configure a separate and independent Recycle Bin on each drive.

If that suggestion seems too extreme, consider this safety/convenience compromise: leave the Recycle Bin safety net in place most of the time, but bypass the Recycle Bin on command only when it seems appropriate.

The trick to skipping the Recycle Bin on a one-shot basis is to press the Shift key while you delete a file. Doing so—and then clicking Yes in the confirmation box—deletes the file permanently, skipping its layover in the Recycle Bin. (The Shift-key trick works for every method of deleting a file: pressing the Delete key, choosing Delete from the shortcut menu, and so on.)

Auto-emptying the Recycle Bin

The Recycle Bin has two advantages over the physical trash cans behind your house: First, it never smells. Second, when it's full, it can empty itself automatically.

To configure this self-emptying feature, you specify a certain fullness limit. When the Recycle Bin contents reach that level, Windows begins deleting files (permanently) as new files arrive in the Recycle Bin. Files that arrived in the Recycle Bin first are deleted first.

Unless you tell it otherwise, Windows reserves 10 percent of your drive to hold Recycle Bin contents. To change that percentage, edit the "Maximum size" number, in megabytes (Figure 3-16). Keeping the percentage low means you're less likely to run out of the disk space you need to install software and create documents. On the other hand, raising the percentage means you'll have more opportunity to restore files you later want to retrieve.

Note: Every disk has its own Recycle Bin, which holds files and folders that you've deleted from that disk. As you can see in the Recycle Bin Properties dialog box, you can give each drive its own trash limit, and change the deletion options shown in Figure 3-16 for each drive independently. Just click the drive's name before changing the settings.

Shortcut Icons
All Versions

A *shortcut* is a link to a file, folder, disk, or program (see Figure 3-17). You might think of it as a duplicate of the thing's icon—but not a duplicate of the thing itself. (A shortcut occupies almost no disk space.) When you double-click the shortcut icon, the original folder, disk, program, or document opens. You can also set up a keystroke for a shortcut icon, so that you can open any program or document just by pressing a certain key combination.

Shortcuts provide quick access to the items you use most often. And because you can make as many shortcuts of a file as you want, and put them anywhere on your PC, you can, in effect, keep an important program or document in more than one folder. Just create a shortcut of each to leave on the desktop in plain sight, or drag

Figure 3-17:
You can distinguish a desktop shortcut (left) from its original in two ways. First, the tiny arrow "badge" identifies it as a shortcut; second, its name contains the word "shortcut." Right: The Properties dialog box for a shortcut indicates which actual file or folder this one "points" to. The Run drop-down menu (shown open) lets you control how the window opens when you double-click the shortcut icon.

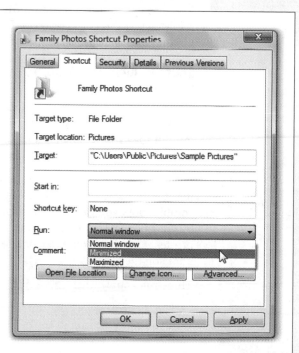

their icons onto the Start button or the Quick Launch toolbar. In fact, everything listed in the Start→All Programs menu *is* a shortcut. So is every link in the top part of your Navigation pane.

Tip: Don't confuse the term *shortcut,* which refers to one of these duplicate-icon pointers, with *shortcut menu,* the context-sensitive menu that appears when you right-click almost anything in Windows. The shortcut *menu* has nothing to do with the shortcut icons feature; maybe that's why it's sometimes called the *context* menu.

Creating and Deleting Shortcuts

To create a shortcut, right-drag an icon from its current location to the desktop. When you release the mouse button, choose Create Shortcuts Here from the menu that appears.

Tip: If you're not in the mood for using a shortcut menu, just left-drag an icon while pressing Alt. A shortcut appears instantly. (And if your keyboard lacks an Alt key—yeah, right—drag while pressing Ctrl+Shift instead.)

You can delete a shortcut the same as any icon, as described in the Recycle Bin discussion earlier in this chapter. (Of course, deleting a shortcut *doesn't* delete the file it points to.)

Unveiling a Shortcut's True Identity

To locate the original icon from which a shortcut was made, right-click the shortcut icon and choose Properties from the shortcut menu. As shown in Figure 3-17, the resulting box shows you where to find the "real" icon. It also offers you a quick way to jump to it, in the form of the Find Target button.

Shortcut Keyboard Triggers

Even after reading all of this gushing prose about the virtues of shortcuts, efficiency experts may still remain skeptical. Sure, shortcuts let you put favored icons everywhere you want to be, such as your Start menu, Quick Launch toolbar, the desktop, and so on. But they still require clicking to open, which means taking your hands off the keyboard—and that, in the grand scheme of things, means slowing down.

Lurking within the Shortcut Properties dialog box is another feature with intriguing ramifications: the Shortcut Key box. By clicking here and then pressing a key combination, you can assign a personalized keystroke for the shortcut. Thereafter, by pressing that keystroke, you can summon the corresponding file, program, folder, printer, networked computer, or disk window to your screen (no matter what you're doing on the PC).

Three rules apply when choosing keystrokes to open your favorite icons:

- The keystrokes work only on shortcuts stored *on your desktop or in the Start menu*. If you stash the icon in any other folder, the keystroke stops working.

- Your keystroke can't incorporate the Space Bar or the Backspace, Delete, Esc, Print Screen, or Tab keys.

- There are no one- or two-key combinations available here. Your combination must include at least two of these three keys—Ctrl, Shift, and Alt—*and* another key.

Windows enforces this rule rigidly. For example, if you type a single letter key into the box (such as *E*), Windows automatically adds the Ctrl and Alt keys to your combination (Ctrl+Alt+E). All of this is the operating system's attempt to prevent you from inadvertently duplicating one of the built-in Windows keyboard shortcuts and thoroughly confusing both you and your computer.

Tip: If you've ever wondered what it's like to be a programmer, try this. In the Shortcut Properties dialog box (Figure 3-17), use the Run drop-down menu at the bottom of the dialog box to choose "Normal window," "Minimized," or "Maximized." By clicking OK, you've just told Windows what kind of window you want to appear when opening this particular shortcut. (See page 86 for a discussion of these window types.)

Controlling your Windows in this way isn't exactly the same as programming Microsoft Excel, but you are, in your own small way, telling Windows what to do.

Compressing Files and Folders
All Versions

Windows is especially effective at compressing files and folders to reduce the space they occupy on your hard drive—which is ironic, considering the fact that hard drives these days have enough capacity to stretch to Bill Gates's house and back three times.

Even so, compressing files and folders can occasionally be useful, especially when hard drive space is running short, or when you want to email files to someone without dooming them to an all-night modem-watching session. Maybe that's why Microsoft has endowed Windows Vista with two different schemes for compressing files and folders: *NTFS compression* and *zipped folders*.

NTFS Compression
Windows Vista, since you asked, requires a hard drive that's formatted using a software scheme called *NTFS* (short for NT file system; see page 621 for details). It's a much more modern formatting scheme than its predecessor, something called FAT32—and among its virtues is, you guessed it, NTFS compression.

This compression scheme is especially likable because it's completely invisible. Windows automatically compresses and decompresses your files, almost instantaneously. At some point, you may even forget you've turned it on. Consider:

- Whenever you open a compressed file, Windows quickly and invisibly expands it to its original form so that you can edit it. When you close the file again, Windows instantly recompresses it.

- If you send compressed files (via disk or email, for example) to a PC whose hard drive doesn't use NTFS formatting, Windows once again decompresses them, quickly and invisibly.

- Any file you copy into a compressed folder or disk is compressed automatically. (If you only *move* it into such a folder from elsewhere on the disk, however, it stays compressed or uncompressed—whichever it was originally.)

There's only one downside to all this: you don't save a *lot* of disk space using NTFS compression (at least not when compared with Zip compression, described in the next section). Even so, if your hard drive is anywhere near full, it might be worth turning on NTFS compression. The space you save could be your own.

Compressing files, folders, or disks

To turn on NTFS compression, right-click the icon for the file, folder, or disk whose contents you want to shrink; from the shortcut menu, choose Properties. Proceed as shown in Figure 3-18.

Figure 3-18:
In the Properties dialog box for any file or folder, click Advanced. Turn on the checkbox that says "Compress drive to save disk space." All the subfolders will be compressed, too.

Your Turn to Drive

Hey, my Dell has two CD/DVD burners. How do I specify which one is the default for burning blank discs?

All in good time, grasshoppa.

Choose Start→Computer. Right-click the icon of the burner you want; from the shortcut menu, choose Properties. Click the recording tab; use the drive menu to choose the one you want to do the heavy lifting. (Authenticate yourself if necessary, as described on page 191.)

Many Windows veterans wind up turning on compression for the entire hard drive, even though it takes Windows several hours to do the job. (If you plan to go see a movie while Windows is working, though, quit all your programs first. Otherwise, the compression process will halt whenever it encounters an open file—waiting for you to close the file or tell Windows to ignore it—and you'll find the job only half done when you return from the cineplex.)

When Windows is finished compressing, their names appear in a different color, a reminder that Windows is doing its part to maximize your disk space.

Note: If they don't change color, somebody—maybe you—must have turned off the "Show encrypted or compressed NTFS files in color" option (see page 85).

Zipped Folders

As noted above, NTFS compression is ideal for freeing up disk space while you're working at your PC. But as soon as you email your files to somebody else or burn them to a CD, the transferred copies bloat right back up to their original sizes.

Fortunately, there's another way to compress files: Zip them. If you've ever used Windows before, you've probably encountered Zip files. Each one is a tiny little suitcase, an *archive*, whose contents have been tightly compressed to keep files together, to save space, and to transfer them online faster (see Figure 3-19). Use this method when

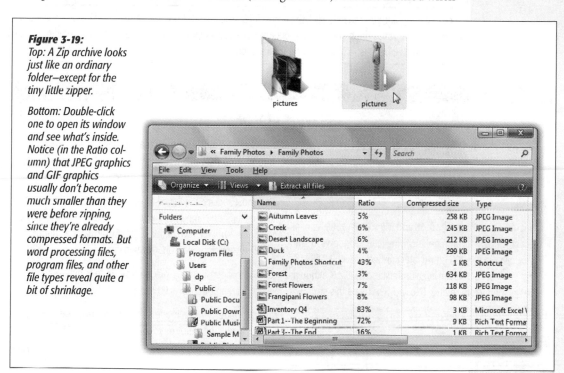

Figure 3-19:
Top: A Zip archive looks just like an ordinary folder—except for the tiny little zipper.

Bottom: Double-click one to open its window and see what's inside. Notice (in the Ratio column) that JPEG graphics and GIF graphics usually don't become much smaller than they were before zipping, since they're already compressed formats. But word processing files, program files, and other file types reveal quite a bit of shrinkage.

you want to email something to someone, or when you want to pack up a completed project and remove it from your hard drive to free up space.

Creating zipped folders

You can create a Zip archive in either of two ways:

- Right-click any blank spot on the desktop or an open window. From the shortcut menu, choose New→Compressed (zipped) Folder. Type a name for your newly created, empty archive, and then press Enter.

  Now, each time you drag a file or folder onto the archive's icon (or into its open window), Windows automatically stuffs a *copy* of it inside.

  Of course, you haven't exactly saved any disk space, since now you have two copies (one zipped, one untouched). If you'd rather *move* a file or folder into the archive—in the process deleting the full-size version and saving disk space—right-drag the file or folder icon onto the archive icon. Now from the shortcut menu, choose Move Here.

- To turn an *existing* file or folder into a Zip archive, right-click its icon. (To zip up a handful of icons, select them first, then right-click any one of them.) Now, from the shortcut menu, choose Send To→Compressed (zipped) Folder. You've just created a new archive folder *and* copied the files or folders into it.

Tip: At this point, you can right-click the zipped folder's icon and choose Send To→Mail Recipient. Windows automatically whips open your email program, creates an outgoing message ready for you to address, and attaches the zipped file to it. It's now set for transport.

WORKAROUND WORKSHOP

Flavors of UDF

Different operating systems understand different versions of UDF:

Windows 98 and Windows 2000 can't understand any version.

Mac OS X (10.3 and 10.4) and Windows 2000 can all recognize UDF 1.5, but not anything later. Windows XP and Windows Server 2003 (and later) are good with UDF 2.01. And Vista, of course, can even understand UDF 2.5, although 2.01 is the factory setting. (Nobody ever said this stuff was gonna be easy.)

In any case, if you learn that your adoring audience requires one UDF format or another, you can let Windows Vista know.

You must specify which version you want to burn in step 3 in the steps on page 153. See the dialog box that appears (Figure 3-20)? When you choose "Show formatting options," you'll see a link called "Change version."

Click it to open a dialog box that offers four different UDF versions, ranging from 1.50 to 2.50.

Click OK after you've made your choice from the pop-up menu. Now, good luck to you.

Working with zipped folders

In many respects, a zipped folder behaves just like any ordinary folder. Double-click it to see what's inside.

If you double-click one of the *files* you find inside, however, Windows opens up a *read-only* copy of it—that is, a copy you can view, but not edit. To make changes to a read-only copy, you must use the File→Save As command and save it somewhere else on your hard drive.

Note: Be sure to navigate to the desktop or Documents folder, for example, before you save your edited document. Otherwise, Windows will save it into an invisible temporary folder, where you may never see it again.

To decompress only some of the icons in a zipped folder, just drag them out of the archive window; they instantly spring back to their original sizes. Or, to decompress the entire archive, right-click its icon and choose Extract All from the shortcut menu (or, if its window is already open, click the "Extract all files" link on the task toolbar). A dialog box asks you to specify where you want the resulting files to wind up.

Burning CDs and DVDs from the Desktop

All Versions

Burning a CD or DVD is great for backing stuff up, transferring stuff to another computer, mailing to somebody, or archiving older files to free up hard drive space. These days, you can buy blank CDs and DVDs very inexpensively in bulk via the Web or discount store.

In ancient times—you know, like 2002—every PC came with a CD-ROM drive. Nowadays, new PCs come with either a *combo drive* (a drive that can burn blank CDs *and* play back DVDs) or a drive that burns *both* CDs and DVDs.

Before you dig in, however, here's a brief chalk talk about CD data formats.

A Tale of Two Formats

Turns out Windows Vista can burn blank CDs and DVDs using your choice of *two* formats.

- **Mastered (ISO).** This is what most of the world is used to. It's what everybody burned before Windows Vista came along.

  You know the drill. You insert the blank disc and then drag files and folders into its window. The PC duplicates each item, parking it in an invisible, temporary holding area until you're ready to burn. You burn all the files and folders at once.

  Trouble is, you're therefore *doubling* the disk-space requirement of the files you intended to burn. If you're burning a DVD to get older files off your hard drive because you're running low on space, you could wind up in a catch-22. You can't free up drive space without burning a DVD first—but you don't have enough drive space to burn a DVD!

Tip: To be fair, you *can* change the location of the temporary holding folder—if you have another hard drive. In your Computer window, right-click your burner's icon; from the shortcut menu, choose Properties. Click the Recording tab; from the drive menu, choose the hard drive you prefer, authenticating (page 191) when you're asked.

At this point, the Mastered format's sole virtue is compatibility. These discs play in just about any computer, including Macs, PCs, and CD or DVD players that play MP3 CDs and digital video.

- **Live File System (UDF).** This newer, more modern format—Vista's new factory setting—is light-years more convenient. It lets you use a blank CD or DVD exactly as though it's a floppy disk or USB flash drive. You can drag files and folders onto it, move icons around on it, rename them, and so on. There's no momentous Moment of Burn; files are copied to the CD in real time, whenever you put them there. You can leave a disc in your drive, dragging stuff onto it throughout the week as it's convenient—without every having to click a Burn button.

What's more, you can the eject the CD, store it or share it—and then, later, put it back into your PC and *burn more stuff onto it.* That's right—you can burn a single CD as many times as you like. And we're talking regular, cheapie CD-R discs, not CD-RW (rewritable).

What Vista creates, in other words, is a *multisession* disc. Each time you burn more material onto it, you create a new disc icon that will appear separately in your Computer window when you insert the CD.

Of course, the downside is that discs you burn this way generally work only in *Windows XP and Windows Vista* computers. Beware, because this is the default setting!

Tip: If it helps you to remember which format is which, here's a mnemonic for you: the last letter of the format name (ISO, UDF) lets you know whether this is the *Older* format or the *Future* one.

Burning, Step by Step

Now that, with luck, you understand the difference between the Mastered (ISO) and File System (UDF) formats, you're ready to proceed.

1. **Insert a blank disc into your PC.**

   The AutoPlay dialog box appears, asking whether you intend for this CD or DVD to hold computer files or music (Figure 3-20, top left). If you want to burn a music CD, skip ahead to Chapter 14.

Note: If you *always* want to create data CDs (or always burn music CDs), turn on "Always do this for blank CDs" to save yourself a step each time.

Vista duly records your preference in the AutoPlay applet of the Control Panel. If you ever change your mind, you can always open that applet and reverse yourself, as described in Chapter 8.

Otherwise, continue to step 2.

2. **Click the "Burn files to disc" link.**

   Windows asks you to name the CD or DVD.

3. **Type a name for the disc.**

   But don't click Next yet. This crucial moment is your only chance to change the disc's format.

   If you're OK with burning in the delicious, newfangled UDF format described above, never mind; skip to step 4.

   If you want this disc to be usable by a Macintosh, a CD or DVD player, or somebody using a version of Windows before Windows XP, though, you'll want to take this moment to change the format. Figure 3-20 shows the full life cycle of a disk you're burning.

   Once that's done, you can go on to step 4.

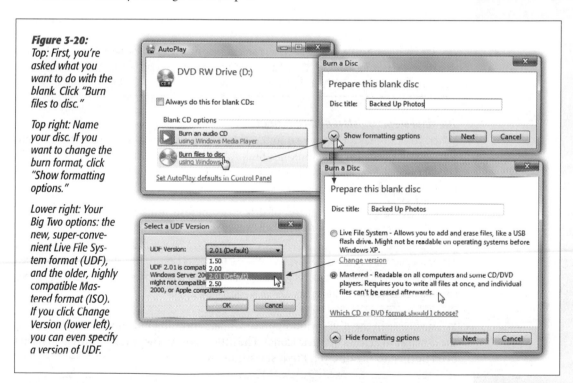

Figure 3-20:
Top: First, you're asked what you want to do with the blank. Click "Burn files to disc."

Top right: Name your disc. If you want to change the burn format, click "Show formatting options."

Lower right: Your Big Two options: the new, super-convenient Live File System format (UDF), and the older, highly compatible Mastered format (ISO). If you click Change Version (lower left), you can even specify a version of UDF.

4. **Click Next.**

   Your PC takes a moment—a long one—to format the blank disc.

When it's finished, it opens a special disc-burning window, which will be the temporary waiting room for files that you want to copy. (If you can't find the window, choose Start→Computer and double-click the name of your CD/DVD drive.)

5. **Begin putting files and folders into the disc's window.**

You can use any combination of these three methods:

First, you can scurry about your hard drive, locating the files and folders you want on the CD. Drag their icons into the open CD/DVD window, or onto the disc burner's icon in the Computer window.

Second, you can highlight the files and folders you want burned onto the CD. Choose Organize→Copy. Click in the CD or DVD's window, and then choose Organize→Paste to copy the material there.

Finally, you can explore your hard drive. Whenever you find a file or folder you'd like backed up, right-click it. From the shortcut menu, choose Send To→DVD/CD-RW Drive (or whatever your burner's name is).

To finish the job, see "The final steps," below, for the kind of disc you're burning.

Tip: The Details pane at the bottom of the window gives you a running tally of the disk space you've filled up so far. (It may say, for example, "223.2 MB of 702.8 used on disc.") At last, you have an effortless way to exploit the blank disc's capacity with precision.

The final steps: Mastered (ISO) format

When you put files and folders into the disc's window, Windows actually *copies* them into a temporary, invisible holding-tank folder. (If you must know, this folder is in your Personal folder→Local Settings→AppData→Local→Microsoft→Windows→Burn→Temporary Burn Folder.)

In other words, you need plenty of disk space before you begin burning a CD—at least double the size of the CD files themselves.

Tip: Remember that a standard CD can hold only about 650 MB of files. To ensure that your files and folders will fit, periodically highlight all the icons in the Computer→CD window (choose Organize→Select All). Then inspect the Details pane to confirm that the size is within the legal limit.

What you see in the disc's window, meanwhile, is nothing but shortcuts (denoted by the downward arrows on their icons). The little down arrows mean, "This icon hasn't been burned to the disc yet. I'm just waiting my turn."

Tip: If you change your mind about including some of the files, highlight their icons in the disc window. On the task toolbar, click "Delete temporary files." You've just reclaimed the disc space those duplicates were using.

At last, when everything looks ready to go, click the "Burn to disc" link in the task toolbar. Or right-click the burner's icon, or any blank spot in its window, and, from the shortcut menu, choose "Burn to disc."

The CD Writing Wizard appears, to guide you through the process of naming and burning the disc. The PC's laser proceeds to record the CD or DVD, which can take some time. Feel free to switch into another program and continue working.

When the burning is over, the disc pops out, and you have a freshly minted CD or DVD, whose files and folders you can open on any PC or even Macintosh.

The final steps: Live File System (UDF) format

If you've been dragging files and folders into the window of a Live File System-formatted disc, the truth is, you *could* stop here. You can keep that CD or DVD in your drive, or eject it and store it—whatever. Whenever you put it back into your PC, you can pick up right where you left off, adding and erasing files as though it's a big flash drive.

To eject the disc, right-click your burner's icon; from the shortcut menu, choose Eject.

Just to make things extra complicated, though, there *may* be a final step to take before you can take your new Live File System disc on the road. You have to take this step, called *closing the session,* only if *all three* of these conditions are true:

- You intend to use this disc in another computer, *and…*

- This disc will be put into another computer's CD-ROM or DVD-ROM drive (playback only), and not a drive that can itself burn this kind of disc, *and…*

- It's a blank disk type that ends with the letter R (and not RW).

Actually, Windows Vista closes each session automatically every time you eject a Live File System disc. Clearly, Microsoft didn't really expect people to remember that elaborate matrix of conditions for requiring the closing step.

Besides, closing the session doesn't mean "freeze this disc forever." Even after you've closed the session, you can still put the disc back into your PC and burn more stuff onto it. (Then you can close *that* session to use the disc *again* on other machines—and so on, until the disc is full.)

So if it's automatic and does no harm, why does Microsoft even bring this closing business to your attention?

Because you eat 20 megabytes of space on the disc—and you wait around for a couple of minutes—every time you close a session.

If you, the power user, would like session-closing to be a decision left up to you, you can make Vista *stop* automatically closing sessions on your –R discs. Right-click the burner's icon in your Computer window; from the shortcut menu, choose Properties. In the dialog box, click the Recording tab, and then the Global Settings button. Now authenticate yourself (page 191). Finally, turn off "Automatically close the current UDF session when the disc is ejected," and then click OK twice.

From now on, Windows won't close your session—or use up 20 megabytes—unless *you* click the "Close session" link on the toolbar. (Or right-click your burner's icon in the Computer window and choose "Close session.") This way, you can maximize the space and speed of CDs and DVDs that you keep on your desk and *don't* distribute to other people.

Tip: If you try the CD or DVD in somebody else's machine and it doesn't work—and you realize that you forgot to close the session—all is not lost. You can always return the disc to your machine and close the session there.

And now, help yourself to some aspirin.

Final Notes

Here are a few final notes on burning CDs and DVDs at the desktop:

- Not sure what kinds of disks your PC can burn? Choose Start→Computer. Study the name of the burner. There it is, plain as day: a list of the formats your machine can read and write (that is, burn). If you have a combo drive (can burn and play CDs, but can only play DVDs), for example, you'll see something like: "DVD/CD-RW Drive." If your burner can *both* play and record *both* CDs and DVDs, it will say "DVD-RW/CD-RW Drive."

- To erase a –RW type disc (rewritable, like CD-RW or DVD-RW), open your Computer window. Right-click the burner's icon; from the shortcut menu, choose Format. Authenticate yourself (page 191), if necessary, change the file-system format if you like, and then turn on Quick Format. Finally, click Start to erase the disc.

Tip: Of course, you don't have to erase the disc completely. You can always select and delete individual icons from it using the Delete key.

- If you do a lot of disc burning, a full-fledged burning program like Nero adds myriad additional options. Only with a commercial CD-burning program can you burn MP3 music CDs, create *mixed-mode* CDs (containing both music and files), create Video CDs (low-quality video discs that play on DVD players), and so on.

Interior Decorating Vista

In designing Windows Vista, Microsoft had three giant goals. First, beef up Windows's security. Second, modernize its features. Third, give it a makeover. That last part was especially important; it drove Microsoft nuts that little old Apple, with its five-percent market share, was getting all the raves for the good looks and modern lines of its Macintosh operating system.

Without a doubt, Vista looks a heck of a lot better than previous versions of Windows. The new system font alone, so much clearer and more graceful than the one that's labeled your icons for decades, contributes to the new look.

And then there's Aero, the new visual design scheme described on page 22. Its transparent window edges may not add much to your productivity, but they do look cool.

Still, all of these changes aren't for everybody. Fortunately, Vista is every bit as tweakable as previous versions of Windows. You can turn off Aero, or just selected parts of it. You can change the picture on your desktop. You can bump up the text size for better reading by over-40 eyeballs. As Microsoft might say, "Where do you want to redesign today?"

Aero or Not

Home Premium • Business • Enterprise • Ultimate

If you ask Microsoft, the whole Aero thing (the look and the features) is a key benefit of Vista. Indeed, those glassy surfaces and see-through window edges are, in large part, where Vista got its name and its breathless marketing slogan ("Bring clarity to your world").

But there's certain to be someone, somewhere, who doesn't care for the new look—and Microsoft rarely takes a step forward without offering a step back to those who want it. You can not only change Vista's color scheme, you can also completely turn off

Windows Aero

Vista Basic

Windows Standard

Figure 4-1:
Most people with fast enough computers use the Aero Glass look of Windows Vista—and that's why the illustrations in this book show Aero Glass. But your computer may look different, especially if you've deliberately turned on one of the other styles.

Your choices are: Vista Basic (middle), which looks a lot like Aero—the window edges are still rounded, and the Start menu still has the new two-tone design, but the window edges aren't transparent. You lose taskbar thumbnails (page 94) and Flip 3D, too (page 90).

With Windows Standard (bottom) and the slightly darker Windows Classic, you lose all semblance of 3-D window elements; windows have sharp, square corners, and the Start menu is solidly gray. You're in a weird cross between Windows Vista and Windows Me.

the Aero look and features, if you so desire. You can substitute any of the three looks depicted in Figure 4-1.

Tip: Aero Glass uses up some of your PC's horsepower, 24 hours a day. Changing your scheme from Aero to Basic (or simply turning off transparency) can give your computer a speed boost, because it no longer has to compute and draw fuzzy images of whatever is behind your window title bars.

Microsoft figures that's not something you'll want to do often, so the controls are a bit buried. But here they are, just in case you're a believer in opaque window edges:

1. **Right-click a blank spot on the desktop. From the shortcut menu, choose Personalize.**

   The Personalization control panel opens.

2. **Click the first link, "Window Color and Appearance."**

   If you've been using the Aero design, you now arrive at the dialog box shown in Figure 4-2. Here's where you can choose a different accent color for your windows, or adjust (or turn off) the degree of window-edge transparency, which will make your PC slightly faster.

   If you've been using one of the other themes, you go directly to the dialog box shown in Figure 4-3; skip to step 4.

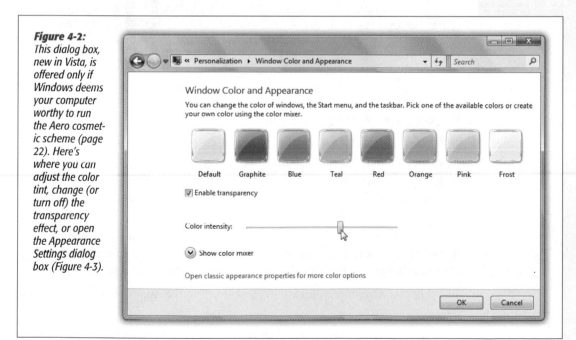

Figure 4-2:
This dialog box, new in Vista, is offered only if Windows deems your computer worthy to run the Aero cosmetic scheme (page 22). Here's where you can adjust the color tint, change (or turn off) the transparency effect, or open the Appearance Settings dialog box (Figure 4-3).

3. **Click "Open classic appearance properties…" at the bottom of the window.**

   The Appearance Settings dialog box opens.

---

4. **In the Color Scheme list, click the Windows design look you prefer: Windows Vista Aero, Windows Vista Basic, Windows Standard, or Windows Classic.**

   With each click, you see a sample at the top of the dialog box. (Figure 4-3 shows the samples more clearly.)

5. **Once you find a design you like, click OK.**

   The screen flickers, thunder rolls somewhere, and your screen changes.

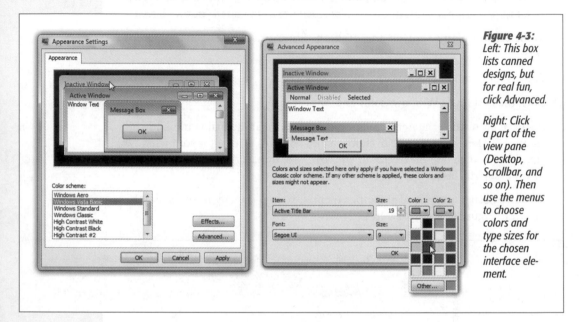

Figure 4-3:
Left: This box lists canned designs, but for real fun, click Advanced.

Right: Click a part of the view pane (Desktop, Scrollbar, and so on). Then use the menus to choose colors and type sizes for the chosen interface element.

Dialing Up Your Own Look
All Versions

As you know from Figure 4-1, Windows includes a number of *color schemes*: predesigned accent-color sets that affect the look of all the windows you open. These color-coordinated design schemes affect the colors and shapes of your window edges, title bars, window fonts, desktop background, and so on.

Turns out, however, that you have far more control than just switching wholesale from one scheme to another. You can actually tweak *individual elements* of a theme: change the font, change the title-bar color, change the icon spacing, and so on.

To begin this adventure, you have to get yourself to the Appearance Settings dialog box:

- **If your computer runs Aero:** Right-click the desktop. From the shortcut menu, choose Personalize. In the control panel that appears, click "Window Color and Appearance," and then click the link that says "Open classic appearance properties for more color options." (You can see this link in Figure 4-2.)

- **If your computer doesn't run Aero:** Right-click the desktop. From the shortcut menu, choose Personalize. When you click "Window Color and Appearance," you get the classic Appearance Settings dialog box right away (Figure 4-3, left), without ever seeing the box in Figure 4-2.

See the "Color scheme" list (Figure 4-3, left)? If you see Windows Aero in this list, great. You can get the full Vista experience, complete with animations, see-through window edges, Flip 3D (page 90), and so on.

If you see only Windows Vista Basic, then you probably have a lower-powered PC (or, rather, a lower-powered graphics card), or you're using the Home Basic edition of Vista. That's not so bad, though. You still get the clean, modern look of Vista windows and buttons, a rounded black glass look for the taskbar and start menu, and so on.

And finally, by choosing Windows Standard or Windows Classic styles from the "Windows and buttons" drop-down list (Figure 4-3, left), you return your PC to the visual look of Windows 2003/Windows 2000. (Strangely, there's no way to restore the nostalgic color scheme of Windows XP.)

Note: The "High Contrast" schemes in the list are designed to help out people with limited vision, who require greater differences in color between window elements. High-contrast schemes do not use any of the Aero features and more closely resemble the squared-off windows and dialog boxes of Windows 2000.

FREQUENTLY ASKED QUESTION

The Solution to Tiny Type

OK, fine—I can adjust things like the standard Windows type size, but only if I choose the old Windows Classic design scheme. Look, I'm over 40, my new laptop has tiny, tiny pixels, and I want to bump up the point size! Isn't there anything I can do without having to give up the new Vista look?

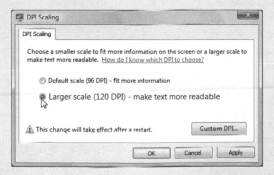

The people have spoken, and they've said, "We want our screens to show more!"

The manufacturers have responded, and they've said, "OK, fine—we'll just make the pixels smaller." These days, text on PC screens (especially laptops) is practically unreadable for over-40 eyes.

Yes, there *is* a way to bump up the standard Windows point size. Right-click the desktop; from the shortcut menu, choose Personalize. Then click the "Adjust font size dpi" link at the left side of the dialog box.

After you authenticate yourself (page 191), you arrive at the DPI Scaling dialog box, where you can scale up the size of the text, at least in programs (like Windows itself) that are modern enough to respond to this control. (The dialog box offers only two choices: default size, or one size bigger. To choose something larger, click the Custom DPI button.)

You, the Interior Designer

The real fun, however, awaits when you choose one of the canned schemes, like Windows Classic (Figure 4-3, left), and *then* click the Advanced button. Now you find yourself in a dialog box that lets you change every single aspect of this scheme independently (Figure 4-3, right).

Note: Microsoft put a lot of work into the new look of Vista, and doesn't especially want people diluting it with their own random changes. "If you want the Vista look," the company is saying, "it's all or nothing." If Windows Vista Basic (or Windows Vista Aero) is selected in the "Windows and buttons" list (Figure 4-3, left), the changes you make in the Advanced box (Figure 4-3, right) may have no effect.

Proceed with your interior-decoration crusade in either of two ways:

- Change the elements of the scheme one at a time. Start by choosing from the Item drop-down list (or by clicking a piece of the illustration at the top half of the dialog box, like a title bar or a button). Then use the Size, Color 1, and Color 2 drop-down lists to tailor the chosen element—such as Desktop or Scrollbar—to suit your artistic urges.

GEM IN THE ROUGH

Effects: The Tiniest Speed Tweaks

If you peer closely at the dialog box shown at left in Figure 4-3, you'll see a button called Effects. It takes you to a dialog box that lets you control what Microsoft calls *special effects* in Vista.

Now, these aren't exactly the kind of special effects they make at Industrial Light and Magic for use in *Star Wars* movies. In fact, they're so subtle, they're practically invisible—and there are far fewer effects in Vista than there were in XP.

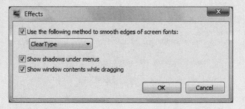

Use the following method to smooth edges of screen fonts. When fonts are enlarged, they become ragged on the curves. But when you turn on this option, Windows Vista softens the curves, making all text look more professional (or slightly blurrier, depending on your point of view).

Using the drop-down list, you can choose a smoothing technology called ClearType. It's designed especially for flat-panel screens, as on laptops. It simulates smoother

edges on the typed characters by using clever color changes on the pixels at the edges of certain letters. *Factory setting:* On, ClearType.

Show shadows under menus. Take a look: In Windows Vista, open menus actually seem to cast faint, light gray drop shadows, as though the menu is floating an eighth of an inch above the surface of the window behind it. It's a cool, but utterly superfluous special effect that saps a tiny bit of speed from the proceedings. This checkbox is the on/off switch. *Factory setting:* On.

Show window contents while dragging. If this option is off, when you drag a window, a faint outline of its border is visible; you don't see all the items *in* the window coming along for the ride. As soon as you stop dragging, the contents reappear. If it's on, however, as you drag a window across your screen, you see all its contents, too—which can slow the dragging process on slower machines. *Factory setting:* On.

- Some of the screen elements named in the Item drop-down list have text associated with them: Icon, Inactive Title Bar, Menu, Message Box, ToolTip, and so on. When you choose one of these text items, the Font drop-down list at the bottom of the dialog box comes to life. Using this menu, you can change the typeface (font, color, and size) used for any of these screen elements. If you have trouble reading the type in dialog boxes (because you have a high-resolution, tiny-type screen), or you wish your icon names showed up a little more boldly, or you'd prefer a more graceful font in your menus, these controls offer the solution.

Tip: If you create an attractive combination of colors and type sizes, remember that you can preserve it for future generations. Click OK to return to the Appearance Settings box. Then return to the Personalization control panel. (For example, right-click the desktop, and then, from the shortcut menu, choose Personalize.)

Now, click the Theme link; in the Theme Settings dialog box, click Save As and name your creation. Thereafter, you'll see its name listed alongside the "official" Microsoft themes.

(A Theme, by the way, isn't the same as a color scheme. A Theme includes much more than visual elements; it also includes sounds, icons, and so on.)

Desktop Background (Wallpaper)
All Versions

Vista has a whole new host of desktop pictures, patterns, and colors for your viewing pleasure. You want widescreen images for your new flat-panel monitor? No problem, Vista's got 'em. Want something gritty, artsy, in black and white? They're there, too. And you can still use any picture you'd like as your background as well.

To change yours, right-click the desktop. From the shortcut menu, choose Personalize. In the Personalization dialog box, click Desktop Background.

Use a Microsoft Photo
Now you're looking at the box shown in Figure 4-4. It starts you off examining the Microsoft-supplied photos that come with Vista. They're organized into categories like Black and White, Light Auras, Paintings, Textures (which take well to being *tiled*—more on that in a moment), Vistas (panoramic nature shots—yes, there had to be some), and Widescreen (designed to fit especially wide monitors).

Tip: If you'd rather have a plain, solid-colored background, choose Solid Colors from the Picture Location pop-up menu. You'll have your choice of a full palette of shades. It's not a bad idea, actually; you'll gain a little bit of speed, and it'll be a little easier to find your icons if they're not lost among the weeds and mountain bushes of a nature photo.

If you see something you like, click it to slap it across the entire background of your desktop. Click OK.

Use Your Photo

It's much more fun, of course, to use one of your *own* pictures on the desktop. That might be an adorable baby photo of your niece, or it might be Britney Spears with half her clothes off; the choice is yours.

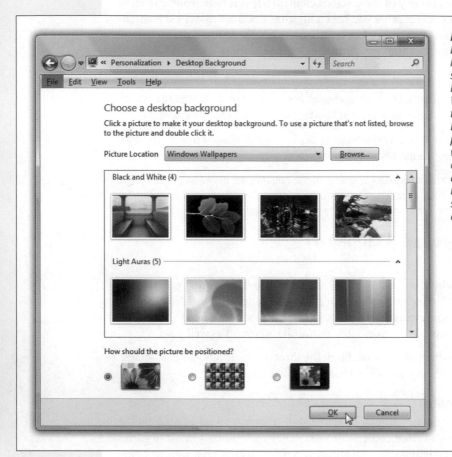

Figure 4-4:
Desktop Backgrounds have come a long way since Windows 3.1. Because of Windows Vista's name, most of the desktop images Desktop Backgrounds points to are, well, vistas—beautiful, expansive, nature images. There are many more to choose from, so feel free to look around.

At the top of the Desktop Background dialog box is a Picture Location pop-up menu. It lists several folders that are likely to contain photos on your PC:

- **Pictures** points to your Pictures folder, so it conveniently shows you all of the pictures saved there—up for grabs for your desktop.

- **Sample Pictures** contains even more great pictures for the desktop. They've been supplied by Microsoft so that, immediately upon installing Vista, you'll have some pix to fool around with.

- **Public Pictures** is a subfolder of the Public folder (page 730). It's expected to be the place you share your pictures with others who have access to your computer. (Ironically, the Public Pictures folder *contains* the Sample Pictures folder.)

Tip: If you store pictures in a folder other than Pictures, you can still use them. That's what the Browse button is for. Click it to select the folder and make its contents appear as thumbnail wallpaper candidates.

Beneath the thumbnails, by the way, Microsoft asks a very good question: "How should the picture be positioned?" What it means, actually, is, "How should the picture be positioned *if* it's too small to fill your screen?"

Your choices are (as represented by the mini-pictures):

- **Fit to screen.** Stretch the picture to fit the desktop, even if distortion may result.

- **Tile.** Place the picture in the upper-left corner of the desktop, and repeat it over and over until the entire desktop is covered.

- **Center.** Plop the picture in the middle of the desktop. If the picture is smaller than the desktop, a colored border fills in the gaps. (You can change the border color by clicking the little "Change background color" link that appears when you choose the Center option.)

Once you have chosen your desktop picture, and the way it will be positioned, apply your new desktop by clicking OK.

Screen Savers
All Versions

You don't technically *need* a screen saver to protect your monitor from burn-in. Today's energy-efficient monitors wouldn't burn an image into the screen unless you left them on continuously, unused, for at least two years, according to the people who design and build them.

No, screen savers are mostly about entertainment, pure and simple—and Windows Vista's built-in screen saver is certainly entertaining.

GEM IN THE ROUGH

Webby Wallpaper

If there's a graphic on the Web that strikes your fancy, *it* can become wallpaper, too. Right-click the image—right there in your Web browser—and choose Set as Background (or Set as Wallpaper) from the shortcut menu. The graphic moves immediately to the middle of your desktop. (You'll probably have to close or minimize your browser window to see it.)

Windows Vista saves the file in an invisible folder (your Personal→AppData→Roaming→Microsoft→Internet Explorer folder, if you must know). Windows names it *Internet Explorer Wallpaper.bmp*. (If you use a Firefox browser, the file is called *Firefox Wallpaper.bmp* and lands in the Mozilla→Firefox folder instead of the Microsoft→Internet Explorer folder.) If you find another Web graphic you like and want to repeat the steps to turn it into wallpaper, be aware that Windows Vista saves the new file with the same name, *replacing* the original file. To have access to both files, change the name of the previous wallpaper file before grabbing a new image.

The idea is simple: A few minutes after you leave your computer, whatever work you were doing is hidden behind the screen saver; passers-by can't see what's on the screen. To exit the screen saver, move the mouse, click a mouse button, or press a key.

Tip: Moving the mouse is the best way to get rid of a screen saver. A mouse click or a key press could trigger an action you didn't intend—such as clicking some button in one of your programs or typing the letter whose key you pressed.

Choosing a Screen Saver

To choose a Windows Vista screen saver, right-click the desktop. From the shortcut menu, choose Personalize. In the resulting window, click Screen Saver.

Now use the Screen Saver drop-down list. A miniature preview appears in the preview monitor on the dialog box (see Figure 4-5).

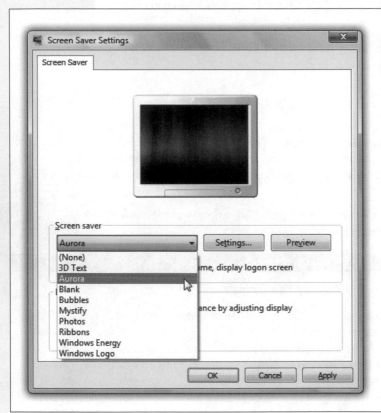

Figure 4-5:
Some screen savers don't work unless you have an Aero-capable PC (page 22): Windows Energy, Ribbons, Mystify, Bubbles, Aurora, and 3D Text. If you don't have an Aero machine, you're left with slim pickings. Of course, the photo sample pictures are nice. (If you have an Aero-capable PC but you've turned off the Aero look, the fancy screen savers are still available.)

To see a *full-screen* preview, click the Preview button. The screen saver display fills your screen and remains there until you move your mouse, click a mouse button, or press a key.

The Wait box determines how long the screen saver waits before kicking in, after the last time you move the mouse or type. Click the Settings button to play with the chosen screen saver module's look and behavior. For example, you may be able to change its colors, texture, or animation style.

At the bottom of this tab, click "Change power settings" to open the Power Options Window described on page 298.

Tip: If you keep graphics files in your Pictures folder, try selecting the Photos screen saver. Then click the Settings button and choose the pictures you want to see. When the screen saver kicks in, Vista puts on a spectacular slide show of your photos, bringing each to the screen with a special effect (flying in from the side, fading in, and so on).

Sounds
All Versions

Windows plays beeps and bloops to celebrate various occasions: closing a program, yanking out a USB drive, logging in or out, getting a new fax, and so on. You can turn these sounds on or off, or choose new sounds for these events; see page 308.

Mouse Makeover
All Versions

If your fondness for the standard Windows arrow cursor begins to wane, you can assert your individuality by choosing a different pointer shape. For starters, you might want to choose a *bigger* arrow cursor—a great solution on today's tinier-pixel, shrunken-cursor monitors.

Begin by right-clicking the desktop and, from the shortcut menu, choosing Personalize. In the dialog box, click Mouse Pointers. You arrive at the dialog box shown in Figure 4-6.

At this point, you can proceed in any of three ways:

POWER USERS' CLINIC

Password-Protecting Screen Savers

If you work in an office, password-protecting your screen saver is a great idea. It means that if you wander away to get coffee, and your screen saver kicks in, your snoopy co-workers can't stop by your desk and wiggle the mouse to see what you were working on.

To set this up, turn on the "On resume, logon screen" checkbox. Now, the act of "awakening" the PC by clicking the mouse or pressing a key merely produces the standard logon screen. Until somebody types the correct password, the data that's currently on your screen is safe from prying eyes.

If you *don't* work in a public place, however, and you're actually *annoyed* that you have to re-log on every time your screen saver kicks in, now you know the solution. Turn *off* the checkbox.

- **Scheme.** Windows has many more cursors than the arrow pointer. At various times, you may also see the spinning circular cursor (which means, "Wait; I'm thinking," or "Wait; I've crashed"), the I-beam cursor (which appears when you're editing text), the little pointing-finger hand made famous by Microsoft's advertising (which appears when you point to a Web page link), and so on.

  All of these cursors come prepackaged into design-coordinated sets called *schemes*. To look over the cursor shapes in a different scheme, use the Scheme drop-down list; the corresponding pointer collection appears in the Customize list box. Some are cute: Dinosaur, for example, displays an animated marching cartoon dinosaur instead of the hourglass cursor. Some are functional: the ones whose names include "large" offer jumbo, magnified cursors ideal for very large screens or failing eyesight. When you find one that seems like an improvement over the Windows Aero (system scheme) set, click OK.

- **Select individual pointers.** You don't have to change to a completely different scheme; you can also replace just one cursor. To do so, click the pointer you want to change, and then click the Browse button. You're shown the vast array of cursor-replacement icons (which are in the Local Disk (C:)→Windows→Cursors folder). Click one to see what it looks like; double-click to select it.

- **Create your own pointer scheme.** Once you've replaced a cursor shape, you've also changed the scheme to which it belongs. At this point, either click OK to activate

Figure 4-6:
Ever lose your mouse pointer while working on a laptop with a dim screen? Maybe pointer trails could help. Or have you ever worked on a desktop computer with a mouse pointer that seems to take forever to move across the desktop? Try increasing the pointer speed.

your change and get back to work, or save the new, improved scheme under its own name, so you can switch back to the original when nostalgia calls. To do so, click the Save As button, name the scheme, and then click OK.

Tip: The "Enable pointer shadow" checkbox at the bottom of this tab is pretty neat. It casts a shadow on whatever's beneath the cursor, as though it's skimming just above the surface of your screen.

Pointer Options

Clicking the Pointer Options tab offers a few more random cursor-related functions (see Figure 4-6).

- **Pointer speed.** It comes as a surprise to many people that the cursor doesn't move five inches when the mouse moves five inches on the desk. Instead, you can set things up so that moving the mouse one *millimeter* moves the pointer one full *inch*—or vice versa—using the Pointer speed slider.

  It may come as even greater surprise that the cursor doesn't generally move *proportionally* to the mouse's movement, regardless of your "Pointer speed" setting. Instead, the cursor moves farther when you move the mouse faster. How *much* farther depends on how you set the "Select a pointer speed" slider.

  The Fast setting is nice if you have an enormous monitor, since it prevents you from needing an equally large mouse pad to get from one corner to another. The Slow setting, on the other hand, can be frustrating, since it forces you to constantly pick up and put down the mouse as you scoot across the screen. (You can also turn off the disproportionate-movement feature completely by turning off "Enhance pointer precision.")

- **Snap To.** A hefty percentage of the times when you reach for the mouse, it's to click a button in a dialog box. If you, like millions of people before you, usually click the *default* (outlined) button—such as OK, Next, or Yes—the Snap To feature can save you the effort of positioning the cursor before clicking.

  When you turn on Snap To, every time a dialog box appears, your mouse pointer jumps automatically to the default button, so that all you need to do is click. (And to click a different button, such as Cancel, you have to move the mouse only slightly to reach it.)

- **Display pointer trails.** The options available for enhancing pointer visibility (or invisibility) are mildly useful under certain circumstances, but mostly, they're just for show.

  If you turn on "Display pointer trails," for example, you get ghost images that trail behind the cursor like a bunch of little ducklings following their mother. In general, this stuttering-cursor effect is irritating. On rare occasions, however, you may find that it helps locate the cursor if you're making a presentation on a low-contrast LCD projector.

- **Hide pointer while typing** is useful if you find that the cursor sometimes gets in the way of the words on your screen. As soon as you use the keyboard, the pointer disappears; just move the mouse to make the pointer reappear.

- **Show location of pointer when I press the CTRL key.** If you've managed to lose the cursor on an LCD projector or a laptop with an inferior screen, this feature helps gain your bearings. When you press and release the Ctrl key after turning on this checkbox, Windows displays an animated concentric ring each subsequent time you press the Ctrl key to pinpoint the cursor's location.

Tip: You can also fatten up the insertion point—the cursor that appears when you're editing text. See page 269.

Change Your Theme
All Versions

You know about color *schemes* from the beginning of this chapter. Now meet the bigger picture: Themes.

A *Theme* is a design scheme that incorporates much more than your color scheme. It also involves the background picture for your desktop, sounds, and even the mouse pointer shape.

Figure 4-7:
You may notice, after specifically applying a theme, that the theme you seem to be using is "Modified Theme." This happens whenever you apply a theme, then change anything, any single component of a theme, including changing your desktop background. Vista takes note and reports the theme you are using as modified.

Theme options let you radically change the look and emotional tenor of your entire PC with a single click (Figure 4-7).

There are only two themes to choose from out of the box: Windows Vista and Windows Classic. Windows Classic theme is the unsnazzy look of Windows 2000; the Windows Vista theme, of course, is what you've been looking at all along.

It's easy enough to design a new Theme of your own, however. Just make any of the other changes described in this chapter. Fiddle with your wallpaper, window fonts, icons, and so on. Then return to the Themes dialog box and click Save As. Finally, give your new theme a name, so you can call it up whenever you like.

Monitor Settings
All Versions

You wouldn't get much work done without a screen on your computer. It follows, then, that you can get *more* work done if you tinker with your screen's settings to make it more appropriate to your tastes and workload. And boy, are there a lot of settings to tinker with.

You can find them by right-clicking the desktop; from the shortcut menu, choose Personalize. In the resulting dialog box, click Display Settings. The window shown in Figure 4-8 appears.

Resolution
The Resolution slider snaps to the various possible *resolution* settings that your monitor's software driver makes available: 800 x 600, 1024 x 768, 1280 x 800, and so on.

When using a low-resolution setting, such as 640 x 480, the size of the pixels (dots) that constitute your screen image increase, thus enlarging the picture—but showing a smaller slice of the page. This setting is ideal, for example, when playing some small-window Web movie, making it fill more of the screen.

FREQUENTLY ASKED QUESTION

Blurry Flat-Panel Screens

Yucko! I tried the 800 x 600 setting on my laptop, and everything got all blurry and fuzzy! How do I fix it?

On any flat-panel screen—not just laptop screens—only one resolution setting looks really great: the maximum one. That's what geeks call the *native* resolution of that screen.

At lower resolutions, the PC does what it can to blur together adjacent pixels, but the effect is fuzzy and unsatisfying. (On a traditional bulky monitor, the electron gun can actually make the pixels larger or smaller, but on flat-panel screens, every pixel is a fixed size.)

At higher resolutions (such as 800 x 600 or 1024 x 768), the pixels decrease, reducing the size of your windows and icons, but showing more overall area. Use this kind of setting when you want to see as much screen area as possible: when working on two-page spreads in a page-layout program, for example.

Colors

Today's monitors offer different *color depth* settings, each of which permits the screen to display a different number of colors simultaneously. This pop-up menu varies by video driver, but generally offers settings such as Medium (16-bit), which was called High Color in previous versions of Windows; High (24-bit), once known as True Color; and Highest (32-bit).

In the early days of computing, higher color settings required a sacrifice in speed. Today, however, there's very little downside to leaving your screen at its highest setting. Photos, in particular, look best when you set your monitor to higher-quality settings.

The Low (8-bit) option—if you even have it—makes photos look blotchy. It displays only 256 colors on the screen, and is therefore useful only for certain computer games that, having been designed to run on ancient PCs, require the lower color setting. (In that case, you shouldn't set your whole system to 256 colors just to run these older games. Instead, you should use the new compatibility mode described on page 236.)

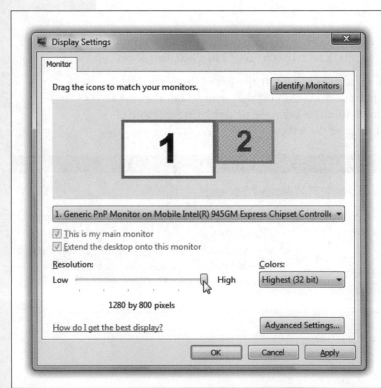

Figure 4-8:
All desktop screens today, and even most laptop screens, can make the screen picture larger or smaller, thus accommodating different kinds of work. Conducting this magnification or reduction entails switching among different resolutions (the number of dots that compose the screen).

Multiple Monitors

If your PC has two or more graphics cards, one graphics card with multiple connections, or a standard laptop video-out connector, you can hook up a second monitor or a projector. You can either display the same picture on both screens (which is what you'd want if your laptop were projecting slides for an audience), or create a gigantic virtual desktop, moving icons or toolbars from one monitor to another (Figure 4-9). The latter setup also lets you keep an eye on Web activity on one monitor while you edit data on another. It's a *glorious* arrangement, even if it does make the occasional family member think you've gone off the deep end with your PC obsession.

To bring about that extended-desktop scenario, click the icon that represents screen 2 (the external one), and then turn on "Extend the desktop onto this monitor." (If you can't figure out which screen is screen 2, click the Identify Monitors button in the upper-right corner.)

Tip: Plugging in a projector generally inspires Windows to present a clean, simple dialog box that asks a simple question: Where do you want to send your screen image? To the PC's screen, to the projector, or to both?

This is an extremely thoughtful touch for laptop luggers, because it avoids the staggeringly confusing keyboard-based system you previously had to use. That's where you'd press, for example, F8 three times to cycle among the three modes: image on laptop only (projector dark), image on projector only (laptop screen dark), or image on both at once. Vista's method is much easier.

Figure 4-9:
When you have multiple monitors, the controls on the Settings tab change; you now see individual icons for each monitor. When you click a screen icon, the settings in the dialog box change to reflect its resolution, color quality, and so on.

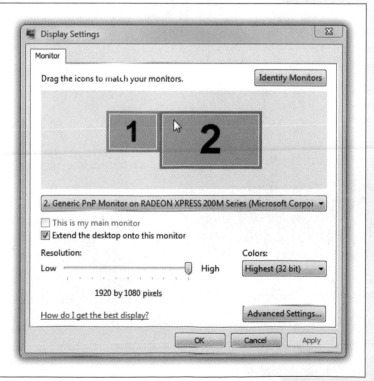

Advanced settings

If you click the Advanced button on the Settings tab, you're offered a collection of technical settings for your particular monitor model. Depending on your video driver, there may be tab controls here that adjust the *refresh rate* to eliminate flicker, install an updated adapter or monitor driver, and so on. In general, you'll rarely need to adjust these controls—except on the advice of a consultant or help-line technician.

Getting Help

W indows Vista may be better than any version of Windows before it, but improving something means *changing* it. And in Windows Vista, a *lot* has changed; otherwise, you probably wouldn't be reading a book about it.

Fortunately, help is just around the corner—of the Start menu, that is. Windows now has a completely new electronic Help system; some of its "articles" even offer links that perform certain tasks *for* you. It may take all weekend, but eventually you should find written information about this or that Windows feature or problem.

This chapter covers not only the Help system, but also some of the ways Vista can help you get help from a more experienced person via your network or the Internet.

Navigating the Help System
All Versions

To open the Help system, choose Start→Help and Support, or press F1. The Help and Support window appears, as shown in Figure 5-1. From here, you can home in on the help screen you want using one of two methods: clicking your way from the Help home page, or using the Search command.

Help Home Page
The home page shown in Figure 5-1 contains three basic areas:

- At the top: buttons for six broad categories of help, like Windows Basics, Security and Maintenance, What's new?, and Troubleshooting.

- In the middle: links to seeking help from other human beings via the Internet.

• At the bottom: links to certain help articles that Microsoft believes answer some of the top questions. At the very bottom of the window are a couple of links to help Web sites.

If one of the broad topics at the top corresponds with your question, click it to see a list of subtopics. The subtopic list leads you to another, more focused list, which in turn leads you to an even narrower list. Eventually you'll arrive at a list that actually produces a help page.

Tip: If you seem to have misplaced your contact lenses, you can adjust the type size used by the Help Center. Click the Options button (top right of the window), and then, from the pop-up menu, choose Text Size. Its submenu offers a choice of five font sizes, from Smallest to Largest.

Figure 5-1:
The Back, Forward, Home, and Search controls on the Help system's toolbar may look like the corresponding tools in a Web browser, but they refer only to your travels within the Help system. Other buttons at the top let you print a help article or change the type size.

Search the Help Pages

By typing a phrase into the Search Help box at the top of the main page and then pressing Enter (or clicking the tiny magnifying glass button), you instruct Windows to rifle through its 10,000 help pages to search for the phrase you typed.

Here are a few pointers:

- When you enter multiple words, Windows assumes that you're looking for help screens that contain *all* of those words. For example, if you search for *video settings,* help screens that contain both the words "video" and "settings" (although not necessarily next to each other) appear.

- If you would rather search for an exact phrase, put quotes around the search phrase ("video settings").

- Once you've clicked your way to an article that looks promising, you can search within that page, too. Open the Options pop-up menu (upper-right corner of the Help window) and choose "Find (on this page)."

Tip: When you're on a laptop at 39,000 feet, you probably don't have an Internet connection. In that case, you may prefer that Windows not attempt to search Microsoft's help site on the Internet. Open the Options pop-up menu (top right), choose Settings, and turn off "Include Windows Online Help and Support when you search for help." Click OK.

GEM IN THE ROUGH

Links in Help

Along with the nicely re-written help information, you'll find, here and there in the Help system, a few clickable links.

Sometimes you'll see a phrase that appears in green type; that's your cue that clicking it will produce a pop-up definition.

Sometimes you'll see blue links to other help screens.

And sometimes you'll see a brand new Vista element: help links that *automate* the

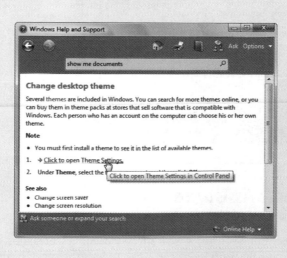

task you're trying to learn. These goodies, denoted by a blue compass icon, offer you two ways of proceeding: either Windows can do the *whole* job for you, or it can show you step by step, using blinking, glowing outlines to show you exactly where to click.

There aren't nearly enough of these automated help topics—but when you stumble onto one, turn down the lights, invite the neighbors, and settle back for an unforgettable five minutes of entertainment.

Drilling Down

If you're not using the same terminology as Microsoft, you won't find your help topic by using the Search box. Sometimes, you may have better luck unearthing a certain help article by drilling down through the Table of Contents.

Start by clicking the little book icon at the top of the window; it's called the Browse button, but it opens a tidy, clickable table of contents. If a topic's icon looks like a little book, that means you'll be treated to even *more* topic listings. If its icon looks like a page with a ? symbol, clicking it opens an actual help article (Figure 5-2).

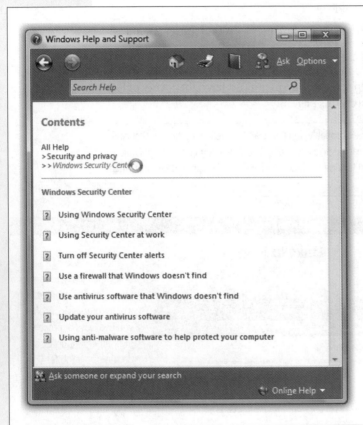

Figure 5-2:
As you arrive on each more finely grained sub-table of sub-contents, you'll see an indented list of topics in the top part of the window. These >> brackets illustrate the levels through which you've descended on your way to this help page; you can backtrack by clicking one of these links.

Remote Assistance
All Versions

You may think you know what stress is: deadlines, breakups, downsizing. But nothing approaches the frustration of an expert trying to help a PC beginner over the phone—for both parties.

The expert is flying blind, using Windows terminology that the beginner doesn't know. Meanwhile, the beginner doesn't know what to look for and describe on the phone.

Every little step takes 20 times longer than it would if the expert were simply seated in front of the machine. Both parties are likely to age ten years in an hour.

Fortunately, that era is at an end. Windows' Remote Assistance feature lets somebody having trouble with the computer extend an invitation to an expert, via the Internet. The expert can actually see the screen of the flaky computer, and even take control of it by remotely operating the mouse and keyboard. The guru can make even the most technical tweaks—running utility software, installing new programs, adjusting hardware drivers, even editing the Registry (Appendix B)—by long-distance remote control. Remote Assistance really *is* the next best thing to being there.

Remote Assistance: Rest Assured

Of course, these days, most people react to the notion of Remote Assistance with stark terror. What's to stop some troubled teenager from tapping into your PC in the middle of the night, rummaging through your files, and reading your innermost thoughts?

Plenty. First of all, you, the help-seeker, must begin the process by sending a specific electronic invitation to the expert. The invitation has a time limit: If the helper doesn't respond within, say, an hour, the electronic door to your PC slams shut again. Second, the remote-control person can only *see* what's on your screen. She can't actually manipulate your computer unless you grant another specific permission.

Finally, you must be present *at your machine* to make this work. The instant you see something fishy going on, a quick tap on your Esc key disconnects the interloper.

Tip: If you still can't stand the idea that there's a tiny keyhole into your PC from the Internet, choose Start→ Control Panel. Click Classic View, if necessary, and then double-click the System icon.

In the System dialog box, click the Remote Settings link (left side), authenticate (page 191), and turn off "Allow Remote Assistance connections to this computer." Click OK. Now you've effectively removed the use of the Remote Assistance feature from Windows.

FREQUENTLY ASKED QUESTION

Compatibility Backward

Is Vista's version of Remote Assistance compatible with Windows XP machines? What about Windows Server 2003?

Well, sort of.

Remote Assistance works between Vista and these earlier systems *if* they initiate the connection. You, the guru using Vista, cannot offer assistance—you can only accept the struggling person's invitation.

Furthermore, Vista's version of Remote Assistance doesn't let you *talk* to the other person. If the XP or Server 2003 victims click the Start Talk button, they'll just be talking to themselves.

If you're a bit picky, and you want to ensure that only true-blue Vista people answer your pleas for help, open the System applet in the Control Panel; click "Remote settings"; authenticate yourself (page 191); click Advanced; and turn on "Create invitations that can only be used from computers running Windows Vista or later." Click OK.

Remote Assistance, Step by Step

Anybody with Windows XP, Server 2003, or Vista can help anyone else with one of those operating systems. The steps, however, are different depending on whether you're the flailer or the helper.

The following steps assume that you're running Windows Vista. (The steps are slightly different if you're using Windows XP or Server 2003—but then you'd be reading a different book, wouldn't you?)

Tip: If you and your guru are both fans of Windows Live Messenger, Microsoft's chat program, you have at your disposal a more direct way of starting a Remote Assistance session. When you see that your guru is online in Messenger, choose Actions→Start Request Remote Assistance.

If the guru accepts, and you accept the acceptance, then a Remote Assistance session begins, without you having to go through all the email rigamarole described below.

Instructions for the novice

If you're the one who wants help, first make sure that your PC has been set up to allow Remote Assistance (and remote control).

Choose Start→Control Panel. Click Classic View; double-click the System icon. In the links at left, click "Remote settings," and then authenticate yourself (page 191).

Here before you is the master switch for permitting remote connections. If you click Advanced (the button, not the tab), you'll find two other key security options:

- **Allow this computer to be controlled remotely.** If this is turned on, your guru will be able to operate your PC, not just see what's onscreen.

- **Invitations.** These options let you specify how quickly an invitation to a guru expires. Of course, nobody can get into your PC without a confirmation by you, while you're seated in front of it. Even so, it may give you an extra level of comfort knowing that after, say, three hours of waiting for your guru to come home and get your invitation, the window of opportunity will close.

Click OK twice to close the dialog boxes.

NOSTALGIA CORNER

Help for Dialog Boxes

In Windows XP, whenever you faced a dialog box containing a cluster of oddly worded options, the "What's This?" feature came to the rescue. It made pop-up captions appear for text boxes, checkboxes, option buttons, and other dialog box elements.

You summoned these pop-up identifiers by clicking the ?

button in the upper-right corner of the dialog box, and then clicking the element you wanted identified.

In Vista, there's still a ? button in some dialog boxes. But it doesn't offer anything like pop-up captions. Instead, it opens an article from the standard Windows Help center that explains the relevant dialog box as a whole.

Now you're ready to send the invitation itself:

1. **Choose Start→Help and Support.**

   The Help and Support Center appears, as described earlier in this chapter.

2. **Click "Windows Remote Assistance."**

   You'll see this item under the "Ask someone" heading. After a moment, a window appears. It wants to know if you're the helper or the helpee.

3. **Click "Invite someone you trust to help you."**

   The phrase "you trust"—new in Windows Vista—is Microsoft's little way of reminding you that whoever you invite will be able to see anything you've got open on the screen. (Those who would rather keep that private know who they are.)

   In any case, now the "How do you want to invite someone?" screen appears.

Tip: If you click "Save this invitation as a file" at this point, Vista invites you to save a *ticket file*—a standalone invitation file—to your hard drive. You'll have to do that if you have a Web-based email account like Google Mail, Hotmail, or Yahoo Mail. (Make up a password first—see step 5, below, for an explanation—and then attach the file you've saved in this step when sending a message to your guru.)

Saving the file is also handy because you can save some steps by resending it to your guru the next time you're feeling lost.

---

4. **Click "Use email to send an invitation."**

   Now Vista wants you to make up a password. It's designed to ensure that your guru, and only your guru, can access your machine. (Of course, you need to find some way of *telling* that person what the password is—maybe calling on the phone or sending a separate email.)

5. **Type a password into both boxes and then click Next.**

   You're going to be sending your invitation via email. If you've never set up email on this PC, Vista automatically opens up Windows Mail and begins the email account-setup wizard. (The window may be *behind* the Remote Assistance window; check your taskbar.)

   Set up your account as described in Chapter 12, because if you don't *have* an account, you're pretty much out of luck with Remote Assistance. Get on the phone and ask your guru to drive over to your place.

   In any case, if you do have working email, then your email program now opens, and Windows actually composes an invitation message *for* you. "Hi," it begins. "I need help with my computer. Would you please use Windows Remote Assistance to connect to my computer so you can help me?"

   You're welcome to edit this message, of course, perhaps to something that does a little less damage to your ego.

---

6. Type your guru's email address into the "To:" box, and then send the message.

Windows sends an electronic invitation to your Good Samaritan.

Now there's nothing to do but sit back, quietly freaking out, and wait for your guru to get the message and connect to your PC. (See the next section.)

If your buddy accepts the invitation to help you, then the message shown at top in Figure 5-3 appears, asking if you're absolutely, positively sure you want someone else to see your screen. If you click Yes, the assistance session begins.

If you get a note that your expert friend wants to take control of your PC (Figure 5-3, bottom), and that's cool with you, click OK.

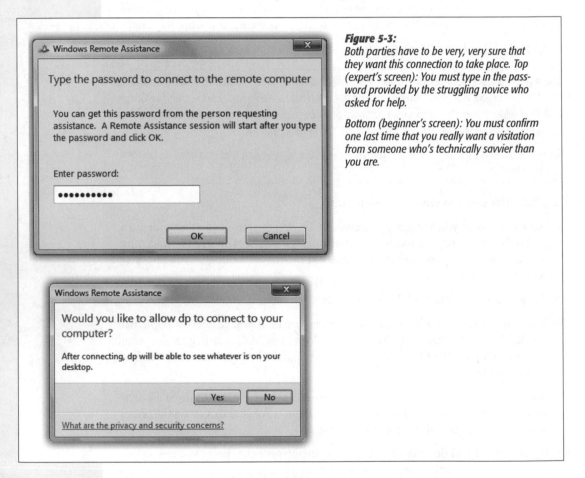

Figure 5-3:
Both parties have to be very, very sure that they want this connection to take place. Top (expert's screen): You must type in the password provided by the struggling novice who asked for help.

Bottom (beginner's screen): You must confirm one last time that you really want a visitation from someone who's technically savvier than you are.

Now watch in amazement and awe as your cursor begins flying around the screen, text types itself, and windows open and close by themselves (Figure 5-4).

As noted earlier, if the expert's explorations of your system begin to unnerve you, feel free to slam the door by clicking the "Stop sharing" button on the screen—or just by pressing the Esc key. Your friend can still see your screen, but can no longer control it. (To close the connection completely, so that your screen isn't even visible anymore, click the Disconnect button.)

Instructions for the expert

When the novice sends you an email invitation, it arrives in your email program with an attachment—a tiny file called RATicket.MsRcIncident. This is your actual invitation, a Remote Assistance *ticket*.

When you open it, you're asked to supply the six-digit password that your helpless newbie created in step 5 above. Once that's done, the online help session can begin.

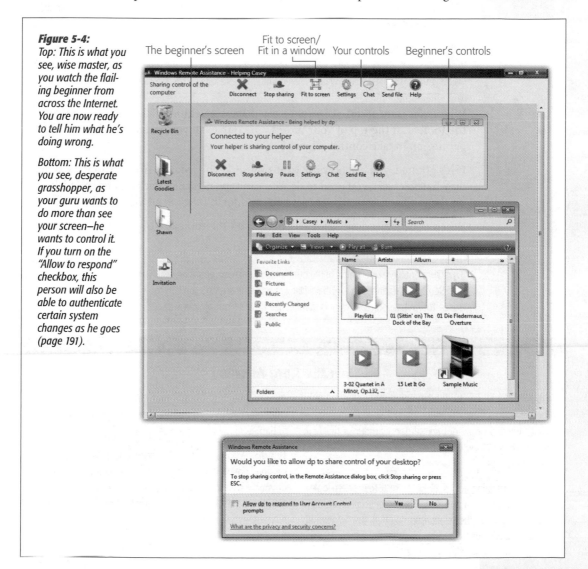

Figure 5-4:
Top: This is what you see, wise master, as you watch the flailing beginner from across the Internet. You are now ready to tell him what he's doing wrong.

Bottom: This is what you see, desperate grasshopper, as your guru wants to do more than see your screen—he wants to control it. If you turn on the "Allow to respond" checkbox, this person will also be able to authenticate certain system changes as he goes (page 191).

The beginner's screen Fit to screen/ Fit in a window Your controls Beginner's controls

Tip: And by the way, if the novice, a trusting individual, sends you a Remote Assistance ticket that doesn't expire for a very long time (99 days, for example), keep it around on your desktop or in your Start menu. From now on, both of you can skip all of the invitation-and-response rigmarole. Now, whenever he needs your help, he can just call you up or email you. And all you have to do is double-click your ticket and wait for the OK from the other side.

At this point, you observe a strange sight: the other person's screen in a special Remote Assistance window (Figure 5-4, top). To communicate with your troubled comrade, chat on the phone, if you like, or click the Chat button to type back and forth.

Tip: If the victim's screen isn't exactly the same size as yours, click the "Fit to screen" button identified in Figure 5-4. With each click on that button, you cycle your display between two modes.

In the first one, the other person's screen is represented at full size, although you may have to scroll around to see all of it. With another click, Windows compresses (or enlarges) the other person's screen image to fit inside your Remote Assistance window, even though the result can be distorted and ugly.

When you want to take control of the distant machine, click "Request control" on the toolbar at the top of your screen. Of course, all you've actually done is just ask *permission* to take control (Figure 5-4, bottom).

If it's granted, you can now use your mouse, keyboard, and troubleshooting skills to do whatever work you need to do. You can type messages back and forth (click Chat on the toolbar) or even send files back and forth (click Send Files on the toolbar).

When your job is done, click Disconnect on the toolbar—or wait for your grateful patient to do so.

Tip: Once you've taken control of the other person's screen, your first instinct might be to close the gargantuan Remote Assistance window that's filling most of the screen. Don't. If that window closes, the connection closes, too. What you really want is to *minimize* it, so it's out of your way but not closed.

TROUBLESHOOTING MOMENT

When the Aero Misses

Transmitting a live video feed from one PC to another across the network or Internet requires a fairly speedy connection. That's why you may not see all the glamour of the Aero design (page 22) when you're connected to someone via Remote Access.

You, the struggling help-seeker, can restore the Aero look, if your connection is fast enough. Click Settings on the Remote Access toolbar. In the resulting dialog box, the "Bandwidth usage" slider controls how complete the visual treats are—and how much data gets used as a result.

(What's especially odd is that you can see the remote computer's Aero design even if *your* computer is too slow to handle Aero!)

This dialog box also offers, by the way, a "Save a log of this session" option. It creates a text file that records every step of your assistance setting. Later, you can inspect it to reassure the paranoid inside of you that no files were deleted or transferred without your awareness by the person you trusted.

Getting Help from Microsoft
All Versions

If you run into trouble with installation—or with any Windows feature—the world of Microsoft is filled with sources of technical help. For example, you can follow any of these avenues, all of which have direct links from the home page of the Help system (choose Start→Help and Support):

- **Windows communities.** This link takes you to some Internet newsgroups (bulletin boards) pertaining to Windows and Windows issues. You can post questions to the multitudes all over the Internet and return later to read the answers.

- **Microsoft Customer Support pages.** This Web site offers a summary of all the different ways you can get help from Microsoft: phone numbers, pricing plans, links to other help sources, and so on.

    You'll discover there that if you bought Vista separately (that is, it didn't come on your computer), you can call Microsoft for free during business hours. The company is especially interested in helping you get Windows installed. In fact, you can call as often as you like on this subject.

    After that, you can call for everyday Windows questions for free—twice. You'll be asked to provide your 20-digit product ID number, which you can look up by right-clicking Computer in your Start menu and clicking the Properties tab. The not-toll-free number is listed in the packaging of your Vista installation DVD.

    (If Windows came preinstalled on your machine, on the other hand, you're supposed to call the computer company with your Windows questions.)

    Once you've used up your two free calls, you can still call Microsoft—for $35 per incident. (They say "per incident" to make it clear that if it takes several phone calls to solve a particular problem, it's still just one problem.) This service is available 24 hours a day; the U.S. number is (800) 936-5700.

Tip: If you're not in the United States, direct your help calls to the local Microsoft office in your country. You'll find a list of these subsidiaries at *http://support.microsoft.com*.

- **Microsoft website for IT professionals.** This link takes you to a special Web site for network administrators, programmers, and other IT (information technology) pros. At this site you'll find special articles on deployment, corporate security, and so on.

- **Windows Online Help and Support.** This is the mother lode: the master Web site for help and instructions on running Windows Vista. You can search it, use its links to other pages, read articles, study FAQs (frequently asked questions), or burrow into special-topic articles.

Of course, a lot of these online articles are built right into the regular Help system described at the beginning of this chapter. Unless you've turned off "Include Windows Online Help and Support when you search for help," you generally don't have to go online to search a second time.

Part Two:
Vista Software

Chapter 6: Programs, Documents, and Gadgets

Chapter 7: The Freebie Software

Chapter 8: The Control Panel

2

Programs, Documents, and Gadgets

When you get right down to it, an operating system like Windows is nothing more than a home base from which to launch *applications* (programs). And you, as a Windows person, are particularly fortunate, since more programs are available for Windows than for any other operating system on earth.

But when you launch a program, you're no longer necessarily in the world Microsoft designed for you. Programs from other software companies work a bit differently, and there's a lot to learn about how Windows handles programs that were born before it was.

This chapter covers everything you need to know about installing, removing, launching, and managing programs; using programs to generate documents; understanding how documents, programs, and Windows communicate with each other; and exploiting Vista's great new hybrid document/program entity, the Sidebar gadget.

Opening Programs
All Versions

Windows lets you launch (open) programs in many different ways:

- Choose a program's name from the Start→All Programs menu.

- Click a program's icon on the Quick Launch toolbar (page 101).

- Double-click an application's program file icon in the Computer→Local Disk (C:)→ Program Files→application folder, or highlight the application's icon and then press Enter.

- Press a key combination you've assigned to be the program's shortcut (page 146).

- Choose Start→Run, type the program file's name in the Open text box, and then press Enter.

- Let Windows launch the program for you, either at startup (page 20) or at a time you've specified (see Task Scheduler, page 606).

- Open a document using any of the above techniques; its "parent" program opens automatically. For example, if you used Microsoft Word to write a file called Last Will and Testament.doc, double-clicking the document's icon launches Word and automatically opens that file.

What happens next depends on the program you're using (and whether or not you opened a document). Most present you with a new, blank, untitled document. Some, such as FileMaker and Microsoft PowerPoint, welcome you instead with a question: do you want to open an existing document or create a new one? And a few oddball programs, like Adobe Photoshop, don't open any window at all when first launched. The appearance of tool palettes is the only evidence that you've even opened a program.

Exiting Programs
All Versions

When you exit, or quit, an application, the memory it was using is returned to the Windows pot for use by other programs.

If you use a particular program several times a day, like a word processor or calendar, you'll save time in the long run by keeping it open all day long. (You can always minimize its window to get it out of the way when you're not using it.)

But if you're done using a program for the day, exit it, especially if it's a memory-hungry one like, say, Photoshop. Do so using one of these techniques:

- Choose File→Exit.

- Click the program window's Close box, or double-click its Control-menu spot (at the upper-left corner of the window).

- Right-click the program's taskbar button; from the shortcut menu, choose Close or Close Group.

- Press Alt+F4 to close the window you're in. (If it's a program that disappears entirely when its last document window closes, you're home.)

- Press Alt+F, then X.

After offering you a chance to save any changes you've made to your document, the program's windows, menus, and toolbars disappear, and you "fall down a layer" into the window that was behind it.

Authenticate Yourself: User Account Control

You can't work in Windows Vista very long before encountering the dialog box shown here. It appears any time you install a new program or try to change an important setting on your PC. (Throughout Vista, a tiny colorful shield icon next to a button or link indicates a change that will produce this message box.)

Clearly, Microsoft chose the name User Account Control (UAC) to put a positive spin on a fairly intrusive security feature; calling it the IYW (Interrupt Your Work) box probably wouldn't have sounded like so much fun.

Why do these boxes pop up? In the olden days before Vista, nasties like spyware and viruses could install themselves invisibly, behind your back. That's because Windows ran in *Administrative* mode all the time, meaning it left the door open for anyone and anything to make important changes to your PC. Unfortunately, that included viruses.

Windows Vista, on the other hand, runs in *Standard* mode all the time. Whenever somebody or some program wants to make a big change to your system—something that ought to have the permission of an *administrator* (page 669)—the UAC box alerts you. If you click Continue, Windows elevates (opens) the program's permissions settings just long enough to make the change.

Most of the time, *you* are the one making the changes, which can make the UAC box a bit annoying. But if that UAC dialog box ever appears *by itself*, you'll know something evil is afoot on your PC, and you'll have the chance to shut it down.

How you get past the UAC box—how you *authenticate yourself*—depends on the kind of account you have (Chapter 23): *standard* or *administrator.*

If you're an administrator, just click Continue to proceed. If you're a Standard account holder, the UAC dialog box

requires the name and password **of** an administrator. You're supposed to call an administrator over to your desk to indicate his permission to proceed by entering his own name and password.

Questions? Yes, you in the back?

Why does the screen go dark around the dialog box?

That's another security step. It's designed to prevent evil software from tricking you by displaying a *fake* Windows dialog box. Windows darkens and freezes everything on the screen except the one, true Windows dialog box: the UAC box. (For your edification, the UAC box appears superimposed on the window of the program that's doing the asking.)

What happens if the program that wants my attention is minimized on the taskbar?

The window's taskbar button blinks to get your attention.

Can I turn off these UAC interruptions?

Yes. In your Control Panel, click Classic View, and double-click User Accounts. Click "Turn User Account Control on or off," authenticate yourself (page 191), and then turn off "Use User Account Control (UAC) to help protect your computer." Click OK.

This really, truly isn't a good idea, though. Really it's not. You're sending your PC right back to the days of Windows XP, when any sneaky old malware could install itself or change your system settings without your knowledge. Do this only on a PC that's not connected to a network or the Internet, for example, or maybe when you, the all-knowing system administrator, are trying to troubleshoot and the UAC interruptions are slowing you down.

When Programs Die: The Task Manager
All Versions

Windows may be a revolution in stability (at least if you're used to, say, Windows Me), but that doesn't mean that *programs* never crash or freeze. They crash, all right—it's just that you rarely have to restart the computer as a result.

When something goes horribly wrong with a program, your primary interest is usually exiting it. But when a program locks up (the cursor moves, but menus and tool palettes don't respond) or when a dialog box tells you that a program has "failed to respond," exiting may not be so easy. After all, how do you choose File→Exit if the File menu itself doesn't open?

As in past versions of Windows, the solution is to invoke the "three-fingered salute": Ctrl+Alt+Delete.

Tip: Actually, there may be a quicker solution. Try right-clicking the frozen program's taskbar button; from the shortcut menu, choose Close. This trick doesn't always work—but when it does, it's much faster than using the Task Manager.

In Vista, however, Ctrl+Alt+Delete no longer opens the fabled Task Manager. Instead, it opens the new Windows Security screen (Figure 6-1).

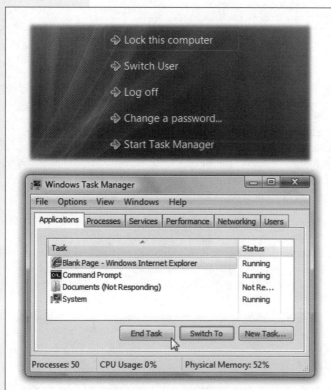

Figure 6-1:
Top: Click the Task Manager button on the Windows Security dialog box to check on the status of a troublesome program.

Bottom: As if you didn't know, one of these programs is "not responding." Highlight its name and then click End Task to slap it out of its misery. Once the program disappears from the list, close the Task Manager and get on with your life. You can even restart the same program right away—no harm done.

From *here* you can get to the Task Manager—by clicking Start Task Manager (Figure 6-1, top). Now you see a list of every open program. The Status column should make clear what you already know: that one of your programs is ignoring you.

Tip: You can also run Task Manager by right-clicking the taskbar and, from the shortcut menu, choosing Task Manager from the shortcut menu. Doing this bypasses the Windows Security dialog box and brings you directly to Windows Task Manager, with the Applications tab selected.

As shown in Figure 6-1, shutting down the troublesome program is fairly easy; just click its name and then click the End Task button. (If yet another dialog box appears, telling you that "This program is not responding," click the End Now button.)

UP TO SPEED

Sending an Error Report to Microsoft

Whenever Windows detects that a program has exited, shall we say, *eccentrically*–for example, it froze and you had to terminate it–your PC quietly sends a report back to Microsoft, the mother ship, via the Internet. It provides the company with the technical details about whatever was going on at the moment of the freeze, crash, or premature termination.

The information includes the name and version number of the program, the date and time, and other details. Microsoft swears that it doesn't collect any information about *you*.

Microsoft says that it has two interests in getting this information. First, it collates the data into gigantic electronic databases, which it then analyzes using special software tools. The idea, of course, is to find trends that emerge from studying hundreds of thousands of such reports. "Oh, my goodness, it looks like people who own both Speak-it Pro 5 and Beekeeper Plus who right-click a document that's currently being printed experience a system lockup," an engineer might announce one day. By analyzing the system glitches of its customers en masse, the company hopes to pinpoint problems and devise software patches with much greater efficiency than before.

Second, Microsoft's computers may also react to the information on the spot and send you a dialog box that lets you know about an available fix.

Windows XP did this report-sending, too, but it asked you *each time* a program crashed. In Vista, the report-sending feature is either turned *on* all the time or *off* all the time.

To adjust the settings, choose Start→Control Panel; click Classic View; open the Problem Reports and Solutions applet. On the left-side task pane, click "Change settings." In the resulting dialog box, click "Advanced settings." There, before you, is the On/Off switch (where it says, "For my programs, problem reporting is:").

This dialog box offers various other privacy controls. For example, you can create a Block list–programs whose crashes won't be reported. (This means you, owners of Music Piracy Plus 4.0.) You can also specify whether crashes are *always* reported, *never* reported, or left to the discretion of each account holder.

Finally, you can see a list of the reports it's sent so far; click "View problem history." For details on the Problems and Solutions system, see Chapter 22.

When you jettison a recalcitrant program this way, Windows generally shuts down the troublemaker gracefully, even offering you the chance to save unsaved changes to your documents.

If even this treatment fails to close the program, you might have to slam the door the hard way. Click the Processes tab, click the name of the program that's giving you grief, and then click the End Process button. (The Processes list includes dozens of programs, including many that Windows runs behind the scenes. Finding the abbreviated name of the program may be the hardest part of this process.)

Using this method, you'll lose any unsaved changes to your documents—but at least the frozen program is finally closed.

Tip: If you click a program's taskbar button but its window doesn't appear, the program may be frozen. In that case, try right-clicking the taskbar button; from the shortcut menu, choose Restore.

Saving Documents
All Versions

In a few programs, such as the Calculator or Solitaire, you don't actually create any documents; when you close the window, no trace of your work remains.

Most programs, however, are designed to create *documents*—files that you can reopen for further editing, send to other people, back up on another disk, and so on.

That's why these programs offer File→Save and File→Open commands, which let you preserve the work you've done, saving it onto the hard drive as a new file icon so that you can return to it later.

The Save Dialog Box
When you choose File→Save for the first time, you're asked where you want the new document stored on your hard drive (Figure 6-2). In Windows Vista, this Save As dialog box is crystal-clear; in fact, for the first time in Windows history it's now a *full Explorer window*, complete with taskbar, Navigation pane, Search box, Views menu, and Organize menu. All of the skills you've picked up working at the desktop come into play here; you can even delete a file or folder right from within the Save or Open box. (The Delete command is in the Organize menu.)

To give it a try, launch any Windows program that has a Save or Export command—WordPad , for example. (Not all programs from other software companies have updated their Save dialog boxes yet.) Type a couple of words and then choose File→Save. The Save As dialog box appears (Figure 6-2).

Saving into Your Documents Folder
The first time you use the File→Save command to save a file, Windows suggests putting your newly created document in your Documents folder.

For many people, this is an excellent suggestion. First, it means that your file won't accidentally fall into some deeply nested folder where you'll never see it again. Instead, it will be waiting in the Documents folder, which is very difficult to lose.

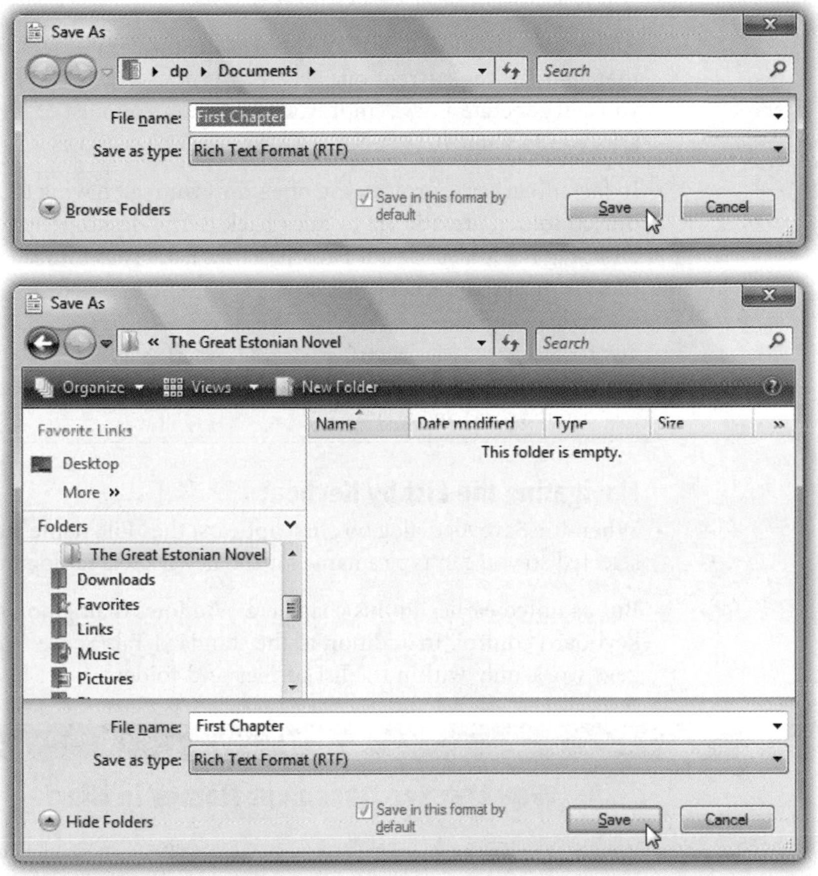

Figure 6-2:
When the Save box first opens, it may appear in the collapsed form shown at top. Click the Browse Folders button to expand it into the full-blown dialog box shown at bottom. Type a name, choose a folder location, and specify the format for the file you're saving.

Second, it's very easy to make a backup copy of your important documents if they're all in one folder. There's a third advantage, too: the Documents folder is also what Windows displays whenever you use a program's File→Open command. In other words, the Documents folder saves you time both when *creating* a new file and when *retrieving* it.

Tip: If the Documents folder becomes cluttered, feel free to make subfolders inside it to hold your various projects. You could even create a different default folder in Documents for each program.

Saving into Other Folders

Still, the now-familiar Navigation pane (page 66) also appears in the Save dialog box. (At least it does in the Save box's expanded from; see Figure 6-2.) So do the Address bar (page 60) and the Search box. You always have direct access to other places where you might want to save a newly created file.

All the usual keyboard shortcuts apply: Alt+up arrow, for example, to open the folder that *contains* the current one. There's even a New Folder button on the toolbar, so you can generate a new, empty folder in the current list of files and folders. Windows asks you to name it.

In fact, if, on some project, you often find yourself having to navigate to some deeply buried folder, press ⊞+D to duck back to the desktop, open any Explorer window, and drag the folder to your Favorite Links list. From now on, you'll have quick access to it from the Save dialog box.

Tip: Many programs let you specify a different folder as the proposed location for saved (and reopened) files. In Microsoft Word, for example, you can change the default folders for the documents you create, where your clip art is stored, and so on.

Navigating the List by Keyboard

When the Save As dialog box first appears, the "File name" text box is automatically selected so you can type a name for the newly created document.

But as noted earlier in this chapter, a Windows dialog box is elaborately rigged for keyboard control. In addition to the standard Tab/Space bar controls, a few special keys work only within the list of files and folders. Start by pressing Shift+Tab (to

---

GEM IN THE ROUGH

Why You See Document Names in Black

In the Save dialog box, Windows displays a list of both folders *and documents* (documents that match the kind you're about to save, that is).

It's easy to understand why *folders* appear here: so that you can double-click one if you want to save your document inside it. But why do *documents* appear here? After all, you can't very well save a document into another document.

Documents are listed here so that you can perform one fairly obscure stunt: If you click a document's name, Windows copies its name into the "File name" text box at the bottom of the window. That's a useful shortcut if you want to *replace*

an existing document with the new one you're saving. By saving a new file with the same name as the existing one, you force Windows to overwrite it (after asking your permission, of course).

This trick also reduces the amount of typing needed to save a document to which you've assigned a different version number. For example, if you click the Thesis Draft 3.1 document in the list, Windows copies that name into the "File name" text box; doing so keeps it separate from earlier drafts. To save your new document as *Thesis Draft 3.2,* you only need to change one character (change the 1 to 2) before clicking the Save button.

---

shift Windows' attention from the "File name" text box to the list of files and folders) and then:

- Press various letter keys to highlight the corresponding file and folder icons. To highlight the Program Files folder, for example, you could type *PR*. (If you type too slowly, your keystrokes are interpreted as separate initiatives—highlighting first the People folder and then the Rodents folder, for example.)

- Press the Page Up or Page Down keys to scroll the list up or down. Press Home or End to highlight the top or bottom item in the list.

- Press the arrow keys (up or down) to highlight successive icons in the list.

- When a folder (or file) is highlighted, you can open it by pressing the Enter key (or double-clicking its icon, or clicking the Open button).

The File Format Drop-Down Menu

The Save As dialog box in many programs offers a menu of file formats (usually referred to as file *types*) below or next to the "File name" text box. Use this drop-down menu when preparing a document for use by somebody whose computer doesn't have the same software.

UP TO SPEED

Dialog Box Basics

To the delight of the powerful Computer Keyboard lobby, you can manipulate almost every element of a Windows dialog box by pressing keys on the keyboard. If you're among those who feel that using the mouse to do something takes longer, you're in luck.

The rule for navigating a dialog box is simple: Press Tab to jump from one set of options to another, or Shift+Tab to move backward. If the dialog box has multiple *tabs,* like the one shown here, press Ctrl+Tab to "click" the next tab, or Ctrl+*Shift*+Tab to "click" the previous one.

Each time you press Tab, the PC's *focus* shifts to a different control or set of controls. Windows reveals which element has the focus by using text highlighting (if it's a text box or drop-down menu), or a dotted-line outline (if it's a button).

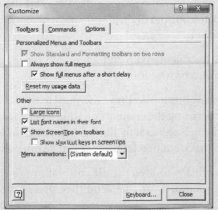

In the illustration shown here, the "Different odd and even" checkbox has the focus.

Once you've highlighted a button or checkbox, simply press the Space bar to "click" it. If you've opened a drop-down list or set of mutually exclusive *option buttons,* or *radio buttons*, press the up or down arrow key. (Once you've highlighted a drop-down list's name, you can also press the F4 key to open it.)

Each dialog box also contains larger, rectangular buttons at the bottom (OK and Cancel, for example). Efficiency fans should remember that tapping the Enter key is always the equivalent of clicking the *default* button—the one with the darkened or thickened outline (the OK button in the illustration here). And pressing Esc almost always means Cancel (or "Close this box").

For example, if you've typed something in Microsoft Word, you can use this menu to generate a Web page document or a Rich Text Format document that you can open with almost any standard word processor or page-layout program.

Closing Documents
All Versions

You close a document window just as you'd close any window, as described in Chapter 2: by clicking the close box (marked by an X) in the upper-right corner of the window, by double-clicking the Control menu spot just to the left of the File menu, or by pressing Alt+F4. If you've done any work to the document since the last time you saved it, Windows offers a "Save changes?" dialog box as a reminder.

Sometimes closing the window also exits the application, and sometimes the application remains running, even with no document windows open. And in a few *really* bizarre cases, it's possible to exit an application (like Windows Mail) while a document window (an email message) remains open on the screen, lingering and abandoned!

The Open Dialog Box
All Versions

To reopen a document you've already saved and named, you can pursue any of these avenues:

- Open your Documents folder (or whichever folder contains the saved file). Double-click the file's icon.

- If you've opened the document recently, choose its name from the Start→Recent Items menu.

- If you're already in the program that created the document, choose File→Open. (Or check the bottom of the File menu, where many programs add a list of recently opened files.)

- Type the document's path and name into the Start→Run box or the Address bar. (You can also browse for it.)

The Open dialog box looks almost identical to the Save As dialog box. Once again, you start out by perusing the contents of your Documents folder; once again, the dialog box otherwise behaves exactly like an Explorer window. For example, you can press Backspace to back *out* of a folder that you've opened.

When you've finally located the file you want to open, double-click it or highlight it (from the keyboard, if you like), and then press Enter.

In general, most people don't encounter the Open dialog box nearly as often as the Save As dialog box. That's because Windows offers many more convenient ways to *open* a file (double-clicking its icon, choosing its name from the Start→Documents command, and so on), but only a single way to *save* a new file.

Moving Data Between Documents

All Versions

You can't paste a picture into your Web browser, and you can't paste MIDI music into your word processor. But you can put graphics into your word processor, paste movies into your database, insert text into Photoshop, and combine a surprising variety of seemingly dissimilar kinds of data. And you can transfer text from Web pages, email messages, and word processing documents to other email and word processing files; in fact, that's one of the most frequently performed tasks in all of computing.

Cut, Copy, and Paste

Most experienced PC users have learned to quickly trigger the Cut, Copy, and Paste commands from the keyboard—without even thinking. Figure 6-3 provides a recap.

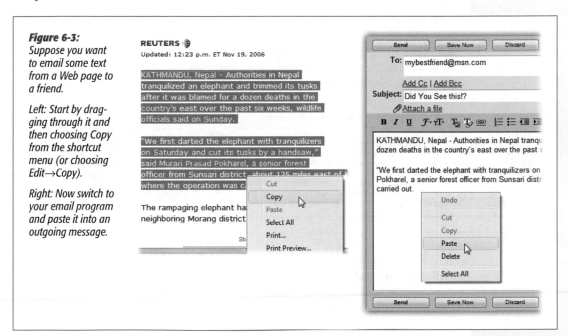

Figure 6-3:
Suppose you want to email some text from a Web page to a friend.

Left: Start by dragging through it and then choosing Copy from the shortcut menu (or choosing Edit→Copy).

Right: Now switch to your email program and paste it into an outgoing message.

Bear in mind that you can cut and copy highlighted material in any of three ways. First, you can use the Cut and Copy commands in the Edit menu; second, you can press Ctrl+X (for Cut) or Ctrl+C (for Copy); and third, you can right-click the highlighted material and, from the shortcut menu, choose Cut or Copy.

When you do so, Windows memorizes the highlighted material, stashing it on an invisible Clipboard. If you choose Copy, nothing visible happens; if you choose Cut, the highlighted material disappears from the original document.

Pasting copied or cut material, once again, is something you can do either from a menu (choose Edit→Paste), from the shortcut menu (right-click and choose Paste), or from the keyboard (press Ctrl+V).

The most recently cut or copied material remains on your Clipboard even after you paste, making it possible to paste the same blob repeatedly. Such a trick can be useful when, for example, you've designed a business card in your drawing program and want to duplicate it enough times to fill a letter-sized printout. On the other hand, whenever you next copy or cut something, whatever was previously on the Clipboard is lost forever.

Drag-and-Drop

As useful and popular as it is, the Copy/Paste routine doesn't win any awards for speed; after all, it requires four steps. In many cases, you can replace that routine with the far more direct (and enjoyable) drag-and-drop method. Figure 6-4 illustrates how it works.

Tip: To drag highlighted material offscreen, drag the cursor until it approaches the top or bottom edge of the window. The document scrolls automatically; as you approach the destination, jerk the mouse away from the edge of the window to stop the scrolling.

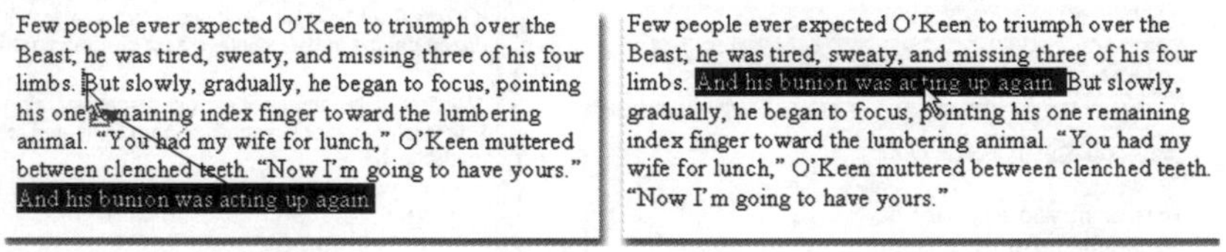

Figure 6-4:
You can drag highlighted text (left) to another place in the document—or a different window or program (right).

Several of the built-in Windows programs work with the drag-and-drop technique, including WordPad and Mail. Most popular commercial programs offer the drag-and-drop feature, too, including email programs and word processors, AOL, Microsoft Office programs, and so on.

Note: Scrap files—bits of text or graphics that you can drag to the desktop for reuse later—no longer exist in Windows Vista.

As illustrated in Figure 6-4, drag-and-drop is ideal for transferring material between windows or between programs. It's especially useful when you've already copied something valuable to your Clipboard, since drag-and-drop doesn't involve (and doesn't erase) the Clipboard.

Its most popular use, however, is rearranging the text in a single document. In, say, Word or WordPad, you can rearrange entire sections, paragraphs, sentences, or even individual letters, just by dragging them—a terrific editing technique.

Tip: Using drag-and-drop to move highlighted text within a document also deletes the text from its original location. By pressing Ctrl as you drag, however, you make a *copy* of the highlighted text.

Export/Import

When it comes to transferring large chunks of information from one program to another—especially address books, spreadsheet cells, and database records—none of the data-transfer methods described so far in this chapter does the trick. For such purposes, use the Export and Import commands found in the File menu of almost every database, spreadsheet, email, and address-book program.

These Export/Import commands aren't part of Windows, so the manuals or help screens of the applications in question should be your source for instructions. For now, however, the power and convenience of this feature are worth noting. Because of these commands, your four years' worth of collected names and addresses in, say, an old address-book program can find its way into a newer program, such as Palm Desktop, in a matter of minutes.

FREQUENTLY ASKED QUESTION

When Formatting Is Lost

How come pasted text doesn't always look the same as what I copied?

When you copy text from Internet Explorer, for example, and then paste it into another program, such as Word, you may be alarmed to note that the formatting of that text (bold, italic, font size, font color, and so on) doesn't reappear intact. In fact, the pasted material may not even inherit the current font settings in the word processor. There could be several reasons for this problem.

For example, not every program *offers* text formatting—Notepad among them. And the Copy command in some programs (such as Web browsers) doesn't pick up the formatting along with the text. So when you copy something from Internet Explorer and paste it into Word or WordPad, you may get plain unformatted text. (There is some good news along these lines, however. Word maintains formatting pasted from the latest Internet Explorer.)

Finally, a note on *text wrapping*. Thanks to limitations built into the architecture of the Internet, email messages aren't like word processor documents. The text doesn't flow continuously from one line of a paragraph to the next, reflowing as you adjust the window size. Instead, email programs insert a press of the Enter key at the end of each line *within* a paragraph.

Most of the time, you don't even notice that your messages consist of dozens of one-line "paragraphs." When you see them in the email program, you can't tell the difference. But if you paste an email message into a word processor, the difference becomes painfully apparent—especially if you then attempt to adjust the margins.

To fix the text, delete the invisible carriage return at the end of each line. (Veteran PC users sometimes use the word processor's search-and-replace function for this purpose.) Or, if you just need a quick look, reduce the point size (or widen the margin) until the text no longer breaks oddly.

Speech Recognition
All Versions

For years, there's been quite a gulf between the promise of computer speech recognition (as seen on *Star Trek*) and the reality (as seen just about everywhere else). You say "oxymoron," it types "ax a moron." (Which is often just what you feel like doing, actually.)

Microsoft has had a speech-recognition department for years. But until recently, it never got the funding and corporate backing it needed to do a really bang-up job.

The speech recognition in Windows Vista, however, is another story. It can't match the accuracy of its chief rival, Dragon NaturallySpeaking, but you might be amazed to discover how elegant its design is now, and how useful it can be to anyone who can't, or doesn't like to, type.

In short, Speech Recognition lets you not only *control* your PC by voice—open programs, click buttons, click Web links, and so on—but also *dictate text* a heck of a lot faster than you can type.

To make this all work, you need a PC with a microphone. The Windows Speech Recognition program can handle just about any kind of mike, even the one built into your laptop's case. But a regular old headset mike—"anything that costs over $20 or so," says Microsoft—will give you the best accuracy.

Take the Tutorial

The easiest way to fire up Speech Recognition for the first time is to open the Start menu and then type *spee*. Using the mouse takes *way* too much time (Start→All Programs→Accessories→Ease of Access→Windows Speech Recognition).

In any case, the first time you open Speech Recognition, you arrive at a very slick, very impressive full-screen tutorial/introduction, featuring a 20-something model in, judging by the gauzy whiteness, what appears to be heaven.

Click your way through the screens. Along the way, you're asked to:

- **Specify what kind of microphone you have. Headset, desktop, array, or built-in?**

- **Read a sample sentence,** about how much Peter loves speech recognition, so your PC can gauge the microphone's volume.

- **Give permission** to Vista to study your documents and email collection. Needless to say, there's no human rooting through your stuff, and none of what Speech Recognition finds is reported back to Microsoft. But granting this permission is a great way to improve your ultimate accuracy, since the kinds of vocabulary and turns of phrase you actually use in your day-to-day work will be built right into Speech Recognition's understanding of your voice.

- **Print the reference card.** This card is critical when you're first learning how to operate Windows by voice. Truth is, however, you don't really need to print it. The same information appears in this chapter, and you can always call the reference card up on the screen by saying into your microphone, "What can I say?"

- **Practice.** The tutorial is excellent; it'll take you about half an hour to complete. It teaches you how to dictate and how to operate buttons, menus, windows, programs, and so on.

Tip: At the outset, Windows is just *simulating* its responses to what you say. But behind the scenes, it's actually studying your real utterances, learning about your voice, and shaping your voice profile. This, in other words, is the "voice training" session you ordinarily have to perform with commercial dictation programs.

Now you're ready to roll. Operating Windows by voice entails knowing three sets of commands:

- Controlling Speech Recognition itself,

- Controlling Windows and its programs, and

- Dictating.

The following sections cover these techniques one at a time.

Controlling Windows Speech Recognition

Slip on your headset, open Windows Speech Recognition, and have a gander at these all-important spoken commands:

- **"Start listening"/"Stop listening."** These commands tell your PC to start and stop listening to you. That's important, because you don't want it to interpret everything you say. It would not be so great if it tried to act when you said to your roommate, "Hey, Chris, close the window."

   So say "Start listening" to turn on your mike—you'll see the microphone button on the speech status palette (Figure 6-5) darken. Say "Stop listening" when you have to take a phone call.

Tip: Once you've opened the Speech Recognition program, you can hit a keystroke to turn listening on and off instead. That key combo is Ctlr+⊞. Get it? "Control Windows"?

- **"What can I say?"** This one's incredibly important. If you can't figure out how to make Windows do something, look it up by saying this. You get the Speech Recognition page of the Vista Help system, complete with a collapsible list of the things you can say.

- **"Show Speech Options."** This command opens the shortcut menu for the Speech palette, as shown in Figure 6-5. From this menu, you can leap into further training, open the "What can I say?" card, go to the Speech Recognition Web site, and so on.

- **"Hide Speech Recognition"/"Show Speech Recognition"** hides or shows the Speech palette itself when screen real estate is at a premium.

Controlling Windows and Its Programs

The beauty of controlling Windows by voice is that you don't have to remember what to say; you just say whatever you would click with the mouse.

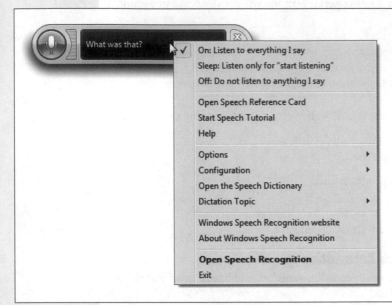

Figure 6-5:
The Speech palette is how Windows holds up its end of the conversation. If it doesn't understand something you said, for example, its text says, "What was that?" The Speech shortcut menu opens when you say "Show Speech Options." It's as though you right-clicked the little palette.

For example, to open the little Calculator program using the mouse, you'd click the **Start** button (to open the Start menu), then **All Programs,** then **Accessories**, and finally **Calculator.** To do the same thing using speech recognition, you just *say* all that: "Start…All Programs…Accessories…Calculator." And presto—the Calculator appears.

Actually, that's a bad example; you can open *any* program just by saying "Start Calculator" (or whatever its name is). But you get the idea.

Here's the cheat sheet for manipulating programs. In this list, any word in *italics* is meant as an example (and other examples that work just as well are in parentheses):

- **Start Calculator (Word, Excel, Internet Explorer…).** Opens the program you named, without you having to touch the mouse. Super convenient.

- **Switch to Word (Excel, Internet Explorer…).** Switches to the program you named.

- **File. Open.** You operate menus by saying whatever you would have clicked with the mouse. For example, say "Edit" to open the Edit menu, then "Select All" to choose that command, and so on.

- **Print (Cancel, Desktop…).** You can also click any button by saying its name—or any tab name in a dialog box.

- **Contact us** (**Archives, Home page…**). You can also click any link on a Web page just by saying its name.

- **Double-click Recycle Bin.** You can tell Windows to "double-click" or "right-click" anything you see.

- **Go to Subject** (**Address, Body…**). In an email message, Web browser, or dialog box, "Go to" puts the insertion point into the text box you name. "Address," for example, means the Address bar.

- **Close that.** Closes the frontmost window. Also "Minimize that," "Maximize that," "Restore that."

- **Scroll up** (**down, left, right**). Scrolls the window. You can say "up," "down," "left," or "right," and you can also append any number from one to 20 to indicate how many lines: "Scroll down 10."

- **Press F** (**Shift-F, capital B, down arrow, X three times…**). Makes Windows press the key you named.

Tip: You don't have to say "Press" before certain critical keys: Delete, Home, End, Space, Tab, Enter, Backspace. Just say the key's name: "Tab."

Show numbers

It's great to know that you can click any button or tab by saying its name. But what if you don't *know* its name? What if it's some cryptic little icon on a toolbar? You can't exactly say, "Click the little thing that looks like a guy putting his head between two rollers."

Figure 6-6:
When you say a number, that number turns green and changes into an OK logo—your clue that you must now say "OK" to confirm the selection. (You can run these utterances together without pausing—for example, "three OK.") Not all programs respond to the "Show numbers" command, alas.

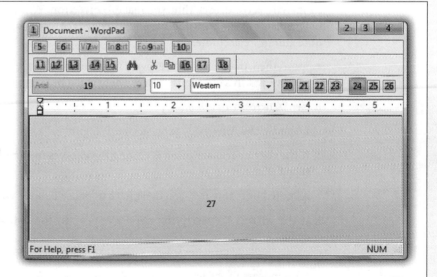

For this purpose, Microsoft has created a clever command called "Show numbers." When you say that, the program overlays *every clickable thing* with superimposed colorful numbers; see Figure 6-6.

The numbers appear automatically if there's more than one button of the same name on the screen, too—several Settings buttons in a dialog box, for example. Say "One OK."

Tip: This trick also works great on Web pages. Say "Show numbers" to see a number label superimposed on every clickable element of the page.

Controlling Dictation

The real Holy Grail for speech recognition, of course, is *dictation*—you speak, and Windows transcribes your words, typing them into any document. (This feature is especially important on Tablet PCs that don't have keyboards.)

Vista's dictation accuracy isn't as good as, say, Dragon NaturallySpeaking's. But it's a close second, it's free, and it's a lot of fun.

It's also very easy. You just talk—at regular speed, into any program where you can type. The only real difference is that you have to *say* the punctuation. You know: "Dear Mom (comma, new line): How are things going (question mark)? Can't believe I'll be home for Thanksgiving in only 24 more weeks (exclamation mark)!"

Correcting errors

Sooner or later—probably sooner—Speech Recognition is going to misunderstand you and type out the wrong thing. It's very important that you correct such glitches—for two reasons. First, you don't want your boss/family/colleagues to think you're incoherent. Second, each time you make a correction, Windows *learns*. It won't make that mistake again. Over time, over hundreds of corrections, Speech Recognition gets more and more accurate.

Suppose, then, that you said, "I enjoyed the ceremony," and Speech Recognition typed out, "I enjoyed this era money." Here's how you'd proceed:

1. Say, "Correct *this era money*."

   Instantly, the Alternates panel pops up (Figure 6-7).

2. **If the correct transcription is among the choices in the list, say its number and then OK.**

   As noted in Figure 6-7, you don't have to pause before "OK."

3. **If the correct transcription *doesn't* appear in the list, speak the correct text again.**

   In this example, you'd say, "the ceremony." Almost always, the version you wanted now appears in the list. Say its number and then OK.

---

4. If the correct transcription *still* doesn't appear in the list, say "Spell it."

You arrive at the Spelling panel; see Figure 6-8.

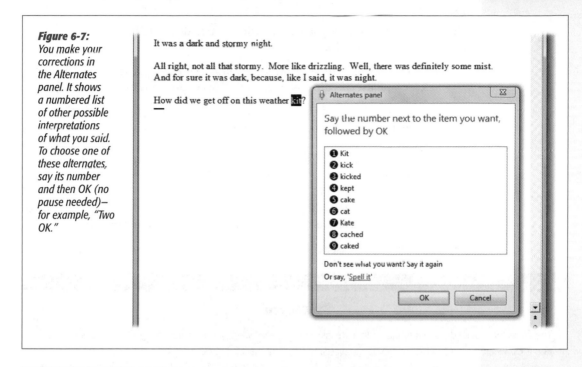

Figure 6-7:
You make your corrections in the Alternates panel. It shows a numbered list of other possible interpretations of what you said. To choose one of these alternates, say its number and then OK (no pause needed)— for example, "Two OK."

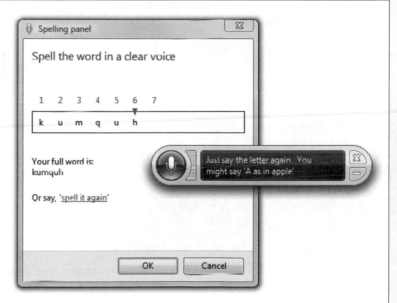

Figure 6-8:
Just spell out the word you really wanted: "F-I-S-H," for example. For greater clarity, you can also use the "pilot's alphabet": Alpha, Bravo, Charlie, Delta, and so on—or even "A as in alliga-tor" (any word you like). If it mishears a letter you've spoken, say the number over it ("three") and then repronounce the letter. Say "OK" once you've gotten the word right.

When you finally exit the Alternates panel, Speech Recognition replaces the corrected text *and* learns from its mistake.

More commands

Here are the other things you can say when you're dictating text. The first few are extremely important to learn.

- **Select *next (previous) two (10, 14, 20...) words (sentences, paragraphs).*** Highlights whatever you just specified—for example, "Select previous five sentences."

  At this point, you're ready to copy, change the font or style, say "Cap that" to capitalize the first words—or just redictate to replace what you wrote.

Tip: If the phrase you want to highlight is long, you can say, "Select *My country* through *land of liberty.*" Windows highlights all of the text *from* the first phrase *through and including* the second one.

- **Correct *ax a moron.*** Highlights the transcribed phrase and opens the Alternates panel, as described above. (You can say a whole phrase or just one word.)

- **Undo.** Undoes the last action.

GEM IN THE ROUGH

Mousegrid

The voice commands described in this section are all well and good when it comes to clicking onscreen objects. But what about *dragging* them?

When you say "Mousegrid," Speech Recognition superimposes an enormous 3 x 3-square grid on your screen, its squares numbered 1 through 9.

Say "five," and a new, much smaller 3 x 3-square grid, also numbered, appears in the space previously occupied by the five square.

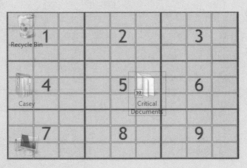

You can keep shrinking the grid in this way until you've pinpointed a precise spot on the screen.

Dragging something–say, an icon across the desktop–is a two-step process.

First, use Mousegrid to home in on the exact spot on the

screen where the icon lies; on your last homing-in, say "four mark." (In this example, the icon you want lies within the four square. "Mark" means "This is what I'm going to want to drag.")

When you say "mark," the Mousegrid springs back to full-screen size; now you're supposed to home in on the *destination* point for your drag. Repeat the grid-shrinking exercise–but in the last step, say "seven click." Watch in amazement as Windows magically grabs the icon at the "mark" position and drags it to the "click" position.

You can use Mousegrid as a last resort for *any* kind of click or drag when the other techniques (like saying button or menu names, or saying "show numbers") don't quite cut it.

- **Scratch that.** Deletes the last thing you dictated. ("Delete that" works, too.)

- **Delete** *your stupid parents.* Instantly deletes the text that you identified.

Tip: If you use commands like *Delete, Select, Capitalize,* or *Add hyphens to* on a word that occurs *more than once* in the open window, Speech Recognition doesn't try to guess. It puts colorful numbered squares on every occurrence of that word. Say "one OK" (or whatever the number is) to tell it *which* occurrence you meant.

- **Go to** *little.* Puts the insertion point right before the word "little."

- **Go after** *lamb.* Puts the insertion point right after the word "lamb."

- **Go to the** *start (end)* **of the** *sentence (paragraph, document).* Puts the insertion point where you said.

- **Caps.** Capitalizes the next word you dictate (no pause is necessary). Saying "All caps" puts the next word ENTIRELY in caps.

- *Ready* **no space** *Boost.* Types ReadyBoost—no space.

- *He typed the word* literal *comma.* The command "literal" tells Speech Recognition to type out the word that follows it ("comma"), rather than transcribing it as a symbol.

- **Add hyphens to** *3D.* Puts a hyphen in the word ("3-D").

- **Start typing** *I, P, C, O, N, F, I, G;* **stop typing.** When you say "Start typing" (and then pause), you enter Typing mode. Now you can spell out anything, letter by letter, in any program on earth. It's a handy way to dictate into programs that don't take dictation well, like PowerPoint and Excel.

GEM IN THE ROUGH

Text to Speech

The big news in Vista is that speech-to-text feature. But Windows can also convert typed text *back* to speech, using a new set of voices of its very own.

To hear them, choose Start→Control Panel. In Classic view, open Speech Recognition Options. In the task pane at left, click "Text to speech." Click Preview Voice to hear the astonishing realism of Microsoft Anna, the new computer voice that debuts with Vista. You can even control her speaking rate using the "Voice speed" slider.

Unfortunately, you won't have many chances to *hear* Microsoft Anna. She's available in Narrator (page 269) to read error messages aloud (woo-hoo!), and Speech Recognition's Speech Options shortcut menu offers a "Speak text in correction dialog" option that makes her read the choices in the Alternates panel.

But Windows offers no way for her to read back *whatever you want,* like stuff you've written or articles you find on the Web.

Note to Microsoft—let Anna free!

Speech Recognition tips

There are zillions of secrets, tips, and tricks lurking in Speech Recognition—but here are a few of the most useful:

- You can teach Speech Recognition new words—unusual last names, oddball terminology—by adding them directly to its dictionary. Say "Show speech options" to open the shortcut menu, and then click (or say) "Open the Speech Dictionary." You're offered the chance to add words, change existing words, or stop certain words from being transcribed.

- When you want to spell out a word, say "Spell it," and then launch right into the spelling: "F, R, E, A, K, A, Z, O, I, D." You don't have to pause between letters or commands.

- In the Spelling window, say the digit over the wrong letter, then say A, or Alpha, or "A as in alligator" (or any word that starts with that letter).

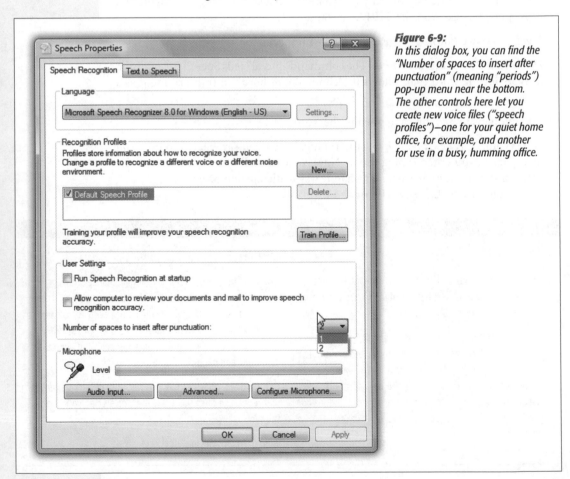

Figure 6-9:
In this dialog box, you can find the "Number of spaces to insert after punctuation" (meaning "periods") pop-up menu near the bottom. The other controls here let you create new voice files ("speech profiles")—one for your quiet home office, for example, and another for use in a busy, humming office.

- Beginning any utterance with "How do I" opens up Windows Help; the next part of your sentence goes into the Search box.

- "Computer" forces the interpretation of your next utterance as a command; "Insert" forces it to be transcribed.

- Out of the box, Speech Recognition puts two spaces after every period—a very 1980s thing to do. Nowadays, that kind of gap looks a little amateurish. Fortunately, you can tell Speech Recognition to use only one space.

  Making this change requires you to visit the little-known Advanced Speech Options dialog box. Choose Start→Control Panel. In Classic view, open Speech Recognition Options. In the task pane at left, click "Advanced speech options" (Figure 6-9).

The Sidebar
All Versions

As you know, the essence of using Windows is running *programs,* which often produce *documents.* In Vista, however, there's a third category: a set of weird hybrid entities that Microsoft calls *gadgets.* They appear, all at once, floating in front of your other windows, at the right side of the screen. They're there when you first fire up Vista, or whenever you press ⊞+Space bar. (You can also open them by choosing Start→All Programs→Accessories→Windows Sidebar.)

Welcome to the new world of the Sidebar (Figure 6-10).

What are these weird hybrid entities, anyway? They're not really programs, because they don't create documents or have listings in the All Programs menu. They're certainly not documents, because you can't name or save them. What they *most* resemble, actually, is little Web pages. They're meant to display information, much of it from the Internet, and they're written using Web programming languages like DHTML, Javascript, VBScript, and XML.

Note: They're generally distributed as .zip files that, when decompressed, have the filename extension *.gadget.*

Vista's starter gadgets include a calculator, current weather reporter, stock ticker, clock, and so on. Mastering the basics of Sidebar won't take you long at all:

- **To move a gadget,** drag it around the screen. It doesn't have to stay in the Sidebar area.

  In fact, you can drag *all* of the gadgets off the Sidebar, if you like, and park them anywhere on the screen. You could even close the now-empty Sidebar—right-click a blank spot and, from the shortcut menu, choose Close Sidebar—and leave the gadgets themselves stranded, floating in place. (If they look too lonely, you can reopen the Sidebar by right-clicking the tiny Windows Sidebar icon in your notification area and, from the shortcut menu, choosing Open.)

Tip: If the gadget doesn't seem to want to move when you drag it, you're probably grabbing it by a clickable portion. Try to find a purely graphical spot—the spiral binding of the calendar, for example.

And if all else fails, right-click the gadget. From the shortcut menu, choose Detach from Sidebar.

- **To close a gadget,** point to it. You'll see the square X button appear at the gadget's top-left corner; click it. (You can also right-click a gadget and choose Close Gadget from its shortcut menu.)

- **To add a gadget to the Sidebar,** click the + button at the top of the screen (Figure 6-10), or right-click any gadget (or the Sidebar notification-area icon) and choose Add Gadget from the Sidebar.

You've just opened the Gadget Gallery, a semi-transparent catalog of all your gadgets, even the ones that aren't currently on the screen (Figure 6-11). Open one by double-clicking its icon, or by dragging it to a blank spot on your Sidebar.

Figure 6-10:
When you summon the Sidebar, you get a fleet of floating miniprograms that convey or convert all kinds of useful information. They appear and disappear all at once, on a tinted translucent sheet.

If you add more gadgets than can fit on the Sidebar, a tiny ▶ appears at the top of the Sidebar. Click it to bring the next "page" full of gadgets into view.

- **To rearrange your gadgets within the Sidebar,** just drag them up or down, using any blank spot as a handle. The other gadgets slide out of the way.

Figure 6-11:
You may have to scroll the Gadget Gallery to see all the gadgets, by clicking the Page arrows at the top left of the window. When you're finished opening new gadgets, close the Gadget Gallery by clicking its X button.

Losing the Sidebar

To get rid of the Sidebar, you have several options.

- **Hide it** by right-clicking a blank spot on the Sidebar. From the shortcut menu, choose Close Sidebar.

  This technique just hides the actual Sidebar rectangle. It doesn't close any gadgets that you've moved onto your screen, and it's still technically running, using memory.

- **Quit it completely,** so it's not using up memory or distracting you, by right-clicking the Windows Sidebar notification-area icon. From the shortcut menu, choose Exit.

- **Make it stop auto-starting** along with Windows by opening the Windows Sidebar Properties control panel. (Quickest way: Right-click the Windows Sidebar icon in your notification area. From the shortcut menu, choose Properties.) Turn off "Start Sidebar when Windows starts." Click OK.

Sidebar Tips

Like most new Vista features, Sidebar is crawling with tips and tricks. Here are a few of the biggies:

- You can open more than one copy of the same gadget. Just double-click its icon more than once in the Gadget Bar. You wind up with multiple copies of it on your screen: three Clocks, two Weather trackers, or whatever. That's a useful trick when, for example, you want to track the time or weather in more than one city, or when you maintain two different stock portfolios.

- If you point to a gadget without clicking, two or three tiny icons appear to its right. One is the X (Close button), which you've already met. The one that looks like a tiny wrench opens the gadget's Settings dialog box, where, for example, you can specify which stocks you want to track, or which town's weather you want to see. The third one, a tiny grid, is a "grip strip" that lets you drag the gadget to a new spot on the screen.

- Once the Sidebar is open, you can "tab" your way through the gadgets, highlighting one after another, by repeatedly pressing ⊞+G. When a certain gadget is highlighted, you can manipulate it. Close it, for example, by pressing Alt+F4.

- The "Search all gadgets" box (top right of the Gadget Gallery) lets you jump directly to a certain gadget, of course—a real sanity saver for the hard-core gadget collector. But if you click the ▾ to its right, the pop-up menu lets you restrict your search to only "Recently installed gadgets" or gadgets that came from Microsoft itself (choose "Microsoft Corporations").

- Many of the gadgets require an Internet connection, preferably an always-on connection like a cable modem.

- Ordinarily, your everyday work windows are allowed to cover up the Sidebar and its gadgets. If you have two monitors, though, or one really huge one, you can reverse that logic; you can tell Vista to put the gadgets on top of all other windows.

  To do that, choose Start→Control Panel→Classic View→Windows Sidebar Properties. Turn on "Sidebar is always on top of other windows."

Tip: The same Control Panel applet lets you place the Sidebar on the *left* side of the screen, if you like, or even specify *which* of your many monitors it should appear on.

Gadget Catalog

Here's a rundown of the standard gadgets that come preinstalled in Vista. True, they look awfully simple, but some of them harbor a few secrets.

Tip: If you right-click an individual gadget, the shortcut menu offers, among other commands, an Opacity control. That is, you can make any individual gadget more or less see-through—something that makes more sense for, say, the clock than the photo slideshow.

Calendar

Sure, you can always find out today's date by pointing to the clock on your taskbar. And this gadget isn't much of a calendar. It doesn't show your appointments, and it doesn't hook into Windows Calendar.

But it's much nicer looking than the taskbar one. And besides, you can use this calendar to look ahead or back. Here's the scheme of things you can click:

- **Click today's red "page"** to open the month-view calendar.

- **Navigate** to a different month by clicking ◄ or ► buttons. Change the year by clicking the current year digits at the top of the month view.

- **Click a date square** to see its "page," identifying its day and date. (Not that you learn much by doing this—clicking Wednesday, June 22 makes the big date squares read "Wednesday, June 22." Ooooh!)

- **Click the red peeking corner** to return to the month-view calendar.

Clock

Sure, this clock shows the current time, but your taskbar does that. The neat part is that you can open up several of these clocks—double-click Clock in the Gadget Gallery repeatedly—and set each one up to show the time in a different city. The result looks like the row of clocks in a hotel lobby, making you look Swiss and precise.

- **Point to the analog clock** without clicking to see a digital rendition of the current time ("5:34 p.m.").

- **Click the Options (wrench) button** for a choice of eight good-looking analog clock faces. The Options dialog box also lets you choose each clock's time zone, add a sweep-second hand, and name this clock—"New York" or "London," for example. This name appears on the clock's face—a handy option when you've opened this gadget more than once, creating different clocks that track different time zones.

Contacts

The concept behind this gadget is, of course, to give you faster access to your own address book. (Trudging off to the actual Contacts folder, described on page 250, takes way too long when you just want to look up a number.)

FREQUENTLY ASKED QUESTION

The Disappearing Notes, Stocks, or Weather

Hey! I filled my Notes gadget with grocery lists and Web addresses, and now they're gone!

Hey! I set up my home city in the Weather gadget, and now it's showing Redmond, Washington!

Hey! I painstakingly typed in all my stocks, and now it's forgotten them all!

Welcome to gadget hell, buddy.

Remember, gadgets are not actually programs. They don't,

therefore, have their own preference files stashed away on the hard drive.

And so—here's the bad news—any time you close a gadget, you *lose all the data you had typed into it.* When you reopen Weather, it always shows Redmond, Washington (Microsoft's home town); when you reopen Stocks, it always shows the NASDAQ and S&P indexes; when you reopen Notes, the sticky notes are always empty; and so on.

And so, a word to the wise: don't click that X button unless you really mean it!

The gadget may look like a simple Rolodex card, but it's actually filled with clickable shortcuts. For example:

- **Search bar.** Type a few letters of somebody's name here. As you type, the gadget homes in on that person's entry from the Contacts program. (Clear the Search bar by clicking the little X.)

- **Names.** Click a name to open this person's Contacts entry, complete with phone number, email address, and so on.

- **Red tab** (**left side**). Click to return to the full master list of contacts.

- **Email address.** Click to fire up the Mail program (or whatever email program you use), complete with a fresh outgoing message already addressed to this person. All you have to do is type your message and click Send.

Tip: This gadget is easier to understand if you drag it off of the Sidebar. Once free on your screen, it appears as a *two*-page binder, with the master list of contacts on the left side of the binding, and the individual Rolodex "page" on the right.

CPU Meter

A power user's dream—now you can watch your PC wheeze and gasp under its load in real time, with statistical accuracy.

The CPU Meter has two gauges. The left-side one shows how hard you're driving your CPU (central processing unit—that is, your Intel or AMD chip), expressed as a percentage of its capacity. The smaller dial shows how much of your computer's RAM (memory) you're using at the moment. Watch the needles rise and fall as you open and close your programs! (Watch them go nuts when you open Microsoft Office!)

Currency

This one's for you, world travelers (or global investors). This little gadget can convert dollars to euros, or shillings to francs, or whatever to whatever.

From the upper pop-up menu, choose the currency type you want to convert *from:* U.S. Dollars, Norwegian Krone, or whatever. Into the text box, type how *many* of those you want to convert.

Use the lower pop-up menu to specify which units you want to convert *to.*

You don't have to click anything or press any key; the conversion is performed for you instantly and automatically as you type. (Never let it be said that technology isn't marching forward.)

Some of Currency's features are available only when you drag this gadget *out* of the Sidebar and into a spot where it has room to expand. For example:

- **See more details** about your currency's current situation by clicking the little ˜ button to the left of each pop-up menu. Your Web browser opens and takes you to the MSN Money Web site, already opened to a details page about that currency and its history.

- **Convert more currencies** at once by clicking the + button (lower-right of the gadget). That is, you can see $20 represented as dinar, baht, and shekels simultaneously.

- **Find out where the data comes from** by clicking the words Data Providers.

Note: This gadget actually does its homework. It goes online to download up-to-the-minute currency rates to ensure that the conversion is accurate.

Feed Headlines

An *RSS feed* is a newfangled Internet feature, in which the headlines from various Web sites are sent to you automatically (see page 380 for details). Internet Explorer 7 can accept RSS feeds, of course—but you don't have to fire it up every time you want to know the news of the world. Just take a look at this little gadget.

Actually, don't look yet; out of the box, this gadget doesn't show much at all. But if you click its "View headlines" link, you get to see 100 recent headlines, all from Microsoft sources: Microsoft news, Microsoft tips, Microsoft articles, and so on.

- **Substitute your own feeds.** This gadget is much more attractive when you fill it with your own favorite feeds—the *New York Times*, sports-score sites, favorite online columnists, and so on. Fortunately, the gadget inherits its list of feeds from those you've subscribed to in Internet Explorer, as described on page 380.

  Once you've subscribed to a feed there, click this gadget's Options (wrench) button. Use the "Display this feed" list to choose the feed you want displayed.

Tip: You can choose only *one* item from the "Display this feed" pop-up menu. Fortunately, that doesn't mean only one feed. If you take the effort to create a *folder* for your favorite feeds when storing them in Internet Explorer, you can choose that *folder's* name in this gadget, thereby getting a rotating list of *multiple* favorite feeds.

- **Scroll the list** by clicking the the ▲ or ▼ buttons.

- **See more of each headline** by dragging this gadget off the sidebar, if you've got the room.

Notes

Notes is a virtual Post-it note that lets you type out random scraps of text—a phone number, a Web address, a grocery list, or whatever.

- **Edit the note** by typing away. Right-click to access Cut, Copy, and Paste commands.

- **Add another page** by clicking the + button (lower right); delete the current page by clicking the X button (lower left). Once you have more than a single page, use the ◄ or ► buttons to move among them.

• **Change the paper color, font, or size** by clicking the Options button (tiny wrench) at the right side of the gadget. Font and Size controls appear there; click the ◄ or ► buttons to see the different pastel paper colors available.

Stocks

Hey, day traders, this one's for you. This gadget lets you build a stock portfolio and watch it rise and fall throughout the day.

It contains your list of stocks, their current prices (well, current as of 20 minutes ago), and the amount they've changed—green if they're up, red if they're down. Click a stock's name to see its chart and other details in a Web page.

To set up your portfolio, proceed like this:

• **Add a stock** by clicking the + button below the list, typing its name or stock abbreviation into the box at the top, and pressing Enter. If there's only one possible match—Microsoft, for example—the gadget adds it to the list instantly. If there's some question about what you typed, or several possible matches, you'll see a pop-up menu listing the alternatives, so you can click the one you want.

Collapse the "Add a stock" dialog box by clicking the + button again, or simply by clicking anywhere else on your screen.

• **Scroll the list** by clicking the ▲ or ▼ buttons.

• **Remove a stock from the list** by clicking the little X button that appears when you point to its name.

• **See company names instead of abbreviations** by clicking the Options (wrench) button and then turning on "Display company name in place of symbol."

Tip: Ordinarily, the gadget displays the ups and downs of each stock as a dollar amount ("+.92" means up 92 cents, for example). But if you turn on "Show change as a percentage"—which also appears when you click the Options button—you'll see these changes represented as percentages of their previous values.

Picture Puzzle

For generations, Microsoft Windows fans had their Solitaire game—and only occasionally looked over the backyard fence to see the Tile Game that their Macintosh friends were playing. The idea, of course, is to click the tiles of the puzzle, using logic to rearrange them back into the original sequence, so that they eventually slide together into the put-together photograph.

• **Change the photo** by clicking the Options (wrench) button.

• **Pause the timer** (upper-left corner) by clicking the tiny clock.

• **See the finished photo,** so you know what the goal is, by holding the cursor down on the little ? button.

- **Give up** by clicking the double-arrow button in the upper-right corner of the puzzle window. (The same button rescrambles the puzzle.)

Weather

This gadget shows a handy current-conditions display for your city (or any other city), and, at your option, even offers a three-day forecast.

Before you get started, the most important step is to click the Options (wrench) button. In the Options dialog box, you'll see where you can specify your city and state or Zip code. Type it in and press Enter; the gadget goes online to retrieve the latest Weather.com info. You can also specify whether you prefer degrees Celsius or degrees Fahrenheit. Click OK.

Now the front of the gadget displays the name of your town, general conditions, and current temperature.

- **See more details** by dragging the gadget out of the Sidebar. Now you see today's predicted high and low, the sky situation (like "Clear"), the current temperature, and the three-day forecast.

- **See the complete weather report** by clicking the underlined location (such as "Central Park, NY") to open your Web browser and call up the full-blown Weather.com page for that location.

Slide Show

So you've got a digital camera and a hard drive crammed with JPEGs. What are you gonna do with 'em all?

Slide Show offers an ingenious way to savor your handiwork all day long. It's just what it says: a small slideshow that presents one photo at a time for a few seconds each. Think of it as an electronic version of the little spouse 'n' kids photo that cubicle dwellers prop up on their desks—except that the picture changes every 15 seconds.

The buttons in the tiny translucent control bar at the bottom of picture correspond to Previous Photo, Pause/Resume, Next Photo, and View (which opens up the picture—much larger now—in Windows Photo Gallery).

- **Substitute your own photos.** When you first install Vista, this gadget presents Microsoft's favorite nature photos. But where's the fun in that? Once you're sick of them, click the Options (wrench) button. In the dialog box, use the Folder controls to choose a folder full of your own pictures.

- **Set up the show timing.** Fifteen seconds is an awfully long time to stare at one photo, of course. Then again, if the pix change too often, they'll be distracting, and you won't get any work done. Nonetheless, the Options dialog box lets you keep each slide on the screen for as little as 5 seconds or as long as 5 minutes.

The Options box also lets you create a crossfade effect as one slide morphs into the next. And the Shuffle checkbox, of course, makes Slide Show present your pix in a random order, rather than their alphabetical order in the folder.

Tip: If you drag this gadget off the Sidebar itself, you get to see your photos at a larger, more pleasant size.

Figure 6-12:
Top: After downloading the new gadget (you'll have to click a couple of confirmation buttons along the way), you see this display. Click Install to install it (or Don't Install, if you think it's evil).

Bottom: Not all good things come from Microsoft. Here's a handful of neat gadgets written by other people.

More Gadgets

The gadgets that come with Vista are meant to be only examples—a starter collection. The real beauty of gadgets is that people can write their own new ones for the whole world to enjoy: gadgets that show your local movie listings, regional gas prices, your email Inbox, upcoming Outlook appointments, and so on (Figure 6-12, bottom).

To see the current list of goodies that have been vetted by Microsoft, click "Get more gadgets online" in the Gadget Gallery described above. That takes you to the Microsoft Gadgets Gallery downloads page. (Alternatively, go straight to *http://gallery. microsoft.com.*)

You should have no problem finding gadgets that tell you local traffic conditions, let you know if your flight will be on time, help you track FedEx packages, provide a word (or joke, or comic strip) of the day, and so on.

Installing a gadget

Downloading and installing a gadget isn't hard, but there are a number of steps. Here's what you'll see if you use Internet Explorer, for example:

- A warning that you're installing software not written by Microsoft (click OK).

- The File Download dialog box (click Save).

- The Save As dialog box, asking where to store the download (click Save).

Unless you interfered, Internet Explorer drops the new gadget into your Personal→ Downloads folder. Open that folder, and then double-click the new gadget to install it. Figure 6-12 illustrates the process.

Uninstalling a gadget

If you decide you don't want a gadget, you can just close it (right-click it; from the shortcut menu, choose Close Gadget). That leaves it on your PC, but dormant.

If, on the other hand, you really doubt you'll ever need it again, open your Gadget Gallery. Right-click the offending gadget; from the shortcut menu, choose Uninstall. Now it's really, truly gone.

Filename Extensions and File Associations

All Versions

Every operating system needs a mechanism to associate documents with the applications that created them. When you double-click a Microsoft Word document icon, for example, Word launches and opens the document.

In Windows, every document comes complete with a normally invisible *filename extension* (or just *file extension*)—a period followed by a suffix that's usually three letters long.

Here are some common examples:

When you double-click this icon...	...this program opens it
Fishing trip**.doc**	Microsoft Word
Quarterly results**.xls**	Microsoft Excel
Home page**.htm**	Internet Explorer
Agenda**.wpd**	Corel WordPerfect
A home movie**.avi**	Windows Media Player
Sudoku**.gadget**	Sidebar gadget
Animation**.dir**	Macromedia Director

Tip: For an exhaustive list of every file extension on the planet, visit *www.whatis.com*; click the link for "Every File Format in the World."

Behind the scenes, Windows maintains a massive table that lists every extension and the program that "owns" it. More on this in a moment.

Displaying Filename Extensions

It's possible to live a long and happy life without knowing much about these extensions. Because file extensions don't feel very user-friendly, Microsoft designed Windows to *hide* the suffixes on most icons (Figure 6-13). If you're new to Windows, you may never have even seen them.

Some people appreciate the way Windows hides the extensions, because the screen becomes less cluttered and less technical-looking. Others make a good argument for the Windows 3.1 days, when every icon appeared with its suffix.

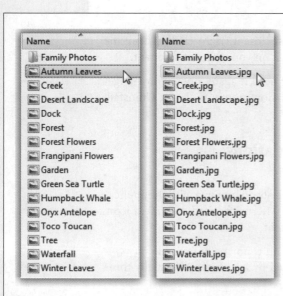

Figure 6-13:
As a rule, Windows shows filename extensions only on files whose extensions it doesn't recognize. The JPEG graphics at left, for example, don't show their suffixes. Right: You can ask Windows to display all extensions, all the time.

For example, in a single Explorer window, suppose one day you discover that three icons all seem to have exactly the same name: PieThrower. Only by making filename extensions appear would you discover the answer to the mystery: that one of them is called PieThrower.ini, another is an Internet-based software updater called PieThrower.upd, and the third is the actual PieThrower program, PieThrower.exe.

If you'd rather have Windows reveal the file suffixes on *all* icons, open an Explorer window. Choose Organize→Folder and Search Options. In the Folder Options dialog box, click the View tab. Turn off "Hide extensions for known file types," and then click OK.

Now the filename extensions for all icons appear (Figure 6-13).

Hooking Up an Unknown File Type

Every now and then, you might try to open a mystery icon—one whose extension is missing, or whose extension Windows doesn't recognize. Maybe you've been sent some weirdo document that was created by a beekeeper or banjo transcriber using a program you don't have, or maybe you're opening a document belonging to an old DOS program that doesn't know about the Windows file-association feature. What will happen when you double-click that file?

Windows *asks* you.

In the dialog box shown in Figure 6-14, Windows offers you two different buttons:

- **Use the Web service to find the appropriate program.** In other words, Windows will take your PC onto the Internet and look up the mystery file extension on the Microsoft Web site.

- **Select the program from a list of installed programs.** Windows displays a dialog box that looks like the one at bottom in Figure 6-14. Click the name of the program you want, and then turn on "Always use the selected program to open this kind of file," if you like.

Hooking up a File Extension to a Different Program

Windows comes with several programs that can open text files with the extension *.txt*—Notepad and WordPad, for example. Windows also comes with several programs (Paint, Photo Gallery) that can open picture files with the extension *.jpg*. So how does it decide *which* program to open when you double-click a .txt or .jpg file?

Easy—it refers to its internal database of preferred *default programs* for various file types. But at any time, you can reassign a particular file type (file extension) to a different application. If you've just bought Photoshop, for example, you might want it to open up your JPEG files, rather than Photo Gallery.

This sort of surgery has always confused beginners. Yet it was important for Microsoft to provide an easy way of reprogramming documents' mother programs; almost everyone ran into programs like RealPlayer that, once installed, "stole" every file association they could. The masses needed a simple way to switch documents back to their preferred programs.

So in Vista, Microsoft ripped up its File Types dialog boxes and started from scratch. Whether or not the *three* new file-association mechanisms are actually superior to the *one* old one—well, you be the judge.

Tip: The File Types tab of the Folder Options dialog box, once the headquarters of document-to-program relationships, no longer exists in Vista.

Figure 6-14:
Top: Sometimes Windows doesn't know what to do with an icon you've just double-clicked. If you're pretty sure your PC has a program that can open it, give it a little help—click "Select a program from a list of installed programs" and then click OK.

Bottom: Use this window to select a program for opening the mystery file. It's sometimes useful to associate a particular document type with a pro-gram that didn't create it, by the way. For example, if you double-click a text file, and the Open With dialog box appears, you might decide that you want such documents to open automatically into WordPad.

Method 1: Start with the document

Often, you'll discover a misaligned file-type association the hard way. You'll double-click a document and the wrong program opens it.

For that reason, Microsoft has added a new way of reprogramming a document—that starts right in Explorer, with the document itself.

Right-click the icon of the file that needs a new parent program. From the shortcut menu, choose Open With.

If you're just trying to open this document into the new program *this once,* you may be able to choose the new program's name from the Open With submenu (Figure 6-15, top). Vista doesn't always offer this submenu, however.

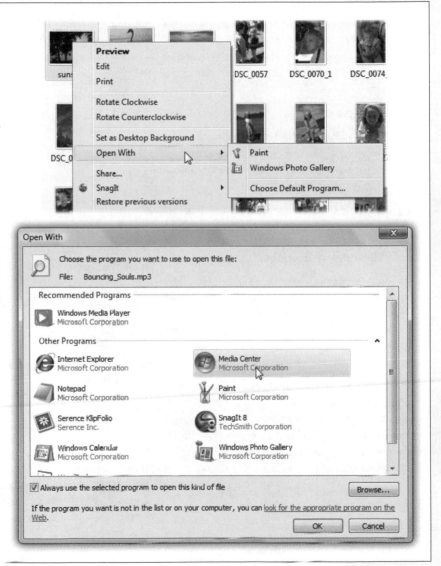

Figure 6-15:
Top: To reassign a document to a new parent program, use its Open With shortcut menu. If you're lucky, you'll get a submenu of available programs that can open the document.

Bottom: Windows is prepared to show you a list of every program that can open the mystery file. Scroll through the list of installed programs to select the one you want. By turning on the checkbox at the bottom of the dialog box, you create a file association that will handle similar files (those with the same file extension) in the future.

If you choose Choose Default Program from the submenu, or if there's no submenu at all, the new Open With dialog box appears, as shown in Figure 6-15 (bottom). It's supposed to list every program on your machine that's capable of opening the document.

And now, a critical decision: Are you trying to make *this document only* open in a different program? Or *all documents of this type?*

FREQUENTLY ASKED QUESTION

Program Access and Defaults

OK, I've just barely understood your description of the new Control Panel applet, where I can hook up documents to programs or programs to documents. So what, exactly, is this other *link in that applet, called "Set program access and computer defaults?"*

Well, it's kind of a long story.

In its 2002 agreement with the U.S. Department of Justice, Microsoft agreed to give other companies a fighting chance at competing with programs like Internet Explorer, Outlook Express, and Windows Media Player.

If you open the Default Programs applet and click "Set program access and computer defaults," you get the dialog box shown here. After you authenticate yourself (page 191), you're offered three or four options:

Microsoft Windows means, "Use all of Microsoft's utility programs, just as Windows has been doing from Day One." You're saying that you prefer Microsoft's Web browser (Internet Explorer), email program (Windows Mail), music/video player (Windows Media Player), and instant messaging program (Windows Messenger).

Selecting this option doesn't *prevent* you from using other browsers, email programs, and so on—you'll still find them listed in the Start→All Programs menu. But this option does put the Internet Explorer and Windows Mail icons, for example, into prime positions at the top of your Start menu for quick and easy access.

Non-Microsoft means, "Use *anything* but Microsoft's programs! Instead, use Netscape Navigator, Eudora, RealPlayer, Sun's Java, or whatever—just nothing from Microsoft."

You should install your preferred alternate programs *before*

selecting this option. Otherwise, the only programs this feature "sees" are Microsoft programs, which would make selecting this option a tad pointless.

As with the "Microsoft" option, choosing this option places your preferred programs' icons at the top of your Start menu. Unlike the "Microsoft" option, however, this option *removes access* to the corresponding Microsoft programs. If you choose a non-Microsoft program as your email program, for example, Windows Mail disappears completely from the All Programs menu and its folder (in C:→Program Files).

Of course, Microsoft's programs aren't really gone—they're just hidden. They pop right back when you choose the "Microsoft Windows" option, or when you choose Custom and then click the associated "Enable access to this program" checkbox. Just remember to click OK to apply your changes.

Computer Manufacturer means, "Use whatever programs are recommended by Dell" (or whoever made the PC and signed deals with AOL, Real, and so on). This option doesn't appear on all PCs.

Custom lets you choose each kind of program independently, whether it comes from Microsoft or not. For example, you can choose Firefox, Internet Explorer, or any other Web browser as your default browser. (They'll all be listed here when you click the double-arrow button to expand the dialog box.)

During your selection process, note the "Enable access to this program" checkbox. It really means, "List this baby at the top of the Start menu, and also put its icon on the Quick Launch toolbar, the Desktop, and wherever else important programs are listed."

If it's just this one, click OK and stop reading. If it's *all* files of this type (all JPEGs, all MP3s, all .doc files…), then also turn on "Always use the selected program to open this kind of file," and click OK.

You should now be able to double-click the original document—and smile as it opens in the program you requested.

Note: If the program isn't listed, click the Browse button and go find it yourself. And if you don't seem to have *any* program on your PC that will open the document, click "look for the appropriate program on the Web." You go online to a File Associations Web page, which lists programs that Microsoft knows can open the file.

Method 2: Start with the program

If you'd prefer to edit Vista's master database of file associations directly, a new Control Panel applet awaits. You can approach the problem from either direction:

- Choose a program and then choose which file types you want it to take over; or

- Choose a filename extension (like .aif or .ico) and then choose a new default program for it.

Here's how to perform the first technique:

1. **Choose Start→Control Panel. Click Classic View→Default Programs.**

   The new Default Programs control panel opens.

2. **Click "Set your default programs."**

   A curious new dialog box appears, as shown in Figure 6-16 at top. It's a list of every program on your machine that's capable of opening multiple file types.

3. **Click the name of a program.**

   For example, suppose a program named FakePlayer 3.0 has performed the dreaded Windows Power Grab, claiming a particular file type for itself without asking you. In fact, suppose it has elected itself King of *All* Audio Files. But you want Windows Media Player to play everything *except* for FakePlayer (.fkpl) files.

   In this step, then, you'd click Windows Media Player.

   If you want Media Player to become the default player for *every* kind of music and video file, you'd click "Set this program as default." But if you want it to open only *some* kinds of files, proceed like this:

4. **Click "Choose defaults for this program."**

   Now yet another dialog box opens (Figure 6-16, bottom). It lists every file type the selected program knows about.

5. **Turn on the checkboxes of the file types for which you want this program to be the default opener.**

Of course, this step requires a certain amount of knowledge that comes from experience—how the heck would the average person know what, say, a .wvx file is?—but it's here for the power user's benefit.

6. Click Save, then OK.

Method 3: Start with the file type

Finally, you can approach the file-association problem a third way: by working through a massive alphabetical list of filename extensions (.aca, .acf, .acs, .aif, and so on) and hooking each one up to a program of your choice.

Figure 6-16:
Top: Each software program you install must register the file types it uses. The link between the file type and the program is called an association. This dialog box displays each program on your PC that's capable of opening documents.

Bottom: If you click "Choose defaults for this program," you get this box, where you can manually inform Windows of which file types the selected program is allowed to open. In this example, the box tells you which types of files will open in QuickTime Player when double-clicked.

1. **Choose Start→Control Panel. Click Classic View→Default Programs.**

   The Default Programs control panel opens.

2. **Click "Associate a file type or protocol with a program."**

   A massive filename extensions list opens, as shown in Figure 6-17.

3. **Select the filename extension you want, and then click "Change program."**

   Now the Open With dialog box appears (the same one shown in Figure 6-16).

4. **Click the name of the new default program.**

   Once again, if you don't see it listed here, you can click Browse to find it yourself.

5. **Click OK and then Close.**

Installing Software
All Versions

As you probably know, Microsoft doesn't actually sell PCs (yet). Therefore, you bought your machine from a different company, which probably installed Windows on it before you took delivery.

POWER USERS' CLINIC

Who Gets the Software?

As you're probably becoming increasingly aware, Microsoft designed Windows to be a *multiuser* operating system, in which each person who logs in enjoys an independent environment—from the desktop pattern to the email in Windows Mail. The question thus arises: when someone installs the new program, does every account holder have equal access to it?

In general, the answer is yes. If an administrator (page 669) installs a new program, it usually shows up on the Start→All Programs menu of *every* account holder.

Occasionally, a program's installer may offer you a choice: install the new software so that it's available *either* to everybody *or* only to you, the currently logged-in account holder.

Also occasionally, certain programs might just install software into your own account, so nobody else who logs in even knows that the program exists.

In that case, you can proceed in either of two ways. First, you can simply log in to each account, one after another, reinstalling the program for each account.

Second, you may be able to get away with moving the program's shortcut from your own personal account folder to the corresponding location in the All Users folder. Windows actually maintains two different types of Programs folders: one that's shared by everybody, and another for each individual account holder.

Here's where that information pays off. Open your Start→All Programs menu; right-click the name of the program you want everyone to be able to access, and choose Copy from the shortcut menu. Now right-click the Start menu; from the shortcut menu, choose Open All Users. In the window that appears, right-click the Programs folder, and then choose Paste from the shortcut menu. The program now appears on the Start menu of everybody who uses the machine.

Many PC companies sweeten the pot by preinstalling other programs, such as Quicken, Microsoft Works, Microsoft Office, more games, educational software, and so on. The great thing about preloaded programs is that they don't need installing. Just double-click their desktop icons, or choose their names from the Start→All Programs menu, and you're off and working.

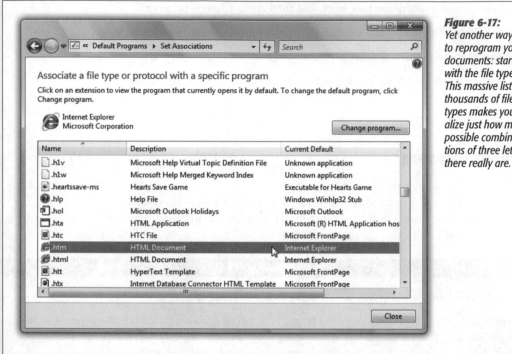

Figure 6-17:
Yet another way to reprogram your documents: start with the file type. This massive list of thousands of file types makes you realize just how many possible combinations of three letters there really are.

Sooner or later, though, you'll probably want to exploit the massive library of Windows software and add to your collection. Today, almost all new software comes to your PC from one of two sources: a disc (CD or DVD) or the Internet.

An installer program generally transfers the software files to the correct places on your hard drive. The installer also adds the new program's name to the Start→All

---

FREQUENTLY ASKED QUESTION

Microsoft InstallShield?

I'm a bit confused. I bought a program from Infinity Workware. But when I run its installer, the Welcome screen says InstallShield. Who actually made my software?

Most of the time, the installer program isn't part of the software you bought or downloaded, and doesn't even

come from the same company. Most software companies pay a license to installer-software companies. That's why, when you're trying to install a new program called, say, JailhouseDoctor, the first screen you see says InstallShield. (InstallShield is the most popular installation software.)

Programs menu, tells Windows about the kinds of files (file extensions) it can open, and makes certain changes to your *Registry* (Appendix B).

The Preinstallation Checklist

You can often get away with blindly installing some new program without heeding the checklist below. But for the healthiest PC and the least time on hold with tech support, answer these questions before you install anything:

- **Are you an administrator?** Windows derives part of its security and stability by handling new software installations with suspicion. For example, you can't install most programs unless you have an *administrator account* (see page 669).

- **Does it run in Windows Vista?** If the software or its Web site specifically says it's compatible with Vista, great. Install away. Otherwise, consult the Microsoft Web site, which includes a list—not a complete one, but a long one—of all Vista-compatible programs.

Tip: See "Running Pre-Vista Programs" later in this chapter for compatibility tips.

- **Is the coast clear?** Exit all your open programs. (One quick way is to right-click the buttons on the taskbar, one at a time, and choose Close or Close Group from the shortcut menu.) You should also turn off your virus-scanning software, which may take the arrival of your new software the wrong way.

- **Am I prepared to backtrack?** If you're at all concerned about the health and safety of the software you're about to install, remember that the System Restore feature (page 648) takes an automatic snapshot of your system just before any software installation. If the new program turns out to be a bit hostile, you can rewind your system to its former happier working condition.

Installing Software from a Disc

Most commercial software these days comes on a CD or DVD. On each one is a program called Setup.exe, which, on most installation discs, runs automatically when you insert the disc into the machine. You're witnessing the *AutoPlay* feature at work.

If AutoPlay is working (page 286), a few seconds after you insert the disc, the "wait" cursor appears. A few seconds later, the Welcome screen for your new software appears, and you may be asked to answer a few onscreen questions (for example, to specify the folder into which you want the new program installed). Along the way, the program may ask you to type in a serial number, which is usually on a sticker on the CD envelope or the registration card.

When the installation is over—and sometimes after restarting the PC—the words All Programs appear with orange highlighting in the Start menu. If you click, the new program's name also appears highlighted in orange, and your Start→All Programs menu is now ready for action.

Installing Downloaded Software

The files you download from the Internet (see Figure 6-18) usually aren't ready-to-use, double-clickable applications. Instead, almost all of them arrive on your PC in the form of a *compressed* file, with all the software pieces crammed together into a single, easily downloaded icon. The first step in savoring your downloaded delights is restoring this compressed file to its natural state, as described on page 149.

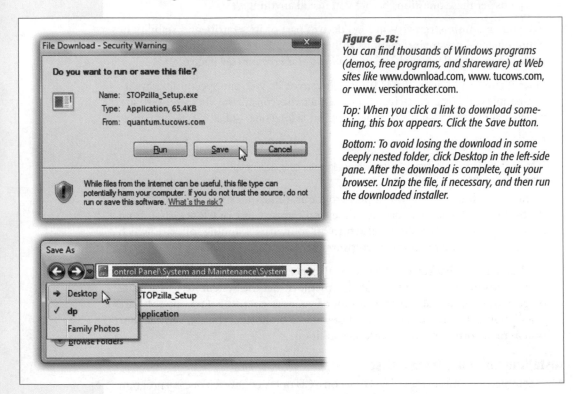

Figure 6-18:
You can find thousands of Windows programs (demos, free programs, and shareware) at Web sites like www.download.com, www. tucows.com, *or* www. versiontracker.com.

Top: When you click a link to download something, this box appears. Click the Save button.

Bottom: To avoid losing the download in some deeply nested folder, click Desktop in the left-side pane. After the download is complete, quit your browser. Unzip the file, if necessary, and then run the downloaded installer.

After unzipping the software (if it doesn't unzip itself), you'll usually find, among the resulting pieces, an installer, just like the ones described in the previous section.

Installing Windows Components

The Windows installer may have dumped over a gigabyte of software onto your hard drive, but it was only warming up. Plenty of second-tier programs and features came on the Vista DVD—stuff that Microsoft didn't want to burden you with right off the bat, but copied to your hard drive just in case.

To see the master list of software components that you have and haven't yet installed, choose Start→Control Panel→Classic View→Programs and Features. Click the "Turn Windows features on or off" link at the left side of the window.

You've just launched the Windows Features Wizard—basically a list of all the optional Windows software chunks. Checkmarks appear next to some of them; these are the ones you already have. The checkboxes that aren't turned on are the options you still haven't installed. As you peruse the list, keep in mind the following:

- To learn what something is, point to it without clicking. A description appears in a tooltip balloon.

- Turn on the checkboxes for software bits you want to install. Clear the checkboxes of elements you already have, but that you'd like Windows to hide.

Note: In Windows Vista, turning off an optional feature *doesn't* remove it from your hard drive, as it did in Windows XP. Turning off a feature simply hides it, and doesn't return any disk space to you. You can make a feature magically reappear just by turning the checkbox back on (without having to hunt down your Vista installation disc).

- Some of these checkboxes' titles are just titles for bigger groups of independent software chunks (see Figure 6-19).

Uninstalling Software
All Versions

When you've had enough of a certain program and want to reclaim the disk space it occupies, don't just delete its folder. The typical application installer tosses its soft-

Figure 6-19:
Most of the optional installations involve networking and administrative tools designed for corporate computer technicians. Still, you might want to turn off Games if you don't have that kind of time to kill, or Tablet PC Optional Components if your computer doesn't have a touch screen.

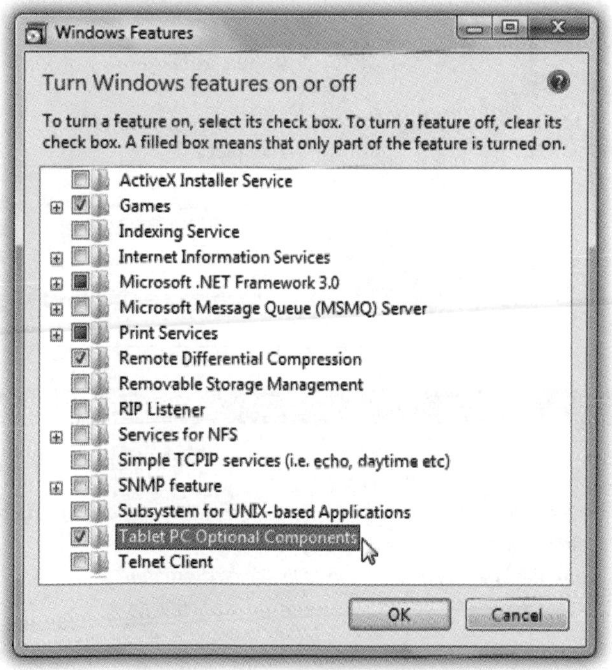

ware components like birdseed all over your hard drive; therefore, only some of the
program is actually in the program's folder.

Instead, ditch software you no longer need using the "Programs and Features" control
panel described above. Click the "Uninstall a program" link at the top left, and then
proceed as shown in Figure 6-20.

Tip: If your computer is a member of a workgroup and you're using Fast User Switching (see page 686), don't
delete a program until you've verified that it isn't running in somebody else's account behind the scenes.

Figure 6-20:
*To vaporize a pro-
gram, click its name
to reveal the toolbar
above it, as shown
here, and then click
the Uninstall button.
Here's a tip—right-
click the column
headings to add or
remove columns. If
you choose More,
you'll see some really
useful ones, like Last
Used On (shows you
the last date you
ran this program)
and Used (how
often you've run
it—Frequently, Rarely,
or whatever).*

FREQUENTLY ASKED QUESTION

This File Is in Use

*Hey, I tried to uninstall a program using Programs and
Features, like you said. But during the process, I got this
scary message saying that one of the deleted program's
files is also needed by other programs. It asked me if I was*
*sure I wanted to delete it! Heck, I wouldn't have the faintest
idea. What should I do?*

Don't delete the file. Leaving it behind does no harm, but
deleting it might render one of your other applications
nonfunctional..

Even after you uninstall a program, the folder that contained it may still exist, especially if it contains configuration files, add-ons, or documents that you created while the program was still alive. If you're sure you won't need those documents, it's safe to remove the folder (discussed later in this section), along with the files inside it.

Note: In Windows XP, the list in this dialog box was cluttered up with dozens upon dozens of "Windows Hotfixes"—the little security patches that Microsoft sends out weekly or monthly via the Internet just to make your life interesting.

In Vista, though, they get a list of their own. Click "View installed updates" (one of the links in the task pane at the left side of Features and Programs). That's useful to remember if you suspect one day that a certain patch has broken something on your PC.

When Uninstalling Goes Wrong

That's the *theory* of uninstalling Windows programs, of course. In practice, you'll probably find that the Programs and Features program should more accurately be called the "Add or I'll-Make-My-Best-Effort-to-Remove-Programs-But-No-

---

GEM IN THE ROUGH

Not Your Father's Keyboard

Keyboards built especially for using Windows contain some extra keys on the bottom row:

On the left, between the Ctrl and Alt keys, you may find a key bearing the Windows logo (⊞). No, this isn't just a tiny Microsoft advertising moment; you can press this key to open the Start menu without having to use the mouse. (On desktop PCs, the Windows key is usually on the bottom row; on laptops, it's sometimes at the top of the keyboard.)

On the right, you may find a duplicate ⊞ key, as well as a key whose icon depicts a tiny menu, complete with a microscopic cursor pointing to a command. Press this key to simulate a right-click at the current location of your cursor.

Even better, the ⊞ key offers a number of useful functions when you press it in conjunction with other keys. For example:

⊞+Space bar opens the Sidebar.

⊞+number key opens the corresponding icon on the Quick Launch toolbar (⊞+1, ⊞+2, etc.).

⊞+D hides or shows all of your application windows (ideal for jumping to the desktop for a bit of housekeeping).

⊞+E opens an Explorer window (Chapter 2).

⊞+F opens the Search window (Chapter 3).

⊞+G cycles through your Sidebar gadgets.

⊞+L locks your screen. Everything you were working on is hidden by the login screen; your password is required to get past it.

⊞+M minimizes all open windows, revealing the desktop. (⊞+D is better, however, since the same keystroke also returns the windows.)

⊞+Shift+M restores all minimized windows.

⊞+R opens the Run command (page 10).

⊞+T cycles through the Taskbar buttons.

⊞+U opens the Ease of Access center (formerly the Universal Access center).

⊞+X opens the new Mobility Center (page 572).

⊞+Tab switches through all the application buttons on the taskbar.

⊞+Break opens the System Properties dialog box.

Guarantees" program. A disappointing percentage of the time, one error message or another pops up, declaring that the installation can't proceed because Windows can't find this or that component.

Most of the time, it's not the fault of Windows. Programs and Features is simply a list of links, like the All Programs section of your Start Menu. When you highlight an entry and click Uninstall, Windows just fires up the program's own uninstaller program. When the uninstaller doesn't work, thanks to some bug or glitch, the fun begins.

The truth is, the world won't end if you just leave the crippled program on board your PC. You can join millions of other PC fans who slog along, hard drives corroded with bits of software they can't seem to remove. Apart from the waste of space and the uneasy feeling that your PC is getting clogged arteries, there's no harm done.

But if you'd rather wipe the slate clean, start by visiting the Web site of the company that made your program. Dig into its support section to see if the company has provided a fix or any removal instructions. (Some companies discover bugs in their uninstaller utilities just like they might in any other part of their programs, and then release patches—or even special removal tools—that let their customers remove their software.)

If that step doesn't lead anywhere, you can get serious by eliminating the stubborn bits by hand. Because the process is manual and technical—and because, heaven willing, you won't need it often—it's been offloaded to a free bonus article called "Removing Stubborn Programs." You can find it on this book's "Missing CD" at *www.missingmanuals.com*.

Running Pre-Vista Programs
All Versions

"You can't make an omelet without breaking a few eggs." If that's not Microsoft's motto, maybe it should be. Each successive version of Windows may be better than the previous one, but inevitably winds up "breaking" hundreds of programs, utilities, and drivers that used to run fine.

To soften the blow, Microsoft has pulled every trick in the book to make older, pre-Vista programs run successfully. For example:

16-Bit Programs
A 16-bit program is one that's so old, it was written when Windows 3.1 roamed the earth and George Bush Sr. was president. (Programs written for Windows 95 and later are known as *32-bit* programs; Vista can even run *64-bit* programs.) But amazingly enough, Windows Vista can run most of these programs. It does so in a kind of software simulator—a DOS-and-Windows 3.1 PC impersonation called a *virtual machine*.

As a result, these programs don't run very fast, they don't understand the long filenames of modern-day Windows, and they may crash whenever they try to "speak" directly to certain components of your hardware. (The simulator stands in their way, in the name of keeping Windows stable.) Furthermore, if just one of your 16-bit programs crashes, *all* of them crash, because they all live in the same memory bubble.

Even so, it's impressive that they run at all, 10 years later.

DOS Programs

These programs are 16-bit programs, too, and therefore they run just fine in Windows, even though DOS no longer lurks beneath the operating system.

To open the black, empty DOS window that's familiar to longtime PC users, choose Start→All Programs→Accessories→Command Prompt. (See page 255.)

Programs Written for Windows 95, 2000, XP, and So On

In principle, programs that were written for recent versions of Windows should run fine in Vista. Unfortunately, some of them contain software code that deliberately sniffs around to find out what Windows version you have. These programs (or even their installer programs) may say, "Windows *what?*"—and refuse to run.

Fortunately, the Properties box of every program (or program shortcut) offers you the opportunity to fool such programs into believing that they're running on a Windows

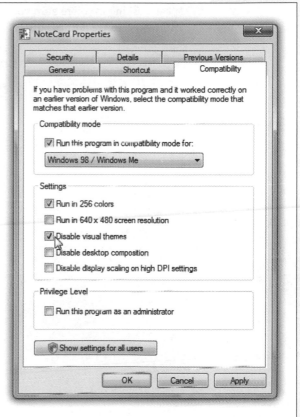

Figure 6-21:
By turning on "Run this program in compatibility mode for" and choosing the name of a previous version of Windows from the drop-down list, you can fool that program into thinking that it's running on Windows 95, Windows Me, Windows NT, or whatever. While you're at it, you can also specify that this program switch your screen to certain settings required by older games—256 colors, 640 x 480 pixel resolution, and so on—or run without the new Windows Vista look (turn on "Disable visual themes").

XP machine, Windows 2000 machine, or whatever. Figure 6-21 details the process, but a few footnotes are in order:

- You're much better off securing an updated version of the program, if it's available. Check the program's Web site to see if a Vista-compatible update is available.

- Don't try this trick with utilities like virus checkers, backup programs, CD burning software, and hard drive utilities. Installing older versions of these with Vista is asking for disaster.

- If the program you're trying to run is on a CD or on a hard drive elsewhere on the network, you won't be able to change its properties using the steps described in Figure 6-21. Instead, choose Start→Control Panel. Click Programs, and then click "Use an older program with this version of Windows." A series of wizard screens explains the concept of compatibility-fooling, and then lets you choose the program you'd like to fool.

- The "Run this program as an Administrator" checkbox (also shown in Figure 6-21) can also be a magical pill that lets an older program run. In effect, though, you're overriding one of Vista's new security features in the process.

   That's why, the next time you open the program, a UAC message (page 191) appears, asking if you're sure you want this program to be allowed to run. Click Allow—if you're *darned* sure.

The Freebie Software

E ven after a fresh installation of Windows Vista, a glance at your Start→All
Programs menu reveals a rich array of preinstalled Windows Vista applications—as an infomercial might put it, they're your *free bonus gifts*. This chapter
offers a crash course in these programs, a few of which could probably merit Missing
Manuals of their own.

For your reference pleasure, they're described here semi-alphabetically—that is, just
as they appear in the All Programs menu (Figure 7-1).

For example, Accessories doesn't appear here first, because it appears way down the
list in your All Programs menu.

Default Programs
All Versions

This item is a link to the Default Programs applet in your Control Panel. It's described
in Chapter 8.

Internet Explorer
All Versions

Yes, it's *that* Internet Explorer—Microsoft's world-famous Web browser. Full details
are in Chapter 11.

Windows Calendar

All Versions

It took until Vista for Microsoft to include a standard calendar program with Windows, but no matter; it's nice to have.

In many ways, Calendar is not so different from those "Hunks of the Midwestern Police Stations" paper calendars people leave hanging on the walls for months past their natural life span. But Calendar offers several advantages over paper calendars. For example:

- It can automate the process of entering repeating events, such as weekly staff meetings or gym workout dates.

- Calendar can give you a gentle nudge (with a dialog box and a sound, if you like) when an important appointment is approaching.

- You can "publish" your calendar on the Internet, so all your family members/classmates/baseball team members/downtrodden employees know the schedule. For example, you can subscribe to your spouse's calendar, thereby finding out when you've been committed to after-dinner drinks on the night the big game's on TV.

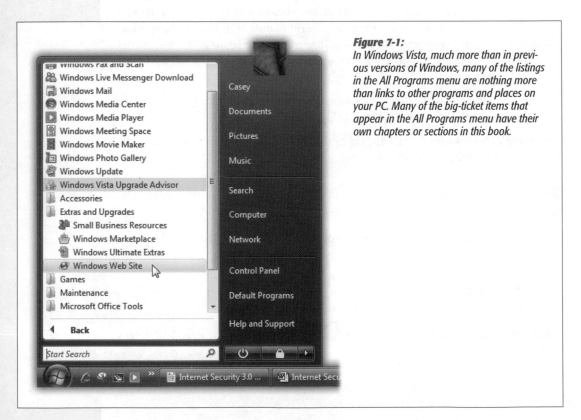

Figure 7-1:
In Windows Vista, much more than in previous versions of Windows, many of the listings in the All Programs menu are nothing more than links to other programs and places on your PC. Many of the big-ticket items that appear in the All Programs menu have their own chapters or sections in this book.

Working with Views

When you open Calendar, you see something like Figure 7-2. By clicking the View button on the toolbar (or using its pop-up menu), you can switch among any of these views:

- **Day** shows the appointments for a single day in the main calendar area, broken down by time slot.

  If you choose File→Options, you can specify what hours constitute a workday. This is ideal both for those annoying power-life people who get up at 4:30 a.m. for 2 hours of calisthenics, as well as for the more reasonable people who sleep until 11 a.m. before rolling out of bed and heading over to the home office in the den.

Tip: Calendar provides a quick way to get to the current day's date: click the Today button on the toolbar.

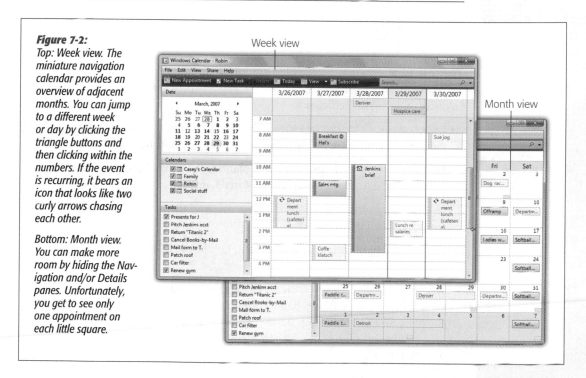

Figure 7-2:
Top: Week view. The miniature navigation calendar provides an overview of adjacent months. You can jump to a different week or day by clicking the triangle buttons and then clicking within the numbers. If the event is recurring, it bears an icon that looks like two curly arrows chasing each other.

Bottom: Month view. You can make more room by hiding the Navigation and/or Details panes. Unfortunately, you get to see only one appointment on each little square.

Week view

Month view

- **Work Week** fills the main display area with five columns, reflecting the current week. (You specify which day begins your work week by choosing File→Options.)

- **Week** fills the main display area with seven columns, reflecting the current week.

- **Month** shows the entire month that contains the current date. Double-click a date number to jump to the day view for that date.

- **Navigation Pane.** See the info panels at the left side of the screen—the mini-calendar, Calendar list, and Tasks list? That's the Navigation pane. You can hide it to save space if necessary.

- **Details Pane** is the rightmost section of the window, where you fill out the details of an appointment (start time, alarm information, and so on).

Tip: Your mouse's scroll wheel can be a great advantage in Calendar. For example, when entering a date, turning the wheel lets you jump forward or backward in time. It also lets you change the priority level of a To Do item you're entering, or even change the time zone as you're setting it.

Making an Appointment

The basic calendar is easy to figure out. After all, with the exception of one unfortunate Gregorian incident, we've been using calendars successfully for centuries.

Even so, there are two ways to record a new appointment: a simple way and a more flexible, elaborate way.

The easy way

You can quickly record an appointment using any of several techniques, listed here in order of decreasing efficiency:

- In Day, Week, or Work Week view, double-click a time slot on the calendar, in any view. A box appears, where you type the name for your new appointment.

- In the Month view, double-click in a blank area of the appropriate date's square, and then type in the newly created colored bar.

- In any view, right-click a date or a time slot, and then choose New Appointment from the shortcut menu.

- Click New Appointment on the toolbar. Or choose File→New Appointment. Or press Ctrl+N.

  A new appointment appears on the currently selected day, regardless of the current view. Unfortunately, it's probably got the time wrong. Change the time by editing the Start time in the Details pane (Figure 7-3), or by dragging the colored "grip strip" at the left edge of the appointment's box. (This grip strip doesn't appear in Month view.)

A new event believes itself to be 1 hour long, but you can adjust its duration by dragging the bottom edge vertically. (Carefully position the cursor until it sprouts double arrows.)

Tip: Newly minted appointments don't *have* to start out being 1 hour long. You can change the factory setting for this duration in the File→Options dialog box.

In many cases, that's all there is to it. You have just specified the day, time, and title of the appointment. You can get on with your life.

The long way

The Details pane shown in Figure 7-3 contains all the information about a certain appointment. Here, you can create far more specific appointments, decked out with far more bells and whistles.

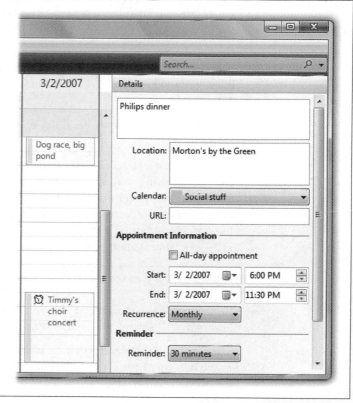

Figure 7-3:
You can open this info pane, if it's not already at the right side of the screen, by choosing View→Details Pane, or by pressing Ctrl+D. Incidentally, you hide the pane the same way.

For each appointment, you can tab your way to the following information areas:

- **Name.** That's the large, unlabeled box at the top—the name of your appointment. For example, you might type *Fly to Phoenix*.

- **Location.** This field makes a lot of sense; if you think about it, almost everyone needs to record *where* a meeting is to take place. You might type a reminder for yourself like *My place*, a specific address like *212 East 23rd,* or some other helpful information like a contact phone number or flight number.

- **Calendar.** A *calendar,* in Calendar's confusing terminology, is a subset—a category—into which you can place various appointments. You can create one for yourself, another for whole-family events, another for book-club appointments, and so on. Later, you'll be able to hide and show these categories at will, adding or removing them from the calendar with a single click. Details begin on page 247.

- **URL.** If there's a Web page that lists details about, for example, some conference you're going to attend, you can type its address here.

- **All-day appointment.** An "all-day" event, of course, is something with no specific time of day associated with it: a holiday, a birthday, a book deadline. When you turn on this box, you'll see the name of the appointment jump to the top of the daily- or weekly-view screen, in the area reserved for this kind of thing (Figure 7-2, top).

- **Start, End.** You can adjust the times shown here by typing, clicking buttons, or both.

For example, start by clicking the hour, and then increase or decrease this number either by pressing your up and down arrow keys, clicking the up or down arrow *buttons,* or by typing a number. Press the right arrow key to highlight the minutes and repeat the up/down business. Finally, press the right arrow again to highlight the AM/PM indicator, and type either *A* or *P*—or press the up or down arrow key—to change it, if necessary.

Tip: If you specify a different ending date, you get a *banner* across the relevant dates in the Month view.

- **Recurrence.** The pop-up menu here contains common options for repeating events: "Every day," "Weekly," and so on. It starts out saying None.

The somewhat goofy part is that if you choose any of those convenient commands in the pop-up menu, Calendar assumes that you want to repeat this event every day/week/month/year *forever.* You don't get any way to specify an end date. You'll be stuck seeing this event repeating on your calendar until the end of time. That may be a good choice for recording your anniversary, especially if your spouse might be consulting the same calendar. But it's not a feature for people who are afraid of long-term commitments.

If you want the freedom to *stop* your weekly gym workouts or monthly car payments, choose Advanced from the pop-up menu instead.

The dialog box that appears offers far more control over how this event repeats itself. You can make the repeating stop after a certain number of times, which is a useful option for car and mortgage payments. And if you choose "Until," you can specify the date that the repetitions come to an end; use this option to indicate the last day of school, for example.

Tip: This dialog box also lets you specify days of the week. For example, you can schedule your morning runs for Monday, Thursday, and Saturday mornings.

- **Reminder.** This pop-up menu tells Calendar that you want to be notified when a certain appointment is about to begin. Use the pop-up menu to specify how much advance notice you want. If it's a TV show you like to watch, you might set up a reminder only five minutes before airtime. If it's a birthday, you might set up a two-day warning to give yourself enough time to buy a present, and so on.

  To get your attention, Calendar generally displays a message on the screen; if you choose File→Options and turn on "Play sound for reminders," you'll get a little audio cue, too.

- **Attendees.** If the appointment is a meeting or some other gathering, you can type the participants' names here. If a name is already in your Windows address book (page 250), you can save time by clicking the Attendees button and double-clicking your guests' names.

  Once you've specified some attendees, an Invite button appears next to the list of names. If you click it, Calendar fires up Windows Mail and prepares ready-to-send messages, each with an .ics attachment: a standard calendar-program invitation file.

  Your guest will get a special email message containing the details of the appointment. If that person has a calendar program that accepts .ics files (like iCal on the Mac or the Google calendar that's affiliated with Gmail), the lucky duck can add it directly to his calendar, right from the email program, or even send an accept/decline response to you.

- **Notes.** Here's your chance to customize your calendar event. You can type, paste, or drag any text that you like in the notes area—driving directions, contact phone numbers, a call history, or whatever.

Your newly scheduled event now shows up on the calendar, complete with the color coding that corresponds to the calendar category you've assigned.

What to Do with an Appointment

Once you've entrusted your agenda to Calendar, you can start putting it to work. Calendar is only too pleased to remind you (via pop-up messages) of your events, reschedule them, print them out, and so on. Here are a few of the possibilities.

Editing events

To edit a calendar event's name or details, double-click it.

Tip: If you simply want to change an appointment from a fixed-duration appointment (running 1 to 2 p.m., for example) to an all-day event, you can bypass the Details pane. Instead, just right-click the appointment's name (or anywhere on its block); from the shortcut menu, choose Make All-day Appointment.

You don't have to bother with this if all you want to do is *reschedule* an event, however, as described next.

Rescheduling events

If an event in your life gets rescheduled, you can move an appointment just by dragging the rectangle that represents it. Drag the event vertically in its column to change its time on the same day, or horizontally to another date in week or month view.

Note: You can't reschedule the *first* occurrence of a recurring event by dragging it—you have to edit the date in the Details pane. You can drag subsequent occurrences, though.

If something is postponed for, say, a month or two, you're in trouble; you can't drag an appointment beyond its month window. You have no choice but to open the Details pane and edit the starting and ending dates or times—or just cut and paste the event to a different date.

Lengthening or shortening events

If a scheduled meeting becomes shorter or your lunch hour becomes a lunch hour-and-a-half (in your dreams), changing the length of the representative calendar event is as easy as dragging the top or bottom border of its block in any column view (see Figure 7-4).

Tip: In Week view, if you've grabbed the top or bottom edge of an appointment's block so the cursor changes, you can drag *horizontally* to make an appointment cross the midnight line and extend into a second day.

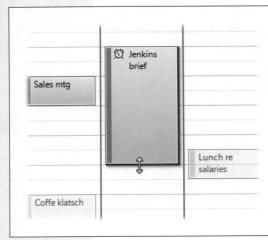

Figure 7-4:
You can resize any calendar event just by dragging its border. As your cursor touches the bottom edge of a calendar event, it turns into a double-headed arrow. You can now drag the event's edge to make it take up more or less time on your calendar.

Printing events

To commit your calendar to paper, choose File→Print, or press Ctrl+P. The resulting Print dialog box lets you specify a range of dates and which view you want (Week, Month, or whatever).

Deleting events

To delete an appointment, just select its box and then press the Delete key. If you delete a recurring event (like a weekly meeting), Calendar asks whether you want to delete only that particular instance of the event or the entire series.

Searching for Events

You should recognize the Search box at the top right of the Calendar screen: it's almost identical to the Start menu's Search box. This one is designed to let you hide all appointments except those matching what you type into it. Figure 7-5 has the details.

The "Calendar" Category Concept

Everyone in your house (or office) can have his own set of appointments on the same calendar, color-coded so he can tell his schedule apart from everyone else's. The red appointments might be yours; the blue ones, your spouse's; the green ones might be your kid's. You can overlay all of them simultaneously to look for conflicts (or mutually available meeting times), if you like.

Each such set of appointments is called, confusingly enough, a *calendar*.

Even if you're not sharing Calendar with a whole family, you still might be able to use these color-coded subsets. You might create calendars (appointment categories) called Home, Work, and TV Reminders. A small business could have categories called Deductible Travel, R&D, and R&R.

To create a calendar, choose File→New Calendar. Type a name that defines the category in your mind.

Tip: Whenever you're about to create an appointment, click a calendar name *first*. That way, the appointment will already belong to the correct calendar.

Hiding Calendars En Masse

Those little calendar categories sure are handy. You can have one color-coded category for each member of your family. Then, when you want to see just the kids' schedules, you can turn off the checkboxes for you and your spouse's calendars.

It would be nicer, though, if you could do all of that with a single click—that is, if you could make *all* your kids' calendars appear at once, and make *all* parental appointments vanish.

That's the point of calendar *groups*—containers that consolidate the appointments from several *other* calendars. Having super-calendars like this make it easier to manage, hide, show, print, and search subsets of your appointments.

To create a calendar group, choose File→New Group. Name the resulting item in the Calendar list; for the most part, it behaves like any other calendar. Drag other calendar names onto it to include them. Click the flippy triangle to hide or show the component calendars.

To change the color-coding of your category, click its name, and then, in the Details pane, use the Color pop-up menu.

You assign an appointment to one of these categories using the pop-up menu on its Details pane. After that, you can hide or show an entire category of appointments at once just by turning on or off the appropriate checkbox in the Calendars list.

Figure 7-5:
As you type into the search box, Calendar opens a Search Results window that lists events with matching text. Double-click anything in this listing to highlight the corresponding rectangle on your calendar (and open its Details pane). Click the little X box (upper-right) to close the search-results box.

"Publishing" Calendars to the Web

One of Calendar's best features is its ability to post your calendar on the Web, so that other people—or you, using a different computer—can subscribe to it, which adds *your* appointments to *their* calendars. For example, you might use this feature to post the meeting schedule for a club that you manage, or to share the agenda for a series of upcoming financial meetings that all of your co-workers will need to consult.

As it turns out, the Web is full of such schedules, ready for adding to your *own* calendar. That's because Windows Calendar is nice enough to understand the common .iCalendar format that sports teams, schools, and other institutions use to post their calendars on the Web.

Publishing

Begin by clicking the calendar category you want in the left-side list. (To publish more than one calendar, create a calendar group.)

Then choose Share→Publish; the dialog box shown at top in Figure 7-6 appears. Here you customize how your saved calendar is going to look and work. You can even turn on "Automatically publish changes made to this calendar," so whenever you edit the calendar, Calendar connects to the Internet and updates the calendar automatically.

When you click Publish, your PC connects to the Web and then shows you the Web address (URL) of the finished page (Figure 7-6).

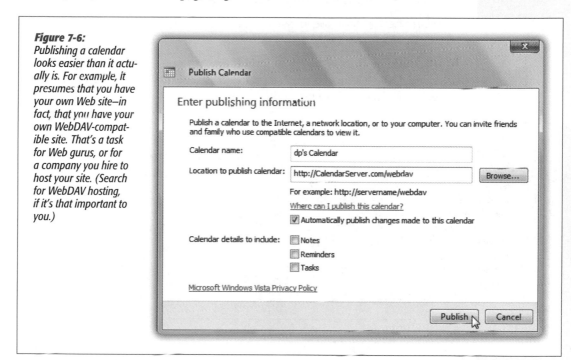

Figure 7-6:
Publishing a calendar looks easier than it actually is. For example, it presumes that you have your own Web site—in fact, that you have your own WebDAV-compatible site. That's a task for Web gurus, or for a company you hire to host your site. (Search for WebDAV hosting, if it's that important to you.)

Subscribing

If somebody else has published a calendar, you subscribe to it by clicking the Subscribe button in the toolbar. In the Subscribe to a Calendar dialog box, type in the Internet address you received from the person who published the calendar.

You can also specify how often you want your own copy to be updated (assuming you have a full-time Internet connection), and whether or not you want to be bothered with the publisher's alarms and notes.

When it's all over, you see a new "calendar" category in your left-side list, representing the published appointments.

Tip: Want to try it out right now? Visit *www.icalshare.com,* a worldwide clearinghouse for sets of Calendar appointments. You can browse calendars for shuttle launches, Mac trade shows, National Hockey League teams, NASCAR races, soccer matches, the *Iron Chef* and *Survivor* TV shows, holidays, and much more.

When you find one you like, click the Download Calendar link that appears just beneath it. When your browser asks if you want to open the file or save it, click Open. Calendar's Import dialog box appears, so that you can specify which calendar (category) should receive it. Finally, click Import.

You'll never suffer from empty-calendar syndrome again.

To Do Lists

Calendar's Tasks feature lets you make a To Do list and shepherds you along by giving you gentle reminders, if you so desire (Figure 7-7).

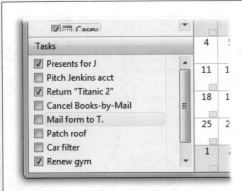

Figure 7-7:
The Tasks list hangs out at the bottom of the Navigation pane.
(Choose View→Navigation Pane if you don't see it.)

Add a new task by clicking New Task in the toolbar. (If nothing happens, it's because you don't have a calendar category selected in the Calendars list.)

Type a name for the to-do item and then press Enter. In the Details pane, you can also specify the task's priority, alarm, and so on. To change a task's priority, use the Priority pop-up menu. Use the checkbox to indicate that you've completed a task; delete a selected task altogether by pressing the Delete key.

Windows Contacts

All Versions

Windows Contacts (Start→All Programs→Windows Contacts) is a new feature in Windows Vista: a central directory for phone numbers, email addresses, and mailing addresses. It's not so much a *program* as a specialized Explorer window, complete with individual icons that represent the people in your social circle.

When you open it (Figure 7-8), click New Contact on the toolbar. You're shown a dialog box with tabbed panels for various categories of contact information. Fill in the name, email address, phone number, and other information for this person.

After you've gone to the trouble of typing in all of this information, Windows Vista repays your efforts in three places, for starters:

- **In Windows Mail.** As Chapter 12 makes clear, a well-informed address book is extremely useful when sending an email message. There's no need to remember that Harold Higgenbottom's email address is *hhiggenbottom@crawl-space.ix.net.de*; instead, you only need to type *hhig*. The program fills in the email address for you automatically.

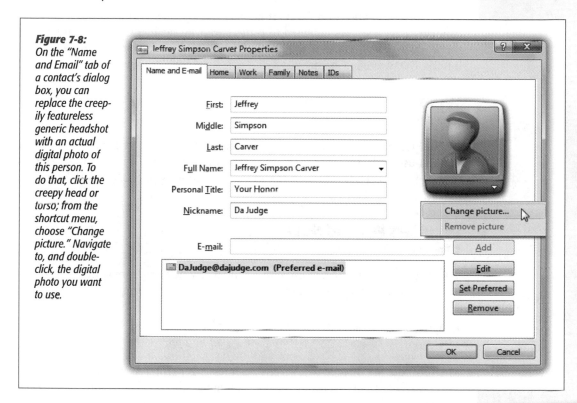

Figure 7-8:
On the "Name and Email" tab of a contact's dialog box, you can replace the creepily featureless generic headshot with an actual digital photo of this person. To do that, click the creepy head or torso; from the shortcut menu, choose "Change picture." Navigate to, and double-click, the digital photo you want to use.

- **In the Search dialog box.** As noted in Chapter 3, you can quickly look up somebody's number using the Start menu's new Search box.

- **In the shortcut menu.** If you right-click someone's name in your Contacts window, the Action submenu (in the shortcut menu) offers two useful options. One is Send Email, which opens up an outgoing, preaddressed message to this person. The other is Call This Contact. If your PC is hooked up to a phone line (and so is your phone), Windows can dial the number for you.

Microsoft's hope is that other software companies will take advantage of Contacts' open design (it's written in XML, a common Web language) so that they, too, can exploit your address book.

Tip: To import address book information from another program, click Import on the toolbar. Windows can inhale the information from any of several popular address-book formats, including CSV, LDFI, vCard, and Windows Address Book (that is, Outlook Express).

Windows Defender
All Versions

This program is Microsoft's way of acknowledging that Windows has a spyware problem (page 341). It's designed to protect your PC against spyware—and, if you think you're *already* infected, to scan the hard drive for infections and remove what it finds. Details are in Chapter 20.

Windows DVD Maker
Home Premium • Ultimate

If your PC has a DVD burner (and the Premium or Ultimate versions of Vista), then you can use DVD Maker to turn your camcorder (or digital-camera) masterpieces into standard DVDs that play on the TVs of your adoring public. Chapter 15 has the details.

Windows Fax and Scan
Business • Enterprise • Ultimate

See Chapter 17 for full details on sending and receiving faxes from your PC—and on scanning documents using a scanner.

Windows Live Messenger Download
All Versions

Microsoft doesn't include its own instant-messenger (Internet chat) program with Windows Vista anymore; it's already had enough dealings with government antitrust lawyers to last it a lifetime.

Still, Microsoft certainly makes Windows Live Messenger (formerly Windows Messenger) easy enough to get. Choose this command to open the Microsoft Web page from which you can download the program.

Windows Mail
All Versions

Windows Mail is the new name for a *very* old standby: Outlook Express. Chapter 12 has the full story.

Windows Media Center
Home Premium • Ultimate

The software that once required a special-edition PC is now available to anyone with the Home Premium or Ultimate editions of Windows Vista. See Chapter 16 for more.

Windows Media Player
All Versions

This massive music and video player is described in Chapter 14.

Windows Meeting Space
Home Premium • Business • Enterprise • Ultimate

Chapter 25 describes this program, which lets you collaborate across a network by seeing what's on each other's screens.

Windows Movie Maker
Home Premium • Ultimate

As a courtesy, Microsoft has thrown in this basic video-editing program, suitable for chopping the dull parts out of your camcorder footage. Chapter 15 has the scoop.

Windows Photo Gallery
All Versions

See Chapter 13 for details on the new Vista digital photography headquarters.

Windows Update
All Versions

This program is Microsoft's system for patching your copy of Windows via the Internet. Full coverage appears in Chapter 20.

Accessories
All Versions

The programs in this suite have two things in common. First, they're all smallish, single-purpose programs (or just links to them) that you'll probably use only occasionally. Second, you get to them from the Start→All Programs→Accessories menu.

Calculator
At first glance, this calculator looks like nothing more than a thinner version of every pocket calculator you've ever seen (Figure 7-9). You can operate it either by clicking the buttons with your mouse or by pressing the corresponding keys on your keyboard.

Tip: Choosing View→Digit Grouping instructs the Calculator to display numbers with commas (123,456,789), making large numbers (123456789) a lot easier to read.

Most of the buttons look just like the ones on the plastic calculator that's probably in your desk drawer at this very moment, but several require special explanation:

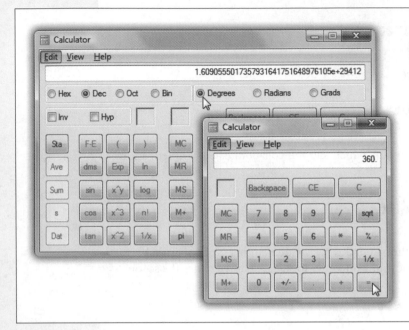

Figure 7-9:
After ducking into a phone booth, the humble Calculator (lower right) emerges as Scientific Calculator (upper left), which contains a hexadecimal/decimal/octal/binary converter for programmers, mathematical functions for scientists, and enough other buttons to impress almost anyone.

- **/.** The slash means "divided by" in computerese.

- ***.** The asterisk is the multiplication symbol.

- **sqrt.** Click this button to find the square root of the currently displayed number.

- **%.** Type in one number, click the * button, type a second number, and then click this button to calculate what percentage the first number is of the second.

FREQUENTLY ASKED QUESTION

Clipboard Viewer

Hey, what happened to the Clipboard Viewer? It used to be in the System Tools group of my Start→Programs→Accessories menu, and now it's gone.

Yes, Clipboard Viewer was a cool little program for seeing the material you'd most recently copied.

It's gone. You can't even use the Run command to issue the *Clipbrd.exe* command any more.

Fortunately, the shareware world is ready to step into the breach. Take a look, for example, at AccelClip (available, among other places, from this book's "Missing CD" page at *www.missingmanuals.com*).

- **1/x.** Here's a Ratio button. It makes the currently displayed number appear as the denominator of a fraction. That is, it turns "4" into ¼, which it expresses as 0.25.

Tip: This calculator may appear to have almost every feature you could desire, but, in fact, it lacks a paper-tape feature—and we all know how easy it is to get lost in the middle of long calculations.

The solution is simple: Type your calculation, such as *34+(56/3)+5676+(34*2)=*, in a word processor. Highlight the calculation you've typed, choose Edit→Copy, switch to the Calculator, and then choose Edit→Paste. The previously typed numbers fly into the Calculator in sequence, finally producing the grand total on its screen. (You can then use the Edit→Copy command to copy the result back out of the Calculator, ready for pasting into another program.)

But by choosing View→Scientific, you turn this humble five-function calculator into a full-fledged scientific number-cruncher, as shown in Figure 7-9.

Command Prompt

The Command Prompt opens a *command line interface:* a black, empty screen with the time-honored *C:>* prompt where you can type out instructions to the computer. This is a world without icons, menus, or dialog boxes; even the mouse is almost useless.

Surely you can appreciate the irony. The whole breakthrough of Windows was that it *eliminated* the DOS command-line interface that was still the ruling party on the computers of the day. Most non-geeks sighed with relief, delighted that they'd never have to memorize commands again. Yet here's Windows Vista, Microsoft's supposedly ultramodern operating system, complete with a command line! What's going on?

Actually, the command line never went away. At universities and corporations worldwide, professional computer nerds kept right on pounding away at the little *C:* prompts, appreciating the efficiency and power such direct computer control afforded them.

You never *have* to use the command line. In fact, Microsoft has swept it far under the rug, obviously expecting that most people will use the beautiful icons and menus of the regular desktop.

Tip: You can also open the command prompt directly from the Start menu. Just type *command* into the Search box and then press Enter.

If you have a little time and curiosity, however, the command prompt opens up a world of possibilities. It lets you access corners of Windows that you can't get to from the regular desktop. (Commands for exploring network diagnostics are especially plentiful—*ping, netstat,* and so on.) It lets you perform certain tasks with much greater speed and efficiency than you'd get by clicking buttons and dragging icons. And it gives you a fascinating glimpse into the minds and moods of people who live and breathe computers.

Here are a few examples:

Command	Purpose	Example
control	Opens a Control Panel applet	*control date/time*
ping	Checks to see if a server is responding	*ping nytimes.com*
ipconfig	Reveals your PC's IP address and other network info	*ipconfig*
mkdir	Make directory (that is, create a folder)	*mkdir \Reports*
copy	Copy files from one folder to another	*copy c:\Reports*.* \Backup*

You can also type the true, secret name of any program to open it, quickly and efficiently, without having to mouse around through the Start menu. For example, you can type *winword* to open Word, or *charmap* to open the Character Map.

To learn a few of the hundreds of DOS commands at your disposal, consult the Internet, which is filled with excellent lists and explanations. To find them, visit a search page like *www.google.com* and search for *DOS command reference*. You'll find numerous ready-to-study Web sites that tell you what to type at the MS-DOS prompt. (A book like *Windows Vista in a Nutshell* is also a good source.)

Tip: You can open a Command Prompt for any folder just by Shift+right-clicking a folder. From the shortcut menu, choose Open Command Window Here.

Connect to a Network Projector

Talk about a program you won't use every day!

This little wizard is designed to detect, and connect your PC to, a *network projector*—a video projector that can project the image from any computer on the network. You, the pitchmaster, can stand in the conference room on the eighth floor (where the projector is), showing your awestruck co-workers a PowerPoint presentation that's actually sitting on your PC in Accounting down on the fourth.

Note: This feature isn't available in the Home Basic or Home Premium versions of Vista.

If such a projector is already set up and turned on, you should be able to find it and connect to it by clicking "Search for a projector." You're asked for a password, if necessary, and whether you want to *mirror* (display the same thing as) or *extend* the screen (act as additional area) of your fourth-floor PC.

If the projector is not on the same *subnet* (chunk of the network), however, the Vista wizard won't see it. In that case, you'll have to click "Enter the projector address" instead. Tap in the projector's network address (supplied by your friendly network administrator, of course).

Note: Don't use videos in your network-projected pitches. They'll show up choppy when transmitted over the network.

Notepad

Notepad is a bargain-basement *text editor,* which means it lets you open, create, and edit files that contain plain, unformatted text, like the Read.txt files that often accompany new programs. You can also use Notepad to write short notes or edit text that you intend to paste into your email program after editing it.

Notepad basics

Notepad opens automatically when you double-click text files (those with the file extension .txt). You can also open Notepad by choosing Start→All Programs→ Accessories→Notepad—or, more efficiently, by typing *notep* into the Start menu's Search box.

You'll quickly discover that Notepad is the world's most frill-free application. Its list of limitations is almost longer than its list of features.

For example, Notepad can't open large files. If you double-click a text file icon that contains more than about 50 KB of text, Windows Vista automatically opens the file in WordPad (described next) instead of Notepad. Furthermore, the Notepad window has no toolbar, and can work only with one file at a time.

Above all, Notepad is a *text* processor, not a *word* processor. That means that you can't use any formatting at all—no bold, italic, centered text, and so on. That's not necessarily bad news, however. The beauty of text files is that any word processor on any kind of computer—Windows, Mac, Unix, whatever—can open plain text files like the ones Notepad creates.

GEM IN THE ROUGH

Notepad Log Files

As stripped-down as it is, Notepad has one surprising feature not available in any other text processor or word processor: automated log files. Every time you open a certain file, Notepad can automatically insert the current date and time at the bottom of the file, creating a tidy record of when you last worked on it—a nifty way to keep any type of a log, like a record of expenditures or a secret diary.

To set this up, create a new Notepad document (choose File→New). Then type the phrase *.LOG* at the top of the new document. (Capitalize LOG, and put nothing, not even

a space, before the period.)

Now save the document (File→Save) wherever you like, and give it a name. (Notepad adds the extension .txt automatically.)

When you next open the file, Notepad types out the date and time automatically, and puts your cursor on the next line. Now you're ready to type the day's entry.

To make your log file easier to read, press the Enter key to insert a blank line after each entry before saving the file.

About Word Wrap

In the old days, Notepad didn't automatically wrap lines of text to make everything fit in its window. As a result, chunks of text often went on forever in a single line of text or got chopped off by the right side of the window, which could produce disastrous results when you were trying to follow, say, a soufflé recipe.

In Windows Vista, lines of text wrap automatically, exactly as they do in a word processor. But you're still seeing nothing more than the effects of the Format→Word Wrap command—an option you can turn off, if you like, by choosing the command again. (You can tell when Word Wrap is on by the presence of a checkmark next to the command in the Format menu.)

Paint

You can use Paint to "paint" simple artwork or to edit graphics files from other sources. You might say that Paint is something like Adobe Photoshop (well, in the same way that you'd say that the local Cub Scout newsletter is like the *New York Times*). Common tasks for this program include making quick sketches, fixing dust specks on scanned photos, and entertaining kids for hours on end.

When you first open Paint, you get a small, empty painting window. Go like this:

1. **Choose Image→Attributes to specify the dimensions of the graphic you want to create. Click OK.**

   Later in your life, you may want to peruse the other commands in this menu, which let you stretch or flip your graphic.

2. **Click a tool on the palette at the left side.**

   If you need help identifying one of these tools, point to it without clicking. A tooltip identifies the icon by name, and a help message appears at the bottom of the window.

3. **If you've selected a painting tool, like the paintbrush, pencil, or line tool, click a "paint" color from the palette at the bottom of the window.**

   You may also want to change the "brush" by choosing from the options located below the tool palette, like the three spray-paint splatter sizes shown in Figure 7-10.

4. **If you've selected one of the enclosed-shape tools at the bottom of palette, right-click a swatch to specify the color you want to fill the inside of that shape.**

   These tools all produce enclosed shapes, like squares and circles. You can specify a different color for the border of these shapes and for the fill color inside.

5. **Finally, drag your cursor in the image area (see Figure 7-10).**

   As you work, don't forget that you can use the Edit→Undo command up to three times in a row, "taking back" the last three painting maneuvers you made. (Just don't screw up *four* times in a row.)

For fine detail work, click the magnifying glass icon, and then click your painting. You've just enlarged it so every dot becomes easily visible.

Paint can open and create several different file formats, including BPP, JPEG, and GIF—every file format you need to save graphics for use on a Web site.

Tip: Paint also offers a nifty way to create wallpaper (see page 163). After you create or edit a graphic, choose File→Set as Background (Tiled) or File→Set as Background (Centered) to transfer your masterpiece to your desktop immediately.

Figure 7-10:
The Paint tools include shapes, pens for special uses (straight lines and curves), and coloring tools (including an airbrush). The top two tools don't draw anything. Instead, they select portions of the image for cutting, copying, or dragging to a new location.

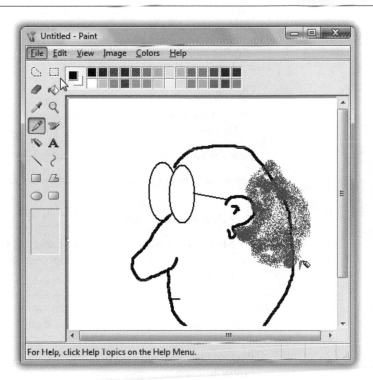

Remote Desktop Connection

Remote Desktop Connection, which comes built into certain Vista versions (Business, Enterprise, and Ultimate), lets you sit at your home PC and operate your office PC by remote control. Details are in Chapter 5.

Run

When you want to open something with just a few keystrokes, the little Run command-line window is there for you. See page 40 for details.

Snipping Tool

Snipping Tool takes pictures of your PC's screen, for use when you're writing up instructions, illustrating a computer book, or collecting proof of some secret screen you found buried in a game. You can take pictures of the entire screen or capture only the contents of a rectangular selection. When you're finished, Snipping Tool displays your snapshot in a new window, which you can print, close without saving, edit, or save (as a JPEG, GIF, PNG, or embedded HTML file), ready for emailing or inserting into a manuscript or page-layout program.

Now, as experienced PC enthusiasts already know, Windows has *always* had shortcuts for capturing screenshots: press PrntScrn to print a picture of the whole screen; add the Alt key to copy it to your Clipboard.

So why use Snipping Tool instead? Because it's infinitely more powerful and flexible. Here's how it works:

1. **Open Snipping Tool.**

   The first time you open it, Vista offers you the chance to add its micro-icon to your Quick Launch toolbar (page 101), so you can get to it faster the next time.

   Now the Snipping palette appears on your screen.

2. **From the New shortcut menu, specify what area of the screen you want to capture.**

   Your choices are:

   Free-form Snip, which means you can drag your cursor in any crazy, jagged, freehand, nonrectangular shape. Snipping Tool conveniently outlines it with a red border.

Tip: You can change the border color in the Options dialog box. It appears when you click Options on the main Snipping palette, or when you choose Tools→Options in the editing window.

   Rectangular Snip lets you drag diagonally across the frozen screen image, thus capturing a square or rectangular area. Unfortunately, you can't adjust the rectangle if your aim was a little off; the instant you release the mouse button, the program captures the image in the rectangle.

   A **Window Snip** neatly captures an entire window, automatically cropping out the entire background. And *which* window does it capture? That's up to you. As you point to each window, a red border appears around it to illustrate what Snipping Tool *thinks* you intend to capture. When the correct one is highlighted, click the mouse to capture.

Tip: A "window," in this context, doesn't have to be a window. It can also be the taskbar, a Sidebar gadget, the Start menu logo, a dialog box, and so on.

And a **Full-screen Snip,** of course, captures the entire screen.

3. **Specify what you want to capture, if necessary.**

   That is, drag across the screen for a Free-form or Rectangular snip, or click the window (object) you want for a Window Snip. (Skip this step if you chose Full-screen Snip. In that case, Snipping Tool pretty much knows what to do.) Now the editing window appears (Figure 7-11).

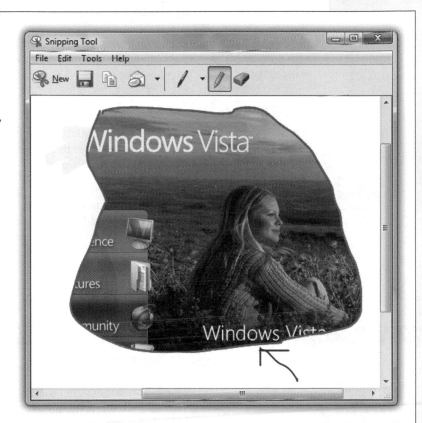

Figure 7-11:
After you capture a snip, the editing window appears, with your screen grab right in the middle of it. The Pen, Highlighter, and Eraser tools are there to help you annotate, draw attention to, or erase parts of your illustration. (The Eraser works only on pen and highlighter strokes— not the snip itself.)

What you do with your finished graphic is up to you. For example:

- **Paste it.** The edited image may be in the window in front of you, but the original, unedited image is *also* on your invisible Windows Clipboard. Close the editing window without saving changes, pop into your graphics, word processing, or email program, and paste (Ctrl+V) what you've copied. Often, that's exactly what you'll want to do.

Tip: On the other hand, the Snipping Tool's tendency to copy everything to the Clipboard can be *bad* if there was already something *on* the Clipboard that you wanted to keep. (The Clipboard can hold only one thing at a time.) If that syndrome is driving you nuts, you can turn off the copy-to-Clipboard feature in Options.

- **Send it.** The little envelope button on the editing-window toolbar automatically prepares an outgoing email message with your graphic already pasted in (or, if your email program is set to send plain, unformatted text messages only, as an attachment).

- **Save it.** If your intention is to save the capture as a file, click the Save (floppy-disk) icon, or choose File→Save, or press Ctrl+S. When the Save As dialog box appears, type a name for your graphic, choose a file format for it (from the "Save as type" pop-up menu), specify a folder location, and then click Save.

Tip: If you capture the screen of a Web page and save it in HTML format, Snipping Tool helpfully prints the original URL (Web address) at the bottom of the image, so you'll know where it came from. You can turn off this "subtitling" feature in the Options dialog box of Snipping Tool.

Sound Recorder

Windows comes with a generous assortment of sound files that you can use as error beeps, as described in Chapter 8. But no error beep is as delightful as one that you've made yourself—of your 2-year-old saying, "Nope!" for example, or your own voice saying, "Dang it!"

Using Sound Recorder (Figure 7-12) requires a sound card, speakers, and a microphone. If your PC is appropriately equipped, you can use this little program to record various snippets of your life, which can serve a number of purposes, including error beeps.

Recording a new sound

Here's how to do it:

POWER USERS' CLINIC

May I Please See a Menu?

Snipping Tool, as you've already seen, is a heck of a lot better than the old PrntScrn keystroke. But at first glance, you might assume that it still can't take a picture of a menu or a shortcut menu. After all, the instant you try to drag to highlight the menu, the menu closes!

Actually, you can capture menus—if you know the secret.

Open Snipping Tool, and then *minimize* it, which hides its window but keeps it running.

Now open the menu you want to capture, using the mouse or keyboard. Once the menu is open, press this all-new Vista keystroke: Ctrl+Print Screen (that is, the PrntScrn key). That's

all it takes; Snipping Tool is smart enough to know that you intend to capture just the menu.

That's workable, but still a bit complicated. That's why, if you're *actually* going to write a computer book or manual, you'll probably want a proper screen-capture program like SnagIt (*www.techsmith.com*). It offers far more flexibility than any of Vista's own screenshot features. For example, you have a greater choice of file formats and capture options, you can dress up the results with arrows or captions, and (with its companion program, Camtasia) you can even capture *movies* of screen activity.

---

1. Choose Start→All Programs→Accessories→Sound Recorder.

   The window shown in Figure 7-12 appears.

2. Click Start Recording. Make the sound, and then click Stop Recording as soon as possible thereafter.

   If you see the green animated bar dance in the Sound Recorder window, great; that's your VU (sound level) meter. It tells you that the PC is hearing you. If you don't see this graphic, however, then the sound isn't getting through. Most likely, the problem is that your PC control panel isn't set to record the appropriate sound source. Visit the Control Panel and open the Sound panel to investigate.

   As soon as you click Stop Recording, the Save As box appears.

Figure 7-12:
Sound Recorder has been lobotomized since the Windows XP version, but it does the job.

UP TO SPEED

Text-Selection Fundamentals

Before doing almost anything to text in a word processor, like making it bold, changing its typeface, or moving it to a new spot in your document, you have to *highlight* the text you want to affect. For millions of people, this entails dragging the cursor extremely carefully, perfectly horizontally, across the desired text. And if they want to capture an entire paragraph or section, they click at the beginning, drag diagonally, and release the mouse button when they reach the end of the passage.

That's all an enormous waste of time. Selecting text is the cornerstone of every editing operation in a word processor, so there are faster and more precise ways of going about it.

For example, double-clicking a word highlights it, instantly and neatly. In fact, by keeping the mouse button pressed on the second click, you can now drag horizontally to highlight text in crisp one-word chunks—a great way to highlight text faster and more precisely. These tricks work anywhere you can type.

In most programs, including Microsoft's, additional shortcuts await. For example, *triple*-clicking anywhere within a paragraph highlights the entire paragraph. (Once again, if you *keep* the button pressed at the end of this maneuver, you can then drag to highlight your document in one-paragraph increments.)

In many programs, including Word and WordPad, you can highlight exactly one sentence by clicking within it while pressing Ctrl.

Finally, here's a universal trick that lets you highlight a large blob of text, even one that's too big to fit on the current screen. Start by clicking to position the insertion point cursor at the very beginning of the text you want to capture. Now scroll, if necessary, so the ending point of the passage is visible. Shift-click there. Windows instantly highlights everything that was in between your click and your Shift-click.

---

3. **Type a name for your sound file in the "File name" text box, choose a folder for it, and then click the Save button.**

   You've just created a .wma file, a standard kind of Windows sound file.

What to do with sounds

When you double-click a .wma file, the file opens in Windows Media Player and plays back immediately. (Press Esc to halt playback.) Sound files are ideal for emailing to other people, posting on Web sites, transferring over the network, and so on. Many a Bart Simpson sound clip proliferates via the Internet in exactly this way.

Sync Center

You're supposed to use this program in conjunction with Windows Mobile cellphones and palmtops. It's also the terminal for the Vista's offline files feature. (This feature is great for laptop owners who want to take work home from the office network, or network domain members who want to keep working on documents even if the server that houses them goes down.) See page 587 for Sync Center details.

Windows Explorer

See page 60 for details on this navigational tool.

Windows Mobility Center

The Mobility Center gives you a single, centralized dashboard for managing laptop features. Here, in one window, you can turn wireless networking on and off, change display settings to suit the environment, change the display orientation, and even sync your palmtop or phone with your PC. Page 572 has the full rundown.

Windows Sidebar

Chapter 6 describes this handy, gadget-filled strip of your screen.

WordPad

WordPad is a very basic word processor (see Figure 7-13). Tragically, the Vista version can no longer create or open Microsoft Word files; Microsoft executives must have thought that WordPad was letting people get away without buying Microsoft Office.

(Little did they know that you can just use Google's online word processor at *http://docs.google.com,* which *can* open and create Word files.)

WordPad is now limited to opening and creating plain text files, Rich Text Format (RTF) documents, and Microsoft Write documents.

Using WordPad

When WordPad first opens, you see an empty sheet of electronic typing paper. Just above the ruler, you'll find drop-down menus and buttons that affect the formatting of your text, as shown in Figure 7-14. As in any word processor, you can apply these formats (like bold, italic, or color) to two kinds of text:

- Text you've highlighted by dragging the mouse across it.

- Text you're *about* to type. In other words, if you click the I button, the next characters you type will be italicized. Click the I button a second time to turn off the italics.

Figure 7-13:
WordPad has menu bars, toolbars, rulers, and plenty of other familiar Windows features. Unlike Notepad, WordPad lets you use bold and italic formatting to enhance the appearance of your text. You can even insert graphics, sounds, and movies. (WordPad can open only one file at a time, however.)

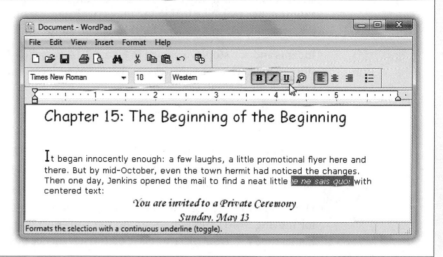

Figure 7-14:
The rightmost buttons make paragraphs flush left, centered, flush right, or bulleted as a list. You can drag through several paragraphs before clicking these buttons, or you can click these buttons to affect just the paragraph where your insertion point already is. The dotted lines in this illustration indicate how each press of the Tab key lines up the text with one of the tab stops you click onto the ruler.

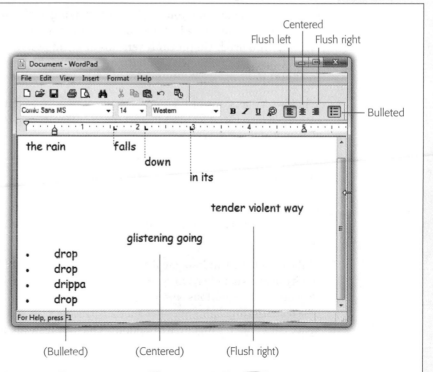

The rightmost formatting buttons affect entire paragraphs, as shown in Figure 7-14.

WordPad doesn't offer big-gun features like spell checking, style sheets, or tables. But it does offer a surprisingly long list of core word processing features. For example:

- **Edit→Find, Edit→Replace.** Using the Find command, you can locate a particular word or phrase instantly, even in a long document. The Replace command takes it a step further, replacing that found phrase with another one (a great way to change the name of your main character throughout an entire novel, for example).

- **Indents and Tab stops.** As shown in Figure 7-14, you click on the ruler to place tab stops there. Each time you press the Tab key, your insertion point cursor jumps in line with the next tab stop.

- **Bulleted lists.** You're reading a bulleted list right now. Either click the rightmost icon on the toolbar or choose Format→Bullet Style.

- **Object Linking and Embedding.** This feature (Insert→Object) lets you create or insert a picture, graph, chart, sound, movie, spreadsheet, or other kind of data into your WordPad document.

- **Drag-and-drop editing.** Instead of using the three-step Copy and Paste routine for moving words and phrases around in your document, you can simply drag highlighted text from place to place on the screen. See page 200164 for details.

Ease of Access

If you have trouble using your keyboard or making out small text on the screen, the programs in the Start→All Programs→Accessories→Ease of Access folder may be just what you need. (In previous versions of Windows, this accessibility center was called Universal Access, which pretty much explains why its keyboard shortcut is still ⊞+U.)

Windows Vista is one of the most disability-friendly operating systems on earth. It includes a long list of features that let the PC magnify, speak, or otherwise boost the elements of the screen.

The Ease of Access item in the Start menu is actually yet another *folder*. It contains these items.

Ease of Access Center

This new control panel gathers together all of Vista's accessibility features under one roof.

At the top of the window, you'll find the triggers for four of Vista's big-ticket accessibility items: Magnifier, On-Screen Keyboard, Narrator, and High Contrast. You can click one of these buttons with your mouse, or, if you can't use the mouse, just wait; a blue rectangle highlights one after another, pausing a few seconds at each stop. Tap the Space bar to open a highlighted option. (The four features are described below.)

At the bottom of the window, you'll find a tidy list of new Vista controls that tweak the PC's audio, visual, mouse, and keyboard settings in special ways to help out people with limited hearing, vision, or mobility. When you click one of these links (such as "Use the computer without a display"), a special, very peculiar window opens, half Explorer window and half dialog box, that's filled with checkboxes. Here's the rundown.

Tip: Not all of these features are useful only to people with disabilities. If you have a flat-panel screen, for example, you may have noticed that everything on the screen is smaller than it might be on a traditional CRT screen. The result is that the cursor is sometimes hard to find, and the text is sometimes hard to read—but these features let you make it more visible.

UP TO SPEED

Mouse Keys, Sticky Keys, Toggle Keys, Filter Keys

The new, improved Ease of Access center offers a single page of options that are designed to make the keyboard easier to use if you have limited dexterity. The four primary features here are:

Mouse Keys lets you use the number keypad to control the arrow cursor. (It's useful if you can't use the mouse, or if you *can* but you want more precision in a graphics program.) Pressing the 2, 4, 6, and 8 keys on this pad moves the mouse around your screen—down, left, up, and right.

If you click "Set up mouse keys," you'll see where you can control how *fast* the cursor moves. You can also turn on "Hold down Ctrl to speed up and Shift to slow down" to do just what it says: make the cursor jump in larger or smaller increments when you press Ctrl or Shift, respectively. As a convenience, you can also indicate that when the NumLock key is tapped, you want the numbers to type *numbers* instead of moving the cursor.

Sticky Keys is for people who have difficulty pressing two keys (such as Ctrl, Alt, and Shift key combinations) at once.

Once this feature has been turned on, you can press keys of a specified combination one at a time instead of simultaneously. To do so, press the first key (Ctrl, Alt, or Shift) *twice,* which makes it "stick." Then press the second key (usually a letter key). Windows responds exactly as though you had pressed the two keys simultaneously.

Here again, a setup page awaits—click "Set up Sticky Keys," Here, you can indicate that you want to be able to turn on Sticky Keys by pressing the Shift key five times in a row. Another option makes Windows beep when a key is double-pressed and "stuck"—a confirmation that you're about to trigger a keyboard shortcut.

Toggle Keys makes the computer beep whenever you press the CapsLock, NumLock, or ScrollLock key. You don't have to be disabled to find this option attractive, since the confirmation beep prevents you from looking up after five minutes of typing to find a page of text tHAT lOOKS lIKE tHIS.

Finally, there's **Filter Keys**. In Windows, holding down a key for longer than a fraction of a second produces repeated keystrokes (such as TTTTTTT). When you turn on FilterKeys, though, Windows treats a repeated key as a *single* keystroke, which can be useful if you have trouble pressing keys lightly and briefly.

The "Set up Filter Keys" link offers an option that lets you use the right-side Shift key as the on/off switch for the filtering mode (by pressing Shift for 8 seconds): "Turn on Filter Keys when right SHIFT [key] is pressed for 8 seconds." It's also the home to the new Bounce Keys option, which helps filter out unwanted keystrokes, and an option that puts a stopwatch-like icon in the Notification Area when you're in FilterKeys mode.

• **Use the computer without a display.** If you have trouble seeing the screen, turn on Narrator here (described on page 269). You can also turn on Audio Description, in which a disembodied voice *describes* the action in movies. (Of course, this assumes that the movie comes with a description *track,* and few do.) This screen also lets you make Windows alert boxes go away by themselves after a while—a solution to a blind person's typical dilemma (the PC doesn't seem to react to anything, because, unbeknownst to you, there's a dialog box on the screen holding up the works).

• **Make the computer easier to see.** Here's the on/off switch for High Contrast mode (Figure 7-15)—or, rather, the on/off switch for the *keystroke* that turns on High Contrast mode (Alt+Left Shift+Prnt Scrn).

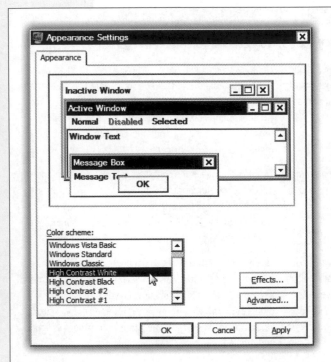

Figure 7-15:
In High Contrast mode, text is white against a black background, and all subtleties and shadings are turned off. The idea is to make the screen easier to read for people with limited vision.

As you can see here, the Settings dialog box actually offers several different variations of High Contrast. Click each (and then Apply) to sample them.

This screen also offers yet another way to turn on Narrator and Magnifier (described later), plus a link to the control panel where you can make text and icons bigger.

Most interesting of all, you can use the options at the bottom of the box to make the "focus" rectangle, or even the blinking word processor insertion point, thicker, to make it easier to see.

• **Use the computer without a mouse or keyboard.** This window offers an on/off switch for the onscreen keyboard (described below), and a link to turn on Speech Recognition (page 202).

- **Make the mouse easier to use.** Very cool: a palette of nine cursor (and insertion-point) styles, in various color schemes and enlarged sizes. One click is all it takes.

  Also on hand is an on/off switch for Mouse Keys, described below, and "Activate a window by hovering over it with the mouse," which lets you switch windows by *pointing* (rather than *clicking*).

- **Make the keyboard easier to use.** These features—Mouse Keys, Sticky Keys, and so on—have been with Windows for several generations, but they finally have a home that makes sense. See the box on page 267 for full details.

- **Use text or visual alternatives for sounds.** If you're deaf, a computer that beeps to get your attention isn't especially helpful. But this feature, formerly called Sound Sentry, instructs Windows to make your screen flash or blink when a sound occurs. You choose which part of the screen you want to use as a warning: the title bar ("caption bar") of the window, the window itself, or the entire desktop.

Note: "Turn on text captions for spoken dialog" refers to subtitles on DVDs and videos. It works only if (a) subtitles have been prepared for the movie you're watching, and (b) the video-playback software is Vista-capable.

- **Make it easier to focus on tasks.** Man, who doesn't occasionally wish it were easier to focus on work?

  Of course, Microsoft has a slightly more literal meaning in mind here. In truth, this page is nothing more than yet *another* set of on/off switches for features that appear on other Ease of Access pages: Narrator, Sticky Keys, Toggle Keys, and so on.

Magnifier

Magnifier is like a software magnifying glass that fills the top portion of your screen. (The actual-size version appears in the bottom half.) The magnified area scrolls as you move your cursor, tab through a dialog box, or type, enlarging whatever part of the screen contains the action. Using the Magnifier Settings dialog box shown in Figure 7-16, you can specify how much magnification you want (one to 16 times), which area of the screen gets magnified, and so on.

Tip: Whenever Magnifier is turned on, you can zoom in or out by pressing Ctrl+plus sign or Ctrl+minus sign, respectively.

Narrator

As the little welcome screen tells you, Narrator is a program that can read aloud whatever text appears on the screen—dialog boxes, error messages, menus, text you've typed, and so on. Narrator doesn't work in all programs, and it sounds a little bit like a Norwegian who's had a few beers. Still, if you have trouble reading text on the screen, or if you just like to hear your email read back to you, it's better than nothing.

In the pre-Vista days, Narrator could read only what you see listed in the Narrator dialog box:

- **User's Keystrokes.** That is, Narrator pronounces each letter as you type it—a handy safeguard if you can't see what you're doing.

Figure 7-16:
Magnifier enlarges whatever part of the screen your cursor is touching. You can adjust the size of the magnification pane by dragging its edge. You can also tear the pane away from the edge of the screen, so it becomes a floating window; just drag anywhere inside it.

- **System Messages** are Windows error messages and other alert boxes.

- **Scroll Notification** means that you'll be told when the screen has scrolled, to better keep your bearings.

In Vista, however, Narrator is quite a bit more flexible. If you click the Quick Help button, you scan scroll down to see an elaborate chart of keystrokes that tell Narrator what to read. Here, however, are a few of the most useful commands:

Read the frontmost window	Ctrl+Shift+Spacebar
Stop reading	Ctrl
Read the selected word	Insert+F4
Read the selected line	Insert+F5
Read the selected paragraph	Insert+F6
Read the whole document	Insert+F8
Read you the details about the highlighted icon	Ctrl+Shift+Enter

Tip: You can fiddle with Anna, if you like. She's the voice of Windows Vista, and she's adjustable.

If you click Voice Settings, you open a dialog box where you can use pop-up menus to make Anna speak faster or slower, louder or softer, and higher or lower.

On-Screen Keyboard

If you're having trouble typing, keep the On-Screen Keyboard program in mind. It lets you type just by clicking the mouse (Figure 7-17)—an option you may find useful in a pinch.

Figure 7-17:
Use the Keyboard menu to choose a different key layout, and the Settings menu to change the typeface that appears on the keys.

Windows Speech Recognition

Windows Vista offers a completely rewritten speech-recognition feature that's far more useful (and accurate) than past versions. You can read all about it in Chapter 6.

System Tools

This folder (Start→All Programs→Accessories→System Tools) is designed to be a toolbox for basic Windows administration, maintenance, and troubleshooting programs. Many of these programs are described elsewhere in this book:

Backup Status and Configuration	Chapter 22
Computer	Chapter 1
Control Panel	Chapter 8
Disk Cleanup	Chapter 20
Disk Defragmenter	Chapter 21
Task Scheduler	Chapter 20
System Information	Chapter 21
System Restore	Chapter 22
Windows Easy Transfer	Appendix A

Two items on this submenu, however, have nothing to do with PC health and fitness, and were stashed here perhaps because Microsoft couldn't find a more logical place to stash them: Character Map and Internet Explorer (No Add-ons).

Character Map

Your computer is capable of creating hundreds of different typographical symbols—the currency symbols for the yen and British pound, diacritical markings for French and Spanish, various scientific symbols, trademark and copyright signs, and so on. Obviously, these symbols don't appear on your keyboard; to provide enough keys, your keyboard would have to be the width of Wyoming. You *can* type the symbols, but they're hidden behind the keys you do see.

The treasure map that reveals their locations is the Character Map. When first opening this program, use the Font pop-up menu to specify the font you want to use (because every font contains a different set of symbols). Now you see every single symbol in the font. As you hold your mouse down on each symbol, a magnified version of it appears to help you distinguish them. See Figure 7-18 for details on transferring a particular symbol to your document.

Tip: *In general, Internet email can't handle the fancy kinds of symbols revealed by the Character Map. Don't be surprised if your copyright symbol turns into a gibberish character when received by your lucky correspondent.*

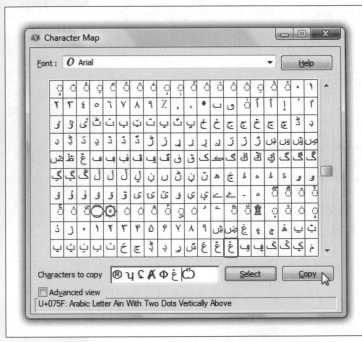

Figure 7-18:
Double-click a character to transfer it to the "Characters to copy" box, as shown here. (Double-click several in a row, if you want to capture a sequence of symbols.) You may have to scroll down quite a bit in some of today's modern Unicode fonts, which contain hundreds of characters. Click Copy, and then Close. When you've returned to your document, choose Edit→Paste to insert the symbols.

Internet Explorer (No Add-ons)

The version of Internet Explorer included with Vista is far more secure than previous versions. Its behavior can still get flaky, however, especially when you go gunking it up with add-ons and plug-ins. There may come a day when your main copy is behaving oddly, but you don't have the time to troubleshoot. In that case, choose this command. It opens a fresh, virginal copy of Internet Explorer, with all of your add-on junk stripped away—a copy that, in theory, should perform as smoothly as the day it was born.

Tablet PC

These links take you to three programs that are especially (or exclusively) useful to people who use PCs with touch screens—Tablet PCs, as they're known. All three—Sticky Notes, Tablet PC Input Panel, and Windows Journal—are described in Chapter 19.

Extras and Upgrades
All Versions

This little grab bag offers a few links to Microsoft-run online stores and storehouses of information:

- **Windows Anytime Upgrade.** As you're probably aware, Windows Vista comes in a number of different editions: Home Premium, Business, Enterprise, and so on. (Details are in the Introduction.)

  But what if you buy, say, the Home Basic version, but you later decide that you really wanted the cool looks and video-editing features of Home Premium? Or maybe you bought Business, but you really crave the backup and encryption features of Ultimate?

  Not to worry; Microsoft has made sure that you'll be taken care of. Using this command, you can *upgrade* your version of Vista to a higher version; all you need is a valid credit-card number and a few bucks in your account.

  When you choose this command, you go online to the Windows Anytime Upgrade Web page. This site detects which Vista version you have now, and offers to show you what kind of happiness awaits when you upgrade to one of the higher-priced versions.

  If you decide to move ahead with the upgrade, you're asked to find your original Windows Vista installation DVD. (Little did you know that it actually includes *all* versions of Vista—but holds back certain features that you haven't paid for.)

  The upgrade process doesn't disturb any of your programs, settings, or documents. Everything remains exactly where it was (although Microsoft does recommend that you make a backup before upgrading, just in case).

- **Windows Marketplace** is Microsoft's online catalog. It's always there when your credit card is feeling under-exercised. (One useful link here: Windows Tested Products. It's a list of programs that Microsoft has certified to be Vista-compatible.)

- **Windows Ultimate Extras** appears only if you're using the Ultimate edition of Windows Vista. One of the perks of Ultimate ownership is, of course, all the bonus goodies that Microsoft intends to offer just for you—and the Ultimate Extras Web site is where you'll find 'em.

Early Ultimate Extras included a poker game, a setup tool for BitLocker (page 637), and DreamScene, which lets you install a *video* as your desktop wallpaper. It comes with several looping scenes, one with breathtaking flowing waterfall.

- **Windows Web Site.** This link is provided for that very small audience, the people who can't remember *www.microsoft.com*.

Games
All Versions

Even if you have a corporate version of Vista, like the Business or Enterprise version, you still get a bunch of games, for your procrastination pleasure. Three of them are new in Vista (Chess Titans, Mahjong Titans, Purble Place), and one (Inkball) used to be available only on Tablet PCs.

Unfortunately, the Games folder may disappoint Windows veterans: Microsoft's games can no longer be played against other people on the Internet. Evidently Microsoft closed that entertainment channel in its pursuit of Internet security.

Here's the Vista complement of games, all of which are listed in the Start→All Programs→Games submenu.

Tip: Complete instructions lurk within the Help menu of each game.

Chess Titans

It's not just chess—it's computer-generated chess on a gorgeously rendered board with a set of realistic 3-D pieces. You can rotate the board in space, as described in Figure 7-19.

Figure 7-19:
How did this chess board get rotated like this? On Aero-capable PCs, you can right-click a corner of the board and rotate it in 3-D space to study your situation from a different angle. (It snaps back to its original angle when you let go—unless, of course, you choose Game→Options and turn off "Rotate board back after free view.") Cool!

When you launch Chess, you're asked what difficulty level you want. Then you're offered a fresh, new game that's set up in Human vs. Computer mode—meaning that you (the Human, with the light-colored pieces) get to play against the Computer (your PC, on the dark side). Drag the chess piece of your choice into position on the board, and the game is afoot.

If you'd rather trade piece colors with the PC, no biggie. Choose Game→Options and select "Play against computer as black."

Tip: Click a piece without dragging to see where it's allowed to move, courtesy of light-up chessboard squares.

If you and a buddy are looking for something to do, you can play against each other. Choose Game→"New game against human," and enjoy the way Windows rotates the chessboard after each person's turn.

Freecell

You might think of this card game as solitaire on steroids. When you choose Game→New Game, the computer deals eight piles of cards before you. The goal is to sort them into four piles of cards—one suit each and sequentially from ace to king—in the spaces (the "Home stacks") at the upper-right corner of the screen. (To move a card, click it once and then click where you want it moved to. You're allowed to move only the bottom card from one of your eight stacks, or the cards in the free cells, described next.)

You can use the upper-left placeholders, the "free cells," as temporary resting places for your cards. From there, cards can go either onto one of the upper-right piles or onto the bottom of one of the eight piles in the second row. However, when moving

---

UP TO SPEED

In Every Game, a Gem

Many of the games in Vista bear the same names as the ones in Windows XP—but they're actually all new. All nine have a consistent look, consistent menus, and consistent options.

Each has two menus, Game and Help. The Game menu always offers a way to start a new game, plus these intriguing options:

Statistics reveals your personal game-playing history: how many times you've won, and so on.

Options lets you turn animations and helpful pop-up tip boxes off if you find them annoying or insulting. Here, too, you'll find checkboxes for "Always save game on exit"

and "Always continue saved game," which can help lend a through line to your otherwise fractured, chaotic life.

And **Change Appearance** lets you redecorate your game world. For example, if, in Chess Titans, you choose Game→Change Appearance, you can choose all kinds of wacky materials for the look of your pieces—Wood, Porcelain, or Frosted Glass—and for your game board (Porcelain, Marble, or Wood).

Use *those* options if you don't have *enough* variety in your life.

---

cards to the eight piles, you must place them alternating red/black, and in descending sequence.

Games Explorer

It's just a standard Explorer window containing all nine of Vista's bonus games.

Hearts

The object of this card game is to get rid of all the hearts you're holding by passing them off to other players. At the end of each round, all players counts up their points: one point for each heart, and thirteen points for the dreaded queen of spades. The winner is the person with the fewest points when the game ends (which is when somebody reaches 100).

What makes it tricky is that even while you're trying to ditch your hearts, somebody else may be secretly trying to collect them. If you can collect *all* of the hearts *and* the queen of spades, you win big-time; everybody else gets 26 big fat points, and you get off scot-free.

You can play Classic Hearts only against Windows, which manages the hands and strategies of three other fictional players to play against you (named North, West, and East).

InkBall

This game is really designed for Tablet PCs, but you can get by with a mouse. You're supposed to draw ink strokes on the screen, frantically building temporary "bumpers"

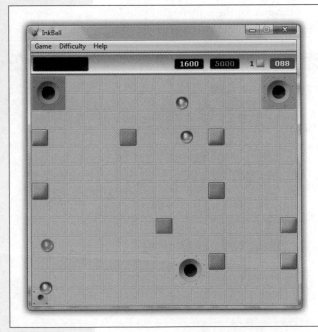

Figure 7-20:
In Inkball, the different colors are worth different numbers of points, ranging from red (200), blue, green, and finally gold (1,600). Gray balls don't win you any points; on the other hand, they're allowed to go into any holes without penalty.

that bounce the balls into matching color-holes—and stop them from going into different-colored holes (Figure 7-20). You have to act fast, because (a) you're racing the clock and (b) each line you draw vanishes if a ball hits it.

Mahjong Titans

Here's yet another kind of solitaire. (Naturally. Now that Microsoft has removed the playing-across-the-Internet features from its games, what other kind of game is there but solitaire?)

In Mahjong, though, you use tiles instead of cards. When the game begins, click the starting tile pile you want to work with. The idea is to click pairs of matching tiles to make them disappear—but only free tiles (not pinned under any others) can disappear.

Most of the time, the tiles have to match *exactly*, both in pattern and in number. Flower tiles let you off easy, though—any flower is considered a match of any other. Season tiles, same deal; any matches any.

Tip: If you get stuck, press the letter H key for a hint. Well, not so much a hint as a blatant giveaway; the next pair of available matching tiles blinks at you.

GEM IN THE ROUGH

Why Mimesweeper Didn't Make the Cut

Vista is the first version of Windows to be written in the age of blogs (Web diaries)—and Microsoft actually permitted its programmers to participate by keeping Windows fans updated on Vista's progress.

Most of the Vista blogs were pretty mundane, filled with programmery stuff. But Microsoft researcher David Vronay had PC nuts splurting their coffee in laughter with this fake posting:

"One of the most common requests I get from people is a list of features that didn't make it [into Windows Vista]. I thought it would be interesting for readers to hear about some of these things.

"As you may know, we have taken flack in the past for Minesweeper and the use of mines. Although we don't have land mines in the USA, in many countries they are experienced in daily life, and not something to make light of in a video game.

"So for Vista, we wanted to replace mines with something that people also wanted to avoid finding. Thus we came up with the concept of Mimesweeper.

"In Mimesweeper, you uncover street intersections on a black-and-white striped grid in which several mimes are hidden. Just like wandering around Paris, the goal is to figure out where all of the mimes are without actually encountering one.

"Unfortunately, beta feedback revealed a tremendous amount of controversy over the use of mimes. Although we do not have many mimes in the USA, apparently there are many countries where running into a mime is common occurrence and not something to make light of in a video game.

"In the end, we pulled the concept and replaced it with a garden of flowers."

Minesweeper

Under some of the grid cells are mines; under others, hints about nearby mines. Your goal: find the mines without blowing yourself up.

When clicking random squares, you run the risk of getting blown up instantly. If that happens, you lose; them's the breaks. But if you get lucky, you uncover little numbers around the square you clicked. Each number reveals how many mines are hidden in the squares surrounding it. Using careful mathematical logic and the process of elimination, you can eventually figure out which squares have mines under them. (To help keep track, you can right-click the squares to plant little flags that mean, "Don't step here.") You win if you mark all the mine squares with flags.

Figure 7-21:
All three of the games here smack of the games you find on educational CDs like Reader Rabbit.

Purble Place

Meet Microsoft's nod to the next generation of Windows fans: Purble Place, which is geared toward the elementary-school (or even preschool) set (Figure 7-21).

Which game you play depends on which of the three Fisher-Price buildings you click first:

- **Purble Pairs.** It's Ye Olde Memory Matching Game. Click any two tiles to reveal what's on their faces. If they match, they disappear. If not, they spin face-down again; as the game goes on, you have to remember where you saw that darned hat, or cake, or whatever. You're racing against the clock.

- **Comfy Cakes.** The TV shows you what kind of cake the chef needs. As the naked cake moves down the assembly lines, you have to click the right pan shape, batter color, frosting flavor, and decoration by clicking the appropriate buttons below the belt. The idea is to make the cake match the one shown on the TV. As you get better, the conveyor belt speeds up (can you say *I Love Lucy*?).

- **Purble Shop.** Your mission is to build a Purble character whose features match the mystery dude (marked by the question mark). Each time you assemble some features from the shelves (eyes, nose, mouth) and click the checkmark button, the game tells you how many of these features you got right—but not which ones. Through trial and error, you're supposed to deduce what the mystery dude actually looks like.

Solitaire

Here it is: the program that started it all, the application that introduced millions of people to the joys of a graphic interface like Windows. (Ask the advanced-beginner Windows fan to identify a good program-file code to type into the Start→Run dialog box, and he might not know *winword* or *msconfig*—but he'll probably know *sol.*)

In Solitaire, the object is to build four piles of cards, one for each suit, in ascending order (starting with aces). To help achieve this, you maintain seven smaller stacks of cards in the second row. You can put cards onto these piles as long as you alternate red and black, and as long as the cards go in descending order (a four of hearts can be placed on a five of spades, for example). Click a face-down card on one of these piles to turn it over. If it helps you to continue the red/black/red/black sequence you've started, remember you can drag around stacks of face-up cards on these piles. And when you can't find any more moves to make, click the deck in the upper-left corner to reveal more cards.

Figure 7-22:
In the easiest level, there's no need to worry about color or suit, because the game gives you only spades. If you run out of imagination, just press the letter M or H key to make the program propose a move. And if even the game can't find a legal move, simply click the deck in the lower-right corner to distribute another round of cards, which opens up a new round of possibilities.

Spider Solitaire

If your spirit needs a good game of solitaire, but you just don't have the time or patience for Solitaire or FreeCell, this kinder, gentler, *easier* game may be just the ticket. Thanks to the built-in cheat mechanism, which suggests the next move with no penalty, you can blow through this game with all of the satisfaction and none of the frustration of traditional solitaire games.

You play with 104 cards. You get ten stacks across the top of the screen, and the rest in a pile in the lower-right corner of the screen (Figure 7-22). All you have to do is create stacks of cards in descending order, from king down to ace, by dragging cards around. As soon as you create such a stack, the cards fly off the playing board. The goal is to remove *all* of the cards from the playing board.

Sticking with the game to the very end delivers an animated fireworks display—and a tiny, budding sense of achievement.

Maintenance

This folder contains four PC maintenance tools that may one day save your bacon:

- **Backup and Restore Center** is described in Chapter 22.
- **Help and Support** is the main online help system for Windows (Chapter 5).
- **Problem Reports and Solutions** lets you let Microsoft know about your problems, in hopes that they'll pay attention.
- **Windows Remote Assistance** is the online connection mechanism that lets a guru see your screen, and even operate your mouse, from afar (page 178).

Startup

The Startup folder contains documents, disks, folders, and programs that you want to run *automatically* when you log in. Maybe you begin your day with an email or calendar check, for example; if so, drop their icons into this folder. Page 29 has the details.

The Control Panel

Like the control panel in the cockpit of an airplane, the Control Panel is an extremely important feature of Windows Vista. It's teeming with miniature applications (or *applets*) that govern every conceivable setting for every conceivable component of your computer. Some are so important, you may use them (or their corresponding notification-area icons) every day. Others are so obscure you'll wonder what on earth inspired Microsoft to create them. This chapter covers them all.

Note: Here and there, within the Control Panel, you'll spot a little Windows security-shield icon. It tells you that you're about to make an important, major change to the operating system, something that will affect everyone who uses this PC—fiddling with its network settings, for example, or changing its clock. To prove your worthiness (and to prove that you're not an evil virus attempting to make a nasty change), you'll be asked to *authenticate* yourself; see the box on page 191 for details.

Home View: The Big Vista Change
All Versions

To have a look at your Control Panel applet collection, choose Start→Control Panel to open the Control Panel window.

You'll see that for the third straight Windows edition, Microsoft has rejiggered the layout in an attempt to make the thing easier to navigate.

The most important change is the pair of links in the task pane at the left side of the window. This task pane indicates that there are two ways to view the window's contents: *Control Panel Home* and *Classic View*.

Control Panel Home is another stab at the Category view featured in Windows XP. This time, however, the categories are much more detailed (Figure 8-1).

To use the Control Panel Home view, you're supposed to drill down. For example, suppose you wanted to delete all your Web browser's cookies (stored Web-page preference files). You might first guess that this task's category would be Network and Internet, or maybe Security; you'd be right either way. (Microsoft has tasks listed in several categories, just in case.) After you click that heading, you see individual tasks like "Delete browsing history and cookies." Clicking that link opens the dialog box that lets you do the deed.

Tip: A list of your most recent Control Panel activities appears under Recent Tasks in the left-side task pane.

Here's a rundown of the new, improved Control Panel Home categories:

- **System and Maintenance.** In this category are system and administrative tasks like backing up and restoring, setting your power options, and viewing performance information.

- **Security.** Look here for all security-related tasks, like maintaining Windows Firewall; blocking spyware; setting Internet options or parental controls; and accessing the Security Center.

- **Network and Internet.** This category contains settings related to network settings, Internet options, offline files (page 589), and Sync Center (to manage synchronizing data between computers, pocket gadgets, and network folders).

- **Hardware and Sound.** Here you'll find everything for managing hardware connected to your computer, as well as some interesting management features. For example, the settings for Sideshow, Tablet PCs, and screen orientation lurk.

UP TO SPEED

Control Panel Terminology Hell

The Control Panel continues to be an object of bafflement for Microsoft, not to mention its customers; from version to version of Windows, this window undergoes more reorganizations than a bankrupt airline.

Vista presents the most inconsistent and oddball arrangement yet. There are far more icons in the Control Panel than ever before—about 50 of them, in fact. But they're not all the same kind of thing.

Some are the traditional *applets,* meaning mini-applications (little programs). Others are nothing more than tabbed dialog boxes. Some open up wizards (interview dialog boxes that walk you through a procedure) or even ordinary Explorer windows. And even among the applets, the look and elements of the Control Panel panels varies widely.

So what are people supposed to call these things? The world needs a general term for the motley assortment of icons in the Control Panel window.

To help you and your well-intentioned authors from going quietly insane, this chapter refers to all of the Control Panel icons as either icons (which they definitely are) or applets (which most of them are—and besides, that's the traditional term for them).

- **Programs.** You'll probably use this one a lot. Here's how you uninstall programs, choose which program is your preferred one (for Web browsing or opening graphics, for example), or turn Windows features on and off.

Figure 8-1:
Top: The Control Panel categories have been expanded and rearranged to make it even easier for novices to find tasks. Clicking a category heading takes you to the associated list of tasks (and their applets). For your convenience, several tasks are listed under more than one category. It seems that even Microsoft couldn't decide where each should definitively go.

Bottom: If you choose any category, you're taken to the category window, which displays the tasks in the selected category (with some likely task settings listed beneath them). A useful list of all other categories appears on the left (in case you didn't find what you were looking for and need to look elsewhere).

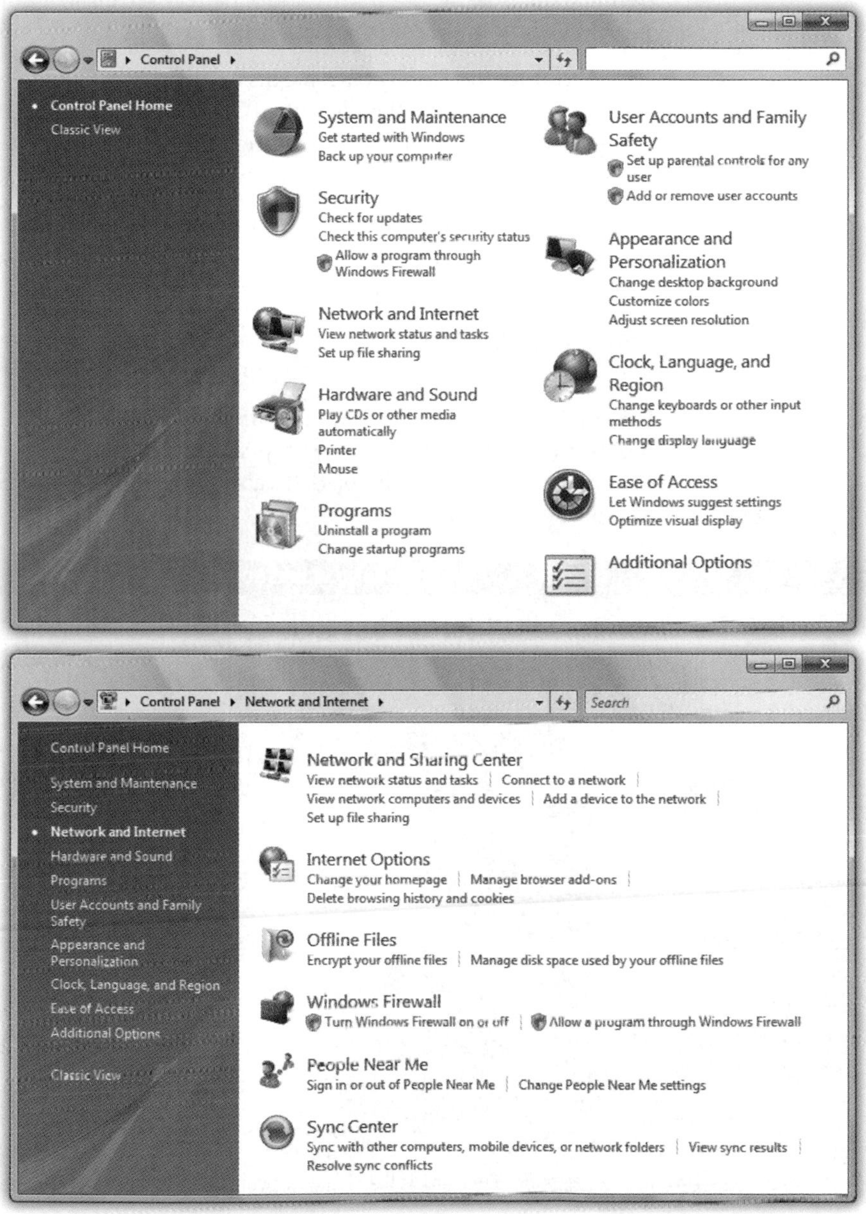

Note: This pane also offers a link called Get Programs Online. Microsoft, it seems, wants you to start buying software online.

- **Mobile PC.** This category shows up only if you are, in fact, using a laptop or another flavor of portable PC. It's mostly about battery settings, options for touch-screen Tablet PCs, and synchronizing data with palmtops and phones.

- **User Accounts and Family Safety.** This category contains the settings you need to manage the accounts on the computer (Chapter 23), including the limited accounts that parents can create for their children. CardSpace (page 313) also shows up in this category.

- **Appearance and Personalization.** Here's a big category indeed. It covers all things cosmetic, from how the desktop looks (plus taskbar, Sidebar, and personalization settings), to folder options, fonts, and ease-of-access settings.

- **Clock, Language, and Region.** These time, language, and clock settings all have one thing in common: they differ according to where in the world you are.

- **Ease of Access.** This revamped category replaces the Accessibility Options dialog box from Windows XP. It's one-stop shopping for every feature Microsoft has dreamed up to assist the disabled. It's also the rabbit hole into Speech Recognition Options.

WORKAROUND WORKSHOP

Where'd I Put that Setting?

Ever try to configure a setting in the Control Panel, but forget which applet it's in? Happens all the time. In the pre-Vista days, there could be some guessing in your future, as you clicked through likely categories, or opened and closed a few applet icons. Now, however, you can use the handy-dandy Search field located in the upper-right corner of the window.

For example, let's say you can't remember exactly where to go to set up Sticky Keys for your keyboard. Is that

a keyboard setting or an Ease of Access setting? Don't worry about it. In Control Panel Home view, type *sticky* into the search box. Presto: you get a list of all tasks that might involve *sticky*. From there, it's easy to go directly to the setting you're looking for.

Unfortunately, this trick doesn't work in Classic view. In Classic view, for some reason, Microsoft allows you to search only by icon name. Otherwise, it gives you a polite suggestion to change your view.

- **Additional Options.** This is a catch-all category. If you install a program that can be controlled through the Control Panel, chances are good that it will show up here.

Classic View
All Versions

Microsoft has attempted to make Home view work by putting every setting into every possible category. A lot of redundancy and repetition results—and you *still* might not be able to find the setting you're looking for. The category concept sounds OK in principle, but it'll drive veterans nuts. You don't want to guess what category Fax wound up in—you just want to open the old Print and Fax control panel, right now.

Fortunately, Classic View is still available. That's where the Control Panel displays all 50 icons in alphabetical order (Figure 8-2). Just double-click the icon of the applet you'd like to use.

Tip: The Icon view, unfortunately, chops off a lot of applets' names. For that reason—and to see more applets in less space—consider switching Classic View into Details view or List view. Do that by right-clicking a blank spot of the window; from the shortcut menu, choose View→Details or View→List.

The same shortcut menu lets you group, stack, and sort the icons to your heart's content.

Figure 8-2:
Classic View might be overwhelming for novices, because the task icons give little indication what settings they actually contain. Here's a hint: remember you can just move your mouse over a task and pause there. A tooltip pops up, giving you an idea what's inside.

The Control Panel, Applet by Applet
All Versions

Classic View is the perfect structure for a chapter that describes each Control Panel applet, since it's organized in alphabetical order. The rest of this chapter assumes that you're looking at the Control Panel in Classic View.

Tip: If you're really a speed freak, even the Classic View method of accessing a particular Control Panel program is fairly inefficient. After all, you must first choose Start→Control Panel and wait for the window to open, then you have to double-click the individual program you want.

To save time, you can do one of two things. Either turn on the feature that lets you choose a certain program's name *directly* from the Start menu, as described on page 45, or, if you don't mind a cluttered desktop, make a shortcut for the programs you access most. Just right-click it and select Create Shortcut from the shortcut menu. It automatically places it on the desktop for you. Or, what the heck—drag an applet right out of the Control Panel *into* the Start menu to install it there!

Add Hardware
This icon isn't really a Control Panel program at all; it's a wizard, and it's described in Chapter 18.

Administrative Tools
This icon is actually a folder containing a suite of very technical administrative utilities. These tools, intended for serious technowizards only, are explained in Chapter 20.

AutoPlay
In Windows XP, when you inserted a CD into the CD player, a dialog box popped up, asking what you wanted to do with it. It gave you a list of common things that Windows can do with a CD or DVD that you've inserted, like playing the music on a CD, opening the CD in an Explorer window to look at its contents, running whatever installer is on the disc, copying the photos on the CD to your Pictures folder, or doing nothing at all.

Unfortunately, if you chose the wrong checkbox (and then turned on "Always do the selected action") you couldn't easily change your mind. And XP didn't take into consideration that not all DVDs and CDs are made equal. Some are audio CDs, some are video CDs, and so on; you might well want each type to have its own standard behavior.

And that's what makes Autoplay so cool (Figure 8-3). Autoplay, new to Vista, finally gives you a single place to configure how you would like your CDs and DVDs (and memory cards, flash drives, and cameras) to be run. And yes, you can specify how audio CDs are handled, versus *enhanced* audio CDs.

Autoplay differentiates between different kinds of audio CDs and DVDs, video CDs and DVDs, programs (like software and games), pictures, video and audio files, blank CDs and DVDs, and even proprietary kinds of disks, like Blu-Ray, HD, and Super

Video. It even lets you manage how externally attached devices (like a camera or USB drive) are handled.

Tip: If you've never liked Autoplay and you don't want Windows to do *anything* when you insert a disc, just turn off "Use autoplay for all media and devices" at the top of the window.

Figure 8-3:
Top: The Autoplay window appears whenever you insert a record-able CD or DVD, memory card, or flash drive. You can say what you want to happen (like "Import pictures" or "Burn files to disc") just for this time, or—by turning on "Always do this"—forever. But what if you want to change your mind?

Bottom: Finally: a single, easy-to-use place to change the automatic actions for all kinds of discs and memory sticks. To set what happens when you insert each type of device or disc, open the adjoining pop-up menu. It displays a list of possible actions, like "Play audio CD," "Rip music from CD," "Open folder to view files," or "Take no action."

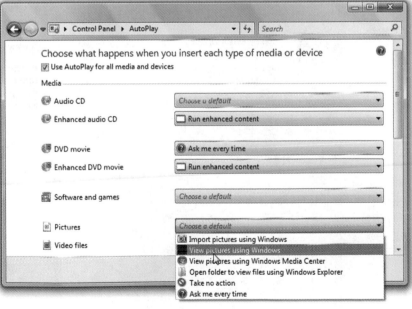

Backup and Restore Center

Backup and Restore Center is a new applet that allows you more control over if and how you back up your computer (and restore it). Check out Chapter 22 for more detailed information.

BitLocker Drive Encryption

BitLocker is a new security feature. It encrypts the data on your drives to keep them from being accessed by the bad guys who might steal your laptop. For details, see Chapter 21.

Color Management

Microsoft created this applet in conjunction with Canon in an effort to make colors more consistent from screen to printer. Details are in Chapter 17.

Date and Time

Your PC's conception of what time it is can be very important. Every file you create or save is stamped with this time, and every email you send or receive is marked with

Figure 8-4:
Top: The Date and Time tab has a lovely analog clock displaying the time. You can't actually use it to set the time, but it looks nice. To make a change to the date or time of the computer, click "Change date and time."

Bottom: At that point, select the correct date by using the calendar. Specify the correct time by typing in the hour, minute, and seconds. Yes, type it; the up and down arrows next to the time field are too inefficient except when you're changing AM to PM or vice versa.

it. When you drag a document into a folder that contains a different draft of the same thing, Windows warns that you're about to replace an older version with a newer one (or vice versa)—but only if your clock is set correctly.

This program offers three tabs:

- **Date and Time.** Here's where you can change the time, date, and time zone for the computer (Figure 8-4)—if, that is, you'd rather not have the computer set its own clock (read on).

Tip: In the Time Zone section of the Date and Time tab, you can find exactly when Vista thinks Daylight Savings Time is going to start (or end, depending on what time of year it is). In addition, there's an option to remind you a week before the time change occurs, so you don't wind up unexpectedly sleep-deprived on the day of your big TV appearance.

- **Additional Clocks.** If you work overseas, or if you have friends, relatives, or clients in different time zones, you'll like this one; it's the only thing that stands between you and waking them up at three in the morning because you forgot what time it is where they live.

  This new Vista feature shows you, at a glance, what time it is in other parts of the world. You can give them any display name you want, like "Paris" or "Mother-in-Law time." Note that the additional clocks' times are based on the PC's own local time. So if the computer's main clock is wrong, the other clocks will be wrong, too.

  Figure 8-5 shows how to check one of your additional clocks.

Tip: If you *click* the time on the taskbar instead of just pointing to it (Figure 8-5), you get three large, beautiful *analog* clocks in a pop-up window.

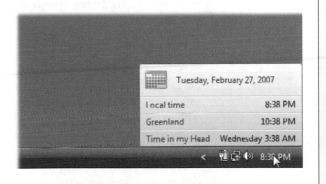

Figure 8-5:
To see the time for the additional clocks, point without clicking over the time in the notification area. You'll get a pop-up displaying the time on the additional clock (or clocks) that you configured.

- **Internet Time.** This option has nothing to do with Swatch Internet Time, a 1998 concept of time that was designed to eliminate the complications of time zones. (Then again, it introduced complications of its own, like dividing up the 24-hour day into 1000 parts called ".beats," each one being 1 minute and 26.4 seconds long.)

Instead, this tab teaches your PC to set its own clock by consulting one of the highly accurate scientific clocks on the Internet. To turn the feature on or off, or to specify which atomic Internet clock you want to use as the master clock, click Change Settings. (No need to worry about Daylight Savings Time, either; the time servers take that into account).

Note: Your PC resets its clock once a week—*if* it's connected to the Internet at the time. If not, it gives up until the following week. If you have a dial-up modem, in other words, you might consider connecting to the Internet every now and then and then using the Update Now button to compensate for all the times your PC unsuccessfully tried to set its own clock.

Default Programs

In an age when Microsoft is often accused of leveraging Windows to take over other realms of software, like Web browsing and graphics, the company created this command center. It's where you choose your preferred Web browser, music-playing program, email program, and so on—which may or may not be the ones provided by Microsoft.

You're offered four links:

- **Set your default programs.** Here's where you teach Vista that you want your own programs to replace the Microsoft versions. For instance, you can tell Vista that, when you double-click a music file, you want to open iTunes and not Windows Media Player. For details, see page 223.

- **Associate a file type or protocol.** This window lets you specify exactly what kind of file you want to have opened by what program. (That's essentially what happens in the background when you set a default program.) File associations are covered in more depth on page 223.

- **Change Autoplay Settings.** This option opens the Autoplay applet described on page 286.

- **Set program access and computer defaults.** Here, you can not only manage what programs are used by default, like browsing with Internet Explorer or getting email with Windows Mail, but also disable certain programs so that they can't be used at all. It's organized in rather combative schemes: you can choose to prefer Micro-soft products (disabling access to the non-Microsoft interlopers), Non-Microsoft Products (pro-third party, anti-Microsoft), or create a Custom scheme, in which you can specifically choose a mix of both. See page 226 for more information.

Device Manager

The Device Manager console shows you where all your hardware money was spent. Here, you or your tech-support person can troubleshoot a flaky device, disable and enable devices, and manage device drivers. If you're comfortable handling these more advanced tasks, then Chapter 18 is for you.

Display

OK, just kidding—the Control Panel doesn't contain an icon for Display anymore. But you're probably used to looking for it here, so consider this a friendly cross-reference to Chapter 4.

Ease of Access Center

The Ease of Access Center is a completely revamped version of the Accessibility Options of Windows versions gone by. It's designed to make computing easier for people with disabilities, although some of the options here can benefit anyone. See page 266 for details.

Folder Options

This program offers three tabs—General, View, and Search—all of which are described in Chapter 2.

Fonts

This icon is a shortcut to a folder; it's not an applet. It opens into a window that reveals all of the typefaces installed on your machine, as described in Chapter 17.

Game Controllers

If you're a serious gamer, the Game Controllers program may interest you. You use it to configure and control the joysticks, steering wheels, game pads, flight yokes, and other controllers you've attached to your PC. After all, if your joysticks and controllers aren't installed and configured properly, you can't pulverize aliens to full capacity.

To get started, install the driver software that came with your gaming device. If it's a modern, USB, Vista-compatible gadget, you may not even need to do that much. Just plug in the device and watch the notification area for a message that Vista has detected it and installed the correct driver. (See Chapter 18 for more on installing gadgetry.)

Next, open the Game Controllers program, where you should see the newly installed controller listed. Click it and then click OK. If your device isn't listed, click the Add button. In the Add Game Controller dialog box, specify the kind of controller you intend to install—"Gravis GamePad Pro (GamePort)," "6-button joystick w/two POVs and throttle," or what have you—and then click OK.

Once you've selected the device, highlight its name in the Controller list box, and then click the Properties button to test and set up its various buttons, wheels, and knobs.

Note: Game controllers generally work only in games that recognize them—not within Windows itself. That USB steering wheel you've installed, for example, will almost certainly work in your racing-car simulator game, but don't expect it to help you drive around the icons on your desktop.

Indexing Options

As noted in Chapter 3, Vista's new Search box is so magnificently fast because it doesn't actually root through all your files. Instead, it roots only through an *index* of your files, an invisible, compact database file that Vista maintains in the background.

This dialog box lets you manage indexing functions and change what gets indexed, and lets you know how many items have been indexed. To learn more about the particulars of indexing and how to use it, see Chapter 3.

Internet Options

A better name for this program would have been "Web Browser Options," since all of its settings apply to Web browsing—and, specifically, to Internet Explorer. As a matter of fact, this is the same dialog box that opens from the Tools→Internet Options menu command within Internet Explorer. Its tabs break down like this:

- **General, Security, Privacy, and Content.** These tabs control your home page, cache files, search field defaults, and history list. They also let you define certain Web pages as off-limits for your kids and manage RSS feeds, as well as block pop-up windows. Details on these options are in Chapter 10.

- **Connections.** Controls when your PC modem dials; see page 328 for details.

- **Programs.** Use this tab to manage browser add-ons, decide whether or not Internet Explorer should warn you whenever it is not the default browser (for your protection, of course), or choose the default programs that open, should you click a link to email someone, open a media file, or view the HTML source of a Web page (View menu→Source).

- **Advanced.** On this tab, you'll find dozens of checkboxes, most of which are useful only in rare circumstances and affect your Web experience only in minor ways. For example, "Enable personalized favorites menu" shortens your list of bookmarks over time, as Internet Explorer hides the names of Web sites you haven't visited in a while. (A click on the arrow at the bottom of the Favorites menu makes them reappear.)

  Similarly, turning off the "Show Go button in Address bar" checkbox hides the Go button at the right of the Address bar. After you've typed a Web address (URL), you must press Enter to open the corresponding Web page instead of clicking a Go button on the screen. And so on.

iSCSI Initiator

This applet is not for the faint of heart. In fact, it requires tech support or your network administrator to set up properly, and is completely useless for computers not on a network. Just opening it could wind up opening holes in your Windows Firewall. You've been warned.

Java

Java is a programming language that's responsible for a lot of the interactive goodies on the Web. This control panel is not, in fact, a Microsoft effort—which may explain why it looks nothing like the other applets—but was contributed by Sun, the company responsible for Java. The controls here are interesting to Web geeks only.

Keyboard

You're probably too young to remember the antique known as a *typewriter*. On some electric versions of this machine, you could hold down the letter X key to type a series of XXXXXXXs—ideal for crossing something out in a contract, for example.

On a PC, *every* key behaves this way. Hold down any key long enough, and it starts spitting out repetitions, making it easy to type, "No WAAAAAY!" or "You go, grrrrrl!" for example. (The same rule applies when you hold down the arrow keys to scroll through the text document, hold down the = key to build a separator line between paragraphs, hold down Backspace to eliminate a word, and so on.) The Speed tab of this dialog box (Figure 8-6) governs the settings.

- **Repeat delay.** This slider determines how long you must hold down the key before it starts repeating (to prevent triggering repetitions accidentally).

- **Repeat rate.** The second slider governs how fast each key spits out letters once the spitting has begun.

POWER USERS' CLINIC

iSCSI Initiator

You've already been warned that iSCSI Initiator is for system administrators, and you still want to know about it?

OK, fine.

iSCSI Initiator is a way of connecting your computer to hard drives on almost any kind of network—even across the Internet.

In the old days, accessing such externally stored data was painfully slow. If you needed a file on that distant hard drive, you didn't dare work on it "live," from across the network; it would be just too slow. So you'd download the files to your computer first, work on it, and then upload it when you were done.

And that's why Microsoft created iSCSI. It's not as fast as using your computer's internal hard drive, but it's a big improvement. Ever walked on one of those moving sidewalks between airport terminals, zooming past the people who are walking on the ground? That's the kind of speed boost iSCSI gives you.

To make this work, your computer *initiates* the process of finding and connecting to the *target* iSCSI storage device across the network. (That's why this applet is called iSCSI Initiator, get it?)

Your computer must have an iSCSI service running on it, and the ports that iSCSI uses must be open on your computer's firewall. (The applet offers to do this part for you.) Once the service is started and the ports are open (or you've cancelled through the prompts), you can get to the iSCSI Initiator dialog box and configure its settings. It's at that point that you really need a highly-paid network professional to configure the settings, because it's filled with such fun settings as CHAP or IPsec authentication, the IP address of the RADIUS server, the IP address of the target device, and more.

After making these adjustments, click the "Click here and hold down a key" test box to try out the new settings.

- **Cursor blink rate.** The "Cursor blink rate" slider actually has nothing to do with the *cursor,* the little arrow that you move around with the mouse. Instead, it governs the blinking rate of the *insertion point,* the blinking marker that indicates where typing will begin when you're word processing, for example. A blink rate that's too slow makes it more difficult to find your insertion point in a window filled with data. A blink rate that's too rapid can be distracting.

Figure 8-6:
How fast do you want your keys to repeat? This dialog box also offers a Hardware tab, but you won't go there very often. You'll use it exclusively when you're trying to troubleshoot your keyboard or its driver.

TROUBLESHOOTING MOMENT

Sharing a Computer Between a Lefty and Righty

If a right-hander and a left-hander share a computer, confusion and marital discord may result. If the mouse is set for the righty, nothing works for the lefty, who then may assume that the PC is broken or cranky.

If you're using individual user accounts (see Chapter 23), Vista can solve the problem by switching the left- and right-button modes automatically when each person logs on.

But if you're not using user accounts, you probably need a quick way to switch the mouse buttons between lefties and righties. The easiest way is to create a shortcut to the Mouse control panel. Be sure to put it on the desktop or the Quick Launch toolbar, so that the button-switching checkbox is only a click away.

Mouse

All of the icons, buttons, and menus in Windows make the mouse a very important tool. And the Mouse dialog box is its configuration headquarters (Figure 8-7).

Figure 8-7:
If you're a southpaw, you've probably realized that the advantages of being left-handed when you play tennis or baseball were lost on the folks who designed the computer mouse. It's no surprise, then, that most mice are shaped poorly for leftics—but at least you can correct the way the buttons work.

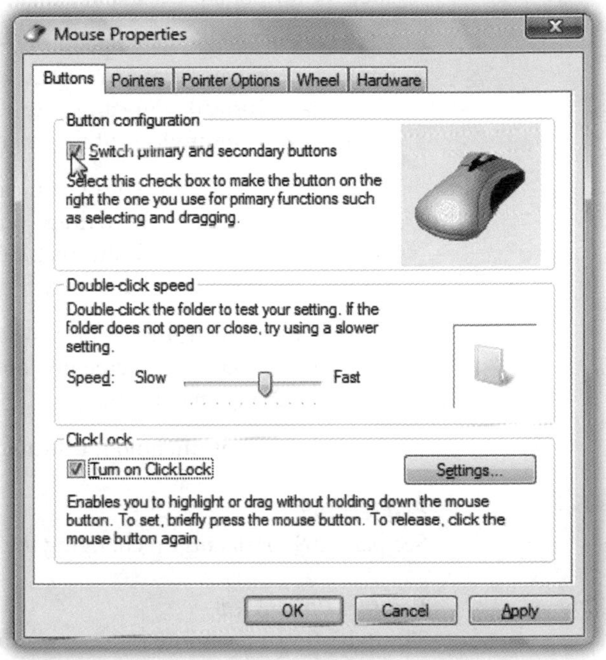

Buttons tab

This tab offers three useful controls: button configuration, double-click speed, and ClickLock.

- **Button configuration.** This checkbox is for people who are left-handed and keep their mouse on the left side of the keyboard. Turning on this checkbox lets you switch the functions of the right and left mouse buttons, so that your index finger naturally rests on the primary button (the one that selects and drags).

- **Double-click speed.** Double-clicking isn't a very natural maneuver. If you double-click too slowly, the icon you're trying to open remains stubbornly closed. Or worse, if you accidentally double-click an icon's name instead of its picture, Windows sees your double-click as two single clicks, which tells Windows that you're trying to rename the icon.

  The difference in time between a double-click and two single clicks is usually well under a second. That's an extremely narrow window, so let Vista know what you consider to be a double-click by adjusting this slider. The left end of the slider bar represents 0.9 seconds, and the right end represents 0.1 seconds. If you need more time between clicks, move the slider to the left; by contrast, if your reflexes are highly tuned (or you drink a lot of coffee), try sliding the slider to the right.

Each time you adjust the slider, remember to test your adjustment by double-clicking the little folder to the right of the Speed slider. If the folder opens, you've successfully double-clicked. If not, adjust the slider again.

- **ClickLock.** ClickLock is for people blessed with large monitors or laptop trackpads who, when dragging icons onscreen, get tired of keeping the mouse button pressed continually. Instead, you can make Vista "hold down" the button automatically, avoiding years of unpleasant finger cramps and messy litigation.

  When ClickLock is turned on, you can drag objects on the screen like this. First, point to the item you want to drag, such as an icon. Press the left mouse or trackpad button for the ClickLock interval. (You can specify this interval by clicking the Settings button in this dialog box.)

  When you release the mouse button, it acts as though it's still pressed. Now you can drag the icon across the screen by moving the mouse (or stroking the trackpad) without holding any button down.

  To release the button, hold it down again for your specified time interval.

Pointers tab

See page 269 for details on changing the shape of your cursor.

Pointers Options tab

This tab offers a few more random cursor-related functions.

- **Pointer speed.** It comes as a surprise to many people that the cursor doesn't move five inches when the mouse moves five inches on the desk. Instead, you can set things up so that moving the mouse one *millimeter* moves the pointer one full *inch*—or vice versa—using the Pointer speed slider.

  It may come as an even greater surprise that the cursor moves farther when you move the mouse faster. How *much* farther depends on how you set the "Select a pointer speed" slider.

  The Fast setting is nice if you have an enormous monitor, since it prevents you from needing an equally large mouse pad to get from one corner to another. The Slow setting, on the other hand, can be frustrating, since it forces you to constantly pick up and put down the mouse as you scoot across the screen. (You can also turn off the disproportionate-movement feature completely by turning off "Enhance pointer precision.")

- **Snap To.** A hefty percentage of the times when you reach for the mouse, it's to click a button in a dialog box. If you, like millions of people before you, usually click the *default* (outlined) button—such as OK, Next, or Yes—the Snap To feature can save you the effort of positioning the cursor before clicking.

When you turn on Snap To, every time a dialog box appears, your mouse pointer jumps automatically to the default button, so that all you need to do is click. (And to click a different button, such as Cancel, you have to move the mouse only slightly to reach it.)

- **Display pointer trails.** *Pointer trails* are ghost images of your mouse pointer that trail behind the pointer like ducklings following their mother. In general, this stuttering-cursor effect is irritating.

- **Hide pointer while typing.** Hiding the mouse pointer while you're typing is useful if you find that it sometimes gets in the way of the words on your screen. As soon as you use the keyboard, the pointer disappears; just move the mouse to make the pointer reappear.

- **Show location of pointer when I press the CTRL key.** If you've managed to lose the cursor on an LCD projector or a laptop with an inferior screen, this feature helps you gain your bearings. When you press and release the Ctrl key after turning on this checkbox, Windows displays an animated concentric ring each subsequent time you press the Ctrl key to pinpoint the cursor's location.

Wheel tab

The scroll wheel on the top of your mouse may be the greatest mouse enhancement since they got rid of the dust-collecting ball on the bottom. It lets you zoom through Web pages, email lists, and documents with a twitch of your index finger.

Use these controls to specify just how *much* each wheel notch scrolls. (You may not see this tab at all if your mouse doesn't have a wheel.)

Hardware tab

The Mouse program provides this tab exclusively for its Properties buttons, which takes you to the Device Manager's device properties dialog box. Useful if you have to troubleshoot a bad driver.

Network and Sharing Center

This network command center is an important step forward in Vista. It offers, among other things, a handy map that shows exactly how your PC is connected to the Internet. It also contains a tidy list of all networking-related features (file sharing, printer sharing, and so on), complete with on/off switches. See Chapter 26 for details.

Offline Files

The Offline Files applet opens into a dialog box where you can manage your offline file folders and access the Sync Center. See Chapter 19.

Parental Controls

This applet lets you, the wise parent, control what your inexperienced or out-of-control loved one (usually a child, but sometimes a spouse) can and cannot do on (or with) the computer. For more information, see Chapter 10.

Pen and Input Devices

This applet opens up a dialog box where you can configure how your stylus (pen) interacts with the desktop and windows. (Yes, stylus. You need this control panel primarily if you have a Tablet PC or a graphics tablet.) For details, see Chapter 19.

People Near Me

When you turn on People Near Me, you can collaborate with other Vista geeks across the network, using programs like Windows Meeting Space. For more information about People Near Me and ad hoc networking, see Chapter 26.

Performance Information and Tools

Vista needs a fast computer. Just how fast is yours? This control panel breaks it down for you, even going so far as giving your PC a grade for speed (page 20).

In addition, this window has convenient links to tabs of several other applets, (like Power Options, Indexing Service, and System Performance), as well as access to the old Disk Cleanup utility. For power users, there's even a kickin' Advanced Tools window stocked with speed-related goodies, logs, and reports. For details, see Chapters 6 and 20.

Personalization

Have you ever admired the family photo or space shuttle picture plastered across a co-worker's PC desktop? Wish the cursor were bigger? Annoyed that you have to log in again every time your screen saver kicks in?

All of these are aspects of the powerful new Personalization applet. It's such a big topic, it gets its own chapter: Chapter 4.

Phone and Modem Options

You'll probably need to access these settings only once: the first time you set up your PC or laptop to dial out. Details in Chapter 9.

Power Options

The Power Options program manages the power consumption of your computer. That's a big deal when you're running off a laptop's battery, of course, but it's also important if you'd like to save money (and the environment) by cutting down on the juice consumed by your *desktop* PC.

The options you see depend on your PC's particular features. Figure 8-8 displays the Power Options for a typical computer.

In Vista, Microsoft has tried to simplify the business of managing the electricity/speed tradeoff in two ways. First, it has abandoned the old name *power scheme* and adopted a new one: *power plan*. You can feel the clouds breaking up already.

(A power plan dictates things like how soon the computer goes to sleep, how bright the screen is, what speed the processor cranks at, and so on.)

Second, it presents you right up front with three premade power plans:

- **Balanced,** which is meant to strike a balance between energy savings and performance. When you're working hard, you'll get all the speed your PC can deliver; when you're thinking or resting, the processor slows down to save juice.

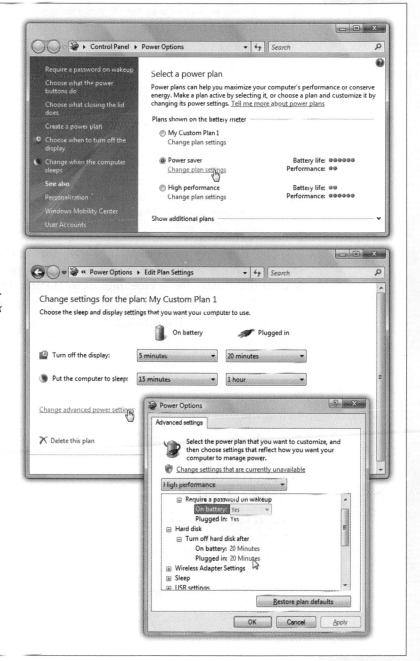

Figure 8-8:

Top: The factory setting power er plan, reasonably enough, is the Balanced plan. To take a look at the settings, click "Change plan settings."

Middle: At first glance, it looks like you can change only a couple of settings, like when the computer sleeps and when the display turns off.

Bottom: But if you click the "Change advanced power settings" link, you can see that the dialog box has more settings. Now you've got the full range of control over your screen, hard drive, wireless antenna, processor, installed PCI cards, and other power-related elements. Click the + sign to expand a topic, and then twiddle with the settings.

- **Power Saver** slows down your computer, but saves power—a handy one for laptop luggers who aren't doing anything more strenuous than word processing.

- **High Performance** sucks power like a black hole, but grants you the computer's highest speed possible.

Tip: You don't have to open the Control Panel to change among these canned plans. On a laptop, for example, you can just click the battery icon on your notification area and choose from the pop-up menu.

Creating your own plan

But adding to Microsoft's canned three plans can be useful, not only because you gain more control, but also because you get to see exactly what a plan is made of.

Start by clicking "Create a power plan" (left side of the window). On the next screen, type a name for your plan (say, PowerPoint Mode), and click Next.

The "Change settings" dialog box now appears. Yeah, yeah, you can use the pop-up menus to specify how soon your PC sleeps and turns off its monitor; if you're using a laptop, you can even specify *different* timings depending on whether you're running on battery power or plugged into the wall. Boring!

But click Create anyway. You return to the "Select a power plan" screen, where your new plan name appears. Finally, you're ready for the real fun: Click "Change plan settings" under its name. Then click "Change advanced power settings" (see Figure 8-8, bottom). Lots of these subsettings are technical and tweaky, but a few are amazingly useful:

- **Require a password on wakeup.** Nice security feature if you're worried about other people in your home or office seeing what you were working on before your machine went to sleep to save power.

- **Hard disk.** Making it stop spinning after a few minutes of inactivity saves a lot of juice. The downside: the PC takes longer to report in for work when you return to it and wake it up.

- **Wireless Adapter Settings.** If you're not using your computer, you can tell it to throttle back on its WiFi wireless networking signals to save juice.

- **Sleep.** How soon should the machine enter low-power sleep state after you've left it idle? And should it sleep or hibernate (page 32)?

- **Power buttons and lid.** What should happen when you close the lid of your laptop or press its Power or Sleep button (if it has one)? What should happen when you choose the Start menu's ⏻ button? Most of the time, you'll want the machine to use Vista's brainy new Sleep option (page 30).

- **PCI Express.** If you've got any adapter cards installed, and they're modern and Vista-aware, they, too, can save you power by sleeping when not in use.

- **Processor power management.** When you're running on battery, just how much are you willing to let your processor slow down to save juice?

- **Search and Indexing.** Remember from Chapter 3 how the Search mechanism is constantly scanning your hard drive to keep its index up to date? That takes power. You might want it to cool its jets a bit when you're running on battery.

- **Display.** These controls govern how fast your monitor turns off to save power.

- **Multimedia settings.** These controls have little to do with electricity, and everything to do with ruining your big PowerPoint pitch. They let you specify that the computer should not sleep if you're in the middle of playing a song, movie, or PowerPoint deck.

- **Battery.** "Critical battery action" dictates what the laptop should do when the battery's all out: hibernate, sleep, or shut down. The other settings here let you govern when Vista's two low-battery warnings appear (that is, at what percentage-remaining levels).

Some of these options also appear in the task pane at the left side of the Power Options control panel, for your convenience. They affect whatever plan is currently selected.

Printers

This one isn't a program at all; it's a shortcut to your Printers folder, described in Chapter 17.

Problem Reports and Solutions

Ever try to install a program that worked on your old computer onto a new computer? Ever have the installation fail mysteriously? Ever experience a hang, freeze, or crash? In Vista, Microsoft continues its efforts to conduct a troubleshooting session on a worldwide scale.

This telling new Windows applet has been designed to reassure you that everything is OK, but to offer more information if you insist.

As you can see in Figure 8-9, the first screen lists solutions that Vista might have found when reporting an error to Microsoft. (It could happen!) Beneath the Solutions to Install area is one called "Information about other problems." Don't let this section fool you; just because it's empty does not, in fact, mean you have no other problems. This section lists the problems for which Microsoft might have a solution requiring more legwork, such as "Call Microsoft."

In the Task Pane of this window are the real links that help you see what glitches, crashes, and freezes your computer's software might be having, and what might be done about it.

- **Check for new solutions.** This link literally checks in with Microsoft and sees if there are any solutions for all of your existing problems.

- **View problem history.** In this window you may see a surprising number of listed problems, grouped by type. They can be displayed in bold, meaning that the problem has not been reported to Microsoft. All problems not in bold are items for which you already sought a solution, so at least they have been reported to Microsoft.

Tip: You change the way the problems listed in the View problem history window are organized. Right-click any column heading. In the shortcut menu, you can choose to group problems by product, problem, and more.

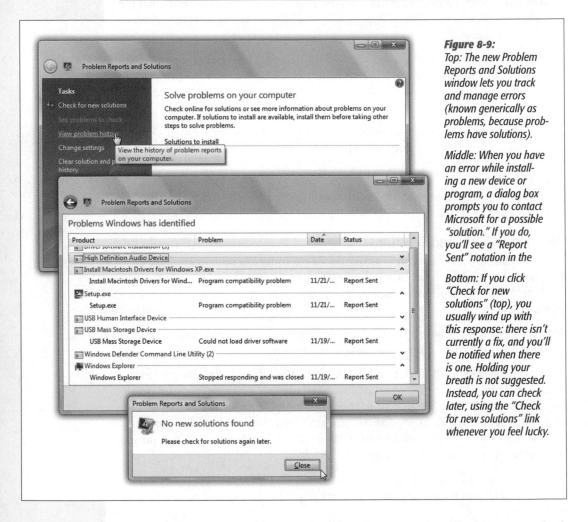

Figure 8-9:
Top: The new Problem Reports and Solutions window lets you track and manage errors (known generically as problems, because problems have solutions).

Middle: When you have an error while installing a new device or program, a dialog box prompts you to contact Microsoft for a possible "solution." If you do, you'll see a "Report Sent" notation in the

Bottom: If you click "Check for new solutions" (top), you usually wind up with this response: there isn't currently a fix, and you'll be notified when there is one. Holding your breath is not suggested. Instead, you can check later, using the "Check for new solutions" link whenever you feel lucky.

- **See problems to check.** Here you see the list of unreported problems. To check online for solutions, turn on the checkboxes for the appropriate problems, and click Check for Solutions.

  Notice that, at the bottom right of the window, there's a checkbox that checks for all other problems while looking for the solution to the problem you selected. (That is, it functions exactly like the "Check for new solutions" link.) It might conveniently find a recent solution for some other unresolved problem on your computer, or it may just vastly increase the time you wait while trying to find a solution to the problem you *were* looking for. If you want to look only for the solution you selected, clear that checkbox.

- **Change settings.** This link takes you to a window where you can change how your computer checks for solutions.

  Notice, by the way, that nowhere in this window is there any way to *disable* problem reporting—something the privacy-conscious might want to do. For that purpose, you need to click the "Advanced settings" link.

  On the Advanced settings screen, you can turn off reporting for yourself, or control problem reporting for the other users of your computer. You can even choose *how* automatically Vista will check for solutions: if it sends reports automatically, asks you first, or sends extra information just to be thorough (Figure 8-10).

Figure 8-10:
In the Advanced settings window, you can disable reporting for both yourself and any other users of this computer. You can even block programs that you know Vista is cranky about so it will stop wasting time reporting their problems.

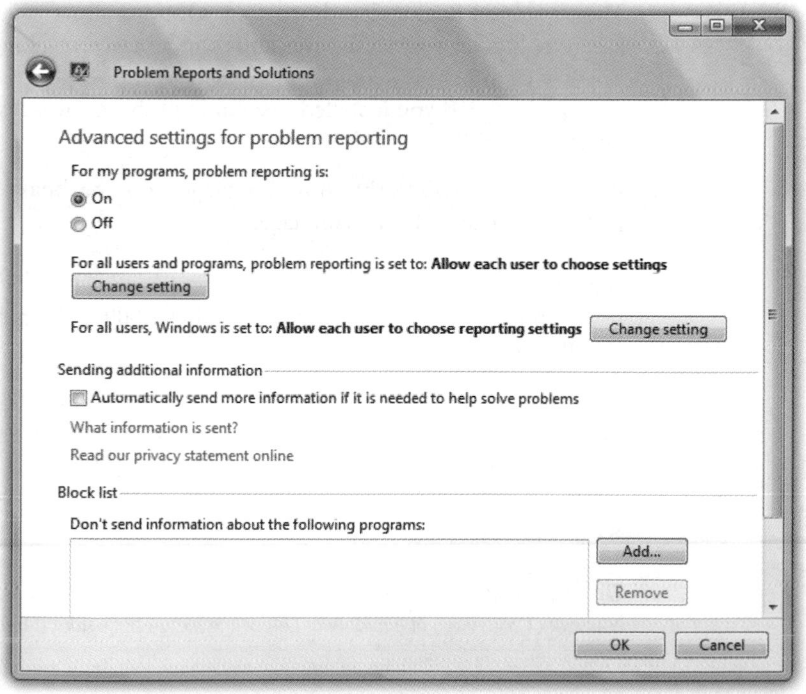

- **Clear solution and problem history.** There may come a time when all problems have been solved and your computer is running so smoothly that you want to clear your history window so you can better identify new problems when they come up. In that circumstance, clearing the solution and problem history will do the job.

Programs and Features

Programs and Features is about managing the software you have installed, managing updates, and buying software online. It replaces the old Add/Remove Programs program. ("Add" was dropped from the name because it was unnecessary; all programs these days come with their own installer. When was the last time you installed a program through Add/Remove Programs?)

This window is useful for fixing (which might simply mean reinstalling), changing, and uninstalling existing programs, and is the only place you can go to turn on (or off) Windows features like Fax and Scan, Games, Meeting Space, and more.

Regional and Language Options

Windows Vista can accommodate any conceivable arrangement of date, currency, and number formats; comes with fonts for dozens of Asian languages; lets you remap your keyboard to type non-English symbols of every ilk; and so on.

The revamped Regional and Language Options allow you to install multiple input language kits on your computer and switch between them when the mood strikes. The key term here is *default input language*; the language for the operating system doesn't change. If you installed Vista in English, you'll still see the menus and dialog boxes in English.

But when you switch the input language, your keyboard can type the characters necessary for the selected language.

Formats tab

If you think that 7/4 means July 4 and that 1.000 is the number of heads you have, skip this section.

But in some countries, 7/4 means April 7, and 1.000 means one thousand. If your PC isn't showing numbers, times, currency symbols, or dates in a familiar way, choose your country from the "Current format" pop-up menu. (Or, if you're a little weird, use the "Customize this format" button to rearrange the sequence of date elements; see Figure 8-11.)

Tip: The Customize Regional Options box (Figure 8-11) is where you can specify whether you prefer a 12-hour clock ("3:05 PM") or a military or European-style, 24-hour clock ("1505").

Location tab

This tab, new to Vista, identifies your computer's location. The point is so that when you go online to check local news and weather, you'll get the *right* news and weather—a handy feature if you're traveling with a laptop.

Keyboards and Languages tab

The symbols you use when you're typing in Swedish aren't the same as when you're typing in English. Microsoft solved this problem by creating different *keyboard layouts*, one for each language (or more, like Qwerty or Dvorak for English). Each keyboard layout rearranges the letters that appear when you press the keys. For example, in the Swedish layout, pressing the semicolon key produces an ö—not a semicolon (;).

There are two buttons on the Keyboards and Languages tab: Change Keyboards and Install/Uninstall Languages.

Figure 8-11:
Top: Regional standard format templates are available from the drop down list in the Formats tab.

Bottom: Once you choose a standard format (like US), then you can customize exactly how numbers, currency, time, and dates are handled. Simply click "Customize this format."

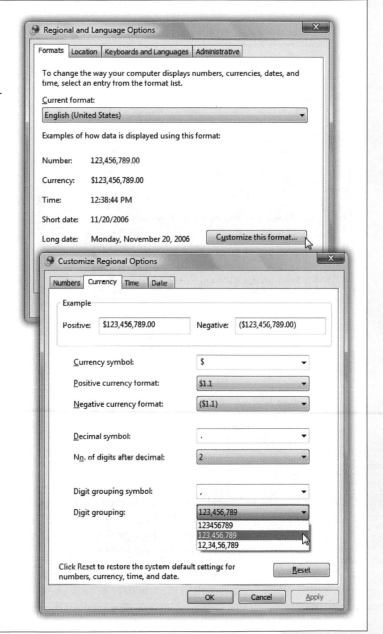

The Install/Uninstall Languages button lets you install additional language packs to your computer (you can download them from Microsoft's Web site). The Change Keyboards button takes you to another dialog box with three tabs:

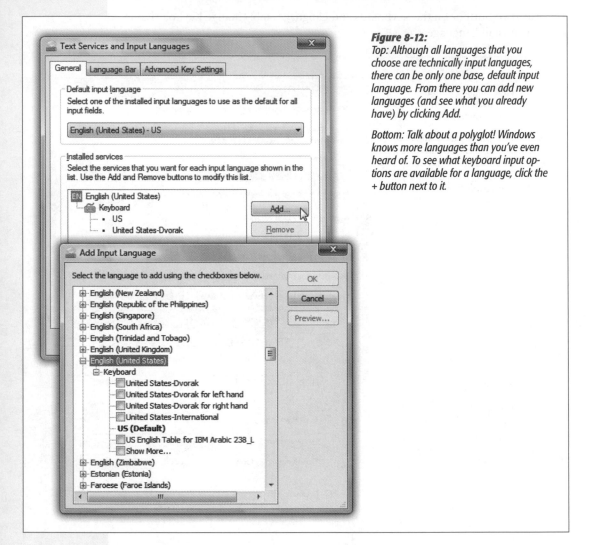

Figure 8-12:
Top: Although all languages that you choose are technically input languages, there can be only one base, default input language. From there you can add new languages (and see what you already have) by clicking Add.

Bottom: Talk about a polyglot! Windows knows more languages than you've even heard of. To see what keyboard input options are available for a language, click the + button next to it.

- **General tab.** In order to even use Windows Vista, you must have an input language. The default is US English. If yours is different, then choose it from the drop-down list. This is the language that Vista will use to communicate with you, and the standard language for your keyboard.

  To change your keyboard language and/or the keyboard layout, click Add, and then scroll to the language of your choice. (Expand the + buttons to see the available keyboard layouts. For English, the traditional QWERTY layout is the factory setting, but you can choose from several Dvorak offerings.)

Once you have selected your keyboard layouts, you need to access them. There are two ways to manage and switch between keyboard layouts: the Language bar, and creating keyboard combinations.

- **Language bar.** The Language bar is a floating toolbar that lets you switch input languages the fly; it appears automatically as soon as you add more than one language or keyboard layout (or when you use handwriting or speech recognition). The options on this tab can make the Language bar transparent, display text labels, and even add additional Language bar icons in the taskbar. See page 102 for more on the Language bar.

- **Advanced Key Settings.** On this tab, you can set up a keyboard combination to use to switch between layouts. The factory setting is the left Alt key+Shift, which scrolls through your layouts sequentially with each press, but you can also assign a combination to each specific layout.

Administrative

The "Change system locale" button on this tab lets you specify which language handles error messages and the occasional dialog box. (Just changing your input language may not do the trick.)

The "Copy to reserved account" button lets the newly configured language settings apply to new user accounts, so anyone who gets a new account on this computer will have your language, format, and keyboard settings conveniently available to them.

Scanners and Cameras

This icon isn't a program at all; it's a shortcut to the Scanners and Cameras window (see Figure 8-13), where there's an icon for each digital camera or scanner you've installed.

Fortunately, Vista largely automates the operation of these gadgets once you've hooked them up. Still, it's nice to have a central window that contains their icons, so that, if nothing else, you can select them to examine their properties. See Chapter 17 for details on scanning in Vista.

Security Center

Chapter 10 covers this command center in detail.

Sound

In Vista, the Sound dialog box has been simplified. It now contains only three tabs that control every aspect of your microphone and speakers: Playback, Record, and Sounds. See Figure 8-14.

Playback and Recording tabs

These tabs simply contain the icons for each attached sound device. To change a device's settings, select it, and then click Configure.

If you are configuring an output ("playback") device like a speaker or headset, then you get a quick wizard that lets you set the speaker configuration (stereo or quadraphonic, for example). If you're configuring a microphone ("recording"), then you're taken to the Speech Recognition page, where you can set up your microphone.

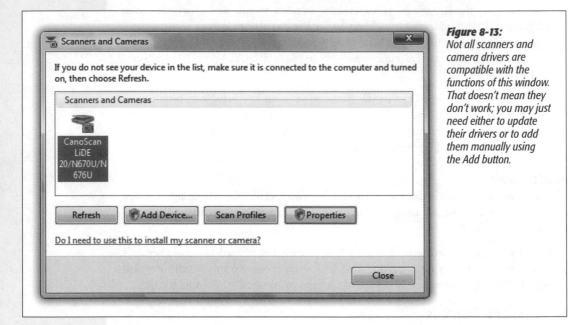

Figure 8-13:
Not all scanners and camera drivers are compatible with the functions of this window. That doesn't mean they don't work; you may just need either to update their drivers or to add them manually using the Add button.

Sounds tab

Windows Vista comes with a new, freshly composed suite of little sound effects—beeps, musical ripples, and chords—that play when you turn on the PC, trigger an error message, empty the Recycle Bin, and so on. And if you like, you can hear them on many other occasions, such as when you open or exit a program, open a menu, restore a window, and so on. This tab lets you specify which sound effect plays for which situation (Figure 8-15).

See the Program list of system events? A speaker icon represents the occasions when a sound will play. If you click the name of some computer event (say, Low Battery Alert), you can:

- Remove a sound from the event by choosing (None) from the Sounds drop-down list.

- Change an assigned sound, or add a sound to an event that doesn't have one, by clicking the Browse button and choosing a new sound file from the list in the Open dialog box.

Tip: When you click the Browse button, Vista opens the Local Disk (C:)→Windows→Media folder, which contains the .wav files that provide sounds. If you drag .wav files into this Media folder, they become available for use as Windows sound effects. Many people download .wav files from the Internet and stash them in the Media folder to make their computing experience quirkier, more fun, and richer in *Austin Powers* sound snippets.

When you select a sound, its filename appears in the Sounds drop-down list. Click the triangular Play button to the right of the box to hear the sound.

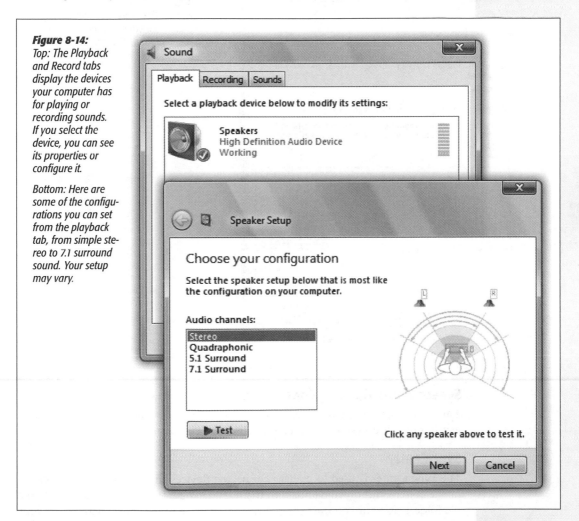

Figure 8-14:
Top: The Playback and Record tabs display the devices your computer has for playing or recording sounds. If you select the device, you can see its properties or configure it.

Bottom: Here are some of the configurations you can set from the playback tab, from simple stereo to 7.1 surround sound. Your setup may vary.

Tip: Each set of sounds is called a sound *scheme*. Sometimes the sound effects in a scheme are even sonically related. (Perhaps the collection is totally hip-hop, classical, or performed on a kazoo.) To switch schemes, use the "Sound scheme" pop-up menu.

You can also define a new scheme of your own. Start by assigning individual sounds to events, and then click the Save As button to save your collection under a name that you create.

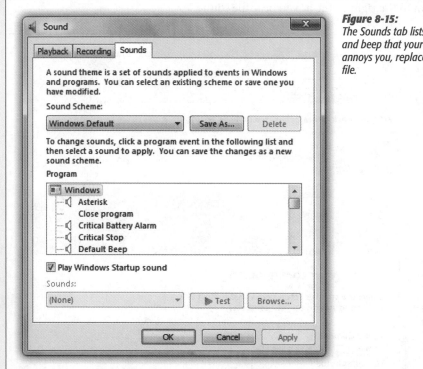

Figure 8-15:
The Sounds tab lists every single bing, bong, and beep that your computer makes. If one annoys you, replace it with your own .wav file.

Speech Recognition Options

This little program, enhanced for Windows Vista, lets you set up all the speech-related features of Windows. See Chapter 6 for complete details.

Sync Center

The Sync Center is used to manage connected devices (like smartphones or palmtops), upload and download data to them, and synchronize their files with offline file folders on your computer. (Finally, an easy place to get those pictures off your Bluetooth phone!)

For details, see Chapter 19.

System

This advanced control panel window is the same one that appears when you right-click your Computer icon and choose Properties from the shortcut menu (or press ⊞+Break key). It's been revamped for Windows Vista, but still contains the various settings that identify every shred of circuitry and equipment inside, or attached to, your PC.

When you open the System icon in Control Panel, you're taken to the System window (Figure 8-16). Here you can find out:

Figure 8-16:
The System window is a one-stop shop for all things computer-related. From your hardware (and what Vista thinks of it) to your product ID key, System's got you covered.

- **What edition of Vista is installed on your computer.** As you know, Vista comes in several editions. Not all editions are made equal; if you're flailing to find some feature that you could have sworn is supposed to be in Vista, it's good to check here. You might find out that the feature you want is available only on higher-priced versions.

- **Your PC's performance rating.** See page 20.

- **The model name and speed of your PC's processor chip** (such as Pentium 4, 2.6 GHz).

- **How much memory your PC has.** That's a very helpful number to know, particularly if you need to improve your computer's speed.

- **Your computer's name, domain or workgroup,** which can be modified with the Change settings. Remember, your computer name and description are primarily useful on a network, since that's how other people will identify your computer. Unless you tell it otherwise, Vista names your computer after your login name, something like Casey Robbins-PC.

- **Whether or not your operating system is activated.** For more on Activation, check Appendix A.

- **What the Product ID key is for your system.** Every legal copy of Vista has a Product ID Key—a long serial number that's required to activate Microsoft software. For more information about Product ID keys, see Appendix A.

Tip: In the Windows Activation section, you can do something unprecedented (and this is a really good thing): you can change your product key without having to reinstall your operating system. Now you can change your product ID simply by choosing to Change product key in the System window. That's progress.

At the left side of the window, you'll find a few links:

- **Device Manager.** This very powerful console lists every component of your PC: CD-ROM, Modem, Mouse, and so on. Double-clicking a component's name (or clicking the + symbol) discloses the brand and model of that component. For more on the Device Manager, see Chapter 18.

- **Remote Settings.** To read about Remote Assistance—the feature that lets a technical help person connect to your PC (via the Internet) to help you troubleshoot—turn to page 178.

- **System Protection.** This link takes you to the System Protection tab in the System dialog box. Here, you can keep track of the automatic system restores (snapshot backups of a system), or even create a new restore point. And if your computer has begun to act like it is possessed, you can go here to restore it to a previous restore point's state. Check out Chapter 22 for more details.

- **Advanced System Settings.** Clicking this link opens the Advanced tab of the System Properties dialog box. This tab is nothing more than a nesting place for four buttons that open other dialog boxes—some of which aren't "advanced" in the least.

The first Settings button opens the **Performance Options** dialog box, described in Chapter 20. The second Settings button opens the **User Profiles** box, which is covered in Chapter 23. The third Settings button opens a **Startup and Recovery** window. It contains advanced options related to *dual-booting* (Appendix A) and what happens when the system crashes.

Finally, the **Environment Variables** button opens a dialog box that will get only technically minded people excited. It identifies, for example, the path to your Windows folder and the number of processors your PC has. If you're not in the computer-administration business, avoid making change here.

Tablet PC Settings

This applet is all about managing a Tablet PC, one of those touchscreen laptop thingies. Here, you'll find settings that focus on tablet display orientation and calibration, handwriting recognition, and configuring pen input. If you don't have a Tablet PC, this dialog box is not for you. Otherwise, flip to Chapter 19.

Taskbar and Start Menu

This program controls every conceivable behavior of the taskbar and Start menu. You can read all about these options—the same ones that appear when you right-click the taskbar or the Start button and choose Properties from the shortcut menu—in Chapters 1 and 2.

Text to Speech

Text to Speech opens the Speech Properties dialog box. (You can also get here from the Speech Recognition applet.)

Here's where you configure the voice of Windows—the robotic voice, called Microsoft Anna—that you hear any time Windows reads text aloud.

The catch, of course, is that Windows never *does* read text aloud, except when you're using Narrator (page 269)—and Narrator has its own set of voice-selection controls. Microsoft Word *can* read text to you, however, and for that reason, you may be happy to know that you can specify Anna's rate of speaking (or that of the other Vista voice options) using this dialog box.

User Accounts

This control panel is the master switch and control center for the user-accounts feature described in Chapter 23. If you're the only one who uses your PC, you can (and should) ignore it.

Welcome Center

The Welcome Center, a new Vista feature, is the window that welcomes you every single time you log in (until you turn off the "Run at startup" checkbox). This window conveniently displays how to get started with Vista and pay Microsoft for more products and services. For a more detailed look at this window and its offerings, see Chapter 1.

(Why is this even in the Control Panel? Well, let's not be nit-picky.)

Windows CardSpace

Ever have to fill out a form on the Internet—name, address, email address—only to go to a different site that requests exactly the same information?

Of course you have. Everyone has, and it's annoying as heck.

CardSpace is Microsoft's attempt to solve that duplication-of-effort problem. You're supposed to create a profile containing this kind of information, like a digital ID card. You show your card at a site, and the site gets your information off of the card, saving you all that retyping.

Before you get too excited, though, there is a catch. CardSpace works only with Web sites that are, ahem, CardSpace-compatible—and there aren't many of them yet.

When you double-click the Windows CardSpace icon the first time, an introductory window appears to let you know what CardSpace is for. The second window actually manages your information (Figure 8-17).

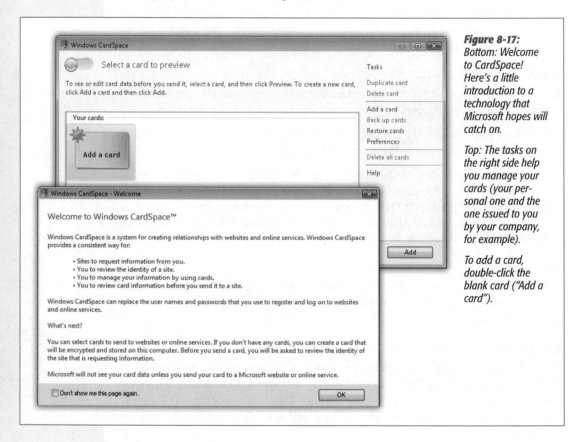

Figure 8-17:
Bottom: Welcome to CardSpace! Here's a little introduction to a technology that Microsoft hopes will catch on.

Top: The tasks on the right side help you manage your cards (your personal one and the one issued to you by your company, for example).

To add a card, double-click the blank card ("Add a card").

CardSpace handles two kinds of information cards: Personal and Managed. Personal cards store your name, email, address, phone, birthday, and so on. You can even add a photo if you wish.

Managed cards are cards given to you by a business or institution, like a bank or credit card company. They contain some information about you, but mostly they point at a company that is managing the card (and is allowed to have a private bit of information, like a credit card number). When you use a Managed card in a transaction with a Web site, the site retrieves private information (such as a credit card number) from the company that issued the CardSpace card. It confirms that you are who you say you are, have the right to use the card, and the right to use the private information the managing company has for you.

Windows Defender

Windows Defender is Microsoft's anti-spyware product, built into Windows Vista (and available for free for Windows XP). For an extensive look at what it can do for you, see Chapter 9.

Windows Firewall

In this age of digital technology, when most people's computers are connected at all times to the Internet (and therefore always exposed and vulnerable to the Internet), it is a good and reasonable idea to have a firewall protecting your computer from possible attacks and exploitation. To learn more about Windows Firewall, see Chapter 10.

Windows Mobility Center

The Windows Mobility Center icon appears only if you have a laptop. It (the Mobility Center, not the laptop) is described on page 572.

Windows Sidebar Properties

Windows Sidebar is the strip of Internet-savvy little gadget programs that's lovingly described on page 211.

POWER USERS' CLINIC

CardSpace Security Matters

As you can see, CardSpace cards can be a serious security worry. Fortunately, Vista lets you back up, restore, and lock the cards.

Locking a card means assigning it a password (a PIN, or personal identification number), so nobody can open or send it without authentication. To lock a card, select it in the CardSpace window. Then click Preview at the bottom of the window (or double-click the card).

On the right side of the Card Details window, under Tasks, click "Lock this card." You're now offered the chance to enter your password; it can be numbers, letters, or symbols. After entering the password (PIN), click the Lock button.

Backing up the card means saving an encrypted copy of it in a file somewhere of your choosing. This should be a very closely guarded location. Cards that have been backed up are encrypted with a password that must be at least eight characters long. Without the password, it cannot be restored. Ever.

To back up a card, click "Back up cards," put a checkmark next to the card (or cards) you want to back up, click Continue, and then navigate to the folder where you want to save the encrypted file of the card. Don't forget to name the file something that you will remember. Finally, click Backup and enter the backup password. Do not forget where you put the backup, what it is called, and what the password is.

Restoring a card means finding the backup of the card and restoring it to the CardSpace for access.

To Restore a card, click "Restore cards," and Browse to wherever you stored the card backup. Once you've selected your backup, click Continue, enter the password to decrypt it, and click Continue to bring up the Restore Cards window. If the card you want to restore is the one in the window (it could be the wrong one; it happens), click the Restore button to restore it to the CardSpace window.

Windows SideShow

As described in Chapter 19, Windows SideShow is a secondary screen, like a tiny text-only display on specially made SideShow-compatible laptops or desktop keyboards. It's designed to offer quick lookups of your email, calendar, Internet news feeds, and so on—without even having to power up the laptop itself.

Microsoft fervently hopes that a cornucopia of SideShow-compatible laptops and keyboards (and cellphones and palmtops, for that matter) will hit the market eventually.

This applet lets you configure which gadgets (mini-programs) are available for displaying on that little screen.

Windows Update

Because Windows is a constant work in progress, Microsoft frequently releases updates, fixes, patches, and drivers, in hopes of constantly improving your computer's speed and security all the time (or at least one Tuesday a month). Windows Update is the tool used to acquire, install, and track those useful fixes. For a more in-depth look at Windows Update, see Chapter 20.

3

Part Three:
Vista Online

Chapter 9: Hooking Up to the Internet

Chapter 10: Online Security

Chapter 11: Internet Explorer 7

Chapter 12: Windows Mail

Hooking Up to the Internet

Plenty of people buy a PC to crunch numbers, scan photos, or cultivate their kids' hand-eye coordination. But for millions of people, Reason One for using a PC is to get on the Internet. Few computer features have the potential to change your life as profoundly as the World Wide Web and email.

If you upgraded to Windows Vista from an earlier version of Windows, then you can already get online, as the Vista installer is thoughtful enough to preserve your old Internet settings. (So is Windows Easy Transfer, described in Appendix A.)

Broadband Connections (Cable Modems and DSL)
All Versions

A growing fraction of the world's Internet citizens get online over *broadband* connections—that is, high-speed connections like cable modems and DSL boxes. These contraptions offer gigantic advantages over dial-up modems. For example:

- **Speed.** These modems operate at 5 to 50 times the speed of a traditional dial-up modem. For example, you might wait 5 minutes to download a 2 MB file with a standard modem—a job that would take about 10 *seconds* with a cable modem.

- **No dialing.** You're hooked up permanently, full time, so you don't waste time connecting or disconnecting—ever. You're *always* online.

- **No weekends lost to setup.** A representative from the phone company (DSL) or cable TV company (cable modems) generally comes to your home or office to install the cable modem or DSL box and configure Windows to use it.

• **Possible savings.** At this writing, cable modems and DSL services cost $30 to $45 a month. That includes the Internet account for which you'd ordinarily pay $20 if you signed up for a traditional ISP. And since you're connecting to the Internet via cable TV wires or unused signal capacity on your telephone lines, you may save even more money by canceling the second phone line you were using for dialup.

Virtually all cable TV companies offer cable modem service, and most phone companies offer DSL (depending on how far you live from the central office).

It's also worth noting that cable modems and DSL modems aren't *always* blazing fast; for example, DSL modems may be slower the farther away you are from the telephone company.

Even so, these devices are always faster than a dial-up modem.

Tip: Technically, neither cable modems nor DSL modems are *modems,* since they don't *mo*dulate or *demo*dulate anything. (That's where the term modems comes from: they convert data into bursts of sound.) But most people call them modems anyway.

So how do you get online once you've got one of these services? You don't—you're *already* online, always and forever (except when the service goes out). Just open up your Web browser, email program, chat program, or whatever—and it just works.

Wireless Networks
All Versions

A broadband connection like a cable modem or DSL is heaven, but it's not the penthouse floor of heaven. These days, the ultimate bliss is connecting without wires, from anywhere in your house or building—or, if you're a laptop warrior, someone *else's* house or building, like Starbucks, McDonald's, airport lounges, hotel lobbies, and anywhere else that a WiFi Internet "hot spot" has been set up.

Those are places where somebody has set up an *WiFi access point* (or base station), which is a glorified antenna for their cable modem or DSL box. Any computer that's been equipped with a corresponding wireless networking card (as most new laptops are these days) can hop online at high speed with only a couple of clicks.

Tip: Whenever you try to get online, Windows Vista automatically hunts for a working connection—wired or wireless. That's a blessing for laptops. When you're at the office plugged into an Ethernet cable, you get the security and speed of a wired network. When you're in some hotel-lobby hot spot, and your laptop can't find the Ethernet cable, it automatically hops onto the wireless network, if possible.

(And how does the dial-up modem enter into all this? That's up to you. Open Internet Options in your Control Panel, click the Connections tab, and turn on, for example, "Dial whenever a network connection is not present" or "Never dial a connection." Keep the "Never dial" option in mind if the Connect dialup dialog box starts popping up every time your WiFi signal hiccups.)

For the basics of setting up your own wireless network, see Chapter 24. But for details on connecting to someone else's wireless network (using a laptop in a hotel lobby, for example), see Figure 9-1.

Tip: In the delightful event that more than one hot spot is available at once, you can tell Windows which ones you want to connect to first. Choose Start→Network; in the toolbar, click "Network and Sharing Center." From the links at left, click "Manage wireless networks" to see the list of all your WiFi networks' names. Drag the networks' names up or down in the list to change their preferred connection order.

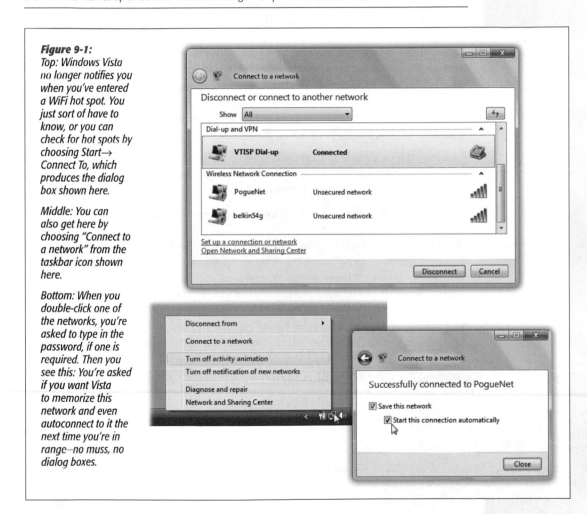

Figure 9-1:
Top: Windows Vista no longer notifies you when you've entered a WiFi hot spot. You just sort of have to know, or you can check for hot spots by choosing Start→ Connect To, which produces the dialog box shown here.

Middle: You can also get here by choosing "Connect to a network" from the taskbar icon shown here.

Bottom: When you double-click one of the networks, you're asked to type in the password, if one is required. Then you see this: You're asked if you want Vista to memorize this network and even autoconnect to it the next time you're in range—no muss, no dialog boxes.

Dial-Up Connections
All Versions

High-speed Internet is where it's at, baby! But there are plenty of reasons why you may be among the 50 percent of the Internet population that connects via dial-up modem, slow though it is. Dial-up is a heck of a lot less expensive than broadband.

And its availability is incredible—you can find a phone jack in almost any room in the civilized world, in places where the closest Ethernet or WiFi network is miles away.

To get online by dial-up, you need a dial-up *account*. You sign up with a company called an Internet service provider (or *ISP*, as insiders and magazines inevitably call them).

Note: America Online (AOL) is still a good avenue for novices and parents of young children, thanks to its extensive parental controls and a lot of freebies. Its services, pages, and tools are free now, as long as you provide your own ISP. Or you can sign up for AOL's own dial-up ISP service for $10 a month.

National ISPs like EarthLink and AT&T have local telephone numbers in every U.S. state and many other countries. If you don't travel much, you may not need such broad coverage. Instead, you may be able to save money by signing up for a local or regional ISP. In fact, you can find ISPs that are absolutely free (if you're willing to look at ads), or that cost as little as $4 per month (if you'll promise not to call for tech support). Google can be your friend here.

Even if you have a cable modem or DSL, you can generally add dial-up access to the same account for another few bucks a month. You'll be happy to have that feature if you travel a lot (unless your cable modem comes with a *really* long cord).

In any case, dialing the Internet is a local call for most people.

Tip: The Internet is filled with Web sites that list, describe, and recommend ISPs. To find such directories, visit Google and search for *ISP listings.* One of the best Web-based listings, for example, can be found at *www.boardwatch.com.* (Of course, until you've actually got your Internet account working, you'll have to conduct this research on a PC that *is* online, like the free terminals available at most public libraries.)

Microsoft no longer tries to steer you to its own MSN service, as it did in Windows XP. Instead, Vista expects that you've contacted an ISP on your own. It assumes that

---

GEM IN THE ROUGH

Cellular Wireless

WiFi hot spots are fast and usually cheap—but they're hot *spots.* Beyond 150 feet away, you're offline.

No wonder laptop luggers across America are getting into *cellular* Internet services. All of the big cellphone companies offer PC cards or ExpressCards that let your laptop get online at high speed *anywhere* in major cities. No hunting for a coffee shop; with a cellular Internet service, you can check your email while zooming down the road in a taxi. (Outside of the metropolitan areas, you can still get online wirelessly, though much more slowly.)

Verizon and Sprint offer the fastest such networks, using a technology called EV-DO. Cingular and T-Mobile's offerings are much slower.

So why isn't the world beating a path to this delicious technology's door? Because it's expensive—$30 to $60 a month on top of your phone bill.

You may also be able to get your laptop online by connecting it to your cellphone with a cable—a lower-priced, slower option. Ask your cellphone carrier.

you're equipped with either (a) a setup CD from that company, or (b) a user name, password, and dial-up phone number from that ISP, which is pretty much all you really need to get online.

Your only remaining task is to plug that information into Windows. (And, of course, to plug your computer into the phone jack on the wall.)

Here's how you do it.

1. **Choose Start→Network.**

   The Network window opens.

2. **On the toolbar, click Network and Sharing Center. In the task list at left, click "Set up a connection or network."**

   It's one of the links at the left side of the window. In any case, the "Choose a connection option" dialog box opens.

3. **Click "Set up a dial-up connection" (Figure 9-2, top), and then click Next.**

   If your modem isn't hooked up to a phone line, you get a "could not detect a dial-up modem" dialog box. Either fix the problem, or click "Set up a connection anyway." Windows will save your settings, and you can connect later, once you've solved your hardware problems.

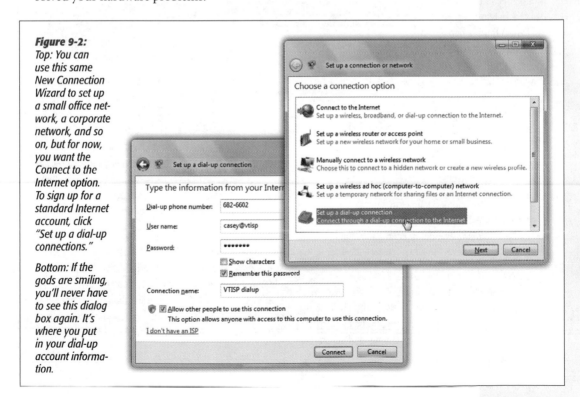

Figure 9-2:
Top: You can use this same New Connection Wizard to set up a small office network, a corporate network, and so on, but for now, you want the Connect to the Internet option. To sign up for a standard Internet account, click "Set up a dial-up connections."

Bottom: If the gods are smiling, you'll never have to see this dialog box again. It's where you put in your dial-up account information.

4. Fill in the phone number, user name, and password your ISP provided
(Figure 9-2, bottom).

You can call your ISP for this information, or consult the literature delivered by
postal mail when you signed up for an ISP account.

Note: *The checkbox called "Allow other people to use this connection" refers to the Windows* accounts
*feature described in Chapter 23, in which various people who share the same computer keep their worlds
of information and settings separate by signing in each time they use the machine. It's asking you: "Is this
the Internet account you want this PC to use no matter who's logged in at the moment?"*

The First Time: Home, Work, or Public Location

This gets a little technical, so hold onto your hat.

The first time you connect to a new network—the first time
you use a wireless hot spot, first time you connect to a dial-
up ISP, first time you plug into an office network—you see
this dialog box.

It's asking you to categorize the network you've
just joined. Is this a *public*
network, like a coffee-
shop hot spot? Is it a Work
network—a corporate net-
work that's likely to be
staffed by security-con-
scious network geeks?
Or is it your own home
network, where you don't
have to worry so much
about hackers?

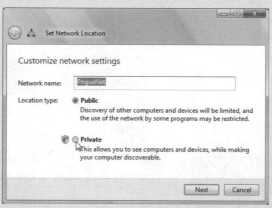

The choice you make here has absolutely nothing to do with
the physical *location,* no matter what the dialog box says.
Instead, it tells Windows how much *security* to apply to the
network you've just joined.

If you choose Public, for example, Windows makes your
computer invisible to other computers nearby. (Technically,
it turns off the Vista feature called *network discovery.*) That's
not ideal for file sharing, printer sharing, and so on—but

it means that hackers have a harder time "sniffing" the
airwaves to detect your presence.

If you say a network is Public, you may be visited quite a
bit by the "Unblock?" messages from the Windows firewall.
That's Windows just be-
ing insecure, asking for
permission every time any
program (like a chat pro-
gram) tries to get through
the firewall.

If those messages are
driving you crazy, maybe
you should change the
location to the Home or
Work settings, which are
less paranoid. In these "location" settings, network
discovery is turned on, so
you and your PCs can see each other on the network and
share files, music, printers, and so on.

To change a connection from one location (that is, security
scenario) to another, connect to the network in question.
Choose Start→Network. On the toolbar, click Network and
Sharing Center. Click Customize, and then click either Public
or Private (meaning home and office networks). Authenticate
yourself (page 191). Click Next, and then Close.

If you were given a setup CD instead, click "I don't have an ISP," and then click "Use the CD I received from an ISP." Insert the disc when you're asked.

Otherwise, complete the final step.

5. Click Connect.

Assuming a phone line is plugged in, your PC dials and makes its connection with the mother ship.

6. Make a decision: is this network Public or Private?

When the "Choose a location" dialog box appears, click Home, Work, or Public after you've read what the heck that means (see the box on the facing page). (Hint—"Public" is the most secure option for dial-up.)

Connection Management
All Versions

No matter what crazy combination of Internet connections you've accumulated on your computer, Windows represents each one as a *connection icon.* You can view them, rename them, change their settings, or just admire them by opening the window shown at top in Figure 9-3.

To get there, choose Start→Network. On the toolbar, click Network and Sharing Center. Click "Manage network connections" (in the left-side task pane).

Tip: If you travel frequently between the same couple of cities, consider making a different dial-up connection icon for each city—with the local access phone number already stored in each. To do that, right-click the first dial-up icon (Figure 9-3); from the shortcut menu, choose Create Copy. Authenticate yourself (page 191), then double-click the newly hatched icon to change its built-in phone number.

These icons are handy because their Properties dialog boxes are crammed with useful information. A dial-up connection icon stores your name, password, phone number, and so on; a broadband icon stores various technical Internet connection details.

In these and other situations, you need a way to make manual changes to your connections. Here, for example, is how you might change the Internet settings for a cable modem, DSL, or wireless connection.

1. Right-click a connection icon; from the shortcut menu, choose Properties. Authenticate yourself (page 191).

(This assumes that you've started in the Network Connections window shown in Figure 9-3.) You get the dialog box shown at top in Figure 9-4, bottom.

2. Double-click the listing that says Internet Protocol Version 4.

An even more intimidating dialog box now appears (Figure 9-4, top).

3. Type in your account information.

Most of the time, your cable or phone company has instructed you to turn on "Obtain an IP address automatically" and "Obtain DNS server address automatically." You don't know how lucky you are—you've been saved from typing in all the other numbers in this dialog box. Otherwise, turn on "Use the following IP address" and type in the appropriate numbers. Do the same with "Use the following DNS server addresses."

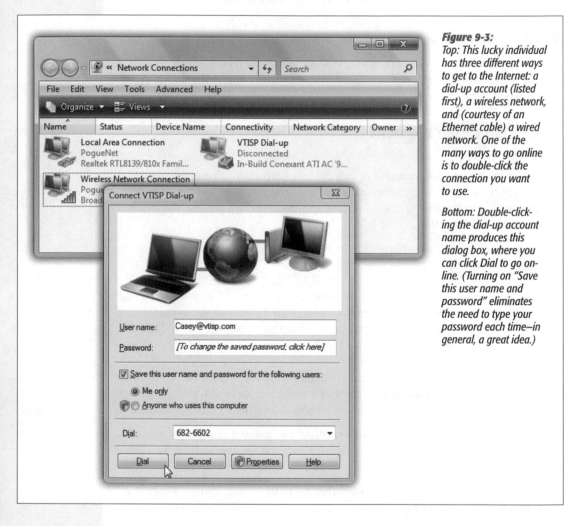

Figure 9-3:
Top: This lucky individual has three different ways to get to the Internet: a dial-up account (listed first), a wireless network, and (courtesy of an Ethernet cable) a wired network. One of the many ways to go online is to double-click the connection you want to use.

Bottom: Double-clicking the dial-up account name produces this dialog box, where you can click Dial to go online. (Turning on "Save this user name and password" eliminates the need to type your password each time—in general, a great idea.)

4. **Click OK.**

   As a courtesy, Vista doesn't make you restart the computer in order for your new network settings to take effect.

The Notification Area Icon

The Network icon in the notification area (Figure 9-5) is a handy status meter, no matter how you're getting online. If it bears a red X, for example, it means that your PC isn't connected to any network at all.

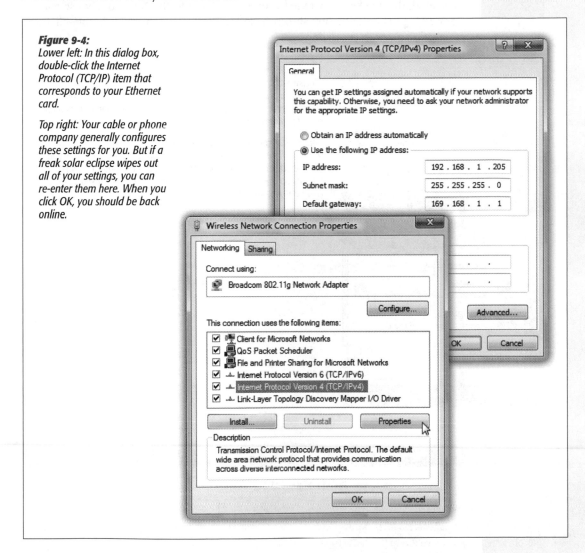

Figure 9-4:
Lower left: In this dialog box, double-click the Internet Protocol (TCP/IP) item that corresponds to your Ethernet card.

Top right: Your cable or phone company generally configures these settings for you. But if a freak solar eclipse wipes out all of your settings, you can re-enter them here. When you click OK, you should be back online.

Details on Dial-Up

All Versions

If you enjoy a full-time Internet connection like a cable modem, DSL, or some wireless variation thereof, you're constantly online. Skip to the next chapter.

If you have a dial-up modem, however, connecting and disconnecting are manual operations.

Manual Connections

In general, the quickest way to tell your PC to dial into the Net is to choose Start→ Connect To. The dialog box shown in Figure 9-1 (top) appears; double-click the connection's row in the dialog box.

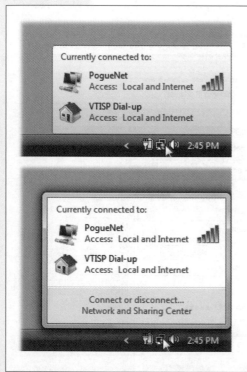

Figure 9-5:
Top: If you point to this icon without clicking, you'll see a tooltip showing your WiFi signal strength and, if you're dialing up, whether or not you're connected.

Bottom: If you click it, you get additional links to key control centers. And if you right-click it, you get a shortcut menu that lets you disconnect, troubleshoot, or display "activity animation"—blinky screens on the two tiny computers, illustrating the transfer of data. (Figure 9-1 shows that one.)

IP Addresses and You

Every computer connected to the Internet, even temporarily, has its own exclusive *IP address* (IP stands for Internet Protocol). When you set up your own Internet account, as described on these pages, you're asked to type in this string of numbers. As you'll see, an IP address always consists of four numbers separated by periods.

Some PCs with high-speed Internet connections (cable modem, DSL) have a permanent, unchanging address called a *fixed* or *static* IP address. Other computers get as-

signed a new address each time they connect (a *dynamic* IP address). That's always the case, for example, when you connect via a dial-up modem. (If you can't figure out whether your machine has a static or fixed address, ask your Internet service provider.)

If nothing else, dynamic addresses are more convenient in some ways, since you don't have to type numbers into the Internet Protocol (TCP/IP) Properties dialog box shown in Figure 9-4.

The Connect To Dial-up dialog box appears (Figure 9-3, bottom). Just press Enter, or click Dial, to go online.

Tip: You can also create a desktop shortcut for your connection. Right-drag its icon out of the window shown in Figure 9-6 (top) and onto the desktop. When you release the mouse button, choose Create Shortcut(s) Here from the shortcut menu. Now just double-click the shortcut whenever you feel the urge to surf. (You can even drag the resulting icon onto your Quick Launch toolbar (page 101).

Automatic Dialing

It's important to understand that when your PC dials, it simply opens up a connection to the Internet. But aside from tying up the phone line, your PC doesn't actually *do* anything until you launch an Internet program, such as an email program or a Web browser. By itself, making your PC dial the Internet is no more useful than dialing a phone number and then not saying anything.

Therefore, using the Internet is generally a two-step procedure: First, open the connection; second, open a program.

Fortunately, Windows offers a method of combining these two steps. You can make the dialing/connecting process begin automatically whenever you launch an Internet program.

To turn on this option, just open your Web browser and try to Web surf. When the PC discovers that it's not, in fact, online, it displays the Dial-up Connection dialog box at top in Figure 9-6. Turn on the "Connect automatically" checkbox, and then click Connect.

From now on, whenever you use a feature that requires an Internet connection, your PC dials automatically. (Examples: specifying a Web address in a window's Address bar, clicking the Send and Receive button in your email program, clicking a link in the Windows Help system, and so on.)

FREQUENTLY ASKED QUESTION

Laptop's Lament: Away from the Cable Modem

When I'm home, I connect my laptop to my cable modem. But when I'm on the road, of course, I have to use my dial-up ISP. Is there any way to automate the switching between these two connection methods?

If there weren't, do you think your question would have even appeared in this chapter?

The feature you're looking for is in the Control Panel. In Classic view, double-click Internet Options, click the Connections tab, and then turn on "Dial whenever a network connection is not present."

From now on, your laptop will use its dial-up modem only when it realizes that it isn't connected to your cable modem.

Disconnecting

Unless you intervene, a dial-up connection never hangs up (unless your ISP hangs up *for* it). It will continue to tie up your phone line until the other family members hunt it down, hours later, furious and brandishing wire cutters.

Therefore, it's worth taking a moment to configure your system so it won't stay online forever.

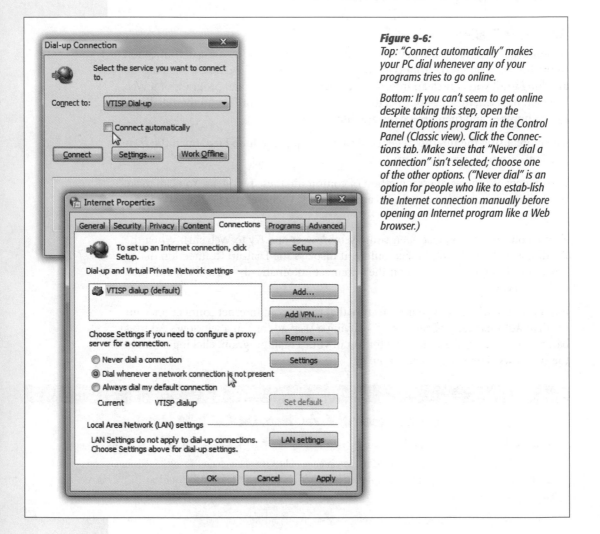

Figure 9-6:
Top: "Connect automatically" makes your PC dial whenever any of your programs tries to go online.

Bottom: If you can't seem to get online despite taking this step, open the Internet Options program in the Control Panel (Classic view). Click the Connections tab. Make sure that "Never dial a connection" isn't selected; choose one of the other options. ("Never dial" is an option for people who like to estab-lish the Internet connection manually before opening an Internet program like a Web browser.)

- **Disconnect manually.** When you're finished using the Internet, the quickest way to end the phone call is by right-clicking the little connection icon on your taskbar. Now choose Disconnect from the shortcut menu (Figure 9-5, bottom).

- **Disconnect automatically.** You can also set up your PC to hang up the phone automatically several minutes after your last activity online.

To find the necessary controls, right-click your connection icon. (A quick way to get to it: Choose Start→Connect To.) From the shortcut menu, choose Properties. Authenticate yourself (page 191).

In the resulting dialog box, click the Options tab. Near the middle of the box, you'll see a drop-down list called "Idle time before hanging up." You can set it to 1 minute, 10 minutes, 24 hours, or whatever.

Advanced Modem Settings

Because so many people consider the Internet such an important PC feature, Windows Vista lets you fine-tune its dialing, modem, and Internet settings to within an inch of their lives. You should consider the rest of this chapter optional—or power-user—reading.

To adjust the settings for your modem's dialing patterns, choose Start→Control Panel. In Classic view, double-click Phone and Modem Options. (See Chapter 8 for more on the Control Panel window.)

The very first time you open this box, you're asked to supply your local area code. When you click OK, you wind up in the dialog box shown in Figure 9-7. It has three major tabs, each serving important functions.

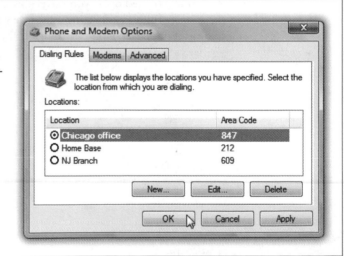

Figure 9-7:
This dialog box has two priorities: to establish rules for dialing out, and to define as many different sets of rules for dialing as you need. If you're setting up dialing properties for a desktop computer, you won't need to change these settings after the first successful call.

Here, for example, you can set up *dialing rules* that automatically dial a 1 or a 9 for an outside line, depending on where you are in your travels. You can even plug in calling-card numbers so that your Internet calls are billed to your boss.

For a complete description of these fairly obscure controls, visit this book's "Missing CD" page at *www.missingmanuals.com* and download the free bonus PDF document, "Dialing Rules.pdf."

Modems Tab

The second tab in the Phone and Modem Options program, called Modems, is simply a list of the modems currently connected to your PC. (Most people not in Oprah's tax bracket see only one modem listed here.)

Double-clicking a modem opens its Properties dialog box, which bursts with technical parameters for your modem. In general, you'll need to visit these dialog boxes only when troubleshooting, following the instructions of some telecommunications geek from your modem company. Two of them, however, are more generally useful:

- **Change the speaker volume.** The modern modem may have revolutionized computer communications, but the squealing sounds it makes could wake the dead—or, worse, the spouse. To turn the speaker off so you no longer hear the shrieks every time you dial, click the Modem tab, and then drag the Speaker volume slider to Off.

Tip: The slider affects the speaker volume only while it's dialing and making a connection to another computer. After the connection is established, the speaker *always* goes silent, so you don't have to listen to all the squawking noises that indicate data transmission.

- **Wait for the dial tone before dialing.** This checkbox (also on the Modem tab) is normally turned on. If you travel abroad with your laptop, however, you may experience trouble connecting if the foreign country's dial tone doesn't sound the same as it does back home. Turning off this checkbox often solves the problem.

Internet Security

I f it weren't for that darned Internet, personal computing would be a lot of fun. After all, it's the Internet that lets all those socially stunted hackers enter our machines, unleashing their viruses, setting up remote hacking tools, feeding us spyware, trying to trick us out of our credit-card numbers, and otherwise making our lives an endless troubleshooting session. It sure would be nice if they'd cultivate some other hobbies.

In the meantime, these low-lifes are doing astronomical damage to businesses and individuals around the world—along the lines of $100 billion a year (the cost to fight viruses, spyware, and spam).

A big part of the problem was the design of Windows itself. In the quaint old-fashioned days of 2000, when Windows XP was designed, these sorts of Internet attacks were far less common. Microsoft left open a number of back doors that were intended for convenience (for example, to let system administrators communicate with your PC from across the network) but wound up being exploited by hackers.

Microsoft wrote Windows Vista for a lot of reasons: to give Windows a cosmetic makeover, to give it up-to-date music and video features, to overhaul its networking plumbing—and, of course, to make money. But Job Number One was making Windows more secure. Evil strangers will still make every attempt to make your life miserable, but one thing is for sure: They'll have a much, much harder time of it.

Note: This chapter focuses on Vista's new self-protection features—all of them. It's only called "Internet Security" because, in fact, virtually all of the infectious unpleasantness that can befall a PC these days comes from the Internet. A PC that never goes online probably won't get infected.

So why is Internet Explorer (IE) the most popular hacking target? First, it's by far the most popular browser on the planet. Second, Internet Explorer includes hooks directly into Windows itself, so a hacker can wreak havoc on Windows by using Internet Explorer as a back door.

Lots of Vista's security improvements are invisible to you. They're deep in the plumbing, with no buttons or controls to show you. If you're scoring at home, they include features called:

- **Application isolation.** A program can't take over important tasks performed by Windows itself.

- **Service hardening.** Windows *services* are programs that run in the background: the print spooler that comes with Windows, virus checkers from other companies, and so on. Service hardening prevents rogue services (or services that have been surreptitiously modified by nasties from the Internet) from making changes to parts of the system they're not supposed to touch; for example, they can't change important system files or the Registry (Appendix B).

- **Protected Mode.** Protected Mode shields the operating system from actions taken by Internet Explorer or its add-ons. So even if a nasty piece of software breaks through all Internet Explorer's security features, it can't do harm to your PC, because Protected Mode locks IE inside a safe box. Put another way, what happens in Internet Explorer stays in Internet Explorer.

- **Address Space Layout Randomization.** When a program is running, it keeps a lot of information in system memory. Because many viruses and worms depend on their author's knowledge of *how* vulnerable programs keep that information organized, ASLR scrambles that information—not so much that the programs can't run—to makes it harder for them to break into your system.

- **Network Access Protection.** On a corporate domain network, this feature prevents you from connecting to an insufficiently protected PC on the network—one lacking virus protection, for example.

- **PatchGuard.** Prevents non-Microsoft software from touching the beating heart of Windows.

- **Code Integrity.** Software is checked before it runs to make sure it hasn't been modified somehow.

The rest of this chapter describes features that *aren't* invisible and automatic—the ones that you can control.

Note, however, that built-in security tools can't do the whole job of keeping your PC safe; you play a role, too. So keep in mind these basic tips before you or your family go online:

- **Don't trust a pretty face.** It doesn't take much expertise to build a snazzy-looking Web site. Just because a Web site looks trustworthy doesn't mean that you can trust it. If you're visiting a little-known Web site, be careful what you do there.

- **Don't download from sites you don't know.** The Web is full of free software offers. But that free software may, in fact, be spyware or other malware. (Malware is a general term for viruses, spyware, and other Bad Software.) So be very careful when downloading anything online.

- **Don't click pop-up ads.** Pop-up ads are more than mere annoyances; some of them, when clicked, download spyware to your PC. As you'll see later in this chapter, Internet Explorer includes a pop-up blocker, but it doesn't block all pop-ups. So to be safe, don't click.

With all that said, you're ready to find out how to keep yourself safe when you go online.

Security Center
All Versions

If you're looking for the best place to go for at-a-glance information about the current state of your Internet security, head to the Security Center, by choosing Control Panel→Security→Security Center, shown in Figure 10-1.

The main part of the screen tells you the state of firewall security, automatic updating, malware protection, and other security settings. Green means you're protected; yellow means you're partially protected; and red means that you're open to attack.

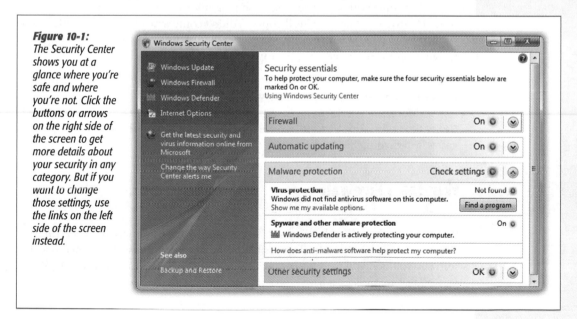

Figure 10-1:
The Security Center shows you at a glance where you're safe and where you're not. Click the buttons or arrows on the right side of the screen to get more details about your security in any category. But if you want to change those settings, use the links on the left side of the screen instead.

In the malware protection area, for example, you'll see green if you're running both Windows Defender (Vista's anti-spyware feature) and antivirus software; yellow if you're running only one of them; and red if neither one is turned on. For details, expand the panel by clicking the colored button or down arrow.

The Security Center isn't just a status display. It also alerts you (using a color-coded icon in the System Tray, plus a pop-up balloon) whenever any of your security settings drops to yellow or red. Double-click the icon to open the Security Center and find out what it's worried about.

Tip: If you, a competent and completely confident power user, would prefer that the Security Center stop nagging you and displaying its colored icons in the System Tray, you can shut it up. In the Security Center, click "Change the way Security Center alerts me." From the screen that appears, select "Don't notify me, but display the icon," or "Don't notify me and don't display the icon (not recommended)."

The Security Center is also a central control panel whose links let you change the most important Internet-related security settings: Windows Firewall, Windows Update, Windows Defender, and general Internet options. (They're all described in this chapter.)

Security Center and Antivirus

The Security Center alerts you when it discovers that you don't have antivirus software on your PC. Since Vista doesn't actually come with any antivirus software, you'll almost certainly see these software nags until you download and install one. (Yes, even with all of Vista's fortifications, it's not invulnerable, and you still need antivirus software.)

Some PCs come with a trial version of some antivirus program; you have to pay an annual fee to keep it up-to-date. If your PC didn't come with any antivirus software at all, or if you've upgraded your PC from an earlier version of Windows, getting some antivirus software should be at the top of your To Do list.

Important: Vista requires antivirus software written especially for Vista. Antivirus software from the Windows XP days won't work.

Tip: Installing antivirus software doesn't necessarily mean paying for it. Several very good antivirus programs are free for personal use, like Avast (*www.avast.com*).

Windows Firewall
All Versions

If you have a broadband, always-on connection, you're connected to the Internet 24 hours a day. It's theoretically possible for some cretin to use automated hacking software to flood you with files or take control of your machine. Fortunately, Vista's *firewall* feature puts up a barrier to such mischief.

The firewall acts as a gatekeeper between you and the Internet. It examines all Internet traffic, and lets through only communications that it knows are safe; all other traffic is turned away at the door.

Tip: Truth is, you may not technically need a software firewall like this. Do you have a *router* that distributes your Internet signal through the house (page 700)? If so, it probably also has a *hardware* firewall already protecting your entire network. Still, there's no harm in having both a hardware and software firewall in place.

How It Works

Every kind of electronic message sent to or from your PC—instant messaging, music sharing, file sharing, and so on—conducts its business on a specific communications channel, or *port*. Ports are numbered tunnels for certain kinds of Internet traffic.

The problem with Windows before Vista came along was that Microsoft left all of your ports *open* for your convenience—and, as it turns out, for the bad guys.` In Vista (and in Windows XP Service Pack 2), all the ports arrive on your PC *closed*.

The firewall blocks or permits signals based on a predefined set of rules. They dictate, for example, which programs are permitted to use your network connection, or which ports can be used for communications.

The big improvement in Vista's firewall was supposed to be that it protected both inbound and outbound traffic. (The Windows XP firewall handled only inbound traffic.)

Now, inbound signals are a much bigger threat than outgoing ones. Still, some spyware, Trojans, and malicious software "phones home"—that is, once secretly installed, it sends out an invisible note telling the world it's ready to be used to attack your PC. Some may try to attack other computers near it. And some turns your PC into a zombie: basically a spam relay station. Your PC could be pumping out millions of junk-mail messages a day, and you wouldn't even know it.

Shortly after Vista debuted, however, the geek community discovered an inconvenient truth about the Windows Vista Firewall: it does not, in fact, block those outbound connections. It's capable of doing so, but only when programmed by a professional. The bottom line: The Windows Firewall is a lot better than nothing. But for maximum protection, you should still install beefier firewall software from another company. (You can find free ones on the Web.)

You don't need to do anything to turn on the Windows Firewall. When you turn on Windows Vista, it's already at work. But the Windows Firewall *can* be turned off. To make sure that it's running properly, choose Control Panel→Security→Windows Firewall. If it's working properly, a green message tells you so. If it's turned off, a red message lets you know. To turn the firewall on and off, click Change settings, and make your selection.

Punching Through the Firewall

The firewall isn't always your friend. It can occasionally block a perfectly harmless program from communicating with the outside world—a chat program, for example.

Fortunately, whenever that happens, Windows lets you know with a message like the one shown in Figure 10-2. Most of the time, you'll know exactly what program it's talking about, because it's a program you just opened *yourself*. In other words, it's not some rogue spyware on your machine trying to talk to the mother ship. Click Unblock and get on with your life.

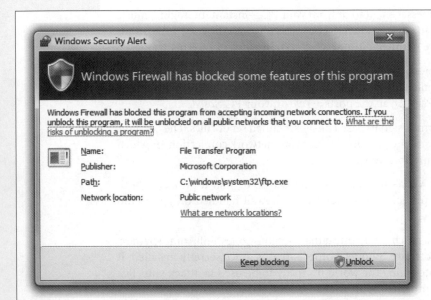

Figure 10-2:
From time to time, your life with Vista will be interrupted by this message. It's your firewall speaking. It's trying to tell you that a program is trying to get online, as though you didn't know. Most of the time, you can just hit Unblock and get on with your life.

Fine-Tuning the Firewall

If you're willing to root around in a little techie underbrush, you can learn a lot, and perfect the firewall, using Windows Firewall settings (Figure 10-3). Get there by going to Control Panel→Security→Windows Firewall→Change Settings, and then authenticate yourself (page 191). Here's what you can do with each tab:

- **General.** Here's where to turn the firewall on and off. You can also completely block all Internet access—for example, to make absolutely sure that nobody's tapping into your laptop when you're in a wireless coffee shop—by turning on "Block all incoming connections."

Tip: Plenty of companies sell more powerful software firewalls (that is, with more geeky options). Never use one at the same time you use the Windows Firewall, however; a troubleshooting nightmare could result. So if you're running a firewall like ZoneAlarm or Norton Personal Firewall, *turn off* the Windows Firewall. (Most firewall programs do that automatically when you install them, but it's a good idea to check.)

- **Exceptions.** Here's the tab to use if you're having problems with a program being blocked by the Windows Firewall. It lets you tell the Windows Firewall to make an "exception" for a particular program, and let it through.

A checkmark means that this program is allowed through the Windows Firewall. Scroll through and see if the problematic program is on the list. If it is, turn on its checkbox, and then click OK. If it's not on the list, click Add program, find and select the program, and then click OK to add it to the list.

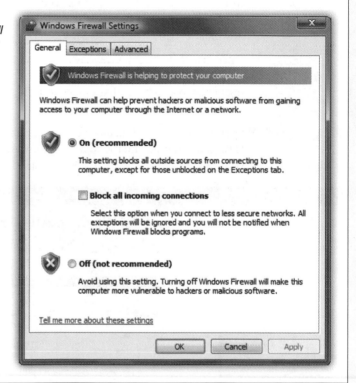

Figure 10-3:
The General screen of the Windows Firewall Settings screen lets you turn the firewall on and off, and even block all Internet access. You'll rarely have any reason to touch the other tabs. But if some program conflicts with the Firewall, head to the Exceptions tab to fix it. The Advanced tab lets you turn the firewall on and off for individual networks to which you connect, such as a home network or a wireless hot spot.

Finally, turn on its checkbox and click OK. It should now work fine with the Windows Firewall.

- **Advanced.** This tab lists all the networks for which the Windows Firewall is providing protection. If you connect to multiple networks, such as at hot spots, home, and so on, they should all be here; the checkmarks indicate which networks are being protected. As a general rule, it's a good idea for the Windows Firewall to protect all your networks.

Windows Defender

All Versions

Spyware is software that you don't know you have. You usually get it in one of two ways. First, a Web site may try to trick you into downloading it. You'll see what looks like an innocent button in what's actually a phony Windows dialog box, or maybe you'll get an empty dialog box—and clicking the Close box actually triggers the installation.

Second, you may get spyware by downloading a program that you *do* want—"cracked" software (commercial programs whose copy protection has been removed) is a classic example—without realizing that a secret program is piggybacking on the download.

Once installed, the spyware may make changes to important system files, install ads on your desktop (even when you're not online) or send information about your surfing habits to a Web site that blitzes your PC with pop-up ads related in some way to your online behavior.

Spyware can do much damage beyond simply tracking what you do on the Internet. It can, for example, hijack your home page or search page, so every time you open your browser, you wind up at a Web page that incapacitates your PC with a blizzard

---

POWER USERS' CLINIC

A More Powerful Way to Customize the Firewall

The Windows Firewall Settings screen gives you a good deal of control over how the Windows Firewall works. But it governs only inbound network traffic, not outbound. It also offers no way to create a log (a text-file record) of all attempts to contact your PC from the network or the Internet, which can be handy when you suspect that some nasty hacker has been visiting you in the middle of the night.

There is, however, an even more powerful Firewall control panel. In an effort to avoid terrifying novices, Microsoft has hidden it, but it's easy enough to open. It's called the Windows Firewall With Advanced Security applet.

To fire it up, type *wf.msc* into the Start menu's Search box, and then double-click the result. It lets you customize outbound as well as inbound connections. You can also make Windows Firewall create a log of all its activities, which you can later read using Notepad or another text editor.

---

of pop-ups. *Keylogger* spyware can record all of your keystrokes, passwords and all, and send them to a snooper.

Fortunately, Microsoft has provided, in Windows Vista, its first-ever anti-spyware program. It's called Windows Defender (Control Panel→Security→Windows Defender).

Note: Defender used to be called Microsoft AntiSpyware. Microsoft changed the name because Defender not only scans your PC looking for spyware, just like several free programs, but also monitors important corners of the operating system that are common spyware targets. The watched areas include startup programs, system preference settings, Internet Explorer settings and downloads, and so on.

Figure 10-4:
This screen tells when you last scanned for spyware, whether Defender found any spyware, and your daily scanning schedule. Pay particular attention to the "Definition version." This tells you how up-to-date your spyware definitions are. If they're more than a week old, use Windows Update (Chapter 20) to get the latest definitions.

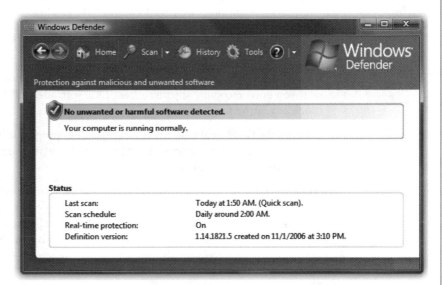

Is It Spyware or Adware?

Spyware has a less-malignant cousin called adware, and the line between the two types is exceedingly thin.

Adware is free software that displays ads (the free version of Eudora, for example). In order to target those ads to your interest, it may transmit reports on your surfing habits to its authors. (Windows Defender doesn't protect against adware.)

So what's the difference between adware and spyware? If it performs malicious actions, like incapacitating your PC with pop-ups, it's spyware for sure.

Proponents of adware say, "Hey—we've gotta put bread on our tables, too! Those ads are how you pay for your free software. Our software doesn't identify you personally when it reports on your surfing habits, so it's not really spyware."

But other people insist that any software that reports on your activities is spyware, no matter what.

Windows Defender protects you against spyware in two ways. First, it's a kind of silent sentinel that sits in the background, watching your system. When it detects a piece of spyware trying to install itself, Defender zaps it. Second, it scans your hard drive for infections every day, and removes what it finds.

You don't need to do anything to turn Windows Defender on. It runs every time you start Windows. And every night at 2 a.m., if your PC is turned on, Defender scans your system, killing any spyware it finds.

To see Windows Defenders' recent activities, select Control Panel→Security→Windows Defender, as shown in Figure 10-4. At a glance, you'll see if your PC is safe.

Most of the time, Windows Defender doesn't find any spyware. If it ever does, Windows lets you know. An alert message pops up and asks if you want to allow the questionable software to keep working, or instead remove it. Here's how you should respond:

- If the alert level is **Severe, High, or Medium,** let Windows Defender remove the spyware immediately.

- If the alert level is **Low,** read the message for details. If you don't like what you read, or if you don't recognize the publisher of the software, tell Windows Defender to block or remove the software.

- **Not yet classified** generally denotes a harmless program. If you recognize the software's name, let it run normally. If not, search the program's name with Google to help you decide whether to let it run or not.

For basic operations, that's all you need to know about Windows Defender. But there's a lot more you can dig into, and it's worthwhile to explore it. Across the top of the screen, you'll see four links: Home, Scan, History, and Tools. You know all about Home already; it's where you are when you first run the program, as shown in Figure 10-4. Here's what you need to know about the rest:

Scan

This link scans your PC for spyware. Click it to start a scan, or click the ▾ button to change the *kind* of scan. Your choices:

- **Quick Scan** is what Windows Defender does every night. It scans those parts of your PC most likely to be infected by spyware, plus any programs you're currently running. (Why would you run a Quick Scan if it already ran last night? Maybe because you've just installed a piece of software, or you've visited a dubious Web site.)

- **The Full Scan** is more thoroughgoing; it looks at every single file on all of your hard disks, as well as any programs currently running. If you suspect you've been infected by spyware, run the Full Scan to whack it. It takes considerably longer than a Quick Scan.

- **The Custom option** lets you specify which folders you want to scan, just in case you think spyware might be lurking in a non-obvious spot.

History

This tab offers a log of all the actions Windows Defender has taken (Figure 10-5). For each program it's taken action on, it lists the name, the alert level, the action it took, the date, and whether the action was successful. Click a listing to find out more details about it, like its location, file name, and description of why Defender considered the program suspicious.

Techies will be glad to see more rarefied information here, such as the Registry key each program uses.

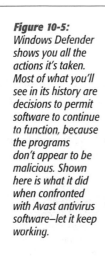

Figure 10-5:
Windows Defender shows you all the actions it's taken. Most of what you'll see in its history are decisions to permit software to continue to function, because the programs don't appear to be malicious. Shown here is what it did when confronted with Avast antivirus software—let it keep working.

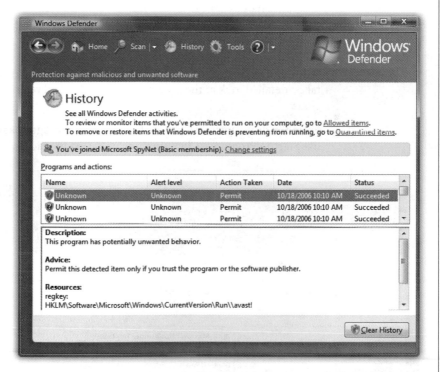

Tools

Here's where Microsoft has assembled Windows Defender's advanced tools:

- **Options.** Schedule how and when Windows Defender should run, and what actions it should take when it comes across suspicious software, among other options.

   The factory setting is to scan your system every night at 2 a.m. Of course, there's a good chance your PC won't be turned on at that hour—so use these options to specify a time when your PC *is* turned on.

   You can also select a Quick Scan or Full Scan. It's set to Quick Scan, but if you set it to run at a time when you're not using the PC, it can't hurt to set it to do a Full Scan. This section also lets you specify what Defender should do when it comes across high-, medium-, and low-alert items. "Default action," which tells Defender to use its own judgment, is the best setting.

- **Quarantined items.** When Defender finds spyware, it puts the offending software into a quarantined area where it can't do any more harm. This tab lets you see the quarantined software, delete it, or restore it (take it out of quarantine). In general, restoring spyware is a foolhardy move.

- **Allowed items.** If Defender announces that it's found a potential piece of malware, but you allow it to run anyway, it's considered an Allowed Item. From now on, Defender ignores it, meaning that you trust that program completely. Allowed programs' names appear on this list.

    If you highlight a program's name and then click Remove From List, it's *gone* from the Allowed list, and therefore Defender monitors it once again.

- **Software Explorer.** This area (Figure 10-6) is primarily for experts who want to take a detailed look at the programs on your PC and remove any that look suspicious.

    From the drop-down list, choose the category of programs you want to examine, like Startup Programs. Click anything in the list to read the name of its publisher,

Figure 10-6:
Plenty of programs configure themselves to run automatically every time you start Windows, but they don't bother to tell you that. This can bog your system down. Software Explorer is a great way to hunt down these programs down. Disable any you don't want to run on startup. You'll still be able to run the program manually, so it won't interfere with running the program whenever you want.

a description, the executable file that runs it—enough details to make your head spin. You can click Remove, Disable, or (if you've already disabled something but want to allow it to run again) Enable. (If these buttons are dimmed, click Show For All Users first.)

- **Microsoft SpyNet.** One of Defender's most potent tricks is learning about emerging spyware types from the Microsoft SpyNet network, which harnesses the collective wisdom of Vista fans all over the Internet.

  Suppose, for example, that Windows Defender can't determine whether or not some new program is spyware. It can send out an online feeler to see how people in the network have handled the same program—for example, if other Vista fans removed it (having determined that it's spyware)—and then use what it finds out to handle your own copy of that program.

  Microsoft says that all of this information is anonymous. If you're OK with that, you can opt in to the SpyNet community here.

Data Execution Prevention

One of Windows Vista's new security features, Data Execution Prevention (DEP), isn't well-known, but it protects you against a variety of threats. It monitors important Windows services (background programs) and programs to make sure that no virus has hijacked them to your PC from within its own system memory. If DEP finds out an attack is underway, it automatically closes the offending service or program.

DEP comes set to protect only Windows itself—not other programs. You can, though, ask DEP to monitor *every* program on your system, or programs that you specify. The upside is better protection; the downside is that DEP could conflict with those programs, causing them to run erratically or not at all. In such cases, though, you can always turn off DEP protection for the affected programs.

(Note: If DEP suddenly starts interfering with important Win-

dows files and features, a recently installed program could be at fault. Try uninstalling it, or inquire if the publisher has a DEP-friendly version; that may solve the problem.)

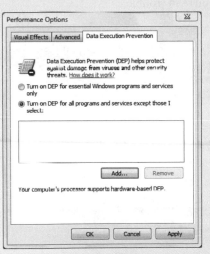

To turn on DEP for some or all programs, open Control Panel→ System and Maintenance→System→"Advanced system settings." In the Performance section, click Settings, and then click the Data Execution Prevention tab, shown here. Select "Turn on DEP for all programs and services except those I select," then click OK.

Should you find that DEP interferes with a program, click Add, then follow the directions for selecting it.

Incidentally, at the bottom of the Data Execution Prevention screen, you can see whether or not your PC offers DEP *circuitry,* which reduces its speed impact. If not, Windows runs a software-based version of DEP.

• **Windows Defender website.** This link takes you to the Windows Defender site, which contains a few moderately useful help resources about spyware.

The Phishing Filter

All Versions

The criminal mind knows no bounds. How else do you explain the clever nefariousness of *phishing* attacks?

In a phishing attack, you're sent what appears to be legitimate email from a bank, eBay, PayPal, or some other financial Web site. The message tells you that the site needs to confirm account information, or warns that your account has been hacked, and needs you to help keep it safe.

If you, responsible citizen that you are, click the provided link to clear up the supposed problem, you wind up on what looks like the bank/eBay/PayPal Web site. But it's a fake, carefully designed to look like the real thing; it's run by a scammer. If you type in your password and login information, as requested, the next thing you know, you're getting credit-card bills for $10,000 charges at high-rolling Las Vegas hotels.

The fake sites look so much like the real ones that it can be extremely difficult to tell them apart. (That's *can* be; on some of the phishing sites, spelling mistakes a fourth grader wouldn't make are a clear giveaway.) To make the site seem more realistic, the scam artist often includes legitimate links alongside phony ones. But if you click the login link, you're in trouble.

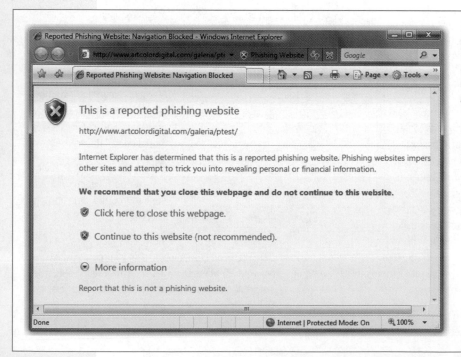

Figure 10-7:
Don't go there: Internet Explorer blocks you from visiting known phishing sites. It uses a variety of methods for determining what's a legitimate site and what's a phishing site, including getting updated lists of known phishing sites.

Internet Explorer 7's new phishing filter protects you from these scams. You don't need to do anything to turn it on; it's always running.

One day, though, when you least expect it, you'll be on your way to visit some Web site—and Internet Explorer will stop you in your tracks with a pop-up warning that you're about to open to a "reported phishing website" (Figure 10-7).

In that situation, click the *green checkmark button* to close the page. Do not click the red X button; it will send you through to the phony site.

If Internet Explorer isn't quite sure about a certain site's phishiness, but it has a funny feeling in its bones, a yellow button appears next to the Address bar that says, "Suspicious Website." Unless you absolutely know the site is legitimate, it's a good idea to head somewhere else.

Phine-Tuning the Phish Philter

There's not much to controlling the phishing-filter feature; you can turn it on and off and check a certain Web site to see if it's legitimate. Choose Tools→Phishing Filter to view the following options:

- **Check this Website.** This command sends the address of the Web site you're visiting to Microsoft's computers, where it's checked against the massive real-time database of phishing sites.

Note: The first time you try this command, you'll get a pop-up message that explains, for the sake of your privacy paranoia, that you're about to transmit anonymous information to Microsoft. Click OK to proceed; if you want the warning to never appear again, check the box next to "Don't show this again."

After a moment, a message appears to let you know whether the site is legitimate, suspicious, or a phishing site. If it's legitimate, a box pops up telling you so (Figure

---

FREQUENTLY ASKED QUESTION

Sherlock Explorer

How does Internet Explorer know what's a phishing site and what's not?

IE uses three bits of information to figure out whether a site is legitimate or a phishing site.

Its first line of defense is a Microsoft-compiled, frequently updated database of known phishing sites that, believe it or not, sits right on your own hard drive. Whenever you head to a Web site, Internet Explorer consults that database. If the Web site appears in the list, you get the warning. (The database is compiled from several phish-tracking companies,

including Cyota, Internet Identity, and MarkMonitor, as well as from direct user feedback.)

Second, Internet Explorer uses heuristics, a sort of low-level artificial intelligence. It compares characteristics of the site you're visiting against common phishing-site characteristics. The heuristics tool helps IE recognize phishing sites that haven't yet made it into the database of known sites.

Finally, Internet Explorer quietly sends addresses of some of the sites you visit to Microsoft, which checks it against a frequently updated list of reported phishing sites (not the database on your PC).

10-8, top); if it's suspicious or a phishing site, the warning appears in the Address Bar (Figure 10-8, bottom).

- **Turn Off/On Automatic Website Checking.** This option sounds as if it turns off the phishing filter, but it really doesn't do that. Instead, it disables one of the lines of defense against phishing sites: sending a list of Web sites that you visit to Microsoft, to check against Microsoft's database.

Note: Actually, Automatic Website Checking sends more than just the address of the site you're visiting to Microsoft. It also sends your computer's IP address, browser type, and phishing filter version number. It's transmitted in encrypted form. No information associated with the site is sent, like search terms you've used, information you've entered into forms, or cookies.

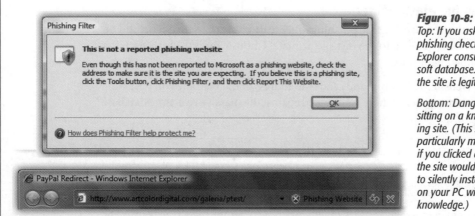

Figure 10-8:
Top: If you ask for a phishing check, Internet Explorer consults a Microsoft database. In this case, the site is legit.

Bottom: Danger! You're sitting on a known phishing site. (This site was a particularly malicious one; if you clicked a link on it, the site would attempt to silently install a virus on your PC without your knowledge.)

However, you'll still be protected by the two other lines of defense (checking your own PC's database of phishing sites and heuristic checking).

Microsoft says that it doesn't save the Web site addresses it collects, and can't associate it with *you* in any way. If you'd prefer not to transmit your whereabouts to Microsoft or anyone else, however, you can turn off this feature—with the understanding that you'll be a little more vulnerable to phishing attacks.

- **Report this Website.** If you stumble onto a Web site that you think is a phishing site, click here. A new browser window opens; turn on "I think this is a phishing Website." Choose the language used by the site, and then click Submit.

Also use this option in the opposite situation: when you're visiting what you *know* is a legitimate site, but that Internet Explorer identifies as a phishing site. Just above the Submit button are two choices: one for reporting that you don't think the Web site is a phishing site, and the other to report that you *know* it's not a phishing hole because you *own* it.

- **Phishing Filter Settings.** When you select this option, the Advanced Internet Options dialog box opens, crammed with Internet Explorer settings covering virtually every aspect of the browser. To see the phishing filter settings, scroll way down, almost to the bottom of the list.

  Choose Disable Phishing Filter if you think you can spot the tricksters perfectly well on your own. The other options provide a second place where you can turn that sending-Web-site-information-to-message ("automatic website checking") on or off.

Privacy and Cookies
All Versions

Cookies are something like Web page preference files. Certain Web sites—particularly commercial ones like Amazon.com—deposit them on your hard drive like little bookmarks, so that they'll remember you the next time you visit. On Amazon, in fact, a greeting says "Hello, Casey" (or whatever your name is), thanks to the cookie it uses to recognize you.

Most cookies are perfectly innocuous—and, in fact, are extremely helpful. They can let your PC log into a site automatically, or let you customize what the site looks like and how you use it.

But fear is on the march, and the media fan the flames with tales of sinister cookies that track your movement on the Web. Some Web sites rely on cookies to record which pages you visit on a site, how long you spend on a site, what kind of information you like to find out, and so on.

POWER USERS' CLINIC

Add-On Manager

Internet Explorer is more than just a browser. In fact, it's practically a kind of mini-operating system that lets lots of little add-on programs run inside of it. The most common category of these plug-ins is called ActiveX controls. They grant all kinds of super-powers to Internet Explorer; for example, the Flash add-on makes possible animations and movies on YouTube and many other sites.

But ActiveX controls and other add-ons can cause problems. Install too many, and your browser can get sluggish. Sometimes add-ons conflict with one another, resulting in an Internet Explorer crash. And some—this is the really nasty part—may actually be malicious code, designed to gum up your browser or your PC.

To help you get a handle on your plug-in situation, choose Tools→Manage Add-ons→Enable or Disable Add-ons. You'll see a list of all your add-ons and ActiveX controls. They're listed in several different categories, like those that are currently loaded into Internet Explorer and ActiveX controls you've downloaded.

Highlight one to read details about it, and to summon the Disable, Enable, and Delete buttons. (Hint: Before clicking any of these buttons, do a Google search on the name or the file name. You'll find out soon enough if the plug-in is trustworthy. Be especially wary of add-ons in the Browser Helper Objects [BHOs] category. These can be useful, but also very dangerous.)

If you're worried about invasions of privacy—and you're willing to trade away some of the conveniences of cookies—Internet Explorer is ready to protect you.

The Terminology of Cookies

Before you begin your cookie-fortification strategy, you'll have to bone up on a little terminology. Here are a few explanations to get you started:

- A **first-party cookie** is created by the site you're currently visiting. These kinds of cookies generally aren't privacy invaders; they're the Amazon type described above, designed to log you in or remember how you've customized, for example, the Google home page.

- **Third-party cookies** are deposited on your hard drive by a site other than the one you're currently visiting—often by an advertiser. Needless to say, this kind of cookie is more objectionable. It can track your browsing habits and create profiles about your interests and behaviors.

- A **compact privacy statement** is a Web site's publicly posted privacy policy that describes how its cookies are used. Here you'll find out why cookies are used, for example, and how long they stay on your PC. (Some cookies are automatically deleted when you leave a Web site, and others stay valid until a specified date.)

- **Explicit consent** means you've granted permission for a Web site to gather information about your online activity; that is, you've "opted in."

- **Implicit consent** means you haven't OK'ed that info gathering, but the site assumes that it's OK with you because you're there on the site. If a Web site uses the implicit-consent policy, it's saying, "Hey, you're fair game, because you haven't opted out."

Cookie Options

Choose Tools→Internet Options→Privacy to get to the Privacy tab shown in Figure 10-9.

POWER USERS' CLINIC

Examine Individual Cookies

Want to see the actual cookies themselves as they sit on your hard drive—the individual cookie files?

They're sitting on your hard drive in your personal folder→ AppData→Roaming→Microsoft→Windows→Cookies folder.

Each is named something like *casey@abcnews.com[1].txt*. The name of the Web site or ad network usually appears after the @, but not always—sometimes you just see a number.

To inspect a cookie, open the file as you would any other text file (in Notepad or WordPad, for example). Usually, there's nothing but a list of numbers and letters inside, but you might occasionally find useful information like your user name and password for the Web site.

If you don't want the cookie on your hard disk, simply delete it as you would any other text file.

Tip: You can also accept or reject cookies on a site-by-site basis. To do that, click the Sites button on the Privacy tab (Figure 10-9). The Per Site Privacy Actions dialog box appears. Type the name of the site in question, and then click either Block or Allow.

The slider on the left side lets you pick your compromise on the convenience/privacy scale, ranging from Accept All Cookies to Block All Cookies. Here are a few examples (and good luck with the terminology):

Figure 10-9:
This screen helps you keep your private information private—it lets you control how your PC works with cookies, which are bits of data put on your hard disk by Web sites. Medium High is a good setting that balances your privacy with Web sites' needs to use cookies for purposes like automated logins.

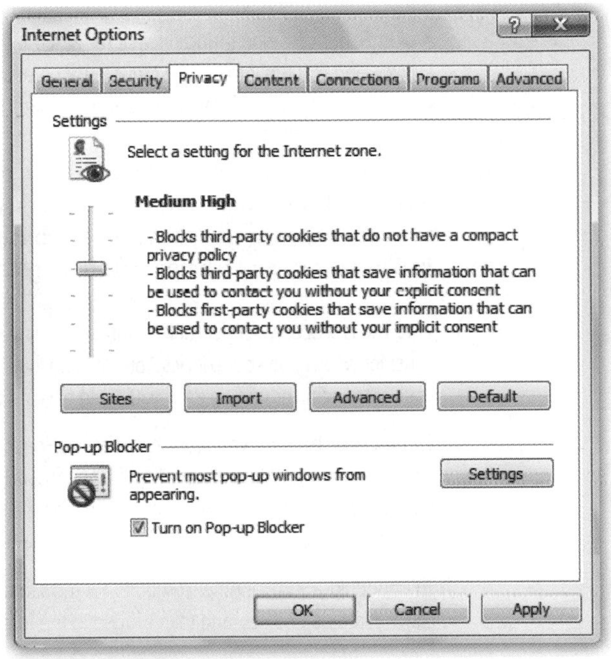

- **Block All Cookies.** No cookies, no exceptions. Web sites can't read existing cookies, either.

- **High.** No cookies from any Web site that doesn't have a compact privacy policy. No cookies from sites that use personally identifiable information without your explicit consent.

- **Medium High.** Blocks third-party cookies from sites that don't have a compact privacy policy or use personally identifiable information without your explicit consent. Blocks first-party cookies that use personally identifiable information without your implicit consent.

- **Medium (Default).** Blocks third-party cookies from sites that don't have a compact privacy policy or that use personally identifiable information without your implicit consent. Accepts first-party cookies from sites that use personally identifiable information without your implicit consent, but deletes them when you close Internet Explorer.

- **Low.** Blocks third-party cookies from sites that don't have a compact privacy policy. Accepts third-party cookies that use personally identifiable information without your implicit consent, but deletes them when you close Internet Explorer.

- **Accept All Cookies.** All cookies OK. Web sites can read existing cookies.

Choose the setting you want, and then click OK, and you're ready to start browsing.

Note: Some sites don't function well (or at all) if you choose to reject all cookies. So if you choose High Privacy, and you run into trouble browsing your favorite sites, return here and change the setting to Medium High. (Internet Explorer's factory setting is Medium.)

If you're ever curious whether a Web site you've visited in your current browser session has placed any cookies on your hard disk, press the Alt key to make Internet Explorer's menu bar appear. Choose View→Web Page Privacy Policy. You'll see a list of the sites you've visited, and whether any have placed cookies on your PC.

Tip: This is probably deeper cookie information than you really wanted to know, but here it is—you may want to consider *backing up* your cookies. You could do that, for example, and transfer your cookies to another PC, for your auto-login convenience. Or you could back up the cookies just in case yours get somehow deleted.

To export or back up your cookies, open Internet Explorer. Press the Alt key to make the menus appear. Then choose File→Import and Export. The Import/Export Wizard launches. Choose Export Cookies and follow the directions. A single text file containing all your cookies is created in your Documents folder (or a folder you specify).

To import cookies to another computer (or the same one after a disaster), launch the Import/Export Wizard, choose Import Cookies, and then browse to the folder where you stashed the backup file.

History: Erasing Your Tracks
All Versions

You'd be surprised and shocked to see the kinds of information Internet Explorer stores about you. Behind the scenes, it logs every Web site you ever visit. It stashes your cookies, of course, plus passwords and information you type into Web forms (your name and address, for example). Your hard drive also keeps cache files—graphics and text files that make up the Web pages themselves, stored on your hard drive to speed up their reappearance if you visit those sites again.

Now, some people find it creepy that Internet Explorer maintains a complete list of every Web site they've seen recently, right there in plain view of any family member or co-worker who wanders by.

Fortunately, you can delete any or all of these tracks easily enough.

- To delete just one particularly incriminating History listing, right-click it in the History list (page 379). From the shortcut menu, choose Delete. You've just rewritten History.

- You can also delete any other organizer icon in the History list: one of the little Web-site folders, or even one of the calendar folders like "Three Weeks Ago."

- To erase the entire History menu, choose Tools→Delete Browsing History, and then click "Delete history."

- The same dialog box (Figure 10-10) offers individual buttons for deleting the other kinds of tracks—the passwords, cache files, and so on. Or, if you really want a clean slate, you can click Delete All to purge all of it at once.

This is good information to know; after all, you might be nominated to the Supreme Court some day.

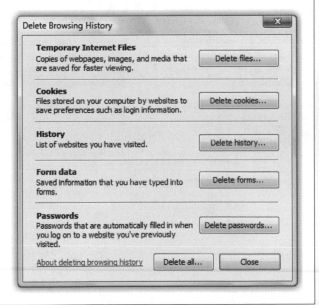

Figure 10-10:
The Delete Browsing History dialog box lets you delete traces of your Internet activities, including your browsing history, cookies, temporary files, passwords, and forms data. Keep in mind that when you delete some of this, it may make Web browsing less convenient. Delete your cookies, for example, and you'll have to enter your name and password again every time you go to a site like Amazon.

The Pop-up Blocker
All Versions

The ad banners at the top of every Web page are annoying enough—but nowadays, they're just the beginning. The world's smarmiest advertisers have begun inundating us with *pop-up* and *pop-under* ads: nasty little windows that appear in front of the browser window, or, worse, behind it, waiting to jump out the moment you close your browser. They're often deceptive, masquerading as error messages or dialog boxes… and they'll do absolutely anything to get you to click inside them (Figure 10-11).

Pop-ups are more than just annoying; they're also potentially dangerous. They're a favorite trick that hackers use to deposit spyware on your PC. Clicking a pop-up can begin the silent downloading process. That's true even if the pop-up seems to serve a legitimate purpose—asking you to participate in a survey, for example.

Internet Explorer, fortunately, has a pop-up *blocker*. It comes automatically turned on; you don't have to do anything. You'll be browsing along, and then one day you'll see the "Pop-up blocked" message in the yellow Information bar (Figure 10-11, top).

Tip: At the outset, IE does more than just show the Info bar message. It also opens a little dialog box–yes, a pop-up–to brag that it's blocked a pop-up (Figure 10-12). For best results, click "Don't show this message again," and then click OK. (The "pop-up blocked" message still shows on the Information bar, so you'll always know when a pop-up is sent into the ether.)

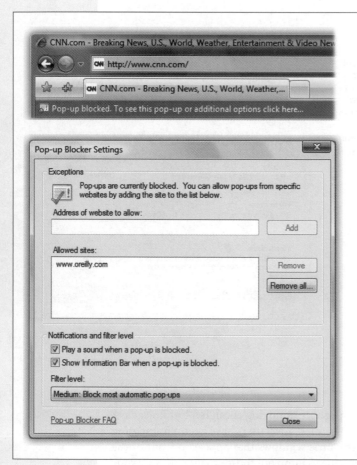

Figure 10-11:
Top: If you click the "pop-up blocked" message, you can choose Temporarily Allow Pop-ups, which lets you see what IE is blocking–or just press Ctrl+Alt. Or if pop-ups are important on a certain page (like the confirmation screen on a travel-booking site), choose Always Allow Pop-ups from This Site.

Bottom: Later, you can always manage the list of "pop-ups permitted" sites by choosing Tools→Pop-up Blocker→Pop-up Blocker Settings. This dialog box appears, listing all pop-up–approved Web sites (and offering a Remove button if you're having second thoughts). Here, too, you can turn off the "blocked pop-up" sound, eliminate the Information bar, or adjust the level of the pop-up filter (High, Medium, or Low).

Note that IE blocks only pop-ups that are spawned *automatically*, not those that appear when you click something (like a seating diagram on a concert-tickets site). And it doesn't block pop-ups from your local network, or from Web sites you've designated as Trusted (choose Tools→Internet Options→Security, click "Trusted sites," and then click Sites).

Tip: As you can read in Figure 10-11, there *is* a High setting that blocks *all* pop-ups, even the ones that appear when you click a link. Even then, you still have a way to see the occasional important pop-up: hold down the Ctrl key as your Web page is loading.

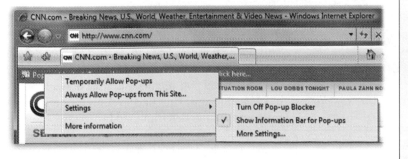

Figure 10-12:
This alert can get annoying after a while, so consider turning it off by clicking "Don't show this message again" and then clicking OK.

Overriding the Pop-up Block

Sometimes, though, you *want* to see the pop-up. Some sites, for example, use pop-up windows as a way to deliver information—a seating chart when you're buying plane or concert tickets, for example.

Tip: When a useful pop-up makes it through the Pop-up Blocker, it usually appears in its own small, separate window. But you can exploit Internet Explorer's new tabbed-browsing feature (page 373) by making the pop-up open in a new tab.

Choose Tools→Internet Options, click the General tab, and then, under the Tabs section, click Settings. In the Tabbed Browsing Settings dialog box, click "Always open pop-ups in a new tab," and then click OK.

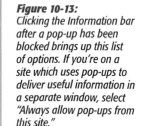

Figure 10-13:
Clicking the Information bar after a pop-up has been blocked brings up this list of options. If you're on a site which uses pop-ups to deliver useful information in a separate window, select "Always allow pop-ups from this site."

In those situations, click the Information Bar. A dialog box appears that lets you manage pop-ups from this particular Web site (Figure 10-13).

Your options:

- **Temporarily Allow Pop-ups** lets this Web site's pop-ups through just for this browsing session. Next time, pop-ups will be blocked again.

- **Always Allow Pop-ups from This Site** does what it says.

- **Settings** lets you configure the Pop-up Blocker. From the menu that appears, select Turn Off Pop-up Blocker to turn the blocker off. Turn off Show Information Bar for Pop-ups if you don't even want the yellow Information bar to appear when a pop-up is blocked. Select More Settings, and a screen appears that lets you always allow or block pop-ups from specific sites (Figure 10-14).

Figure 10-14:
Here's another way to specify Web sites whose pop-ups are always OK by you: type an address and then click Add. (This is the same screen that appears if you click the Information bar after a pop-up is blocked, and then select Setting.)

This dialog box also lets you control how you're notified in the event of a pop-up: with a sound, with a note in the Information bar, or neither. You can also use the Filter Level pop-up menu to tone down Internet Explorer's aggressiveness in blocking pop-ups. The High level, for example, blocks *all* pop-ups, even ones that Internet Explorer determines to be necessary for the site to run properly.

Tip: If you've installed some other company's pop-up blocker, you can turn off IE's version by choosing Tools→Pop-up Blocker→Turn Off Pop-up Blocker.

Internet Security Zones

All Versions

In the real world, you usually have a pretty good sense of where the bad parts of town are, and how to avoid them after dark. On the Web, it's not so easy. The most elegant-looking Web page may be a setup, a trick by sleazy hackers to install viruses on your PC.

Security zones is yet another (pre-Vista) Internet Explorer feature that was designed to limit the number of paths the bad guys have into your PC. It's fairly confusing, which is why not many people bother with it.

Under this scheme, if you have tons of time, you can place individual Web sites into different classifications (zones) according to how much you trust them. Internet Explorer refuses to download potential bad stuff (like those ActiveX plug-instruments) from sites in the seedier zones. Your PC, sanitized for your protection.

For example, internal company Web sites, right there on the corporate network, are pretty unlikely to be booby-trapped with spyware and viruses (unless you have a really twisted network administrator). Such internal sites are automatically part of the low-security **Local intranet** zone. If you maintain a Web site at home, it's in that zone, too.

There are also zones called **Trusted sites** (medium security) and **Restricted sites** (high security), but you have to put Web sites into these zones manually, as described in a moment. Any site you haven't manually placed into a zone automatically belongs to the **Internet zone** (medium security).

To see your options, choose Tools→Internet Options→Security from within Internet Explorer (Figure 10-15).

FREQUENTLY ASKED QUESTION

The Wisdom of Internet Explorer

How does the Pop-up Blocker know a good pop-up from a bad one, anyway?

Internet Explorer generally tries to distinguish between pop-ups it considers necessary for a site to run, and those it considers annoying or dangerous.

Although it doesn't always succeed, there is some logic behind its thinking.

At the factory setting, some pop-ups get through. For example, it allows pop-ups that contain "active content" for

example, important features, brought to you by ActiveX controls and browser add-ons, that are integral to the proper functioning of a Web site: seating charts, flight-details screens, and so on.

The blocker doesn't block pop-ups from sites in your Local intranet or Trusted sites zones, either.

Finally, if you already have a spyware infection, pop-ups may appear constantly; the Pop-up Blocker isn't designed to block spyware pop-ups.

Security Levels

And what, exactly, is meant by "medium security" or "high security"? These settings control what can and can't be done when you're visiting such a site. For example, they

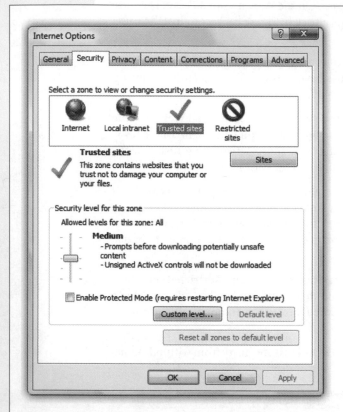

Figure 10-15:
The Internet Options Security tab lets you control Internet Explorer's security settings for browsing the Web. You can customize the settings for each zone by moving the slider up for more security, or down for less security.

POWER USERS' CLINIC

Customizing Ad Infinitum

If you don't like the security settings for each of the zones, you can change them. You could, for example, become a more trusting person and tell Internet Explorer to treat the Internet zone with Medium-low security.

In Internet Explorer, choose Tools→Internet Options→Security, shown in Figure 10-15. For Local intranet and Trusted sites, click the zone and then drag the slider. For Internet and Restricted Sites, click the zone. Then click Custom Level; in the Security Settings dialog box, from the "Reset to" drop-

down box, select the new security level and then click OK.

And speaking of tweaks not many people will make, you can also change the *definition* of a zone—that is, what kinds of online activities it permits—rather than relying on the canned High, Medium, Medium-Low, and Low levels.

Click any zone and then select Custom Level. The Security Settings dialog box appears. Pick your options, such as whether a site should be allowed to install desktop items, how to handle ActiveX controls, and so on. Then click OK.

---

govern whether or not you're allowed to download files, and whether or not Internet Explorer runs little embedded Web-page programs like Java applets or ActiveX controls. (Java applets are little programs that offer interactivity on Web sites, like games and interactive weather maps.)

Here's the cheat sheet:

- **High** security blocks all kinds of features that could conceivably be avenues for bad guys to infect your browser: ActiveX controls, Java and Java applets, and downloads.

- **Medium** security means that whenever a Web site triggers an ActiveX control to run, you're asked for permission. Unsigned ActiveX controls—those whose origins aren't clear to Internet Explorer—don't get run at all. Downloads and Java applets are OK.

- **Medium-Low.** Same as Medium, but some ActiveX programs run without first checking with you.

- **Low.** Runs all ActiveX controls and other little Web programs. Rarely asks you for permission for things.

Classifying Sites by Hand

You don't have to rely on Microsoft's judgment about which Web sites belong in which zones—you can classify them yourself. For example, if you know and trust a certain Web site, you can put it in the Trusted sites zone.

To do that, select a zone, click Sites, and then, in the dialog box that appears, click Advanced. In the *next* dialog box, type in the Web site's URL and then click Add.

Hot Spot Security
All Versions

One of the greatest computing conveniences of the new millennium is the almighty public wireless hot spot, where and your WiFi laptop can connect to the Internet at high speed, often for free. There are thousands of them at cafés, hotels, airports, and other public locations (see *www.jiwire.com* for a national directory).

But unless you're careful, you'll get more than a skinny latte from your local café if you connect to their hot spot—you may get eavesdropped on as well. It's theoretically possible for someone sitting nearby, using free and easy-to-find shareware programs, to "sniff" the transmissions from your laptop. He can intercept email messages you send, names and passwords, and even the images from the Web pages you're visiting.

Now, there's no cause for alarm; you don't have to sell your laptop and move to the Amish country over this. There are, however, a few simple steps that will go a long way toward keeping yourself safe:

- **Tell Windows it's a public network.** When you first connect to a wireless network, Windows Vista asks whether it's a public or private one. Choosing Public gives you extra built-in protection. Technically speaking, Vista turns off *network discovery*, the feature that makes your PC announce its presence to others on the network. (Unfortunately, lurking criminals using special scanning software can still find you if they're determined.)

- **Turn off file sharing.** You certainly don't want any of your over-caffeinated neighbors to get access to your files. Open the Control Panel Control, click "Set up file sharing," and turn off file sharing and Public folder sharing.

- **Watch for the padlock.** You generally don't have to worry about online stores and banks. Whenever you see the little padlock icon in Internet Explorer (or whenever the URL in the Address bar begins with https instead of http), you're visiting a secure Web site. Your transmissions are encrypted in both directions, and can't be snooped.

- **Look over your shoulder.** Hacking isn't always high-tech stuff; it can be as simple as "shoulder surfing," in which someone looks over your shoulder to see the password you're typing. Make sure no one can look at what you're typing.

- **Don't leave your laptop alone.** Coffee has a way of moving through your system fast, but if you have to leave for the rest room, don't leave your laptop unattended. Pack it up into its case and take it with you, or bring along a lock that you can use to lock your laptop to a table.

- **Use a Virtual Private Network (VPN).** Even if somebody intercepts your "hi, Mom" email, it may not be the end of the world. If you're doing serious corporate work, though, and you want maximum safety, you can pay for wireless virtual private network (VPN) software that encrypts all of the data that you're sending and receiving. Nobody will be able to grab it out of the air using snooping software at a hot spot.

  For example, HotSpotVPN (*www.hotspotvpn.com*) costs $3.88 per day or $8.88 per month. You get a password, user name, and the Internet address of a VPN server.

  Go to Control Panel→Network and Internet→Network and Sharing Center→"Set up a connection or network." Select "Connect to workplace" and follow the prompts for creating a new VPN connection with the information provided to you by HotSpotVPN.

Protect Your Home Wireless Network
All Versions

Public wireless hot spots aren't the only ones that present a theoretical security risk; your wireless network at home harbors hacker potential, too. It's possible, though rare, for so-called war drivers (people who drive around with laptops, looking for unprotected home WiFi networks) to piggyback onto home networks to download child pornography or send out spam.

This one's easy to nip in the bud:

- **Turn on wireless encryption.** When you first set up your WiFi router (also called a base station or access point), you're offered the chance to create a password for your network. Take the chance. (Modern wireless routers offer two different types of password-protected encryption, called WEP and WPA. If it's available, choose the more modern, more secure one, which is WPA.)

  You'll then need to use matching encryption on each wireless PC on your network. Go to Control Panel→Network and Internet→Network and Sharing Center→ Manage Wireless Networks, and then right-click your network adapter. Choose Properties→Security. Type in the encryption information that matches what you entered on your router.

Note: You won't have to type this password every time you want to get onto your own network! Vista offers to memorize it for you.

- **Ban unwanted PCs.** Many routers include a feature that lets you limit network access to specific wireless computers. Any PC that's not on the list won't be allowed in. The feature is called MAC address filtering, although it has nothing to do with Macintosh computers. (A MAC address is a serial number that uniquely identifies a piece of networking hardware.)

  Not all routers can do this, and how you do it varies from router to router, so check the documentation. In a Linksys SRX 400, for example, you log into the router's administrator's screen using your Web browser, and then select Wireless→Wireless Network Access. On the screen full of empty boxes, type the MAC address of the PC that you want to be allowed to get onto the network.

Tip: To find out the MAC address of a PC, press ⊞+R to open the Run dialog box, type *ipconfig /all*, and press Enter. In the resulting info screen, look for the Physical Address entry. That's the MAC address.

  Type all the MAC addresses into the boxes on the Linksys router, click Save Settings, and you're all done.

- **Place your router properly.** Placing your WiFi router centrally in the house minimizes the "leaking" of the signal into the surrounding neighborhood.

Parental Controls
All Versions

Many parents reasonably worry that it's far too easy for kids to find upsetting material on the Internet, accidentally or not: violence, pornography, hate speech, illegal drug sites, and so on.

A new Vista feature gives you a fighting chance at keeping this stuff off your PC: parental controls. They're easy to use and fairly complete.

Go to Control Panel→"Set up Parental Controls for any users" (in the User Accounts and Family Safety category). Authenticate yourself (page 191).

The dialog box shown in Figure 10-16 appears, listing all the user *accounts* on the PC (Chapter 23). One of the key advantages of the accounts system is that you can set up separate "worlds" for each person in your family—and now comes the payoff.

Click your kid's account to open up its parental controls screen. (If you haven't yet created accounts for your kids, you can create them here first.)

Figure 10-16:
Parental Controls lets you control how your children use the PC and the Internet. Most parents will be most interested in the Windows Vista Web Filter, which lets you filter out objectionable Web sites, and lets you stop children from downloading software.

Under the Parental Controls setting, click "On, enforce current settings"—the master switch. You can now set up these limits for your offspring's PC use:

- **Windows Vista Web Filter** blocks access to objectionable Web sites—and prevents any Web downloads.

  When you click the link, you're sent to a configuration screen that lets you select how restrictive you want the controls to be. You'll have the chance to turn on *automatic* blocking based on what's on each site, using canned settings like High, Medium, None, or Custom (Figure 10-17).

Tip: The High setting permits Internet Explorer to open *only* Web sites that are specifically designed for children.

  Alternatively, you can type in the addresses of *individual* Web sites that you want to declare off-limits by turning on "Only allow websites which are on the allow list," and then clicking "Edit the Allow and Block list."

Finally, don't miss the "Block file downloads" checkbox. If you really want a safe PC, turn this one on. Your kid won't be able to download anything from the Web at all: no songs, games, videos—and no viruses, spyware, or worms.

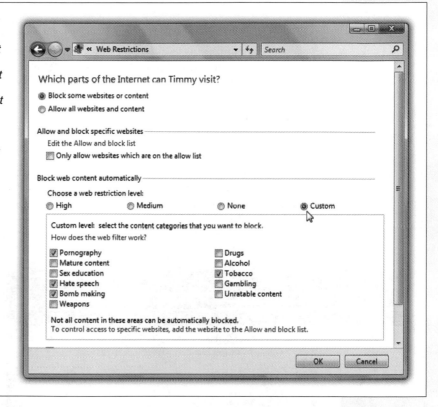

Figure 10-17:
The Custom option lets you specify exactly what you consider objectionable. After all, you might find Weapons OK for your 12-year-old, but not Pornography or Bomb making. Don't let the 12-year-old actually see this list, however; it may serve as an inspiration rather than a deterrent.

Content Advisor

There's one more Internet Explorer security feature worth mentioning, or maybe not: the Content Advisor.

It was an earlier Microsoft stab at giving parents a way to control what their children view on the Web. You can specify sites you approve, as well as sites you want to block. If somebody tries to visit a Web site that you've declared off-limits using this feature, he'll see a message saying that the site isn't available.

There's not much point in learning about the Content Advisor. It's not as useful or easy to figure out as Parental Con-

trols, described above. Not as effective, either; part of it relies on Web site *ratings,* which are something like movie ratings except that Web sites are supposed to rate *themselves.* As you can well imagine, the resulting ratings feature isn't exactly a foolproof (or even half-finished) system.

If you're interested in this feature—say, for your work as a historian—you can read more about it in the free downloadable bonus excerpt from this chapter called Content Advisor.pdf. You'll find it on this book's "Missing CD" at *www.missingmanuals.com.*

- **Time Limits** lets you set the days and times of the week that your little tyke can use the Internet. You might, for example, decide to keep your kids off the PC on school nights. When you click "Time limits," a calendar opens, where you can block times by selecting them.

- **Games** prevents your youngsters from playing games altogether, or lets you specify which kinds of games they can play: Early Childhood, say, or Adults Only. You can even customize any level, by blocking specific upsetting depictions within the games—everything from "Animated Blood" to "Use of Drugs" and everything in between.

Note: To make this feature work, Vista consults a tiny GDF (game definition file) that software companies can put into their game. Game companies usually use ratings bestowed by a ratings board like the Entertainment Software Ratings Board (ESRB).

If a publisher uses information from a different ratings board, or doesn't have a rating file (GDF) at all, Vista consults Microsoft's own 2,000-game database. And if even *that* source draws a blank, Vista considers the game unrated. You may have noticed that the Games screen in Parental Controls offers a "Block games with no rating" option, which is designed just for such situations.

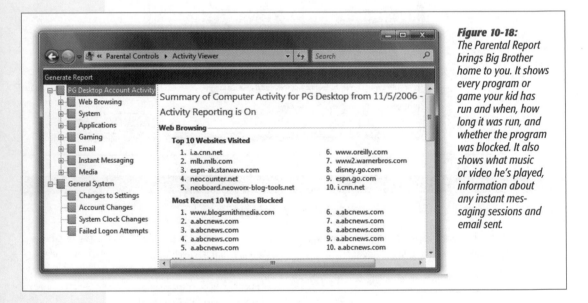

Figure 10-18:
The Parental Report brings Big Brother home to you. It shows every program or game your kid has run and when, how long it was run, and whether the program was blocked. It also shows what music or video he's played, information about any instant messaging sessions and email sent.

- **Allow and block specific programs** lets you declare individual programs on your PC to be off-limits. On the configuration screen, turn on "Casey [or whoever] can only use the programs I allow." Windows presents you with a staggering list of every single program on your PC; turn on the checkboxes of the programs that you consider appropriate for your kid. Click OK.

If your lovable young ruffian does attempt to run an off-limits program, a box appears that says, "Parental Controls has blocked this program." If he clicks "Ask an administrator for permission," the UAC box appears (page 191), so that he can call you or some other older, wiser account holder over to the PC. You can type in a name and administrator password to "unlock" the program—just for this time.

- **View activity reports.** Parental Controls reports are exceptionally detailed; they let you see pretty much everything that your kids have been doing on the PC. For example, it shows the 10 most popular Web sites they've each visited, the most recent Web sites blocked, files downloaded, and file downloads blocked. You also see how when your kid logged onto the PC, and the amount of time spent during each session. And that's just the beginning (Figure 10-18).

The final step is explaining the new limits to the young account holder. (Windows Vista has no new features to help you with that one.)

Internet Explorer 7

Microsoft has gone to great lengths to integrate the Internet into every nook and cranny of Windows. Links and buttons that take you online are everywhere: on the Help screens, in the Windows freebie programs, and even in the "Send error report to Microsoft?" dialog boxes that appear after a program crashes. Once you've got your Internet connection working (Chapter 9), you may find that it's easier to go online than it is *not* to.

Internet Explorer (or IE, as it's often abbreviated) is the most famous Web browser on earth, thanks to several years of Justice-department scrutiny and newspaper headlines.

The greatly revamped version 7 offers boatloads of new features. A *huge* number of them are related to security, since most bugs and viruses enter your PC from the Internet: the new phishing filter, pop-up blocker, download blocker, Windows Defender, cookies manager, ActiveX blocking, Protected Mode, parental controls, and so on.

There's so much of this stuff, in fact, that they'd weigh this chapter down with all their negative energy. They've been offloaded to Chapter 10.

There are lots of great new productivity features, too, though: an RSS reader, tabbed browsing, a new Search bar, a new interface design, and so on. *This* chapter is all about using Internet Explorer to surf the Web.

(Hey, it could happen.)

IE7: The Grand Tour

All Versions

You can open Internet Explorer in a number of ways:

- Choose its name from the Start menu.

- Click its shortcut on the Quick Launch toolbar.

- Type a Web address—its *URL* (Uniform Resource Locator)—into a window's Address bar. A Web page URL usually begins with the prefix *http://*, but you can leave that part off when typing into the Address bar.

- Click a blue, underlined link on a Windows Help screen.

… and so on.

As you can see in Figure 11-1, the Internet Explorer window is filled with tools that are designed to facilitate a smooth trip around the World Wide Web.

Figure 11-1:
The Internet Explorer window offers tools and features that let you navigate the Web almost effortlessly; these various toolbars and status indicators are described in this chapter. Chief among them: the Address bar, which displays the address (URL) of the Web page you're currently seeing, and the standard buttons, which let you control the Web-page loading process.

A link (or hyperlink) is a bit of text, or a little graphic, that's been programmed to serve as a button. When you click a link, you're transported from one Web page to another. One may be the home page of General Motors; another might have baby pictures posted by a parent in Omaha. About a billion pages await your visit.

Tip: Text links aren't always blue and underlined. In fact, modern Web designers sometimes make it very difficult to tell which text is clickable, and which is just text. When in doubt, move your cursor over some text. If the arrow changes to a pointing-finger cursor, you've found yourself a link.

Actually, you can choose to hide *all* underlines, a trick that makes Web pages look cleaner and more attractive. Underlines appear only when you point to a link (and wait a moment). If that arrangement appeals to you, open Internet Explorer. Choose Tools→Internet Options, click the Advanced tab, scroll down to "Underline links," select the Hover option, then click OK.

Menus and Gizmos

Internet Explorer 7 no longer has a traditional menu bar (although you can make the old one come back if you press Alt or F10). Instead, it offers five tiny menu *icons* at the upper-right corner. Each little ▾ is, in fact, a menu.

Here's a look at the other basic controls—the doodads that surround your browser window.

The Address Bar

When you type a new Web page address (URL) into this strip and press Enter, the corresponding Web site appears. (If only an error message results, then you may have mistyped the address, or the Web page may have been moved or dismantled—a relatively frequent occurrence.)

Because typing out Internet addresses is so central to the Internet experience and such a typo-prone hassle, the Address bar is rich with features that minimize keystrokes. For example:

- You don't have to click in the Address bar before typing; just press Alt+D.

GEM IN THE ROUGH

Let AutoFill Do the Typing

Internet Explorer can remember the user names and passwords you type into those "please sign in" Web sites.

You can't miss this feature; each time you type a password into a Web page, this dialog box appears.

It's a great time- and brain-saver, even though it doesn't work on all Web sites. (Of course, use it with caution if you share an account on your PC with other people.)

When you want IE to "forget" your passwords–for security reasons, for example–choose Tools→Options. Click the Content tab, click Settings, and click OK.

Here in this dialog box, you'll also find checkboxes that control *what* Internet Explorer memorizes: Web addresses (autocomplete in the Address bar), forms (your name, address, and so on), and user names and passwords.

- You don't have to type out the whole Internet address. You can omit the *http://www* and *.com* portions if you press Ctrl+Enter after typing the name; Internet Explorer fills in those standard address bits for you.

  To visit Amazon.com, for example, a speed freak might press Alt+D to highlight the Address bar, type *amazon,* and then press Ctrl+Enter.

- Even without the Ctrl+Enter trick, you can still omit the *http://* from any Web address. (Most of the time, you can omit the *www.,* too.) To jump to today's Dilbert cartoon, type *dilbert.com* and then press Enter.

- When you begin to type into the Address bar, the AutoComplete feature compares what you're typing against a list of Web sites you've recently visited. IE displays a drop-down list of Web addresses that seem to match what you're typing. To spare yourself the tedium of typing out the whole thing, just click the correct complete address with your mouse, or use the down arrow key to reach the desired listing and then press Enter. The complete address you selected then pops into the Address bar.

  (To make AutoComplete *forget* the Web sites you've visited recently—so that nobody will see what you've been up to—delete your History list, as described on page 352.)

- Press F4 (or click the ▾ inside the right end of the Address bar) to view a list of URLs you've visited recently—your History list, in other words. Once again, you can click the one you want—or press the up or down arrow keys to highlight one, and the Enter key to select it.

Topside Doodads

Around the Address bar, you'll find several important buttons. Some of them lack text labels, but all offer *tooltip* labels:

- **Back button, Forward button.** Click the Back button to revisit the page you were just on. (*Keyboard shortcut:* Backspace and Shift+Backspace, or Alt+left arrow and Alt+right arrow.)

Tip: Pressing Shift as you turn your mouse's scroll wheel up or down also navigates forward and back. Cool.

  Once you've clicked Back, you can then click the Forward button (or press Alt+right arrow) to return to the page you were on *before* you clicked the Back button. Click the ▾ button for a drop-down list of all the Web pages you've visited during this online session (that is, within this browser window, as opposed to your long-term History list).

- **Refresh button.** Click this double-arrow button (just to the right of the Address bar) if a page doesn't look or work quite right, or if you want to see the updated version of a Web page (such as a stock ticker) that changes constantly. This button forces Internet Explorer to redownload the Web page and reinterpret its text and graphics.

- **Stop (X) button.** Click this button, at the far right end of the Address bar, to interrupt the downloading of a Web page you've just requested (by mistake, for example). (*Keyboard shortcut:* Esc.)

- **Search bar.** There's no tidy card catalog of every Web page. Because Web pages appear and disappear hourly by the hundreds of thousands, such an exercise would be futile.

    The best you can do is to use a search engine, a Web site that searches *other* Web sites. You might have heard of the little engine called Google, for example.

    But why waste your time plugging in *www.google.com?* Here's one of Internet Explorer's most profoundly useful features—a Search box that accesses Google automatically—or any other search page you like. Type something you're looking for into this box—*electric drapes*, say—and then press Enter. You go straight to the Google results page.

    Actually, the factory setting is Microsoft's own search page, Live.com, not Google. It takes a moment to reprogram the Search box so that it uses Google or another search service, but it's worth the effort. From the ▾ button to the right of the magnifying glass icon, choose Find More Providers. See Figure 11-2 for the next steps.

Tip: Truth is, it's often faster to type your search phrase into the *Address bar itself,* if for no other reason than you have a keyboard shortcut to get your cursor in there (Alt+D). When you press Enter, IE does a Web search for that term, using the same search service you've set up for the Search box.

Window Controls

These last items wrap up your grand tour of Internet Explorer's window gizmos:

- **Scroll bars.** Use the scroll bar, or the scroll wheel on your mouse, to move up and down the page—or to save mousing, press the Space bar each time you want to see more. Press Shift+Space bar to scroll *up*. (The Space bar has its traditional, space-making function only when the insertion point is blinking in a text box or the Address bar.)

    You can also press your up and down arrow keys to scroll. Page Up and Page Down scroll in full-screen increments, while Home and End whisk you to the top or bottom of the current Web page.

- **Home button.** Click to bring up the Web page you've designated as your home page—your starter page.

    And which page is that? Whichever one you designate. Open a good startup page (Google, NYTimes.com, Dilbert.com, whatever), and then choose Add or Change Home Page from this icon's pop-up menu.

- **Status bar.** The status bar at the bottom of the window tells you what Internet Explorer is doing (such as "Opening page…" or "Done"). When you point to a link without clicking, the status bar also tells you which URL will open if you click it.

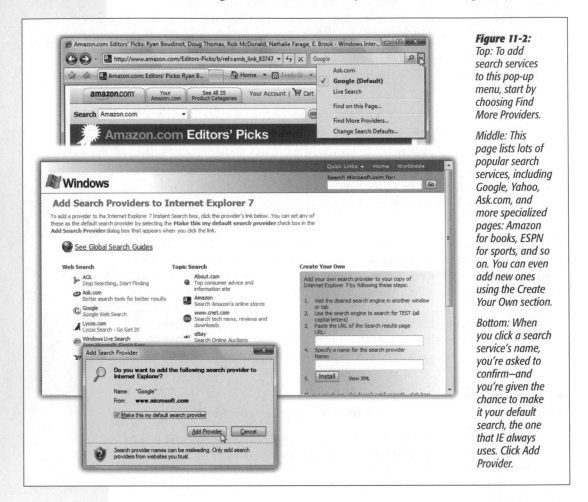

Figure 11-2:
Top: To add search services to this pop-up menu, start by choosing Find More Providers.

Middle: This page lists lots of popular search services, including Google, Yahoo, Ask.com, and more specialized pages: Amazon for books, ESPN for sports, and so on. You can even add new ones using the Create Your Own section.

Bottom: When you click a search service's name, you're asked to confirm—and you're given the chance to make it your default search, the one that IE always uses. Click Add Provider.

And when you're opening a new page, a graph appears here, showing that your PC is still downloading (receiving) the information and graphics on the Web page. In other words, you're not seeing everything yet.

If you consult all this information only rarely, you may prefer to hide this bar, thus increasing the amount of space actually devoted to showing you Web pages. To do so, choose View→Status Bar from the Classic menu bar (press Alt). The checkmark disappears from the bar's name in the View menu to indicate that the status bar is hidden.

Tabbed Browsing

All Versions

Beloved by hard-core surfers the world over, *tabbed browsing* is a way to keep a bunch of Web pages open simultaneously—in a single, neat window, without cluttering up your taskbar with a million buttons.

Figure 11-3 illustrates.

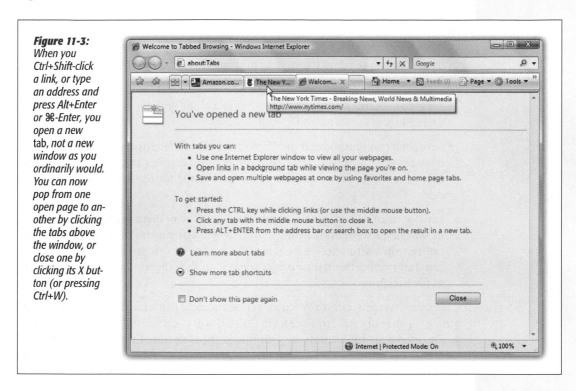

Figure 11-3:
When you Ctrl+Shift-click a link, or type an address and press Alt+Enter or ⌘-Enter, you open a new tab, not a new window as you ordinarily would. You can now pop from one open page to another by clicking the tabs above the window, or close one by clicking its X button (or pressing Ctrl+W).

Shortcut-O-Rama

Turning on tabbed browsing unlocks a whole raft of Internet Explorer shortcuts and tricks, which are just the sort of thing power surfers gulp down like Gatorade:

- **To open a new, empty tab** in front of all others, press Ctrl+T (for tab), or click the New Tab stub identified in Figure 11-3, or double-click anywhere in the empty area of the tab row. From the empty tab that appears, you can navigate to any site you want.

- **To open a link into a new tab,** Ctrl-click it. Or click it with your mouse wheel.

  Or, if you're especially slow, right-click it and, from the shortcut menu, choose Open in New Tab.

Note: Ctrl-clicking a link opens that page in a tab *behind* the one you're reading. That's a fantastic trick when you're reading a Web page and see a reference you want to set aside for reading next, but you don't want to interrupt whatever you're reading.

But if you want the new tab to appear in *front,* add the Shift key.

- **To close a tab,** either click the X on it, press Ctrl+W, press Alt+F4, or click the tab with your mouse wheel or middle mouse button, if you have one.

Tip: If you press Ctrl+Alt+4, you close all tabs *except* the one that's in front.

- **Switch from one tab to the next** by pressing Ctrl+Tab. Add the Shift key to move backwards through them.

- **Jump to a specific tab** by pressing its number along with the Ctrl key. For example, Ctrl+3 brings the third tab forward.

- **Save a tab configuration.** If there's a certain set of Web sites you like to visit daily, open them all into tabs. Then click the Add to Favorites button; from its menu, choose Add Tab Group to Favorites. Type a name for the group, and then click Add.

  Later, you can recreate your current setup—with all of them in a tabbed window— by selecting the resulting listing in the Favorites menu and then clicking the blue right-arrow button beside its name. The beauty of this arrangement is that you can start reading the first Web page while all of the others load into their own tabs in the background.

One more note to tab fans: When you close Internet Explorer, a dialog box appears asking if you really want to close *all* the tabs. If you click Show Options at this point, you're offered an opportunity to "Open these the next time I use Internet Explorer." Turn that on and click Close Tabs; the next time you go a-browsing, you'll pick up right from the tabs where you left off.

Note: If you find all this tabby business confusing and unnecessary, you can turn off the whole feature. In Internet Explorer, choose Tools→Internet Options. Click the General tab; under Tabs, click Settings. Turn off Enable Tabbed Browsing, and then click OK twice.

Quick Tabs (Thumbnails)

Once you've got a bunch of tabs open, you may face a horizontal screen-space crunch. How much, exactly, of the text "Welcome to Bass World—The Internet's Global Resource for Bass Fisherfolk" can you see on a half-inch tab?

Not much. But how, then, are you supposed to tell your tabs apart?

By using another new Internet Explorer feature called Quick Tabs. Figure 11-4 shows all.

Tip: You can *close* a tab directly from the Quick Tabs screen, too—just click the X button in the upper-right corner of the thumbnail.

Tab Settings

People get really, *really* obsessive over tabs for some reason. They want tabs to behave *just* the way they expect, or it's back to Firefox they go.

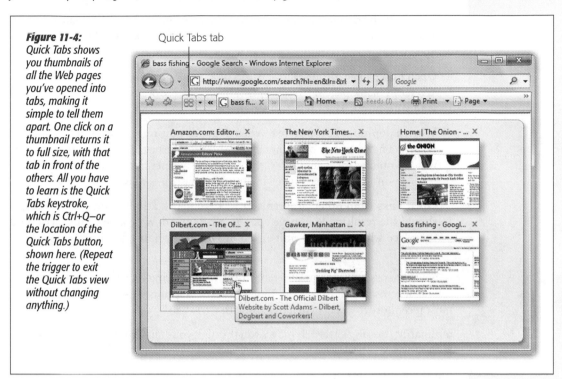

Figure 11-4:
Quick Tabs shows you thumbnails of all the Web pages you've opened into tabs, making it simple to tell them apart. One click on a thumbnail returns it to full size, with that tab in front of the others. All you have to learn is the Quick Tabs keystroke, which is Ctrl+Q—or the location of the Quick Tabs button, shown here. (Repeat the trigger to exit the Quick Tabs view without changing anything.)

Quick Tabs tab

No worries—Internet Explorer lets you customize tabs' behavior to within an inch of their lives. Start by choosing Tools→Internet Options→General; in the Tabs section of the dialog box, click Settings. Here's the most useful of what you'll find:

- **Enable Tabbed Browsing.** This is the on/off switch for the whole tab feature.

- **Warn me when closing multiple tabs.** If tabs are open when you close Internet Explorer, a confirmation box appears: "Do you want to close all tabs?" It's semi-annoying but semi-useful, because you may not realize that you're about to close all your tabs.

  You can turn on "Do not show me this dialog again" right in that box, or you can turn off this checkbox.

- **Always switch to new tabs when they are created.** Makes every new tab appear in front of the others, even if you Ctrl-click a link rather than Ctrl+Shift-click it.

(Even if you leave this option off, though, Ctrl+Shift-clicking a link still opens the tab in front.)

- **Enable Quick Tabs.** This is the on/off switch for the feature shown in Figure 11-4.

- **Open new tabs next to the current tab.** Ordinarily, IE creates a new tab right next to the one you're on, thus shoving all the other tabs off to the right. If you turn off this checkbox, new tabs appear to the right of all open tabs.

- **Load only the first home page when Internet Explorer starts.** Got a tab group set as your home page (page 384)? Turn on this box if you want only the first tab to open when IE starts, rather than the whole tab group.

- **Open home page for new tabs instead of a blank page.** When you click the New Tab tab, a blank page normally opens. If you instead want the new tab to appear with your home page on it, turn on this box.

- **When a pop-up is encountered.** When a "good" pop-up window opens, should it open in a new window or a new tab? Or should Internet Explorer try to figure out which would be most helpful? (If the Web programmer has specified a specific size for the pop-up, it appears in a window; otherwise, in a new tab.)

- **Open links from other programs in….** If you click a link in an email message, should the resulting Web page open in a new window or a new tab? Or should it replace whatever's currently in the frontmost window or tab? Only you can decide.

Actually, there's one more useful tabbed-browsing setting that's *not* here—for some reason, Microsoft stuck it on the Tools→Internet Options→Advanced tab. It's "Use most recent order when switching tabs with Ctrl+Tab."

Ordinarily, pressing Ctrl+Tab moves you through your tabs from left to right; adding Shift moves you backward.

But if you turn this option on, Ctrl+Tab jumps through the tabs you've visited in *reverse chronological order.* It's just the way Alt+Tab works when you're switching between Windows programs. This arrangement makes it very easy to compare two Web pages, because pressing Ctrl+Tab bounces you back and forth between the last two you've visited.

Note: This option also affects what happens when you hit Ctrl+W repeatedly to *close* tabs. They close in reverse chronological order.

Favorites (Bookmarks)
All Versions

When you find a Web page you might like to visit again, press Ctrl+D. That's the keyboard shortcut for the Add to Favorites command. (The long way is to click the Add to Favorites button identified in Figure 11-5.) Type a shorter or more memorable name, if you like, and click Add.

The Web page's name appears instantly in the "Favorites center," which is the menu indicated by the yellow star (Figure 11-5). The next time you want to visit that page, open this menu—or press Alt+C—and click the Web site's name in the list.

Tip: You can send your list of Favorites to or from other browsers or other PCs, which can save you a lot of time.

To do that, open the Add to Favorites menu (Figure 11-5); choose Import and Export. The Import/Export wizard appears to guide you through the process. Consider saving them onto, for example, a flash drive, for ease in transporting to another location or computer.

Figure 11-5:
Top: When you want to flag a Web page for visiting later, using this menu is one way to do it.

Bottom: Internet Explorer offers to add this Web page's name (or a shorter name that you specify for it) either to the Favorites menu itself, or to a "folder" (category) within that menu. The next time you want to visit that page, just select its name from the star-shaped menu at the top left of the window.

You can rearrange the commands in your Favorites menu easily enough. Open the Favorites center (Figure 11-6), and then drag the bookmarks up and down in the list.

Or, for more elaborate organizing tasks—creating and deleting folders, renaming sites, and so on—click the Add to Favorites button (Figure 11-5) and, from the shortcut menu, choose Organize Favorites. You get a little dialog box that makes all of those tasks easy.

Tip: If you *Shift*-click the Organize Favorites command, you open a standard Explorer window that lists your favorites as though they're standard computer files (which they are). Technically, you're now inside your Personal→Favorites folder. Now you can use standard Windows techniques to delete, rename, copy, paste, and otherwise manipulate your Favorites. You can even back them up, copy them to a flash drive, and so on.

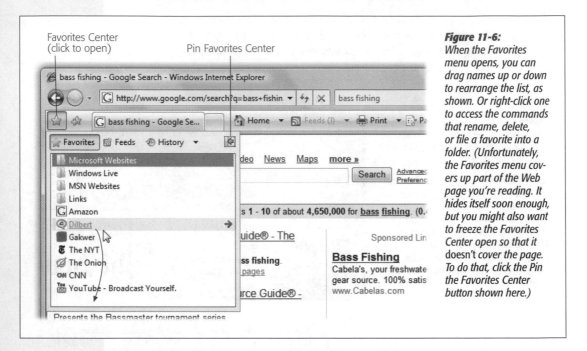

Favorites Center (click to open)

Pin Favorites Center

Figure 11-6:
When the Favorites menu opens, you can drag names up or down to rearrange the list, as shown. Or right-click one to access the commands that rename, delete, or file a favorite into a folder. (Unfortunately, the Favorites menu covers up part of the Web page you're reading. It hides itself soon enough, but you might also want to freeze the Favorites Center open so that it doesn't cover the page. *To do that, click the Pin the Favorites Center button shown here.)*

The Links Toolbar

The Favorites pane is one way to maintain a list of Web sites you visit frequently. But opening a Web page in that pane requires *two mouse clicks*—an exorbitant expenditure of energy. The Links toolbar, on the other hand, lets you summon a few, very select, *very* favorite Web pages with only *one* click.

You make the Links toolbar appear by choosing Tools→Toolbars→Links. Figure 11-7 illustrates how to add buttons to, and remove them from, this toolbar. Once they're there, you can rearrange these buttons simply by dragging them horizontally.

Tip: As shown in Figure 11-7, you can drag a link from a Web page onto your Links toolbar. But you can also drag it directly to the desktop, where it turns into a special Internet shortcut icon. To launch your browser and visit the associated Web page, just double-click this icon whenever you like.

Better yet, stash a few of these icons in your Start menu or Quick Launch toolbar for even easier access. (Moreover, if you open your Computer→C: drive→Users→ [Your Name]→Favorites folder, you'll see these shortcut icons for *all* your favorite links. Feel free to drag them to the desktop, Quick Launch toolbar, Links toolbar, or wherever you like.)

History List

All Versions

This *history* is a list of the Web sites you've visited. It's the heart of three IE features: AutoComplete, described at the beginning of this chapter; the drop-down list at the right side of the Address bar; and the History list itself.

Figure 11-7:
Once you've got a juicy Web page on the screen, you can turn it into a Link by dragging the tiny page icon directly to the Links bar, as shown here. (You can also drag any link from a Web page onto the toolbar.) If you right-click a link, you can choose Rename (to pick a shorter name that fits better).

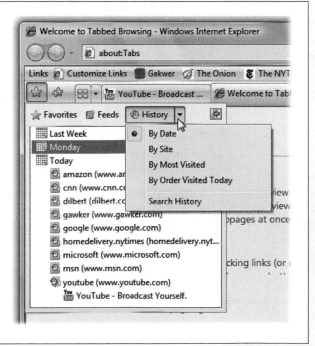

Figure 11-8:
If you click the little ▾ button next to the word History, you'll see that you can view the list sorted by Web site, date, frequency of visits—or you can see only the sites you've visited today, in order. The same little pop-up menu offers a command called Search History, so that you can search for text in the History list—not the actual text on those pages, but text within the page addresses and descriptions.

That's the pane that appears when you click the Favorites (star) button and then click History—or just press Ctrl+H. Figure 11-8 presents the world's shortest History class.

The History pane lists the Web sites you've visited in the last week or so, neatly organized into subfolders like "Today" and "Last Week." These are great features if you can't recall the URL for a Web site that you remember having visited recently.

Click one of the time-period icons to see the Web sites you visited during that era. Click the name of a Web site to view a list of each visited page *within* that site—and click an actual URL to reopen that Web page in the main window.

You can configure the number of days for which you want your Web visits tracked. To do so, choose Tools→Internet Options→General; where it says "Browsing history," click Settings. At the bottom of the dialog box, you'll see the "Days to keep pages in history" control.

For details on *erasing* your History list for security purposes, see page 352.

Tip: The more days IE tracks, the easier it is for you to refer to those addresses quickly. On the other hand, the more days you keep, the longer the list becomes, which may make it harder to use the list easily and efficiently.

Oh. and if you set "Days to keep pages in history" to 0, Internet Explorer won't track your movements at all. (You know who you are.)

RSS: The Missing Manual

All Versions

In the beginning, the Internet was an informational Garden of Eden. There were no banner ads, pop-ups, flashy animations, or spam messages. People thought the Internet was just the greatest.

Those days, unfortunately, are long gone. Web browsing now entails a constant battle against intrusive advertising and annoying animations. And with the proliferation of Web sites and blogs, just reading your favorite sites can become a full-time job.

Enter RSS, a technology that lets you subscribe to *feeds*—summary blurbs provided by thousands of sources around the world, from Reuters to Microsoft to your nerdy next-door neighbor. News and blog sites usually publish RSS feeds, but RSS can also bring you podcasts (recorded audio broadcasts), photos, and even videos.

You used to need a special RSS *reader* program to tune into them—but no longer. Internet Explorer 7 can "subscribe" to updates from such feeds, so you can read any new articles or postings at your leisure.

The result? You spare yourself the tedium of checking for updates manually, plus you get to read short summaries of new articles without ads and blinking animations. And if you want to read a full article, you can click its link in the RSS feed to jump straight to the main Web site.

Note: RSS either stands for Rich Site Summary or Really Simple Syndication. Each abbreviation explains one aspect of RSS—either its summarizing talent or its simplicity. (Web feeds and XML feeds are the same thing.)

Viewing an RSS Feed

So how do you sign up for these free, automatic RSS "broadcasts"? Watch your tab bar as you're surfing the Web. When Internet Explorer's Feeds button (Figure 11-9) turns orange, IE is telling you, "This site has an RSS feed available."

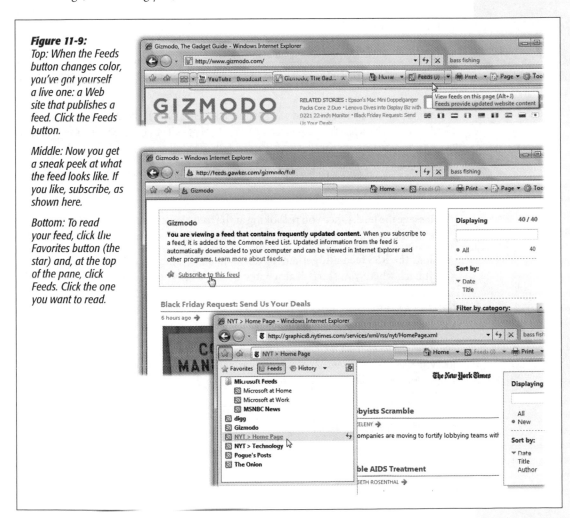

Figure 11-9:
Top: When the Feeds button changes color, you've got yourself a live one: a Web site that publishes a feed. Click the Feeds button.

Middle: Now you get a sneak peek at what the feed looks like. If you like, subscribe, as shown here.

Bottom: To read your feed, click the Favorites button (the star) and, at the top of the pane, click Feeds. Click the one you want to read.

(Sometimes, in fact, the site has *multiple* feeds available—for example, in different formats—in which case you can choose among them using the ▼ menu next to the RSS icon.)

Tip: To find more RSS feeds, visit a site like *www.feedster.com* or *www.syndic8.com*.

By the way, Internet Explorer isn't the only RSS reader. If you catch the RSS bug, you might want to try out a more powerful RSS reader. Visit *www.downloads.com,* for example, and search for *RSS readers,* or try a Web-based one like *www.reader.google.com.*

To see what the fuss is all about, click that button. Internet Explorer switches into RSS-viewing mode, as shown in Figure 11-9.

At this point, you have three choices:

- **Subscribe.** Click the Add to Favorites button, and then click Subscribe to This Feed. From now on, you'll be able to see whether the RSS feed has had any new articles posted—without actually having to visit the site. Figure 11-9 has the details.

Note: Once you've subscribed to a feed, Internet Explorer checks the originating Web site once a day for updates.

You can make it check a bit more obsessively, if you like (as often as every 15 minutes), or cool its jets (once a week). To adjust the schedule, choose Tools→Internet Options→Content; click Settings at the bottom of the dialog box. Use the "Every:" pop-up menu to specify the frequency.

While you're here, turn on "Play a sound" if you want a little sonic heads-up, too, when IE finds that a Web page you've just opened has an available RSS feed.

- **Massage the feed.** Once you're looking at the feed, you can sort the headline items by date, title, and author, or use the Search box to find text among all the articles.

- **Close the RSS feed altogether.** To do so, just click the Feeds button again. You're left back where you started, at whatever Web page you were visiting.

Tip: Once you've subscribed to some feeds, you don't actually have to fire up Internet Explorer just to see what's new in your world. Remember the Sidebar? The Gadgets described in Chapter 7?

One of them, you may recall, is called Feed Headlines. Yes, right there on your desktop, you'll see headlines from your subscribed Web sites, updating themselves as the news breaks. Click a headline to open a mini-preview window; double-click to open Internet Explorer and view the actual Web page.

Tips for Better Surfing
All Versions

Internet Explorer is filled with shortcuts and tricks for better speed and more pleasant surfing. For example:

Full-Screen Browsing

IE7's toolbars and other screen doodads take up less space in the Vista version than in previous versions, but they still eat up screen space. The Web is supposed to be a *visual* experience; this encroachment of your monitor's real estate isn't necessarily a good thing.

But if you press F11 (or choose View→Full Screen from the Classic menus), all is forgiven. The browser window explodes to the very borders of your monitor, hiding the Explorer bar, toolbars, and all. The Web page you're viewing fills your screen, edge to edge—a glorious, liberating experience.

You can return to the usual crowded, toolbar-mad arrangement by pressing F11 again—but you'll be tempted never to do so.

Picking a Home Page

The first Web site you encounter when IE connects to the Internet is a Microsoft Web site—or Dell, or EarthLink; the point is, *you* didn't choose it. This site is your factory-set *home page*.

Unless you actually work for Microsoft, Dell, or EarthLink, however, you'll probably find Web browsing more fun if you specify your *own* favorite Web page as your startup page.

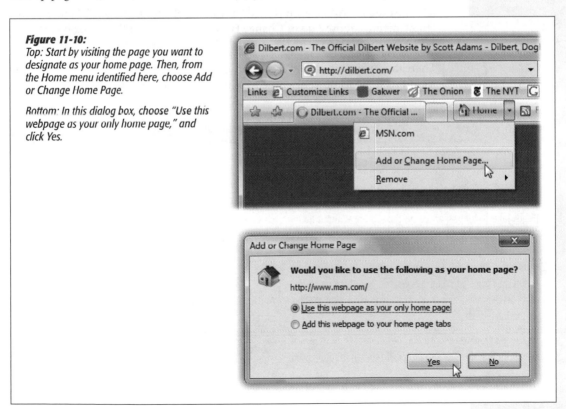

Figure 11-10:
Top: Start by visiting the page you want to designate as your home page. Then, from the Home menu identified here, choose Add or Change Home Page.

Bottom: In this dialog box, choose "Use this webpage as your only home page," and click Yes.

The easiest way to go about it is to follow the instructions shown in Figure 11-10.

Google makes a nice home page; so does a news site. But here are a couple of possibilities that might not have occurred to you:

- **A blank page.** If you can't decide on a home page, or your mood changes from day to day, set up a blank—empty—home page. This setup makes IE load very quickly when you first launch it. Once this window opens, *then* you can tell the browser where you want to go today.

  To set this up, open the Home menu (Figure 11-10) and choose Remove→Remove All; in the confirmation box, click Yes.

- **Multiple home page tabs.** This is a cool one. Now that Internet Explorer can display tabs, you can designate a bunch of them to open all at once each time you fire up Internet Explorer. It's a great way to avoid wasting time by calling up one site after another, because they'll all be loading in the background as you read the first one.

Note: Choose "Tab settings" on page 375; a few settings there pertain exclusively to home page tab groups.

The quickest way to set up a Home tab set: Open all the Web sites into their own tabs, just the way you'll want IE to do automatically in the future. Then, from the Home menu, choose Add or Change Home Page. Next, in the dialog box (Figure 11-10, bottom), select "Use the current tab set as your home page," and click Yes.

Thereafter, you can always add additional tabs to this starter set by choosing "Add this webpage to your home page tabs," the bottom option shown in Figure 11-10.

UP TO SPEED

Faster Browsing Without Graphics

Sure, sure, graphics are part of what makes the Web so compelling. But they're also responsible for making Web pages take so long to arrive on the screen. Without them, Web pages appear almost instantaneously. You still get fully laid-out Web pages; you still see all the text and headlines. But wherever a picture would normally be, you see an empty rectangle containing a generic "graphic goes here" logo, usually with a caption explaining what that graphic would have been.

To turn off graphics, choose Tools→Internet Options, which opens the Internet Options dialog box. Click the Advanced

tab, scroll down halfway into the list of checkboxes, and turn off "Show pictures" (in the Multimedia category of checkboxes).

Now try visiting a few Web pages. You'll feel a substantial speed boost, especially if you're connected by dial-up modem.

And if you wind up on a Web page that's nothing without its pictures, you can choose to summon an individual picture. Just right-click its box and choose Show Picture from the shortcut menu.

Note: Although it's a little more effort, you can also edit your home page (or home page tab sets) manually in a dialog box, rather than opening them up first.

Choose Tools→Internet Options→General. In the "Home page" text box, type each address, complete with *http://* and so on. If you want to create a home page tab set, type each address on its own line. (Leave the box empty for a blank home page.) Click OK, OK?

Bigger Text, Smaller Text

When your eyes are tired, you might like to make the text bigger. When you visit a site designed for Macintosh computers (whose text tends to look too large on PC screens), you might want a smaller size. You can adjust the point size of a Web page's text using the Page→Text Size commands.

Zooming In and Out

So much for magnifying the *text;* what about the whole Web page?

There are plenty of ways to zoom in or out of the whole affair:

- If you have a scroll-wheel mouse, press the Ctrl key as you turn the mouse's wheel. (This works in Microsoft Office programs, too.)

- Press Ctlr+plus or Ctrl+minus on your keyboard.

- Use the pop-up menu in the lower-right corner of the window (where it probably says "100%" at the moment). Just clicking the digits repeatedly cycles the page among 100, 125, and 150 percent of actual size. Alternatively, you can use its ≥ menu to choose any degree of zoom from 50 to 400 percent—or choose Custom to type anything in between.

Online Photos

Internet Explorer is loaded with features for handling graphics online. Right-clicking an image on a Web page, for example, produces a shortcut menu that offers commands like Save Picture As, E-mail Picture, Print Picture, and Set as Background (that is, wallpaper).

Tip: To turn off IE's picture-shrinking feature, choose Tools→Internet Options. Click the Advanced tab, scroll down to the Multimedia heading, and turn off "Enable Automatic Image Resizing." Click OK

By the way, when you see a picture you'd like to keep, right-click it and choose Save Picture As from the shortcut menu. After you name the picture and then click the Save button, the result is a new graphics file on your hard drive containing the picture you saved. (You can also choose Set as Background, which makes the picture part of your desktop image itself.)

Saving Pages

You can make Internet Explorer *store* a certain Web page on your hard drive so that you can peruse it later—on your laptop during your commute, for example.

The short way is to choose Page→Save As. For greatest simplicity, choose "Web Archive, single file (*.mht)" from the "Save as type" drop-down list. (The other options here save the Web page as multiple files on your hard drive—a handy feature if you intend to edit them, but less convenient if you just want to read them later.) Name the file and click the Save button. You've just preserved the Web page as a file on your hard drive, which you can open later by double-clicking it.

Sending Pages

Internet Explorer provides two different ways of telling a friend about the page you're looking at. You might find that useful when you come across a particularly interesting news story, op-ed piece, or burrito recipe.

- **The send-the-whole-page method.** While looking at a page, choose Page→Send Page by E-Mail to open a new Mail message with a copy of the actual Web page in the body. Address the message and click Send.

  Not all recipients, however, will be able to see the message; some email programs can't display HTML messages like this one. (Such programs show only plain-text messages.)

- **The send-a-link method.** To send just a link to the page you're looking at, choose Page→Send Link by E-mail. Then proceed as usual, addressing the message and clicking Send. All your recipients have to do is click the link to open it in their Web browsers.

Tip: The Page menu also offers the curious Edit with Notepad command. It opens the raw, underlying HTML coding of the page in Notepad, so that you can inspect and make changes to it—a great way to make emergency changes to the text of your own Web page when you're on the road and have no other editing tools on hand.

Printing Pages

Printing has been *vastly* improved in Internet Explorer 7. The decade of chopped-off printouts is over.

Now, when you choose Print (the little printer icon) *all* of the Web page's text is auto-shrunk to fit within the page.

Tip: You can print only *part* of a page, too. Drag through the portion you want, press Ctrl+P, click Selection, and then click Print.

Better yet, if you choose Print→Print Preview, you get a handsome preview of the end result. The icons in the Print Preview window include buttons like these:

- **Portrait, Landscape** (Alt-O, Alt+P) controls the page orientation: upright or sideways.

- **Turn headers and footers on or off** (Alt+E) hides or shows the header (the text at the top of the printout, which usually identifies the name of the Web site you're printing and the number of pages) and the footer (the URL of the Web page, and the date).

- **View Full Width** (Alt+W) blows up the preview to fill your screen, even if it means you'll have to scroll down to see the whole page. (This option has no effect on the printout itself.)

- **View Full Page** (Alt+1) restores the original view, where the entire printout preview is shrunk down to fit your screen.

- **1 Page View pop-up menu** governs how many pages fit in the preview window at a time.

- **Change Print Size** pop-up menu affects the size of the image on the printed pages. Shrink to Fit adjusts the printout so that it won't be chopped off, but you can manually magnify or reduce the printed image by choosing the other percentage options in this menu.

Tip: Lots of Web sites have their own "Print this Page" buttons. When they're available, use them instead of Internet Explorer's own Print command. The Web site's Print feature not only makes sure the printout won't be chopped off, but it also eliminates ads, includes the entire article (even if it's split across multiple Web pages), and so on.

Turn Off Animations

If blinking ads make it tough to concentrate as you read a Web-based article, choose Tools→Internet Options→Advanced tab, and then scroll down to the Multimedia heading (Figure 11-11). Turn off "Play animations in web pages" to stifle most animated ads. Alas, it doesn't stop *all* animations; the jerks of the ad-design world have grown too clever for this option.

Take a moment, too, to look over the other annoying Web page elements that you can turn off, including sounds.

Internet Options

Internet Explorer's Options dialog box offers roughly 68,000 tabs, buttons, and nested dialog boxes. Most of the useful options have been described, in this chapter, with their appropriate topics (like Tabbed Browsing). Still, by spending a few minutes adjusting Internet Explorer's settings, you can make it more fun (or less annoying) to use.

To open this cornucopia of options, choose Tools→Internet Options (Figure 11-11).

The Keyboard Shortcut Master List
All Versions

Before you set off into the Internet Explorer sunset, it's worth admitting that surfing the Web is one of the things most people do *most* with their PCs. And as long as you're going to spend so much time in this single program, it's worth mastering its keyboard shortcuts. Once you've learned a few, you save yourself time and fumbling.

Here it is, then: the complete master list of every Internet Explorer keyboard shortcut known to Microsoft. Clip and save.

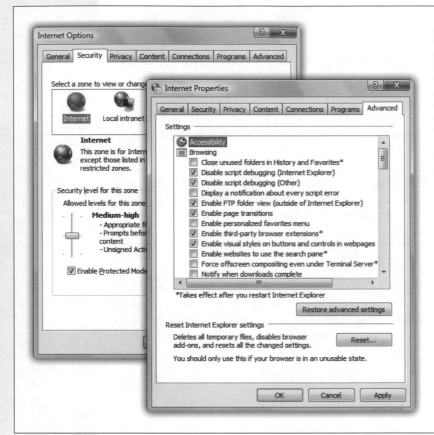

Figure 11-11:
Choosing Tools→Internet Options opens this dialog box, the identical twin of the Internet Options program in the Control Panel. Two of its tabs are shown here. Double-click one of the headings (like "Accessibility") to collapse all of its check-boxes. Your sanity is the winner here.

Viewing

Full Screen mode (on/off)	F11
Cycle through links on a page	Tab
Search the text on a page	Ctrl+F
Open the current page in a new window	Ctrl+N
Print this page	Ctrl+P
Select all items on the page	Ctrl+A
Zoom in/out by 10 percent	Ctrl+plus, Ctrl+minus
Zoom to 100%	Ctrl+0
Override pop-up blocker	Ctrl+Alt
Shut up this Web page's background sounds	Esc

Bars and Menus

Highlight the Address bar	Alt+D
Add *http://www.* and *.com* to the text in Address Bar	Ctrl+Enter
Add *http://www.* and *.net* or *.org* to the text in Address Bar	Ctrl+Shift+Enter
Open URL in the Address Bar in new tab	Alt+Enter
View previously typed addresses	F4
Highlight the Information bar	Alt+N
Open Home menu	Alt+M
Open Feeds menu	Alt+J
Open Print menu	Alt+R
Open Page menu	Alt+P
Open Tools menu	Alt+O
Open Help menu	Alt+L
Open Favorites menu	Alt+C, Ctrl+I
Open Favorites in pinned mode (won't auto-close)	Ctrl+Shift+I
Organize Favorites dialog box	Ctrl+B
Open Feeds list	Ctrl+J
Open Feeds in pinned mode	Ctrl+Shift+J
Open History	Ctrl+H
Open History in pinned mode	Ctrl+Shift+H

Navigation

Scroll down a screenful	Space bar (or Page Down)
Scroll up a screenful	Shift+Space bar (or Page Up)
Go to home page	Alt+Home
Go back a page	Alt+left
Go forward a page	Alt+right
Refresh page	F5
Super refresh (ignore any cached elements)	Ctrl+F5
Stop downloading this page	ESC
Open link in a new window	Shift-click
Add current page to Favorites	Ctrl+D
"Right-click" any highlighted item	Shift+F10
Search bar	
Highlight the Search Bar	Ctrl+E
Open list of search services	Ctrl+down
Open search results in new tab	Alt+Enter

Tabbed Browsing

Open link in new background tab	Ctrl-click*
Open link in new foreground tab (left or middle button)	Ctrl+Shift-click
Close tab (closes window if only one tab is open)	Ctrl+W, Ctrl+F4*
Quick Tab view	Ctrl+Q
Open new empty tab	Ctrl+T

View list of open tabs	Ctrl+Shift+Q
Switch to next tab	Ctrl+Tab
Switch to previous tab	Ctrl+Shift+Tab
Switch to tab #1, #2, etc.	Ctrl+1, Ctrl+2, etc.
Switch to last tab	Ctrl+9

* or scroll wheel-click, or middle button-click

Windows Mail

Email is a fast, cheap, convenient communication medium; these days, it's almost embarrassing to admit that you don't have an email address. To spare you that humiliation, Windows Vista includes Windows Mail 7, a renamed, revamped version of Outlook Express. It lets you receive and send email and read *newsgroups* (Internet bulletin boards).

If you do have an email address, or several, Mail can help you manage your email accounts, messages, and contacts better than ever.

To use Mail, you need several technical pieces of information: an email address, an email server address, and an Internet address for sending email. Your Internet

---

UP TO SPEED

What's New, Besides the Name

Let's face it: Windows Mail is really Outlook Express in a new outfit.

Microsoft says that it changed the name because so many people got Outlook Express (the free program) confused with Outlook (the expensive one).

It's not exactly the same, though. Mail has much better junk-mail filtering, as described later in this chapter. Messages are now stored on the hard drive as individual files, rather than a

single, big, seething database of them, which makes possible the lightning-fast searching described in Chapter 3.

One Outlook Express feature that's *missing* from Mail, however, is the ability to check free Hotmail accounts online; Microsoft mutters something about making it too easy for spammers.

But that's life. Microsoft giveth, and Microsoft taketh away.

---

service provider or your network administrator is supposed to provide all of these ingredients.

Setting Up Windows Mail
All Versions

The first time you use Mail (Start→All Programs→Windows Mail), you're prompted to plug in the necessary Internet addresses and codes that tell the program where to find your email. The first thing you'll see is shown in Figure 12-1.

Note: If you used the Easy Transfer Wizard (page 783) to bring over your files and settings from an older PC, Windows Mail is probably already set up quite nicely. If that's the case, skip to the next section.

Figure 12-1:
To set up an email account in Windows Mail, start by filling in the Display Name. This is the name people will see when you send them email, in the "From:" field. It does not have to be the same as your email address; it can be your full name, a nickname, or anything you like. When you're done, click Next to continue.

Click Next to step through the wizard's interview process, during which you'll provide the following information:

- **Display Name.** The name that should appear in the "From:" field of the email you send.

- **Email Address.** The email address you chose when you signed up for Internet services, such as *billg@microsoft.com.*

- **Mail Servers.** Enter the information your ISP provided about its mail servers: the type of server, the name of the incoming mail server, and the name of the outgoing mail server. Most of the time, the incoming server is a *POP3 server* and its name is connected to the name of your ISP. It might be *popmail.mindspring.com,* for example, or *mail.comcast.net.*

  The outgoing mail server (the *SMTP server*) usually looks something like *mail. mindspring.com* or *smpt.comcast.net.*

- **Logon Name and Password.** Enter the name and password provided by your ISP. This is generally your full email address and the password you already created.

  If you wish, turn on "Remember password," so that you won't have to enter it each time you want to collect mail. (Turn on Secure Password Authentication [SPA] only if instructed by your ISP or network administrator.)

Click Finish to close the wizard and open Windows Mail.

Tip: If you want to add a second email account, choose Tools→Accounts in Windows Mail. In the resulting dialog box, click Add; the wizard you worked through previously reappears.

Sending Email

When you finally arrive at the main Mail screen, you've already got mail; the Inbox contains a message for you (Figure 12-2). The message is a welcome from Microsoft, but it wasn't actually transmitted over the Internet; it's a starter message just to tease you. Fortunately, all your future mail will come via the Internet.

In order to receive and send new mail, you must use the Send & Receive command. You can trigger it in any of several ways:

UP TO SPEED

POP, IMAP, and Web-based Mail

When it comes to email, there are three flavors of accounts (not counting America Online mail, which is a mutant breed and not something that Windows Mail can talk to): POP (also known as POP3), IMAP (also known as IMAP4), and Web-based. Each has its own distinct feeling, with different strengths and weaknesses.

POP accounts are the most common. A POP server transfers your incoming mail to your hard drive before you read it, and then deletes the original copies on the Internet. From now on, those messages live on your computer, and it's up to you to save them, back them up, or delete them. (You can configure Windows Mail not to delete the messages from the server, but most ISPs don't give you much disk space. If your mailbox gets too full, the server may begin rejecting your incoming messages.)

IMAP servers are newer than, and have more features than, POP servers, but as a result, they don't enjoy as much popularity or support. IMAP servers are Internet computers that store all of your mail for you, rather than making you download it each time you connect. The benefit? You can access the same mail regardless of which computer you use. IMAP servers remember which messages you've read and sent, too.

One downside to this approach, of course, is that you can't work with your email except when you're online, because all your mail is on an Internet server, not on your hard drive. And if you don't conscientiously delete mail manually after you've read it, your online mailbox eventually overflows. Sooner or later, the system starts bouncing fresh messages back to their senders, annoying your friends and depriving you of the chance to read what they have to say.

Free, Web-based servers like Hotmail also store your mail on the Internet. You can use a Web browser on any computer to read and send messages; then again, most POP accounts these days offer that feature, too. Web email is slower and more cumbersome to use than "regular" email accounts

---

- Click the Send/Receive button on the toolbar. (It's shown in Figure 12-3, which also shows how you can specify *which* account you want to check.)

- Choose Tools→Send and Receive→Send and Receive All.

- Press Ctrl+M (for Mail).

Tip: You can set up Mail to check your email accounts automatically according to a schedule. Just choose Tools→Options. On the General tab, you'll see the "Check for new messages every ___ minutes" checkbox, which you can change to your liking.

Figure 12-2:
Meet Windows Mail. You should see a Welcome to Windows Mail email that looks similar to this one. The email contains information about Windows Mail, its features, and how to use it.

GEM IN THE ROUGH

Checking a Specific Email Account

You don't have to check *all* of your email accounts whenever you want to get mail. Suppose, for example, that you want to send a message to *yourself*—from your work account to your home account. In that case, you'd want to send/receive mail only from your office account. (If, in the same pass, Windows Mail also downloaded messages *from* your home account, you'd wind up with the same message in your office PC's copy of Mail, defeating the whole purpose of the exercise.)

Excluding an account (or several accounts) from the "Send and Receive All" routine is easy enough. Open the Accounts window (Tools→Accounts), select the account to turn off, and then click Properties. Turn off "Include this account when receiving Mail or synchronizing," click OK, and, finally, close the Accounts window.

Now suppose you *usually* want to check all accounts, but *occasionally* want to check only one of them. On such an occasion, click the ▾ beside the Send/Receive button and choose that account's name from the pop-up menu. (Alternatively, choose the account name from the Tools→Send and Receive submenu.)

Now Windows Mail contacts the mail servers listed in the account list, retrieving new messages and downloading any files attached to those messages. It also sends any outgoing messages and their attachments.

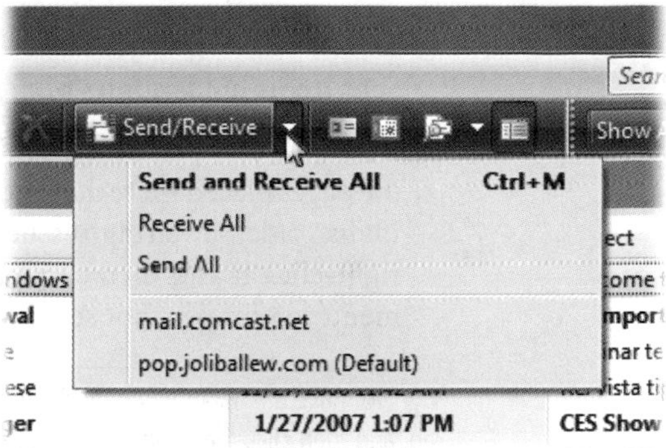

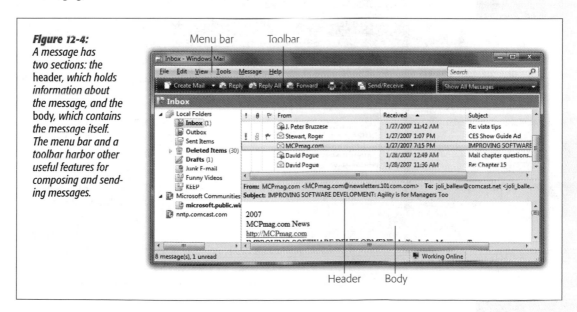

Figure 12-3:
The Send and Receive button is located on the toolbar in Windows Mail. The arrow beside it lets you choose which mail you'd like to get, if you don't want to check all of your accounts.

In the list on the right side of your screen, the names of new messages show up in bold type; folders containing new messages show up in bold type, too (in the Folders list at the left side of the screen). The bold number in parentheses after the word "Inbox" represents how many messages you haven't read yet.

Finally, after messages are downloaded, Windows Mail applies its *mail filters*—what it calls *rules*—to all new messages (to screen out junk mail, for example). More on rules on page 407.

Figure 12-4:
A message has two sections: the header, *which holds information about the message, and the* body, *which contains the message itself. The menu bar and a toolbar harbor other useful features for composing and sending messages.*

Menu bar   Toolbar

Header   Body

Mail folders in Windows Mail

At the left side of the screen, Windows Mail organizes your email into *folders*. To see what's in a folder, click it once:

- **Inbox** holds mail you've received.

- **Outbox** holds mail you've written but haven't sent yet.

- **Sent Items** holds copies of messages you've sent.

- **Deleted Items** holds mail you've deleted. It works a lot like the Recycle Bin, in that messages placed there don't actually disappear. Instead, they remain in the Deleted Items folder, awaiting rescue if you opt to retrieve them. To empty this folder, right-click it and then choose "Empty 'Deleted Items' Folder" from the shortcut menu (or simply choose Edit→Empty 'Deleted Items' Folder).

Tip: To make the folder empty itself every time you exit Mail, choose Tools→Options, click the Advanced tab, and then click the Maintenance button. From the Maintenance dialog box, turn on "Empty messages from the 'Deleted Items' folder on exit."

POWER USERS' CLINIC

The Mighty Morphing Interface

You don't have to be content with the factory-installed design of the Windows Mail screen; you can control which panes are visible, how big they are, and which columns show up in list views.

To change the size of a pane, drag its border to make it larger or smaller, as shown here. You can also hide or show the toolbar, folder list, status bar, search bar, or preview pane using the View→Layout command; in the dialog box, turn off the checkboxes for the window elements you could do without.

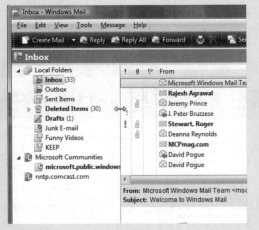

The View→Layout command also lets you control where the preview pane appears: under the message list, as usual, or to its right—a great arrangement if you have a very wide screen.

Mail lets you decide what columns are displayed in the list pane. For example, if you don't particularly care about seeing the Flag column, you can hide it, leaving more space for the Subject and Received columns. To switch columns on or off, choose from the list in the View→Columns dialog box.

You can also *rearrange* the columns, which can be handy if you'd rather see the Subject column first instead of the sender, for example. Just drag the column's name header horizontally; release when the vertical dotted line is where you want the column to wind up. To make a column wider or narrower, drag the short black divider line between column names horizontally, much the way you'd resize a folder window list-view column.

- **Drafts** holds messages you've started but haven't finished—and don't want to send just yet.

- **Junk E-Mail** holds messages deemed as junk (spam) by Mail's Junk E-Mail Protection. (More about that later.)

You can also add to this list, creating folders for your own organizational pleasure—Family Mail, Work Mail, or whatever. See page 405.

Composing and sending messages

To send a message, click Create Mail on the toolbar (or press Ctrl+N, or choose Message→New Message). The New Message form opens (Figure 12-5).

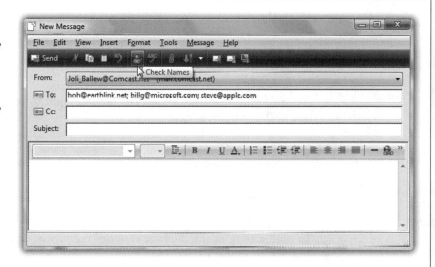

Figure 12-5:
In the New Message window, type the name of the recipients, separated by semicolons, in the "To:" field. If Windows Mail doesn't automatically complete the name for you (by consulting your address book and recent recipients list), click Check Names.

GEM IN THE ROUGH

The Quick Contacts Gadget

To get to your contacts quickly, add the Contacts gadget to the Sidebar.

Thereafter, when you want to send an email message, call up the lucky recipient's name by typing a few letters of his name into the gadget; it

appears in the Contacts gadget list, as shown here.

Now, to send an email to that person, click the email address shown on the right. A new message opens, preaddressed and ready to write and send.

Composing the message requires several steps:

1. **Type the email address of the recipient into the "To:" field.**

   If you want to send a message to more than one person, separate their email addresses using semicolons, like this: *bob@earthlink.net; billg@microsoft.com; steve@apple.com.*

   There's no need to type out all those complicated email addresses, either. As you begin typing the person's plain-English name, the program attempts to guess who you mean (if it's somebody in your Contacts list)—and fills in the email address automatically.

   If it guesses the correct name, great; press Tab to move on to the next text box. If it guesses wrong, just keep typing. The program quickly retracts its suggestion and watches what you type next.

   As in most Windows dialog boxes, you can jump from blank to blank in this window (from the "To:" field to the "CC:" field, for example) by pressing the Tab key.

2. **To send a copy of the message to other recipients, enter the additional email address(es) in the "CC:" field.**

   CC stands for *carbon copy*. There's very little difference between putting all your addressees on the "To:" line (separated by semicolons) and putting them on the "CC:" line. The only difference is that using the "CC:" line implies, "I sent you a copy because I thought you'd want to know about this correspondence, but I'm not expecting you to reply."

   Press Tab when you're finished.

3. **Type the topic of the message in the "Subject:" field.**

   Some people get bombarded with email. That's why it's courteous to put some thought into the Subject line. (For example, use "Change in plans for next week" instead of "Hi.")

   Press the Tab key to move your cursor into the message area.

4. **Choose a format (HTML or plain text), if you like.**

   When it comes to formatting a message's body text, you have two choices: *plain text* or *HTML* (Hypertext Markup Language).

Plain text means that you can't format your text with bold type, color, specified font sizes, and so on. HTML, on the other hand, is the language used to create Web pages, and it lets you use formatting commands (such as font sizes, colors, and bold or italic text).

But there's a catch: a handful of older email programs can't read HTML-formatted email. Also, HTML mail is much larger, and therefore slower to download, than plain-text messages.

So which should you choose? Plain text tends to feel more professional, never irritates anybody—and you're guaranteed that the recipient will see exactly what was sent.

If you send an HTML message to someone whose email program can't handle HTML, all is not lost—your message appears in a friendly, plain-text format that anyone can read. Still, certain Internetters remain fairly hostile toward heavily formatted email.

To specify which format Windows Mail *proposes* for all new messages (plain text or HTML), choose Tools→Options. Click the Send tab. Next, in the section labeled Mail Sending Format, choose either the HTML or Plain Text button, and then click OK.

No matter which setting you specify there, however, you can always switch a *particular* message to the opposite format. Just choose Format→Rich Text (HTML), or Format→Plain Text, in the New Message window.

If you choose the HTML option, clicking in the message area activates the HTML toolbar, whose various buttons control the formatting, font, size, color, paragraph indentation, line spacing, and other word processor–like formatting controls (Figure 12-6).

Just remember: less is more. If you go hog-wild formatting your email, the message may be difficult to read, especially if you apply stationery (a background).

5. **Enter the message in the message box (the bottom half of the message window).**

   You can use all standard editing techniques, including Cut, Copy, and Paste, to rearrange the text as you write it.

Tip: If Microsoft Word is installed on your PC, you can also spell check your outgoing mail. Just choose Tools→Spelling (or press F7) in the new message window.

---

6. **Add a signature, if you wish.**

   Signatures are bits of text that get stamped at the bottom of outgoing email messages. They typically contain a name, a mailing address, or a Star Trek quote.

   To create a signature, choose Tools→Options, click the Signatures tab, and then click the New button. The easiest way to compose your signature is to type it into the Edit Signatures text box at the bottom of the window. (If you poke around long enough in this box, you'll realize that you can actually create multiple signatures—and even assign each one to a different outgoing email account.)

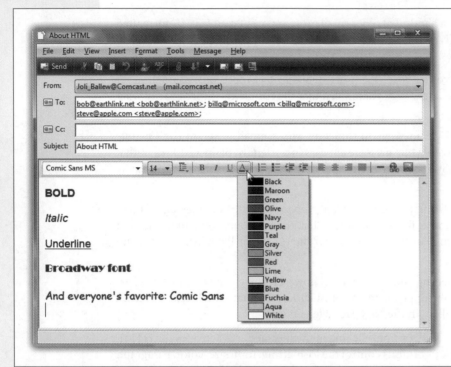

Figure 12-6:
When you're composing an email using the HTML format, the New Message window gives you options for choosing fonts, formatting options like Bold, Italic, and Underline, and colors (from a handy color palette).

UP TO SPEED

Blind Carbon Copies

A *blind carbon copy* is a secret copy. This feature lets you send a copy of a message to somebody secretly, without any of the other recipients knowing. The names in the "To:" and "CC:" fields appear at the top of the message for all recipients to see, but nobody can see the names you typed into the "BCC:" box. To view this box, choose View→All Headers in the New Message window.

You can use the "BCC:" field to quietly signal a third party that a message has been sent. For example, if you send your co-worker a message that says, "Chris, it bothers me that you've been cheating the customers," you could BCC your boss or supervisor to clue her in without getting into

trouble with Chris.

The BCC box is useful in other ways, too. Many people send email messages (containing jokes, for example) to a long list of recipients. You, the recipient, must scroll through a very long list of names the sender placed in the "To:" or "CC:" field.

But if the sender uses the "BCC:" field to hold all the recipients' email addresses, you, the recipient, won't see any names but your own at the top of the email. (Unfortunately, spammers—the miserable cretins who send you junk mail—have also learned this trick.)

Once you've created a signature (or several), you can tack it onto your outgoing mail for all messages (by turning on "Add signatures to all outgoing messages" at the top of this box) or on a message-by-message basis (by choosing Insert→Signature in the New Message window).

7. **Click the Send button.**

Alternatively, press Alt+S, or choose File→Send Message. Your PC connects to the Internet and sends the message.

Tip: If you seem to be able to receive mail but can't send it, your Internet service provider might require Mail to log into its server before sending email. To try that approach, first click Tools→Accounts. From there, click your account's name, and then the Properties ›Servers tab. Turn on "My server requires authentication." Click OK, and then Close.

If you're working offline, you might prefer Mail to place each message you write in the Outbox folder, saving them up until you click the Send/Receive button on the toolbar; see "Send tab," on page 415.

The Contacts list

Accumulating names in a Contacts list—the same one described on page 250—eliminates the need to enter complete email addresses whenever you want to send a message. Click the Contacts button on the toolbar; then, to begin adding names and email addresses, click New Contact.

Tip: Windows Mail offers a convenient timesaving feature: the Tools→Add Sender to Contacts command. Whenever you choose it, Mail automatically stores the email address of the person whose message is on the screen. (Alternatively, you can right-click an email address in the message and choose "Add Sender to Contacts" from the shortcut menu.)

Attaching files to messages

Sending little text messages is fine, but it's not much help when you want to send somebody a photograph, a sound recording, a Word or Excel document, and so on. Fortunately, attaching such files to email messages is one of the world's most popular email features.

To attach a file to a message, use either of two methods:

- **The long way.** Click the Attach button (the paper-clip icon) on the New Message dialog box toolbar. Alternatively, you could select Insert→File Attachment. When the Open dialog box appears, locate the file and select it. (In the resulting navigation window, Ctrl-click multiple files to attach them all at once.)

  Now the name of the attached file appears in the message, in the Attach text box. When you send the message, the file tags along.

Note: If you have a high-speed connection like a cable modem, have pity on your recipients if they don't. A big picture or movie file might take you only seconds to send, but tie up your correspondent's modem for hours.

- **The short way.** If you can see the icon of the file you want to attach—in its folder window behind the Mail window, on the Desktop, or wherever—then attach it by *dragging* its icon directly into the message window. That's a handy technique when you're attaching many different files.

Tip: To remove a file from an outgoing message before you've sent it, click it and then press the Delete key.

Reading Email
All Versions

Just seeing a list of the *names* of new messages in Mail is like getting wrapped presents—the best part's yet to come. There are two ways to read a message: using the preview pane, and opening the message into its own window.

To preview a message, click its name in the list pane; the body of the message appears in the preview pane below. Don't forget that you can adjust the relative sizes of the list and preview panes by dragging the gray border between them up or down.

To open a message into a window of its own, double-click its name in the list pane. An open message has its own toolbar, along with Previous and Next message buttons (which look like upward- and downward-pointing arrows).

Once you've read a message, you can view the next one in the list either by pressing Ctrl +U (for the next *unread* message), or by clicking its name in the list pane. (If you're using preview mode, and haven't opened a message into its own window, you can also press the up or down arrow key to move from one message to the next.)

Tip: To mark a message that you've read as an *unread* message, so that its name remains bolded, right-click its name in the list pane and then choose Mark as Unread from the shortcut menu.

Here's another timesaver: To hide all the messages you've already read, just choose View→Current View→Hide Read Messages. Now, only unread messages are visible in the selected folder. To bring the hidden messages back, choose View→Current View→Show All Messages.

When Pictures are Part of the Message
Sending pictures in email is a globally popular activity—but Mail doesn't want you to see them.

Mail comes set up to block images, because these images sometimes serve as "bugs" that silently report back to the sender whether you received and opened the message. At that point, the spammers know that they've found a live, working email address—and, better yet, a sucker who opens mail from strangers. And presto, you're on their "safe senders" list, and the spam flood *really* begins.

You'll know if pictures were meant to appear in the body of a message; see the strip that appears at the top in Figure 12-7.

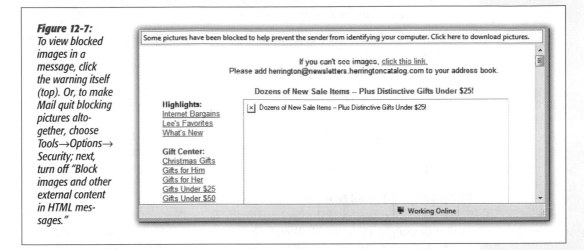

Figure 12-7:
To view blocked images in a message, click the warning itself (top). Or, to make Mail quit blocking pictures altogether, choose Tools→Options→Security; next, turn off "Block images and other external content in HTML messages."

How to Process a Message

Once you've read a message and savored the feeling of awe brought on by the miracle of instantaneous electronic communication, you can handle the message in any of several ways.

Deleting messages

Sometimes it's junk mail, sometimes you're just done with it; either way, it's a snap to delete a message. Click the Delete button on the toolbar, press the Delete key, or choose Edit→Delete. (You can also delete a batch of selected messages simultaneously.)

UP TO SPEED

Selecting Messages

In order to process a group of messages simultaneously—to delete, move, or forward them, for example—you must first master the art of multiple message selection.

To select two or more messages that appear consecutively in your message list, click the first message, then Shift-click the last. Known as a *contiguous selection*, this trick selects every message between the two that you clicked.

To select two or more messages that *aren't* adjacent in the list (that is, skipping a few messages between selected ones), Ctrl-click the messages you want. Only the messages you click get selected—no filling in of messages in between, this time.

After using either technique, you can also *deselect* messages you've managed to highlight—just Ctrl-click them again.

The messages don't actually disappear. Instead, they move to the Deleted Items folder. If you like, click this folder to view a list of the messages you've deleted. You can even rescue some simply by dragging them into another folder (even right back into the Inbox).

Mail doesn't truly vaporize messages in the Deleted Items folder until you "empty the trash." You can empty it in any of several ways:

- Right-click the Deleted Items folder. Choose "Empty 'Deleted Items' Folder" from the shortcut menu.

- Click a message, or a folder, within the Deleted Items Folder list and then click the Delete button on the toolbar (or press the Delete key). You're asked to confirm its permanent deletion.

- Set up Mail to delete messages automatically when you quit the program. To do so, choose Tools→Options→Advanced. Click the Maintenance button, and then turn on "Empty messages from the 'Deleted Items' folder on exit." Click OK.

Replying to Messages

To reply to a message, click the Reply button in the toolbar, or choose Message→Reply to Sender, or press Ctrl+R. Mail creates a new, outgoing email message, preaddressed to the sender's return address. (If the message was sent to you *and* a few other people, and you'd like to reply to all of them at once, click Reply All in the toolbar.)

To save additional time, Mail pastes the entire original message at the bottom of your reply (either indented, if it's HTML mail, or marked with the > brackets that serve as Internet quoting marks); that's to help your correspondent figure out what you're talking about.

Note: To turn off this feature, choose Tools→Options, click the Send tab, and then turn off "Include message in reply."

Mail even tacks *Re:* ("regarding") onto the front of the subject line.

UP TO SPEED

About Mailing Lists

During your email experiments, you're likely to come across something called a mailing list—a discussion group conducted via email. By searching Yahoo.com or other Web directories, you can find mailing lists covering just about every conceivable topic.

You can send a message to all members of such a group by sending a message to a single address—the list's address. The list is actually maintained on a special mail server. Everything

sent to the list gets sent to the server, which forwards the message to all of the individual list members.

That's why you have to be careful if you're actually trying to reply to *one person* in the discussion group; if you reply to the list and not to a specific person, you'll send your reply to every address on the list—sometimes with disastrous consequences.

Your insertion point appears at the top of the message box. Now, just begin typing your reply. You can also add recipients, remove recipients, edit the subject line or the message, and so on.

Tip: Use the Enter key to create blank lines within the bracketed original message in order to place your own text within it. Using this method, you can splice your own comments into the paragraphs of the original message, replying point by point. The brackets preceding each line of the original message help your correspondent keep straight what's yours and what's hers. Also, if you're using HTML formatting for the message, you can format what you've written in bold, italic, underlined, or even in another color for easier reading.

Forwarding Messages

Instead of replying to the person who sent you a message, you may sometimes want to *forward* the message—pass it on—to a third person.

To do so, click Forward in the toolbar, choose Message→Forward, or press Ctrl+F. A new message opens, looking a lot like the one that appears when you reply. Once again, before forwarding the message, you have the option of editing the subject or the message. (For example, you may wish to precede the original message with a comment of your own, along the lines of: "Frank: I thought you'd be interested in this joke about Congress.")

All that remains is for you to specify who receives the forwarded message. Just address it as you would any outgoing piece of mail.

Printing Messages

Sometimes there's no substitute for a printout of an email message—an area where Mail shines. Click Print in the toolbar, choose File→Print, or press Ctrl+P. The standard Windows Print dialog box pops up, so that you can specify how many copies you want, what range of pages, and so on. Make your selections, and then click Print.

Filing Messages

Mail lets you create new folders in the Folders list; by dragging messages from your Inbox onto one of these folder icons, you can file away your messages into appropriate cubbies. You might create one folder for important messages, another for order confirmations from shopping on the Web, still another for friends and family, and so on. In fact, you can even create folders *inside* these folders, a feature beloved by the hopelessly organized.

To create a new folder, see Figure 12-8.

Tip: To rename an existing folder, right-click it and choose Rename from the shortcut menu.

To move a message into a folder, proceed like this:

• Drag it out of the list pane and onto the folder icon. You can use any part of a message's "row" in the list as a handle. You can also drag messages en masse onto a folder after selecting them.

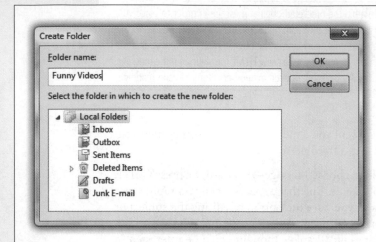

Figure 12-8:
To create a new folder, choose File→Folder→New, or right-click the Local Folders icon (in the folder list), and choose New Folder from the shortcut menu. Either way, this window appears. Name the folder and then, by clicking, indicate which folder you want this one to appear in. Usually, you'll want to click Local Folders (that is, not inside any other folder).

• Right-click a message (or one of several that you've highlighted). From the shortcut menu, choose Move to Folder. In a dialog box, the folder list appears; select the one you want, and then press Enter or click OK.

Tip: When you click a arrow in the Folder list, you see all folders contained within that folder, exactly like in Windows Explorer. You can drag folders inside other folders, nesting them to create a nice hierarchical folder structure. (To drag a nested folder back into the list of "main" folders, just drag it to the Local Folders icon.)

You can also drag messages between folders; just drag one from the message list onto the desired folder at the left side of the screen.

This can be a useful trick when you apply it to a message in your Outbox. If you decide to postpone sending it, drag it into any other folder. Windows Mail won't send it until you drag it *back* into the Outbox.

Flagging Messages

Sometimes, you'll receive an email message that prompts you to some sort of action, but you may not have the time or the fortitude to face the task at the moment. ("Hi there…it's me, your accountant. Would you mind rounding up your expenses for 1993 through 2001 and sending me a list by email?")

That's why Mail lets you *flag* a message, positioning a small, red flag in the corresponding column next to a message's name. These little flags are visual indicators that mean whatever you want them to mean. You can bring all flagged messages to the top of the list by choosing View→Sort By→Flag.

To flag a message in this way, select the message (or several messages) and choose Message→Flag Message. (Use the same command again to clear a flag from a message.)

Opening Attachments

Just as you can attach files to a message, people can send files to you. You know when a message has an attachment because a paper-clip icon appears next to its name in the Inbox.

To free an attached file from its message, releasing it to the wilds of your hard drive, use one of the following methods:

- Click the attachment icon, select Save Attachments from the shortcut menu, and then specify the folder in which you want the file saved (Figure 12-9).

Figure 12-9:
One way to rescue an attachment from an email message is to click the paper-clip icon and choose Save Attachments. You can also drag an attachment's icon onto your desktop. Either way, you take the file out of the Mail world and into your standard Windows world, where you can file it, trash it, open it, or manipulate it as you would any file.

- Click the attachment icon, and select the attachment to open. Choose the name of the attachment in order to open the file directly (in Word, Excel, or whatever).

- If you've double-clicked the message so it appears in its own window, drag the attachment icon out of the message window and onto any visible portion of your desktop.

- Again, if you've opened the message into its own window, you can double-click the attachment's icon in the message. Once again, you're asked whether you want to open the file or save it to the disk.

Message Rules

Once you know how to create folders, the next step in managing your email is to set up *message rules*. These are filters that can file, answer, or delete an incoming message *automatically* based on its subject, address, or size.

Message rules require you to think like the distant relative of a programmer, but the mental effort can reward you many times over. In fact, message rules can turn Mail into a surprisingly smart and efficient secretary.

Setting up message rules

Now that you're thoroughly intrigued about the magic of message rules, here's how to set one up:

1. **Choose Tools→Message Rules→Mail.**

   If you've never created a message rule, you'll see what's shown in Figure 12-10.

   If you *have* created message rules before, you see the Message Rules window first. Click New to open the New Mail Rule window shown in Figure 12-10.

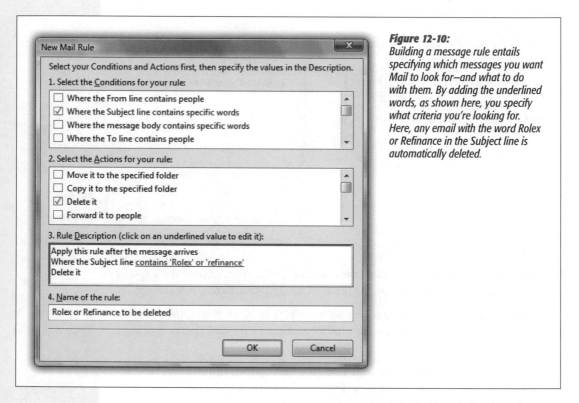

Figure 12-10:
Building a message rule entails specifying which messages you want Mail to look for—and what to do with them. By adding the underlined words, as shown here, you specify what criteria you're looking for. Here, any email with the word Rolex or Refinance in the Subject line is automatically deleted.

2. **Use the top options to specify how Mail should select messages to process.**

   For example, if you'd like Mail to watch out for messages from a particular person, you would choose, "Where the From line contains people."

   To flag messages containing *loan, $$$$, XXXX, !!!!*, and so on (favorites of spammers), choose, "Where the Subject line contains specific words."

If you turn on more than one checkbox, you can set up another condition for your message rule. For example, you can set up the first criterion to find messages *from* your uncle, and a second that watches for subject lines that contain "joke." Now, only jokes sent by your uncle get placed in, say, Deleted Items. Figure 12-11 shows the word "and," plus a few other items you'll learn about shortly.

Figure 12-11:
If you've set up more than one criterion, you'll see the under-lined word and *at the bottom of the dialog box. It indicates that the message rule should apply only if* all *of the conditions are true. Click the* and *to produce a little dialog box, where you have the option to apply the rule if* any *of the conditions are met.*

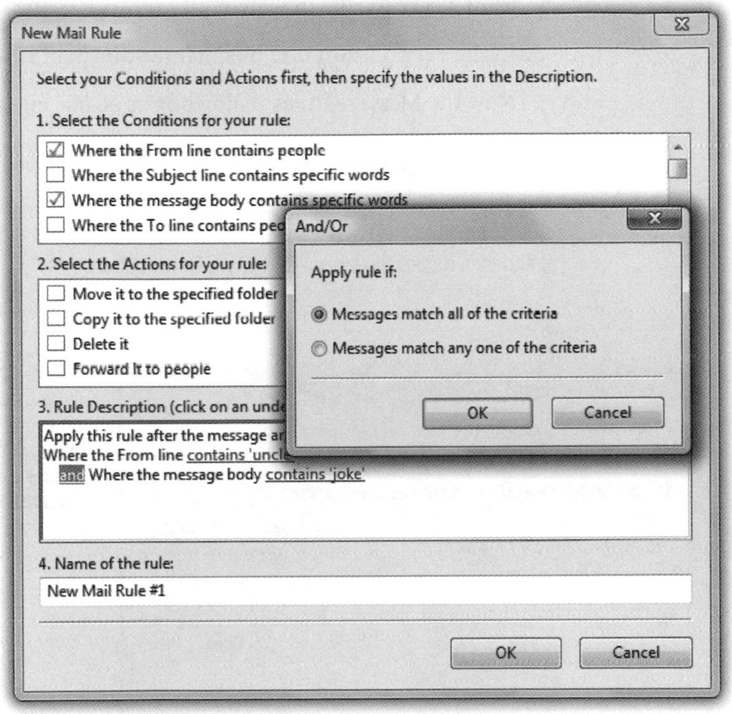

3. **Using the second set of checkboxes, specify what you want to happen to messages that match the criteria.**

   If, in step 2, you told your rule to watch for messages from your uncle containing the word "joke" somewhere in the message body, here's where you can tell Mail to delete or move the message into, say, a Spam folder.

   With a little imagination, you'll see how these checkboxes can perform absolutely amazing functions with your incoming email. Windows Mail can delete, move, or print messages; forward or redirect them to somebody; automatically reply to certain messages; and even avoid downloading files bigger than a certain number of kilobytes (ideal for laptop lovers on slow hotel room connections).

4. **Specify *which* words or people you want the message rule to watch out for.**

In the bottom of the dialog box, you can click any of the underlined phrases to specify which people, which specific words, which file sizes you want Mail to watch out for—a person's name, or *XXX*, in the previous examples.

If you click "contains people," for example, a dialog box appears that lets you open your Contacts list to select certain individuals whose messages you want handled by this rule. If you click "contains specific words," you can type in the words you want a certain rule to watch out for. And so on.

5. **In the very bottom text box, name your mail rule. Click OK.**

Now the Message Rules dialog box appears (Figure 12-12).

Tip: Windows Mail applies rules as they appear—from top to bottom—in the Message Rules window. If a rule doesn't seem to be working properly, it may be that an earlier rule is intercepting and processing the message before the "broken" rule even sees it. To fix this, try moving the rule up or down in the list by selecting it and then clicking the Move Up or Move Down buttons.

Figure 12-12:
Once a rule is created, it lands in the Message Rules window under the Mail tab. Here, you can manage the rules you've created, choose a sequence for them (those at the top get applied first), and apply them to existing messages (by clicking Apply Now).

Two sneaky message-rule tricks

You can use message rules for many different purposes. But here are two of the best:

- **File mail from specific people.** For instance, if you have a few friends who constantly forward their idea of funny messages, create a rule that sends any email from them to a specific folder automatically. At the end of the day, look through the folder just to make sure you haven't missed anything, and if you have time, read the "most excellent funny emails in the whole wide world."

- **The email answering machine.** If you're going on vacation, turn on "For all messages" in step 2, and then "Reply with message" in step 3. In other words, you can turn Windows Mail into an email answering machine that automatically sends a canned "I'm away until the 15th" message to everyone who writes you.

Tip: Unsubscribe from, or turn off, any email mailing lists before you turn on "For all messages." Otherwise, you'll incur the wrath of the other list members by littering their email discussion groups with copies of your autoreply message.

Junk Email
All Versions

Windows Mail now offers Junk E-Mail Options, a feature that was glaringly absent in Outlook Express.

The Junk filter automatically channels what it believes to be spam into the Junk E-Mail folder in the folder list. Its factory setting is Low, meaning that only the most obvious spam gets sent to the Junk E-Mail folder. You'll probably still get a ton of spam, but at least almost no legitimate mail will get mistakenly classified as spam.

Figure 12-13:
To visit this dialog box, choose Tools→Junk E-Mail Options. Choose No Automatic Filtering, Low, High, or Safe List Only. You can also opt to permanently delete suspected spam instead of moving it to the Junk E-Mail folder. No matter what setting you choose, though, always go through the Junk E-Mail folder every few days to make sure you haven't missed any important messages that were flagged as spam incorrectly.

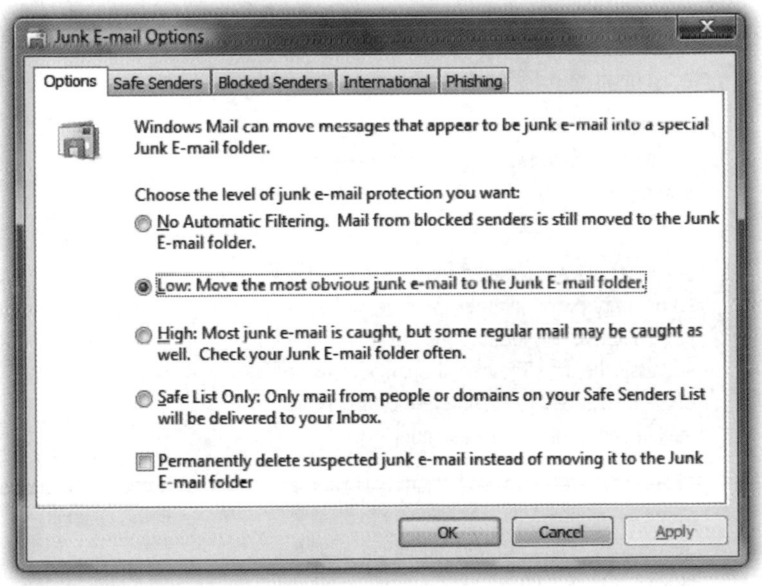

You can configure the level of security you want in the Junk E-Mail Options window, shown in Figure 12-13.

Junk E-Mail Options

Junk E-Mail options offers five tabs. The Options tab is shown in Figure 12-13. The other tabs are:

- **Safe Senders.** Messages from any contacts, email addresses, or domain names that you add to this list are never treated as junk email. (A domain name is what comes after the @ sign in an email address, as in bob@*herbalviagra.com*.) Click Add to begin.

Tip: The two checkboxes below the list are also useful in preventing "false positives." The first, "Also trust e-mail from my Windows Contacts," means that anyone in your own address book is not a spammer. The second, "Automatically add people I e-mail to the Safe Sender's list," means that if you send mail *to* somebody, it's someone you don't consider a spammer.

- **Blocked Senders.** This one's the flip side of Safe Senders: it's a list of contacts, email addresses, and domain names that you always want flagged as spam.

Canning Spam

Help! I'm awash in junk email! How do I get out of this mess?

Spam is a much-hated form of advertising that involves sending unsolicited emails to thousands of people. While there's no instant cure for spam, you can take certain steps to protect yourself from it.

1. Use one email account for online shopping, Web site and software registration, and newsgroup posting; use a second one for person-to-person email.

   Spammers have automated software robots that scour every public Internet message and Web page, automatically locating and recording email addresses they find. These are the primary sources of spam, so at least you're now restricting the junk mail to one secondary mail account.

2. Whenever you receive a piece of junk mail, choose Message→Junk E-Mail→Add Sender to Blocked Senders List. Windows Mail no longer accepts email from that sender.

3. When filling out forms or registering products online, look for checkboxes requesting permission for the company to send you email or share your email address with its "partners." Just say no.

4. When posting messages in a newsgroup, insert the letters NOSPAM, SPAMISBAD, or something similar somewhere into the email address you've specified in the News Account dialog box (page 420). Anyone replying to you via email must manually remove it from your email address, which, while a hassle, keeps your email address away from the spammer's robots. (They're getting smarter every day, though; a trickier insert may be required, along the lines of REMOVETOEMAIL or SPAMMERSARESCUM.)

5. Create *message rules* to filter out messages containing typical advertising words such as *casino, Rolex, herbal,* and so forth. (You'll find instructions in this chapter.)

6. Buy an antispam program like SpamAssassin.

- **International.** You can also block email in foreign languages, or that originate overseas. (A huge percentage of spam originates overseas, since U.S. antispam laws have no jurisdiction there.) See Figure 12-14.

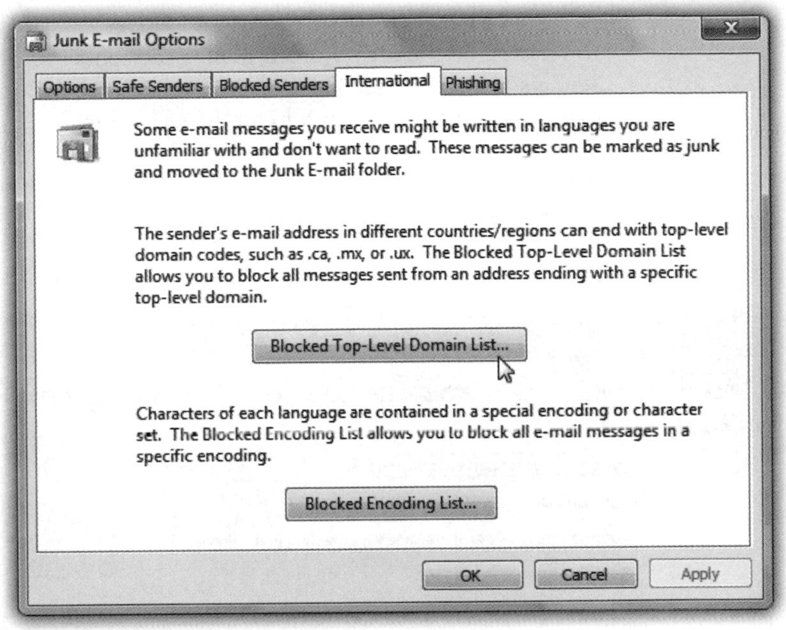

Figure 12-14:
If you find you're getting email from specific countries or domains, you can select the top-level domains (.ca for Canadian mail, .uk for British mail, and so on) for those countries. All email from those domains now gets treated as junk email.

- **Phishing.** For a complete description of phishing scams, see page 346. In brief, phishing email is designed to look like it came from your bank, eBay, or PayPal—but it's a trick to get you to surrender your account information so the bad guys can steal your identity.

Windows Mail keeps phishing email out of your Inbox unless you turn off this feature on this tab.

When the Junk Filter Goes Wrong

Windows Mail doesn't always get it right. It labels some good messages as junk, and some spam messages as OK.

Over time, though, it's supposed to get better—*if* you patiently help it along. Every time you see a good piece of email in the Junk E-Mail folder, click it, and then click Not Junk on the Toolbar.

Better yet, use the Message→Junk E-Mail submenu to choose one of these two options:

- **Add Sender to Safe Senders List.** No future mail from this person will be misfiled.

- **Add Sender's Domain to Safe Senders List.** No future mail from this person's entire company or ISP will be marked as spam.

The news isn't so good if you find a piece of spam in your Inbox; incredibly, there's no This is Junk button on the toolbar, or even a similar command in the Message menu.

You can use the Message→Junk E-Mail→Add Sender (or Sender's Domain) to Blocked Senders List, of course. But since spammers rarely use the same address or domain twice, it's probably faster just to hit the Delete key.

> **Note:** Microsoft intends to continue improving the quality of its spam filter through regular Windows Update updates (page 614).

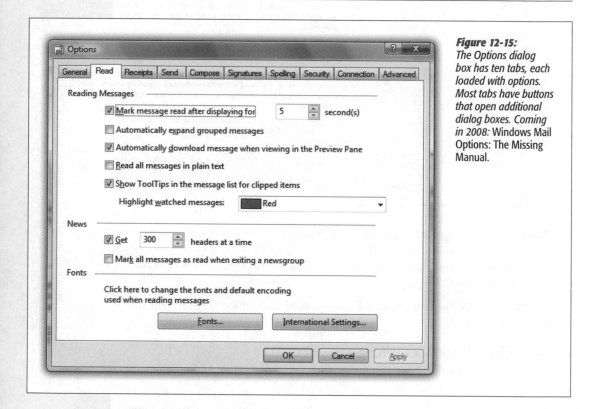

Figure 12-15:
The Options dialog box has ten tabs, each loaded with options. Most tabs have buttons that open additional dialog boxes. Coming in 2008: Windows Mail Options: The Missing Manual.

Configuring Windows Mail
All Versions

Mail has enough features and configuration options to fill a very thick book. You can see them for yourself by choosing Tools→Options. Here's a brief overview of some of the most useful options (Figure 12-15).

General Tab

Most of the controls here govern what Mail does when you first open the program. Take note of the options to connect automatically; you can opt to have Mail check for messages every few minutes, and then use the drop-down list to say how, and whether, to connect at that time if you're not already online.

Read Tab

Use these options to establish how the program handles messages in the Inbox. One of these options marks a message as having been read—changing its typeface from bold to non-bold—if you leave it highlighted in the list for five seconds or more, even without opening it. That's one option you may want to consider turning off. (This tab is also where you choose the font you want to use for the messages you're reading, which is an important consideration.)

Receipts tab

You can add a *return receipt* to messages you send. When the recipient reads your message, a notification message (receipt) is emailed back to you under two conditions: *if* the recipient agrees to send a return receipt to you, and *if* the recipient's email program offers a similar feature. (Windows Mail, Outlook, and Eudora all do.)

Send Tab

The options here govern outgoing messages. One option to consider turning *off* here is the factory-set option, "Send messages immediately." That's because as soon as you click the Send button, Mail sends messages immediately, even if you haven't fully had time to consider the consequences of the rant inside it—aimed at an ex, a boss, or a co-worker—which could land you in hot water.

It's also a good choice if you're on a dial-up connection. All of this dialing—and *waiting* for the dialing—drives some people crazy, especially in households with only one phone line.

If you turn this option off, clicking the Send button simply places a newly written message into the Outbox. As you reply to messages and compose new ones, the Outbox collects them. They're not sent until you click the Send/Receive button, or press Ctrl+M. Only at that point does Mail send your email. If you're on dial-up, it sends all the waiting outgoing mail at once.

Tip: To see the messages waiting in your Outbox, click the Outbox icon at the left side of the screen. At this point, you can click a message's name (in the upper-right pane of the screen) to view the message itself in the *lower*-right pane, exactly as with messages in your Inbox.

Don't bother to try *editing* an outgoing message in this way, however; Mail won't let you do so. Only by double-clicking a message's name (in the upper-right pane), thus opening it into a separate window, can you make changes to a piece of outgoing mail.

The Send tab also includes features for configuring replies. For example, you can disable the function that includes the message in the reply.

Finally, the "Automatically put people I reply to in my Contacts list" option can be a real timesaver. Each time you reply to somebody, his email address is automatically saved in your Contacts list. The next time you want to write him a note, you won't need to look up the address—just type the first few letters of it in the "To:" box.

Compose Tab

Here's where you specify the font you want to use when writing messages and newsgroup messages.

This is also the control center for *stationery* (custom-designed templates, complete with fonts, colors, backgrounds, borders, and other formatting elements that you can use for all outgoing email). Needless to say, sending a message formatted with stationery means that you're using HTML formatting, as described earlier, complete with its potential downsides.

To choose a stationery style for all outgoing messages, turn on the Mail checkbox, and then click the Select button. You're offered a folder full of Microsoft stationery templates; click one to see its preview. You can also click the Create New button, which launches a wizard that walks you through the process of creating your own background design.

Tip: You don't have to use one particular stationery style for all outgoing messages. When sending a message, instead of clicking the Create Mail button on the Mail toolbar, just click the ▾ *next* to it. Doing so opens a window that lists several stationery styles, letting you choose one on a message-by-message basis.

Signatures Tab

As noted earlier in this chapter, you use this tab to design a *signature* for your messages. By clicking the New button and entering more signature material in the text box, you can create several *different* signatures: one for business messages, one for your buddies, and so on.

To insert a signature into an outgoing message, choose Insert→Signature, and then choose the one you want from the list that appears.

Spelling Tab

The Spelling tab offers configuration options for the Mail spell-checking feature (which requires that you have Microsoft Word). You can even force the spell checker to correct errors in the *original* message when you send a reply, although your correspondent may not appreciate it.

Security Tab

This tab contains options for sending secure mail, using digital IDs, and encryption. If you're using Mail in a business that requires secure email, the system administrator will provide instructions. Otherwise, you'll find that most of these settings have no effect.

A few settings worth exploring appear under "Virus Protection" and "Download Images," shown in Figure 12-16.

Tip: One of these options is very useful in the modern age: "Warn me when other applications try to send mail as me." That's a thinly veiled reference to viruses that, behind the scenes, send out hundreds of infected emails to everybody in your Contacts list. This option ensures that if some software—not you—tries to send messages, you'll know about it.

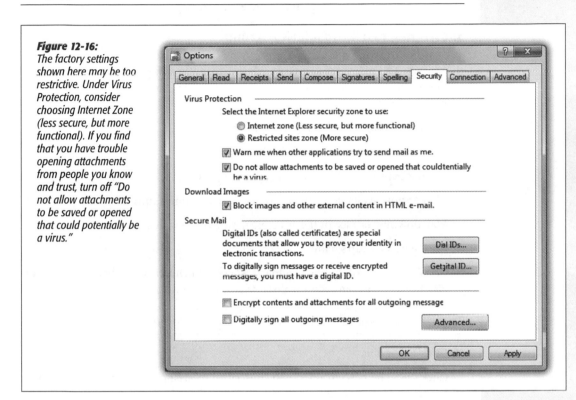

Figure 12-16:
The factory settings shown here may be too restrictive. Under Virus Protection, consider choosing Internet Zone (less secure, but more functional). If you find that you have trouble opening attachments from people you know and trust, turn off "Do not allow attachments to be saved or opened that could potentially be a virus."

Connection Tab

Here, you can tell Mail to hang up automatically after sending and receiving messages (and reconnect the next time you want to perform the same tasks). As noted in the dialog box, though, Mail otherwise uses the same Internet settings described in Chapter 9.

Advanced Tab

This tab is your housekeeping and settings center for Mail. You can configure what you want Mail to do with your contact's vCards (virtual business cards), if you want to compose your replies at the bottom of emails instead of the top, and whether or not you want to mark message threads in newsgroups as "watched."

Don't miss the Maintenance button. It lets you clear out old deleted messages, clean up downloads, purge newsgroup messages, and so on.

Newsgroups
All Versions

Newsgroups have nothing to do with news; in fact, they're Internet bulletin boards. There are hundreds of thousands of them, on every conceivable topic: pop culture, computers, politics, and every other special (and *very* special) interest; in fact, there are thousands just about Windows. You can use Mail to read and reply to these messages almost exactly as though they were email messages.

Subscribing to a Microsoft Newsgroup

Subscribing to your first newsgroup can be quite an experience, simply because there are just so many newsgroups to choose from. Mail has a link to the Microsoft Communities newsgroups built right in—a good way, though nerdy, to get started with newsgroups.

To join a Microsoft Community newsgroup:

1. **Click Microsoft Communities in the folder list.**

   A "Subscribe to newsgroups" dialog box appears.

2. **Click "Show available newsgroups and turn on communities."**

   Mail downloads a list of the available newsgroups, which may take a while.

3. **Click a newsgroup's name.**

   Consider Microsoft.public.windows.vista.general, for example; here, you can post questions and get answers for Vista-related questions.

Tip: You can select more than one newsgroup by Control-clicking their names.

---

4. **Click Subscribe.**

   Click OK. The newsgroup(s) you subscribed to are now available in Mail, under Microsoft Communities.

UP TO SPEED

Newsgroups Explained

Newsgroups (often called *Usenet*) started out as a way for people to conduct discussions via a bulletin-board-like system, in which a message is posted for all to see and reply to. These public discussions are divided into categories called newsgroups, which cover the gamut from miscellaneous photographic techniques to naval aviation.

These days, Usenet has a certain seedy reputation as a place to exchange pornography, pirated software, and MP3 files with doubtful copyright pedigrees. Even so, there are tens of thousands of interesting, informative discussions going on, and newsgroups are great places to get help with troubleshooting, exchange recipes, or just to see what's on the minds of your fellow Usenet fans.

Reading Messages

Once you've subscribed to a newsgroup, the next time you connect to the Internet and select the newsgroup from the newsgroup list, Mail downloads all of the message summaries in the discussions to which you've subscribed. (There may be just a few messages, or several hundred; they may go back only a few days or a couple of weeks, depending on the amount of "traffic" in each discussion and the storage space on the news server.)

To read the messages in a newsgroup, either click an entry in the list of messages to download the contents of the message and display it in the preview window (Figure 12-17), or double-click an entry to open the list of messages in a new window.

Tip: You can set up message rules for newsgroups to screen out messages from certain people, messages with certain phrases in their Subject lines, and so on. It works exactly like the message rules for email, as described earlier in this chapter. Just go to Tools→Message Rules→News.

Figure 12-17:
If you've been using Mail for email, the newsgroup interface should look familiar. The Folders pane lists news servers to which you've subscribed, the top-right pane lists the names of messages in a selected newsgroup, and the bottom-right pane displays the actual text of the message you've highlighted in the message list.

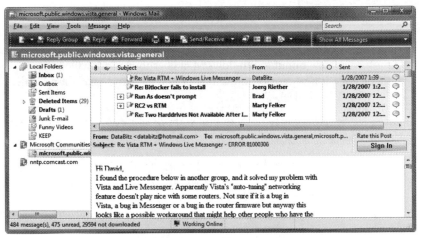

Replying, Composing, and Forwarding Messages

Working with newsgroup messages is very similar to working with email messages, except that you must be conscious of whether you're replying to the individual sender of a message or to the entire group. Otherwise, you can reply to messages, forward them, or compose them exactly as described earlier in this chapter. As with email, you can use plain text or (if you don't mind annoying the other Internet citizens) HTML formatting. You can include file attachments, too, by, for example, using the Attach toolbar button.

Tip: Aside from posting ads and HTML-formatted messages, the best way to irritate everyone on a newsgroup is to ask a question that has already been answered recently on the newsgroup. Before asking a question, spend five minutes reading the recent newsgroup messages to see whether someone has already answered your question. Also consider visiting the Groups tab at *www.google.com,* a Web site that lets you search all newsgroups for particular topics.

Subscribing to Other Newsgroups

What if you don't want to subscribe to a Microsoft computer-geek-filled newsgroup, but would rather subscribe to a newsgroup about cats?

To find a newsgroup on a specific topic, choose Tools→Accounts; click Microsoft Communities (default), and then click the Add button. On the next screen, click Newsgroup Account. Now a wizard steps you through the process of creating a news account in Mail. You're asked for your name, your email address, and—this may be the hard part—the address of your news server. You have to get that tidbit from whatever company provides your Internet connection.

Download the List of Newsgroups

When you're finished with the wizard, Mail invites you to download a list of newsgroups available on your server. Click the Yes button, and then wait patiently for a few minutes. Windows Mail goes to work downloading the list, which can be quite long—tens of thousands of entries—and take a long time. Fortunately, it's a one-time deal.

Now you're ready to find yourself some good online discussions; see Figure 12-18.

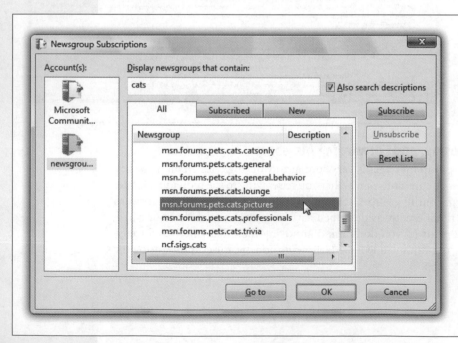

Figure 12-18:
In the box at the top, type the term you're hoping to find in a newsgroup's title (such as kittensandcats—in cyberspace, nobody can hear you use the Space bar). If you turn up a good-sounding topic in the gigantic list beneath, click its name and click Subscribe to subscribe to it. Now, each time you connect, Mail will download the latest messages on that topic.

Part Four: Pictures, Movies, and Media Center

4

Chapter 13: Windows Photo Gallery

Chapter 14: Windows Media Player

Chapter 15: Movie Maker and DVD Maker

Chapter 16: Media Center

Windows Photo Gallery

Your digital camera is brimming with photos. You've snapped the perfect gradu-
ation portrait, captured that jaw-dropping sunset over the Pacific, or compiled
an unforgettable photo essay of your 2-year-old attempting to eat a bowl of
spaghetti. It's time to use your PC to gather, organize, and tweak all these photos so
you can share them with the rest of the world.

Until Vista came along, all Windows offered for digital photos was Paint. That's right,
Paint—a feeble holdover from 1985 that sat in your Programs→Accessories folder
and opened one picture at a time. Barely.

Microsoft has addressed photo organizing/editing with a vengeance in Vista. Pathetic
little Paint is still there, for the benefit of change-phobic Windows veterans. But now
there's also Windows Photo Gallery, a beautiful, full-blown digital camera companion
that has nothing to be ashamed of.

Photo Gallery: The Application
All Versions

Photo Gallery approaches digital photo management as a four-step process: importing the photos to your Pictures folder; organizing, tagging, and rating them; editing
them; and sharing them (via prints, onscreen slideshows, design DVD slideshows,
email, screen saver, and so on).

To open Photo Gallery, choose its name from the Start→Programs menu, or double-
click a photo in your Pictures folder. You arrive at the program's main window, the
basic elements of which are shown in Figure 13-1.

Getting Pictures into Photo Gallery

All Versions

You're probably most interested in getting fresh photos off your digital camera. But if you've been taking digital photos for some time, you may also have photo files already crammed into folders on your hard drive or on CDs. If you shoot pictures with a traditional film camera and use a scanner to digitize them, you've probably got piles of JPEG or TIFF images stashed away on disk already.

Navigation tree   Thumbnails   Details pane

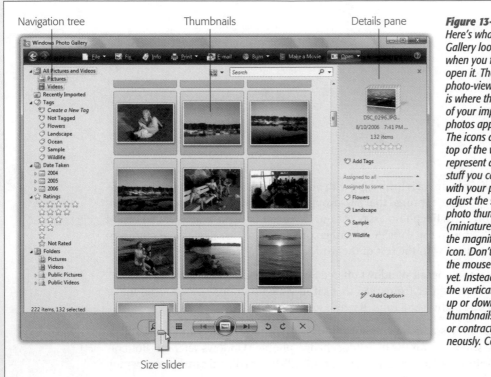

Figure 13-1:
Here's what Photo Gallery looks like when you first open it. The large photo-viewing area is where thumbnails of your imported photos appear. The icons at the top of the window represent all the stuff you can do with your photos. To adjust the size of the photo thumbnails (miniatures), click the magnifying-glass icon. Don't release the mouse button yet. Instead, drag the vertical slider up or down. All the thumbnails expand or contract simulta-neously. Cool!

Size slider

This section explains how to transfer files from each of these sources into Photo Gallery itself.

Photos from Your PC

The very first time you open it, Photo Gallery displays all the digital photos it can find in your Pictures folder (Start→Pictures).

This is important: you're looking at the *actual files* on your hard drive. If you delete a picture from Photo Gallery, you've just deleted it from your PC. (Well, OK, you've actually moved it to your Recycle Bin. But still, that's a step closer to oblivion.)

If you store your photos in other folders, you can make Photo Gallery aware of those, too. You can go about this task in either of two ways:

- **The menu way.** Choose File→Add Folder to Gallery; navigate to and select the additional folder, and then click OK. (You'll see the additional folder listed in the Folders category of the left-side master list.)

- **The draggy way.** Find the folder on your desktop or in any Explorer folder. Drag the folder itself directly onto the word Folders in the left-side list, as shown in Figure 13-2.

Note: Don't add your whole hard drive or Windows folder to Photo Gallery's list. You'll wind up adding literally *thousands* of little graphics—not actual photos, but bits of Web pages, button images, and other random visual detritus that Windows uses to display your programs and windows. Photo Gallery will grind to a halt.

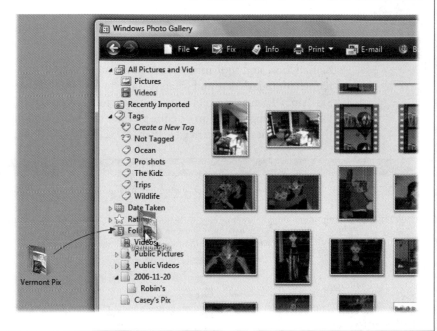

Figure 13-2:
You can add a "watched folder" to Photo Gallery by dragging it off the desktop (or any folder window) right onto the Folders heading, as shown here. The cursor changes to a + symbol to let you know that Photo Gallery understands your intention.

You can also drag individual photo or video files directly into Photo Gallery's window (from the desktop or an Explorer window, for example). Windows not only makes it appear in Photo Gallery, but also copies it to your Pictures folder for safekeeping.

Note: This trick works only with JPEG files. Graphics in other formats, and, in fact, anything else other than videos, wind up getting copied to your Pictures folder but don't show up in Photo Gallery.

Photos from a Digital Camera

Every modern camera comes with a USB cable that connects to your PC. That's handy, because it makes the photo-transfer process happen practically by itself.

- **If Photo Gallery is already running:** Choose File→Import from Camera or Scanner. In the dialog box that appears, click the name of your camera, and then click Import.

- **If Photo Gallery isn't yet running:** Connect the camera to one of your PC's USB jacks. At this point, you see the message shown in Figure 13-3. Click "Import using Windows." (After the importing is finished, Photo Gallery opens automatically to show your newly acquired pix—unless you've turned off this feature in Photo Gallery's Options.)

Either way, unless you've turned off this option in Options, Photo Gallery now invites you to apply a *tag* to each of the incoming photos. Typing in a name for each new batch—*Disney, First Weekend* or *Baby Meets Lasagna,* for example—will help you organize and find your pictures later on.

In either case, Windows sets about sucking in all the photos from the camera and placing them into your Pictures folder.

Not all loose and squirming—that'd be a mess. Instead, it neatly creates subfolders, named for today's date and whatever tag you gave this batch (for example, "2007-2-15 Ski Trip"). Each photo gets auto-renamed, too, according to the tag (Ski Trip 001.jpg, Ski Trip 002.jpg, and so on), on the premise that you'll find *those* names more helpful than the names the *camera* gave them (DSC_IMG_0023.jpg, for example).

GEM IN THE ROUGH

Auto Card Erase

Ordinarily, each time your camera's card is full, you'll want to dump all of the pictures onto your PC.

And ordinarily, each time you've finished dumping them, you'll want to erase the memory card so that it's empty and ready to reuse.

Windows can do that for you, but it doesn't want to take you by surprise. That's why the "Erase after importing" checkbox appears in the "Importing Pictures and Videos" status box during the importing process.

If you *always* want your photos erased, though, you can save yourself that step.

In Photo Gallery, choose File→ Options. Click the Import tab. There you'll see the "Always erase from camera after importing" checkbox.

Incidentally, Photo Gallery doesn't delete your pictures until *after* it has successfully copied them all to the Pictures folder. In other words, letting Windows erase your card is perfectly safe, and can spare your camera a little battery power.

This "Tag these pictures" dialog box also offers a direct link to the Options box shown in the box on the facing page.

Tip: You can fiddle with Vista's folder and photo naming conventions by choosing File→Options→Import in Photo Gallery. For example, you can opt to have the subfolder named after the date the pictures were *taken* instead of the date they were *imported.*

Figure 13-3:
When you connect a digital camera, Vista offers to import the photos from it. After the import, turn off the camera, and then unplug it from the USB cable.

UP TO SPEED

Scanning Photos

In Vista, Microsoft has outsourced the task of scanning to two different programs. When you want to scan documents, you're supposed to use Windows Fax and Scan. When you want to scan photos, though, stay right where you are—in Photo Gallery.

When a scanner is turned on and connected to the PC, choose File→Import from Camera or Scanner, clicking the scanner's name in the next dialog box, and then clicking Import. The New Scan dialog box appears. From the Profile list, choose Photo. You can also specify a color format, file format, resolution, and so on.

Click Preview to see what lies ahead. If it all looks good, click Scan.

As usual, Photo Gallery offers to tag the picture; click Import. After a moment, the freshly scanned photo pops up in the Photo Gallery viewer, ready for you to fix and organize it.

Behind the scenes, Photo Gallery dumps the scanned file into the Pictures folder. (You can override this setting by choosing File→Options→Import tab within Photo Gallery. Click "Settings for," choose Scanners, click Browse, and then find the folder you prefer.)

Photos from a USB Card Reader

A USB *memory card reader* offers another convenient way to transfer photos into Photo Gallery. Most of these card readers, which look like tiny disk drives, are under $20; some can read more than one kind of memory card.

If you have a reader, then instead of connecting the camera to the PC, you can slip the camera's memory card directly into the reader. Windows, or Photo Gallery, recognizes the reader as though it's a camera and offers to import the photos, just as described on the previous pages.

This method offers several advantages over the camera-connection method. First, it eliminates the considerable battery drain involved in pumping the photos straight off the camera. Second, it's less hassle to pull a memory card out of your camera and slip it into your card reader (which you can leave always plugged in) than it is to constantly plug and unplug camera cables. Finally, this method lets you use almost *any* digital camera with Photo Gallery, even those too old to include a USB cable connector.

The File Format Factor

Photo Gallery is a bit finicky about digital pictures' file formats. It's not a universal graphics manager by any means; in fact, it really prefers JPEG and TIFF files. Here are the details.

Common graphics formats

Photo Gallery recognizes the most common photo file formats—but not all of them. Here's the rundown:

- **JPEG.** Just about every digital camera on earth saves photos as JPEG files—and Photo Gallery handles this format beautifully. JPEG is the world's most popular file format for photos, because even though a JPEG photo is compressed to occupy a *lot* less disk space than it would otherwise, the visual quality is still very high. JPEG is also the most common format for photos on the Web.

Note: While most digital photos you work with are probably JPEG files, they're not always *called* JPEG files. You may also see JPEG referred to as JPG or *JFIF* (JPEG File Interchange Format). Bottom line: The terms JPEG, JFIF, JPEG JFIF, and JPEG 2000 all mean the same thing.

- **TIFF.** Some cameras offer you the chance to leave your photos *uncompressed* on the camera, in what's called TIFF format. These files are huge—in fact, you'll be lucky if you can fit *one* TIFF file on the memory card that came with the camera. Fortunately, they retain 100 percent of the picture's original quality.

  Along with JPEG, TIFF is Photo Gallery's other favorite photo format.

- **GIF** is the most common format used for non-photographic images on Web pages (borders, backgrounds, and logos). Unfortunately, Photo Gallery doesn't much care for GIF files. In fact, it can't display them at all.

- **PNG** files are also used in Web design, though not nearly as often as JPEG and GIF. They often display more complex graphic elements. Photo Gallery can show you PNG files, but can't edit them.

- **BMP** was once a popular graphics file format in Windows. Its files are big and bloated by today's standards, though, so Microsoft is trying to dissociate itself from them. Photo Gallery can't open or fix them.

- **WPD** is a new Microsoft graphics protocol intended for cellphones and palmtops. (Actually, only the technology is called WPD; the images are still labeled .jpg.)

- **Photoshop** refers to Adobe Photoshop, the world's most popular image-editing and photo-retouching program. Photo Gallery can't recognize, open, or fix Photoshop files.

Movies

In addition to still photos, most consumer digital cameras these days can also capture cute little digital movies. Some are jittery, silent affairs the size of a Wheat Thin; others are full-blown, 30-frames-per-second, fill-your-screen movies (that eat up a memory card plenty fast). Either way, Photo Gallery can import and organize them, as long as they're in .wmv, .asf, .mpeg, or .avi format. (Unfortunately, that list doesn't include .mov, a common movie format of digital cameras.)

You don't have to do anything special to import movies; they get slurped in automatically. To play one of these movies once they're in Photo Gallery, see Figure 13-4.

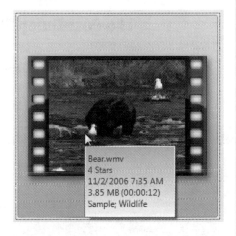

Figure 13-4:
The first frame of each video clip shows up as though it's a photo in your library. Your only clues that it's a movie and not a photo are the film sprocket holes along the sides and the tooltip that identifies the movie's running time. If you double-click one, it opens up and begins to play immediately.

Bear.wmv
4 Stars
11/2/2006 7:35 AM
3.85 MB (00:00:12)
Sample; Wildlife

RAW format

Most digital cameras work like this: when you squeeze the shutter button, the camera studies the data picked up by its sensors. The circuitry then makes decisions about sharpening level, contrast, saturation, white balance, and so on—and then saves the processed image as a compressed JPEG file on your memory card.

For millions of people, the result is just fine, even terrific. But all that in-camera processing drives professionals nuts. They'd much rather preserve every last shred of original picture information, no matter how huge the resulting file—and then process the file *by hand* once it's been safely transferred to the PC, using a program like Photoshop.

That's the idea behind the RAW file format, an option in many pricier digital cameras. (RAW stands for nothing in particular.) A RAW image isn't processed at all; it's a complete record of all the data passed along by the camera's sensors. As a result, each RAW photo takes up much more space on your memory card.

But once RAW files open up on the PC, image-manipulation nerds can perform astounding acts of editing to them. They can actually change the lighting of the scene—retroactively! And they don't lose a speck of image quality along the way.

Most people use a program like Photoshop or Photoshop Elements to do this kind of editing. But humble little Photo Gallery can at least open and organize them—usually. Its success at this depends on *which* kind of RAW files you've added to your Pictures folder. Each camera company (Canon, Nikon, and so on) has created a different flavor of RAW files, and it's up to Microsoft to keep Photo Gallery updated. If there are RAW files in your Pictures folder but they're not showing up in Photo Gallery, well, now you know the reason.

Note: You can open a RAW file for editing in Photo Gallery, but you're never making changes to the original file. Photo Gallery automatically creates a *copy* of the photo—in JPEG format—and lets you edit *that*.

The Post-Dump Slideshow
All Versions

If you're like most people, the first thing you want to do after dumping the photos from your camera into your PC is to see them at full size, filling your screen. That's the beauty of Photo Gallery's slideshow feature.

POWER USERS' CLINIC

Regedit for a Glimpse at the Themes

If your PC's graphics score isn't at least 3.0, you're locked out of seeing the full set of slideshow themes Microsoft has toiled countless nights to create. A shame, really.

Fortunately, if you're handy with regedit (page 788), you can still make them appear, as long as you have either the Home Premium or Ultimate version of Vista. These slideshows may not run especially smoothly; in fact, they'll probably look horrible. Remember, these themes are hidden from you

because your PC doesn't have the horsepower. But at least you can see what all the fuss is about.

To make this change, fire up regedit. Open the HKCU\Software\Microsoft\Windows Photo Gallery\SlideShow key.

Set the_Type to *DWORD Value,* the_Name to *WinSATScore,* and the_Value to *300.* Save your changes, reopen Photo Gallery, and check out the newly blossomed Themes menu.

To begin the slideshow, specify which pictures you want to see. For example:

- To see the pictures you most recently imported, click Recently Imported.

- Click a folder, tag, rating row, or another heading in the Navigation tree at the left side of the screen.

- If "All Pictures and Videos" (your whole library) is selected, click one of the photo-batch headings in the main window—for example, "2007—35 items."

Now click the unlabeled Play button at the bottom of the window (see Figure 13-5)—or just hit F11. Photo Gallery fades out of view, and a big, brilliant, full-screen slideshow of the new photos—and even self-playing videos—begins.

What's really useful is the slideshow control bar shown in Figure 13-5. You make it appear by wiggling your mouse as the show begins.

Click Exit, or press any key, to end the slideshow.

Note: Photo Gallery can't play music with your slides. (Bummer.) Microsoft cheerfully suggests that if you want music, you can first pop into another program (like Windows Media Player) to start playback, then return to Photo Gallery to start the slides. If that's what's going on, you can always click the Mute command in the gear pop-up menu.

Figure 13-5:
As the slideshow progresses, you can pause the show, go backward, rotate a photo, or change the transition effects, all courtesy of this control bar.

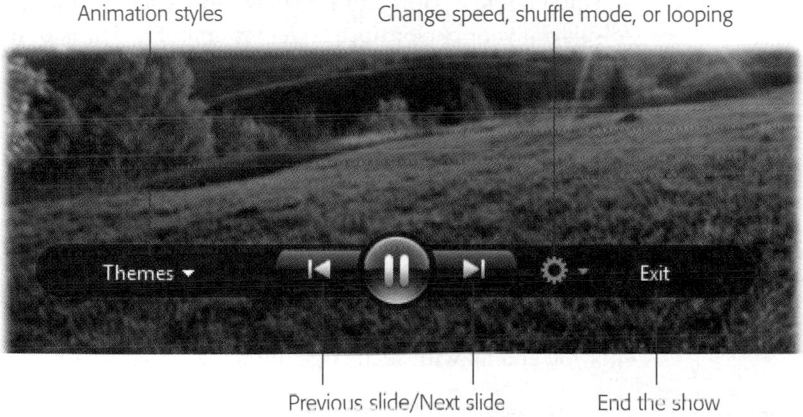

Animation styles

Change speed, shuffle mode, or looping

Themes ▾   Exit

Previous slide/Next slide   End the show

Slideshow Themes

If you wiggle the mouse during a slideshow to make the control bar appear, you'll see an odd little button called Themes at the left side.

A Theme is a canned special-effect set for a slideshow. On a powerful PC, you can call up slideshows with multiple photos parading into and out of view, with special backdrops filling in the gaps. (How do you know your PC is fast enough? The Experience Index score for your graphics card has to be 3.0 or better. See page 20 for your Experience Index score.)

If your PC doesn't have the horsepower for such elaborate effects, your Themes menu is much shorter. You can give the show an old-tyme, mottled brown or monochrome look by choosing "Sepia" or "Black and white" from the Themes menu.

Choosing "Pan and Zoom" instead makes the pictures smoothly cross-fade, panning and zooming as they go, as in a Ken Burns documentary on PBS. Your other choices include "Fade," meaning a crossfade, and "Classic," meaning Windows XP style: no transition effect at all.

The Digital Shoebox
All Versions

If you've imported your photos into Photo Gallery using any of the methods described above, you should now see a neatly arranged grid of thumbnails in Photo Gallery's main photo-viewing area. This is, presumably, your entire photo collection, including every last picture you've ever imported—the digital equivalent of that old shoebox you've had stuffed in the closet for the last 10 years.

Your journey out of chaos has begun. From here, you can sort your photos, give them titles, group them into smaller sub-collections (called *albums*), and tag them with keywords so you can find them quickly.

The Bigger Picture

If you point to a photo thumbnail without clicking, Photo Gallery is kind enough to display, at your cursor tip, a larger version of it. Think of it as a digital version of the magnifying loupe that art experts use to inspect gemstones and paintings.

Tip: If this feature gets on your nerves, choose File→Options, and then turn off "Show picture and video previews in tooltips."

You can also make *all* the thumbnails in Photo Gallery grow or shrink using the Size Control slider—click the blue magnifying-glass pop-up menu at the bottom of the Photo Gallery window. Drag the slider all the way down, and you get micro-thumbnails so small that you can fit 200 or more of them in the window. If you drag it all the way up, you end up with such large thumbnails that only a few fit the screen at a time.

For the biggest view of all, though, double-click a thumbnail. It opens all the way, filling the window. At this point, you can edit the picture, too, as described below.

The Navigation Tree

Even before you start naming your photos, assigning them keywords, or organizing them into albums, Photo Gallery imposes an order of its own on your digital shoebox.

The key to understanding it is the *Navigation tree* at the left side of the Photo Gallery window. This list grows as you import more pictures and organize them—but right off the bat, you'll find icons like these:

- **All Pictures and Videos.** The first icon in the Navigation tree is a very reassuring little icon, because no matter how confused you may get in working with subsets of photos later in your Photo Gallery life, clicking this icon returns you to your entire picture collection. It makes *all* of your photos and videos appear in the viewing area.

  Click the Pictures or Videos subhead to filter out the thumbnails so that *only* photos or *only* videos are visible.

- **Recently imported.** Most of the time, you'll probably work with the photos that you just downloaded from your camera. Conveniently, Photo Gallery always tracks your most recently added batch, so you can view its contents without much scrolling.

- **Tags.** As you work with your photos, you'll soon discover the convenience of adding *tags* (keywords) to them, like Family, Trips, or Baby Pix. Then, with one click on one of the tag labels in this list, you can see *only* the photos in your collection that match that keyword.

Tip: You can Ctrl-click several items in the Tags list at once. For example, if you want to see both Family photos *and* Vacation photos, click Family, then Ctrl-click Vacation.

This trick also works to select multiple months, years, star-rating categories, or folders (described below).

- **Date Taken.** Photo Gallery's navigation tree also offers miniature calendar icons named for the years (2005, 2006, 2007, and so on).

Figure 13-6:
The year and month icons are very helpful when you're creating a slideshow or trying to pinpoint one certain photo. After all, you usually can remember what year you took a vacation or when someone's birthday was. These icons help you narrow down your search without requiring that you scroll through your entire library.

When you import photos, the program files each photo by the date you took it. You can click, say, the 2005 icon to see just the ones you took during that year.

By clicking the flippy triangle next to a year's name, furthermore, you expand the list to reveal the individual *months* in that year; click a month's flippy triangle to see the individual *dates* within that month. Photo Gallery shows *only* the months and dates in which you actually took pictures; that's why 2006, for example, may show only April, July, and October (Figure 13-6).

- **Ratings.** As you'll read in a moment, you can give your pictures star ratings: one star (or none) for the turkeys, five stars for the really great ones that are shoo-ins for your Web page or annual year-end calendar.

  These little rows of stars make it easy to sort your entire collection by rating. Click the row of five stars, for example, to see *only* your five-starrers.

- **Folders.** At the bottom of the list, you'll see a collapsible list of the actual folders, sitting out there on your hard drive, that hold your photos and video clips. At the outset, you'll see only your Pictures and Videos folders (and maybe the Public versions of those, for use on a network). But as you add "watched folders" as described on page 425, this list will grow.

Working with Your Photos

All right: Enough touring Photo Gallery's main window. Now it's time to start *using* it.

Browsing, selecting, and opening photos is straightforward. Here's everything you need to know:

- Use the vertical scroll bar, or your mouse's scroll wheel, to navigate through your thumbnails.

- To create the most expansive photo-viewing area possible, you can temporarily hide the details pane at the right side of the window. To do so, click the tiny X button at its top—just *under* the ? button. (The red X *above* the Help button closes Photo Gallery.) Bring the Info pane back by clicking Info in the toolbar.

Category Groupings

Each time you import a new set of photos into Photo Gallery—whether from your hard drive, a camera, or a memory card—it appears with its own heading in Photo Gallery. Each batch is like one film roll you've had developed. Photo Gallery starts out sorting your Photo Library chronologically, meaning that the most recently imported photos appear at the top of the window.

Tip: If you'd prefer that the most recent items appear at the *bottom* of the Photo Gallery window instead of the top, open the Thumbnail View pop-up menu (Figure 13-7). From the pop-up menu, choose Sort By→Descending.

You can exploit these mini-categories within Photo Gallery in several ways:

- For speed in scrolling through a big photo collection, you can *collapse* these groupings so only their names are visible. To do that, just click the tiny ▲ button at the right end of each horizontal line.

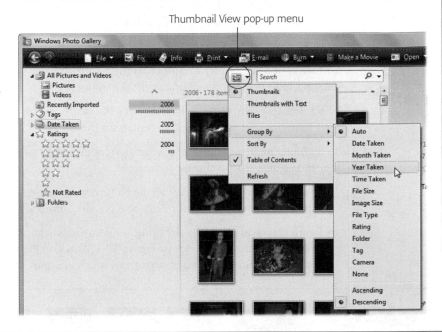

Figure 13-7:
This unlabeled pop-up menu is the master control for the display of photos. You can use it to sort, group, and hide the labels of your photos. Note, too, that you can click the triangle to the right of each header to expand or collapse the category group

Thumbnail View pop-up menu

- The "categories" don't have to be chronological. You can also ask Photo Gallery to cluster your photos into other logical groups: by rating (all the five-starrers together), by camera model, by month taken, and so on.

FREQUENTLY ASKED QUESTION

Your Own Personal Sorting Order

I want to put my photos in my own order. I'm making a slideshow, and I want to dictate the sequence. How do I do that?

You can't.

At least not without a lot of effort—namely, by manually renaming the photos so that their names are 000 Beach, 001 Sunset, and so on.

To rename a photo, click it once. See the Info pane at the right side of the window? (If not, click Info in the toolbar.) Click the photo's name to open its photo-editing box.

If you want to *drag* photos into a new order—say, for the purposes of a slideshow movie—you have to do it in Movie Maker.

To fiddle with the groupings, open the Thumbnail View pop-up menu (identified in Figure 13-7). Choose the grouping criterion you want from the Group By submenu.

- *Within* each group, you can specify how you want the photos sorted: chronologically by date taken or date modified, by file size, by rating, alphabetically by name, or whatever. These options, too, are hiding in the Thumbnail View pop-up menu—this time, in the Sort By submenu.

Selecting Photos

To highlight a single picture in preparation for printing, opening, duplicating, or deleting, click the thumbnail once with the mouse.

That much may seem obvious. But first-time PC users may not know how to manipulate *more* than one icon at a time—an essential survival skill.

To highlight multiple photos in preparation for deleting, moving, duplicating, printing, and so on, use one of these techniques:

- **To select all the photos.** Select all the pictures in the set you're viewing by pressing Ctrl+A (the equivalent of the Edit→Select All command).

- **To select several photos by dragging.** You can drag diagonally to highlight a group of nearby photos, as shown in Figure 13-8. You don't even have to enclose the thumbnails completely; your cursor can touch any part of any icon to highlight

Figure 13-8:
You can highlight several photos simultaneously by dragging a box around them. To do so, start from somewhere outside of the target
photos and drag diagonally across them, creating a whitish enclosure rectangle as you go. Any photos touched by this rectangle are selected when you release the mouse.

it. In fact, if you keep dragging past the edge of the window, the window scrolls automatically.

- **To select consecutive photos.** Click the first thumbnail you want to highlight, and then Shift click the last one. All the files in between are automatically selected, along with the two photos you clicked (Figure 13-9, top). This trick mirrors the way Shift-clicking works in a word processor, the Finder, and many other kinds of programs.

- **To select random photos.** If you only want to highlight, for example, the first, third, and seventh photos in a window, start by clicking photo icon No. 1. Then Ctrl-click each of the others. Each thumbnail sprouts colored shading to indicate that you've selected it (Figure 13-9, bottom).

Figure 13-9:
Top: To select a block of photos (as indicated by the faint colored border on each one), click the first one, and then Shift-click the last one. Photo Gallery selects all the files in between your clicks.

Bottom: To select nonadjacent photos, Ctrl-click them. (To remove one of the photos from your selection, Ctrl-click it.)

If you're highlighting a long string of photos and then click one by mistake, you don't have to start over. Instead, just Ctrl-click it again, and the dark highlighting disappears. (If you do want to start over from the beginning, however, just deselect all selected photos by clicking any empty part of the window.)

The Ctrl-key trick is especially handy if you want to select *almost* all the photos in a window. Press Ctrl+A to select everything in the folder, then Ctrl-click any unwanted photos to deselect them. You'll save a lot of time and clicking.

Tip: You can also combine the Ctrl-clicking business with the Shift-clicking trick. For instance, you could click the first photo, then Shift-click the tenth, to highlight the first 10. Next, you could Ctrl-click photos 2, 5, and 9 to *remove* them from the selection.

Once you've highlighted multiple photos, you can manipulate them all at once. For example, you can drag them en masse out of the window and onto your desktop—a quick way to export them.

In addition, when multiple photos are selected, the commands in the shortcut menu (right-click any *one* of them) apply to all of them simultaneously—like Rotate, Copy, Delete, Rename, or Properties.

Deleting Photos

As every photographer knows—make that every *good* photographer—not every photo is a keeper. You can relegate items to the Recycle Bin by selecting one or more thumbnails, and then performing one of the following:

- Right-click a photo, and then choose Delete from the shortcut menu.
- Click the red, slashy X button at the bottom of the window.
- Press the Delete key on your keyboard.

If you suddenly decide you don't really want to get rid of any of these trashed photos, it's easy to resurrect them. Switch to the desktop, open the Recycle Bin, and then drag the thumbnails out of the window and back into your Pictures folder.

(Of course, if you haven't deleted the imported pictures from your camera, you can still recover the original files and reimport them even after you empty the Recycle Bin.)

Duplicating a Photo

It's often useful to have two copies of a picture. For example, a photo whose dimensions are appropriate for a slideshow or desktop picture (that is, a 4:3 proportion) isn't proportioned correctly for ordering prints (4 x 6, 8 x 10, or whatever). To use the same photo for both purposes, you really need to crop two copies independently.

To make a copy of a photo, double-click its thumbnail to open it. Then choose File→Make a Copy. You're asked to name the duplicate and choose a folder location for it. Do so, and then click Save.

The Info Panel

Behind the scenes, Photo Gallery stores a wealth of information about each individual photo in your collection. To take a peek, highlight a thumbnail, and then click the Info button on the toolbar. A new pane appears at the right side of the window (Figure 13-10), or It reveals that picture's name, rating, creation time and date, dimensions (in pixels), file size, and any comments you've typed into the Captions area.

Figure 13-10:
The Info pane isn't just a place to look at the details of your pictures. You can also edit a lot of it. You can even change the date a photo was taken—a good tip to remember if you're a defense attorney.

- When multiple photos are selected, you see how many photos are selected.

- When no photos are selected, the Info area displays how many pictures or movies are in the currently selected container in the Navigation tree—the current album or film roll, for example.

How does Photo Gallery know so much about how your photos were taken? Most digital cameras embed a wealth of image, camera, lens, and exposure information in the photo files they create, using a standard data format called *XMP* or *EXIF* (Exchangeable Image Format). With that in mind, Photo Gallery automatically scans photos for XMP or EXIF data as it imports them (see Figure 13-11).

Note: Some cameras do a better job than others at embedding EXIF data in photo files. Photo Gallery can extract this information only if it's been properly stored by the camera when the digital photo is created. Of course, most of this information is missing altogether if your photos didn't come from a digital camera (if they were scanned in, for example).

Titles

You can rename a photo easily enough. Just click its existing name in the Info panel, and then retype.

Tip: Most people find this feature especially valuable when it comes to individual photographs. When you import them from your digital camera, the pictures bear useless gibberish names like CRS000321.JPG, CRS000322.JPG, and so on. If you highlight a *bunch* of photos and then change the title, you're renaming *all* of them at once. Photo Gallery even numbers them (Snowstorm 1.jpg, Snowstorm 2.jpg, and so on).

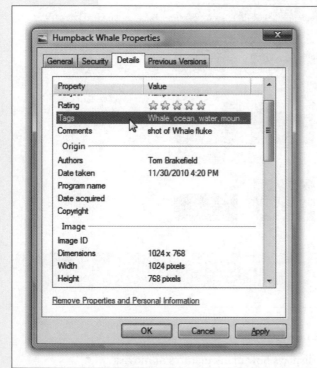

Figure 13-11:
The Properties dialog box reports details about your photos by reading the XMP or EXIF tags that your camera secretly embeds in your files. This is even more information than you see in the Info pane (Figure 13-10).

To open this box, right-click any photo in Photo Gallery. From the shortcut menu, choose Properties.

While you can make a photo's title as long as you want, it's smart to keep it short (about 10 characters or so). This way, you can see all or most of the title in the Title field (or under the thumbnails).

Tip: Once you've gone to the trouble of naming your photos, remember that you can make these names appear right beneath the thumbnails for convenient reference. Use the Thumbnail View pop-up menu (Figure 13-7) to make it so.

Dates

Weirdly enough, you can even edit the dates the pictures were taken—a handy fix if, for example, the camera's clock wasn't set right. Just click the date or time, and then either retype the date digits or click the ▾ button to open a clickable calendar.

Captions

Sometimes you need more than a one- or two-word title to describe a picture. If you want to add a lengthier description, you can type it in the Captions area of the Info pane (click where it says <Add Caption>). The box shows only two lines of text at a time, but it scrolls as necessary if you type more.

Even if you don't write full-blown captions for your pictures, you can use the Captions box to store little details such as the names, places, dates, and events associated with your photos.

The best thing about adding comments is that they're searchable. After you've entered all this free-form data, you can use it to quickly locate a photo using Photo Gallery's search command.

The Table of Contents (Quantity Graph)

You might not know the file names of the pictures you took during your trip to Canada a few years ago. You might not even remember which month it was exactly. But one thing's for sure—you know you took a ton of pictures in a very short time a couple summers ago. The Table of Contents view can show them to you.

You make the timeline appear by clicking the Thumbnail View icon (Figure 13-7), and then choosing Table of Contents from the pop-up menu. See Figure 13-12 for more details.

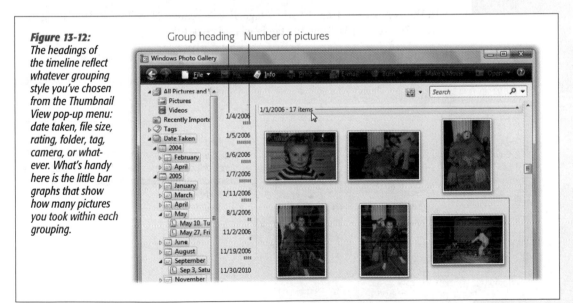

Figure 13-12:
The headings of the timeline reflect whatever grouping style you've chosen from the Thumbnail View pop-up menu: date taken, file size, rating, folder, tag, camera, or whatever. What's handy here is the little bar graphs that show how many pictures you took within each grouping.

The resulting list of years shows you how *many* photos you took within each grouping (that is, each month, with each camera, within each rating group, and so on), thanks to the little bar graphs. As on a cellphone, the more bars you see, the greater the signal (that is, the more photos in that group).

Click a heading to see the photos in that category.

Tags and Ratings
All Versions

Tags are descriptive keywords—like *family*, *vacation*, or *kids*—that you can use to label and categorize your photos and videos. Ratings are, of course, star ratings from 0 to 5, meaning that you can categorize your pictures by how great they are.

The beauty of tags and ratings is that they're searchable. Want to comb through all the photos in your library to find every closeup taken of your children during summer vacation? Instead of browsing through dozens of folders, just click the tags *kids*, *vacation*, *closeup*, and *summer in the Navigation tree*. You'll have the results in seconds.

Or want to gather only the cream of the crop into a slideshow or DVD? Let Photo Gallery produce a display of only your five-star photos.

Editing Tags

Microsoft offers you a few sample entries in the Tags list to get you rolling: Landscape, Travel, and so on. But these are intended only as starting points. You can add as many new tag labels as you want to create a meaningful, customized list.

To build your list, you can operate in either of two ways:

- **In the Navigation tree.** To add a tag, click "Create a New Tag" in the Navigation tree (Figure 13-13). Type the tag label and click OK.

- **In the Info pane.** Click Info in the toolbar. In the Info pane, click Add Tag.

To edit or delete a tag, right-click it, and then, from the shortcut menu, choose Delete or Rename.

Figure 13-13:
You can drag thumbnails onto tags one at a time, or you can select the whole batch first, using any of the selection techniques described on page 436.

Note: Be careful about renaming tags after you've started using them; the results can be messy. If you've already applied the keyword *Fishing* to a batch of photos, but later decide to replace it with *Romantic* in your keyword list, all the Fishing photos automatically inherit the keyword Romantic. Depending on you and your interests, this may not be what you intended.

It may take some time to develop a really good master set of keywords. The idea is to assign labels that are general enough to apply across your entire photo collection, but specific enough to be meaningful when conducting searches.

Applying Tags and Ratings

Photo Gallery offers two methods of applying tags and ratings to your pictures:

- **Method 1: Drag the picture.** One way to apply tags to photos is, paradoxically, to apply the *photos* to the *tags*.

  That is, drag relevant photos directly onto the tags in the Navigation tree, as shown in Figure 13-13.

  To give a photo a new star rating, drag its thumbnail onto the appropriate row in the Navigation tree.

Tip: You can apply as many tags to an individual photo as you like. A picture of your cousin Rachel at a hot dog–eating contest in London might bear all these keywords: Relatives, Travel, Food, Humor, and Medical Crises. Later, you'll be able to find that photo no matter which of these categories you're hunting for.

This method is best when you want to apply a whole bunch of pictures to one or two keywords. It's pretty tedious, however, when you want to apply a lot of different keywords to a single photo. That's why Microsoft has given you a second method, described next.

- **Method 2: Info Pane.** Highlight a thumbnail, and then click Info in the toolbar to open the Info panel. Here, you find a simple list of all tags you've applied to this

---

POWER USERS' CLINIC

Nested Tags

Tags, in essence, are a way to place your pictures into categories. And the only thing that could be more useful than that is being able to put them in *subcategories*.

Fortunately, you can do exactly that using *nested tags*. Within the Trips tag, for example, you can have Hawaii, Vermont, and The Zoo.

To create a sub-tag, just begin a tag's name with a backslash character (\). That's it: you've just created a sub-tag.

Later, when you're applying a tag to a group of photos in the Info pane, you can specify the subcategory just by typing the backslash and the first part of its name.

For example, you might type *tri,* and smile as Photo Gallery's autocomplete feature proposes the rest of the word *Trips.* Type the \ symbol, and then type *ver.* Photo Gallery proposes *Trips\Vermont;* hit Enter to confirm its choice.

(You can use any sub-tag with any main tag. That is, *Family\Vermont* is just as legitimate as *Trips\Vermont.*)

---

photo. Add a tag by clicking Add Tag, and then typing a tag name (or as much as necessary for Photo Gallery to autocomplete it). To change the photo's rating, click the number of stars you want.

The beauty of this system is that you can keep the little Info pane open on the screen as you move through your photo collection. Each time you click a photo—or, in fact, select a group of them—the tags list updates itself to reflect the tags of whatever is now selected.

(To *remove* tag assignments from a certain picture, right-click the name of the tag. From the shortcut menu, choose Remove Tag.)

Tip: You can drag thumbnails onto other Navigation-tree elements, too—not just tags and ratings. For example, you can drag them onto a different month or year to *change* their internal records of when they were taken. You can also drag them onto folders in the Folder list to sort them into different folders. (Yes, you can actually move them around the hard drive this way.)

Using Tags and Ratings

The big payoff for your diligence arrives when you need to get your hands on a specific set of photos, because Photo Gallery lets you *isolate* them with one quick click.

To round up all the photos with, say, the Kids tag, just click Kids in the Navigation tree at the left side of the window. Photo Gallery immediately rounds up all photos labeled with that tag, displays them in the photo-viewing area, and hides all others. Or, to find all your five-star photos, click the row of five stars in the Navigation tree.

TROUBLESHOOTING MOMENT

When Good Tags Go Bad

When you drag some photos onto a tag in Photo Gallery, they seem to take on that tag instantaneously.

That speed, however, is a fakeout—a cosmetic trick. Behind the scenes, it takes Windows quite awhile to make changes to your files, because it's actually saving each *entire photo file,* all 5 or 8 or 13 megapixels of it, back onto the hard drive. If you tag a bunch of photos all at once, that saving process is anything *but* instantaneous.

While the saving process is going on, a little blue pencil-on-paper indicator appears in the lower-left corner of the Photo Gallery window. If you point to it without clicking, a tooltip lets you know how many more files Vista has to process. Until the blue icon disappears entirely—meaning that the job is done—the tags you apply in Photo Gallery might not appear in Explorer windows and other programs.

What Vista is saving is *metadata:* generally hidden text tags that hold all kinds of information about each file. Some file formats, however, aren't capable of storing this extra layer of data—and unfortunately, several of them are picture and movie formats that you'd *think* would be natural candidates for this kind of information.

For example, Windows can't embed metadata (and therefore tags or star ratings) to BMP, PNG, GIF, and MPEG files. Actually, you can apply such identifying information to those file types *in Photo Gallery,* but it won't show up in Explorer windows or anywhere else in Windows (like the Photo Viewer program).

You also won't be able to apply Windows-wide metadata to files that are locked, in use by another program, or corrupted.

More tips:

- To find photos that match multiple keywords, Ctrl-click additional tag labels. For example, if you click Travel, and then Ctrl-click Holidays, Photo Gallery reveals all the pictures that have *either* of those keywords. (There's no way to perform an "and" keyword roundup—that is, to find pictures that have *both* Travel *and* Holidays tags.)

- You can also Ctrl-click *unrelated branches* of the Navigation tree. For example, you can click the Casey tag, and then Ctrl-click the five-star rating row, to find only the very best pictures of Casey. You could then even Ctrl-click "2006" in the Navigation tree to further restrict the photos you're seeing.

  But why stop there? Ctrl-click Videos at the top of the Navigation tree, and now you're seeing only the five-star *videos* of Casey in 2006.

- If you click tag heading (like "Trips"), Photo Gallery automatically selects all of the subheading tags ("Vermont," "Hawaii"). If you don't want to select the sub-tags, *right*-click the top-level tag; from the shortcut menu, choose "Select top-level tag."

- You can drag tags up or down in the Navigation tree (to rearrange them) or even left and right (to turn them into sub-headings within a main tag). As the tag list grows, remember that you can collapse any branch of the tree by clicking its flippy triangle.

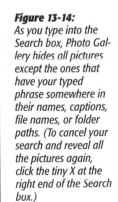

Figure 13-14:
As you type into the Search box, Photo Gallery hides all pictures except the ones that have your typed phrase somewhere in their names, captions, file names, or folder paths. (To cancel your search and reveal all the pictures again, click the tiny X at the right end of the Search box.)

Searching for Photos by Text

The tag mechanism described above is an adequate way to add textual descriptions to your pictures, but there are other ways. The name you give a picture might be significant, and so might the picture's caption or its folder location (that is, its folder *path*).

The Search box at the top of Photo Gallery searches *all* of these text tidbits. It works essentially like the Start menu's Search box:

- Just start typing. As you type, you filter the thumbnails down to just the pictures that match what you've typed so far. You don't have to finish a word, press Enter, or use wildcard characters (*).

- You can type two words (or parts of words) to find pictures that match both. To find all photos of Zelda in Brazil, typing *zel br* will probably do the trick.

- Only beginnings of words count. Typing *llweg* won't find pictures of Renee Zellweger, but *zell* will.

Editing Your Shots
All Versions

Straight from the camera, digital snapshots often need a little bit of help. A photo may be too dark or too light. The colors may be too bluish or too yellowish. The focus may be a little blurry, the camera may have been tilted slightly, or the composition may be somewhat off.

Fortunately, Photo Gallery lets you fine-tune digital images in ways that, in the world of traditional photography, would require a fully equipped darkroom, several bottles of smelly chemicals, and an X-Acto knife.

Note: Photo Gallery can edit photos in only three graphics formats: JPEG, TIFF, and WPD.

You can't paint in additional elements, mask out unwanted backgrounds, or apply 50 different special effects filters in Photo Gallery, as you can with editing programs like Photoshop and Photoshop Elements. Nonetheless, Photo Gallery is designed to handle basic photo fix-up tasks, many of which work with a single click.

All Photo Gallery editing is performed in a special editing mode, in which the photo appears at nearly full-screen size, and tool icons appear at the top (Figure 13-15). You enter Edit mode by double-clicking a photo's thumbnail, either in Photo Gallery or in an Explorer window, and then clicking the Fix button on the toolbar.

You exit Edit mode by clicking "Back To Gallery" (top left of the window).

Ways to Zoom
Before you get deeply immersed in the editing process, it's well worth knowing how to zoom and scroll around, since chances are you'll be doing quite a bit of it.

- **Maximize.** One way to zoom is to change the size of the window itself. Maximize Photo Gallery to enlarge the image.

- **The Size pop-up menu.** Click the magnifying-glass button below the photo and use its slider to zoom in or out.

- **The mouse wheel.** If your mouse has a scroll wheel on the top, you can zoom in or out by turning that wheel, which is surely the most efficient way of all.

Note: The second icon on the toolbar below the photo means, "Fit the photo in the window once again, no matter how much zooming I did."

Figure 13-15:
Photo Gallery's editing tools appear in a special toolbar. There's no Save command. Any changes you make to a photo are automatically saved. But don't worry; Photo Gallery always keeps the untouched, unedited original behind the scenes.

Ordinarily, when you zoom into an open photo, the cursor changes to a friendly little white glove—your clue that you can now scroll the photo in any direction just by dragging. That's more direct than fussing with two independent scroll bars.

But when the Fix pane is open, you have to press the *Alt key* to drag-scroll.

Ten Levels of Undo

As long as you remain in Edit mode, you can back out of your last 10 changes. To change your mind about the *last* change you made, just click the Undo button at the *bottom* of the Fix pane.

To retrace even more of your steps, click the ▾ button next to the Undo button. The resulting pop-up menu lists your last 10 editing steps. Choose how far you want to "rewind," or click Undo All to back out of everything you've done since opening the photo.

But once you leave Edit mode—by returning to the gallery—you lose the ability to undo your individual edits. At this point, the only way to restore your photo is to use the Revert command, which removes all the edits you've made to the photo since importing it (page 454).

Auto Adjust

The Auto Adjust button provides a simple way to improve the appearance of less-than-perfect digital photos. One click makes colors brighter, skin tones warmer, and details sharper. (If you've used Photoshop, the Enhance button is a lot like the Auto Levels command.)

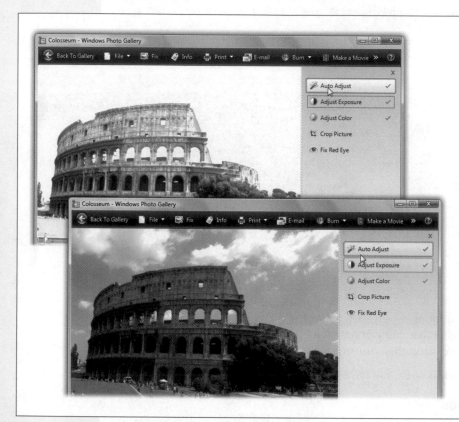

Figure 13-16:
The Auto Adjust command works particularly well on photos that are slightly dark and that lack good contrast, like the original photo on the top. Using Photo Gallery's Brightness and Contrast sliders alone might have helped a little, but the Enhance button produces a faster and overall better result, as shown at the bottom.

It works by analyzing the relative brightness of all the pixels in your photo and attempting to balance the image by dialing the brightness or contrast up or down and intensifying dull or grayish-looking color. Usually, this approach at least makes pictures look somewhat richer and more vivid.

To enhance a photo, just click the Auto Adjust button in the Fix pane. That's it...there's nothing to select first, and no controls to adjust.

As you use the Auto Adjust button, remember that Photo Gallery's image-correcting algorithms are simply best guesses at what your photo is supposed to look like. It has no way of knowing whether you've shot an overexposed, washed-out picture of a vividly colored sailboat, or a perfectly exposed picture of a pale-colored sailboat on an overcast day.

Consequently, you may find that Auto Adjust has no real effect on some photos and only minimally improves others. Remember, too, that you can't enhance just one part of a photo. If you want to selectively adjust specific portions of a picture, you need a true photo-editing program like Photoshop Elements.

Cropping

Think of Photo Gallery's cropping tool as a digital paper cutter. It neatly shaves off unnecessary portions of a photo, leaving behind only the part of the picture you really want.

You'd be surprised at how many photographs can benefit from selective cropping. You can eliminate parts of a photo you just don't want, improve a photo's composition (filling the frame with your subject often has greater impact), or fit a photo to specific proportions (an important step if you're going to turn your photos into standard-size prints).

Here are the steps for cropping a photo:

1. **Open the photo for editing.**

   For example, double-click it, and then click Fix on the toolbar.

Figure 13-17:
When you crop a picture, you draw a rectangle in any direction using the crosshair pointer to define the part of the photo you want to keep. (To deselect this area—when you want to start over, for example—click anywhere in the dimmed area.) Once you've drawn the rectangle and clicked Crop, the excess falls to the digital cutting room floor, thus enlarging your subject.

Choose a standard print size

2. **In the Fix pane, click Crop.**

   The Crop controls appear.

3. **Make a selection from the Proportion pop-up menu, if you like (Figure 13-17).**

   The Proportion pop-up menu controls the behavior of the cropping tool. When the menu is set to Original, you can draw a cropping rectangle of any size and proportion, in essence going freehand.

   When you choose one of the other options in the pop-up menu, however, Photo Gallery constrains the rectangle you draw to preset proportions. It prevents you from coloring outside the lines, so to speak.

   The Proportion feature is especially important if you plan to order prints of your photos. Most digital cameras produce photos whose proportions are 4 to 3 (width to height). This size is ideal for onscreen slideshows and DVDs, because most PC screens and TVs use 4 to 3 dimensions, too—but it doesn't divide evenly into standard print photograph sizes.

   That's why the Proportion pop-up menu offers canned choices like 4 x 6, 5 x 7, and so on. Limiting your cropping to one of these preset sizes guarantees that your cropped photos will fit perfectly into Kodak (or Shutterfly) prints. (If you don't constrain your cropping this way, Kodak—not you—will decide how to crop them to fit.)

   As soon as you make a selection from this pop-up menu, Photo Gallery draws a preliminary cropping rectangle—of the proper dimensions—on the screen, turning everything outside it slightly dim.

   In general, this rectangle always appears in landscape (horizontal) orientation. To make it vertical, click "Rotate frame" just below the Proportion pop-up menu.

   Often, you'll want to give the cropping job the benefit of your years of training and artistic sensibility by *redrawing* the cropping area. Here's how:

4. **Drag the tiny white control handles to reshape the cropping rectangle.**

   Drag inside the rectangle to move it relative to the photo itself.

5. **When the cropping rectangle is just the way you want, click Apply.**

   Photo Gallery throws away all the pixels outside the rectangle. Of course, the Undo and Revert commands are always there if you change your mind.

Note: Remember that cropping always shrinks your photos. Remove too many pixels, and your photo may end up too small (that is, with a resolution too low to print or display properly).

Red-Eye

You snap a near-perfect family portrait: the focus is sharp, the composition is balanced, everyone's smiling. And then you notice it: Uncle Mitch, standing dead center in the picture, looks like a vampire bat. His eyes are glowing red, as though illuminated by the evil within.

Red-eye is light reflected back from your subject's eyes. The bright light of your flash passes through the pupil of each eye, illuminating and bouncing off of the blood-red retinal tissue at the back of the eye. Red-eye problems worsen when you shoot pictures in a dim room, because your subject's pupils are dilated wider, allowing even more light from the flash to shine on the retina.

The best course of action is to avoid red-eye to begin with—by using an external flash, for example. But if it's too late for that, and people's eyes are already glowing demonically, there's always Photo Gallery's Red-Eye tool. It lets you alleviate red-eye problems by digitally removing the offending red pixels. Figure 13-18 shows how.

Truth be told, the Red-Eye tool doesn't know an eyeball from a pinkie toe. It just turns any red pixels black, regardless of what body part they're associated with. Friends and family members look more attractive—and less like Star Trek characters—after you touch up their phosphorescent red eyes with Photo Gallery.

Figure 13-18:
Top: To fix red-eye, zoom in and scroll so that you have a closeup view of the eye with the red-eye problem. Click the Red-Eye button, and then drag a box around each affected eye.

Bottom: With each click, Photo Gallery neutralizes the red pixels, painting the pupils solid black. Of course, this means that everybody winds up looking like they have black eyes instead of red ones—but at least they look a little less like the walking undead.

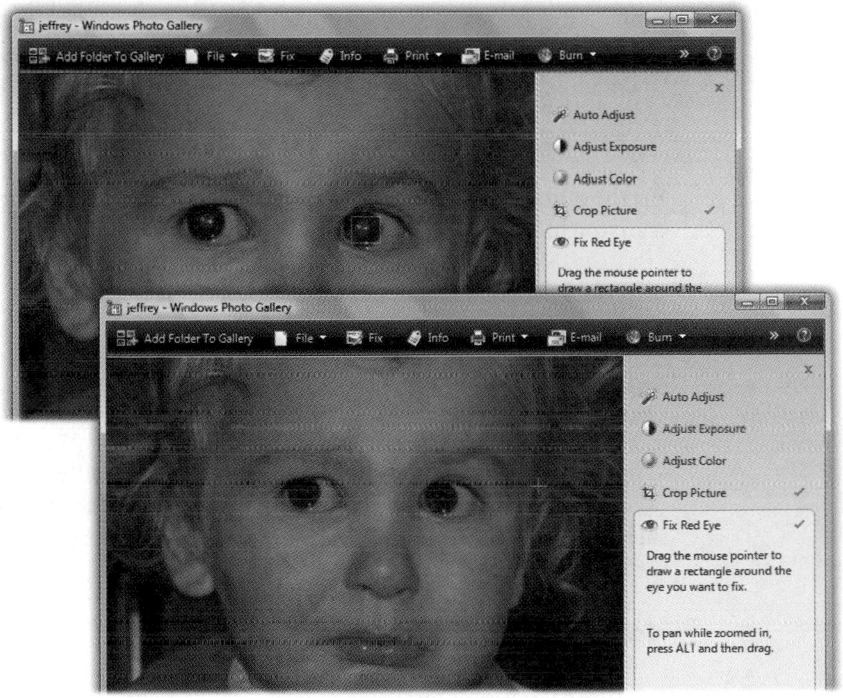

Rotate

Unless your digital camera has a built-in orientation sensor, Photo Gallery imports all photos in landscape orientation (wider than they are tall). The program has no way of knowing if you turned the camera 90 degrees when you took your pictures.

You can use either of these methods to turn them right-side up:

- Click one of the blue Rotate buttons at the bottom of the main Photo Gallery window.

- Right-click a thumbnail; from the shortcut menu, choose Rotate Clockwise (or Counterclockwise).

Tip: After importing a batch of photos, you can save a lot of time and mousing if you first select *all* the thumbnails that need rotating (by Ctrl-clicking each, for example). Then use one of the rotation commands above to fix all the selected photos in one fell swoop.

Exposure and Color Adjustments

Plenty of photos need no help at all. They look fantastic right out of the camera. And plenty of others are ready for prime time after only a single click on the Auto Adjust button, as described earlier.

If you click Exposure or Adjust Color on the Fix pane, though, you can make *gradations* of the changes that the Auto Adjust button makes. For example, if a photo looks too dark and murky, you can bring details out of the shadows without blowing out the highlights. If the snow in a skiing shot looks too bluish, you can de-blue it. If the colors don't pop quite enough in the prize-winning-soccer-goal shot, you can boost their saturation levels.

In short, there are fixes the Adjust panels can make that no one-click magic button can touch.

Exposure (Brightness and Contrast)

When you move the Brightness slider, you're making the *entire* image lighter or darker. In other words, if the picture's contrast is already exactly as you want it, but the whole picture could use darkening or lightening, Brightness should be your tool of choice.

The Contrast slider, on the other hand, affects the difference between the darkest and lightest tones in your picture. If you increase the contrast, you create darker blacks and brighter whites. If you decrease the contrast (too much), you create flat or muddy tones.

Color Balance

One of the most common failings of digital cameras (and scanners) is that they don't capture color very accurately. Digital photos sometimes have a slightly bluish or greenish tinge, producing dull colors, lower contrast, and sickly-looking skin tones. In fact, the whole thing might have a faint green or magenta cast. Or maybe you just want to take color adjustment into your own hands, not only to get the colors right, but to also create a specific mood for an image—icy blue for a freezing day, for example.

The Adjust Color panel offers three sliders that wield power over this sort of thing:

- **Color Temperature.** This slider adjusts the photo along the blue-orange spectrum. Move the slider to the left to make the image "cooler," or slightly bluish—a good way to improve overly yellowish scenes shot in incandescent lighting. Move the slider to the right to warm up the tones, or make them more orange—a particularly handy technique for breathing life back into subjects that have been bleached white with a flash.

Figure 13-19:
You can drag the handle of a slider, of course, but that doesn't give you much accuracy. Sometimes you may prefer to click directly on the slider, which makes the handle jump to the spot. The checkmark means, "You've fooled with this parameter."

Originals-Folder Auto-Cleanup

Let me get this straight: every time I edit a photo, even slightly, I wind up with a duplicate copy of it in some hidden folder on my hard drive? Seems like that's a recipe for wasting a lot of disk space.

True enough: the auto-backup feature means that you wind up with *two* copies of every photo you ever edit, the edited one visible in Photo Gallery, and the original that's stashed on your hard drive. If left unchecked, all of those originals could wind up eating up a distressingly large chunk of your hard drive.

For that reason, Photo Gallery can auto-delete the secret originals after a certain amount of time has passed. If it's been a year since you touched a photo, after all, you're probably happy with the changes you made to it, and you may not need the space-eating safety net any more.

To turn on this feature, choose File→Options within Photo Gallery. In the Options dialog box, under the Original Images heading, you can specify how long Vista should keep those unedited originals on hand.

- **Tint.** If you've ever fiddled with the tint control on a color TV, you already have a decent idea how this slider works. It adjusts the photo's overall tint along the red-green spectrum. Nudge the slider to the right to add a greenish tint, left to add red.

  Adjusting this slider is particularly helpful for correcting skin tones and compensating for difficult lighting situations, like pictures you took under fluorescent lighting.

- **Saturation.** When you increase the saturation of a photo's colors, you make them more vivid; you make them "pop" more. You can also improve photos that have harsh, garish colors by dialing *down* the saturation, so that the colors end up looking a little less intense than they appeared in the original snapshot. That's a useful trick in photos whose *composition* is so strong that the colors are almost distracting.

Tint: Drag the Saturation slider all the way to the left for an instant black-and-white rendition of your shot.

Reverting to the Original

Photo Gallery includes built-in protection against overzealous editing—a feature that can save you much grief. If you end up cropping a photo too much, or cranking up the brightness of a picture until it seems washed out, or accidentally turning someone's lips black with the Red-Eye tool, you can undo all your edits at once with the Revert command. Revert strips away *every change you've ever made* since the picture arrived from the camera. It leaves you with your original, unedited photo—even if it's been months or years since you made the changes.

The secret of the Revert command: whenever you use any editing tools, Photo Gallery—without prompting and without informing you—instantly makes a duplicate of your original file. With an original version safely tucked away, Photo Gallery lets you go wild on the copy. Consequently, you can remain secure in the knowledge that in a pinch, Photo Gallery can always restore an image to the state it was in when you first imported it.

No longer must you make copies of your photos just so you'll have a safety copy if your edits don't work out, or dream up some elaborate naming and folder-filing scheme to accommodate them.

Note: Vista keeps your unedited original photos in your Personal→AppData→Local→Microsoft→Windows→Original Images folder. (It's OK to open this folder to inspect its contents and even open photos inside, but don't delete, move, or rename any of them; you'll wind up completely confusing Photo Gallery.)

If you back up your PC using Vista Backup (page 641), turning on the option to back up photos and images ensures that these originals are backed up.

To restore an original photo, undoing all cropping, rotation, brightness adjustments, and so on, double-click the thumbnail of an edited photo. Click Fix on the toolbar, and then click Revert (at the bottom of the Fix pane). Photo Gallery asks you to confirm the change—after all, you're about to throw away all the editing you've done to this photo, which could represent a lot of time and effort—and then, if you click OK, swaps in the original version of the photo. You're back where you started.

___

Tip: Clearly, Photo Gallery has all the basics covered. But if you want more editing control–for example, if you want to edit only *part* of an image, or you want to add text or something–you'll have to rely on another program.

Fortunately, Photo Gallery plays well with others. Once you've opened a photo, you can use the Open pop-up menu (on the toolbar) to send it off to any other graphics program–say, Photoshop Elements–for additional tweaking.

You're still protected by the warmth and security of the Revert to Original command.

___

Finding Your Audience
All Versions

The last stop on your digital photos' cycle of greatness is, of course, a showing for other people. Photo Gallery offers several ways to make that happen.

___

Tip: A subset of these options, including Slide Show, Print, E-mail, and Burn, are available right in the toolbar of your Pictures window. That is, you don't have to open Photo Gallery first (although in most cases, all you're doing is handing off the task *to* Photo Gallery).

___

Make Prints
If you highlight some photo thumbnails, and then click Print (in the Photo Gallery toolbar), the pop-up menu offers you two choices:

- **Print.** The dialog box shown in Figure 13-20 appears. Here, you can specify what printer, paper, and quality options you want in order to print your own pictures at home—on an inkjet printer, for example.

- **Order Prints.** Even if you don't have a high-quality color printer, traditional prints of your digital photos are only a few clicks away—if you're willing to spend a little money, that is. Figure 13-21 has the details.

___

Tip: If you plan to order prints, first crop your photos to the proper proportions (4 x 6, for example), using the Crop tool described earlier in this chapter. Most digital cameras produce photos whose shape doesn't quite match standard photo-paper dimensions. If you send photos to Shutterfly uncropped, you're leaving it up to Shutterfly to decide which parts of your pictures to lop off to make them fit. (More than one PC fan has opened the envelope to find loved ones missing the tops of their skulls.) You can always restore the photos to their original uncropped versions using the Revert command.

___

Here's how the print-buying process works:

1. **Select the thumbnails of the pictures you want to print. From the toolbar, choose Print→Order Prints.**

Now Vista goes online. (If the PC can't make an Internet connection at all, the Order Prints window doesn't open.)

The "Select a printing company" dialog box appears. It lists Shutterfly at the very least, and may list other companies as Microsoft's marketing gurus do their thing over time.

Figure 13-20:
This very special edition of the Print dialog box shows you exactly how your photos will be cropped when you print them on your home printer. The Options link (lower right) offers advanced settings that govern color management, special printer features, and automatic photo-sharpening.

2. **Click the name of the company you want, and then click Send Pictures.**

   Photo Gallery asks if you're sure you want to expose the intimate details of your photographic life with a bunch of strangers over at Shutterfly. Click Send.

   Now the order form appears (Figure 13-21).

3. **Select the sizes and quantities you want.**

   If you want 4 x 6 or 5 x 7 prints of every photo, just use the checkboxes at the top of the dialog box.

   For more control over sizes and quantities of individual photos, ignore that pop-up menu. Instead, fill in the numbers individually for each photo, scrolling down through the dialog box as necessary. The total cost of your order is updated as you make selections.

As you order, pay heed to the "Suggested" checkmarks. If you *don't* see one next to a photo size, Photo Gallery is pointing out a photo that doesn't have a high enough resolution to be printed at the specified sizes. A photo that looks great at 5 x 7 may look terrible as a 16 x 20 enlargement. Unless you're the kind of person who thrives on disappointment, *never* order prints in a size that's doesn't have the checkmark.

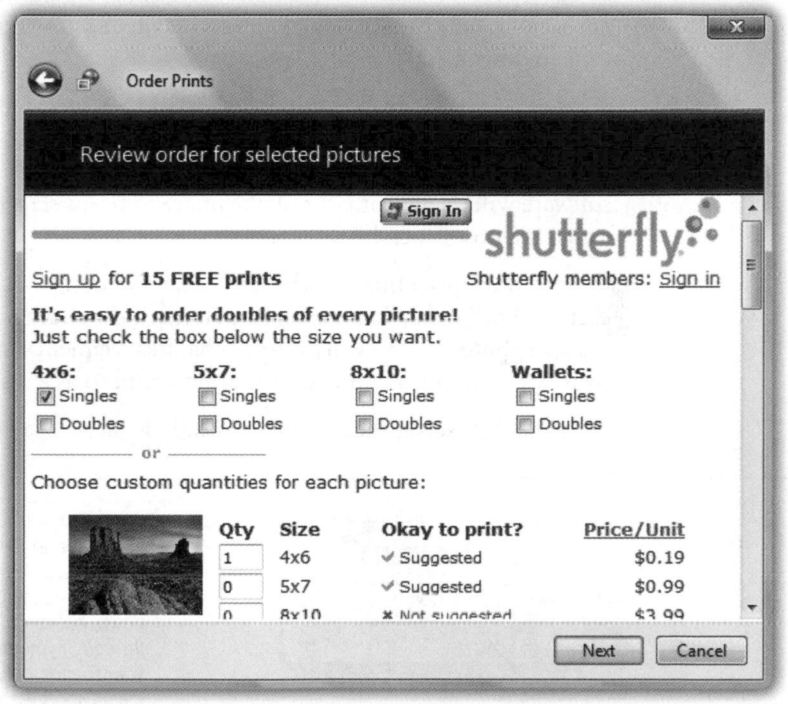

Figure 13-21:
Thanks to a deal between Microsoft and Shutterfly, you can order prints directly from within Photo Gallery. After you select the size and quantity of the pictures you want printed, one click is all it takes to transmit your photos and bill your credit card for the order. The rates range from 19 cents for a single 4 x 6 print to about $4 for 8 x 10s. Within a couple of days, Shutterfly sends you finished photos printed on high-quality glossy photographic paper.

4. Click your way through the rest of the wizard.

You'll be asked for your shipping information, credit-card number, and so on. Finally, you're shown the reference number for your order.

A batch of 24 standard 4 x 6 snapshots costs about $4.50, plus shipping, which is about what you'd pay for processing a roll of film at the local drugstore.

Better yet, you get to print only the prints that you actually want, rather than developing a roll of 36 prints only to find that only two of them are any good.

Slideshows
See "The Post-Dump Slideshow" on page 430.

Email

The most important thing to know about emailing photos is this: *full-size photos are usually too big to email.*

Suppose, for example, that you want to send three photos along to some friends—terrific shots you captured with your 8-megapixel camera.

First, a little math—a typical 8-megapixel shot might consume three or four megabytes of disk space. So sending along just three shots would make at least a 9-megabyte package. It will take you a long time to send, and it will take your recipient a long time to download.

Worse, the average high-resolution shot is much too big for the screen. It does you no good to email somebody an 8-megapixel photo (3264 x 2448 pixels) when his monitor's maximum resolution is only 1900 x 1200. If you're lucky, his graphics software will intelligently shrink the image to fit his screen; otherwise, he'll see only a gigantic nose filling his screen.

Besides, the typical Internet account has a limited mailbox size. If the mail collection exceeds 5 MB or so, that mailbox is automatically shut down until it's emptied. Your massive photo package will push your hapless recipient's mailbox over its limit. She'll miss out on important messages that get bounced as a result.

Photo Gallery solves these problems neatly, as shown in Figure 13-22.

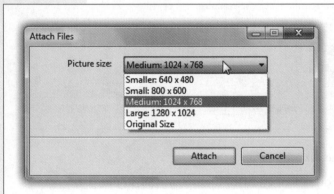

Figure 13-22:
Instead of unquestioningly attaching a multimegabyte graphic to an email message, it offers you the opportunity to send a scaled-down, reasonably sized version of your photo instead. If you take advantage of this feature, your friends will savor the thrill of seeing your digital shots without enduring the agony of a half-hour email download.

Here's how the process works:

1. **Select the thumbnails of the photo(s) you want to email.**

   You can use any of the picture-selecting techniques described on page 436.

2. **Click the Email icon on the toolbar.**

   The dialog box shown in Figure 13-23 appears.

3. **Choose a size for your photo(s).**

This is the critical moment. The "Picture size" pop-up menu in the Attach Files dialog box offers four choices. **Small** and **Smaller** yield a file that will fill a nice chunk of your recipient's screen, with plenty of detail. It's even enough data to produce a small print. Even so, the file size (and download time) remains reasonable.

Use **Medium** and **Large** options sparingly. Save them for friends who have a cable modem or DSL. Even then, these big files may still overflow their email boxes.

Despite all the cautions above, there may be times when a photo is worth sending at **Original Size,** like when you're submitting a photo for printing or publication—and you both have high-speed Internet connections.

No matter which you choose, keep an eye on the "Total estimated size" readout in the dialog box. Most email systems can't accept attachments greater than 5 MB.

4. **Click Attach.**

   At this point, Photo Gallery processes your photos—converting them to JPEG format and, if you requested it, resizing them. It then launches your email program, creates a new message, and attaches your photos to it.

5. **Type your recipient's email address into the "To:" box, and then click Send.**

Figure 13-23:
Below the horizontal line, you'll find three options that govern screen saver special effects, speed, and randomness. Click Save when it all looks good.

Your photos are on their merry way.

Burn to a Disc

If you highlight some photo thumbnails, and then click Burn (in the Photo Gallery toolbar), the pop-up menu offers you two choices:

- **Data disc.** If you now insert a blank CD or DVD, Photo Gallery makes a *backup* of the selected photos. That is, it turns the disc into a data disc that works only in computers. It's a great way to back up or archive your pictures and movies.

- **Video DVD.** This option hands off the photos to DVD Maker for burning to a DVD, so you can share your masterpieces on your friends' TV sets. (Of course, this option is available only if your Vista edition came with DVD Maker, which means Home Premium or Ultimate.) Chapter 15 has step-by-step instructions for rearranging and mastering your DVD slideshow.

Make a Slideshow Movie

If you highlight some photo thumbnails and then click Make a Movie in the toolbar, Vista automatically hands them off to Windows Movie Maker (Chapter 15) and lays them out in the timeline as a slideshow, all ready to go.

All you have left to do is rearrange them, add music and credits, and save as a digital movie file for distribution to your hip friends or publishing online.

Build a Photo Screen Saver

This feature's really nice. You can turn any random batch of photos into your PC's very own screen saver. After half an hour (or whatever) of inactivity, the screen darkens, thunder rolls, and your friends and family begin to appear, gracefully panning and zooming and cross-fading, as your co-workers spill their coffee in admiration and amazement.

The hard part is specifying *which* pictures you want to be part of the show; you can't just highlight a bunch of them and say, "Use these."

Instead, you have to isolate your screen saver–bound shots, either by giving them a certain tag, applying a certain rating, or confining them to a certain folder.

Here are the details. Begin by opening the Screen Saver applet in the Control Panel, using one of these tactics:

- Right-click the desktop. From the shortcut menu, choose Personalize. In the Personalization control panel, click Screen Saver.

- From within Photo Gallery, choose File→Screen Saver Settings.

Either way, the Screen Saver Settings dialog box appears. From the "Screen saver" pop-up menu, choose Photos. Then click Settings to view the options shown in Figure 13-23.

Now you can choose how you want your photos selected for their big moment in the spotlight.

- **Show everything.** If you turn on "Use all pictures and videos from Photo Gallery," then, by golly, everything in Photo Gallery is fair game.

- **By tag.** If you've tagged your screen saver–bound pictures, turn on "Use all pictures and videos from Photo Gallery" and then, in the "With this tag" box, type the tag you want. (Vista autocompletes whatever you start to type.)

Tip: If it's easier to say which photos you *don't* want to see, turn on "Don't show items tagged," and then specify which tags you want to keep out.

- **By rating.** You can also use the "With this rating or higher" to limit the photos by star rating—whether or not you also limited the selection by tag.

- **By folder.** If you keep your screen saver–worthy pix in a folder by themselves, turn on "Use pictures and videos from," and then click Browse to find the folder.

When you've finished setting up the slideshow—that is, screen saver—click Save. When you return to the Screen Saver Settings dialog box, you can either click Preview to manually trigger the screen saver for your inspection, or click OK and wait 20 minutes for the screen saver to kick in by itself.

Windows Media Player

I n the beginning, Windows Media Player was the headquarters for music and video on your PC. It was the Grand Central Terminal for things like music CDs (you could play 'em, copy songs off 'em, and burn 'em); MP3 files and other digital songs (you could sort 'em, buy 'em online, and file 'em into playlists); pocket music players of the non-iPod variety (fill 'em up, manage their playlists); Internet radio stations; DVD movies (watch 'em); and so on.

Media Player still does all that, and more. But it's no longer clear that this is the program you'll use for these activities. Gradually, the Media Player audience is splintering. Nowadays, a certain percentage of people is using alternative programs like:

- **iTunes.** If you have an iPod, you use Apple's iTunes software to do your music and video organizing.

- **Zune software.** If you have a Zune music player, you have to use yet *another* jukebox program—the software that came with it—for loading up and organizing your player.

- **Media Center.** As noted in Chapter 14, many of Media Player's functions are now duplicated in Windows Media *Center,* the vast playback engine described in Chapter 16.

Still, most of the Windows world continues to use Windows Media Player as their music-file database. It's worth getting to know.

Note: In its insatiable quest to dominate the world of digital music and video, Microsoft keeps updating Windows Media Player, usually redesigning it beyond recognition with each update. For example, this chapter describes Media Player version 11, included with Windows Vista out of the gate. But sure as shootin', version 12 will be coming your way within a year or so. (Vista's automatic-update feature will let you know when version 12 is fully baked and ready to download.)

The Lay of the Land
All Versions

The modern Media Player looks quite a bit different from its predecessors. In fact, if you've perused the previous chapter, you'll realize that Media Player and Photo Gallery share a very similar design.

Down the left side of the window is a Navigation tree—a list of the music, videos, and playlists in your collection. The flippy triangles next to the major headings make it easy to collapse sections of the list. Under the Library headings, you can click Artist, Album, Songs, Genre, or whatever, to see your entire music library sorted by that criterion (Figure 14-1). (The Navigation tree isn't visible in some views—more on this in a moment.)

Media Player's top edge, as you may have noticed, offers several primary tabs, which cover the essential functions of Media Player. They're described in more detail in the following pages, but here's a quick overview:

- **Now Playing.** Click this tab while music or video is playing from any source. This is where you can see a list of songs on the CD, a graphic equalizer, and a wild, psychedelic screen saver that pulses in time to the music. Here, too, is where you change the volume and other audio settings.

Tip: To start playing a song, album, playlist, or whatever, just double-click its name. You can use the Space bar to pause or resume playback.

UP TO SPEED

Custom Express

The first time you open Media Player, a welcome message appears. It offers you two choices:

Express Settings. This option is "Recommended" because it makes Media Player the main music and video player for your PC; sends Microsoft anonymous details about what you buy and listen to; and downloads track lists and other details from the Internet when you insert a CD or DVD.

Custom Settings. If you'd rather be a little less free with your private information, or you'd like Media Player not to do quite such a big land grab of your multimedia playback rights, choose this option. You're taken to settings screens where you can tone down Media Player's ambitions.

- **Library.** This screen lists every piece of music or video your copy of Media Player "knows about" on your hard drive; use the Navigation tree to sort and group the lists. This is also where you can sort your songs into subsets called *playlists*.

Figure 14-1:
When you click a label at left, the main portion of the window changes to show you your music collection, using the actual album-cover artwork as their icons. It's very visual, but not especially stingy with screen space. Fortunately, you also have a more compact list view available—choose Details from the View Options pop-up menu identified here.

Navigation pane   Tabs

View Options pop-up menu

List pane

NOSTALGIA CORNER

Returning to the Classic Menus

In an attempt to make Media Player less intimidating, Microsoft gave it a makeover in version 11. It basically went through the menus and hid a lot of the commands that it felt people didn't use much. The remaining commands still appear as menus that pop out of the six main tabs (Now Playing, Library, and so on).

Unfortunately, some really nice features got completely hidden in the process—like Skins.

In this chapter, you'll read several references to the Classic menus. That's where

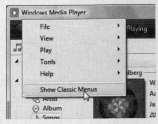

you'll find the *complete* list of Media Player functions.

To make the old menu bar return, press the Alt key. The Classic menu bar returns for the moment, although in a vertical orientation at the left side of the screen.

If you'd rather bring the Classic menu back for good, click the little icon shown here; from the shortcut menu, choose Show Classic Menus.

Now the old menu bar is back—in its former horizontal orientation, just as in the good old days.

- **Rip.** Use this screen to copy songs from one of your music CDs onto your hard drive, as described later in this chapter.

- **Burn.** After transferring some songs to your hard drive—from the Internet or your own music CD collection—you can then burn your own CDs. This screen is the loading dock.

- **Sync.** Here's where you line up music or video that you'd like transferred to a portable music or video player, if you have one that Media Player understands.

- **Urge.** This page is a rabbit hole into Alice in Marketingland. It's the gateway to online music stores—MTV's Urge store is, obviously, the featured one—where you can buy songs for $1 each, or download all you want for $15 a month, with the understanding that you're just renting them; when you stop paying, you lose them all.

Playing Music CDs

For its first trick, Media Player can simulate a $25 CD player. To fire it up, just insert an audio CD into your computer's CD or DVD drive.

If this is the first time you've ever taken this dramatic action, you see the dialog box shown in Figure 14-2. It asks how you want Windows to handle inserted CDs. Do you want it to *play* them? Or *rip* them (start copying their songs to your hard drive)? And if you said "play," do you want to use Media Player or Media *Center*, if you have it?

For now, click "Play audio CD using Windows Media Player."

Media Player opens and the CD begins to play automatically. The screen even fills with a shimmering, laser-light show (called a *visualization*) that pulses along with the music. Ta-da!

Tip: If all the fancy dancy graphics are slowing down your machine as you try to work in other programs, you can always turn them off. Click the tiny ▾ button under the words Now Playing to open the Now Playing menu. Choose Visualizations→No Visualization.

Fun with Media Player

When your everyday work leaves you uninspired, here are a few of the experiments you can conduct on the Media Player screen design:

- **Switch visualizations.** To try a different visualization, Ctrl-click the window (to see the next style) or Shift+Ctrl-click (for the previous one).

  And if you tire of the displays built into Windows, simply download more of them from the Internet by choosing Now Playing→ Visualizations→ Download Visualizations.

Tip: One of the most interesting choices is Album Art, which displays a picture of the album cover for whichever song is now playing.

- **Shrink the window to show some skin.** If the Media Player window is taking up too much screen space, making it harder for you to work on that crucial business plan as you listen to Eminem, press Ctrl+2 to shrink the window (Figure 14-4), or choose View→Skin Mode from the Classic menu (page 465).

Press Ctrl+1 to return the Media Player window to its full-sized glory.

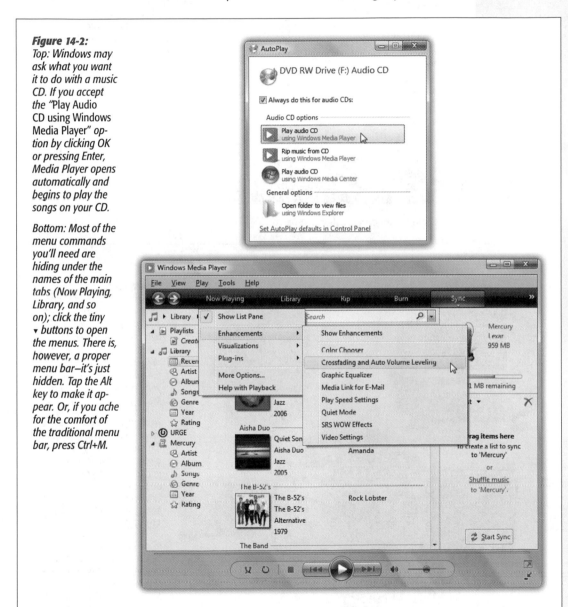

Figure 14-2:
Top: Windows may ask what you want it to do with a music CD. If you accept the "Play Audio CD using Windows Media Player" option by clicking OK or pressing Enter, Media Player opens automatically and begins to play the songs on your CD.

Bottom: Most of the menu commands you'll need are hiding under the names of the main tabs (Now Playing, Library, and so on); click the tiny ▼ buttons to open the menus. There is, however, a proper menu bar—it's just hidden. Tap the Alt key to make it appear. Or, if you ache for the comfort of the traditional menu bar, press Ctrl+M.

Tip: Of course, you can also just minimize Media Player, as you would any window. In fact, the first time you do so, Vista offers to turn on the Media Player *toolbar,* shown in Figure 14-3.

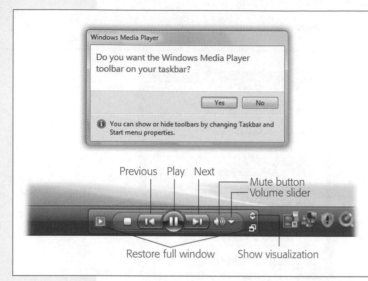

Figure 14-3:
When the Media Player toolbar is on your screen, you have a very tiny set of playback controls available at all times, no matter what program you're using.

Previous Play Next

Mute button
Volume slider

Restore full window Show visualization

Figure 14-4:
In Skin Mode, Media Player takes up less space on your screen and can use radical new design schemes. To return to the full-size window, press Ctrl+1, or hunt through the buttons on your skin until you find the Return to Full Mode button.

To change the skin, choose View→Skin Chooser from the Classic menu (page 465). A directory of available skins appears; it's empty at the outset. Click More Skins; Windows sends you online to Microsoft's grisly-sounding Skin Gallery.

Not all skins are, shall we say, masterpieces of intuitive design; it may take you several minutes just to find the Stop button. When you find a skin you like, click Apply Skin (above the list).

- **Expand the window.** On the other hand, if your PC is briefly serving as a glorified stereo system at a cocktail party, double-click the visualization display itself (or press Alt+Enter). The screen saver effect now fills the entire screen, hiding all text, buttons, and controls. If you have an available laptop and a coffee table to put it on, you've got yourself a great atmospheric effect. (When the party's over, just double-click again, or press Alt+Enter again, to make the standard controls reappear.)

- **Change the skin.** In hopes of riding the world's craze for MP3 files, Microsoft has helped itself to one of WinAmp's most interesting features: *skins.* Definitions: An MP3 file (MPEG Audio Layer-3) is a compact, downloadable, CD-quality sound file format. WinAmp is a popular MP3-playing program. And a skin is a design scheme that completely changes the look of Windows Media Player, as shown in Figure 14-4.

GEM IN THE ROUGH

Playing Across the Network

If you've taken the trouble to set up a home network, you can share songs and playlists with other networked Windows Vista computers. You could, for example, tap into your roommates' jazz collection without getting up from your desk, and they can sample the zydeco and tejano tunes from your world beat playlist. The music you decide to share is streamed over the network to the other computer—or even an XBox 360. Even store-bought, copy-protected songs are OK to share.

You can't share music across the Internet, only within your own home or office network. (Technically speaking, the computers must be on the same *subnet.* And you must have designated your network as *private* [page 359].)

To make your music available to others, choose Library→ Media Sharing. In the dialog box, turn on "Share my media."

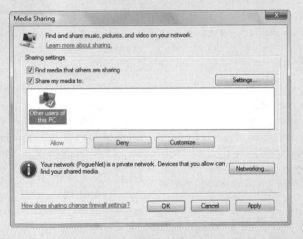

When you click OK, your buddies will find your Media Player collection listed in their Navigation trees, ready to play. (That's *if* they have turned on "Find media that others are sharing" in the same dialog box.)

If you don't want to share with *everyone,* re-choose the Library→ Media Sharing command. This time, you'll see icons that represent the individual PCs on your network. Click a PC's icon and then click either Allow or Deny.

While you're fooling around with the settings, click Settings. You'll see options that let you limit the *kind* of stuff you share (music, photos, videos); restrict the sharing to stuff with a certain star rating or parental rating; or confirm sharing on a PC-by-PC basis. (To set up the last, turn off "Allow new devices and computers automatically.")

Happy sharing!

To choose a new skin, choose View→Skin Chooser from the Classic menu (page 465). Then click each of the available skins, listed down the left side, to see a preview of its appearance. When you click the Apply Skin button (at the top-left corner of the window), your player takes on the look of the skin you chose *and* shrinks down into the compact Skin mode, as described in the previous tip.

- **Fool around with the playback sequence.** You can make the songs on the CD play back in a random order, just as though you'd pushed the Shuffle button on a CD player. To do this, click the Shuffle button or press Ctrl+H. And if you love a particular CD so much that you'd like to hear it over and over again (instead of stopping at the end), press Ctrl+T—the shortcut for Repeat.

Tip: These tricks work for whatever playlist you've currently selected—not just an audio CD. (Playlists are described later in this chapter.)

- **Fool around with the sound.** Don't miss the graphic equalizer, a little row of sliders that lets you adjust the bass, treble, and other frequencies to suit your particular

---

GEM IN THE ROUGH

Filling in Track Names

Precious few audio CDs come programmed to know their own names (and song titles). Every day, millions of people insert music CDs into their computers and see the songs listed as nothing more than "Track 1," "Track 2," and so on—and the album itself goes by the catchy name Unknown Album.

Fix #1. If your PC is online when you insert a certain music CD—you lucky thing—you'll bypass that entire situation. Windows takes a quick glance at your CD, sends a query to *www.allmusic.com* (a massive database on the Web containing information on over 200,000 CDs), and downloads the track list and a picture of the album cover for your particular disc.

Fix #2. If *allmusic.com* draws a blank, as it often does for classical recordings, no big deal. Media Player makes it easy to search the Web for this information at a later time. On the Library tab, right-click an album cover, and then, from the shortcut menu, choose Find Album Info. (Alternatively, you can highlight the names of the *tracks* with missing information; right-click one and then choose Find Album Info.)

Fix #3. You can also type in the names of your songs manually. Once again, begin on the Library tab. Select the tracks you want to edit. (By Shift-clicking or Ctrl-clicking, you can add information to multiple tracks simultaneously—for example, if they all came from the same album.)

Now right-click the *specific column* you want to edit—Artist, Album, or whatever. See the box on page 74 for details on hiding or showing columns, and remember that you may have to scroll horizontally to see them all. From the shortcut menu, choose Edit. A little text box opens so that you can type in the track information manually.

Fix #4. This is pretty cool: In the Navigation tree (Library tab), click the criterion that's missing, like Artist or Album. Now you can *drag* an incorrectly labeled track or album *onto* one with the correct labeling—and marvel as Media Player copies the correct info onto the dragged item.

No matter how the track names and album art get onto your PC, Windows saves this information in your music library (see "Ripping CDs to Your Hard Drive" earlier in this chapter). Therefore, the next time you insert this CD, the Media Player will recognize it and display the track names and album information automatically.

---

speakers and your particular ears. Choose Now Playing→Enhancements→Graphic Equalizer.

The same submenu offers a number of other audio effects, including Quiet Mode (smoothes out the highs and the lows so that sudden blasts don't wake up the kids) and something called SRS WOW, which simulates a 3-D sound experience through nothing more than stereo speakers or headphones.

- **Fool around with the speed.** If you're in a hurry to get through an album, or just think the tempo's too slow, right-click the Play/Pause button below the screen. You're offered commands that speed up or slow down your music—a weird and wonderful feature. (This shortcut menu also lets you know that there are keyboard shortcuts for these commands, like Ctrl+Shift+G for faster playback.)

Ripping CDs to Your Hard Drive

You can copy an album, or selected tracks, to your hard drive in the form of standalone music files that play when double-clicked. The process is called *ripping,* much to the consternation of sleepless record executives who think that it's short for *ripping off.*

Having CD songs on your hard drive is handy because:

- You can listen to your songs without having to hunt for the CDs they came from.
- You can listen to music even if you're using the CD-ROM drive for something else (like a CD-based game).
- You can build your own *playlists* (sets of favorite songs) consisting of tracks from different albums.
- You can compress the file in the process, so that each song takes up much less disk space.
- You can transfer the songs to a portable player or burn them onto a homemade CD.

If you're sold on the idea, open the Rip tab's pop-up menu. Inspect your settings. For example, unless you intervene by clicking the Change button near the top, Windows copies your song files into your Personal→Music folder.

Note, too, that Microsoft has designed Windows Media Player to generate files in the company's own format, called Windows Media Audio (.wma) format. But many people prefer, and even require, MP3 files. For example, most recent CD players and portable music players (including the iPod) can play back MP3 files—but won't know what to do with WMA files.

If you'd prefer the more universally compatible MP3 files, Rip→Format→MP3 (Figure 14-5).

Tip: If you have a stack of CDs to rip, don't miss the two commands in the Rip menu: "Rip CD Automatically When Inserted→Always" and "Eject CD After Ripping." Together, they turn your PC into an automated ripping machine, leaving nothing for you to do but feed it CDs and watch TV.

Finally, the Rip→Bit Rate submenu controls the tradeoff, in the resulting sound files, between audio quality and file size. At 128 kbps, for example, a three-minute MP3 file

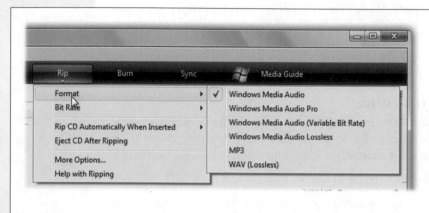

Figure 14-5:
Using this submenu, tell Windows how much to compress the song files (and sacrifice sound quality). If you don't need MP3 compatibility, Windows Media Audio (Variable Bit Rate) maximizes quality and minimizes file size by continuously adjusting the data rate along the song's length.

might consume about 2.8 megabytes. At 192 kbps, the same file sounds much better, but it eats up about 4.2 MB. And at a full 320 kbps, the file's roughly 7 MB.

These are important considerations if you're ripping for a portable MP3 player, like the iPod. For instance, if your music player contains a 20 GB hard drive, it can hold 142 hours of music you've ripped at 320 kbps, or 357 hours at 128 kbps.

For MP3 files, most people find the 192 Kbps setting (on the "Audio quality" slider) to produce great-sounding, relatively compact files. For WMA, 128 Kbps might be a good starting point. Needless to say, let your ears (and the capacity of your portable music player) be your guide.

Here's how you rip:

1. **Insert the music CD. Click the Rip tab in Media Player.**

   The list of songs on the CD appears.

2. **Turn on the checkboxes of the tracks you want to copy.**

   You've waited all your life for this: at last, you have the power to eliminate any annoying songs and keep only the good ones.

3. **Click Start Rip.**

   You'll find this button at the lower-right corner of the window.

   Windows begins to copy the songs onto your hard drive. The Start Rip button changes to Stop Rip, which you can click to interrupt the process.

Organizing Your Music Library

Every CD transferred to your hard drive winds up with an entry on the Library tab, visible in Figure 14-6. You can sort your collection by performer, album, year released, or whatever, just by clicking the corresponding icons in the Navigation tree. Whenever you want to play back some music, just double-click its name in this list—there's no need to hunt around in your shoeboxes for the original CD the songs came from.

But that's just the beginning of Media Player's organizational tools; see Figure 14-6.

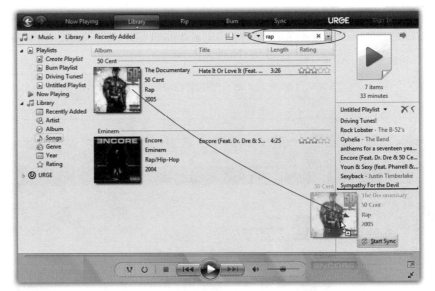

Figure 14-6:
On the Library tab, the Navigation tree (left) lists your playlists. Under the Library heading, you see various ways to sort your collection. To build a playlist, drag songs or CD names into the right panel. Don't miss the Search box at the top, which searches all text related to your songs and videos as you type, hiding all entries that don't match.

Transferring CD songs to your hard drive isn't the only way to log your files in the Media Player database. You can also add sound and video files to this master list using any of these methods:

- Use the Library→Add to Library command (or press F3). Media Player helps you choose more folders to be "watched folders"—that is, folders whose contents will always be reflected in Media Player's lists.

Note: Any song, video, or photo that you ever play in Media Player gets automatically added to its Library—*if* it's on your hard drive or the Internet. If it's on another PC on the network, or on a removable disk like a CD, Media Player doesn't bother adding it, because it probably won't be there the next time you want it.

- Drag sound or video files directly from your desktop or folder windows into the Media Player window.

- The Internet is crawling with online music stores that sell music that you can download straight into Media Player. Page 520 has the details.

Playlists

Microsoft recognizes that you may not want to listen to *all* your songs every time you need some tunes. That's why Media Player lets you create *playlists*—folders in the Navigation list that contain only certain songs. In effect, you can devise your own albums, mixing and matching songs from different albums for different purposes: one called Downer Tunes, another called Makeout Music, and so on.

To create a new playlist, start on the Library tab. The Playlist pane, at the right side of your screen, is empty. It says, "Drag items here to create a playlist." Well, hey—it's worth a try. See Figure 14-7.

Once you've created a playlist, click Save Playlist at the bottom of the pane. Type a name for your playlist, and thrill to the appearance of a new icon in My Playlists "category" of the Navigation tree.

Note: To create another playlist right away, close the first one by clicking the red X beside its name.

Figure 14-7:
To create a playlist, just start dragging tracks or whole albums to the Playlist pane. Switch views, or use the Search box, as necessary to find the tracks you want. Drag songs up and down in the Playlist pane to reorder them. Use the pop-up menu (where it now says Untitled Playlist) to scramble, sort, rename, or save the playlist.

Deleting things

Whenever you want to delete a selected song, playlist, or almost anything else, press the Delete key. Media Player generally asks if you want it deleted only from the library, or if you really want it gone from your computer.

Burning Your Own CDs

All Versions

The beauty of a CD burner is that it frees you from the stifling restrictions put on your musical tastes by the record companies. You can create your own "best of" CDs that play in any CD player—and that contain only your favorite songs in your favorite order. The procedure goes like this:

1. **Click the Burn tab. Insert a blank CD.**

   On the right side of the screen, the Burn pane appears. If your PC has more than one disc burner, click Next Drive until Media Player identifies the correct one.

Note: If you've inserted a rewriteable disc like a CD-RW, and you've burned it before, right-click its icon in the Navigation tree, and then, from the shortcut menu, choose "Erase disc" before you proceed.

---

2. **Specify which songs you want to burn by dragging them into the Burn List (where it says "Drag items here" in the Burn pane).**

   You can add music to your CD-to-be in just about any kind of chunk: individual songs, whole albums, playlists, random audio files on your hard drive, and so on; see Figure 14-8.

Figure 14-8:
Use the Navigation tree to pull up the display you want. For example, to see a complete list of your songs or albums, click Songs or Albums, and then drag individual songs or albums directly into the Burn list. To add a playlist to the Burn List, drag the name of the playlist right across the screen from the Navigation tree. To add a file that's not already in Media Player, drag it out of its Explorer window directly into the Burn List.

As you go, keep an eye on the "time remaining" readout at the top of the Burn List. It lets you know how much more your CD can hold. If you go over the limit, Media Player will burn additional CDs as necessary.

Tip: Media Player adds two seconds of silence between each song, which might explain why you may not be able to fit that one last song onto the disc even though it seems like it should fit.

---

3. **Click Start Burn.**

   It takes a while to burn a CD. To wind up with the fewest "coasters" (mis-burned CDs that you have to throw away), allow your PC's full attention to focus on the task. Don't play music, for example.

Copying Music or Video to a Portable Player

If you have a pocket gizmo that's capable of playing music (like a SanDisk Sansa or a Pocket PC) or even videos (like a Portable Media Center), the process for loading your favorite material onto it is very similar to burning your own CD. The only difference in the procedure is that you do your work on the Sync tab instead of the Burn tab.

If you attach a player with a capacity greater than 4 gigabytes, Media Player automatically copies your entire collection onto it (assuming it will fit). If it's smaller, or if your whole library won't fit, Media Player switches into manual-sync mode, in which you hand-pick what gets copied.

POWER USERS' CLINIC

CD and DVD Format Fun

Most of the time, you'll probably want to burn a regular audio CD, of the type that plays in the world's 687 quintillion CD players. But you can also use the Burn tab to make a *data* CD or DVD—a disc designed to play in *computers*. That's a good way, for example, to make a backup of your tunes.

Actually, some modern CD players can also play *MP3 CDs,* which are basically data CDs filled with MP3 files. That's a great feature, because a single MP3 CD can hold 100 songs or more. (A few can even play *WMA CDs,* meaning CDs containing files in Microsoft's own audio format.)

You specify what kind of disc you intend to burn by choosing its name from the Burn menu (top of the screen).

If you're ever in doubt about how you burned a certain CD (audio or data?), here's a trick: insert it into your PC, open its window, and examine its contents. If you see files with the suffix .cda, you've got yourself an audio CD; if it's full of other kinds of files, like .mp3, .wma, or even .jpg and .doc, it's a data CD.

And now, some other notes about burning discs:

CD-RW. Erasable discs like CD-RW are super-handy, but not all CD players can play them when you've burned them as audio CDs. Test and beware.

DVD. Remember that there are, annoyingly, two different kinds of blank DVD, called DVD+R and DVD-R. Buy the kind that matches your PC's burner, or you'll be making a trip back to the store with your receipt.

Tip: Media Player can play videos with the extensions .wmv, .wvx, .avi, .mpeg, .mpg, .mpe, .m1v, .mp2, .mpa, and .ivf.

As you may have noticed, this list doesn't recognize two of the most popular video-file formats, QuickTime and RealVideo. To play these files, you'll need the free QuickTime Player (available from *www.apple.com/ quicktime*) or RealPlayer (from *www.real.com*).

Automatic sync

Connect the player. Media Player announces that it will perform an automatic sync. Click Finish. Smile. Wait.

From now on, just connecting the player to Media Player brings it up-to-date with whatever songs you've added or deleted on your PC. As your library grows, shrinks, or gets edited, you can sleep soundly, knowing that your portable gadget's contents will be updated automatically the next time you hook it up to your PC's USB port.

Manual sync

Connect the player. Read the dialog box. Click Finish.

In Media Player, click the Sync tab. Drag songs, videos, playlists, or albums into the List pane, exactly as you would do when preparing to burn a CD (something like Figure 14-8). Click Start Sync.

Tip: If you'd like to surrender to the serendipity of Shuffle mode, you can let Media Player choose the songs you get. From the Sync menu, choose the name of your player; from the submenu, choose Shuffle. Each time you sync, you'll get a different random selection from your collection.

Online Music Stores
All Versions

Right from within Media Player, you can search or browse for millions of pop songs, classical pieces, and even comedy excerpts—and then buy them or rent them. (You can pay $1 per song to own it, or about $15 per month to download as many songs as you want, with the understanding that they'll all go *poof!* if you ever stop paying the fee.)

At first, the Online Store tab features Urge, which is MTV's music store. But with a little effort, you can also access Napster, eMusic, XM Satellite Radio, and other music and movie stores.

Note: Two stores you *can't* get to from here are iTunes and Zune Marketplace. You have to get to those using the software that came with your iPod or Zune, as noted at the beginning of this chapter.

To look over your options, open the Urge menu and then choose Browse All Online Stores. Now Media Player window ducks into a phone booth and becomes a Web browser, filled with company logos. Anything you buy gets gulped right into your

Library, ready for burning to a CD or syncing with an audio player, if the store's copy-protection scheme allows it.

The stores fall into three categories:

- **Deliciously integrated.** Some of the online stores, like Urge, are well integrated with Media Player. Once you sign up, the store gets its own icon in the Navigation tree. You can drag songs right out of its lists into a playlist or a Burn list, and you can use Media Player's Search box to search the entire store.

- **Web-page-type stores.** Other stores, like Music Giants, show up as Web sites right within Media Player's main window. They're not built into the Navigation tree, but at least you don't need to switch to a Web browser to see them.

- **Not-at-all integrated stores.** A few stores, like Napster, require you to download and install a separate program.

Figure 14-9:
Top: In the list at the right side of Media Guide, click Internet Radio.

Bottom: Click through the music genres to find what you're up for. Click a station that looks interesting, and then click the little Play button beneath its listing. (The higher the number in the Speed column, the better the sound quality. Note, though, that 128 Kbps is generally too rich for dial-up modems, and may sputter.) Wait for your PC to connect to the Internet site, and then let the music begin!

Tip: If you think you'll be visiting a store again, open its tab menu (click the ▾ button where it once said Urge) and then choose "Add current service to menu." Next time, you'll be able to jump to it without having to choose "Browse all Online Stores" first.

Restrictions

Songs from most online stores are copy-protected—gently. For example, the $1-a-song sites generally permit you to play the songs on up to five computers at once, and to burn a playlist containing the songs 10 times.

The $15-a-month rental (subscription) plans generally don't let you burn CDs at all.

Internet Radio

The 21st century's twist on listening to the radio as you work is listening *without* a radio. Media Player itself can tune in to hundreds of Internet-based radio stations all over the world, which may turn out to be the most convenient music source of all. They're free, they play 24 hours a day, and their music collections make yours look like a drop in the bucket.

For radio, use the rightmost tab (the Online Stores tab). Click the ▾ button; from the menu, choose Media Guide.

Media Guide is a window onto *www.windowsmedia.com*. It's a sort of promotional/ news site that plugs new movies, songs, and videos, displays movie trailers and music videos, and so on.

And it lists radio stations. See Figure 14-9 for details.

Note: Unfortunately, there's no easy way to capture Internet broadcasts or save them onto your hard drive.

DVD Movies

All Versions

If your PC has a drive that's capable of playing DVDs, you're in for a treat. Media Player can play rented or purchased Hollywood movies on DVD as though it was born for the job. (If you have the Home Premium or Ultimate editions of Windows Vista, of course, you may prefer Windows Media *Center* for this task; see Chapter 16.)

You can even play *high-definition* DVDs (HD-DVD or Blu-Ray format), provided your PC has the right kind of DVD drive *and* accompanying software (drivers, decoder software, and player software).

Note: If your PC came with a DVD drive built in, then the manufacturer probably did you the courtesy of installing DVD *decoding software* too. If not, or if you've installed your own DVD drive, you'll have to spring a few bucks for DVD decoding software like DVD XPack (*www.intervideo.com*, $15), NVidia DVD Decoder (*www.nvidia.com*, $20), or PowerDVD (*www.gocyberlink.com*, $15).

Watching movies on your screen couldn't be simpler. Just insert the DVD. Windows automatically detects that it's a video DVD—as opposed to, say, one that's just filled with files.

The dialog box shown in Figure 14-10 appears, or at least it does the very first time you insert a DVD. Click "Play DVD movie using Windows Media Player"— if, indeed, that's the program you want to play the DVD. You may have other programs that can play DVDs, with their own buttons in this dialog box.

Figure 14-10:
Once the DVD is playing, you control the playback using the standard Media Player controls (bottom edge of the window). To switch to a different "chapter," click the ▶▶ button. To change language or parental-control options, right-click the screen; from the shortcut menu, choose Audio and Language Tracks. When you're playing the movie full-screen, the playback controls reappear when you move the mouse a bit.

Now Media Player opens, and your movie begins playing, full-screen. Most of the time, there's nothing for you to do now but watch. But if you're the interactive sort, you can also take action like this:

- **Switch between full-screen mode and window mode** by pressing Alt+Enter. In window mode, the movie plays within the Media Player window, surrounded by the usual controls. The pane at the right side of the window lists the DVD chapters (scenes), which is handy if you want to jump around in the DVD.

- **Pause, skip, adjust the volume** by wiggling your mouse. Playback controls appear for a few seconds at the bottom of the screen, permitting you to pause, adjust the volume, or skip backward or forward, and then fade away so as not to obscure Arnold Schwarzenegger's face.

Alternatively, you can right-click anywhere on the "movie screen" itself to reveal a menu of disc-navigation features.

Tip: For real fun, turn on *English* subtitles but switch the *soundtrack* to a foreign language. No matter how trashy the movie, you'll gain respect from your friends when you say you're watching a foreign film.

Ditching the remote control

When the remote control is hidden, you can always return it to the screen just by moving your mouse. But the true DVD master would never bother with such a sissy technique. The secret keystrokes of Media Player are all you really need to know:

Function	Keystroke
play	Ctrl+P
stop	Ctrl+S
fast forward, rewind	Ctrl+Shift+F, Ctrl+Shift+B
quieter, louder	F9, F10
slower, faster	Ctrl+Shift+S, Ctrl+Shift+G
normal speed	Ctrl+Shift+N
mute	F8
next/previous "chapter"	Ctrl+F, Ctrl+B
full-screen mode	Alt+Enter
eject	Ctrl+E

Of course, watching a movie while sitting in front of your PC is not exactly the great American movie-watching dream. To enhance your viewing experience, you can always connect the video-output jacks of your DVD-equipped PC (most models) to your TV. Details are in Chapter 16.

Figure 14-11:
In Pictures mode, you see thumbnails of your photo collection. The Navigation tree offers one-click grouping mechanisms like Keywords (tags), Rating, Date Taken, and Folder. Double-click a photo to open it and begin a slideshow of it and its neighbors.

"Select a category" icon

View as icons/tiles/list

Pictures and Videos

Microsoft may like to think that music, photos, and videos are all equally important in Media Player. Truth is, though, Media Player is really all about music—those other file types are just gravy.

Nonetheless, Media Player does indeed help you manage your pictures and videos. There's not a whole lot of point to it, considering the fact that Windows Photo Gallery (Chapter 13) is infinitely better suited to the task; for example, you can't edit photos or apply tags within Media Player.

Nevertheless, here's the rundown.

Start by clicking the tiny "Select a category" icon shown in Figure 14-11; from the pop-up menu, choose Pictures or Videos. The screen changes to something that closely resembles Photo Gallery.

Here's what you can do in Pictures or Videos mode:

- **See a photo or video at full size** by double-clicking it. The video plays, or a slide-show begins automatically, showing that photo and the others in its group.

- **Rate a photo or video** by right-clicking it and, from the shortcut menu, choosing Rate→4 Stars (or whatever).

Tip: In Tiles view, it's easier to rate pictures and videos, because a row of stars appears next to each thumbnail. You just click the third star (for example). Use the View Options pop-up menu (Figure 14-11) to switch to Tiles view.

- **Create a playlist** by dragging thumbnails into the List pane at right (on the Library tab). In the context of photos or videos, a playlist basically means a slideshow or sequence of self-playing videos. Click the Play button at the bottom of the screen to see it.

- **Delete a photo or video** by clicking its thumbnail and then pressing the Delete key. Media Player asks if you want it removed only from the library, or from your computer altogether.

Movie Maker and DVD Maker

You want to know why home video's gotten a bad name? It's because nobody bothers to *edit* it. A video involving the baby and an upturned bowl of spaghetti? A laugh riot—for about 30 seconds. But 25 minutes of it? Chinese Water Torture, dude.

But this is the amateur-video era. Web sites like YouTube and Google Video have made short, tightly crafted videos an essential form of self-expression (and sometimes, instant celebrity).

Fortunately, Windows Vista comes equipped with the tools—basic, but real—for editing the video from a camcorder or digital camera, trimming out the boring parts, and dressing it up with credits, music, and so on.

Vista even includes a basic DVD menu-design program, so you can burn your own DVDs, complete with scene-selection screens. Let the creativity begin.

Note: Movie Maker comes only with the Home Basic, Home Premium, and Ultimate editions of Windows Vista, and DVD Maker comes only with Home Premium and Ultimate. Apparently, people in companies don't have cameras.

Importing Video, Music, and Photos
Home Basic • Home Premium • Ultimate

You open Movie Maker by choosing Start→All Programs→Windows Movie Maker. (If you're using the Business or Enterprise version of Vista, you're out of luck. You're obviously far too busy with big corporate projects to be mucking around with movies.)

The Movie Maker screen appears, as shown in Figure 15-1. Its left-side Tasks pane indicates the three major steps you'll take to put a movie together: Import, Edit, and Publish To.

Tasks pane   Clips   Thumbnail view   Preview window

Timeline/Storyboard

Figure 15-1:
Windows Movie Maker's Tasks pane provides quick access to the most-used menu options. The other major working areas of the program are all identified here. You'll do most of your work in the Storyboard or Timeline view at the bottom of the screen.

Behind the scenes, Windows creates a folder called Videos in your Personal folder. This is where you'll find icons representing the various video clips that you capture from your camcorder. (You'll also find a Sample Videos folder there to fool around with until you get your equipment-buying act together.)

The first step is to bring in some video to edit. Proceed in either of these ways:

- **From a camcorder.** The best quality comes when you import video from a digital (DV) camcorder, one that records on MiniDV cassettes.

  Next, you need a *FireWire card* (about $60), if your PC didn't come with a built-in FireWire port. (It may be called an IEEE-1394 or i.Link port.) On the side of almost every digital camcorder model is a special connector, a FireWire port, that connects to the FireWire card with a FireWire *cable.* This single cable communicates both sound and video between the PC and the camcorder, in both directions.

  Prepare to dedicate a *lot* of hard drive space. Digital video footage takes up 3.6 MB *per second* of video—enough to fill up 13 GB per hour of tape.

The Vista version of Movie Maker can even import *high-definition* video from one of the new consumer HD camcorders. Keep in mind, however, that this video takes up even more space on the hard drive and is much slower to work with.

Note: In Vista, Movie Maker can no longer import analog video (from a VCR, for example) through a video capture card you've installed. You can *edit* such videos, but only if you first import them using whatever software came with your card.

Movie Maker is also not much good at importing video from camcorders that use wacky formats like miniature DVDs or hard drives. Here again, you're left on your own to get that video onto the hard drive—then you can import it as files, as described next.

- **Use existing pictures or movies.** You can use Movie Maker to edit movie files you've imported from your digital camera or downloaded from the Internet, too; in fact, you can drag them in directly from Photo Gallery (Chapter 13). You can even splice together still photos to create a living photo album.

Tip: Actually, there's another great way to use Movie Maker: highlight a bunch of pictures in Photo Gallery (Chapter 13) and then click "Make a Movie" on its toolbar. Presto! A new Movie Maker project opens, with all of the photos imported and ready to drag to the Timeline.

Most intriguingly of all, you can also import TV shows you've recorded in Media Center (Chapter 16) and edit them. Chop out the ads, the recaps, and the credits, and maybe save the result to a DVD for watching (or, rather, your kids' watching) on road trips.

Capturing Footage from a Camcorder

To capture footage, hook up your digital camcorder to the PC's FireWire jack. (Some models also work with a USB 2.0 jack.) Then:

1. **Put the camcorder in Playback mode.**

   This primary switch may also be labeled VCR or VTR.

2. **In the task list, under Import, click "From digital video camera."**

   The Import Video wizard appears.

3. **Type a name for the video file you're about to create, and choose a folder for saving it. (Vista proposes your Videos folder.) Click Next. Specify whether you want the whole tape or just selected scenes, and then click Next.**

   If you opted for the whole tape, the camcorder rewinds and begins to play its entire contents into your PC.

   Otherwise, you arrive on the control screen shown in Figure 15-2. You can now control the camcorder by remote control. You can inspect the video as it arrives on your hard drive by watching it in the Preview window.

4. **As the video plays, click Start Video Import and Stop Video Import, as necessary, so that you capture only the scenes you want to edit.**

   You can tap the S key to start and stop importing, too.

5. **When you've reached the end of the good stuff, click Finish.**

   Repeat this process until you've captured all the pieces needed to create your masterpiece.

When it's all over, you wind up back in Movie Maker, where each imported scene appears as its own thumbnail. Skip ahead to "Editing Video."

Figure 15-2:
Use the Play, Stop, Rewind, Fast Forward, and Pause buttons to find the scenes on the camcorder that are worth importing. Once you've got everything cued up, use the Start Video Import (Stop Video Import) button to control the transfer of footage to your hard drive.

Importing Pictures, Movies, and Sounds from the Hard Drive

You don't necessarily need a camcorder to fool around with Movie Maker. You can also bring any movie or picture file on your hard drive into your Movie Maker project; just click the appropriate link in the task pane, in the Import setting (Videos, Pictures, Audio or Music).

At that point, the standard Open File dialog box opens. Find and import the files you want to work with.

Tip: Remember the usual shortcuts that let you select multiple files at once. To grab a sequential batch in the dialog box, click the first file, then Shift-click the last. You can also Ctrl-click to select or deselect individual files (the first, third, and fifth, for example).

Movie Maker turns each imported file into a clip, which you can edit, chop up, or manipulate, as described in the following paragraphs.

Tip: To the ancient question, "What is the sound of one hand clapping?" you can now add, "What is the duration of a still picture?" As far as Windows is concerned, the answer is, "Five seconds." When you drag a still-image clip into your Timeline, as described below, Windows gives it a 5-second proposed duration. To make a still image stay on the screen for a longer or shorter interval, simply drag its right-hand triangle on the ruler, as shown in Figure 15-3.

As your cinematic career flourishes, you can create multiple folders in the pane at left to hold the clips from various projects. Choose View→Collections (to replace the Tasks pane with the Collections pane); right-click "Imported media"; then, from the shortcut menu, choose New Collection Folder. You can drag clips from one folder to another to suit your obsessive tendencies.

Editing Video

Home Basic • Home Premium • Ultimate

Once you've accumulated a few clips, it's time to conduct some general organization—rearranging the clips; trimming off excess footage from the ends; adding credits, music, and effects, and so on.

Phase 1: Organize Your Clips

Icons for the clips you've imported gather in the Collection area at the center of the screen. (Behind the scenes, they're really in your Personal→Videos folder.)

Double-click a clip to see it play in the monitor window. The Space bar (or the letter K key) pauses and resumes playback. Press F2 to rename a clip.

Tip: The scroll wheel on your mouse is a scrubbing wheel. Turn it to shuttle backward and forward in a clip that's playing for precise cursor positioning.

Phase 2: Drag Them into the Storyboard

Your real job here, though, is assembling your clips into a coherent, complete video masterpiece by dragging them into the timeline at the bottom of the screen. Movie Maker can display this horizontal strip in either of two ways, depending on your current selection in the View pop-up menu (Figure 15-3):

- **Storyboard.** In this view, each clip appears as an icon, like a slide on a slide viewer. Each is the same size, even if one is eight minutes long and the next is only two.

- **Timeline.** In this view, each clip is represented by a horizontal bar whose width represents the clip's playback duration. Additional parallel "tracks" represent soundtracks playing simultaneously, titles and credits, and transition effects.

Whichever view you choose, this is where you'll organize the scenes of your movie. Drag the clips from the Clips area (shown in Figure 15-1) down into this area to place them in the order you want. You can rearrange them once they're there, too, simply by dragging. You can also trim unwanted material off the beginning or end of each clip by dragging the triangles in each icon.

As you go, you can preview your film in progress by choosing Play→Play Storyboard or Play Timeline, depending on which window you're working with; either way, the keyboard shortcut is Ctrl+W. As usual, the Space bar pauses or resumes playback.

Tip: Choose View→Full Screen (or press Alt+Enter) to make the movie fill your monitor as it plays back. Unless you're working with digital video, the blotchy, blurry enlargement may trigger your innate demand-your-money-back instincts. But this trick is useful, for example, when showing your finished movie to a group of people in a room. From a few feet away, the poor picture quality isn't as noticeable.

Phase 3: Chop Up the Clips

As you work, you may frequently find it useful to cut your clips into smaller pieces, thereby eliminating boring material. You can do this in either of two ways:

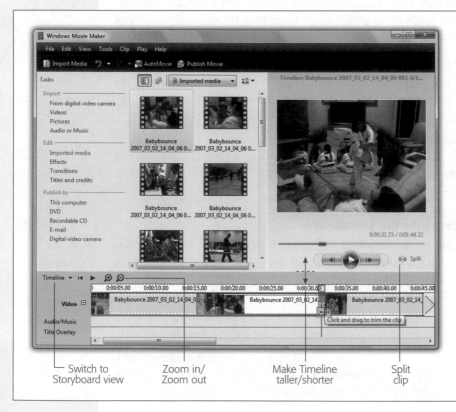

Figure 15-3:
The filmstrip at the bottom of the window offers two different views. Switch between them using the View pop-up shown here at lower left. In Timeline view (bottom), you see the relative lengths of your clips; Storyboard view often provides a better feel for the overall shape of your movie.

Switch to Storyboard view

Zoom in/ Zoom out

Make Timeline taller/shorter

Split clip

- **Split a clip.** After aligning the scroll bar underneath the Preview pane with the spot where you want the clip chopped, choose Clip→Split, press M, or click the Split button (shown in Figure 15-3). Movie Maker turns the single clip into two different clips, adding a number to the name of the second one.

- **Trim a clip.** Sometimes you just want to trim off unwanted footage from either end of a clip—a task Movie Maker lets you perform only after you've added a clip to the Timeline. Then drag the triangle handles, which you can see in Figure 15-3.

Phase 4: Add Video Transitions

What happens when one clip ends and the next one begins? In about 99.99 percent of all movies, music videos, and commercials, you get a *cut.* That's the technical term for "nothing special happens at all." One scene ends, and the next one begins immediately.

Professional film and video editors, however, have at their disposal a wide range of *transitions*—special effects that smooth the juncture between one clip and the next. For example, the world's most popular transition is the *crossfade* or *dissolve,* in which the end of one clip gradually fades away as the next one fades in. The crossfade is so popular because it's so effective. It gives a feeling of softness and grace to the transition, and yet it's so subtle that the viewer might not even be conscious of its presence.

Like all DV editing programs, Movie Maker offers a long list of transitions, of which crossfades are only the beginning. Movie Maker makes adding such effects incredibly easy, and the results look awesomely assured and professional.

To see the catalog of these fancy transitions, click Tools→ Transitions (or click the Transitions link in the Tasks pane). The available transitions—about 60 of them—appear in the Transitions pane, shown in Figure 15-4. You can double-click any of these icons to see what the transition looks like. To use one in your movie, drag its icon down between two clips in either the Storyboard or the Timeline window. (It's easier to drag transition icons when you're in the Storyboard view, because you have such a big target, the big square between the clips, shown in Figure 15-3.)

Tip: Most transitions make your movie shorter. To superimpose the ends of two adjacent clips, Movie Maker is forced to slide the right-hand clip to the left, making the overall movie end sooner.

Having your overall project shortened is a serious problem, especially when you've been synchronizing your footage to an existing music track. Having these transitions slide all of your clips to the left can result in chaos, throwing off the synchronization work you've done.

Sometimes you can get around this problem by adding the music *after* the video editing is complete.

Phase 5: Add Video Effects

A video effect is a special effect: a color filter, frame rotation, slow motion, artificial zooms (in or out), and so on. As with transitions, using them with abandon risks making your movie look junky and sophomoric—but every now and then, a special effect may be just what you need for videographic impact.

To view your choices, choose Tools→Effects (or click Effects in the Tasks pane). You preview, apply, edit, and delete them exactly as you do transitions (Figure 15-4). For example, you drag an effect square just *to the left of* the clip that you want to affect—but it affects the entire clip.

Click to see transition choices

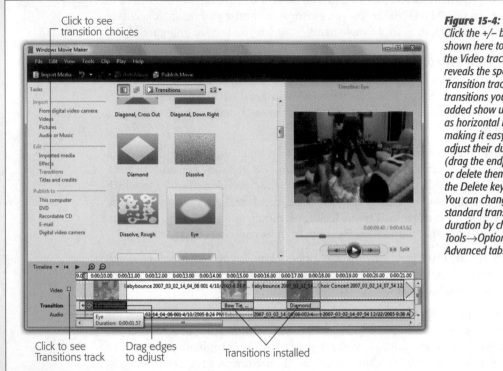

Figure 15-4:
Click the +/– button shown here to expand the Video track so it reveals the special Transition track. Any transitions you've added show up here as horizontal blocks, making it easy to adjust their durations (drag the endpoints) or delete them (press the Delete key).
You can change the standard transition duration by choosing Tools→Options→ Advanced tab.

Click to see Transitions track

Drag edges to adjust

Transitions installed

If you really intend to go to town with effects on a certain clip, right-click it in either the Storyboard or the Timeline window, then choose Effects from the shortcut menu. The Add or Remove Effects dialog box appears. If you promise to use good taste, you can even pile up multiple effects on a single clip and rearrange the order in which they're applied.

Phase 6: Add Titles and Credits

Text superimposed over footage is incredibly common in the film and video worlds. You'd be hard-pressed to find a single movie, TV show, or commercial that doesn't have titles, captions, or credits. In fact, it's the *absence* of superimposed text that pegs most camcorder videos as amateur efforts.

To add this kind of text in Movie Maker, begin by choosing Tools→Titles and Credits (or click "Titles and Credits" in the Tasks pane).

As shown in Figure 15-5, you're offered four places to put text: at the beginning of the movie, at the end of the movie, before a clip, or on a clip.

Figure 15-5:
Top: The titles and credits option offers several different placements for titles and a way to enter credits for your video.

Second from top: On the next screen, you're supposed to type up the actual text of the credits.

Third: Here's where you choose an animation style for the text: how will it fly onto the screen? The result can look—well, if not professional, then at least familiar.

Bottom: Adjust superimposed titles' duration by dragging their end handles in the Title Overlay track.

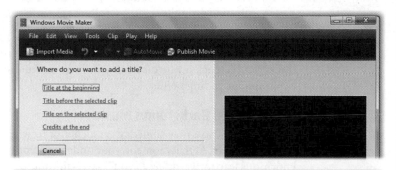

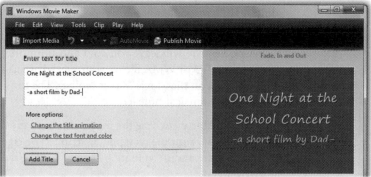

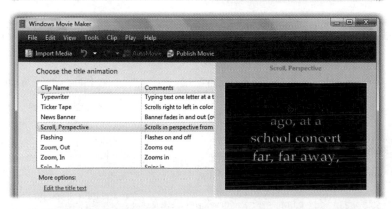

Once you've clicked your choice, you can type the actual text. This screen also offers "Change the title animation" and "Change the text font and color" links, which affect how the titles or credits drift across the screen (and in what type style). The animation effects duplicate just about every common TV-title style: letters flying onto the screen, spinning onto the screen, scrolling across the screen, and so on.

When you click Add Title, the program switches to Timeline view and adds your text to the film in progress (Figure 15-5, bottom). On the Timeline, text gets its own track; double-click a title block to edit it. You can also drag its ends to change the beginning or ending points.

Phase 7: Add Background Music

If you're lucky, you may someday get a chance to watch a movie whose soundtrack isn't finished yet. At that moment, your understanding of the film medium will take an enormous leap forward. "Jeez," you'll say, "without music and sound effects, this $200 million Hollywood film has no more emotional impact than…my home movies!"

And you'll be right. Without music, sound effects, and sound editing, even the best Hollywood movie will leave you cold and unimpressed. Fortunately, Movie Maker can use any MP3 or WMA file on your hard drive as a musical soundtrack. Just click Import Media on the Movie Maker toolbar. The music file appears among your clips with a special musical-note icon.

Now, in Timeline view, drag the music clip onto the track marked Audio/Music. You can drag the appropriate rectangular strip left or right to control where it starts and ends; adjust the audio's volume by right-clicking it and choosing Volume from the shortcut menu.

GEM IN THE ROUGH

AutoMovie

AutoMovie might sound like a synonym for "drive-in theater," but it really means "automatically assembled movie." This feature purports to do all of the editing for you. You just show it which clips or clip collections you want assembled, and the program does the rest.

"The rest," in this case, primarily consists of adding transitions and a few video effects between the clips. Don't expect the software to add a narrative arc and develop characters.

To use AutoMovie, click AutoMovie on the toolbar. A box appears, listing several canned style choices: Flip and Slide, Highlights Movie, Music Video, Old Movie, and so on—and

links that let you insert a title or choose a soundtrack.

Unfortunately, there's no way to preview these canned editorial decisions. You have no choice but to click "Create AutoMovie," take a look at the result, and then choose Edit→Undo AutoMovie if you'd like to try a different variation.

The truth is, you probably won't use AutoMovie very often. Video editing is an art, and letting a computer do the editing usually isn't any more successful than letting a computer write your term paper for you. But it sure looks good at trade show demos.

Unfortunately, you can't create variations along the music's length (to make it softer when someone's talking, for example); you can, however, use the Tools→Audio Levels command to adjust its overall volume relative to the camcorder sound.

Tip: Even if you don't own a camcorder, one of the nicest things you can do with Movie Maker is produce a slide show with sound. After importing still images as described earlier, import a pop song to lay underneath it. You'll be surprised at how much impact the result has.

Phase 8: Save the Movie

When your flick looks and sounds good, you can save it as a standalone file on your hard drive, which you can then double-click to play, or send to potential investors.

To save the file, click a link in the "Publish to" section of the task pane (or choose File→Publish Movie, or press Ctrl+P). You have five options:

- **This computer.** Choose this option if you want to preserve the complete movie as a file on your hard drive. You can choose from several different compression formats and frame proportions (that is, widescreen vs. standard).

Tip: If you have the Home Premium or Ultimate edition of Vista, you'll even see three high-definition export options here: Windows Media HD (in 720p or 1080p format) and Windows Media HD for XBox 360. If your source material was also HD video, these formats preserve all of the high-def quality. Note that the resulting files are huge, and generally play back only on high-end PCs.

- **DVD.** If you do, in fact, have DVD Maker on your PC (this means you, owners of the Home Premium or Ultimate editions of Vista), clicking this link saves and closes your Movie Maker file and hands the whole thing off to DVD Maker so you can design your menus. (DVD Maker is described later in this chapter.)

- **Recordable CD.** A wizard appears to walk you through the process of saving a lower-resolution movie onto a blank CD, so you can distribute it to friends for

---

GEM IN THE ROUGH

The Narrator Speaks

If your PC has a microphone, you can narrate your own "voice-over" soundtrack as the video plays—a great way to create a reminiscence or identify the scene. Unfortunately, you can't add *both* music *and* narration; Movie Maker can tolerate only one added audio track.

In Timeline view, choose Tools→Narrate Timeline; the Narrate Timeline pane appears. Drag the playback indicator to an empty point on the Audio/Music track and then click the

Start Narration button. You can watch the video play as you speak into your microphone.

Click Stop Narration to wrap it up. You're asked to name and save your narration file (it gets a .wma filename extension). At this point, you can adjust the volume or starting/ending points of the narration track just as you would a music track: by adjusting its bar in the Audio/Music track.

---

playback on their PCs. (These disks will also play back on CD and DVD players that bear Microsoft's "HighMAT" logo—of which there are very few.)

- **E-mail.** Video really isn't a good match for email distribution; video files are huge and slow to download. This wizard, therefore, guides you through making a very low-quality, small-framed, slightly jittery movie whose file size is small enough to transmit via the Internet.

- **Digital video camera.** If you don't have a DVD burner and DVD Maker, this is by far the most useful "publish" option. It's the only version that preserves every shred of crisp, clear, smooth-motioned video that was in the original footage. (All other options wind up compressing the video, making it jerkier, smaller-framed, and lower quality.)

Tip: You can turn any individual frame from your movie into a still picture (a JPEG file). In the Preview pane, watch the footage until you see the frame you want to capture, and then choose Tools→Take Picture from Preview. Windows asks you to name your newly created graphics file and save it, and then imports the still photo into the Movie Maker project.

DVD Maker

Home Premium • Ultimate

DVD Maker, a new program, debuts with Windows Vista, and then only with the Premium or Ultimate editions. It's very bare-bones, but it does let you turn your digital photos or camcorder movies into DVDs that work on any DVD player, complete with menus, slideshow controls, and other navigation features. DVD Maker handles the technology; you control the style.

Sure, you can export your finished Movie Maker project as a digital file, or save it to a good old VHS cassette. But preserving your work on a DVD gives you a boatload of benefits, including better durability than tape, dramatically better quality than a movie file, no need for rewinding, duplication without quality loss, and cheaper shipping. (And besides, you can fit a lot more DVDs on a shelf than VHS tapes.)

Note: DVD players sold since 2002 are generally a safe bet for playing back homemade DVDs, but check the master player compatibility list at *www.dvdrhelp.com* if you're ever in doubt. Some players are fussy about which DVD-R brand discs they play, too.

To open DVD Maker, choose its name from the Start→All Programs menu. Or just insert a blank DVD—and when the AutoPlay dialog box appears, click "Burn a DVD video disc using Windows DVD Maker."

Phase 1: Import Videos and Pictures

Click "Add items" on the toolbar (Figure 15-6) to scrounge around on your hard drive for the video files and picture files you want to play on the DVD. (This assumes, of course, that you haven't already added a Movie Maker masterpiece to this list as described above.)

As you build the list of files, keep these points in mind:

- Drag the videos up and down to change their playback sequence.

- Watch the minutes-remaining counter at the lower-left corner. It shows you how full your DVD is so far.

- Use the "Remove items" button on the toolbar to get rid of material you change your mind about.

- Name the DVD in the "Disc title" box.

Figure 15-6:
DVD Maker may be the Notepad of DVD-burning software—so stripped down, it's almost nonexistent. But it does offer the essentials. First, load it up with the videos and photos you want it to show; second, choose a menu design.

Phase 2: Choose What You See First

When you rent a Hollywood DVD, the first thing you see is usually a main-menu screen. Music plays, video clips loop, and buttons like Play and Scene Selection await.

DVD Maker can give *your* DVD a main-menu screen, too. In fact, that's what it will do unless you intervene.

It does, however, offer two other useful possibilities:

- **Start playing automatically.** This is a great option if you don't have multiple scenes to choose from, or if the recipients of your DVD are stark, raving, technophobic novices (see Figure 15-7).

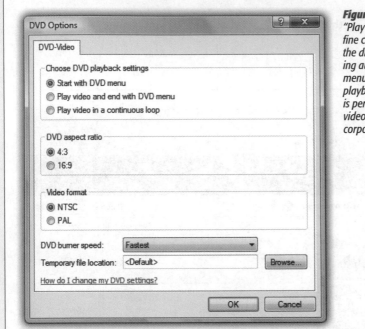

Figure 15-7:
"Play video and end with DVD menu" is a fine choice for technophobes. They'll stick the disc in the player, and it will begin playing automatically. It won't display the main menu screen until it gets to the end of the playback. "Play video in a continuous loop" is perfect for slideshows-of-the-couple's-life videos that play at wedding receptions, or corporate booths at trade shows..

- **Loop.** This one's the same idea, but when the video gets to the end, it repeats from the beginning endlessly, or until you hit the Menu button on your DVD player's remote. At that point, you'll arrive at the main menu screen.

Choose which of these options you want by clicking Options (Figure 15-6), and then making your selection in the dialog box shown in Figure 15-7.

Tip: The dialog box shown in Figure 15-7 is also where you specify the *proportions* of the DVD playback. If it's going to be played on a standard TV, choose 4:3; if you expect it to be played on an HDTV or another widescreen set, choose 16:9.

Once you've made your decision, click OK (to close DVD Options) and then click Next.

Phase 3: Design the Main Menu

Now comes the part where you choose the breathtaking, animated backdrop that will dress up your main menu screen. A wide range of canned themes awaits your inspection, with all kinds of emotional overtones. Some are modern and hip; others look antique and subtle.

Scroll through the list of designs on the right side of the window, clicking each one to see what it looks like in the main work area (Figure 15-8). Note that most designs feature "cutouts" where *your* pictures and videos play, making each DVD unmistakably yours.

Figure 15-8:
Select a design by clicking its thumbnail. The main menu screen takes on your chosen theme instantly. You can't really see the full, animated effect, however, until you click Preview in the toolbar.

Each main menu design comes with three buttons:

- **Play.** On the finished DVD, this button will mean, "Play the movie from the beginning."

- **Scenes.** On the finished DVD, this button will take your audience to a second screen, filled with individual buttons for the individual files you imported.

- **Notes.** When your audience clicks this button, they'll get a special Notes page where they can read whatever information you've supplied about the DVD: background, inspiration, instructions, copyright notices, order form for more copies, whatever.

To make the design even *more* yours, click "Customize menu" in the toolbar. In the resulting dialog box (Figure 15-9), you can go to town like this:

- **Change the font for your title and button labels** using the pop-up menu at the top. Change the color (or add bold or italic) using the three little buttons just below it.

- **Choose different videos or background photos.** Ordinarily, DVD Maker takes care of the cutouts itself, using snippets of your DVD's material to fill the holes. But you can grab totally unrelated pictures or videos from your hard drive to play there instead. Click "Customize menu" on the toolbar. In the resulting dialog box, click the Browse button next to "Foreground video" or "Background video." The Open dialog box appears, so that you can navigate your hard drive and find picture or video files to replace what's on the main menu.

Note: Not all themes include background videos that you can change. And in some designs, the video labeled "background video" is, in fact, a sort of *preroll* video, one that plays *before* the main menu appears.

Figure 15-9:
It's a little tricky trying to envision what effect the changes you make here will have on the final DVD, but trial and error—and the almighty Preview button—will be your guide.

- **Change the button shapes** using the "Scene button styles" pop-up menu. The buttons in question here are the thumbnails that show representative frames of the individual movies, as they appear on the Scenes sub-menu screen.

- **Add some background music** by clicking the Browse button next to "Menu audio" and choosing a music file from your stash. Music makes a huge difference to the feeling of elegance and anticipation your DVD menu creates.

Tip: Once you've tweaked a design to perfection, you can save it for reuse later by clicking "Save as new style" at the top of the Customize dialog box.

When it all looks good, click "Menu text" in the toolbar. It opens the ingeniously titled "Change the DVD menu text" dialog box, where you can specify the name of the DVD as it will appear on the main menu. You can also rewrite the names of the Play and Scenes buttons, if you so desire.

Phase 4: Burn the DVD

Once your menu screens are looking pretty good, you're almost ready to burn the DVD. Before you go using up a blank disc, however, you should test your creation to make sure that it works on the virtual DVD player known as the PC.

The Preview button lets you test your menu system to avoid unpleasant surprises. When you click it, DVD Maker enters Preview mode, which simulates how your DVD works on a standalone set-top DVD player. You even get simulated remote-control buttons (Play, Pause, Next/Previous, Menu, plus arrow buttons) to help you navigate. Click OK to return to the design mode.

To burn the DVD, insert a blank DVD into your PC. Click Burn. After a while, or a bit more than a while, a freshly burned DVD automatically ejects from your drive. The "Your disc is ready" screen offers you the opportunity to burn another copy, which should take a lot less time because DVD Maker has already done the heavy computations.

Note: If the DVD-burning experience left you with little more than a shiny plastic coaster—that is, it didn't work—try burning at a slower speed. In Figure 15-7, you can see the "DVD burner speed" pop-up menu, which governs the speed; sometimes slowing things down results in better luck burning.

GEM IN THE ROUGH

The DVD Slideshow

Here it is, folks—the ultimate gift, the one that will never wind up being sold on eBay or at a garage sale: the DVD slideshow.

If, in Phase 1, you loaded some digital photos onto your DVD, then now, while you're designing the menu screens, you can click "Slide show" in the toolbar. This dialog box appears. Here, you can click Add Music to load up some song files to serve as background music for the slideshow, and choose their playback sequence.

Here, too, is where you specify how long each picture will hang around on the screen. (Hint: 7 seconds is *way* too long; even 3 is pushing it.)

Alternatively, you can turn on "Change slide show length to match music length," meaning that the photos' time on the stage will be determined by the length of the music. If there's 5 minutes of music and 50 slides, each picture will get 10 seconds.

Using the Transition pop-up menu, you can specify what kind of cross-fade you want to see from one photo to the next. Turning on "Use pan and zoom" makes your photos gently slide, grow, and shrink as they appear, as though in a Ken Burns documentary. It's a lovely effect, although it does have a tendency to chop off parts of people's scalps.

When the setup looks perfect, click Change Slide Show.

Media Center

Talk about a digital hub: Media Center is digital-hubbier than any other computer you can buy. This Vista program is the master storage and viewing center for all of your pictures, home movies, music, and TV shows (recorded or downloaded). Better still, it turns your PC into a full-blown digital video recorder, like a TiVo. It lets you watch TV, pause it, rewind and then fast-forward it, record it, and even burn the result to a DVD.

In fact, if you exploit Media Center to its extreme potential, you could ultimately sell every piece of entertainment hardware you own, including DVD players, televisions, and stereos, as well as your membership to the neighborhood movie rental store. With the right version of Vista, always-on Internet, and a well-endowed media center PC, you can simplify and organize your life, and unclutter your home at the same time—all with a single piece of equipment.

The good news is that you no longer need a special "Media Center Edition PC" to get all of this multimedia power; any PC can do this stuff, as long as it's running the *Home Premium or Ultimate* versions of Vista (see Figure 16-1). (The other editions don't include Media Center. Sorry, cubicle dwellers.)

Your Gear List
Home Premium • Ultimate

Even though Media Center works on the lowliest Vista PC, it reserves its best tricks for people whose computers have these high-end luxuries:

- **A TV tuner and cable connection.** You'll need these extras if you want to watch and record live TV on your PC. If your PC didn't come with a TV tuner, you can add one, either in the form of an external USB box or as an expansion card, for under $100.

  Even without a TV tuner, you can use all of Media Center's other features. Media Center works with TV shows you download from the Internet, your home videos, your pictures, and your music.

- **A DVD burner.** It's really great to be able to burn your recorded or downloaded TV shows to a DVD so you can watch them away from home.

- **A connection to your TV.** You can always curl up at your desk to watch TV and movies, but a lot of people find that setup a bit too geeky for their tastes. In a perfect world, you'd connect the PC to your television.

  The easiest way to do that is to run an S-video cable from the PC to the TV, although there are various other ways to do the job.

- **A remote control.** If you're going to connect your PC to a TV, you don't want to have to scramble across the room every time you want to make an adjustment. That's why some computers come with remote controls, so you can run the whole show from your couch. (A wireless keyboard and mouse are useful, too.)

Setup

Premium • Ultimate

Open Media Center by choosing its name from the Start→All Programs menu. You can also just type "Media" into the Start Menu; Windows then shows you all programs on your computer with "Media" in their name. If Media Center offers a little hello that says "Welcome!" and "Select Next to begin," then you've never opened the

---

POWER USERS' CLINIC

Media Center Extender

Q: What could possibly be better than running a cable from your PC to a TV, bringing all your Media Center videos and slideshows to the big screen?

A: *Not* running a cable.

That's right: you can connect the PC to the TV wirelessly–*if* you have an XBox 360, Microsoft's game console. The XBox has something called Media Center Extender technology built right in.

And if buying an XBox isn't in your future, companies like HP and Linksys offer dedicated Media Center devices. They

connect to your home network either wirelessly, using WiFi, or, um, *wirefully,* using Ethernet.

To add a Media Center Extender to your PC, open Media Center, scroll down to Tasks, then scroll across to Add Extender. The Extender Setup walks you through the process of setting up the Extender.

Along the way, you'll be asked to enter the Media Center Extender's 8-digit serial number on your PC. That's a security measure that ties *your* Extender to *your* PC. (You wouldn't want your next-door neighbor enjoying your pictures and TV shows without your knowledge, would you?)

---

program before, and you'll have to set it up. That's what this section is about. (If you don't get the "Click next to begin" greeting, Media Player is already set up. Skip to the next section.)

Tip: You can always repeat the setup process later if necessary. Open Media Center. Then, from the main menu (in the middle of the screen, not the top), choose Tasks→Settings→General→Windows Media Center Setup→Run Media Center Setup Again.

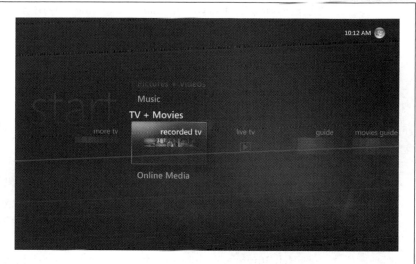

Figure 16-1:
This is what you see once Media Center is set up. You can now buy music online and organize your existing music library, burn a CD of your favorite pictures, pause and re-wind live TV, or schedule a program to record weekly.

As you go, you'll notice that the Media Center *looks* nothing like normal Windows programs. There are no standard windows or menus. And the fonts are *huge*—they look like they've been designed to be read by someone 10 feet away.

In fact, they have. The Media Center interface is designed to be operated from a couch across the room from the TV; normal-size Windows text would be too small to read.

UP TO SPEED

Media Center vs. Media Center PCs

Don't confuse Vista's Media Center software with a "media center PC."

Media center PCs are usually high-dollar investments. They almost always come with TV tuners, high-end video cards, speaker systems, DVD burners, and large monitors. Their TV tuners may even be HDTV capable and accept input from other sources, like video cameras and old VCR players.

You can connect a media center PC to a television in your family room.

Media Center, on the other hand, is just a program. It runs on any PC that has the Home Premium or Ultimate edition of Vista. You could even run Media Center *on* a "media center PC" and then connect it to a TV and other external devices—a dreamy setup indeed for the high-end couch potato.

If you're actually operating the PC from a chair right in front of it, as usual, the whole thing might strike you as a little weird. But you'll remember the plight of the people who *are* sitting 10 feet away, and you'll thank Microsoft on their behalf.

Required Setup

The setup sequence walks you, first of all, through the Required Setup, where you'll see the following options:

- **Join a Wireless Network.** If Media Center decides that your PC can get on a wireless network, it offers you the chance to use the cleverly named Join Wireless Network Wizard to join a wireless network. (If you're already connected to a network or wireless connection, you don't see this step.)

Tip: Although an Internet connection is not required to watch live TV, an always-on Internet connection is very useful. Without it, you won't get the TV guide listings you'll need for the TV-recording portion of Media Center's repertoire.

- **Internet Connection.** If you decline the wireless setup, you're offered the chance to specify some other kind of Internet connection.

- **Test.** Click a button. Test your Internet connection. Hope it works.

- **Privacy Statement.** Click "View the privacy statement online" to see Microsoft's privacy rules and regulations—boring reading, but a must if you worry about those types of things.

- **Help Improve Windows Media Center.** Choose to join or not to join the Customer Improvement Program. If you join, Media Center will send anonymous information to Microsoft about your Media Center use and how reliable Media Center is on your end.

Figure 16-2:
While setting up the required components, you'll configure your Internet connection, test it, and then decide if you want Media Center to connect to the Internet automatically to obtain information about your media and offer you additional media options. Yes is selected here.

- **Get the Most from Windows Media Center.** Allow Media Center to automatically go online to get music, album art, and other media information (Figure 16-2).

Optional TV Setup

To configure Media Center, you'll set up the optional components last. Figure 16-3 shows the Optional Setup screen.

Note: These options appear *only* if your PC has a TV tuner card.

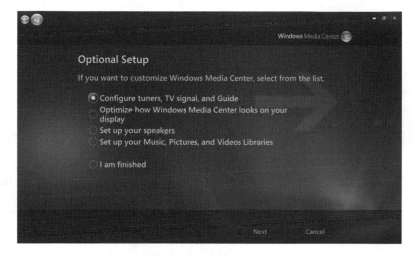

Figure 16-3:
Optional Setup choices vary depending on what hardware is installed. The first option, "Configure tuners, TV signal, and Guide," is displayed only if your Media Center has a working TV tuner card and is otherwise ready for television viewing. If you don't see this option, your PC needs a little work in the hardware department. Click Next to continue (as you'll do throughout this chapter after a task is done.)

Confirm your region

Confirming your region is just another step in the setup process. Choose "Yes, use this region to configure TV services" if the region shown matches your own (for instance, United States). If it does not match, select "No, I want to select a different region" and follow the instructions.

If you don't choose the right region, Media Center won't be able to access the information it needs to configure itself correctly, like the type of cable connection you use, where you want your TV listings to come from, and more.

TV setup options

Wait. It'll take a few minutes for Media Center to download the latest TV setup options for your region. During this process, Media Center tries to detect and configure your TV signal based on what it expects to find in your region. Most of the time it succeeds.

When that step is complete, you're asked to choose "Configure my TV signal automatically (recommended)" or "I will manually configure my TV signal." Select the former. (You can set it up manually, but why ask for trouble?)

When you choose to let Media Center configure your TV signal automatically, Media Center scans for a set-top box signal, a satellite signal, an antenna signal, or a direct cable signal, and configures it automatically.

TV signal configuration result

What you see and do here depends on what kind of connection you have for your television signal. Here are a few options:

- **Antenna.** You have an antenna connected directly to your TV tuner, probably taped to a window next to your PC for better reception. Newer antennas are flexible and can be discreetly hidden behind a curtain or stapled to the outside of a doorjamb.

- **Direct cable connection.** You have a coaxial cable that connects a jack on the wall to your TV tuner. As noted earlier, you may have an external TV tuner or one that's directly installed inside your PC.

- **Set-top box.** Choose this option if you have a cable box from the cable company in between the wall and your PC.

- **Satellite.** You use a satellite connection for your TV. The satellite connection is made via your TV tuner.

If Media Center reports that it can't find a connection, there's probably something wrong with your hardware setup. Make sure the TV tuner is plugged in and turned on, and verify the connections to the tuner. If problems persist, stop the Media Center setup and reboot the computer (and the tuner and cable box for good measure).

If, on the other hand, the program correctly identifies your TV-signal source, click Yes. Work through the wizard until you've successfully chosen the hardware and connections that match your computer's configuration.

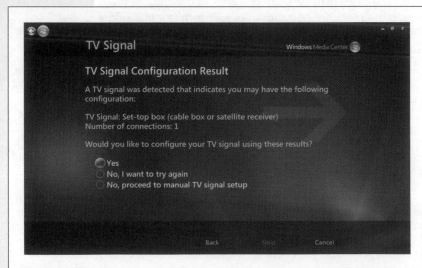

Figure 16-4:
The choices you see here and in the rest of the setup screens depend on which hardware is installed on your PC, like whether or not you have a remote control, set-top box, cable or satellite connections; if you want to use the Guide; and how you want to change channels with the remote. You may also be prompted for a Zip code to configure the Guide, if you've decided to use it. Just keep at it...it'll all be over soon enough.

Along the way, you may be asked to make a few additional decisions. For example, if you have an Internet connection, you'll need to decide if you want to use the online TV guide for your program listings. If so, you'll be prompted to input your Zip code. The Guide will show you everything that's going to be on TV in the next two weeks, making it simple for you to record stuff.

You may also be prompted to select your TV signal provider—Time Warner Cable or Comcast, for example. If you have a remote control, you'll be asked to configure it as well.

Figure 16-4 shows a best case scenario.

Optional Display Setup

After you've completed the setup for the TV tuner, signal, and Guide, the Optional Setup page reappears. It offers three additional branches to the setup labyrinth.

Optimize how Windows Media Center looks on your display

During this setup cycle, you can specify how you want video to look on your PC monitor or a connected television. After all, even if you're already happy with how data looks on your computer screen, watching TV and movies is a whole different ballgame.

This setup step is a lot more fun than most, thanks to the professionally produced *video* that walks you through the steps. When you click Watch Video, a roomful of thin, 30-something models sit around an IKEA-furnished apartment and demonstrate various concepts relating to black levels, color cast, and so on.

Tip: Don't click the X in the top-right corner when the video is playing to stop it. If you do, the entire Media Center Setup closes and you'll have to start over!

During the display setup, you're asked to specify:

- **Which screen you want to use for Media Center's display, if you have more than one.** Choose the highest quality one. You'll get a great picture if you have your PC connected to a real television via an S-video cable, or, better yet, a DVI or HDMI cable (for HDTV sets).

- **What type of monitor you have.** You wouldn't want to tell Media Center you're using a CRT (tube) monitor when you actually have a high-end flat screen.

- **The type of connection that you use to connect your computer to your display.** This step appears only if you've connected an external screen to your PC; it tells Media Center how that TV or monitor is connected to the computer.

  Your choices are Composite or S-video; DVI, VGA, or HDMI; or Component (YpbPr).

  If you don't already know what kind of cable you've used, you may have to get on your hands and knees and peek behind your PC. Choose the connector that offers the best video quality. (See the box on page 508.)

- **What aspect ratio (shape) your screen has.** It's either 4:3 (the shape of traditional TV screens) or 16:9 (widescreen, like a high-def TV).

- **What screen resolution you want.** If the screen looks fine, just click Yes and keep going. If it looks squished or elongated, click No and fiddle with the pixel-resolution settings.

  Remember that, while a higher resolution makes for a better picture, it also requires more PC horsepower. If you choose too high a resolution setting, your video card may offer no picture at all, and programs in the background might wind up making DVDs skip or stutter during playback. Experiment with various settings to see what you like the best.

Optional Speaker Setup

You won't get very far in Audio/Video Land without some speakers. If you haven't already set them up, this phase of Media Center setup is ready when you are. You're asked to specify:

- **Speaker Connection Type.** This very helpful window lets you indicate how you've connected your speakers to your computer—whether via MiniPlug (analog), Dual RCA (analog), Single RCA (digital), or Toslink (digital) jacks. (Built-in laptop speakers are an option, too.)

- **Number of Speakers.** Select the appropriate number of speakers. Choices include 2 Speakers, 5.1 Surround Sound, and 7.1 Surround Sound. Test your speakers when prompted by Media Center.

Select "Set up your speakers" to continue the optional setup process. During the process you'll state how many speakers you have and test sound quality.

UP TO SPEED

It's Good to Have Connections

How can a PC be connected to a TV? Let us count the ways. Each connection type has a distinctly shaped jack, requires a different kind of cable, and offers different video quality. Here are your choices:

S-video. Generally used for connecting DVDs players, TVs, satellite receivers, and cable TV boxes. Also used on computers with TV outputs. Very good picture quality.

DVI. A more modern jack, frequently found on HDTV sets, that's capable of excellent video.

VGA. The oldest connection type, offering the poorest video quality of all. The connection is the old monitor-to-PC 15-pin cable.

HDMI. What's great about this slim, very modern jack is that it carries *both* audio and video (high-def video, in fact) over a single cable. HDMI jacks appear on high-end equipment including HDTVs, projectors, plasmas, and more. It's the best option, if you have it.

Component. Found mostly on HDTVs and newer DVD players. Excellent video, including high-definition, but a hassle because you have to connect three wires on each end (color-coded red, green, and blue). Component cables are being phased out in favor of digital connections.

Optional Libraries Setup

It's finally time to set up your media *library*—that is, your collection of music, videos, movies, pictures, and so on. If this is the first PC you've ever used, you might not have very much media to work with. It's more likely, however, that you've used the Easy Transfer Wizard (page 783) to transfer all of these files from another PC, or upgraded to Vista from an earlier version of Windows.

Tip: If this business about importing your music and videos sounds familiar, it may be because you've already done this job using Windows Media *Player* (not the same thing as Windows Media *Center*), as described in Chapter 14. In that case, you can skip this section; your library should already be in place, since Player and Center share the same library folders.

There isn't much involved in setting up the media library. In fact, if your pictures, music, and videos are already in the Pictures, Music, and Videos folders, you should be good to go. You have to intervene only if you want Media Center to catalog and "watch" *other* folders—folders you've created, folders on other drives, or data on other computers on your network.

In that situation, click "Add folder to watch," and then browse to the folders when prompted. (If you're adding a folder on another PC on the network, select "Add shared folders from another computer." Note that you'll be able to "see" only folders that you've explicitly *shared,* as described on page 729.)

Click the proper folder, and then click OK. When finished, select "I am finished" from the setup page.

TV: Your PC as TiVo

Home Premium • Ultimate

There's nothing as cool as controlling TV: pausing it, rewinding to watch a football pass (or fumble) again, and fast-forwarding through commercials, all right there on your PC. Eat your heart out, TiVo owners!

GEM IN THE ROUGH

Just Move It

If there's more than one computer in your house, consider this radical suggestion—move *all* of your music, picture, and video files to the proper folders on your main Vista computer.

You may wind up duplicating those files in the process. But now you can stop worrying about backing up other networked PCs, monitoring additional folders across a network, and not being able to find a certain song because it's on the wrong computer.

In a nutshell: Move all your music to the Music folder; move all of your pictures to the Pictures folder; and move all of your videos to the Videos folder. Create subfolders by all means, but get all of your media in one place!

When all of these files are all in one place, they're easier to back up, easier to find, easier to access, and faster to open. Moving media to your super-powered Vista PC also frees up space on older, capacity-challenged PCs.

(What's even more fun is taping *Jeopardy!*, watching it to learn the answers, and then playing it again "for the first time" when your spouse gets home.)

If you've equipped your PC with a TV tuner card (or tuner box), that's exactly what Media Center offers. And after you've tasted life with a DVR (digital video recorder), you'll find the commercials, rehashes, and previews of *live* TV to be excruciating.

Explore TV Features

The TV + Movies section of Media Center has lots of options. Open Media Center, select TV + Movies from the main menu, and browse away:

- **More TV.** Select an option (like Showcase, TV & Movies, Music & Radio, News & Sports, Games, and Lifestyle) to view subcategories of online and television shows. Showcase brings up TV channels, including Comedy Central and ABC Family, while TV & Movies offers ABC Enhanced TV, TitanTV, and shows like *American Chopper*. There's nothing like watching *American Chopper* any time you want!

- **Recorded TV.** This delicious category is the home of every TV show you've scheduled Media Center to record automatically, as described below.

  If you haven't recorded anything, you can at least play around with the short movie ads that Microsoft has provided for your experimentation pleasure.

- **Live TV.** This option says, "I just want to watch TV. I don't care about all of this other stuff." (See "Tricks with Live TV" on the facing page.)

- **Guide.** Here's the TV listing for your Zip code, specific to your cable or satellite company. The guide is downloaded automatically (if that's the way you configured it). Figure 16-5 shows an example.

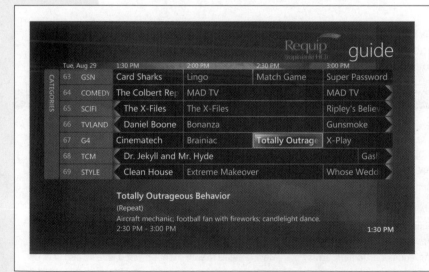

Figure 16-5:
Use your remote control, mouse, or keyboard to navigate through the guide. Type a number into the remote's keypad to change channels. Click Skip (or something similar) to move forward in the Guide. Run the mouse over a show's title to read a short synopsis of the show. Right-click any show title (or use the remote's Info button) to get more program info, record the program, or record the series.

- **Movies Guide.** This guide lists movies available through your TV connection—a part of the Guide that comes with Media Center.

- **Play DVD.** Not much ambiguity here. It's the controls for playing movie DVDs that you insert into your PC.

- **Search.** This tool helps you pluck one show out of your TV-guide haystack. For instance, from Search, select Title, type *South Park,* and find out instantly when the next *South Park* airs. Choose Categories→Educational to find something really boring for your kids to watch. Choose Movie Actor and type *Goldie Hawn* to see what movies or TV shows are coming up with her in the cast.

If you get any "hits," recording them is just a button-click away.

The Media Center Menu System

Already, you're probably mastering the master menu plan for Media Center. You navigate its menus just by using the arrow keys and the OK button on your remote control—or, if you're sitting up close to the PC, using the arrow keys and the Enter key on your keyboard.

Move vertically to highlight a main-menu selection (Pictures+Videos, TV+Movies, Music), and then move horizontally to explore the details of that area. For example, once you select Pictures+Videos, you can move the highlighting left or right to get to More Pictures, Picture Library, Play All, and Video Library.

Tip: At any time, you can return to the main menu by clicking the round, glowing ⊞ button at the top of your screen.

Tricks with Live TV

Open Media Center, choose TV+Movies, and select Live TV. If you have a TV tuner installed, television starts automatically. With Media Center, watching TV is anything but a passive activity. As Figure 16-6 shows, several buttons await.

Note: If you have a cable box connected to your PC, you should be able to get anything on Media Center that you can get when the box is plugged into a television. That includes premium channels and on-demand movies.

Plenty of people just plug the cable directly into the TV tuner, though. They don't get the premium channels, but can still tune in to 30 or so standard cable stations. Doing without a cable box simplifies the setup and saves another monthly fee.

OK, that all seems reasonable—except for the Rewind and Fast-forward buttons, and well, Pause. How is it possible to rewind a live TV broadcast? Or fast-forward it? Or pause it?

When live TV comes into the computer, Media Center saves *(caches)* the show that's playing. Even if you haven't explicitly asked for it to be recorded, it caches the most recent 60 minutes or so. (You can see how full this *buffer* of temporarily recorded TV has become, as shown in Figure 16-13.)

Once it's cached, you can rewind what you've already watched (or what has been cached), and fast-forward through what you don't want to see, like commercials. If you hit the Pause button, your PC freezes the frame. Behind the scenes, it's still recording, saving up what's coming in live, so that you can fast-forward again when you're back from the bathroom or answering the door.

Note: You can't fast-forward into a live TV show until after you've paused or rewound it. Even Microsoft hasn't figured out a way to let you fast-forward into part of a TV show that hasn't yet been broadcast.

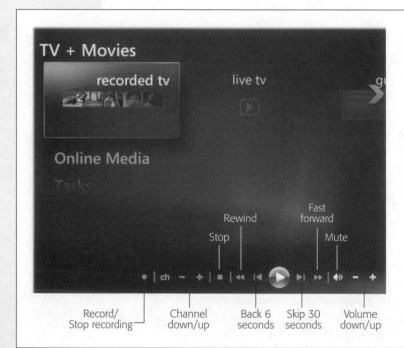

Figure 16-6:
If you're remoteless, move your mouse to the lower-right corner of the screen to summon these TV controls—everything you need for your DVR (digital video recorder) enjoyment. If course, if you have a remote control, you can use it instead.

Either way, the controls here all pertain to a show that's on the air right now.

A typical Media Center maven learns to harness this caching business in order to skip the ads. For example, you might turn on *Judge Judy* at 4 p.m., pause it, and then come back around 4:12, start it from the beginning and fast-forward through all the commercials when they appear. You'll be done by 4:30 and you can watch something else. (Or watch a trivia show like *Ben Stein's Money* for 30 minutes, rewind it to the beginning, and then watch it with someone you want to impress!)

Record a Show or a Season of Shows

To program your PC to record a show, you need a TV with a tuner, as described earlier. Then, do a little browsing for the show you want:

1. **Choose Start→Windows Media Center. Scroll to TV+Movies; choose Guide.**

   Your TV listings appear on the screen.

2. **Locate the show to record.**

   Use your remote control, the mouse, or the keyboard to locate the show you want. Position your mouse in the lower-right corner of the screen to summon the mouse-clickable controls, or use the arrow keys on the remote or keyboard to move through the programs.

Tip: Some special Media Center remote controls and keyboards offer a button that lets you scroll a day at a time; with the mouse, you're pretty much stuck scrolling hour by hour.

---

3. **Record the show.**

   Once you've found the show to record, click it once with the mouse, hit Return or Enter on the keyboard, or click OK on the remote control. The Program Info screen appears (Figure 16-7).

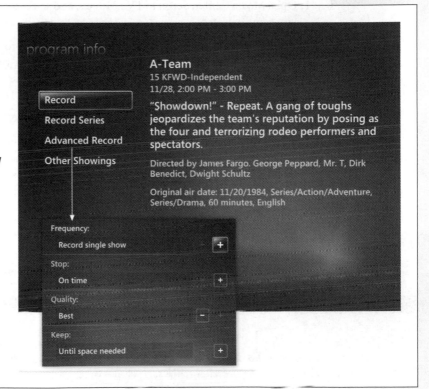

Figure 16-7:
Record means, "record this episode." Record Series makes your PC record every episode of the selected show—a significant advance from the VCR days.

And then there's Advanced Record, which opens up some very useful settings for recording, like Frequency, quality, and adjustments to the start and stop time (to compensate for irregular broadcast times, also known as network audience-retention tactics).

From here, you can choose **Advanced Record**, which contains not-at-all advanced settings for recording, like Frequency (just this show, or the whole series?); Stop time (lets you end the recording between 5 minutes and 3 hours after it's scheduled to end, so that you don't miss the ends of football games that run long); Quality (higher qualities require more hard drive space); and Keep (how long to keep the show on the hard drive before it's auto-deleted—Until Space Needed, For One Week, Until I Watch, Until I Delete).

The Program Info screen also offers a link called **Other Showings,** which lets you see when the selected show will be aired again. This is a good option when a conflict arises between two shows you want to record at the same time. If you find out that one of the shows will be aired in the next day or two, you can work through the conflict by recording the later airing.

Tip: Once a show is scheduled to record, you can right-click its name in the TV guide to set options quickly. You can also right-click any program to record it on the fly, without having to wade through any options at all—a convenient option when you're trying to get out the door.

Watching Recorded TV

To watch a show you've previously recorded, proceed like this:

1. **Open Media Center. Scroll to TV+Movies, and select Recorded TV. Find the show you want to watch.**

   Use the remote control, the mouse, or the keyboard to work through the list of recorded shows. Position your mouse in the bottom-right corner of the screen to access controls for use with the mouse, or use the arrows on the remote or keyboard.

2. **Click the program once. On the next screen, click Play.**

   While you're watching the show, you can use your remote, the keyboard, or the mouse to fast-forward through the commercials, rewind to review a scene, or pause to get a bite to eat. As usual, if you're using the mouse, point to the lower-right corner to make the controls appear. Otherwise, use the keys and buttons on the keyboard or remote.

3. **Delete the program (or resume or restart it).**

   If you stopped the program before it was finished playing, you're offered a Resume command. If the program has ended, or if you've had enough of it before it's over,

---

UP TO SPEED

Managing Recorded TV

Recorded shows can really suck up a lot of hard drive space. Recording your favorite series and *Star Trek* reruns can bleed even the biggest hard drive dry in a matter of months. The next thing you know, you're struggling to grasp why you can't install a game of Tetris for lack of space.

That's why you'll want to watch and then delete shows as often as you can. For the ones you'd like to keep for a while, like a good movie or the last season of *The Sopranos* on HBO, consider burning them to DVD and then deleting the hard drive copy.

---

you can choose Delete, Restart, Keep Until, or Burn CD/DVD. You may see other options too, like Cast and More, or Extras.

Save a Show onto a DVD

If you've found something you really like and want to burn it to a DVD (suggestion: the movie *Time Bandits*)—assuming your PC *has* a DVD burner—follow these directions:

1. **Open Media Center. Insert a blank DVD. Go to Tasks→"Burn CD/DVD."**

   You're offered several DVD formats to burn, like Data DVD, Video DVD, or DVD Slide Show. To make a *backup* of your TV shows, for example (for use in a PC), you'd opt for the Data DVD. To save a TV show or movie onto a regular old DVD for playback in a DVD player, you want the regular Video DVD format.

2. **Select Video DVD. Click Next.**

   Now you're asked to name the DVD. If you have a remote control that has only number keys, you can use the clever little cellphone-like dialing pad to tap out alphabet letters. For example, to enter *Shrek,* you'd tap 7777 (for the letter S), 44, 777, 33, 55.

3. **Type out a name, and then click Next.**

   Now you're asked to choose *what* you want to burn onto your DVD. You can choose either Recorded TV or Video Library (which means any video files on your hard drive that *didn't* come from your TV tuner—your camcorder imports, for example).

4. **Click Recorded TV, and then click Next.**

   Media Center displays what's in your Recorded TV Library. Each show appears as a giant thumbnail image, complete with a checkbox in the lower-right corner.

5. **Turn on the checkboxes of the shows you want to transfer to DVD.**

   You can also use the Select All, Clear All, "by name," and "by date" controls for help in selecting or sorting the videos.

6. **Click Next.**

   You're offered one final chance to review and edit the list of shows. Here, you can click the up or down arrow buttons to rearrange their sequence on the DVD, rename a show, and so on.

7. **Click Burn DVD.**

   The burning process can take quite a while, depending on how much data you've added and how fast your CD/DVD burner is. Once the burn is finished, eject the disc and reinsert it to make sure it works.

Overall, though, this is a great way to get that must-see television show from your computer to the living room, or even those scintillating vacation pictures of Mexico, if you don't have a Media Center Extender!

Tip: You can follow these same steps to burn a slideshow onto a DVD, except, of course, that you should choose DVD Slide Show in step 2.

In fact, you can also insert a regular blank *CD*, although your options in that case are limited to making data discs or burning music CDs.

Renting and Buying Online Movies

Sure, you could drive to the video store, rent a movie (or even buy one), drive back home, and then try to bring the family together to watch it (because it's due back in a couple of days). But if you don't mind a little loss of picture quality, a smaller movie selection, few DVD extras, and a slightly shorter deadline, your Media Center can get you movies without the two trips to the video store. That's because Media Center is tied into MovieLink and CinemaNow, two online downloadable-movie companies.

To get started, you have to register. Open Media Center, select Online Media, select What's New, select TV & Movies, and then select the movie-download store you want. Once you sign up, log in, click Browse All Movies, and find a movie worth watching, you can finally click Rent Now to begin downloading it.

Note: Some movies, on some online stores, can be bought instead of rented. Buying a movie costs four or five times as much as renting it, but at least you can burn it to a DVD for permanence.

You have to wait for the download to finish before you can watch the movie; that's 10 or 20 minutes with high-speed cable. To watch a rented video, you have to install special CinemaNow or MovieLink software.

After the movie has downloaded, you can watch it by clicking Watch Movie. Then, click Play Download.

TROUBLESHOOTING MOMENT

Figure Out What's Not Working

Every month or so, it's a good idea to take inventory, to see how the Media Center TV recording empire is going. Perhaps you thought *American Idol* was a good program to record, but it turns out that everyone in your family watches it live, and nobody deletes the recorded episodes. Perhaps you thought you'd watch *Survivor,* but decided after a few shows that you just weren't into it. Every now and then, in other words, you should revisit your automatic recording schedule.

One way to take inventory is to see what's not being deleted (because it's not being watched). If you have 10 episodes of *Pimp My Ride,* for example, it may be because your kids are watching it at someone else's house; get it off of the Recorded TV list.

To cancel any recording, navigate to Recorded TV. Right-click the show you no longer want to record. Click Program Info, then Series Info, then Cancel Series.

Music: Your PC as Jukebox

Home Premium • Ultimate

You'll probably be listening to a lot of music in Media Center. If you'd rather use Windows Media Player, that's fine, but you can do a lot more with music in Media Center—like using a remote control.

Tip: Media Center music—any music, actually—sounds best on good speakers. To get the most out of your sound system, though, you'll need to connect them correctly, take the room's size and layout into consideration, and consider equalization options. If you'd like some guidance, you can download a free bonus appendix to this chapter that describes how to set up a surround-sound system step by step. It's called Surround Sound Setup.pdf, and it's available on this book's "Missing CD" at *www.missingmanuals.com*.

Use the arrow keys (on the keyboard or remote) to scroll through the main Media Center menu (Music, TV+Movies, and so on). Select Music to get started, and then, from the Music options, select Music Library. (The Music Library is, wildly enough, where your music is stored.) If Media Center asks you to set up the Music library automatically, select OK.

Once setup is complete, you're ready to rock and roll!

Your Music Library

Sooner or later, it will occur to you that your copy of Windows Vista actually comes with *two* massive music- and video-playing programs: Windows Media Center and Windows Media Player. Inevitably, there's quite a bit of duplication.

Fortunately, your PC has only *one* video and music library, which serves up the same music and movies to *both* Media Center and Media Player. If you've already added music to Media Player (Chapter 14), then it shows up in Media Center, too.

Ripping CDs

To *rip* a CD means to copy its songs onto your computer. You now have two different programs that can do the ripping—Media Center and Media Player.

Truth is, Media Player is the better program to use for ripping CDs. For one thing, it lets you rip only *some* of the songs from a CD. For another, you can configure Media Player to start ripping automatically whenever you insert a CD into your drive. And you're not wasting any effort, since all CD music winds up in the same central PC music library, whether Media Player or Media Center does the work.

Still, Media Center *can* rip CDs if you're so inclined. Here's how it works:

1. **Open Media Center and insert a CD.**

   The CD starts playing. If you want to listen to the CD, that's fine; it can keep playing while you rip the tunes. If you don't want to listen to the CD, move the mouse to the lower right of the screen and click the Pause button.

2. **Click Copy CD. When asked if you're sure, click Yes.**

Ripping an entire CD (that is, copying it to your hard drive) takes about 5 minutes. Once the ripping process is done, nothing happens at all; you see only a little note that the ripping process is complete. To rip another CD, eject the first one and insert another.

After all the ripping is finished, click the Back button (top-left corner of Media Center). You arrive at the main Music screen (Figure 16-8). Here, you can view the song list, view the queue, and select Visualize to listen to the music with wild, laser-light-show graphics.

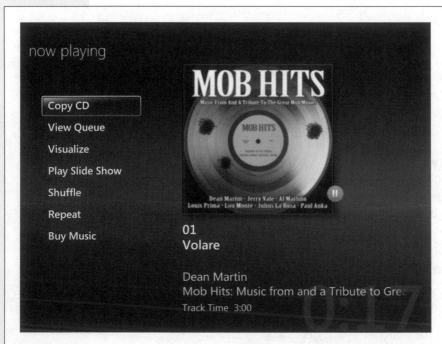

Figure 16-8:
When you insert a CD while Media Center is on, the CD plays automatically. Several choices are then displayed on the left side: Copy CD, View Queue, Visualize, Play Slide Show, Shuffle, Repeat, and Buy Music. To rip the CD to your PC, select Copy CD.

To return to the Music Library, click Back *again*; select Music, and then Music Library. (Media Center remote controls usually have a Music button that shortens those steps.)

Tip: You can edit album or song information from the queue list as detailed in the previous section, or you can edit them directly from the Music Library. To edit a song, album, or album artist, locate the item to edit in the library, right-click that item, and select Edit. You can change the album title, artist name, and genre. This is particularly helpful for songs that are listed in the wrong genre or for a remake or live version of a song you already have on your hard drive.

Playing Music

The first thing you'll notice when you open the Music part of Media Center is that there are songs in there—but not all of them are yours! In fact, if you've never worked with music before, you may have a dozen or so songs in there you've never heard of.

Consider them a little gift from Microsoft, presumably so that you can start fooling around with the Media Center even if you've never downloaded or ripped a single song in your life. Figure 16-9 shows you how.

Tip: Figure 16-9 shows that you can return to the Artists list by repeatedly clicking the Back button. Depending on your PC model, though, there might be a more efficient way.

Your keyboard or remote control may offer a button for Music or Music Library. If so, clicking it takes you back to the main Music Library menu page.

Figure 16-9:
Use the arrow keys to highlight the sort criterion you want (albums, artists…), and then use the down arrow to browse your collection. You can then play the entire album or one song, burn the album to a CD, delete a song from the list, add the song to a queue, and more. Return to the Artists list by repeatedly clicking the Back button.

Music you've ripped shows up in the list illustrated in Figure 16-9, too. You can burrow to it through any of the criteria headings: Artist, Genre, whatever.

When you've drilled all the way down to a song's name, you'll see a list of options at the left side of the screen:

- **Play Song (or Play Album).** If you have a special media-control keyboard, or a remote control, you can use it to skip songs, pause and play, control the volume, and so on. If not, position the mouse at the bottom-right corner of the screen, and use the playback controls that pop up there.

- **Add to Queue.** This option presumes that some other song is already playing; it means, "line up this song to play next."

- **Buy Music.** Takes you online so you can pay for more tunes. (As you'll discover, the music store is not designed to be operated from across the room. You'll have to move close to the screen and use the keyboard and mouse.)

- **Edit Info.** Change the song's title, rating, and so on. (The cellphone-like number pad at the right side is intended to help you input text using only your remote control. It ain't pretty, but it works.)

- **Delete.** In other words, you've had quite enough of this song.

Buy or "Rent" Music Online

Ripping music from your CD collection is one legal way to build up your library. Buying it online is another (see Figure 16-10).

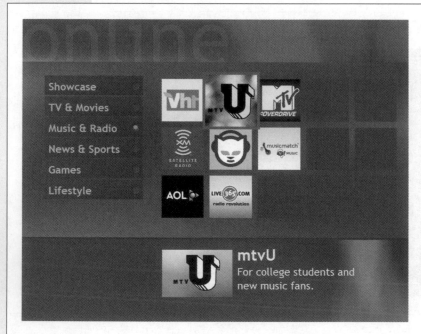

Figure 16-10:
To see what's available in the way of online media, open Media Center, select Music, and select More Music. Now choose Music & Radio. There are lots of choices, including VH1, MTV Overdrive, XM Satellite Radio, Napster, Musicmatch, AOL Music, and Live365.com. To obtain music from any of them, click the one you like best and work through the subscription process. Once you've done that, follow the directions from the media's Web site to select and download music. Many of these music services also give you access to Internet radio.

You'll soon discover that the online music-store racket has evolved into two different business models:

- **Buy the songs for $1 each.** These songs are copy-protected, but you can copy them to up to four other PCs, burn them to CD, or download them to a pocket music player. Usually.

- **Rent the songs.** You pay $10 or $15 a month for the right to download all the music you want—flat fee, baby. The only downside is that when you stop paying the fee, all your music self-destructs. You're left with nothing but memories.

(One of the most heavily promoted of such services is MTV's Urge service, described on page 477.)

Note: Songs from rental services don't look or play any differently than music you've ripped from your CD collection, or music you've purchased. The only difference you'll notice is that you can't burn the downloaded rental music onto a DVD or CD. If you try, you'll get a message that says, "Some of the music in your burn list has been protected with media usage rights. Protected files will play on portable music players, but cannot be burned to a CD or DVD. Would you like to continue?"

You can thank the record company lawyers for that one.

Search the Library

With Media Center you have the option to search for what you want using your remote control, keyboard, or mouse, as with just about any other task in Media Center. In Media Center, select Music, select Search, and then enter a search term by typing letters using the numeric keypad, your remote control, or your keyboard. Clear letters using the Clear button on the remote or the Backspace key on the keyboard. Click the Mode button to change from symbols, to lowercase, to uppercase letters. The search is refined as more letters are added.

Playlists

A *playlist* is a set of songs that you've hand-picked and hand-sequenced. They might have originated on a whole bunch of different CDs, but *you* think they go well together. You can read more about playlists in the Media Player chapter (page 473)—because guess what? Windows Vista is smart enough to make the same playlists show up in *both* programs. Any playlists you create in Media Player appear in Media Center, and vice versa.

Auto Playlists are self-building, self-updating lists of songs that change as you listen, download, and change ratings. These, too, are described in Chapter 14—but unlike Media Player, Media *Center* comes prestocked with Auto Playlists. Here you'll find playlists of music you listen to the most, music you've listened to in the last month, music rated at four or five stars, and so on. As your preferences and playback habits change, so do the items in the playlists.

Note: Media Center has playlists for videos and pictures, too

To view all of your playlists—ones you made, and Auto Playlists Microsoft made—select Music→Music Library→Playlists within Media Center.

Click Play to play a highlighted playlist immediately, or click Add to Queue to play it after whatever's currently playing. You can also delete a playlist by selecting Delete.

Creating Playlists

You can create playlists of your own in Media Center, but it's a little bit awkward. You start the process by assembling a *queue,* as described next. Once you have a queue in place, select Save As Playlist, name the playlist, and click Save. Your playlists are listed (in a playlist *list*, of course) on the Playlists tab of Media Center.

All of this explains why you'll probably be a lot happier building your playlists in Media *Player*, as described in Chapter 14. The playlists you build there also show up in Media Center.

Tip: Once you've set up a playlist, you can immortalize it by burning it to a new, custom CD. Suddenly, you're a one-person record company. Any songs you've imported from your own CD collection or bought for $1 apiece online are fair game. (You generally can't burn songs you've only "rented," using one of those online-music-store monthly subscription programs.)

The Music Queue

A *queue* is a waiting line, whether it's the one at the Department of Motor Vehicles or the list of songs you've lined up to play in Media Center. The music queue is a way to set it and forget it—to slate certain songs, albums, or playlists to play all afternoon without your intervention.

Creating a Queue

You can add music to your Media Center queue in any of three chunks:

- **An album at a time.** Select Music→Music Library→Album, and click an album to add. Click Add to Queue.

- **A song at a time.** Select Music→Music Library. Select a song's name, right-click it, and, from the shortcut menu, choose Add to Queue.

Tip: A remote control, of course, doesn't have a right mouse button. It does, however, have a More Info button, which does the same thing.

- **A playlist at a time.** Select Music→Music Library→Playlist. Click a playlist; click Add to Queue.

GEM IN THE ROUGH

Listen to the Radio

If your PC contains a radio-tuner card—most *TV* tuner cards include radio tuners, too—Media Center's Music Library also offers an option called Radio. That's not Internet radio—we're talking genuine, bona fide, over-the-air FM radio.

Open Media Center and select Music→Radio. Use the Seek buttons to find the station you want. You can also select Save

as Preset to save the station for easier access next time.

(If you *don't* have a radio tuner, you can still listen to hundreds of *Internet* radio stations—but not with Media Center; you need Windows Media Player 11 for that. See Chapter 14.)

Managing the queue

The queue begins to play the minute you add something to it. If you want to edit, clear, or get info on it, select "Now Playing and Queue" in Media Center's main menu. Select Music→View Queue.

Tip: While a song is playing, you can also view and edit the queue by clicking once on the album's icon in the bottom-left corner of the screen.

At this point, you can delve in using three different methods:

- **Edit the queue.** From the Queue page, select Edit Queue. You can now delete any song from the list by clicking the X, or change the order of the queue by clicking the up and down arrows next to any song. When you're finished, click Done.

- **Scramble the queue.** From the Queue page, select Shuffle. The songs in the list now play in random order.

- **Empty the queue.** From the Queue page, select Clear Queue. (No songs are actually deleted from your hard drive or library.)

- **Manage the queue.** Right-click any song in the queue list (or click the More Info button on your remote) and select View Details. Choose Play Song to play the song now. Choose Delete to permanently delete the song from the computer. Click Edit to change details about the song, like the song name, artist name, and rating.

Photos and Video

Home Premium • Ultimate

Just above Music in Media Center's blue-toned main menu is the intriguing entry, Pictures+Videos. Here you'll find a list of all the digital photos and video clips that Media Center found when you first showed it which folders you wanted it to watch.

UP TO SPEED

Videos

Media Center can also handle video clips, like the masterpieces you make with Movie Maker (Chapter 15). A Videos category is also listed in the Pictures+Videos mode. As it turns out, you navigate your Videos and Pictures folders in exactly the same way:

Find a video by drilling down to it.

Sort the videos by clicking a heading above them: Folders, Date Taken, Tags, and so on. (Tags are keywords that you make up; see Chapter 13.)

Play a video by highlighting its icon and pressing Enter or Play.

Control playback using your remote control, if you have one. If not, use the buttons that appear when your mouse approaches the lower-right corner of the screen.

After a video plays, you're offered a Finished screen with three choices: Done, Restart (meaning play again), and Delete. The fourth option—Back—appears only when you mouse your way to the top-left corner of the screen.

Once again, Microsoft starts you off with some basic pictures and vids, so that, at the very least, you can practice navigating the system.

To view some photos, select Pictures+Videos, and open Picture Library. From here, you can view sample photos, as shown in Figure 16-11.

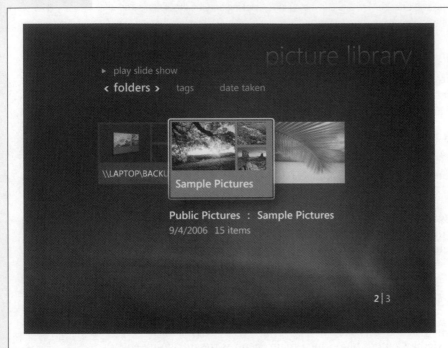

Figure 16-11:
To navigate the Picture Library, run your mouse across the titles in the Picture Library and highlight Folders. Once highlighted, move your mouse to the area underneath Folders, and hover your mouse over Sample Pictures, shown here.

Once again, you work this mode by drilling down. Highlight a folder (Sample Pictures, say) and then press Enter. If you then highlight an individual photo, clicking Enter makes it fill your screen.

Tip: To close the picture, click the Back button. (Don't click the X button at the top right of the screen—you'll shut down the entire Media Center!)

Slideshows

Alternatively, click "Play slide show" at the top of the screen to trigger a magnificent full-screen display. To control its playback using a remote control, use its buttons; if you're using the mouse, move the cursor to the bottom-right corner of the screen to make the playback controls appear. You can also manually move from one image to another using the Fast-forward and Rewind buttons.

Click the Back button in the top-left corner to close the slideshow.

Adding music

Of course, just about any slideshow is more compelling if there's music playing in the background. In Media Center, that's an easy effect:

1. **Start the music playing.**

   In Media Center, click Music→Music Library. Select an album, playlist, or other music grouping, and then click Play.

2. **Return to the Pictures+Videos screen.**

   To do that, click the Back button enough times to return to Media Center's main menu, and then select Pictures+Videos.

3. **Select Picture Library, select a photos folder, and then hit Play Slideshow.**

   The music you started continues as the slideshow proceeds.

Slideshow settings

Unless you change the settings, the standard slideshow presents your pix in random order, a new photo every 12 seconds, with a standard crossfade (transition) effect.

Frankly, however, 12 seconds per photo is an *eternity* if you're anyone but the subject of the photo (or you're in love with that subject). Fortunately, you can change the settings easily enough; see page 529.

Editing Pictures

If you really want to edit your photos, of course, Microsoft has a specialized new Vista tool just for you: Photo Gallery (Chapter 13).

But sometimes you spot a misrotated photo, a picture that needs cropping, or some red-eye in a portrait that you just want to fix quickly without exiting Media Center. Sure enough, you can actually perform basic photo editing from the comfort of your own living room couch.

Start at the thumbnails page. Right-click the problem photo; next, from the shortcut menu, choose Picture Details.

Now you arrive at a new screen that lists tasks at the left side. You can click Rotate to rotate the photo 90 degrees clockwise—a great way to fix a photo that you took with your camera turned vertically.

The real fun, though, awaits when you click Touch Up. On this new screen, these more powerful editing options beckon:

- **Red Eye** is a fully automatic tool. Click the words Red Eye to trigger Vista's "Do your best to remove the reddish retinal reflection from the subject of this flash photo so my loved one doesn't look so much like the spawn of Satan" function.

- **Contrast** is another fully automated feature. One click makes Media Center attempt to improve the tonal range of the photo—the brights and darks.

• **Crop** places a smaller rectangle within the larger frame of your photo, indicating which part of the photo it plans to keep. Everything in the dimmed, foggy outer margins will shortly be hacked away. Click the directional arrow buttons to position the crop box, the magnifying glass buttons to shrink or enlarge the cropping rectangle, or the far-right button to rotate the cropping rectangle by 90 degrees. The actual crop doesn't take place until you click Save (described next).

When you're finished, click Save. You're asked if you want to replace the original; click Yes. There is no other option for saving.

Tip: Click Next and Previous to edit additional pictures.

Burn a CD of Pictures or Videos

Burning photos or videos to a CD or DVD is a handy way to make a backup of them, and it's also a convenient way of taking them with you to a friend's house or a party.

Note: You're not actually creating a music CD that will play in a CD player, or a video DVD that plays in a DVD player. You're basically creating backup discs that hold a lot of computer files—and that are designed to go into another *computer*.

If you want to burn a music CD or video DVD, see Chapters 14 and 15.

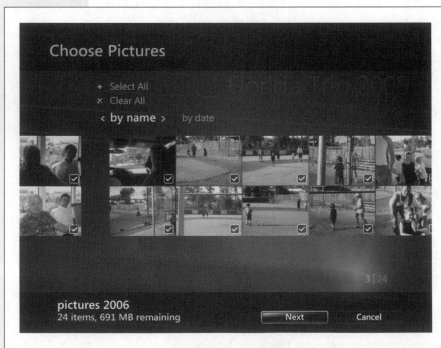

Figure 16-12:
Drill down into the Picture Library subfolders to select pictures you want to add. You can select entire folders or single images. Once you've selected a picture, a folder of pictures, or a mishmash of pictures in any one subfolder, click Next.

Start on the Media Center main menu. Choose Tasks→Burn CD/DVD.

Vista asks you to insert a blank CD or DVD, if you haven't done so already. (What it *actually* says is, "Insert media," but it means a blank disc; nobody expects you to insert *CBS News* or the *New York Times*.)

Insert a blank disc and then click Retry; choose the CD or DVD type (Data CD or Audio CD); type a name; choose the photos folder or music album you want to back up (Figure 16-12); and then click Burn CD (or Burn DVD).

Tip: During the Burn CD/DVD process, Vista invites you to click OK if you want to do other work while the disc is being burned. Light background work like typing or Web surfing should be no problem. Heavy work (Photoshop, video editing) can interfere with the burning, however, resulting in a half burned, failed disc—yet another Frisbee for the yard!

Advanced Settings

Home Premium • Ultimate

Once you've had a little experience with Media Center, the elaborate preferences screens will make a lot more sense. To access the advanced settings, select Tasks on the main Media Center menu, and then select Settings. Here, you'll find all sorts of ways to personalize Media Center.

Most are self-explanatory, but here are a few items worthy of special note:

General

On the General options screen, you can change the following:

- **Startup and Windows Behavior.** Should Media Center always stay on top of other windows, start up automatically when Windows starts, or allow alert messages to appear?

- **Parental Controls.** You can set up a four-digit password that stands between your kids and TV, movies, and DVDs that you consider too violent or racy for them.

- **Optimization.** Schedule a time to run these hard drive tune-up tasks, and they'll run automatically. You should configure this for a time when you won't be using the Media Center, but when the computer is also on and idle.

TV

From the TV options page, you can change the following:

- **Recorder.** You can specify what drive your PC saves TV shows onto, the maximum TV limit, and recording quality. Figure 16-13 shows an example.

  There are plenty of options under Recording Defaults on this page. The ones you'll likely be most interested in are how to record TV series (do you want to record reruns or not?), how many shows you want to keep for a series before writing over the older ones, and when to start and stop program recordings (that is, a few minutes before or after the scheduled time).

- **Guide.** If you're having issues with the TV guide, visit this screen. You can edit the channel list, add channels, get the latest Guide listings and more.

- **Set Up TV Signal.** Don't go here unless you need to make changes to your TV signal setup. You might have to add or remove a set-top box, change cable or satellite companies, or upgrade your television service, for example.

- **Configure Your TV or Monitor.** If you're unhappy with how your display looks or if you've purchased a different display type, tell Media Center about it here.

- **Closed Captioning.** "Closed captioning" refers to subtitles that appear at the bottom of the TV screen. Closed captioning is a free service (paid for by the TV networks) and is great for loud rec rooms, workout rooms, parties, and anyone who's hard of hearing or learning to read. (If you tune into the football game with closed captioning on, people can follow it while listening to music. Loudly.)

Note that even if you turn on closed captioning, not all television shows or television channels offer it.

Tip: The Closed Captioning setting in TV Signal options doesn't affect DVDs.

To make captions appear on DVDs, visit Tasks→Settings→DVD→Closed Captioning. Even then, if your DVD doesn't show captions, you may have to open DVD Setup, described below, and turn on subtitles in your own language.

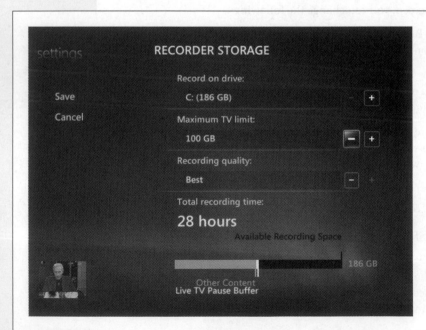

Figure 16-13:
Use the + and – buttons to adjust the amount of storage you want to allot on your PC to hold media. This is an important option. Otherwise, you may one day discover that your PC keeps hanging because your 200 GB drive has 195 GB of Lost in Space *or* Star Trek *on it. If you really want to record season after season of shows, consider changing the quality from Best to something else, or archiving them to DVDs and then erasing the hard-drive copies to free up space.*

Pictures

In Tasks→Pictures, you'll find options like these:

- **Show pictures in random order, Show pictures in subfolders, Show caption.** The only option that needs explanation here is "Show caption." It makes each photo's filename and date taken appear in the slideshow along with the picture.

- **Show song information at the beginning or end of a song, Always, Never.** That is, when you've added background music, do you want the name of the currently playing song (and the performer, album, and so on) to appear on the screen during the slideshow?

- **Transition type.** You have a couple of options for the way one photo fades into the next.

- **Transition time** can be between 2 seconds and a minute. Two or 3 seconds per photo is usually plenty.

- **Slideshow background color** can be black, white, or 50 percent gray. (If the photo fills the screen, of course, you don't see this background color. It appears only when the photo is, for example, an upright shot that leaves empty space on either side of your wide screen.)

Music

From the Music options, you have only two choices:

- **Visualizations.** If you like to trip with the daisies while listening to music, check all of the visualizations (music-driven screen savers) here.

- **Visualization Options.** Make visualizations play every time music plays. Show song information at the beginning and end of a song, always, or never.

DVD

From the DVD options, you can change the following:

- **DVD Language.** If you're into foreign films or want to learn a new language, change these options. Leave subtitles enabled or disable them, change the audio track to another language, and change the DVD menus to another language. For kicks, change the Menu language to Albanian.

- **Closed Captioning.** Again, easy enough. Turn on closed captioning when the media is muted, turn it off completely, or turn it on so it's on all the time.

- **Remote Control Options.** Change the Skip and Replay buttons to skip chapters, skip forward and back, or to change angles.

Library Setup

On this screen, you can tell Media Center to "watch" a new folder (that is, to add the video, photo, or music contents of a folder on your hard drive to its listings automatically) or to stop watching one.

Part Five:
Hardware and Peripherals

Chapter 17: Fax, Print, and Scan

Chapter 18: Expanding Your Hardware

Chapter 19: Laptops, Tablets, and Palmtops

5

Fax, Print, and Scan

Technologists got pretty excited about "the paperless office" in the 1980s, but the PC explosion had exactly the opposite effect. Thanks to the proliferation of inexpensive, high-quality PC printers, the world generates far more printouts than ever. Fortunately, there's not much to printing from Windows Vista.

Installing a Printer
All Versions

A printer is a peripheral device—something outside of the PC—and as such, it won't work without a piece of driver software explaining the new hardware to Windows. In general, getting this driver installed is a simple process. It's described in more detail in Chapter 18; here are a few notes on the process to get you started.

USB Printers

If the technology gods are smiling, then installing the driver for a typical inkjet USB printer works just as described in Chapter 18: you connect the printer, turn it on, and marvel as Vista autodetects it and autoinstalls the driver, thanks to its secret cache of hundreds of printer drivers (Figure 17-1).

If you have a really old printer, its drivers might not be Vista-compatible. Check the manufacturer's Web site, such as *www.epson.com* or *www.lexmark.com,* or a central driver repository like *www.windrivers.com,* to see if there's anything newer.

Network Printers

If you work in an office where people on the network share a single printer (usually a laser printer), the printer usually isn't connected directly to your computer. Instead, it's elsewhere on the network; your PC's Ethernet cable or wireless antenna connects you to it indirectly.

In general, there's very little involved in ensuring that your PC "sees" this printer. Its icon simply shows up in the Start→Control Panel→Printer folder. (If you don't see it, click "Add a printer" in the toolbar. On the wizard's second screen, you're offered the chance to "Add a network, wireless or Bluetooth printer." That's the one you want.)

Note: As you've probably guessed, that's also how you install a wireless or Bluetooth printer.

Figure 17-1:
You got lucky. Windows dug into its own bag of included drivers and installed the correct one. Let the printing begin.

Parallel, Serial, and Infrared Printers

Although USB printers are the world's most popular type today, there was, believe it or not, a time before USB. In those days, most home printers fell into one of these categories:

• **Parallel.** Before USB changed the world, most printers connected to PCs using a printer cable or *parallel cable*. The cable connects to your PC's parallel port, which Microsoft's help screens call the LPT1 port—a 25-pin, D-shaped jack. (On many PCs, this connector is marked with a printer icon on the back panel.)

• **Serial.** Other older printers use a cable connected to one of your computer's *serial* (or *COM*) ports, the connectors that often accommodate an external modem. The primary advantage of a serial connection is the extended cable length—parallel cables must be no more than nine feet long, while serial cables up to 50 feet long work fine.

Tip: To protect its innards, turn off the PC before connecting or disconnecting a parallel or serial cable.

- **Infrared.** Certain printers from HP, Canon, Citizen, and other companies print using *infrared* technology—that is, there's no cable at all. Instead, if your PC has an infrared lens (a few aging laptops may still have them), it can communicate with the printer's similar lens wirelessly, as long as the printer and PC are within sight of, and relatively close to, each other.

Sometimes you get lucky, and these printers work just like modern USB printers: you connect the printer, turn on your PC, and delight in the "Found new hardware" message that appears on your taskbar. You're ready to print.

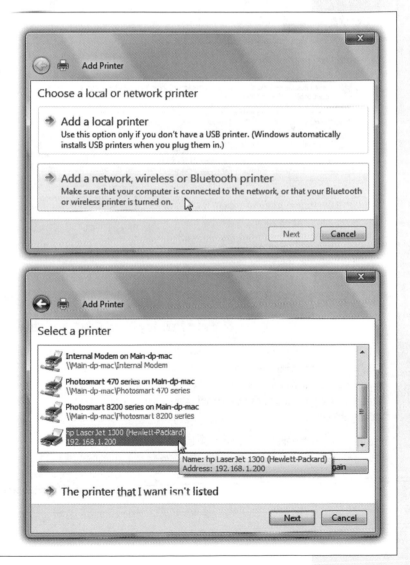

Figure 17-2:
Top: As the note explains, use the Add Printer Wizard only if your printer doesn't connect to your USB port.

Bottom: Hurrah! Windows has found the laser printer on the network. In the following screens, you're asked to name the printer and offered the chance to print a test page.

But if Windows doesn't recognize the printer model you've hooked up, it can't install its drivers automatically.

In that case, you'll have to call upon the mighty powers of the Add Printer Wizard (Figure 17-2). Choose Start→Control Panel; click Classic View→Printers, and click "Add a printer" on the toolbar—if indeed the Add Printer wizard hasn't appeared automatically. Click Next to walk through the questions until you've correctly identified your printer (Figure 17-3), told Windows which it's connected to, and installed the appropriate software.

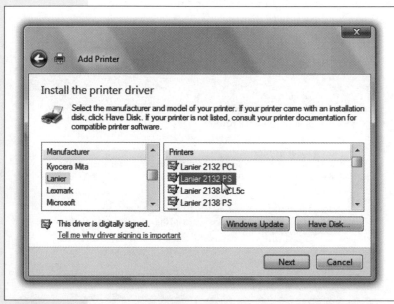

Figure 17-3:
The left pane lists every printer manufacturer Microsoft has ever heard of. Once you've selected your printer's manufacturer, a list of all the printer models from that manufacturer (that Windows knows about) appears in the right pane. Click the Have Disk button if your printer's driver is on a disc supplied by the manufacturer.

TROUBLESHOOTING MOMENT

If Your Printer Model Isn't Listed

If your printer model isn't in the list of printers (Figure 17-3), then Windows doesn't have a driver for it. Your printer model may be very new (more recent than Windows Vista, that is) or very old. You have two choices for getting around this roadblock.

First, you can contact the manufacturer (or its Web site) to get the drivers. Then install the driver software as described in the previous section.

Second, you can use the *printer emulation* feature. As it turns out, many printers work with one of several standard drivers that come from other companies. For example, many laser printers work fine with the HP LaserJet driver. (These laser printers are not, in fact, HP LaserJets, but they *emulate* one.)

The instructions that came with your printer should have a section on emulation; the manufacturer's help line can also tell you which popular printer yours can impersonate.

The Printer Icon

If your driver-installation efforts are ultimately successful, you're rewarded by the appearance of an icon that represents your printer.

This icon appears in the *Printers* window—an important window that you'll be reading about over and over again in this chapter. Exactly how you arrive there depends on how you've set up Vista:

- If you've set up your Start menu to display a submenu for the Control Panel (page 45), just choose Start→Control Panel→Printers.

- Choose Start→Control Panel, then click Printer (in the Hardware and Sound category).

- If you view your Control Panel in *Classic* view (page 281), choose Start→Control Panel, and then open the Printers icon.

- You can also make the Printers window show up in your Start menu, which saves you some burrowing if you use this feature a lot. To put it there, right-click the Start button. From the shortcut menu, choose Properties. On the Start Menu tab, click Customize. Scroll down in the list of checkboxes, and finally turn on the Printers checkbox. Click OK twice.

GEM IN THE ROUGH

Installing Fake Printers

If your printer has two paper trays, switching to the secondary one is something of a hassle. You must spend time making the changes in the Print dialog box, as described later in this chapter. Similarly, switching the printout resolution from, say, 300 dpi to 600 dpi when printing important graphic documents is a multistep procedure.

That's why you may find it useful to create several different icons for *the same printer*. The beauty of this stunt is that you can set up different settings for each of these icons. One might store canned settings for 600 dpi printouts from the top paper tray, another might represent 300 dpi printouts from the bottom one, and so on. When it comes time to print, you can switch between these virtual printers quickly and easily.

To create another icon, just run the Add Printer Wizard a second time, as described on the preceding pages. At the point in the installation where you name the printer, invent a name that describes this printer's alternate settings, like *HP6-600 dpi* or *Lexmark-Legal Size*.

When the installation process is complete, you'll see both printer icons—the old and the new—in the Printers window. Right-click the new "printer" icon, choose Printing Preferences from the shortcut menu, and change the settings to match its role.

To specify which one you want as your *default* printer—the one you use most of the time—right-click the appropriate icon and choose Set as Default Printer from the shortcut menu.

Thereafter, whenever you want to switch to the other set of printer settings—when you need better graphics, a different paper tray, or other special options for a document—just select the appropriate printer from the Printer Name drop-down list in the Print dialog box (Figure 17-5, top). You've just saved yourself a half-dozen additional mouse clicks and settings changes.

In any case, the Printers window now contains an icon bearing the name you gave your printer during installation (Figure 17-4). This printer icon comes in handy in several different situations, as the rest of this chapter clarifies.

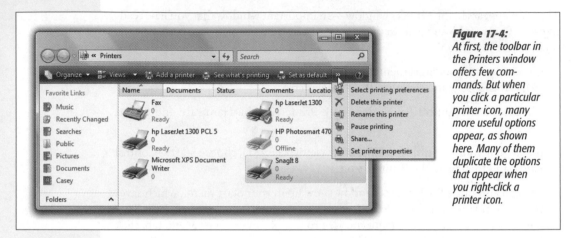

Figure 17-4:
At first, the toolbar in the Printers window offers few commands. But when you click a particular printer icon, many more useful options appear, as shown here. Many of them duplicate the options that appear when you right-click a printer icon.

Printing

Fortunately, the setup described so far in this chapter is a one-time-only task. Once it's over, printing is little more than a one-click operation.

Printing from Programs

After you've created a document you want to see on paper, choose File→Print (or press Ctrl+P). The Print dialog box appears, as shown at top in Figure 17-5.

This box, too, changes depending on the program you're using—the Print dialog box in Microsoft Word looks a lot more intimidating than the WordPad version—but here are the basics:

- **Name.** If your PC is connected to several printers, or if you've created several differently configured icons for the same printer, choose the one you want from this list of printers.

- **Preferences/Properties.** Clicking this button opens a version of the printer's Properties dialog box, as shown in Figure 17-6.

- **Page range** controls which pages of the document you want to print. If you want to print only some of the pages, click the Pages option and type in the page numbers you want (with a hyphen, like *3-6* to print pages 3 through 6).

Tip: You can also type in individual page numbers with commas, like *2, 4, 9* to print only those three pages—or even add hyphens to the mix, like this: *1-3, 5-6, 13-18*.

Click Current Page to print only the page that contains the blinking insertion point. Click Selection to print only the text you selected (highlighted) before opening the Print dialog box. (If this option button is dimmed, it's because you didn't highlight any text—or because you're using a program that doesn't offer this feature.)

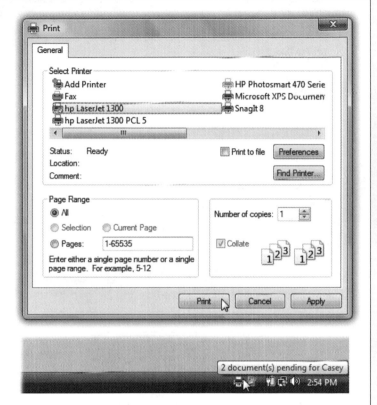

Figure 17-5:
Top: The options in the Print dialog box are different for each printer model and each application, so your Print dialog box may look slightly different. For example, here are the Print dialog boxes from Microsoft Word and WordPad. Most of the time, the factory settings shown here are what you want (one copy, print all pages). Just click OK or Print (or press Enter) to close this dialog box and send the document to the printer.

Bottom: During printing, the tiny icon of a printer appears in your notification area. Pointing to it without clicking produces a pop-up tooltip, like this one, that reveals the background printing activity.

- **Number of copies.** To print out several copies of the same thing, use this box to specify the exact amount. You'll get several copies of page 1, then several copies of page 2, and so on—*unless* you also turn on the Collate checkbox, which produces complete sets of pages, in order.

- **Print.** The Print drop-down list that may appear in the lower-left section of the dialog box offers three options: "All pages in range," "Odd pages," and "Even pages."

Use the Odd and Even pages options when you have to print on both sides of the paper, but your printer has no special feature for this purpose. You'll have to print all the odd pages, turn the stack of printouts over, and run the pages through the printer again to print even pages.

• **Application-specific options.** The particular program you're using may add a few extra options of its own to an Options tab in this dialog box. For example, Internet Explorer offers an Options tab (Figure 17-7).

Figure 17-6:
When you open Properties from the Print dialog box, you can specify the paper size you're using, whether you want to print sideways on the page ("Landscape" orientation), what kind of photo paper you're using, and so on. Here, you're making changes only for a particular printout; you're not changing any settings for the printer itself. (The specific features of this dialog box depend on the program you're using.)

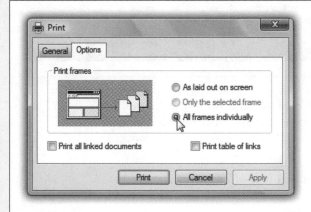

Figure 17-7:
Say you're printing something from Internet Explorer. The Web page about to be printed uses frames (individual, independent, rectangular sections). The Print dialog box in Internet Explorer recognizes frames, and lets you specify exactly which frame or frames you want to print. If the page contains links to other Web pages (and these days, what Web page doesn't?), you can print those Web pages, too, or just print a table of the links (a list of the URL addresses).

When you've finished making changes to the print job, click OK or Print, or press Enter. Thanks to the miracle of *background printing*, you don't have to wait for the document to emerge from the printer before returning to work on your PC. In fact, you can even exit the application while the printout is still under way, generally speaking. (Just don't put your machine to sleep until it's finished printing.)

Printing from the Desktop

You don't necessarily have to print a document while it's open in front of you. You can, if you wish, print it directly from the desktop or an Explorer window in any of three ways:

- Right-click the document icon, and then choose Print from the shortcut menu. Windows launches the program that created it—Word or Excel, for example. The Print dialog box appears, letting you specify how many copies you want and which pages you want printed. When you click Print, your printer springs into action, and then the program quits automatically (if it wasn't open when you started the process).

- If you've opened the Printers window, you can drag a document's icon directly onto a printer icon.

- If you've opened the printer's own print queue window (Figure 17-8) by double-clicking the Printers icon in your Printers window, you can drag any document icon directly into the list of waiting printouts. Its name joins the others on the list.

FREQUENTLY ASKED QUESTIONS

Microsoft XPS = Adobe PDF

What, exactly, is Microsoft XPS? I see an icon for it in my Print dialog box.

Well, you know how Microsoft always comes up with its own version of anything popular? PalmPilot, iPod, Web browser, whatever?

Its latest target is the PDF document, the brainchild of Adobe.

A PDF document, of course, is a file that opens up on any kind of computer—Mac, Windows, Unix, anything—looking exactly the way it did when it was created, complete with fonts, graphics, and other layout niceties. The recipient can't generally make changes to it, but can search it, copy text from it, print it, and so on. It's made life a lot easier for millions of people because it's easy, free, and automatic.

And now Microsoft wants a piece o' dat. Its new Microsoft XPS document format is pretty much the same idea as PDF, only it's Microsoft's instead of Adobe's.

To turn any Windows document into an XPS document, just choose File→Print. In the Print dialog box, choose Microsoft XPS Document Writer as the "printer," and then click Print. You're asked to name it and save it.

The result, when double-clicked, opens up in Internet Explorer. (Yes, Internet Explorer is the new Acrobat Reader.) You might not even notice the two tiny toolbars that appear above and below the main browser window, but they offer the usual PDF-type options: save a copy, find a phrase, jump to a page, zoom in or out, switch to double-page view, and so on.

Microsoft plans to release XPS readers for other versions of Windows—and, eventually, other kinds of computers. Even so, Microsoft has a long battle ahead if it hopes to make the XPS format as commonplace as Acrobat.

But then again, long battles have never fazed it before.

These last two methods bypass the Print dialog box, and therefore give you no way to specify which pages you want to print, nor how many copies. You just get one copy of the entire document.

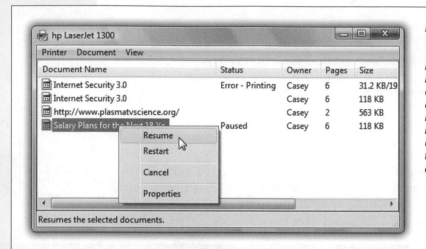

Figure 17-8:
The first document, called "Internet Security 3.0," has begun printing; the bottom one, you've put on hold. Several other documents are waiting. By right-clicking documents in this list, you can pause or cancel any document in the queue—or all of them at once.

Controlling Printouts
All Versions

Between the moment when you click OK in the Print dialog box and the arrival of the first page in the printer's tray, there's a delay. Usually, it's very brief, but when you're printing a complex document with lots of graphics, the delay can be considerable.

Fortunately, the waiting doesn't necessarily make you less productive, since you can return to work on your PC, or even quit the application and go watch TV. An invisible program called the *print spooler* supervises this background printing process. The spooler collects the document that's being sent to the printer, along with all the codes the printer expects to receive, and then sends this information, little by little, to the printer.

Note: The spooler program creates huge temporary printer files, so a hard drive that's nearly full can wreak havoc with background printing.

To see the list of documents waiting to be printed—the ones that have been stored by the spooler—open the Printers window, and then double-click your printer's icon to open its window.

Tip: While the printer is printing, a printer icon appears in the notification area. As a shortcut to opening the printer's window, just double-click that icon.

The printer's window lists the documents currently printing and waiting; this list is called the *print queue* (or just the *queue*), as shown in Figure 17-8. (Documents in the list print in top-to-bottom order.)

You can manipulate documents in a print queue in any of the following ways during printing:

- **Put one on hold.** To pause a document (put it on hold), right-click its name, and then choose Pause from the shortcut menu. When you're ready to let the paused document continue to print, right-click its listing and choose Resume (Figure 17-8).

- **Put them all on hold.** To pause the printer, choose Printer→Pause Printing from the window's menu bar. You might do this when, for example, you need to change the paper in the printer's tray. (Choose Printer→Pause Printing again when you want the printing to pick up from where it left off.)

Note: You can also pause the printer by right-clicking its icon in the Printers window and choosing Pause Printing from the shortcut menu. (To undo this procedure, right-click the icon and choose Resume Printing.)

- **Add another one.** As noted earlier, you can drag any document icon directly *from its disk or folder window* into the printer queue. Its name joins the list of printouts-in-waiting.

- **Cancel one.** To cancel a printout, click its name and then press the Delete key. If you click Yes in the confirmation box, the document disappears from the queue; it'll never print out.

- **Cancel all of them.** To cancel the printing of all the documents in the queue, choose Printer→Cancel All Documents.

Note: A page or so may still print after you've paused or canceled a printout. Your printer has its own memory (the *buffer*), which stores the printout as it's sent from your PC. If you pause or cancel printing, you're only stopping the spooler from sending *more* data to the printer.

- **Rearrange them.** If you're used to, say, Windows Me, it may take you a moment—or an afternoon—to figure out why you can't simply drag documents up or down in the list of waiting printouts to rearrange their printing order. In Windows Vista, the procedure is slightly more involved.

    Start by right-clicking the name of one of the printouts-in-waiting; from the shortcut menu, choose Properties. On the General tab, drag the Priority slider left or right. Documents with higher priorities print first.

Note: When you're finished with a printer—when you sell it, for example—you can eliminate its icon from your Printers window. Right-click its icon; from the shortcut menu, choose Delete.

Fancy Printer Tricks

The masses of Windows users generally slog through life choosing File→Print, clicking OK, and then drumming their fingers as they wait for the paper to slide out of the printer. But your printer can do more than that—much more. Here are just a few of the stunts that await the savvy PC fan.

Printing at 39,000 Feet

Printing any document is really a two-step procedure. First, Windows converts the document into a seething mass of printer codes in the form of a *spool file* on your hard drive. Second, it feeds that mass of code to the printer.

When you're not connected to your printer—for example, when you're sitting in seat 23B several miles over Detroit—you can separate these two tasks. You can do the time-consuming part of the printing operation (creating the spool files) right there on the plane. Then, later, upon your happy reunion with the printer, you can simply unleash the flood of stored spool files, which then print very quickly.

To set this up, right-click the icon for your printer in the Printers window (Figure 17-4). From the shortcut menu, choose Pause Printing. That's all there is to it. Now you can merrily "print" your documents, 100 percent free of error messages. Windows quietly stores all the half-finished printouts as files on your hard drive.

When the printer is reconnected to your machine, right-click its icon once again—but this time, choose Resume Printing from its shortcut menu. The printer springs to life almost immediately, spewing forth your stored printouts with impressive speed.

Sharing a Printer

If you have more than one PC connected to a network, as described in Chapter 24, they all can use the same printer. In the old days, this convenience was restricted to expensive network printers like laser printers. But in Windows Vista, you can share even the cheapest little inkjet that's connected to the USB port of one computer.

To begin, sit down at the computer to which the printer is attached. Choose Start→Network; in the Network window, click "Network and Sharing Center" on the toolbar. Proceed as described in Figure 17-9.

Note: If you're an old-timer who remembers what it's like to turn on sharing one printer at a time, you should know that that method is still available. In the Printers window, right-click the printer's icon and, from the shortcut menu, choose Sharing. In the resulting dialog box, click Change Sharing Options. Authenticate yourself (page 191), and then turn on "Share this printer."

Once you've *shared* the printer, other people on the network can add it to their own Printers windows. Before you begin, though, be aware that nobody can hook into the shared-printer PC without an *account* on that PC (Chapter 23)—one with a password. Printer sharing doesn't work with blank-password accounts.

1. **Choose Start→Control Panel. Click "Hardware and Sound," then "Printer," then "Add a printer."**

   The "Choose a local or network printer" window appears.

2. **Click "Add a network, wireless or Bluetooth printer."**

   After a pause while your PC searches, you see a window populated by all the printers that are available to the other PC.

5. **Click the icon of the printer you want to use, and then click Next. On the "which driver" page, click Next again. Finally, type a name for the printer (as you want it to appear on your PC), and then click Next. On the final screen, click Finish.**

   The shared printer appears in *your* Printers window, even though it's not directly connected to your machine. It's now available for any printing you want to do.

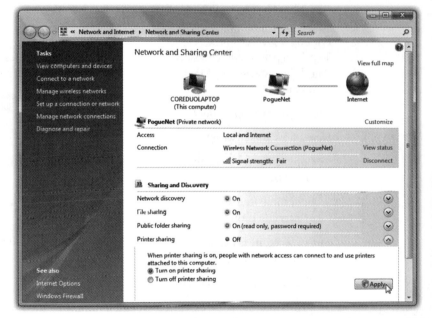

Figure 17-9:
How to turn on printer sharing: Expand the V-shaped arrow where it says "Printer sharing," and click "Turn on printer sharing." Click Apply. Authenticate yourself (page 191).

Printing to a File

When it comes to printing, most of the time you probably think of printing onto paper. In certain circumstances, however, you may not actually want a printout. Instead, you might want to create an electronic printer file on your hard drive, which can be printed later. You might want to do so, for example, when:

- You're working on a document at home, and you've got only a cheesy $49 inkjet printer. By creating a printer file, you can delay printing until tomorrow, in order to use the office's $4,000 color laser printer.

- You plan to send your finished work to a service bureau—that is, a professional typesetting shop. Sending a finished printer file avoids incompatibilities of applications, fonts, layout programs, and so on.

- You want to give a document to someone who doesn't have the program you used to create it, but has the same printer. If you email the *printer file* to her, she'll get to see your glorious design work slide out of her printer nonetheless.

Creating a printer file

To create such a printer file, choose File→Print, just as you would print any document. The Print dialog box appears; now turn on the "Print to file" option. When you then click OK or Print, the Print to File dialog box opens.

Some programs let you choose *where* you want to save the file; others ask you only to name the file itself. In that case, your saved printout goes automatically into your Documents folder. The file type for a document printing to a file is a Printer File, which has the file extension .prn.

Printing a printer file

To print a printer file, choose Start→All Programs→Accessories→Command Prompt. You've just started an MS-DOS command session; your cursor is blinking on the command line.

Now type this: *copy c:\foldername\filename.prn lpt1: /b*

Here's how this instruction breaks down:

- **Copy** is the name of the command you use to print the file—notice that it's followed by a space.

- **C:** is the letter of the drive that contains your printer file. Omit this part if the printer file is on the current drive (usually C:).

- **\foldername** is the name of the folder into which you saved the printer file (Documents, for example).

- **\filename** is the name you gave the file.

- **.prn** is the filename extension (which Windows added to the file automatically when you saved the printer file).

- **lpt1:** is the port to which the printer is connected. Note the colon following the name, and also note there's a space *before* this part of the command. If the printer is attached to LPT2, substitute that port name.

- **/b** tells the Copy command that the file is *binary* (containing formatting and other codes), not simply text.

Note: A printer file (a .prn file) can only be printed on the same printer model that was selected in the Print dialog box when the file was generated. If you want to create a printer file for that color printer at work, in other words, be sure to first install its driver on your computer.

Limiting Hours of Access

If it's just you, your Dell, and a color inkjet, then you're entitled to feel baffled by this feature, which lets you declare your printer off-limits during certain hours of the day. But if you're the manager of some office whose expensive color laser printer makes printouts that cost a dollar apiece, you may welcome a feature that prevents employees from hanging around after hours in order to print out 500 copies of their head shots.

To specify such an access schedule for a certain printer, follow the instructions in Figure 17-10.

POWER USERS' CLINIC

Color Management

As you may have discovered through painful experience, computers aren't great with color. That's because each device you use to create and print digital images "sees" color a little bit differently, which explains why the deep amber captured by your scanner may be rendered as brownish on your monitor, but come out as a bit orangey on your Epson inkjet printer. Since every gadget defines and renders color in its own way, colors are often inconsistent as a print job moves from design to proof to press.

The Windows *color management system* (CMS) attempts to sort out this mess, serving as a translator among all the different pieces of hardware in your workflow. For this to work, each device (scanner, monitor, printer, copier, and so on) must be calibrated with a unique *CMS profile*—a file that tells your PC exactly how your particular monitor (or scanner, or printer, or digital camera) defines colors. Armed with the knowledge contained within the profiles, the CMS software can make on-the-fly color corrections, compensating for the various quirks of the different devices.

Most of the people who lose sleep over color fidelity do

commercial color scanning and printing, where "off" colors are a big deal—after all, a customer might return a product after discovering, for example, that the actual product color doesn't match the photo on a Web site. Furthermore, not every gadget comes with a CMS profile, and not every gadget can even accommodate one. (If yours does, you'll see a tab called Color Management in the Properties dialog box for your printer, as shown here.)

If you're interested in this topic, open the Color Management tab for your printer. (Opening the Color Management applet in the Control Panel gets you to the same place, shown here.) The Automatic setting usually means that Windows came with its own profile for your printer, which it has automatically assigned. If you click Manual, you can override this decision and apply a new color profile (that you downloaded from the printer company's Web site, for example).

Remember to follow the same procedure for the other pieces of your color chain—monitors, scanners, and so on. Look for the Color Management tab or dialog box, accessible from their respective Properties dialog boxes.

Add a Separator Page

If your PC is on a network whose other members bombard a single laser printer with printouts, you might find *separator pages* useful—the printer version of fax cover sheets. A separator page is generated before each printout, identifying the document and its owner.

This option, too, is accessible from the Advanced tab of the printer's Properties dialog box (Figure 17-10). Click the Separator Page button at the bottom of the dialog box. In the Separator Page dialog box, click the Browse button to choose a .sep (separator page) file.

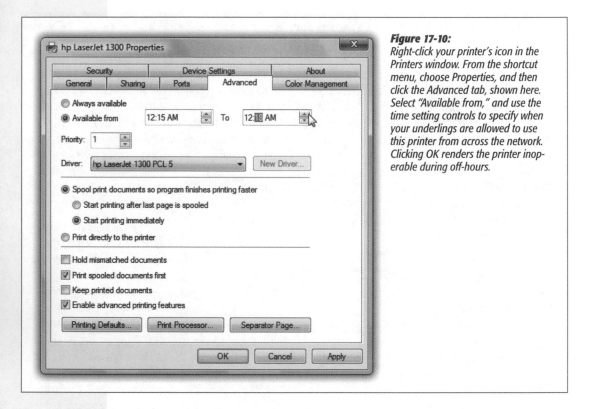

Figure 17-10:
Right-click your printer's icon in the Printers window. From the shortcut menu, choose Properties, and then click the Advanced tab, shown here. Select "Available from," and use the time setting controls to specify when your underlings are allowed to use this printer from across the network. Clicking OK renders the printer inoperable during off-hours.

If you scroll to the very bottom of the resulting list of geeky Windows folder names, you'll find four of them:

- **Sysprint.sep** is the one you probably want. Not only does this page include the name, date, time, and so on, but it also automatically switches the laser printer to PostScript mode—if it's not already in that mode, and if it's a PostScript printer.

- **Pcl.sep** is the same idea, except that it switches the laser printer to PCL mode—commonly found on HP printers—before printing. (PostScript and PCL are the two most common languages understood by office laser printers.)

- **Pscript.sep** switches the printer to PostScript mode, but doesn't print out a separator page.

- **Sysprtj.sep** prints a separator page, switches the printer to PostScript mode, and sets Japanese fonts, if they're available on your printer.

Printer Troubleshooting
All Versions

If you're having a problem printing, the first diagnosis you must make is whether the problem is related to *software* or *hardware*. A software problem means the driver files have become damaged. A hardware problem means there's something wrong with the printer, the port, or the cable.

Test the printer by sending it a generic text file from the command line. To perform such a test, locate a text file or create one in Notepad. Then choose Start→All Programs→Accessories→Command Prompt; send the file to the printer by typing *copy filename.txt prn* and then pressing Enter. (Of course, remember to type the file's actual name and three-letter extension instead of *filename.txt*.)

If the file prints, the printing problem is software-related. If it doesn't work, the problem is hardware-related.

For software problems, reinstall the printer driver. Open the Printers window, right-click the printer's icon, and then choose Delete from the shortcut menu. Then reinstall the printer as described at the beginning of this chapter.

If the problem seems to be hardware-related, try these steps in sequence:

- Check the lights or the LED panel readout on the printer. If you see anything besides the normal "Ready" indicator, check the printer's manual to diagnose the problem.

- Turn the printer off and on to clear any memory problems.

- Check the printer's manual to learn how to print a test page.

- Check the cable to make sure both ends are firmly and securely plugged into the correct ports.

- Test the cable. Use another cable, or take your cable to another computer/printer combination.

Another way to check all of these conditions is to use the built-in Windows *troubleshooter*—a wizard specifically designed to help you solve printing problems. To run, choose Start→Help and Support. Type *printing troubleshooting* into the search box and press Enter. Click "Troubleshoot printer problems" to open that article.

If none of these steps leads to an accurate diagnosis, you may have a problem with the port, which is more complicated. Or even worse, the problem may originate from your PC's motherboard (main circuit board), or the printer's. In that case, your computer (or printer) needs professional attention.

Fonts
All Versions

Some extremely sophisticated programming has gone into the typefaces that are listed in the Fonts dialog boxes of your word processor and other programs. They use *OpenType* and *TrueType* technology, meaning that no matter what point size you select for these fonts, they look smooth and professional—both on the screen and when you print.

Managing Your Fonts

Windows comes with several dozen great-looking fonts: Arial, Book Antiqua, Times New Roman, and so on. But the world is filled with additional fonts. You may find them on Web sites or in the catalogs of commercial typeface companies. Sometimes you'll find new fonts on your system after installing a new program, courtesy of its installer.

To review the files that represent your typefaces, open the Fonts icon in the Control Panel. As Figure 17-11 illustrates, it's easy and enlightening to explore this folder.

Tip: The Fonts icon in your Control Panel window is only a shortcut to the *real* folder, which is in your Local Disk (C:) →Windows→Fonts folder.

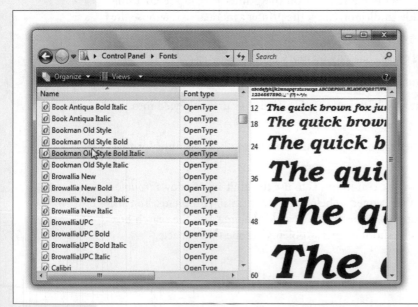

Figure 17-11:
All of your fonts sit in the Fonts folder. You'll frequently find an independent font file for each style of a font: bold, italic, bold italic, and so on. Click a font's name to see how it looks at various sizes. Double-click a font's icon to open that preview into a window of its own.

To remove a font from your system, drag its file icon out of this window, right-click it and then choose Delete from the shortcut menu, or highlight it and then choose File→Delete. To install a new font, drag its file icon into this window (or choose File→Install New Font, and then navigate to, and select, the font files you want to install).

Either way, you'll see the changes immediately reflected in your programs' Font dialog boxes.

Faxing

Business • Enterprise • Ultimate

One of Vista's most spectacular features is its ability to turn your PC's built-in fax modem into a fax machine. This feature works like a charm, saves all kinds of money on paper and fax cartridges, and may even spare you the expense of buying a physical fax machine.

Faxing in Windows Vista is a much more official feature than it was in Windows XP, where it wasn't even installed automatically. Now there's a new program just dedicated to faxing: Windows Fax and Scan.

Sending a fax is even easier on a PC than on a real fax machine; you just use the regular File→Print command, exactly as though you're making a printout of the onscreen document. When faxes come *in*, you can opt to have them printed automatically, or you can simply read them on the screen.

Tip: The similarity with printing doesn't stop there; your Printers folder even contains a Fax icon that works just like a printer icon.

Sending a Fax from Any Program

Now, the one big limitation of PC-based faxing is that you can only transmit documents that are, in fact, *on the computer.* That pretty much rules out faxing notes scribbled on a legal pad, clippings from *People* magazine, and so on (unless you scan them first).

If you're still undaunted, the procedure for sending a fax is very easy.

1. **Open up whatever document you want to fax. Choose File →Print.**

    The Print dialog box appears.

2. **Click the Fax icon (or choose Fax from the Name drop-down list, as shown in Figure 17-12), and then click OK or Print.**

    The very first time you try faxing, you encounter the Fax Setup Wizard. It first asks you to type a name for your fax modem.

Next, it wants you to specify what happens when someone sends a fax to *you* (that is, when the phone line that your PC is connected to "rings"). Click Automatically if you want Windows to answer incoming calls after five rings, assuming that if you haven't picked up by that time, the incoming call is probably a fax.

If you choose "Notify me," each incoming call triggers an onscreen message, asking you whether you want the PC to answer as a fax machine. And if you choose

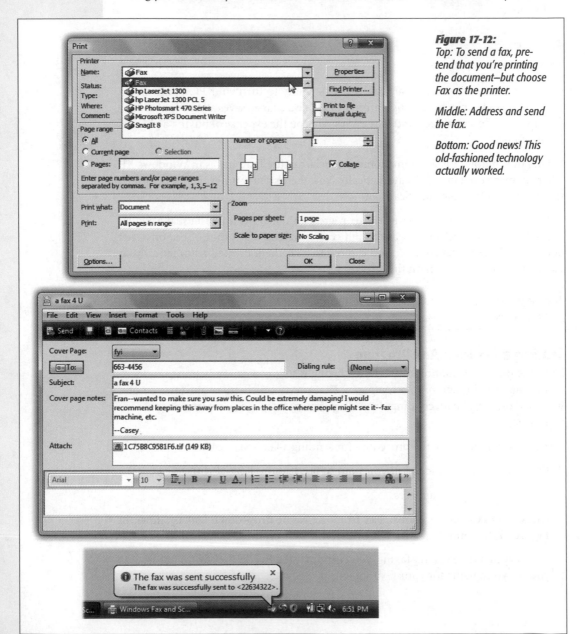

Figure 17-12:
Top: To send a fax, pretend that you're printing the document—but choose Fax as the printer.

Middle: Address and send the fax.

Bottom: Good news! This old-fashioned technology actually worked.

"I'll choose later," you can postpone the decision and get on with sending your first fax.

Note: At this point, the Windows Firewall, rather stupidly, may interrupt to ask if it's OK for Windows Fax and Scan to run. Click Unblock.

Finally, you arrive in a new Vista program called Windows Fax and Scan. It looks a heck of a lot like an email program, complete with an Inbox, a Sent Items folder, and so on. In fact, a New Fax window (like a New Message window) awaits you (Figure 17-12, middle).

POWER USERS' CLINIC

Cover Page Art Class

You don't have to be content with the handful of fax cover pages that Microsoft provides. The Fax and Scan program comes with its own little cover page design studio. To get started, choose Tools→Cover Pages.

At this point, you could click the New button to call up a pure, empty, virginal cover page. But by far the easiest way to get going is to open one of the existing cover pages, make changes to it, and then save it under a different name.

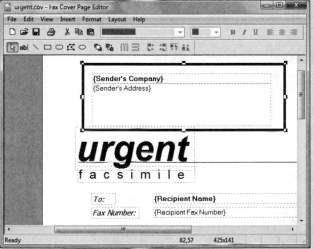

To do so, click the Copy button now in front of you, and then open one of the four cover page templates that Windows presents. Windows puts it into what's now a one-item list. Click Rename to give it a new name, if you like, and then click Open to begin work on your redesign.

The design program works like any standard drawing program. In order to type text that won't change—a confidentiality notice, for example—click the Text tool on the toolbar (which looks like this: **ab|**), and then click the page. Use the commands in the Insert menu to plop placeholder text boxes onto the page—special rectangles that, on the actual cover sheet, will be filled by your name, fax number, the number of pages, and so on. You can transfer your own company logo onto the page just by pasting it there (Edit→Paste).

Every item that you place on the page—a text block, a graphic, and so on—is a separate object that you can move around independently using the arrow tool.

In fact, you can even move a selected object in front of, or behind, other objects, using the commands in the Layout menu.

When you're finished with your masterpiece, choose File→Save. It gets saved into your Documents→Fax→Personal Cover Pages folder (meaning that only you have access to it—not other people who share the PC and log in with their own accounts).

---

3. **Type the recipient's fax number into the "To:" box.**

Or click the tiny envelope next to "To:" to open up your Windows Contacts list. Double-click the name of the fax-equipped buddy you want.

Figure 17-13:
Top: Click the General tab, and then turn on "Allow device to receive fax calls." If you choose "Automatically answer," you can also specify how many rings you want to go by before the PC answers; you don't want it answering regular incoming voice calls before you've had a chance to pick up.

Second from top: Uh-oh! You're getting a call! Click the balloon itself if you think it's a fax.

Third from top: Windows Fax and Scan takes over and begins to download the fax. This window is cleverly known as the Fax Status Monitor.

Bottom: The incoming fax winds up in your Inbox, just as though it's a particularly old-fashioned email message.

4. **If you want a cover page, choose a cover-page design from the Cover Page pop-up menu.**

   If you do, then a new text box opens up, where you can type a little note, which also appears on the cover page.

Note: You can ignore the main message box at the bottom of the window for now. It's intended for creating faxes from thin air, as described below, rather than faxes that began life as documents on your PC.

At this point, you may want to choose View→Preview (or click the tiny Preview icon on the toolbar) to give it a final inspection before it goes forth over the airwaves. When you're finished looking it over, click Send in the toolbar.

5. **Click Send.**

   Your modem dials, and the fax goes on its merry way. A status dialog box appears (although its progress bar doesn't actually indicate how much time remains). You can go do other work on the PC; when the fax goes through, a cheerful message appears in your notification area (Figure 17-12, bottom).

Your recipient is in for a real treat. Faxes you send straight from your PC's brain emerge at the receiving fax machine looking twice as crisp and clean as faxes sent from a standalone fax machine. After all, you never scanned them through a typical fax machine's crude scanner on your end.

Faxing Using Windows Fax and Scan

If you just have a few quick words to fax to somebody, you can use Fax and Scan by itself, without first opening a document on your PC. Open the Fax and Scan program from your Start→All Programs menu.

Click New Fax in the toolbar, fill in the fax number, and choose a cover page as described in the preceding steps. This time, however, you can use the broad message area at the bottom of the window to type the body of your text.

Tip: Cover pages automatically include your name, fax number, and so on. And how does it know all this? Because, in Fax and Scan, you choose Tools→Send Information and fill it out.

Receiving Faxes

There are several reasons why you may *not* want your PC to receive faxes. Maybe you already have a standalone fax machine that you use for receiving them. Maybe your house only has one phone line, whose number you don't want to give out to people who might blast your ear with fax tones.

But receiving faxes on the PC has a number of advantages, too. You don't pay a cent for paper or ink cartridges, for example, and you have a handy, organized software program that helps you track every fax you've ever received.

Note: The discussion here applies to normal people who send faxes using a computer's built-in fax modem. If you work in a corporation where the network geeks have installed a *fax server,* life is even easier. Incoming faxes automatically arrive in the Inbox of the Fax and Scan program.

Exactly what happens when a fax comes in is up to you. Start by opening Windows Fax and Scan; then choose Tools→Fax Settings. Authenticate yourself (page 191), and proceed as shown in Figure 17-13.

You'll see that you have two options for receiving faxes:

- **Manual.** This option is an almost-perfect solution if your PC and your telephone share the same phone line—that is, if you use the line mostly for talking, but occasionally receive a fax. From now on, every time the phone rings, a balloon in your notification area announces: "Incoming call from [the phone number]. Click here to answer this call as a fax call." (See Figure 17-13, middle.)

  When you do so, your PC answers the phone and begins to receive the fax. To see it, open Fax and Scan.

- **Answer automatically.** Use this option if your PC has a phone line all to itself. In this case, incoming faxes produce a telephone-ringing sound, but there's otherwise no activity on your screen until the fax has been safely received. Once again, received faxes secrete themselves away in your Fax Console program.

While you're setting things up in the Fax Settings dialog box, don't miss the "More options" button. It's the gateway to two useful features:

- **Print a copy to.** If you like, Windows can print out each incoming fax, using the printer you specify here. Of course, doing so defeats the environmental and cost advantages of viewing your faxes onscreen, but at least you've got something you can hold in your hand.

- **Save a copy to.** Ordinarily, incoming faxes are transferred to your Fax and Scan program. If you turn on this option, however, you can direct Windows to place a *duplicate* copy of each one—stored as a graphics file—in a folder of your choice.

FREQUENTLY ASKED QUESTION

Scanning Text—and Then Editing It

I scanned an article from a magazine. How do I copy a couple of paragraphs from it into my word processor?

When you scan an article or book, you're not capturing text; you're just taking a *picture* of text. You can no more copy and paste a paragraph out of the resulting graphic file than you can copy text out of a photograph. Your PC sees everything on the scanned page as one gigantic graphic.

If you want to edit text that you've scanned, then you need

optical character recognition (OCR) software, which comes free with certain scanners. This kind of software analyzes the patterns of dots in each scanned graphics file, and does a fairly good job of turning it into a word processor document that contains the original text. When businesses decide to convert old paper documents into computer files (insurance policies, research papers, and so on), OCR software is what they use.

(Either way, it's handy to know that these are standard TIFF graphics files that you can email to somebody else—or even edit.)

To look at the faxes you've received, open Fax and Scan. Click the Inbox to see a list of faxes that have come in—and then double-click one to open it up (Figure 17-13, bottom).

Tip: Another great way to capitalize on the power of your PC for fax purposes is to sign up for J2 or eFax (*www.j2.com* and *www.efax.com*). These services issue you your own personal fax number. And here's the twist–all faxes sent to that number arrive at your PC as email attachments.

The brilliance of the system, of course, is that you don't need another phone line for this, and you can get these faxes anywhere in the world, even on the road. And here's the best part: as of this writing, both of these services are absolutely free. (You might consider reserving a separate email address just for your J2 or eFax account, however, since waves of junk mail are part of the "free" bargain.)

Scanning Documents
Business • Enterprise • Ultimate

You already know that Windows Fax and Scan makes a great little fax center. But faxing is only one technology that turns paper into digital bits. Scanning is the other—and that, too, is a talent of Fax and Scan.

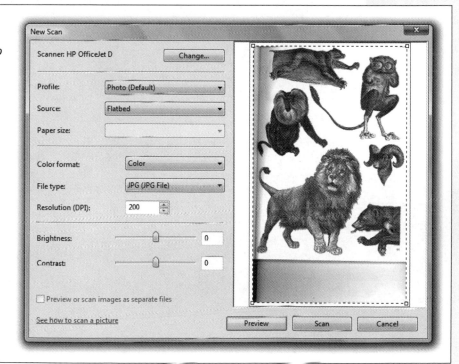

Figure 17-14:
In this box, you have the chance to specify what sort of thing you want to scan–picture? document?–and specify its resolution and color settings.

First, install your scanner (and its driver) as described in Chapter 18.

Load it up with the page you want to scan. In Fax and Scan, click New Scan. The New Scan dialog box appears (Figure 17-14).

Click Preview to trigger a quick, temporary scan so that you can see how the document will look after the scan. If it all looks good, click Scan.

Once the document has magically turned into a graphic in your Scan list, you can do all kinds of neat things with it: forward it as an email attachment or a fax (click "Forward as Fax" or "Forward as E-mail" on the toolbar); export it as a JPEG, GIF, BMP, TIFF, or PNG document (click "Save as" on the toolbar); print it; or delete it.

Hardware

A PC contains several pounds of wires, slots, cards, and chips—enough hardware to open a TrueValue store. Fortunately, you don't have to worry about making all of your PC's preinstalled components work together. In theory, at least, the PC maker did that part for you. (Unless you built the machine yourself, that is. In that case, best of luck.)

But adding *new* gear to your computer is another story. For the power user, hard drives, flash drives, cameras, printers, scanners, network cards, video cards, keyboards, monitors, game controllers, palmtop cradles, and other accessories all make life worth

---

UP TO SPEED

The Master Compatibility List

Remember that Windows Vista is much different from Windows XP. Discovering that a piece of your existing equipment is now flaky or nonfunctional is par for the course.

If you'd like to eliminate every glitch and every shred of troubleshooting inconvenience, limit your add-on gear to products that pass the test—the one administered by the Vista Upgrade Advisor. That's a little program you can download from this Web site:

www.microsoft.com/windowsvista/getready/upgradeadvisor

It runs fine in Vista. However, it's really designed to run in Windows XP, on the premise that you'll want to know how many of your peripherals won't work *before* you install Vista. (The Upgrade Advisor takes the place of the old Hardware Compatibility List [HCL], an online list of every gadget and program on earth that had been shown to work with Windows XP.)

After you download the Advisor program, plug in all your external gadgets—scanners, printers, hard drives, and so on—and then run the program.

---

living. When you introduce a new piece of equipment to the PC, you must hook it up and install its *driver*, the software that lets a new gadget talk to the rest of the PC.

The driver issue is a chronic, nagging worry for the average Windows fan, however. Drivers conflict; drivers are missing; drivers go bad; drivers go out of date.

Fortunately, in Vista, Microsoft continues to hammer away at the driver problem. Vista comes with thousands upon thousands of drivers for common products already built in, and Microsoft deposits dozens more on your hard drive, behind the scenes, with every Windows Update (page 614). Chances are good that you'll live a long and happy life with Windows Vista without ever having to lose a Saturday manually configuring new gizmos you buy for it, as your forefathers did.

This chapter guides you through installing accessory gadgets and their drivers—and counsels you on what to do when the built-in, auto-recognizing drivers don't do the trick.

Note: Chapter 17 contains additional hardware-installation details specific to printers.

External Gadgets
All Versions

Over the years, various engineering organizations have devised an almost silly number of different connectors for printers, scanners, and other *peripherals* (Figure 18-1 shows a typical assortment). The back panel—or front, or even side panel—of your PC may include any of these connector varieties.

USB Jacks
Man, you gotta love USB (Universal Serial Bus). The more of these jacks your PC has, the better.

UP TO SPEED

Of Hubs and Power

If your PC doesn't have enough built-in USB jacks to handle all your USB devices, you can also attach a USB *hub* (with, for example, four or eight additional USB ports), in order to attach multiple USB devices simultaneously.

Whether the jacks are built-in or on a hub, though, you have to be aware of whether or not they're *powered* or *unpowered* jacks.

Unpowered ones just transmit communication signals with the USB gadget. These kinds of USB gadgets work fine with unpowered jacks: mice, keyboards, flash drives, and anything with its own power cord (like printers).

Powered USB jacks also supply current to whatever's plugged in. You need that for scanners, Webcams, hard drives, and other gadgets that don't have their own power cords but transmit lots of data.

The bottom line? If a gadget isn't working, it may be because it requires a powered jack and you've given it an unpowered one.

The USB jack itself is a compact, thin, rectangular connector that's easy to plug and unplug. It often provides power to the gadget, saving you one more cord and one more bit of clutter. And it's hot-pluggable, so you don't have to turn off the gadget (or the PC) before connecting or disconnecting it.

Tip: Be careful, though, not to yank a USB flash drive or hard drive out of the PC when it might be in the middle of copying files.

USB accommodates a huge variety of gadgets: USB scanners, mice, phones, keyboards, printers, palmtop cradles, digital cameras, camcorders, hard drives, and so on.

Most modern PCs come with two or more USB ports, often on both the front and back panels.

Figure 18-1:
The back panel of a typical PC. Not every computer has every kind of jack, and the standard assortment is evolving But these days, you can generally count on a basic collection like the one shown here.

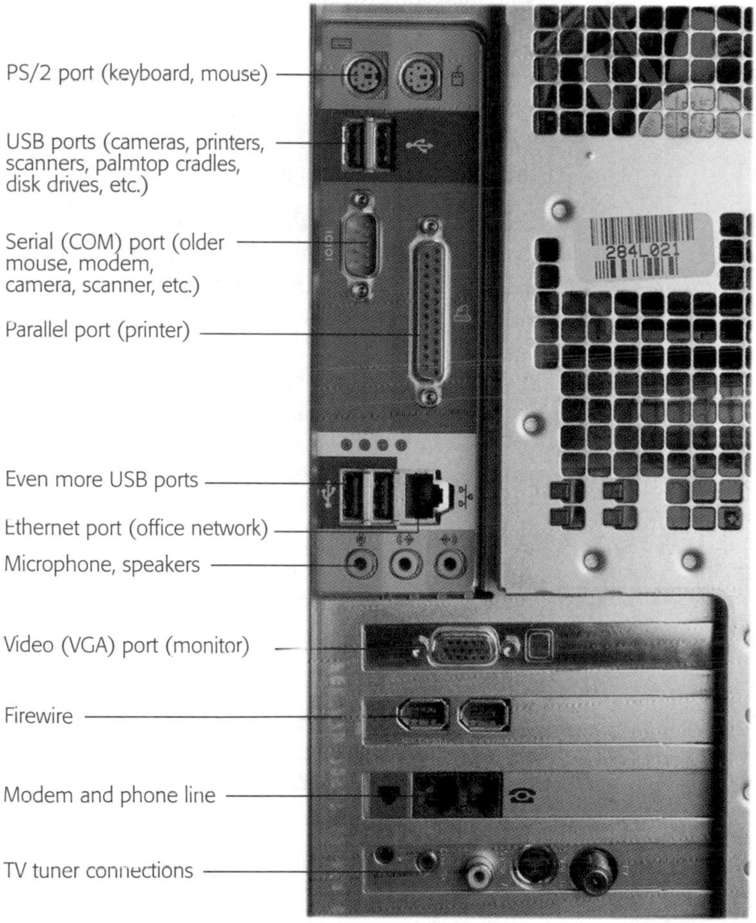

PS/2 port (keyboard, mouse)

USB ports (cameras, printers, scanners, palmtop cradles, disk drives, etc.)

Serial (COM) port (older mouse, modem, camera, scanner, etc.)

Parallel port (printer)

Even more USB ports

Ethernet port (office network)

Microphone, speakers

Video (VGA) port (monitor)

Firewire

Modem and phone line

TV tuner connections

Other Jacks

At one time, the backs of PC were pockmarked with all manner of crazy jacks: serial ports, PS/2 ports, SCSI ports, parallel ports, keyboard ports. Today, all of these connectors are rapidly disappearing, thanks to the all-powerful superiority of the USB jack.

Here's what else you may find on the modern PC, though:

- **FireWire port.** Not all PCs come with this special, rectangle-with-one-V-shaped-end jack, but it's a winner nevertheless. (Various companies may also call it IEEE 1394 or i.Link.) It's a hot-pluggable, extremely high-speed connector that's ideal for digital camcorders (for video editing) and external hard drives.

- **Bluetooth adapters.** Bluetooth is a fascinating short-range wireless technology. Don't think of it as a networking scheme—it's intended for the elimination of *cable clutter.* Once you've equipped your printer, PC, and Palm organizer with Bluetooth adapters, your computer can print to the printer, or HotSync with your Palm, from up to 30 feet away.

- **PC card or ExpressCard slot.** These slots are found primarily on laptops. They accommodate miniature expansion cards, which look like metal Visa cards. Each card adds a useful feature to your laptop: an Ethernet port, a cellular high-speed modem, a WiFi networking antenna, and so on.

Tip: Hundreds of PC cards are available, for thousands of laptop models. The industry is now pushing a narrower type of card, however, called ExpressCard, which fits into a narrower kind of slot. (Actually, there are *two* ExpressCard types—one narrow, and one *really* narrow.) Just make sure, before you buy any card, that it fits the kind of slot your laptop has.

- **Video (VGA) or DVI port.** The VGA connector is a narrow female port with fifteen holes along three rows. Most monitors are designed to plug into either a VGA jack or the more modern DVI (digital visual interface) jack, which has a total of 28 pins and is designed for modern digital LCD screens.

- **Game port.** This connector, which is usually part of a sound card, is a wide female port that accepts joysticks and steering wheels.

Connecting New Gadgets

In books, magazines, and online chatter about Windows, you'll frequently hear people talk about *installing* a new component. In many cases, they aren't talking about physically hooking it up to the PC—they're talking about installing its driver software.

The really good news is that Vista comes equipped with thousands of drivers for gadgets, especially USB gadgets. When you plug the thing into the PC for the first time, Vista autodetects its presence, digs into its trunk for the driver, and installs it automatically. Only a flurry of balloons in the notification area lets you know what's going on (Figure 18-2).

Figure 18-2:
Installing a USB gadget is usually no more involved than plugging it into the PC. Vista takes it from there. All you have to do is wait for the "successfully installed message"–and all of this is a one-time ritual for a given device.

If Windows can't find the driver, a dialog box appears, suggesting that you insert whatever software-installation disc came with the gadget.

And now, the fine print:

- Usually the process shown in Figure 18-2 is all it takes—that is, you start by plugging the device in. Sometimes, though, you're supposed to install the driver before connecting the gizmo. (Check the manual.)

- Usually, the device should be turned on before you plug it in. Again, though, check the manual, because some of them are supposed to be switched on during the installation.

In either case, your gear is now completely installed—both its hardware and its software—and ready to use.

Installing Cards in Expansion Slots
All Versions

Modems and adapter cards for video, TV, sound, network cabling, disk drives, and tape drives generally take the form of circuit boards, or *cards*, that you install inside your PC's case. These slots are connected to your PC's *bus*, an electrical conduit that connects all the components of the machine to the brains of the outfit: the processor and memory.

The two common (and mutually incompatible) kinds of slots are called *ISA* and *PCI*. The ISA bus (Industry Standard Architecture) has been around since the dawn of the PC in the early 1980s. PCI (Peripheral Component Interconnect) is newer and offers much better speed. Most computers in use today have both kinds of slots.

Note: There's also a third type of slot in many of today's computers, called AGP (Accelerated Graphics Port). This slot is almost always occupied by a graphics card.

Knowing the characteristics of the different bus types isn't especially important. What *is* important is knowing what type of slots your computer has free, so you can purchase the correct type of expansion card. To do this, you'll have to open your PC's case to see which type of slots are empty:

- The plastic wall around an ISA slot is usually black. It has metal pins or teeth in the center and a small crossbar about two-thirds of the way down the slot. On some older computers, there may be shorter-length ISA slots with no divider.

- The plastic wall around a PCI slot is usually white or off-white, and shorter than an ISA slot. A PCI slot has a metal center and a crossbar about three-quarters of the way along its length.

Installing a card usually involves removing a narrow plate (the *slot cover*) from the back panel of your PC, which allows the card's connector to peek through to the outside world. After unplugging the PC and touching something metal to discharge static, unwrap the card, and then carefully push it into its slot until it's fully seated.

Note: Depending on the type of card, you may have to insert one end first, and then press the other end down with considerable force to get it into the slot. A friendly suggestion, however: don't press so hard that you flex and crack the motherboard.

Troubleshooting Newly Installed Gear
All Versions

If, when you connect a new component, Windows doesn't display a "successfully installed" message like the one at the bottom of Figure 18-2, it probably can't "see" your new device.

FREQUENTLY ASKED QUESTION

Driver vs. Driver

Which is better: the drivers that come with Windows, or the drivers I've downloaded from the manufacturer's Web site?

In many cases, they're the same thing. The drivers included with Windows usually did come from the hardware's manufacturer, which gave them to Microsoft. However, you should still use the drivers that came from your gadget's manufacturer whenever possible, especially if you got them from the manufacturer's Web site. They're likely to be newer versions than the ones that came with Windows.

- If you've installed an internal card, make sure that it's seated in the slot firmly (after shutting down your computer, of course).

- If you attached something external, make sure that it's turned on, has power (if it came with a power cord), and is correctly connected to the PC.

In either case, before panicking, try restarting the PC. If you still have no luck, try the Add New Hardware Wizard described in the box on page 566. (And if even *that* doesn't work, call the manufacturer.)

If your new gadget didn't come with a disk (or maybe just a disk with drivers, but no installer), then hooking it up may produce a "Found New Hardware" balloon in the notification area, but no message about happy success. In that case, click the balloon to make the New Hardware Wizard appear.

Proceed as shown in Figure 18-3.

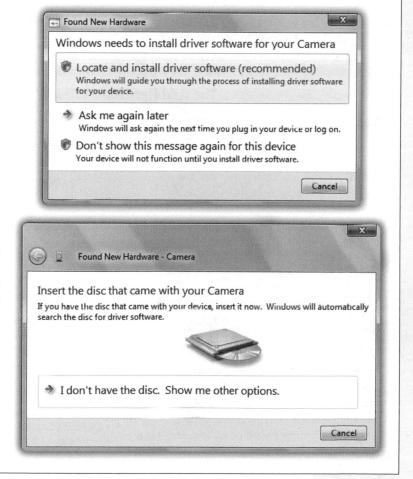

Figure 18-3:
Top: If you have the drivers on a CD from the manufacturer, select the first option, "Locate and install driver software."

Bottom: Now Windows asks for the driver CD. Windows either finds the compatible driver and installs it automatically, or offers you a choice of several. If you do not, in fact, have the CD, click "I don't have the disc." You'll be offered two final, fatalistic options: "Check for a solution" (Windows dials the mother ship on the off chance that a driver has miraculously cropped up since its last update), or "Browse my computer," designed for people who have downloaded a driver from the Web on their own.

Driver Signing

All Versions

Every now and then, when you try to install the software for one new gadget or another, you'll see a warning box that says, "Windows can't verify the publisher of this driver software."

It's not really as scary as it sounds. It's just telling you that Microsoft has not tested this driver for Windows Vista compatibility and programming solidity. (Technically speaking, Microsoft has not put its digital signature on that driver; it's an *unsigned driver.*)

Note: In very rare circumstances, you may also see messages that say, "This driver software has been altered" or "Windows cannot install this driver software." In those cases, go directly to the hardware maker's Web site to download the official driver software; Windows is trying to warn you that hackers may have gotten their hands on the driver version you're trying to install.

In theory, you're supposed to drop everything and contact the manufacturer or its Web site to find out if a Vista-certified driver is now available.

WORKAROUND WORKSHOP

The Add Hardware Wizard

Microsoft really, really hopes that you'll never need the Add Hardware Wizard. (But if you do, choose Start→Control Panel; in Classic view, double-click Add Hardware.)

This little program is a holdover from Windows past, designed for very old, pre-Plug-and-Play gadgets that Windows doesn't autorecognize when you plug them in.

Begin by connecting the new gear; turn off the computer first, if necessary. Turn the machine on again, and then open the Add Hardware Wizard program.

The wizard makes another attempt to detect the new equipment and install its driver. If a happy little "Found New Hardware" balloon appears in your notification area, all is well; the wizard's work is done. If not, you're walked through the process of specifying exactly *what* kind of gadget seems to have gone missing, choosing its manufacturer, inserting

its driver disc, and so on.

Install the hardware that I manually select from a list. If you choose this option and click Next (or if the previous option fails), the wizard displays a list of device types, as shown here. From that list, find and select the type of hardware you want to install—"Imaging devices" for a digital camera or a scanner, for example, "PCMCIA adapters" for a PC card, and so on. (Click Show All Devices if you can't figure out which category to choose.)

Click Next to forge on through the wizard pages. You may be asked to select a port or configure other settings. When you click the Finish button on the last screen, Windows transfers the drivers to your hard drive. (Along the way, you may be instructed to insert the Windows Vista DVD.) As a final step, you may be asked to restart the PC.

In practice, just because a driver isn't signed doesn't mean it's no good; it may be that the manufacturer simply didn't pony up the testing fee required by Microsoft's Windows Hardware Quality Labs. After all, sometimes checking with the manufacturer isn't even possible—for example, it may have gone to that great dot-com in the sky.

So most people just plow ahead. If the installation winds up making your system slower or less stable, you can always uninstall it, or rewind your entire operating system to its condition before you installed the questionable driver. (Use System Restore, described on page 648, for that purpose. Windows automatically takes a snapshot of your working system just before you install any unsigned driver.)

Tip: There is no way to turn off off the "unsigned driver" messages permanently in Vista, much to the dismay of Windows veterans who want to be left alone. (If you Google this problem, you'll find some hacks that purport to do the trick—but you'll also find reports that they don't actually work.) There *is* a way to turn off the messages, but you have to repeat it each time you turn on your PC. See page 658.

The Device Manager
All Versions

The Device Manager is an extremely powerful tool that lets you troubleshoot and update drivers for gear you've already installed. It's a master list of every component that makes up your PC: floppy drive, CD-ROM drive, keyboard, modem, and so on (Figure 18-4). It's also a status screen that lets you know which drivers are working properly, and which ones need some attention.

You can open the Device Manager in any of three ways:

- Right-click Computer (in your Start menu or on the desktop); choose Properties from the shortcut menu. In the Systems Properties dialog box, click the Device Manager link at top left.

- Choose Start→Control Panel; in Classic view, double-click Device Manager.

- Choose Start→Run. In the Run dialog box, type *devmgmt.msc* and press Enter.

In each of these cases, you're asked to authenticate yourself (page 191). You then arrive at the screen shown in Figure 18-4.

Red Xs and Yellow !s: Resolving Conflicts

A yellow exclamation point next to the name indicates a problem with the device's driver. It could mean that either you or Windows installed the *wrong* driver, or that the device is fighting for resources being used by another component. It could also mean that a driver can't find the equipment it's supposed to control. That's what happens to your Webcam driver, for example, if you've detached the Webcam.

A red X next to a component's name usually indicates either that it just isn't working, or that you've deliberately disabled it, as described below. At other times, the X is the result of a serious incompatibility between the component and your computer, or the component and Windows. In that case, a call to the manufacturer's help line is almost certainly in your future.

Tip: To find out which company actually created a certain driver, double-click the component's name in the Device Manager. In the resulting Properties dialog box, click the Driver tab, where you'll see the name of the company, the date the driver was created, the version of the driver, and so on.

Properties ⌐   Update driver software ⌐   ⌐ Disable

Figure 18-4:
The Device Manager lists types of equipment; to see the actual model(s) in each category, you must expand each sublist by clicking the + symbol. A device that's having problems is easy to spot, thanks to the red Xs and yellow exclamation points.

Duplicate devices

If the Device Manager displays icons for duplicate devices (for example, two modems), remove *both* of them. (Right-click each, and then choose Uninstall from the shortcut menu.) If you remove only one, Windows will find it again the next time the PC starts up, and you'll have duplicate devices again.

If Windows asks if you want to restart your computer after you remove the first icon, click No, and then delete the second one. Windows won't ask again after you remove the second incarnation; you have to restart your computer manually.

When the PC starts up again, Windows finds the hardware device and installs it (only once this time). Open the Device Manager and make sure that there's only one of everything. If not, contact the manufacturer's help line.

Resolving resource conflicts

If the "red X" problem isn't caused by a duplicate component, double-click the component's name. Here you'll find an explanation of the problem, which is often a conflict in resources (see Figure 18-5).

Figure 18-5:
The General tab should have all the information you need to resolve a problem. Any resource with a conflict is marked with a red X "not working" icon. If you click "Check for solutions," your PC sends a silent signal back to the mother ship, Microsoft, in hopes of finding that there's a newer driver or a compatibility patch available for downloading.

Turning Components Off

If you click to select the name of a component, the icons at the top of the Device Manager window spring to life. The one on the far right is the Disable button (Figure 18-4), which makes your PC treat the component in question as though it's not even there.

You can use this function to test device conflicts. For example, if a red X indicates that there's a resource conflict, you can disable one of the two gadgets, which may clear up a problem with its competitor.

When you disable a component, a red X appears next to the component's listing in the Device Manager. To undo your action, click the device's name and click the Enable button in the toolbar (formerly the Disable button).

Updating Drivers

If you get your hands on a new, more powerful (or more reliable) driver for a device, you can use the Device Manager to install it.

Tip: Newer isn't *always* better, however; in the world of Windows, the rule "If it ain't broke, don't fix it" contains a grain of truth the size of Texas.

In the Device Manager, click the component's name, and then click the Update Driver Software button in the toolbar (identified in Figure 18-4). The Update Device Driver Wizard walks you through the process.

Along the way, the wizard offers to search for a better driver, or to display a list of drivers in a certain folder so you can make your own selection. In either case, you may have to restart the PC to put the newly installed driver into service.

Driver Rollback

Suppose that you, the increasingly proficient PC user, have indeed downloaded a new driver for some component—your scanner, say—and successfully installed it using the instructions in the previous paragraphs. Life is sweet—until you discover that your scanner no longer scans in color.

In this situation, you'd probably give quite a bit for the chance to return to the previous driver, which, though older, seemed to work better. That's the beauty of Driver Rollback. To find it, open the Device Manager (page 567), click the component in question, and then click the Properties button. There, you'll find the Roll Back Driver button (shown in Figure 18-6).

Figure 18-6:
When you double-click a component listed in your Device Manager and then click the Driver tab, you find four buttons and a lot of information. The Driver Provider information, for example, lets you know who is responsible for your current driver—Microsoft or the maker of the component. Click the Driver Details button to find out where on your hard drive the actual driver file is. Or click Update Driver to install a newer version, the Roll Back Driver button to reinstate the earlier version, or the Uninstall button to remove the driver from your system entirely—a drastic decision.

Incidentally, you can also get to the Roll Back Driver button in the Properties dialog box for a device. To get there, double-click the component's name, and then click the Driver tab shown here.

Windows Vista, forgiving as always, instantly undoes the installation of the newer driver, and reinstates the previous driver.

Laptops, Tablets, and Palmtops

I n Windows Vista, Microsoft makes its biggest nod yet to a raging trend in computing: portability. Laptop sales are trouncing desktop PC sales. In some industries, palmtops or touch-screen PCs are even replacing laptops. And for millions of people, the computing platform of choice isn't a computer at all—it's a cellphone.

That's why Vista is crammed with special features for the peripatetic PC. For example, it has new features for laptops, including a way to change your power-consumption configuration with a quick click on the battery icon in the Notification Area, and a new Mobility Center that lets you switch quickly among networks and workplaces.

Working with a Tablet PC (a touch-screen laptop or slate) is now easier than ever, too, thanks to new or beefed-up features like pen control, digital ink text input, handwriting recognition, and more. (This stuff used to be available only in a special Tablet PC edition of Windows; for the first time, it's part of the basic operating system.)

And finally, if you're a fan of Pocket PC palmtops, Windows Mobile smartphones, or Ultra-Mobile PCs, Vista offers the new Sync Center. It keeps your address book, to-do lists, and email synchronized with your main PC.

Laptops
All Versions

As you can read on page 298, Vista has a full-blown control panel that's dedicated to managing battery power. You can control the screen brightness, wireless antenna strength, and other features, all in the name of saving juice.

That's not the only gift to laptoppers in Vista, however. Read on for all the good stuff.

Battery Meter

The notification area (system tray) has always displayed a little battery meter that shows how your laptop's battery charge is doing. Its icon looks like a battery with a plug beside it when it's plugged into a power outlet, or a battery alone when it's not.

If you point to this icon without clicking, a tooltip displays the status of your laptop's battery, including the current battery charge and what power plan (page 298) you're using. There's more to it than that, though, as you can see in Figure 19-1.

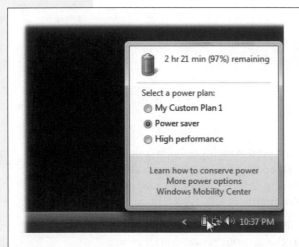

Figure 19-1:
To change the power configuration plan on the fly, click the Battery Meter icon once, and click again on the power plan you'd like to use.

If you click the battery meter icon, you can choose these options from the pop-up menu:

- **Learn how to conserve power**. Opens Windows Help and Support to the "Conserving battery power" page, where you can read how to get the most out of your laptop's battery.

- **More power options**. Opens Power Options window (in the Control Panel), where you can change the plan on the Battery Meter and change plan settings.

- **Windows Mobility Center**. Opens the new Mobility Center, described next.

Mobility Center

This new Vista program appears in your Start→All Programs→Accessories menu no matter what kind of computer you have, but it's intended primarily for laptops. It's a handy, centralized hub for everything that makes a laptop a laptop (Figure 19-2): battery, wireless networking, external projector connection, and so on.

Each setting is illustrated with a cute little icon—but don't be fooled. It's so much more than an icon! It's also a *button* that, when double-clicked, opens up a Control Panel applet or configuration page.

Tip: You can also open one of these icons entirely from the keyboard. See the underlined letter beneath each panel, such as Battery Status or Wireless Network? Press Alt+that letter to highlight the icon, and then press Enter.

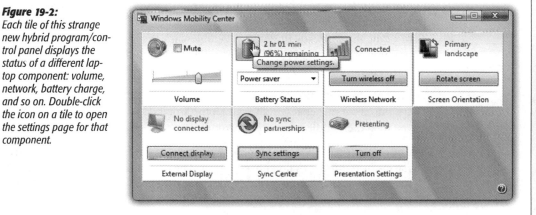

Figure 19-2:
Each tile of this strange new hybrid program/control panel displays the status of a different laptop component: volume, network, battery charge, and so on. Double-click the icon on a tile to open the settings page for that component.

Here's the complete list of tiles that might appear in your Mobility Center. (You may not have all of them, depending on what kind of computer you're using and what components it has.)

- **Brightness.** The slider dims your screen for this work session only, which can save enormous amounts of battery power. Double-click the icon to open the Power Options control panel, where you can make brightness changes that are always in effect.

- **Volume.** Change your speakers' volume, or mute them entirely. Double-click the icon to open the Sound control panel (page 307).

- **Battery Status.** This is your battery's "fuel gauge." The pop-up menu lets you choose a canned setting like "High performance" (your PC doesn't go to sleep, but uses up battery power faster) or "Power saver" (the laptop goes to sleep sooner to conserve juice). Double-click the icon to open the Power Options control panel, where you can change the battery-plan settings for good.

- **Wireless Network.** Turns your WiFi circuitry on or off (which saves power and makes flight attendants happy), and shows how many bars of signal you have. Double-click the icon to open the "Connect to a network" dialog box, which lists all wireless networks within your range.

- **Screen Rotation.** This one shows up only on Tablet PCs. It lets you turn the screen image 90 degrees. Double-click the icon to open the Display Settings control panel for additional screen settings.

- **External Display.** Have you hooked up a second monitor? If so, click "Connect display" to make Vista aware of its new responsibilities. This tile also reveals whether or not Vista "sees" the second screen. Double-click the icon to open the Display Settings control panel, where you can configure the resolution and other settings of the second monitor.

- **Sync Center.** The Sync Center is the communications hub for palmtops and other gizmos that synchronize their data with Windows. This tile shows you the status of a sync that's already under way. Double-click the icon to open the Sync Center program, where you can set up new sync "partnerships" between your PC and your extra gizmos (page 587).

- **Presentation Settings.** This feature is the answer to a million PowerPoint pitchers' prayers: it makes sure that your laptop won't do anything embarrassing while you're in the middle of your boardroom presentation.

Click "Turn on." When the tile says "Presenting," your laptop won't go to sleep. No alarms or reminder dialog boxes appear. The screen saver doesn't kick in. You're free to give your pitch in peace. Double-click the icon to open the new Presentation Settings dialog box shown in Figure 19-3.

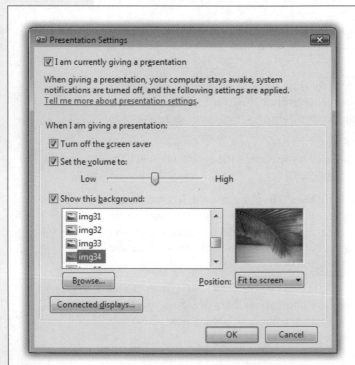

Figure 19-3:
When you're in presentation mode, your screen saver and system notifications won't appear, and your laptop won't go to sleep. You might also want to specify a piece of uncontroversial artwork for your desktop wallpaper, so your bosses and potential employers won't accidentally spot the HotBikiniBabes.com JPEG that you usually use.

Note: You also enter presentation mode when you hook up a network projector (page 256), or when you connect an external monitor. (A New Display Detected dialog box appears, complete with an option to turn on presentation mode.)

Tablet PCs

Home Premium • Business • Enterprise • Ultimate

A Tablet PC is like a laptop with a key difference—it has a touch screen. In theory, that design means that a Tablet PC can be thinner and lighter than a laptop, because it can do without a keyboard.

When Microsoft unveiled its concept for the Tablet PC in 2002, it was convinced that the tablet was the future. "Within five years, I predict it will be the most popular form of PC sold in America," Bill Gates told the crowd at a keynote speech.

Clearly, that never happened. The Tablet PC isn't exactly dead, but its popularity centers on fairly rarefied circles: health care, insurance, and so on.

Maybe Vista will give the whole thing a boost. For the first time, the Tablet PC's features are right there in the main version of Windows (it used to require a specialized version): pen features, touch-screen features, digital ink, handwriting recognition, and so on.

The Mobile PC Control Panel

Almost all of the goodies waiting for you, the tablet fan, are available in the Mobile PC applet of the Control Panel.

If you have a tablet, you can make life easier for yourself by adding the Mobile PC control panel to the top of your Start menu, where it's easy to get to. Figure 19-4 shows the result you're after.

Handwriting Recognition

The accuracy and convenience of Vista's handwriting recognition have come a very long way—which is fortunate indeed, since some Tablet PCs don't have keyboards (or have keyboards that you can detach). You can tell Vista if you're left- or right-handed, use the Handwriting Recognizer to help Vista recognize your handwriting nuances, and turn on Automatic Learning, so Vista learns about you as you learn about it. Hey, if Tablet PCs can decipher doctors' handwriting, surely you can get your Tablet PC to recognize yours.

Using a pop-up transcription window called the Input panel, you can enter text anywhere you can type: Word, email programs, your Web browser, and so on. Vista also comes with a special program called Windows Journal that's a note-taking module designed expressly for tablets.

Teaching Vista how you write

The Handwriting Recognizer increases the chances that Vista will recognize your handwriting correctly. You provide samples of your handwriting, and Vista studies your style. Figure 19-6 shows you how to start the process.

Figure 19-4:
Click Start→Control Panel. Drag Mobile PC—either the little laptop icon itself or the words "Mobile PC"—to the Start button. Without releasing the mouse, wait for the Start menu to open, and then drop the Mobile PC icon at the top-right corner of the Start menu. You can now get to the settings quickly.

You're offered the chance to write either sentences or numbers, symbols, and letters; for best accuracy, you should work through both. More than once, in fact. (They're not brief exercises—the Sentences option involves about 50 screens—but the effort's for a good cause.) Write just the way you would on paper—in cursive, printing, or a mixture of both.

After working through the Handwriting Recognizer, you can start using handwriting recognition.

Tip: If you turn on Automatic Learning, Vista learns more and more about your handwriting the more you use it. To do that, open the Mobile PC control panel. Click Tablet PC Settings→Enable or Disable Handwriting Personalization→Handwriting Recognition tab. Turn on Use Automatic Learning (Recommended).

Handwriting anywhere

To make Vista recognize your handwriting, open any program where you would otherwise type—a word processor, for example.

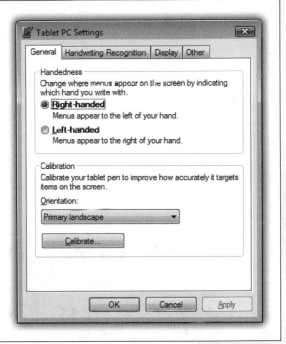

Figure 19-5:
In Tablet PC Settings, you can tell Vista if you're left- or right-handed, calibrate the screen, and select an orientation. Landscape is the "long way," larger on the horizontal side, and Portrait is the "tall way," larger on the vertical side. Calibrating the screen guides you through tapping a crosshair until the screen is fully aligned.

Now open the Input panel, which is a floating handwriting window that automatically converts anything you write into typed text (Figure 19-7). You can summon the Input panel in several ways:

- Tap to put the insertion point in a text-entry area—an empty word processor document or email message, for example, or the Address bar of a Web browser. A tiny Input panel *icon* appears right by the insertion point (Figure 19-7, top); tap it.

- Tap the Input panel *tab*, which peeks out from the left edge of the screen (Figure 19-7, middle).

Tip: If you're left-handed, you'll probably want to move the panel to the *right* side of the screen, which you can do by dragging its outer edge.

- Use the Input panel *gesture*. Most gestures (page 578) involve quick strokes on the tablet's surface; this one, however, is a quick, side-to-side movement of your pen *just above* the surface of, but not touching, the screen.

To turn on this option, open the Mobile PC control panel (page 575), and, under "Pen and Input Devices," click "Change tablet pen settings." On the Pen Options tab, click Start Tablet PC Input panel, click Settings, and turn on "Enable start Input panel gesture." Click OK.

Tip: Even after you've turned on this option, summoning the Input panel with a gesture can be tricky. Try four to six fast, diagonal, four-inch motions of the pen, just above the surface of the screen. Experiment with speed and distance, and keep in mind that the panel won't open if it's already open. (Duh!)

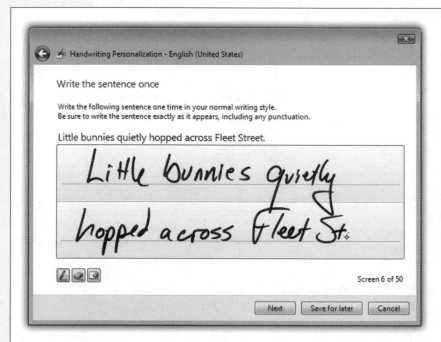

Figure 19-6:
To find the Handwriting Recognizer tool, tap Start, and in the Search window, type Hand. The results in the Start menu include "Personalize handwriting recognition." (Or, if you're a mouser, choose Start→All Programs→Tablet PC→Tablet PC→"Personalize handwriting recognition.") Select it. From the options, choose "Teach the recognizer your handwriting style."

Once the Input panel is open, the buttons in the top-left corner offer three ways to enter text. (Point without clicking to see their names, or consult Figure 19-8.

The Writing pad is by far the most convenient method. To use it, just start writing on the line. Use your normal writing style.

At first, the "digital ink" just sits there where you wrote it. The input panel expands, adding new lines as necessary, as you write. But when you tap the little Insert button, the ink vanishes—and the converted, typed text appears in your document or dialog box.

Gestures

In the pen-computing world, a *gesture* is a quick pen movement that lets you "type" a Space (a long, quick line to the right), a Backspace (long and quick to the left), a press of the Enter key, or a Tab (Figure 19-9).

To try out a gesture or two, make sure the input panel is *completely empty.* You're going to draw one of these special shapes in the input panel, but you'll see its *effect* in whatever Windows program you're using. You don't have to tap Insert or wait, as you do when writing; Vista recognizes the gestures instantly.

You can also scratch out text in the input pad *before* it gets transcribed. Just scribble it out, just as you'd scratch out handwriting on a real piece of paper (Figure 19-7). You can draw a straight line through what you've written, scribble out with an M or W motion, draw looping scribbles, and so on. The text disappears from the pad.

Figure 19-7:
Top: You can open the Input panel by tapping the Input panel icon that appears next to any selected text box.

Middle: You can also tap the tiny tab that hugs the edge of the screen.

Bottom: Once the Input panel is open, you can use it to enter text into any program at all. If you make an error before hitting the Insert button, you can just scribble it out to make it disappear. (Hint: You can customize the heck out of the Input panel—ink thickness, tab appearance, and so on—by choosing Tools→Options within the panel.)

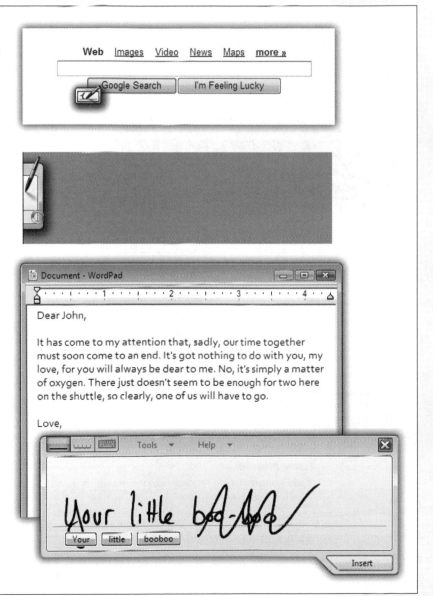

Tip: In Windows XP Tablet Edition, there was only one scratch-out gesture: a Z-shaped scratch-out. If you'd like to return to those halcyon days, choose Tools→Options in the Input panel. From the Gestures tab, select "Only the Z-shaped scratch-out gesture that was available in Microsoft Windows XP Tablet Edition" (Figure 19-9).

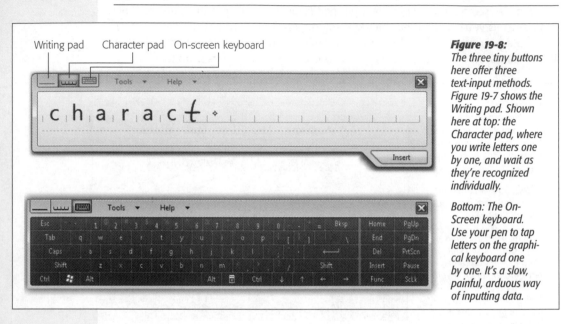

Writing pad   Character pad   On-screen keyboard

Figure 19-8:
The three tiny buttons here offer three text-input methods. Figure 19-7 shows the Writing pad. Shown here at top: the Character pad, where you write letters one by one, and wait as they're recognized individually.

Bottom: The On-Screen keyboard. Use your pen to tap letters on the graphical keyboard one by one. It's a slow, painful, arduous way of inputting data.

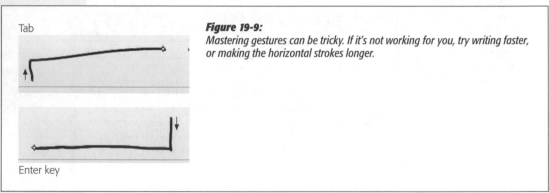

Tab

Enter key

Figure 19-9:
Mastering gestures can be tricky. If it's not working for you, try writing faster, or making the horizontal strokes longer.

Fixing mistakes

Vista's handwriting recognition is amazingly accurate. It is not, however, perfect—in part because your handwriting isn't either.

Correcting a mistake is important for two reasons. First, it fixes the error in your document—and second, it *teaches* Vista so that it's less likely to make that mistake again. Figure 19-10 shows the steps.

The finer points of handwriting recognition

The handwriting recognition feature in Vista is considerably better than it was on the old Windows XP Tablet Edition. Here are a few reasons why:

- **AutoComplete.** As you write in the Input panel, AutoComplete attempts to save you time by guessing what you're going for. If it's right, tap the guess and enjoy how Windows finishes your word.

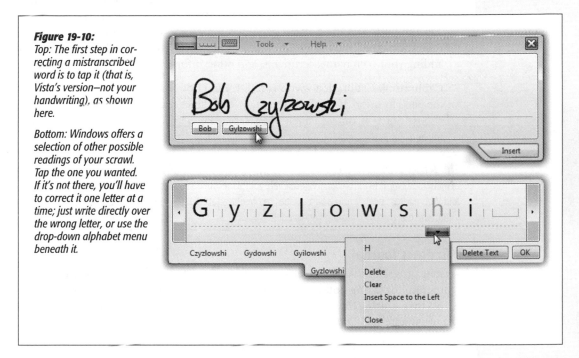

Figure 19-10:
Top: The first step in correcting a mistranscribed word is to tap it (that is, Vista's version—not your handwriting), as shown here.

Bottom: Windows offers a selection of other possible readings of your scrawl. Tap the one you wanted. If it's not there, you'll have to correct it one letter at a time; just write directly over the wrong letter, or use the drop-down alphabet menu beneath it.

- **Scratch-out gestures.** As mentioned earlier, scratch-out gestures let you use your pen to erase anything you've handwritten by scratching it out with the pen. You can customize Scratch-Out Gestures from the Input panel's Tools→Options→Gestures tab.

- **Back-of-pen erase.** Some tablet pens have an "eraser end" that lets you erase text you've written. To find out if your pen is so equipped, flip it upside-down and drag across something you've written. If an eraser icon appears—and your text disappears—then you're one of the lucky ones.

- **Web quick keys.** The Web button in the Input panel opens a panel filled with one-tap bits of Web addresses: http://, www., .com, and so on. It's a lifesaver when you're using your tablet with a Web browser.

Note: Anything you tap on the Num, Sym, or Web panels gets deposited directly into your document. It doesn't first appear in the Input panel, like your handwriting does. After all, Windows is already *sure* of what you intended to type; there's no need for you to approve or correct it.

Some of the old features, meanwhile, are still useful:

- **Numbers and symbols.** The Input panel displays buttons for Bksp (Backspace), Del (Delete), Tab, Enter, Space, and left and right arrow keys. For ease in entering numbers and symbols, special number and symbol pads are available, too (tap Num or Sym).

- **Add words to the Handwriting Dictionary.** To add a word to the Handwriting Dictionary, write the word neatly in the Writing Pad, and correct it if necessary. Tap the button at the bottom edge that represents Vista's transcription. In the correction panel, tap the tiny dictionary icon; select "Add to dictionary." Consider adding your own name, acronyms, and other information you use often.

- **Calibrating.** Calibration involves fine-tuning how accurately your tablet detects the pen's location. If you feel as though your Tablet could benefit from calibration, choose Start→Control Panel; open Tablet PC Settings, and then Calibrate The Screen.

Tip: Windows Help is full of tips and tricks for getting better handwriting recognition. You've just read some of them (add words to the dictionary, recalibrate your screen, use the pads of shortcuts for numbers, symbols, and Web address bits). It also advises lefties to open the Tablet PC Settings applet of the Control Panel to inform the machine by choosing Left-Handed.

Windows Journal

Among programs that work well with handwriting, few can top Windows Journal. It's a program for taking notes, keeping a journal, or recording info-tidbits as you come across them during the work day. It's a great tool for students, since it does away with the usual note-taking tools (notebooks, pens, and paper).

When you choose Start→All Programs→Windows Journal, you're presented with a blank page of what looks like the lined paper of an old spiral notebook.

So why not just make your scribbles, doodles, and math equations in a program like Word? Because Word doesn't accept handwriting—only typed text *converted* from handwriting. Windows Journal, on the other hand, stores the actual graphic representation of anything you write (Figure 19-11).

As you write along, keep in mind that your notes and sketches aren't locked in Journal forever. For example:

- Mail it. Choose Mail→Send to Mail Recipient to send a page by email. The result is very cool. It looks like someone scribbled a handwritten note to you right in the body of the message.

  Of course, there are a couple of problems with this approach. Some people's email programs don't display graphics at all, meaning that they'll see nothing but a big, empty window. And a fully graphic email message is one that can't be searched, annotated, or edited.

Fortunately, you can also select a swath of handwriting and choose Action→Convert Select to E-Mail. Journal does its best to convert the handwriting to text, which it then pastes into an open outgoing email message.

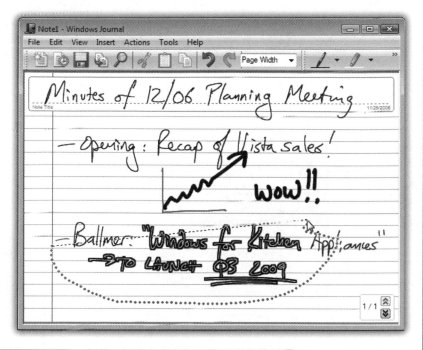

Figure 19-11:
Windows Journal stores your handwriting as digital ink, without attempting to convert everything to typed text. Still, it's not stupid. You can, for example, search your reams of notes for a certain word or phrase. You can also use the Selection tool (looks like a rope lasso) to select text to move, transcribe, or format.

- Export it to a Web archive or a TIFF graphics file (File→Export As).

- Convert parts of it to text. See Figure 19-12.

Tip: Pressing the button on the side of your stylus automatically puts it into Selection mode, saving you a trip to the toolbar or Edit menu.

- Change your "pen." Choose Edit→Format Ink to the thickness, color, and other attributes of the ink style.

Flicks

Pen Flicks, new in Vista, let you navigate documents and manipulate data using your stylus alone. With a flick of the wrist, you can scroll a page at a time, copy, paste, delete, undo, and so on. You have a total of eight pen flicks available to you: up, down, left, right, and the four diagonals.

(So what's the difference between a *flick* and a *gesture*? Very little, except that to make a flick, you draw an invisible line across your *document*, rather than in the input panel.)

To turn on this feature, choose Start→Control Panel. Click Mobile PC, then "Change tablet pen settings" (under the heading Pen and Input Devices). Once the dialog box opens, click the Flicks tab.

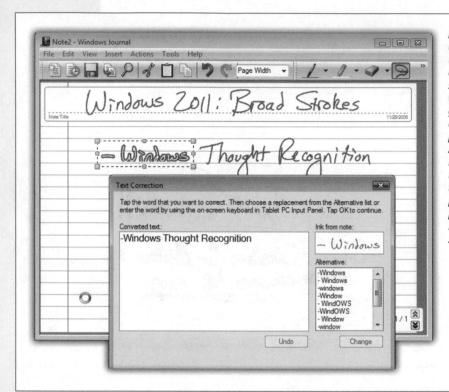

Figure 19-12:
Use the Selection tool (the rope lasso icon on the toolbar) to select any text you've written (by dragging a circle or oval around it); at that point, you can choose Action→Convert Handwriting to Text to turn the writing into typed text, suitable for pasting into another program or depositing right there on the Journal page.

The Flicks tab opens. Turn on "Use flicks…" at the top of the dialog box. At this point, you get only four flicks: up and down (for scrolling) and left and right (for Back and Forward). If you turn on "Navigational flicks and editing flicks," however, you add the diagonal options, making flicks even more useful.

At the bottom, click "Practice using flicks." The Pen Flicks Training dialog box opens, probably startling you with the sudden appearance of an actual *video* that shows someone scrolling with the pen.

When you click Next, you're offered the opportunity to practice the flicking technique. It suggests that you draw short lines "as though you were brushing something off the screen with the tip of the pen," which is well put.

Figure 19-13 shows the built-in flick movements for Page Up and Down, Forward and Back, Delete, Copy, Paste, and Undo. You can change these assignments if you'd prefer, either rearranging the flick directions or assigning entirely different functions to them: Save, Open, Print, press the Alt key (or Ctrl, Shift, or ⊞), and so on. Figure 19-13 shows how.

Tablet settings

If you get into flicking, you should know that, since Microsoft is Microsoft, you have a long list of customizations and tweaks available to you.

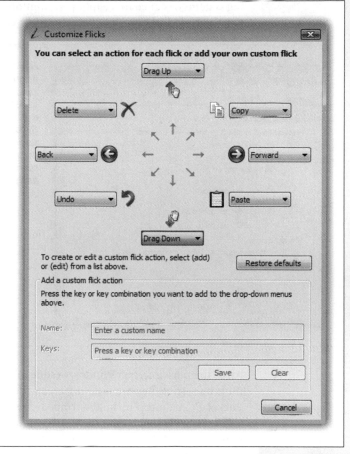

Figure 19-13:
In Control Panel→Mobile PC→Pen and Input Devices→Flicks, click Customize. You get this dialog box, where you can remap the flick directions so that they perform other functions. If you choose Add from one of the little pop-up menus, in fact, the controls at the bottom actually let you map a keystroke to a flick, so that an upward flick triggers, for example, Alt+F4.

Open the Mobile PC control panel (page 575), and, under "Pen and Input Devices," click "Change tablet pen settings." The tabs of the resulting dialog box offers options like these:

- What happens when you double-tap the screen or hold down the pen on the screen (which ordinarily means a right-click). On the Pen Options tab, click one of the pen actions and then click Settings.

- What you see on the screen at the spot where you tap it (Figure 19-14). Make these changes on the Pointer Options tab.

Windows Mobile Devices

All Versions

Windows Mobile isn't really Windows. It's a much smaller, simpler series of operating systems designed for cellphones, palmtops, ultra-mobile PCs and portable Media Centers (handheld music/video/photo players).

Figure 19-14:
Before Vista came along, it was often difficult to know what you were doing when you tapped the screen with the pen on a Tablet PC. Vista makes that a lot easier with visual cues. Here on the Pointer Options tab, you can see the visual feedback for a single tap, a double tap, pressing the pen button, and pressing the pen button and tapping at the same time. If you'd rather not see these visual cues, turn them off.

All of them have certain Windows-esque interface elements—a Start menu is a common one—but they are not, in fact, all the same. For instance, a Windows Mobile Pocket PC palmtop includes stripped-down versions of Word, Excel, PowerPoint, and Internet Explorer; you can manage folders and subfolders, create files, and play, download, and manage music and video. A Windows cellphone, on the other hand, has far fewer features.

Vista's new Sync Center is designed to keep Windows Mobile gadgets up to date with the latest info on your Vista PC, including your email, address book, and calendar. (More information about the Sync Center follows.) It's probably not as full-featured as the software that came with your device. It's primarily designed to:

• Sync up a gadget with Microsoft Outlook, and

• Sync up a laptop with a network server's files, in a feature called offline files.

The Sync Center

All Versions

Syncing is the process of keeping files that are stored in two places matched up with each other. If you add some paragraphs to your novel manuscript on your office PC, you're going to want the copy on your home PC to reflect those changes. You'll want the two computers synced.

Same thing on mobile devices. If you add a new person to your Pocket PC's address book, syncing can copy it into your Outlook address book on your desktop PC.

That's what the Sync Center is designed to handle.

Sync Partnerships

Before you can synchronize your device with Vista's Sync Center, you need to set up a sync partnership for it. The procedure goes like this:

1. **Connect your Windows Mobile cellphone, or your Pocket PC, to your computer. Install the software that came with it.**

NOSTALGIA CORNER

The Briefcase

The trouble with progress is that it entails change—and when you change things, somebody, somewhere is going to be upset. Just ask Microsoft's Windows division.

Anyway, Windows Vista may have the Sync Center, but it also still has the Briefcase, which is something like its predecessor. Microsoft plays it *way* down, to the point of invisibility. But it still does one thing that the Sync Center can't do. It keeps your files straight between *two PCs* (as opposed to one PC and a network server). That's handy when you transport files from desktop to laptop, or from home to work. If you learn to use the Briefcase, you'll be less likely to lose track of which copies of your documents are the most current.

To use the Briefcase, start by adding a briefcase icon on your desktop. To do so, right-click any spot on the desktop; from the shortcut menu, choose New→Briefcase. A new icon appears, called New Briefcase. (If you're feeling inspired, rename it as you would any folder.)

Now round up the icons of the documents you'll work on when away from your main PC. Drag them onto the Briefcase icon. Windows copies the files into this special temporary holding tank.

Now connect your laptop to the desktop PC, if you haven't already. (See Chapter 24 for tips on connecting machines.) Or, if you plan to take your files with you on a USB flash drive, insert it. Drag the Briefcase icon onto the laptop or the flash drive.

You're ready to leave your office. When you get to wherever you're going, open and edit the documents in the copied Briefcase "folder" icon. Whatever you do, don't move those files. (For example, work on the documents right on the flash drive.)

If the copied Briefcase is actually on the laptop's hard drive (not a flash drive), Windows can keep track of changes made to the documents on *both* computers, the original and the copy.

When you return to your main PC, reconnect the laptop or reinsert the flash drive. Now all of your careful step-following is about to pay off.

Right-click the briefcase icon; from the shortcut menu, choose Update All. Windows copies the edited files back to their original folders on your desktop-PC hard drive, automatically replacing the older, original copies.

This is generally an easy task; all recent Windows Mobile devices are Vista-compatible. Some even connect to your PC wirelessly; consult the manual.

Unfortunately, it's not a sure bet by any means that Vista will recognize the gadget you've just connected. If Vista doesn't report that it found a driver for your device and installed it properly, you probably won't see the device in Sync Center. That doesn't mean you can't sync the gadget with Vista, only that you can't use Sync Center to do it. You'll have to use the software that came with the device.

If Vista does announce that it's found a driver and installed it correctly, then you can proceed.

2. **Open Sync Center. In the left pane, click "Set up new sync partnerships."**

The main window lists whatever Sync Center–compatible gadgets Vista can see.

3. **Click the device you want to synchronize. Click Set Up.**

Figure 19-15 shows what you'll see at this stage.

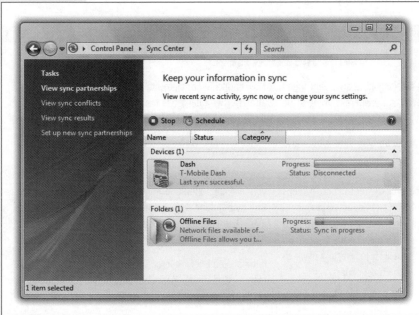

Figure 19-15:
Sync Center doesn't work with all kinds of pocket gadgets, but it's a start. It's also the home base for the Offline Files feature described in the following pages.

4. **Select the settings and schedule to specify how and when your device should sync.**

For example, you might indicate that you want the synchronization to take place every time the device is connected to the PC.

5. **Click Sync to start a manual sync.**

Vista uses its best artificial intelligence to determine what to copy where. For example, if a file has been created on Machine A since your last sync, it gets copied to Machine B. If a file has been deleted, it's deleted on the other machine. And if a file has been changed on *both* machines since the last sync, a dialog box presents you with the decision about which file "wins." (These examples assume that you've set up a *two-way* sync. A one-way sync is much simpler: everything on Machine A always replaces what's on Machine B.)

Offline Files

Business • Enterprise • Ultimate

The *offline files* feature is designed primarily for laptop lovers. It lets you carry off files that generally live on your office network, so you can get some work done while you're away.

Then, when you return and connect your laptop to the office network, Windows automatically copies your edited, updated documents back to their original locations on the network, intelligently keeping straight which copies are the most recent. (And vice versa—if people changed the network copies while you were away, Windows copies them onto your laptop.)

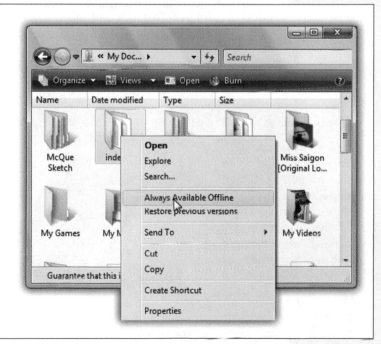

Figure 19-16:
Right-click the icon of a file or folder that's on another computer on the network. From the shortcut menu, choose Always Available Offline. (A checkmark appears. To stop making this file or folder available offline, choose the same command again.) Your PC takes a quick moment to copy the files onto your own hard drive (that is, on the client machine—your laptop).

It's a great feature for corporate workers, which explains why it's not available in the Home Basic and Home Premium versions of Vista. And it's been greatly simplified since the Windows XP version. For example, reconnecting to the network now triggers an automatic, seamless, invisible synchronization of the files you worked on while you were away—there's no more alert balloon, no need to shut down all programs and manually trigger the sync, and so on.

Note: Although Microsoft developed Offline Files primarily for laptops that sometimes leave the network, it can also be a useful feature for *desktop* computers that belong to a network that isn't always up and running. Even so, this chapter refers to your computer as "the laptop," to avoid having to repeat "the laptop or desktop computer that isn't always on the network" 50 million times.

Preparing to Leave the Network

To tell Windows which files and folders you want to take away with you on the laptop, find them on the network. Proceed as shown in Figure 19-13.

Note: If you can't seem to make this work, it may be because the Offline Files master switch has been turned off. To see it, choose Start→Control Panel. In Classic view, double-click Offline Files. On the General tab of the resulting dialog box, you'll see the Enable Offline Files checkbox.

Normally, Windows copies the selected files and folders to your laptop rather slowly. It works in the background, between your mouse clicks and keystrokes.

If you're about to catch a flight, however, and you're nervous that you might not have the latest versions of all the network files you need, you can force Vista to do the entire copying job *right now*. To do that, choose Start→All Programs→Accessories→Sync

---

GEM IN THE ROUGH

Windows SideShow

Laptop lovers, take note—the best is yet to come.

SideShow, a new Vista feature, is a tiny screen built right into the lids or undersides of certain new laptop, tablet, and palmtop models. The cool thing is that it shows you certain kinds of important information—your calendar, new email, the time or weather, your address book—even if the laptop is turned off or asleep.

This external screen uses practically no battery power; it's like having a little PalmPilot built

into the laptop. When SideShow machines arrive on the market, you'll be able to specify which gadget (mini-program) you want to see. It can serve as an alarm that notifies you about an imminent meeting, play songs from your Media Player collection, check a flight time, and so on—without ever having to open the laptop lid.

Will Microsoft's master Side-Show plan find acceptance in the marketplace? Let's meet back on this page in two years and discuss.

Center. Click the Offline Files partnership in the main window, and then click Sync on the toolbar.

> **Tip:** You can also sync only one particular folder. Just open it into a window and then click Sync on the toolbar. (In fact, you can even sync *one individual file* if you have to. Right-click it; from the shortcut menu, choose Sync.)

Working Offline

Now suppose you're untethered from the network, and you have a moment to get some work done. Open Sync Center and double-click the Offline Files icon (shown in Figure 19-15). There, before you, is a list of all the folders to which you "subscribed" before you left the network. See Figure 19-17 for details.

Figure 19-17:
Top: When you open Sync Center, double-clicking Offline Files shows you a list of the folders you added to your offline list.

Bottom: Double-click one of them to see this surprising sight: icons for all the folders that were in that networked folder. Only the ones you explicitly requested are available, however; the rest display Xs.

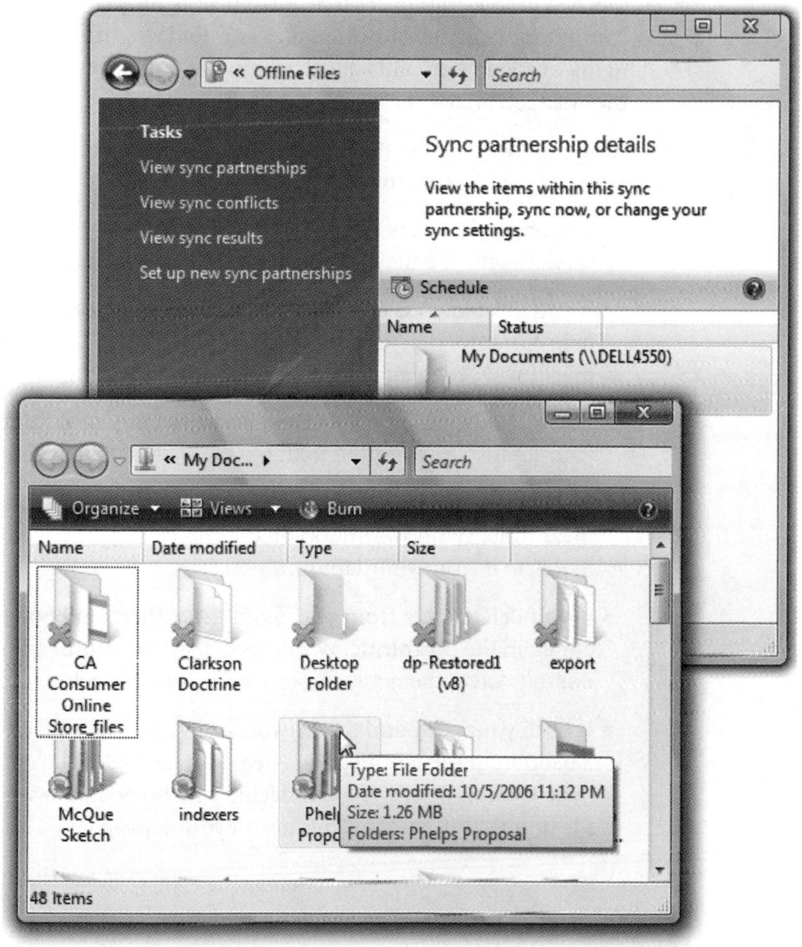

You're free to work with offline files and folders exactly as you would if you were still connected to the network. You can revise, edit, and duplicate files, and even create new documents inside offline folders. The permissions remain the same as when you connect to the network.

Tip: There may be times when you want to work with your own laptop copies (rather than the network copies) even if you're still *on* the network—if, say, the network connection is not so much absent as slow and frustrating. To do that, open the folder on the network that contains the offline files. On its toolbar, click "Work offline." (This button appears only in folders that you've made available offline.)

Reconnecting to the Network

Now suppose you return from your jaunt away from the office. You plop your laptop down on your desk and reconnect the network cable.

Once Windows discovers that it's home again, it whirls into action, automatically comparing your set of offline files and folders with the master set on the network. (This process is much faster than it was in Windows XP, because Vista copies only the changed *pieces* of each file—not the entire file.)

Along the way, Vista attempts to handle discrepancies between the two sets of files as best it can. For example:

- If your copy and a network copy of a file don't match, Windows wipes out the older version with the newer version, so both locations have exactly the same edition.

- If you deleted your copy of a file, or somebody on the network deleted the original, Windows deletes the corresponding file so that it no longer exists on either machine. (That's assuming that nobody edited the file in the meantime.)

- If somebody added a file to the network copy of a folder, you get a copy of it in your laptop's copy of the folder.

- If you've edited an offline file that somebody on the network has deleted in the meantime, Windows offers you the choice to save your version on the network or to delete it from your laptop.

- If you delete a file from your hard drive that somebody else on the network has edited in the meantime, Windows deletes the offline file from your hard drive but doesn't delete the network copy from the network.

- If both your copy and the network copy of a file were edited while you were away, a balloon in the Notification Area notifies you of the conflict. Click it to open the Sync Center, where you can decide which version "wins." (Until you do that, the file in question remains offline, on your laptop.)

Part Six:
PC Health

Chapter 20: Maintenance and Speed Tweaks

Chapter 21: The Disk Chapter

Chapter 22: Backups and Troubleshooting

6

Maintenance and Speed Tweaks

Your computer requires periodic checkups and preventive maintenance—pretty much like you, its human sidekick. Fortunately, Microsoft has put quite a bit of effort into equipping Windows Vista with special tools, all dedicated to the preservation of what Microsoft calls PC Health. Here's a crash course in keeping your PC—and its hard drive—humming.

Disk Cleanup
All Versions

As you use your computer, Windows litters your hard drive with temporary files. Programs, utilities, and Web sites scatter disposable files everywhere. If you could see your hard drive surface, it would eventually look like the floor of a minivan whose owners eat a lot of fast food.

To run Windows Vista's built-in housekeeper program, choose your favorite method:

- **Open the Start menu.** Type *disk cl* in the Search box. Double-click Disk Cleanup in the results list.

- **Open the Start menu.** Click All Programs→Accessories→System Tools→Disk Cleanup.

- **Open the Control Panel.** Click "System and Maintenance," scroll down to the bottom of the window, and, under the Administrative Tools heading, click "Free up disk space."

Vista asks if you want it to clean up only your files, or the files of everyone who uses the computer. When you make your choice, you're then asked which hard drive you want cleaned. When you finally click OK, the program dives right in, inspecting your drive and reporting on files you can safely remove.

The Disk Cleanup dialog box shown in Figure 20-1 appears when the inspection is over. Turn on the checkboxes of the file categories you'd like to have cleaned out, and then click OK to send them to the digital landfill. It's like getting a bigger hard drive for free.

Tip: The More Options tab of the dialog box shown in Figure 20-1 provides links to three other cleanup programs of Windows. Its two "Clean up" buttons take you to the "Uninstall or change a program" window (which lets you delete programs you no longer want) and to a confirmation box that lets you delete all but the latest *restore point,* described in Chapter 22.

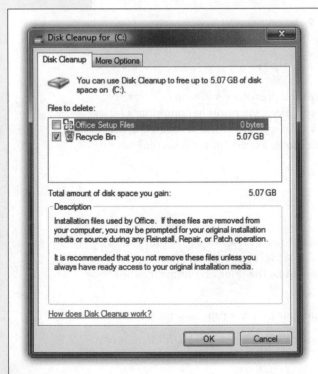

Figure 20-1:
Disk Cleanup announces how much free space you stand to gain. Links on the More Options tab lead to several uninstall functions, for quick removal of programs and restore points.

Disk Defragmenter

All Versions

When you save a new file, Windows records its information onto the hard drive in small pieces called *blocks*. On a new PC, Windows lays the blocks end-to-end on the hard drive surface. Later, when you type more data into a document (thus enlarging it), the file no longer fits in the same space. Windows puts as much of the file in the original location as can fit, but may have to store a few of its blocks in the next empty spot on the hard drive.

Ordinarily, you'll never even notice that your files are getting chopped up in this way, since they open promptly and seamlessly. Windows keeps track of where it has stored the various pieces, and reconstitutes them when necessary.

As your drive fills up, though, the free space that's left is made up of smaller and smaller groups of blocks. Eventually, a new file may not fit in a single "parking place" on the hard drive surface, since there are no free spaces left that are large enough to hold it. Windows may have to store a file in several different areas of the disk, or even hundreds.

When you later try to open such a *fragmented* file, the drive heads (which read the disk) must scamper all over the disk surface, rounding up each block in turn, which is slower than reading contiguous blocks one after the other. Over time, this *file fragmentation* gets worse and worse. Eventually, you wind up griping to your buddies or spouse that you need a new computer, because this one seems to have gotten *so slow*.

The solution: Disk Defragmenter, a program that puts together pieces of files that have become fragmented (split into pieces) on your drive. The "defragger" also rearranges the files on your drives to make the operating system and programs load more quickly. A freshly defragged PC feels faster and more responsive than a heavily fragmented one.

The big news in Windows Vista is that its disk-defragging software runs *automatically* at regular intervals, in the tiny moments when you're not actually typing or clicking. It's like having someone take out your garbage for you whenever the can is full. Slow-PC syndrome should, therefore, be a much less frequent occurrence.

Tip: Fragmentation doesn't become noticeable except on hard drives that have been very full for quite a while. Don't bother defragmenting your drive unless you've actually noticed it slowing down. The time you'll spend waiting for Disk Defragmenter to do its job is much longer than the fractions of seconds caused by a little bit of file fragmentation.

Defragging Settings

Even though Vista defrags your hard drive automatically in the background, you can still exert some control. For example, you can change the schedule, and you can trigger a defragmentation manually when you're feeling like a control freak.

Start by opening the Disk Defragmenter main screen, using any of these techniques:

- Choose Start→Control Panel. Click System and Maintenance→"Defragment your hard drive." (That last link is at the bottom of the window, under the Administrative Tools heading.)

- Right-click the icon of a hard drive in Windows Explorer; from the shortcut menu, choose Properties. In the Properties window, click the Tools tab, and then click Defragment Now.

Note: The button may say Defragment Now, but it won't actually start defragmenting when you click the button. You'll first pay a visit to the main Disk Defragmenter screen.

- In the Start menu's search box, or at a command prompt, type *dfrgui.exe* and press Enter.

Tip: Throughout Windows, and throughout its book and magazine literature, disks are referred to as *volumes.* Usually, volume means disk. But technically, it refers to *anything with its own disk icon* in the Computer window—including disk *partitions* (page 601), DVDs, and so on.

You're asked to authenticate yourself (page 191), and then the Disk Defragmenter window opens (Figure 20-2). From here, you can either adjust the schedule or trigger defragmentation manually.

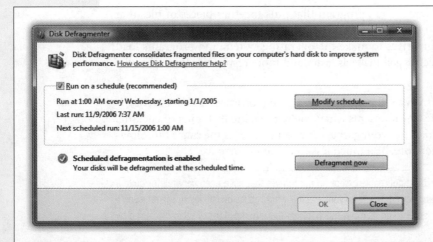

Figure 20-2:
Unless there's a good reason you don't want to schedule defragmentation, it's a good idea to have Windows do it for you automatically—it's like getting someone to take out your trash.

Beyond Disk Defragmenter

Disk Defragmenter isn't the only tool for the defrag job; the world is full of disk-defragmenting programs that offer additional features.

For example, some of them track how often you use the various files on your drive, so they can store the most frequently used files at the beginning of the disk for quicker access. In some programs, you can even *choose* which files go at the beginning of the disk.

Do these additional features actually produce a measurable improvement over Windows Vista's built-in defragger? That's hard to say, especially when you remember the biggest advantage of Disk Defragmenter—it's free.

- Adjust the schedule. Click Modify Schedule. A screen appears, showing that Vista ordinarily defrags your disk late every Tuesday night (1:00 a.m., in fact). You can use the pop-up menus here to specify a Weekly, Daily, or Monthly schedule, complete with day-of-week and time-of-day options. Click OK and then OK again.

- Manually. Click Defragment Now; the defragmenter does its work. Depending on the size of your hard disk, your processor speed, and the amount of fragmentation, it will take anywhere from several minutes to several hours.

Tip: During the defragmentation process, Windows picks up pieces of your files and temporarily sets them down in a different spot, like somebody trying to solve a jigsaw puzzle. If your hard drive is very full, defragmenting will take a lot longer than if you have some empty space available—and if there's less than 15 percent free, Windows can't do the job completely. Before you run Disk Defragmenter, use Disk Cleanup and make as much free disk space as possible.

Hard Drive Checkups
All Versions

Every time you shut down the computer, Windows tidies up, ensuring all files are saved properly on the drive. When all is well, Windows turns off the machine. (All Vista-compatible PCs can turn themselves off; the days of messages telling you that, "It is now safe to turn off your computer" are over.) The time that elapses between your Turn Off Computer command and the actual power-down moment is the "tidying up" period.

But sometimes, thanks to a system crash, power outage, or toddler playing with your surge suppressor, your computer gets turned off without warning—and without the usual shutdown checks. In the olden days, way back even before Windows XP, restarting the PC after such a *dirty shutdown* automatically ran a program called ScanDisk, a utility designed to detect and, when possible, repair drive damage that may have occurred as a result of an improper shutdown.

ScanDisk doesn't exist in Windows Vista, but its functions have been reincarnated. You get to this feature by right-clicking the icon of the hard drive you want to check (in the Computer window). From the shortcut menu, choose Properties; click the Tools tab, and click Check Now. Authenticate yourself (page 191).

Note: Geeks fondly refer to the feature described here as *chkdsk* (apparently named by someone with no vowels on his keyboard). You can also get to it by typing *chkdsk* into the Start menu's Search box. But the method described here is much better-looking.

As shown in Figure 20-3, a box appears, offering two options:

- **Automatically fix file system errors.** Clearly, you want this option turned on, so that any problems Windows finds are taken care of automatically.

Note: Even though the button you clicked was called Check Now, Vista cannot, in fact, check for errors now; that'd be like a surgeon operating on herself. When you click Start, a message cheerfully informs you that Windows will be happy to run this error check the next time it starts up. And indeed it will. Click "Schedule disk check" to make it so.

Figure 20-3:
Checking your disk for errors regularly will go a long way toward making sure that your files won't get corrupted. If you use the "fix file errors" option, the check occurs at the next startup; the "scan" option goes into effect immediately.

• **Scan for and attempt recovery of bad sectors.** If you turn on this option, whenever the scan finds a damaged section of a drive, it moves any files located there elsewhere on the drive. Then the program surrounds that hard-disk area with the

---

FREQUENTLY ASKED QUESTION

When Good Drives Go Bad

I was surprised when the Check Disk dialog box found some problems with my hard drive. I don't understand what could have gone wrong. I treat my PC with respect, talk to it often, and never take it swimming. Why did my hard drive get flaky?

All kinds of things can cause problems with your hard drive, but the most common are low voltage, power outages, voltage spikes, and mechanical problems with the drive controller or the drive itself.

An inexpensive gadget called a *line conditioner* (sold at computer stores) can solve the low-voltage problem. A more expensive gizmo known as an *Uninterruptible Power Supply* (UPS) maintains enough backup battery power to keep your computer going when the power goes out completely—for a few minutes, anyway, so that you can shut down the computer properly. The more expensive models have line

conditioning built in. A UPS is also the answer to power outages, if they're common in your area.

Voltage spikes are the most dangerous to your PC. They frequently occur during the first seconds when the power comes back on after a power failure. A surge suppressor is the logical defense here. But remember that the very cheap devices often sold as surge suppressors are actually little more than extension cords. Furthermore, some of the models that do provide adequate protection are designed to sacrifice themselves in battle. After a spike, you may have to replace them.

If you care about your computer (or the money you spent on it), buy a good surge suppressor, at the very least. The best ones come with a guarantee that the company will replace your equipment (up to a certain dollar value) if the unit fails to provide adequate protection.

digital equivalent of a yellow "Police Line—Do Not Cross" tape, so that Windows won't use the damaged area for storing files in the future.

When you've made your choice, click Start. If you selected only the "Scan" option, the procedure begins immediately; otherwise, the test is performed at the next startup.

Disk Management
All Versions

"Disk management" isn't just a cool, professional-sounding skill—it's the name of a built-in Windows maintenance program that lets you perform all kinds of operations on your hard disk.

To open this technical database of information about your disks and drives, you can use either of these two methods:

- Choose Start→Control Panel. Click System and Maintenance→"Create and format hard disk partitions." (It's at the very bottom of the window.)

- In the Start menu's Search box or at a command prompt, type *diskmgmt.msc* and then press Enter.

In either case, you arrive at the window shown in Figure 20-4. At first glance, it appears to be nothing more than a table of every disk (and *partition* of every disk) currently connected to your PC. In truth, the Disk Management window is a software toolkit that lets you *operate* on these drives.

Figure 20-4:
The Drive Management window does more than just display your drives; you can also operate on them by right-clicking them. Don't miss the View menu, by the way, which lets you change either the top or the bottom display. For example, you can make them display all of your disks instead of your volumes. (There's a difference; see page 622.)

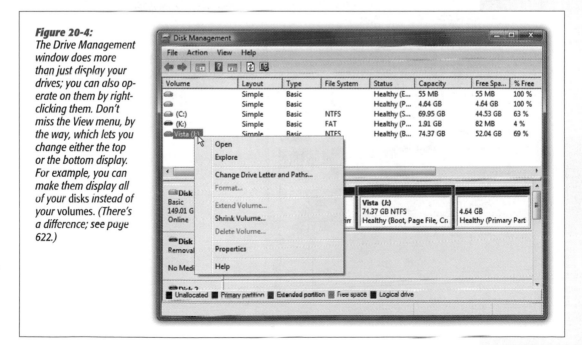

Change a Drive Letter

As you've probably noticed, Windows assigns a drive letter to each disk drive associated with your PC. In the age of floppy disks, the floppy drive was always A:. The primary internal hard drive is generally C:; your CD/DVD drive may be D: or E:; and so on. Among other places, you see these letters in parentheses following the names of your drives in the Start→Computer window.

Windows generally assigns these letters in the order that you install new drives to your system. You're not allowed to change the drive letter of the floppy drive or any startup hard drive (the C: drive and, if you're set up for dual booting, any other boot drives). You can, however, override the *other* drives' unimaginative Windows letter assignments easily enough, as shown in Figure 20-5.

Note: If Windows Vista is currently using files on the disk whose drive letter you're trying to change, Disk Management might create the new drive letter assignment but leave the old one intact until the next time you restart the computer. This is an effort not to pull the rug out from under any open files.

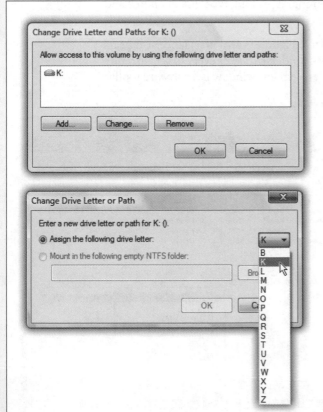

Figure 20-5:
Right-click a drive icon. From the shortcut menu, choose Change Drive Letter and Paths.

Top: In this dialog box, click Change.

Bottom: Next, choose a letter that hasn't already been assigned. Click OK, and then approve your action in the confirmation box.

Partition a New Drive

The vast majority of Windows PCs have only one hard drive, represented in the Computer window as a single icon.

Plenty of power users, however, delight in *partitioning* the hard drive—dividing its surface so that it appears on the screen as two different icons with two different names. At that point, you can live like a king, enjoying the following advantages just like people who have two separate hard drives:

- You can keep Windows Vista on one of them and Windows XP (for example) on the other, so that you can switch between the two at startup time. (This feature, called *dual booting,* is described on page 623.)

- Two partitions make life much easier if you frequently install and reinstall the operating system, or different versions of it. Doing so allows you to keep all your files safely on one partition, confining all the installing/uninstalling activity to the other.

- You can use multiple partitions to keep your operating system(s) separate from folders and files. In this way, you can perform a *clean install* of Windows (page 779) onto one partition without having to worry about losing any of your important files or installation programs.

Now, until Vista came along, partitioning a hard drive using the tools built into Windows required first erasing the hard drive completely. Fortunately, Vista's new Disk Management console (page 601) can save you from that hassle, although making a backup before you begin is still a smart idea. (The short version: Right-click the disk's icon in Disk Management; from the shortcut menu, choose Shrink Volume. In the Shrink dialog box, specify how much space you want to free up, and then click Shrink. Then turn the free space into a new volume, as described next.)

Creating a partition

In the Disk Management window, free space (suitable for turning into a partition of its own) shows up with a black bar and the label Unallocated.

To create a new partition, right-click one of these unallocated segments. From the shortcut menu, choose New Partition. A wizard appears; its screens ask you:

- **What kind of partition you want to create.** (You'll usually want Primary.)

- **How big you want the partition to be.** If you're dividing up a 120 GB drive, for example, you might decide to make the first partition 40 GB and the second 80 GB. Begin by creating the 40 GB partition (right-clicking the big "Unallocated" bar in Figure 20-4). When that's done, you'll see a smaller "Unallocated" chunk still left in the Disk Management window. Right-click it and choose New Partition *again,* this time accepting the partition size the wizard proposes (which is *all* the remaining free space).

- **What drive letter you want to assign to it.** Most of the alphabet is at your disposal.

- **What disk-formatting scheme you want to apply to it.** Windows Vista requires NTFS. But if you're just using the drive to store data (and not to contain a copy of Windows Vista), the old FAT32 format is fine. In fact, if you plan to dual-boot Vista with Linux, Mac OS X, or an old version of Windows, FAT32 might be the only file system that all of those OSes can recognize simultaneously.

When the wizard is through with you, it's safe to close the window. A quick look at your Computer window will confirm that you now have new "disks" (actually partitions of the same disk), which you can use for different purposes.

Turn a Drive into a Folder

Talk about techie! Most people could go their entire lives without needing this feature, or even imagining that it exists. But it's there if you're a power user and you want it.

Using the Paths feature of Disk Management, you can actually turn a hard drive (or partition) into a *folder* on another hard drive (or partition). Each of these disks-disguised-as-folders is technically known as a *mounted drive, junction point,* or *drive path.*

This arrangement affords the following unique possibilities:

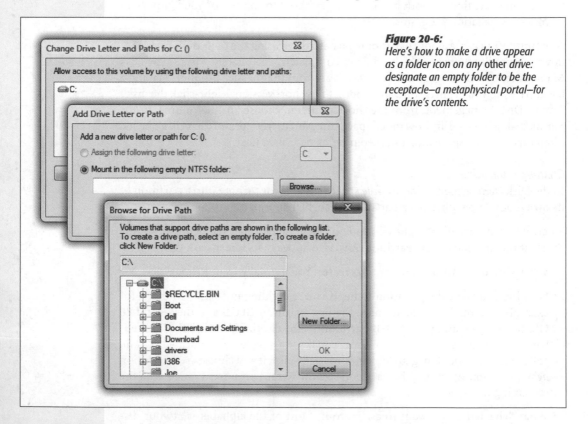

Figure 20-6:
Here's how to make a drive appear as a folder icon on any other drive: designate an empty folder to be the receptacle—a metaphysical portal—for the drive's contents.

- In effect, you can greatly expand the capacity of your main hard drive—by installing a second hard drive that masquerades as a folder on the first one.

- You can turn a burned CD or DVD into a folder on your main hard drive, too—a handy way to fool your programs into thinking that the files they're looking for are still in the same old place on your hard drive. (You could pull this stunt in a crisis—when the "real" folder has become corrupted or has been thrown away.)

- If you're a *power* power user with lots of partitions, disks, and drives, you may feel hemmed in by the limitation of only 26 assignable letters (A through Z). Turning one of your disks into a mounted volume bypasses that limitation, because a mounted volume doesn't need a drive letter at all.

- A certain disk can be made to appear in more than one place at once. You could put all your MP3 files on a certain disk or partition—and then make it show up as a folder in the Music folder of everyone who uses the computer.

Note: You can only create a mounted volume on an *NTFS-formatted* hard drive.

To bring about this arrangement, visit the Disk Management window, and then right-click the icon of the disk or partition that you want to turn into a mounted volume. From the shortcut menu, choose Change Drive Letter and Paths.

In the Change Drive Letter and Paths dialog box, click Add (Figure 20-6, top); in the next dialog box, click Browse. Navigate to and select an empty folder—the one that will represent the disk. (Click New Folder, shown at right in Figure 20-6, if you didn't create one in advance.) Finally, click OK.

Once the deed is done, take time to note a few special characteristics of a mounted volume:

- The mounted volume may behave just like a folder, but its icon is a dead giveaway, since it still looks like a hard drive (or CD drive, or DVD drive, or whatever).

  Still, if you're in doubt about what it is, you can right-click it and choose Properties from the shortcut menu. You'll see that the Type information says "Mounted Volume," and the Target line identifies the disk from which it was made.

- Avoid circular references, in which you turn two drives into folders on *each other*. Otherwise, you risk throwing programs into a spasm of infinite-loop thrashing.

- To undo your mounted-drive effect, return to the Disk Management program and choose View→Drive Paths. You're shown a list of all the drives you've turned into folders; click one and then click Remove.

  You've just turned that special, "I'm really a drive" folder into an ordinary empty folder.

Task Scheduler

All Versions

The Task Scheduler, another power-user trick for techies, lets you set up programs and tasks (like disk defragmentation) so they run automatically according to a schedule that you specify.

Figure 20-7:
It's easy to automate many different kinds of tasks using the Task Scheduler, but when you open it, don't be surprised to see many tasks there already. Windows Vista does a lot of housekeeping work in the background, and uses the Task Scheduler to run a lot of tasks without you having to know the details.

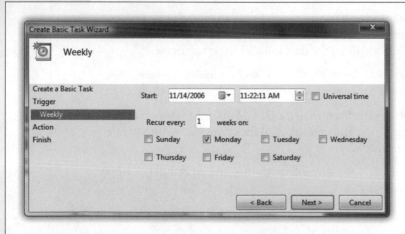

Figure 20-8:
This screen lets you set a schedule for your task. Depending on the trigger you set, you may see a completely different screen here, because the options are determined by the trigger you choose.

This feature has been greatly beefed up and user-friendlified in Vista, to the point that both mere mortals and power geeks may actually find it useful. For example:

- Create an email message that gets sent to your boss each morning, with yesterday's sales figures attached automatically.

- Have the Recycle Bin emptied automatically once a month.

- Create a phony dialog box that appears every time the office know-it-all's PC starts up. Make it say: "The radiation shield on your PC has failed. Please keep back seven feet." You get the idea.

Adding a Task

Here's how you add a new task:

1. **Open the Task Scheduler (Figure 20-7).**

   One way to get there is to choose Start→Control Panel. Click System and Maintenance, then Schedule Tasks (which appears at the bottom of the window). Authenticate yourself (page 191).

2. **Click Create Basic Task.**

   This link appears on the right-hand pane of the Task Scheduler. A wizard appears.

3. **Type a name for the task and a description, and then click Next.**

   Now you're supposed to choose what Windows Vista calls a "trigger"—in plain English, when to run the task (Figure 20-8). You can specify that it run daily, weekly, monthly, or just once; every time the computer starts or every time you log in; or when a specific event occurs—like when a program starts.

4. **Choose a trigger and then click Next.**

   The next screen varies according to the trigger you chose. If you chose to run the task on a daily, weekly, or monthly basis, you're now asked to specify *when* during that day, week, or month. Once that's done, click Next.

   You now wind up at the Action screen. This is where you'll say *what* you want to happen at the appointed time. Your choices are "Start a program," "Send an e-mail," or "Display a message."

5. **Choose an action; click Next.**

   Now you're supposed to say *what* program, email, or message you want the PC to fire up.

   If you chose the email option, you now fill out a form with the recipient's name, address, subject line, message body, and so on; you can even specify an attachment.

   If you chose to run a program, you now browse to select the program. At this point, programmers can also add *arguments*, which are codes that customize how the program starts.

And if you opted to display a message, you get to type a name and text for the message. At the appointed time, an actual Windows dialog box will appear on the screen—except that it will contain text that *you* wrote.

6. **Complete the details about the email, program, or phony dialog box, and then click Next.**

Finally, a screen appears, summarizing the task, when it will run, and so on. To edit it, click the Back button.

7. **To confirm the automated task, click Finish.**

You return to the Task Scheduler window. Although you may have to scroll down to see it, your new task appears in the Active Tasks list at the bottom of the window. If all goes well, Vista will fire it up at the moment you specified.

Editing Scheduled Tasks

To change a scheduled task, you first need to find it in Task Scheduler Library, which is on the left side of the window. Click Task Scheduler Library, and then look at the topmost pane in the middle part of your screen (Figure 20-9). You'll see a list of scheduled tasks. Highlight the one you want to change.

Delete the task by simply hitting the Delete key. To edit a task, click it and then click the Properties link at the right side of the screen. The tabs in the resulting dialog box (General, Triggers, and so on) may sound familiar, but they actually give you far more control over how each task runs than the basic controls you saw when you first set the task up.

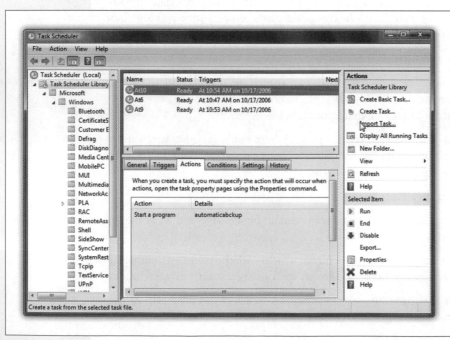

Figure 20-9:
This screen lets you do more than just edit a task. Look at the right-hand pane; you'll see links that let you run the task right now, end the task if it's already started, and disable the task, among others.

Here are some examples of what you can do on each tab:

- **General.** Select which user account should run the task, and tell Windows whether or not to run when the user is logged in.

- **Triggers.** You can delay the task's execution by a few minutes or until a certain date; have it repeat automatically at regular intervals; stop it after a certain time period; and so on. The "Begin the task" pop-up menu offers a wealth of new triggers, like "On idle" and "On workstation unlock."

- **Actions.** Change the action.

- **Conditions.** Specify that the task will run only under certain conditions—for example, after the computer has been idle for a certain amount of time, when the computer is on AC power, or when it switches to battery power, and so on. You can even say that you want to run the task if the PC is sleeping (by waking it first).

- **Settings.** Here's a miscellaneous batch of additional preferences: what actions to take if the task doesn't work, what to do if the computer was turned off at the appointed time, and so on.

- **History.** On this tab, you get to see the task's life story: when it ran and whether each attempt was successful.

Note: Lots of tasks are already present on your PC. Microsoft set them up to ensure the proper running of your computer. To see them all, expand the flippy triangle next to the words Task Schedules Library, and then expand Microsoft, and then Windows. You'll see dozens of tasks in many different categories. In other words, your PC is very busy even when you're not there.

Four Speed Tricks
All Versions

It's a fact of computing. Every PC seems to get slower the longer you own it.

There are plenty of reasons, mostly having to do with the fact that a computer is fastest when it's new and empty:

- The hard drive has loads of free space and zero fragmentation (page 596).

- The boot process hasn't yet been cluttered up by startup code deposited by your programs.

- Few background programs are constantly running, eating up your memory.

- You haven't yet drained away horsepower with antivirus and automatic backup programs.

- Every year, the programs you buy or download are more demanding than the previous year's software.

Some of the usual advice about speeding up your PC applies here, of course: install more memory or a faster hard drive.

But in Windows Vista, here and there, nestled among the 50 million lines of Vista code, you'll find some *free* tricks and tips for giving your PC a speed boost. For example:

SuperFetch

Your PC can grab data from RAM (memory) hundreds of times faster than from the hard drive. That's why it uses a *cache,* a portion of memory that holds bits of software code that you've used recently. After all, if you've used some feature or command once, you may want to use it again soon—and this way, Windows is ready for you. It can deliver that bit of code nearly instantaneously the next time.

When you leave your PC for a while, however, background programs (virus checkers, backup programs, disk utilities) take advantage of the idle time. They run themselves when you're not around—and push out whatever was in the cache.

That's why, when you come back from lunch (or sit down first thing in the morning), your PC is especially sluggish. All the good stuff—*your* stuff—has been flushed from the cache and returned to the much slower hard drive, to make room for those background utilities.

SuperFetch attempts to reverse that cycle. It attempts to keep your most frequently used programs in the cache all the time. In fact, it actually *tracks you* and your cycle of work. If you generally fire up the computer at 9 a.m., for example, or return to it at 1:30 p.m., SuperFetch will anticipate you by restoring frequently used programs and documents to the cache.

There's no on/off switch for SuperFetch, and nothing for you to configure. It's on all the time, automatic, and very sweet.

ReadyBoost

Your PC can get to data in RAM (memory) hundreds of times faster than it can fetch something from the hard drive. That's why it uses a *cache,* a portion of memory that holds bits of software code that you've used recently. (Does this paragraph sound familiar?)

The more memory your machine has, the more that's available for the cache, and the faster things should feel to you. Truth is, though, you may have a bunch of memory sitting around your desk at this moment that's *completely wasted*—namely, USB flash drives. That's perfectly good RAM that your PC can't even touch if it's sitting in a drawer.

Note: ReadyBoost can also work with memory cards, like SD and Compact Flash cards from digital cameras—but *only if* your PC has a built-in card slot. External card readers don't work. (All of the descriptions below apply equally to these memory cards.)

PlaysForSure music players don't work, either—although Apple's iPod Shuffle does!

That's the whole point of ReadyBoost: to use a flash drive as described above as additional cache storage. You can achieve the same effect by installing more RAM, of course, but that job can be technical (especially on laptops), forbidden (by your corporate masters), or impossible (because you've used up all your PC's RAM slots already).

Note: You won't run into problems if you yank out the flash drive; ReadyBoost stores a *copy* of the hard drive's data on the card/flash drive.

You also don't have to worry that somebody can steal your flash drive and, by snooping around the cache files, read about your top-secret plans for world domination. Vista encrypts the data using CIA-quality algorithms.

To take advantage of this speed-boosting feature, just plug a USB flash drive into your computer's USB jack.

Note: Both the flash drive *and* your PC must have USB 2.0 or later. USB 1.1 is too slow for this trick to work.

In any case, the AutoPlay dialog box now opens, as shown in Figure 20-10 (top). Click "Speed up my system"; in the flash device's Properties dialog box (which opens automatically), turn on "Use this device." That box is shown in Figure 20-10, bottom.

That's all there is to it. Your PC will now use the flash drive as an annex to its own built-in RAM, and you will, in theory, enjoy a tiny speed lift as a result.

And now, the fine print:

- Not all flash drives are equally fast, and therefore not all work with ReadyBoost. Look closely at the drive's packaging to see if there's a Vista ReadyBoost logo. (Technically speaking—very technically—its throughput must be capable of 2.5 MB per second for 4 K random reads, and 1.75 MB per second for 512 K random writes.)

- ReadyBoost works only with memory gadgets with capacities from 256 megabytes to 4 gigabytes.

- Vista makes its own suggestions about how much of the drive's capacity to dedicate to ReadyBoost; but if you're the meddlesome type, you can return to the dialog box shown at bottom in Figure 20-10 and change how much of it is used for cache storage. Open Start→Computer and right-click the flash drive's icon. From the shortcut menu, choose Properties. Click the ReadyBoost tab, and configure away (Figure 20-10).

- Once you've set aside space on the flash drive for ReadyBoost, you can't use it for storing everyday files. (Unless, of course, you change the settings in its Properties dialog box or reformat it.)

- You can use one flash drive per PC, and one PC per flash drive.

- Ordinarily, saving files and then erasing them over and over again shortens a flash drive's life. Microsoft insists, however, that you can get 10 years out of one flash drive using ReadyBoost.

- The biggest speed gains appear when you have a 1-to-1 ratio between real PC memory and your flash drive. For example, if your PC has 1 gigabyte of RAM, adding a 1-gig flash drive should give you a noticeable speed boost.

The speed gains evaporate as you approach a 2.5-to-1 ratio. For example, suppose your PC has 1 gigabyte of RAM and you add a 256-megabyte flash drive. That's an 8-to-1 ratio, and you won't feel any acceleration at all.

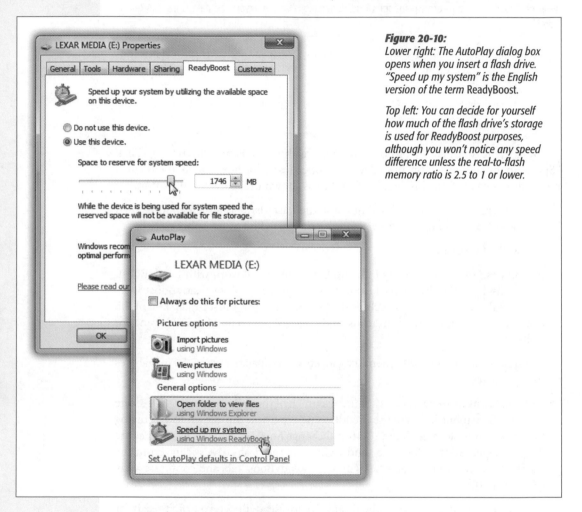

Figure 20-10:
Lower right: The AutoPlay dialog box opens when you insert a flash drive. "Speed up my system" is the English version of the term ReadyBoost.

Top left: You can decide for yourself how much of the flash drive's storage is used for ReadyBoost purposes, although you won't notice any speed difference unless the real-to-flash memory ratio is 2.5 to 1 or lower.

Shutting Off Bells and Whistles

Vista, as you know, is all dressed up for "Where do you want to go today?" It's loaded with glitz, glamour, special effects, and animations. And every one of them saps away a little bit of speed.

With any luck, your PC is a mighty fortress of seething gigahertz that brushes off that kind of resource-sapping as though it were a mere cloud of gnats. But when things start to bog down, remember that you can turn off some of the bells and whistles—and recover the speed they were using.

Here's how.

Open the Start menu. Right-click Computer; from the shortcut menu, choose Properties. In the System control panel that appears, click "Advanced system settings" at left. Authenticate yourself (page 191).

Now, on the Advanced tab (Figure 20-11, top), click the uppermost Settings button. You've just found, in the belly of the beast, the complete list of the little animations that make up Vista's Windows dressing (Figure 20-11, bottom). For example, "Animate windows when minimizing and maximizing" makes Windows present a half-second animation showing your window actually shrinking down onto the taskbar when you minimize it. "Show shadows under mouse pointer" produces a tiny shadow beneath your cursor, as though it were floating a quarter-inch above the surface of your screen.

With one click—on "Adjust for best performance"— you can turn off all of these effects. Or, if there are some you can't live without—and let's face it, tooltips just aren't the same if they don't *fade* into view—click Custom, and then turn off the individual checkboxes for the features you don't need.

Toning Down the Aero

Aero is the new visual look of Windows Vista, but the power for its visual effects—drop shadows, transparency, glitz—doesn't grow on trees. If you can do without some of it, you gain another itty-bitty speed boost. See page 161 for instructions.

UP TO SPEED

Windows ReadyDrive

Microsoft's speed-boosting features seem to be in such a hurry, the programmers didn't even have time to hit the Space bar when naming them (ReadyBoost, SuperFetch). And here's another one: ReadyDrive.

Windows Vista comes ready for a new kind of hard drive: a *hybrid* hard drive, co-designed with Samsung, that, in addition to the usual spinning platters, also contain a chunk of RAM. (It's *nonvolatile flash memory,* meaning that—unlike the memory in your PC—it doesn't die when the power goes off.)

Hybrid hard drives bless you with three advantages:

Save battery power. Windows stores your data in the drive's flash memory, so the hard drive doesn't have to use power by spinning up.

Wake up faster. A hybrid-drive laptop also wakes from Sleep almost instantly—again, because its memory is much faster than its hard drive.

Protect the hard drive. Flash memory has no moving parts, so it doesn't care if your laptop gets jostled in the middle of saving a file. As a result, hybrid drives are less prone to hard drive damage.

Now then, back to the question—what, exactly, is ReadyDrive? That's Microsoft's name for the Vista technology that takes advantage of the new age of hybrid hard drives. At this writing, nobody knows if or when hybrid hard drives will catch on. But when they do, Vista will be ready.

Windows Update

All Versions

Windows Vista is far more secure than previous versions of Windows, but you may have noticed that Microsoft isn't going so far as to say, "You don't need an antivirus program anymore." The hackers will have a *much* harder time of it, but with 50 million lines of code to explore, they're sure to break in somehow.

Microsoft and other security researchers constantly find new security holes—and as soon as they're found, Microsoft rushes a patch out the door to fix it. But creating a patch is one thing; actually getting that patch installed on multiple millions of copies of Windows Vista around the world is another thing entirely.

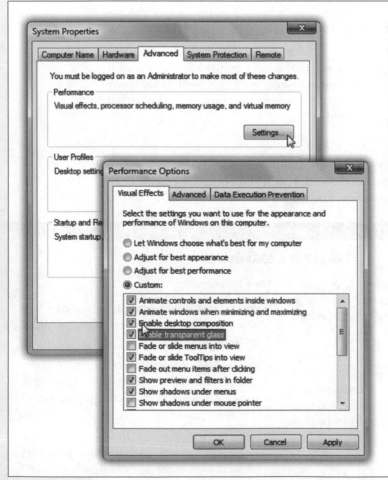

Figure 20-11:
Top left: The Advanced tab of the System Properties dialog box offers three Settings buttons. The one you want is at the top.

Bottom right: Depending on the speed and age of your machine, you may find that turning off all of these checkboxes produces a snappier, more responsive PC–if a bit less Macintosh-esque. (Leave "Use visual styles on windows and buttons" turned on, however, if you like the new, glossy look of Windows Vista.)

Note: In fact, it's Microsoft's *patches* that usually alert hackers to the presence of the security hole in the first place! They exploit the fact that not everyone has the patch in place instantly. (Which brings up the question: should Microsoft even be creating the patches? But that's another conversation.)

That's where Windows Update comes in. When Microsoft releases a security fix, it gets delivered straight to your PC and automatically installed. (If you want, you can first review the fix before installing it, although few people have enough knowledge to judge its value.)

In Vista, Windows Update's job has been expanded. It doesn't just deliver patches to Windows itself; it can also send you better drivers for your hardware and patches to other Microsoft products, notably Office.

If you bought a PC with Windows Vista already on it, Windows Update has already been turned on. And if you upgraded to Windows Vista, you were asked a series of questions about how you wanted Windows Update to work, although you may have forgotten by now.

FREQUENTLY ASKED QUESTION

Moving Virtual Memory

So how do you move the virtual memory swap file for more speed?

Well, you don't, really.

Virtual memory is a trick that computers use to keep a lot of programs open at once—more, in fact, than they technically have enough memory (RAM) for. How do they manage keeping so many software balls in the air? Easy—they set some of them down on the hard drive.

When you bring Photoshop to the front, for example, Windows frees up the necessary memory for it by storing some of the *background* programs' code on the hard drive. When you switch back to, say, Microsoft Word, Windows swaps Photoshop for the Word code it needs from the hard drive, so that the frontmost program always has full command of your actual memory.

In the days of yore, power geeks argued that you could eke out a little extra speed by relocating this setting-down area—the *swap file*—to another hard drive. A clean, fast, dedicated drive, for example.

These days, though, that's a lot of effort for very little noticeable speed boost, if any. Today's hard drives are a lot faster than they once were, and a lot better at handling multiple simultaneous requests for data.

Anyone who really wants to move the swap file to a different drive is probably the kind of power user who'd go whole hog, adding a RAID 0 or RAID 0+1 hard drive setup (and if you know what that is, you're enough of a techie to know how to set it up). That would speed up a lot of other aspects of the PC, too.

If you're still determined to move the swap file, though, you can do it. Open the System Properties dialog box. (Right-click Computer in the Start menu; choose Properties.) Click "Advanced system settings." Click the Advanced tab.

In the Performance section, click Settings. In the next dialog box, click the Advanced tab. (Are you getting the idea that this is an *advanced* technique?) Under "Virtual memory," click Change.

Turn off "Automatically manage paging size for all drives," highlight the new destination hard drive for the swap file, and click OK.

Fiddling with Windows Update

To adjust Windows Update, choose Start→Control Panel. Click System and Maintenance→Windows Update. If there are any available updates that you haven't yet installed, you'll see them here (Figure 20-12).

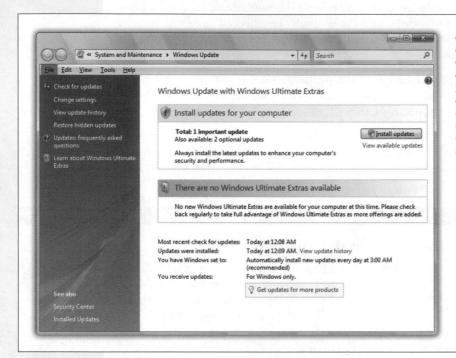

Figure 20-12:
If there are any available updates that you haven't yet installed, you can install them by clicking "Install updates." To get details about an update, click "View available updates."

If you click Change settings, the screen pictured in Figure 20-13 appears. The four options here correspond to four levels of trust people have in Microsoft, the mother ship:

- **Install updates automatically (recommended).** Translation: "Download and install all patches automatically. We trust in thee, Microsoft, that thou knowest what thou do-est." (All of this will take place in the middle of the night—or according to whatever schedule you set on this screen—so as not to inconvenience you.)

- **Download updates but let me choose whether to install them.** The downloading takes place in the background, and doesn't interfere with anything you're downloading for yourself. But instead of installing the newly downloaded patch, Windows asks your permission.

- **Check for updates but let me choose whether to download and install them.** When Windows detects that a patch has become available, a note pops up from your system tray, telling you that an update is available. Click the icon in the system tray to indicate which updates to download and then install.

- **Never check for updates (Not recommended). Microsoft** will leave your copy of Windows completely alone—and completely vulnerable to attacks from the Internet.

Microsoft hates when people choose anything but the first option, because it leaves you potentially open to security holes. On the other hand, patches have sometimes been known to be a bit buggy, so some people like to do a Google search on any new patch before installing it.

Figure 20-13:
Windows Vista's auto-update feature can ask that you be notified either before the software patch is downloaded (third choice) or after it's been downloaded and is ready to install (second choice). You can also permit the updates to be updated and then installed automatically, on a schedule that you specify (top choice).

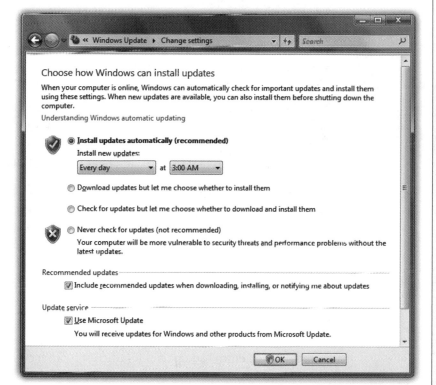

DON'T PANIC

What Ever Happened to the Windows Update Sites?

In previous versions of Windows, you could forgo automatic updates entirely, and instead get your updates via Microsoft's Windows Update site. You'd get there via *http://windowsupdate.microsoft.com,* or by choosing Start→All Programs→Windows Update.

But if you try these tactics in Windows Vista, you'll head to a Web site–that just opens the Windows Update screen on your PC. Updates via the Web site are a thing of the past; it's all done on your PC now.

Notice, at the bottom of Figure 20-13, that there are two sections, one for Recommended updates, and one for Update service. A *recommended update*, in Microsoft lingo, is an update that isn't required to keep your PC safe or to keep your operating system from blowing up, but that can solve "non-critical problems and help enhance your computing experience." That's usually an updated driver or a Windows bug fix or feature enhancement. Turn on Recommended updates if you want them to be included in Windows Update.

The *Update service* section delivers updates for other Microsoft software on your PC, notably Microsoft Office.

Beyond the Basics

There's a lot more to Windows Update than these basics, though. You can take a look at all the updates installed on your PC, for example, and you can even uninstall an update. And you can also restore the mysterious-sounding "hidden updates."

To begin, get back to the screen shown in Figure 20-12. (Choose Control Panel→System and Maintenance→Windows Update to get there.) The left side of the screen includes these links:

- **Check for updates** checks for updates right now, and installs them, if you want.

- **Change settings** works as described earlier.

- **View update history** shows you a list of all the updates that have been downloaded and installed. You see the date of each update, whether it was successful, the type of update, and its purpose. Double-click one to get more details.

- **Restore hidden updates.** As noted below, you can *hide* an update to get it out of your hair. When you click "Restore hidden updates," they reappear so you can reinstall them.

- **Get updates for more products.** This link, at the bottom of the screen, sends you to the Microsoft Update site; the site then downloads an installer onto your system that lets you download updates for Microsoft products like Office. The installer works right inside Windows Updates, so you'll never have to visit Microsoft Update again.

Removing Updates

If an update winds up making life with your PC worse instead of better, you can remove it. Head to Control Panel→Programs→View Installed Updates, right-click an update, and then select Remove.

Note: You can't remove all updates, however. Security-related updates are usually nonremovable.

There's one problem with this action. The next time Windows Updates does it job, it will *re*install the update you just removed.

The workaround is to *hide* the update so that it doesn't get downloaded and installed again. Open Windows Update, and then click "Check for updates."

After Windows finds updates, click "View available updates." Right-click the update you don't want; select "Hide update." From now on, Windows Update ignores the update.

If, later, you change your mind, click "Restore hidden updates," select the update you want installed, and then click Restore.

The Disk Chapter

Files and folders, as you've probably noticed, have a tendency to multiply. Creating new documents, installing new software, and downloading new files can fill up even the largest disk drives in no time—especially if, as Microsoft fervently hopes, you get heavily into music, pictures, and video.

Fortunately, Vista offers a number of ways to manage and expand the amount of space on your hard drives. You can subdivide your drives' storage into individual partitions (sections), save space using disk compression, encrypt the contents of your drives for security, and so on.

You can skip this entire chapter, if you wish, and get along quite well without using any of these features. They're strictly optional. But if you aspire to wear the Power User T-shirt, read on.

Note: Three of the features described in this chapter—dynamic disks, disk compression, and EFS (encryption file system)—all require the *NTFS file system* on your computer's disk drives. That's probably what you're using on your main hard drive, because Windows Vista requires it.

But other kinds of disks—memory cards, iPods, external USB disks, and so on—probably use the older FAT 32 file system instead. You won't be able to use NTFS tricks on them.

Dynamic Disks
Business • Enterprise • Ultimate

Suppose you've run out of space on the hard drive you use to store movies and music, and you've installed another one to collect the overflow. Thanks to a Windows Vista feature called *dynamic disks,* you don't have to move files to the new drive or reorganize your folder scheme. Instead, you can make the new drive fold its space seamlessly with the first drive's, so you suddenly have more disk space on your "one" combo drive.

If you're working with very large files (like those home movies you spend all your free time editing), you can do something similar; instead of folding one drive into another, you can tell Vista to treat a pair of disks as a single disk.

Windows can then save data onto them in an alternating pattern. This makes everything a lot faster, because Vista doesn't have to wait until the first disk finishes saving a chunk of a file to start saving the next chunk. Instead, it can save (or open) files two chunks at a time, on two disks simultaneously.

Note: Unfortunately, you can't extend your startup drive (the C: drive that contains your Windows Vista installation). If you're running out of disk space on your C: drive, you can move your large documents and media files onto another drive you've installed. You can also save a lot of space by uninstalling large programs from the C: drive, and then reinstalling them on the other drive. (If you do this with a game, though, be sure to back up your saved games when you uninstall and restore them when you reinstall; see the support forums or FAQ for the game before you proceed).

How Dynamic Disks Work

If this setup intrigues you, a bit more technical explanation is required.

When you (or your PC maker) first installed Windows, it configured each drive as a *basic disk*—a disk with its own drive letter. But before you can combine two actual drives into one volume, you must first convert them into a more flexible format that Microsoft calls a *dynamic disk.*

UP TO SPEED

Volumes Defined

You won't get far in this chapter, or at PC user group meetings, without understanding a key piece of Windows terminology: *volume.*

For most people, most of the time, volume means "disk." But technically, there's more to it than that—a distinction that becomes crucial if you explore the techniques described in this chapter.

If you open your Computer window, you'll see that each disk has its own icon and drive letter (C:, for example). But each icon isn't necessarily a separate disk. It's possible that you, or somebody in charge of your PC, has split a single drive into multiple *partitions* (Appendix A), each with a separate icon and drive letter. Clearly, the world needs a term for "an icon/drive letter in the Computer window, whether it's a whole disk or not." That term is *volume.*

With Windows Vista's dynamic disks, you can do more than partition one hard drive into multiple volumes—you can also do the reverse, as described in this chapter. If you've installed more than one hard drive, you can actually request that Windows represent them on the screen as *one* volume. This way, you can have as many hard disk drives in your computer as you want and combine their storage space into a unit, represented by one icon and drive letter.

The good news is that you can convert a basic disk into a dynamic disk without losing any data on the drive. The bad news is that you can't change a dynamic disk *back* to a basic disk unless you erase all of the data stored there.

And why would you want to? Because dynamic disks, for all their flexibility, also have some limitations. Before you proceed with converting basic disks to dynamic disks, assume a reclining position and read the following fine print:

- Once you've combined two physical disks into an über-disk (technically called a *spanned volume*), a fatal problem on *one* of the two hard drives will make you lose all of the data on *both* drives—an event that can ruin your whole morning. Keeping regular backups of your spanned volume is critically important (see Chapter 22).

- Dynamic disks are a specialty of Vista Business, Enterprise, and Ultimate. No other version of Windows can read them (not even other Vista versions).

- A dynamic disk can contain only one operating system. You can't *dual boot* from another partition on a dynamic disk, as you can with basic disks. (Dual booting means choosing which of two operating systems to use each time you turn on the PC.) Since you can't extend your boot drive, it's unlikely that you'd want to turn it into a dynamic disk, but you should keep this limitation in mind if you decide to install another operating system, such as Linux, onto the disks you want to convert to dynamic disks.

Note: You might have a dual-boot system and not even know it. Many manufacturers hide a bootable operating system on the hard drive whose sole purpose is to restore your computer to its original configuration when things go wrong.

For example, Dell puts a copy of MS-DOS on a small partition. If you hold down F11 as the computer is starting up, it launches into DOS, loads Norton Ghost, and uses it to restore your hard drive using files from yet another partition—this time, a hidden 3.5 GB partition.

If you convert your drive to a dynamic disk, you will lose the ability to invoke this rescue mode.

- To convert a hard drive to a dynamic disk, it must set aside an invisible storage area to hold a *dynamic disk database*. If you partitioned the drive using Windows XP Professional or Vista, then Windows already reserved enough space for this purpose. But if the drive was partitioned with another operating system, you may have to erase it before converting it to a dynamic disk.

- Dynamic disks generally don't work on laptops, removable disks, disks connected by USB cables or IEEE 1394 (FireWire) cables, or disks connected to shared SCSI or Fibre Channel buses. If your disks fall into any of these categories, Windows Vista won't let you convert them to dynamic disks.

Extending onto Another Disk

If you've installed a new hard drive, Windows Vista treats it as *unallocated space*—disk space that doesn't belong to any volume yet. It's just sitting there, unaccounted for, unusable, waiting for you to make it part of one volume or another. And whenever you find yourself with unallocated space, you can savor the flexibility of dynamic disks.

If you haven't yet been scared off by the cautions in the previous section, and are ready to extend one of your existing disks onto another, the procedure is simple. First, back up your computer. Tragedy isn't likely to befall you, but it's a good idea to back up before performing any kind of traumatic surgery to the disks in your computer.

Next, log onto the computer as a user with Administrative privileges (page 669), and exit any programs that might be running on the disk you plan to convert.

You convert disks and manage the dynamic volumes on them using a special window called the Disk Management console. To open it, use either of these methods:

- Choose Start→Control Panel→System and Maintenance and scroll down to the Administrative Tools section. Click the "Create and format hard disk partitions" link.

- Type *diskmgmt.msc* into the Start menu's Search box, and then press Enter.

Once this window is before you, you see a display of your drives and the partitions on them, as shown in Figure 21-1.

Note: If you've just installed an additional hard drive, Disk Management notices the next time you start it up. It prompts you to initialize the new disks; select the partition style you want to use. In most cases, you should choose the proposed format, MBR (Master Boot Record, which has been used by Windows and MS-DOS for years). The dialog box will tell you when the other choice, GPT (the newfangled GUID Partition Table, used by PCs that are designed around a replacement for the venerable PC BIOS called EFI), is appropriate. Click OK.

The top part of the window lists the partitions on your computer. The bottom part contains a horizontal box representing each drive on your computer, with smaller boxes inside indicating the partitions on each drive. Notice that the header box for

Extending a Volume

One big advantage of dynamic disks is that you can extend an existing volume whenever you feel like it, just by allocating additional disk space to it. If, for example, you run out of space on a volume you've named Data, and you still have some unallocated space on some other disk, you can simply add it to the Data volume to make it bigger. The unallocated space you specify becomes a permanent part of the Data volume. (Note that this is a one-way trip. Once you've added free space to a dynamic volume, it becomes

part of that volume permanently, or at least until you delete the volume—and its data—and recreate it.)

The disk space you use to extend the volume can come from either the same disk or another dynamic disk (in which case you create a *spanned* volume). Note, though, that you can't extend the *system* volume, nor any volume that was originally a partition created by another operating system.

each drive indicates the number of the drive in your system, its capacity, whether or not it's online, and the word "Basic" (indicating that it's currently a basic disk).

Next, you need to decide how you want to expand the disk. You have a choice between *spanning* and *striping*. You can also choose to create a simple dynamic disk, but that won't let you combine two disks into one.

Tip: You can delete a dynamic volume as easily as you created it. Just right-click it in the Disk Management window and select Delete Volume from the shortcut menu. Doing so deletes the entire volume, erasing all the data on it and removing its space from any spanned or striped space on other disks.

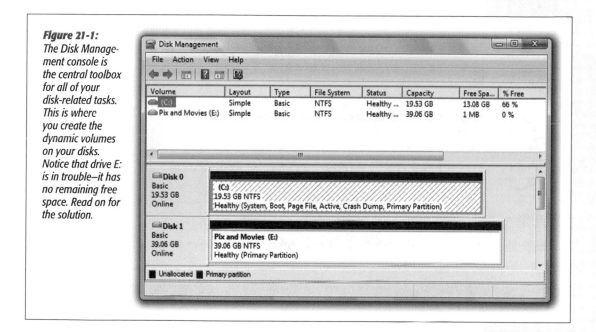

Figure 21-1:
The Disk Management console is the central toolbox for all of your disk-related tasks. This is where you create the dynamic volumes on your disks. Notice that drive E: is in trouble—it has no remaining free space. Read on for the solution.

Here's a rundown of each:

Extending into a spanned volume

Suppose you've managed to shoehorn every byte of data you possibly can onto the hard drive you use for holding video files. You decide to install a second hard drive, to give you more space.

But then what? You don't want to spoil the carefully organized folder structure on your old hard drive by moving parts of it to the new drive; you just want to continue to build on your folders as they are.

The solution, as you know if you read the beginning of this chapter, is to create a *spanned volume*, a single disk icon (and drive letter) that's actually composed of the space from both your old and new drives.

The first order of business (after restarting the computer) is to make sure that Windows has recognized the new drive. When you launch the Disk Management console, a new drive appears in the list, with a great big block of unallocated space for you to fill, as shown in Figure 21-2.

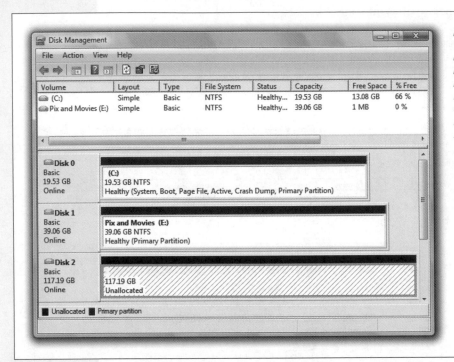

Figure 21-2:
When you install a new hard drive in your computer, it appears in the Disk Management console as a large block of unallocated space. Of course, you'll notice that the new drive is a basic drive; therefore, all you can do is create a basic partition on it.

GEM IN THE ROUGH

What About Extending Basic Disks?

Windows Vista allows you to extend (and shrink) basic disks as well as dynamic disks. Previously, you'd have to buy a program like Partition Magic to perform this kind of operation.

But why would you want to resize your basic disk? In most cases, your basic disk already takes up the entire physical disk drive. However, many computer manufacturers devote several gigabytes of precious disk space to storing *restore images* so you can quickly and easily restore your computer to its factory-fresh state (minus the new-computer smell).

You may not need these restore images. Maybe your PC manufacturer provided a utility program that can generate a set of installation discs, or will sell you a set for a small

fee, or maybe you bought a full retail copy of Windows Vista (not an upgrade version). The point is, though, that if you're sure you'll never need the volume that contains your restore images, you may be able to delete it and extend your C: drive into the space you freed up.

To delete a partition, right-click it in the Disk Management window; from the shortcut menu, choose Delete Volume (this is a good time to pause and think about how fresh your backups are). Once you've done that, you can right-click your C: drive and select Extend Volume.

You can just as easily *shrink* your C: drive, perhaps to make room for dual-booting another operating system such as Linux.

To use the new drive to enlarge your existing volume, right-click your almost-full volume (drive E: in this example), and select Extend Volume from the shortcut menu. The Extend Volumes Wizard appears. Click Next to begin.

When the Select Disks screen appears (Figure 21-3), you'll see that the only available unallocated space in your computer is on your new drive. Select it in the Available column and click Add to add it to the Selected column. Specify how much of the new drive you want to add to the volume (or, to add *all* of it to your original drive, do nothing). Finally, click Next and then Finish.

Note: This operation doesn't erase any of your existing data. Still, this sort of major change is not without risk. So, now is the time to ask yourself, "Do I feel lucky?" If not, make that backup before you do something we'll all regret.

This process converts both disks into a dynamic disk and creates a spanned volume. You'll get a warning from Disk Management about the consequences of converting to a dynamic disk, as described earlier in this chapter. Click Yes to continue.

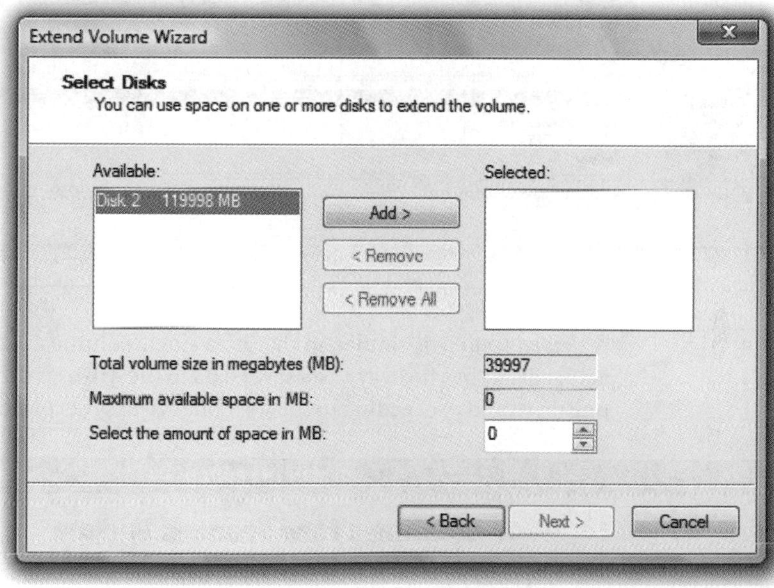

Figure 21-3:
When extending a volume to another disk, click its name in the Available column before adding it to the Selected column.

Notice now that your original volume and your new drive both have a purple header bar and use the same drive letter, as shown in Figure 21-4. You now have a spanned volume using space on both of your hard drives. Your hard drive is now effectively bigger (117 GB of free space out of a combined total of 156 GB), and you can continue to amass new files at your accustomed rate.

Creating a striped volume

As you now know, a *spanned volume* is like a virtual hard drive made up of storage space from more than one dynamic disk. When Windows saves data onto a spanned volume, it completely fills up the allotted space on one drive, then proceeds to the next drive in the volume, until the allotted space on all of the drives is full.

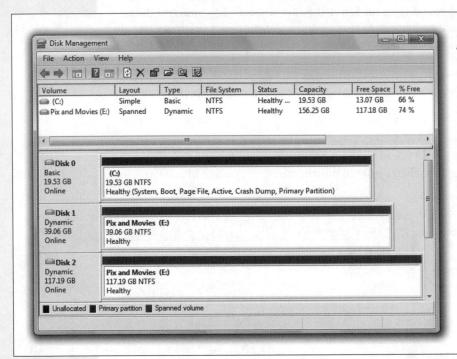

Figure 21-4:
A dynamic volume extended to another disk appears in the Disk Management console with the same color header bar and the same drive letter. Note, too, that the volume list in the top of this dialog box identifies this volume as "Spanned."

A *striped volume* is similar, in that it's a single volume made up of space from several actual disks, but the way Vista saves data to the drives is different. Instead of filling up one drive and proceeding to the next one, Vista saves pieces of each file on more than

---

GEM IN THE ROUGH

Creating a New Spanned Volume

The flexibility of dynamic disks never ends. If you find yourself with bits of unallocated space on two or more dynamic disks, you can actually sweep these scraps together into a single new volume—a spanned volume—that behaves, in Windows, as though it's a single hard drive.

To do this, start in the Disk Management window (Figure 21-1). Right-click any unallocated space on any of the disks and select New Spanned Volume from the shortcut menu. On the Select Disks screen, the unallocated space you clicked appears in the Selected column, and any unallocated space on other dynamic disks appears in the Available column. Add the unallocated space you want to use, and proceed through the wizard to create the new volume.

---

one disk. Because more than one hard drive is saving and reading data in parallel, a speed benefit can theoretically result.

The truth is, though, that for the sorts of small files most people work with, the differences are measured in milliseconds—thousandths of a second—so it's generally not worth creating striped volumes on everyday PC workstations. (On corporate file servers that handle hundreds or thousands of file access requests per minute, or video-editing workstations, it's a different story. The cumulative savings in access times can be significant.)

If you're still tempted to create a striped-volume set, the process is nearly identical to creating a new *spanned* volume (see the box on the facing page), except that, when you right-click, you select New Striped Volume instead of New Spanned Volume. You must also use the same amount of space on each of the drives you select. For example, if you have 100 gigabytes of unallocated space on Disk 0 and 50 gigabytes of unallocated space on Disk 1, your striped volume can be no larger than 100 gigabytes—50 from each drive.

Compressing Files and Folders
All Versions

The hard drives made these days have greater capacities than ever, but programs and files are much bigger, too. Running out of disk space is still a common problem. Fortunately, Vista is especially effective at compressing files and folders to take up less disk space.

Compressing files and folders can also be useful when you want to email files to someone without dooming them to an all-night modem-watching session. That's why Microsoft has endowed Windows Vista with two different schemes for compressing

---

UP TO SPEED

Data Compression

Data compression is the process of replacing repetitive material in a file with shorthand symbols. For example, if a speech you've written contains the phrase *going forward* 21 times, a compression scheme like the one in NTFS may replace each occurrence with a single symbol, making the file that much smaller. When you reopen the file later, the operating system almost instantaneously restores the original, expanded material.

The degree to which a file can be compressed depends on what kind of data the file contains and whether it's already been compressed by another program. For example, programs (executable files) often shrink by half when

compressed. Bitmapped graphics like TIFF files squish down to as little as one-seventh their original size, saving a great deal more space.

The PNG and JPEG graphics files so popular on the Web, however, are already compressed (which is why they're so popular—they take relatively little time to download). As a result, they don't get much smaller if you try to compress them manually. That's one of the main rules of data compression: data can only be compressed once.

In short, there's no way to predict just how much disk space you'll save by using NTFS compression on your drives. It all depends on what you have stored there.

---

files and folders: *NTFS compression* for storing files on your hard drive, and *zipped folders* for files that might have to be transferred.

NTFS Compression

If Windows Vista was installed on your PC when you bought it, or if you upgraded your PC from Windows XP, or if you erased your hard drive before installing Windows Vista, then your hard drive is probably formatted using a file system called *NTFS* (short for *NT file system*).

Most people can live a long and happy life without knowing anything about NTFS. If you work in a corporation, you might be grateful for the additional security it offers to Windows Vista fans (Chapter 23), and leave it at that. Now and then, however, you'll read about other features that are available *only* if your hard drive was prepared using NTFS—and this is one of those cases.

Tip: The hard drive that's running Vista has the NTFS format; Vista requires it. To find out what formatting some other drive uses (a flash drive or external hard drive, for example), choose Start→Computer. Right-click the hard drive icon; from the shortcut menu, choose Properties. In the resulting dialog box, you'll see either "File system: NTFS" or "File system: FAT 32." Unfortunately, special NTFS features like automatic compression aren't available to you unless you upgrade the drive formatting to NTFS. For instructions, download the free appendix to this chapter from this book's "Missing CD" page at *www.missingmanuals.com*. The file is called NTFS Upgrade.PDF. (Note, however, that if you convert a flash drive to NTFS, you may no longer be able to use it with non-Windows computers and devices like digital cameras and palmtops.)

The NTFS compression scheme is especially likable because it's completely invisible to you. Windows automatically compresses and decompresses your files, almost instantaneously. At some point, you may even forget you've turned it on. Consider:

- Whenever you open a compressed file, Windows quickly and invisibly expands it to its original form so that you can read or edit it. When you close the file again, Windows instantly recompresses it.

- If you send compressed files via email or copy them to a PC whose hard drive doesn't use NTFS compression, Windows Vista once again decompresses them, quickly and invisibly.

- Any file you copy into a compressed folder or disk is compressed automatically. (If you only *move* it into such a folder from elsewhere on the disk, however, it stays compressed or uncompressed—whichever it was originally.)

Compressing files, folders, or disks

To turn on NTFS compression, right-click the icon for the file, folder, or disk whose contents you want to shrink. Choose Properties from the shortcut menu. Click the Advanced button, and in the resulting dialog box, turn on "Compress contents to save disk space" (Figure 21-5), click OK and then click Apply or OK when you return to the Properties dialog box. If you have selected a folder for compression, you're prompted as to whether you also want to compress the files and subfolders within it.

Many Windows veterans wind up turning on compression for the entire hard drive. It can take Windows Vista several hours to perform the initial compression of every file on the drive.

If you do this, or even if you try to compress a large folder such as *C:\Program Files*, you will invariably run into a few files that can't be compressed because they're currently in use. Short of opening up the Task Manager and shutting down nearly every process on your system (not recommended), you won't be able to avoid a few of these. Your best bet is to select Ignore All the first time Windows Vista notifies you about this problem. Then you can safely walk away from your computer and let the compression continue.

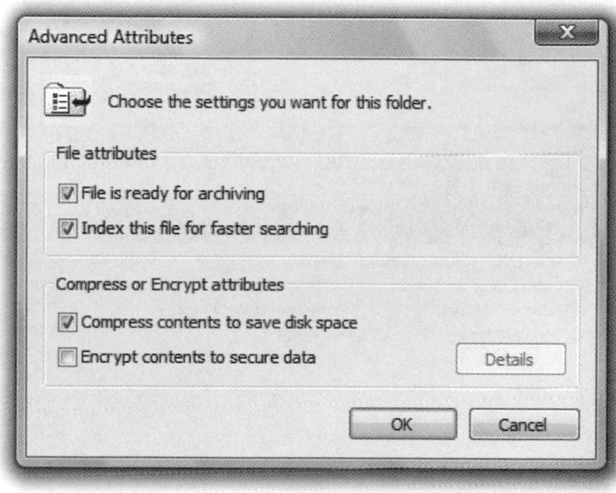

Figure 21-5:
If you don't see the "Compress contents to save disk space" checkbox (highlighted here), then your hard drive probably doesn't use the NTFS formatting scheme.

When Windows is finished compressing, the compressed file and folder icons appear in a different color, a reminder that Windows is doing its part to maximize your disk space. (If they don't change color, then somebody—maybe you—must have turned off the "Show encrypted or compressed NTFS files in color" option described on page 85.)

When you look at the Properties dialog box for a compressed file (right-click the file and choose Properties from the shortcut menu), you can see two file sizes. The Size value indicates the actual (uncompressed) size of the file, while the Size On Disk value is the compressed size of the file—that is, the amount of disk space it's occupying.

Zipped Folders

As noted above, NTFS compression is great for freeing up disk space while you're working at your PC. But when you email your files to somebody else or burn them to a CD, Windows Vista always decompresses them back to their original sizes first.

Fortunately, there's another way to compress files: Zip them. If you've ever used Windows before, you've probably encountered Zip files. Each one is a tiny little suitcase, an *archive*, whose contents have been tightly compressed to keep files together, to save space, and to transfer them online faster (see Figure 21-6). Use Zip files when you want to email something to someone, or when you want to pack up a completed project and remove it from your hard drive to free up space.

Creating zipped folders

In Vista, you don't even need a shareware program like PKZip or WinZip to create or open Zip files. You can create a Zip archive in either of two ways:

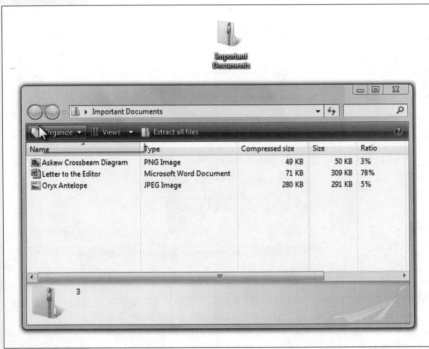

Figure 21-6:
Top: A Zip archive looks like an ordinary folder—except for the tiny zipper.

Bottom: Double-click one to open its window and see what's inside. Notice (in the Ratio column) that JPEG graphics and PNG graphics usually don't become much smaller than they were before zipping, since they're already compressed formats. But word processing files, program files, and other file types undergo quite a bit of shrinkage.

HISTORY CLASS

PKZip

The Zip archive format was developed in the late 1980s by Phil Katz, a pioneer of PC compression technology. Katz's original product, PKZip, was a DOS-based archiving program that soon became an industry standard.

There have been many other archive compression standards over the years, but none of them became as ubiquitous as the Zip format. Every program today that creates or manipulates Zip files, including Windows Vista, owes a debt of thanks—if not a free T-shirt or two—to Phil Katz.

- Right-click any blank spot on the desktop or an open window. From the shortcut menu, choose New→Compressed (zipped) Folder. Type a name for your newly created, empty archive, and then press Enter.

  Now, each time you drag a file or folder onto the archive's icon (or into its open window), Windows automatically stuffs a *copy* of it inside.

  Of course, you haven't actually saved any disk space, since now you have two copies of the original material (one zipped, one untouched). If you'd rather *move* a file or folder into the archive—in the process deleting the full-size version and saving disk space—right-drag the file or folder icon onto the *archive* icon. Now from the shortcut menu, choose Move Here.

- To turn an existing file or folder *into* a zipped archive, right-click its icon. (To zip up a handful of icons, select them first, then right-click any *one* of them.) Now, from the shortcut menu, choose Send To→Compressed (zipped) Folder. You've just created a new archive folder *and* copied the files or folders into it.

Tip: At this point, you can right-click the zipped folder's icon and choose Send To→Mail Recipient. Vista automatically whips open your email program, creates an outgoing message ready for you to address, and attaches the zipped file to it—which is now set for transport.

Working with zipped folders

In many respects, a zipped folder behaves just like any ordinary folder, in that you double-click it to see what's inside.

If you double-click one of the *files* you find inside, however, Vista opens up a *read-only* copy of it—that is, a copy you can view, but not edit. To make changes to a read-only copy, you must use the File→Save As command and save it somewhere else on your hard drive.

Note: Be sure to navigate to the desktop or the Documents folder, for example, before you save your edited document. Otherwise, Windows saves it into an invisible temporary folder, where you may never see it again.

To decompress only some of the icons in a zipped folder, just drag them out of the archive window; they instantly spring back to their original sizes. To decompress the entire archive, right-click its icon and choose Extract All from the shortcut menu (or, if its window is already open, click the "Extract all files" link on the toolbar). A wizard asks you to specify where you want the resulting files to wind up.

Encrypting Files and Folders

Business • Enterprise • Ultimate

If your Documents folder contains nothing but laundry lists and letters to your mom, data security is probably not a major concern for you. But if there's some stuff on your hard drive that you'd rather keep private—you know who you are—Windows

(Business Edition and higher) can help you out. The Encrypting File System (EFS) is an NTFS feature that stores your data in a coded format that only you can read.

The beauty of EFS is that it's effortless and invisible to you, the authorized owner. Windows Vista automatically encrypts your files before storing them on the drive, and decrypts them again when you want to read or modify them. Anyone else who logs on to your computer, however, will find these files locked and off-limits.

If you've read ahead to Chapter 23, of course, you might be frowning in confusion at this point. Isn't keeping private files private the whole point of Vista's *accounts* feature? Don't Vista's *NTFS permissions* (page 692) keep busybodies out already?

POWER USERS' CLINIC

Disk Quotas

Does one of your account holders have a tendency to become a bit overzealous about downloading stuff from the Web, threatening to overrun your hard drive with shareware junk and MP3 files? Fortunately, it's easy enough for you, the wise administrator, to curb such behavior among holders of Standard accounts.

Just choose Start→Computer. Right-click the hard drive icon; from the shortcut menu, choose Properties. In the Properties dialog box, click the Quota tab (shown here). Click Show Quota Settings to bring up the Quota Settings dialog box, and then turn on Enable Quota Management.

You might start by turning on "Deny disk space to users exceeding quota limit." This, of course, is exactly the kind of muzzle you were hoping to place on out-of-control downloaders. The instant they try to save or download a file that pushes their stuff over the limit, an "Insufficient disk space" message appears. They'll simply have to delete some of their other files to make room.

Use the "Limit disk space to ___" controls to specify the cap you want to put on each account holder. Using these controls, you can specify a certain number of kilobytes (KB), megabytes (MB), gigabytes (GB)—or even terabytes (TB), petabytes (PB), or exabytes (EB). (Then write a letter to *PC World* and tell the editors where you bought a multiexabyte hard drive.)

You can also set up a disk-space limit ("Set warning level to ___") that will make a *warning* appear—not to the mad downloader, but to you, the administrator. By clicking the Quota Entries button, you get a little report that shows exactly how much disk space each of your account holders has used up. (This is where you'll see the warning as a written notation.)

If you just want to track your underlings' disk usage without actually limiting them, set the warning level to the desired value, but set the Limit Disk Space value to something impossibly high, like several exabytes.

When you click OK, Windows warns you that it's about to take some time to calculate just how much disk space each account holder has used so far.

Yes, but encryption provides additional security. If, for example, you're a top-level agent assigned to protect your government's most closely guarded egg salad recipe, you can use NTFS permissions to deny all other users access to the file containing the information. Nobody but you can open the file in Windows Vista.

However, a determined intruder from a foreign nation could conceivably boot the computer using *another* operating system—one that doesn't recognize the NTFS permissions system—and access the hard drive using a special program that reads the raw data stored there. If, however, you had encrypted the file using EFS, that raw data would appear as gibberish, foiling your crafty nemesis.

Using EFS

You use EFS to encrypt your folders and files in much the same way that you use NTFS compression. To encrypt a file or a folder, you open its Properties dialog box, click the Advanced button, turn on the "Encrypt contents to secure data" checkbox, and click OK (see Figure 21-7). (For a quicker way, see page 791.)

Figure 21-7:
To encrypt a file or folder using EFS, turn on the "Encrypt contents to secure data" checkbox (at the bottom of its Properties dialog box). If you've selected a folder, a Confirm Attribute Changes dialog box appears, asking if you want to encrypt just that folder or everything inside it, too.

Depending on how much data you've selected, it may take some time for the encryption process to complete. Once the folders and files are encrypted, they appear in a different color from your compressed files (unless, once again, you've turned off the "Show encrypted or compressed NTFS files in color" option).

Note: You can't encrypt certain files and folders, such as system files, or any files in the system *root folder* (usually the Windows folder). You can't encrypt files and folders on FAT 32 drives, either.

Finally, note that you can't both encrypt *and* compress the same file or folder. If you attempt to encrypt a compressed file or folder, Windows Vista needs to decompress it first. You can, however, encrypt files that have been compressed using another technology, such as Zip files or compressed image files.

After your files have been encrypted, you may be surprised to see that, other than their color change, nothing seems to have changed. You can open them the same way you always did, change them, and save them as usual. Vista is just doing its job: protecting these files with minimum inconvenience to you.

Still, if you're having difficulty believing that your files are now protected by an invisible force field, try logging off and back on again with a different user name and password. When you try to open an encrypted file now, a message cheerfully informs you that you don't have the proper permissions to access the file. (For more on Windows Vista security, see Chapter 10.)

EFS Rules

Any files or folders that you move *into* an EFS-encrypted folder get encrypted, too. But dragging a file *out* of it doesn't unprotect it; it remains encrypted as long as it's on an NTFS drive. A protected file loses its encryption only when:

- You manually decrypt the file (by turning off the corresponding checkbox in its Properties dialog box).

- You move it to a FAT 32 drive.

- You transmit it via a network or email—when you attach the file to an email or send it across the network, Vista will decrypt the file before sending it on its way.

By the way, EFS doesn't protect files from being deleted. Even if passing evildoers can't *open* your private file, they can still *delete* it—unless you've protected it using Vista's permissions feature (Chapter 23). Here, again, truly protecting important material involves using several security mechanisms in combination.

GEM IN THE ROUGH

Recovering Encrypted Data

Every now and then, encrypted data becomes inaccessible. Maybe a hard drive crash nukes your password, and therefore your ability to open your own encrypted files. Or maybe a disgruntled employee quits, deliberately refusing to divulge his password or decrypt his important files first.

The first time you encrypt a file, Vista puts a prompt in the notification area suggesting that you back up your encryption key. Click the prompt to start the process of backing up your key (that is, your password).

You can also back up your key by right-clicking an encrypted file and selecting Properties. In the Properties dialog box, click Advanced, and then click Details. You can then select your user name and click Back Up Keys to start the process.

Once you've backed it up to a CD or flash drive, keep it secret, keep it safe, and don't make multiple copies of it. If you lose your key, you can restore it by double-clicking on this file and then going through the Certificate Import Wizard. You'll need to provide the password you supplied when you backed up the key, so don't forget it!

If all else fails, Windows Vista has a fallback mechanism—a back door. The local Administrator account on a PC can be designated as a *recover agent* for users, which gives the administrator the ability to decrypt their files in case of an emergency. For instructions on setting up this feature, see *http://support.microsoft.com/kb/887414*.

BitLocker Drive Encryption

Enterprise • Ultimate

If you think EFS sounds like a great way to keep prying eyes out of your files, you ain't seen nothing yet!

Vista's standard protections—your account password, the encryption of certain files, and so on—are all very nice.

But when million-dollar corporate secrets are at stake, they're not going to stop a determined, knowledgeable thief. The guy could swipe your laptop or even steal the hard drive out of your desktop PC.

If security is that important for you, then you'll be happy to know about BitLocker Drive Encryption, a new Vista feature. When you turn on this feature, your PC automatically *encrypts* (scrambles) everything on your *entire system hard drive,* including all of Windows itself.

If the bad guy tries any industrial-strength tricks to get into the drive—trying to reprogram the startup routines, for example, or starting up from a different hard drive—BitLocker presents a steel-reinforced password screen. No password, no decryption.

You won't notice much difference when BitLocker is turned on. You log in as usual, clicking your name and typing your password.

We're talking hard-core, corporate-level security—with hard-core, corporate-level requirements:

- The Enterprise or Ultimate edition of Vista.

- Two NTFS hard drives or drive partitions on your system: one that will be encrypted, and one that Vista will use to boot the system. (It won't move your Windows folder there, but it will use that drive to hold the files needed to boot up a PC whose C: drive is encrypted.)

  The bad news is that the second drive needs to come *before* your C: drive, and must be configured as the active partition (the partition that the system boots from). It's unlikely that you've set your system up with such a configuration, so if you want to use BitLocker, you'll need to reinstall Vista from scratch.

- You generally need a *Trusted Platform Module (TPM),* a special circuit that's built onto the system boards of BitLocker-compatible PCs, although there's a sneaky workaround if your PC doesn't have this item. Details in a moment.

To find out if the planets are aligned and all the components are installed for you to use BitLocker, choose Start→Control Panel. Open the Security applet and click BitLocker Drive Encryption.

If you see an option there to "Turn on BitLocker" (Figure 21-9), well, great! You're ready to step up to the strongest encryption Vista has to offer. Click that link, and wait while Vista encrypts your hard drive. Oh, and don't forget the password you provide.

Reinstalling Vista on Two Partitions

If, on the other hand, you see a note there explaining why you can't use BitLocker (Figure 21-8), proceed like this:

- If you don't have two partitions, you'll need to back up your data, dig out your Vista installation DVD, create the partitions, and reinstall.

- If you don't have a TPM, you'll need a USB flash drive. With some tweaks to Vista's configuration, you can use this as the "ignition key" to bootstrap BitLocker's strong encryption, eliminating the need for the TPM.

  The USB flash drive option works only on PCs whose BIOS can *see* flash drives in the "pre-OS environment"—that is, before Windows has actually loaded at startup.

Note: Microsoft may one day release a software tool that eliminates the need to manually repartition your system. Keep an eye on the BitLocker team blog for updates: *http://blogs.technet.com/bitlocker/*

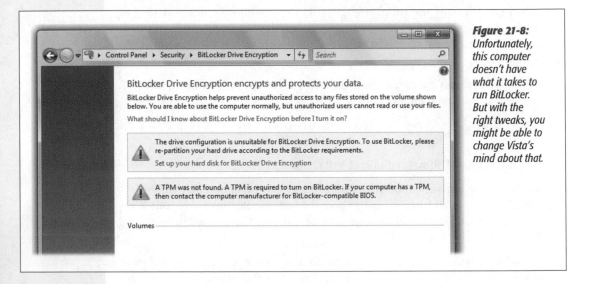

Figure 21-8:
Unfortunately, this computer doesn't have what it takes to run BitLocker. But with the right tweaks, you might be able to change Vista's mind about that.

Here's what you need to do to reinstall Vista with two partitions for BitLocker:

1. **Start up from the Vista installation DVD.**

   Sooner or later, the Install Windows screen appears.

2. **Choose "Repair Your Computer."**

   You arrive at a screen where you can choose an operating system to recover. If you're installing Vista on a brand-new hard drive, you won't see anything listed here. Otherwise, select your currently installed operating system and click Next.

   Now you've got a bunch of recovery tools to choose from.

3. **Choose Command Prompt.**

Here's where you have to get your hands dirty at the command line.

4. **Type *diskpart* at the Command Prompt and press Enter.**

The DISKPART> prompt appears. The next step will create one drive (with drive letter S:) that meets the BitLocker minimum size (1.5 GB), set it as active, and then create a C: drive with the remaining space. This will *erase everything on your hard drive*, so you'd better have backed things up!

5. **Type the following commands:**

```
select disk 0
clean
create partition primary size=1500
assign letter=S
active
create partition primary
assign letter=C
exit
```

Now you're back at the Command Prompt. You have to format the two drives you created:

6. **Type these commands:**

```
format S: /y /q/ fs:NTFS /V:BITLOCKER
format C: /y /q /fs:NTFS /V:VISTA
```

As usual, press Enter after each command.

7. **Type *exit* to close the Command Prompt, click the X in the upper-right corner of the list of System Recovery Tools (don't click Shut Down or Restart), and install Vista onto the C: drive you just formatted.**

If there's a TPM chip in your PC, you should now be able to turn on BitLocker on your drive (see Figure 21-9).

The Flash-Drive Workaround

Of course, a TPM is a special circuit that you either have in your PC or you don't. Fortunately, there's a clever workaround that, believe it or not, lets you use an ordinary USB flash drive instead of a TPM:

1. **Open the Start menu. In the search box, type *gpedit.msc*. Press Enter.**

You've just opened the Group Policy Object Editor, a program you can use to configure advanced settings on Windows.

2. **Drill down to Local Computer Policy ›Computer Configuration→Administrative Templates→Windows Components→BitLocker Drive Encryption.**

Examine the right side of the window.

3. Find "Control Panel Setup: Advanced Setup Options," and double-click it.

The Properties dialog box appears.

4. Select Enabled. Make sure "Allow BitLocker without a compatible TPM (requires a startup key on a USB flash drive)" is turned on. Click OK.

Reboot your computer.

Turning on BitLocker

Now reopen the Control Panel, and select Security→BitLocker Drive Encryption; the window should now look like Figure 21-9. Click Turn On BitLocker, follow the instructions, and let Windows encrypt your drive; this can take some time. You're now protected, even from the most determined and knowledgeable hard drive thieves.

Note: Along the way, BitLocker asks you to save your password somewhere. Be sure to keep it secret and keep it safe. You're going to need it if Vista decides that you've done something that makes it think you're a hacker trying to get in, like installing a second operating system in a dual-boot configuration.

Figure 21-9:
You're now ready to encrypt your drive to keep it safe from prying eyes.

Backups and Troubleshooting

PC troubleshooting is among the most difficult propositions on earth, in part because your machine has so many cooks. Microsoft made the operating system, another company made the computer, and dozens of others contributed the programs you use every day. The number of conflicts that can arise and the number of problems you may encounter is nearly infinite. That's why, if you were lucky, you bought your PC from a company that offers a toll-free, 24-hour help line. You may need it.

In the meantime, Vista is crawling with special diagnostic modes, software tools, and workarounds designed to revive a gasping or dead PC. Some are clearly intended only for licensed geeks. Others, however, are available even to mere mortals armed with no more information than, "It's not working right."

Whether you get it working or not, however, there's one constant that applies to novices and programmers alike—you're always better off if you have a backup copy of your files. Fortunately, Windows Vista comes with not one but three different backup systems. This chapter tells all.

Automatic Backups
All Versions

Consider that the proximity of your drive's spinning platters to the head that reads them is roughly the same proportion as the wheels of an airliner flying at 500 miles per hour, 12 inches off the ground. It's amazing that hard drives work as well, and as long, as they do.

Still, a hard drive is nothing more than a mass of moving parts in delicate alignment, so it should come as no surprise that every now and then, disaster strikes. That's why backing up your data (making a safety copy) on a regular basis is an essential part of using a PC. Even if computers aren't your career, there's probably a lot of valuable stuff on your hard drive: all of your photos, the addresses and phone numbers you've spent hours typing in, a lifetime's worth of email, the Web sites in your Favorites folder, and so on.

If you use Vista in a corporation, you probably don't even have to think about backing up your stuff. A network administrator generally does the backing up for you and your co-workers.

But if you use Windows Vista at home, or in a smaller company that doesn't have network nerds running around to ensure your files' safety, you'll be happy to know about the Backup and Restore feature. It's a brand-new Vista feature that makes it simple to do your own backups.

Tip: There was a Backup program included with Windows XP, but it wasn't part of the standard installation, and it couldn't even back up your stuff onto CDs or DVDs.

Backup Hardware

If you have a home or small business network, backing up to a folder on another PC on your network is a wise idea. An inexpensive external hard drive makes a super-convenient backup disk, too.

The advantage of blank CDs and DVDs, though, is that you can store them somewhere else: in a fireproof box, a safe deposit box at the bank, or the trunk of your

---

UP TO SPEED

Good News, Bad Software News

There's good news and bad news about Backup and Restore. The good news is that it's very easy to use, and you can also use it to make a backup of your *entire* PC. If it crashes, you can restore your entire computer, including the operating system, your settings, and your data files.

The bad news is—there's no diplomatic way to put this—that it's not, ahem, Microsoft's finest work.

For example, it doesn't let you specify individual files and folders to back up—only broad categories of files like Documents, Pictures, or Music. You therefore have to back up every single file in every single folder that meets those broad categories of the files. If you choose to back up compressed

files, not only will you back up your own compressed .zip files, but you'll back up every single compressed file that Windows uses for installation. If you choose Pictures, you wind up backing up every single graphic on your hard disk, including all the graphics that Windows uses itself (icons, dialog box symbols, and so on).

So even if there are only, say, 30 megabytes of files from a few folders that you want backed up, you're forced to back up several hundred megabytes of files for which you have absolutely no use.

Maybe Microsoft didn't want to offend all the software companies that make *good* backup software.

---

car. Keep them anywhere except in your office, so your data is safe even in the case of fire or burglary.

Tip: You can't back up a laptop's files when it's running on battery power. The program won't let you—it's too worried about losing juice in the middle of the operation.

Creating a Backup Job

Once you've decided to back up your PC and also figured out what you're going to back it up *onto,* proceed like this:

1. **Choose Start→Control Panel. Under the System and Maintenance heading, click "Back up your computer."**

   Now Backup and Restore Center opens (Figure 22-1).

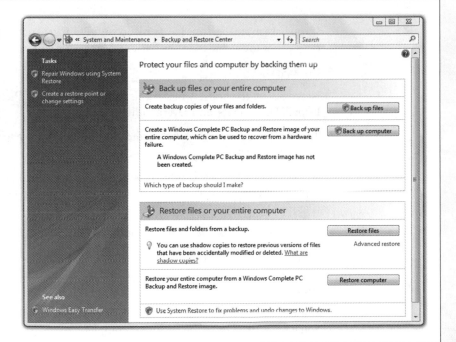

Figure 22-1:
The primary purpose of this screen is to back up and restore your PC. But on the left-hand side, you'll also find links for creating a restore point, and for using System Restore to revert your PC to a previous time.

2. **Click "Back up files."**

   "Back up files" is what most people use most of the time. It can back up your photos, music, videos, email, documents, compressed files, and just about anything else *except* for your programs—and Windows itself.

   ("Back up computer," the other option you may see here, is described on page 647.)

3. **Authenticate yourself (page 191).**

Now Windows looks through your system, locating hard disks and removable drives. The Back Up Files screen appears, offering you the chance to specify where you want to store the backup copies.

4. **Choose a backup drive.**

If you're backing up to a hard disk or removable disk, select "On a hard disk, CD, or DVD." From the drop-down list, choose the drive you want to back up to.

Tip: USB flash drives and memory cards show up in this list, too. Flash drives make particularly handy backup disks because they're small, inexpensive, and can store several gigabytes of data.

If you're backing up to a folder that's shared on a networked PC (page 729), select "On a network," then browse to the folder. You may have to type in a user name and password to use that folder, depending on how you've set up sharing on the PC.

If you have more than one hard disk on your PC, you're now asked to choose which ones you want included in the backup. Make your choice.

5. **Click Next.**

Now you get to choose which *kinds* of files to back up: Pictures, Music, Videos, E-mail, Documents, and several others.

6. **Turn on the checkboxes for the kinds of files you want backed up (Figure 22-2, top). Click Next.**

You can now set up a schedule for automatic, unattended backups, which should bring *enormous* peace of mind to anyone who's been, until now, living dangerously (Figure 22-2, bottom).

7. **Click "Save settings and start backup."**

Backup goes to work, copying your files to their new backup location. The process may take several seconds or several hours, depending on how much you're copying.

You can continue to work on your PC; copying takes place in the background. You'll be notified once the backup is complete.

From now on, your PC backs itself up, on the schedule you set for it. When Windows Vista creates a new backup, it only backs up new files or files that have changed since the last backup; it doesn't waste its time backing up files that haven't been touched.

Note: If you've set your PC to back up to CDs or DVDs, make sure that there's a blank disc available at the appointed time; otherwise, the backup won't happen.

If you want to change your backup settings—back up on a different schedule, say, or add or take away file types—return to the Backup and Restore Center, and click "Change backup settings." From here, you can change anything about your backup.

Restoring Files from a Backup

When your good luck runs out, and you find yourself with a virus/drive crash/meddle-some toddler who threw out an important folder, you'll be glad indeed that you had a backup. This is the payoff.

Figure 22-2:
Top: As noted earlier in this chapter, Vista intends to back up all files of that generic file type—so Documents backs up Word .doc files, Excel .xls files, PowerPoint .ppt files, Adobe .pdf files, and others. You can't specify that you want only certain files or folders backed up.

Bottom: Choose a schedule for the automatic backups. For best results, choose times of day when you know that the computer will be turned on.

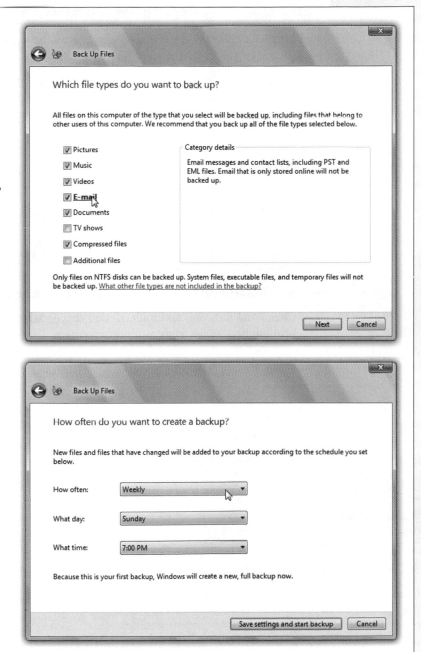

Fortunately, Vista lets you restore individual files and folders—you don't have to restore all files in one fell swoop.

Tip: Perform regular test restores to make sure your data is retrievable from the backup disks. (Consider restoring your files to a test folder–not the folder where the files came from–so you don't wind up with duplicates.) There's no other way to be absolutely sure that your backups are working properly.

Here are the steps. (They assume that, if your whole hard drive did indeed die, you have already replaced it and reinstalled Windows Vista.)

1. **Choose Start→Control Panel. Under the System and Maintenance heading, click "Back up your computer."**

   You're back at the Backup and Restore Center.

2. **Click "Restore files."**

   A screen appears, asking whether you want to restore files from your most recent backup, or from a previous backup.

3. **Click "Files from the latest backup" or "Files from an older backup" and click Next.**

   If you choose to restore from a previous backup, you'll be shown a list of backup dates; choose the one you want.

   Now you arrive at the weird little screen shown in Figure 22-3.

4. **Click "Add files" or "Add folders," and specify what files and folders you want brought back to life from your backup copies.**

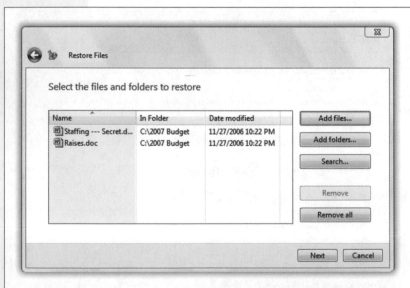

Figure 22-3:
When you restore files, you don't have to restore every single file you've backed up. Click Add Files or Add Folders (shown here), and a screen appears where you can select the specific files or folders you want to restore.

Click "Add files" to restore individual files, or "Add folders" to restore individual folders. Note that at this point, although it may look like you're browsing through your hard disk, you're not. You're only browsing the backup that you made.

You can also *search* for files, if you're not sure where a file is that you want to back up. Click Search, type what you're looking for, and then add the file or files.

5. **Click Next. Indicate where you want the restored files put.**

   You can restore files to their original locations, or to a different folder on your PC.

6. **Click "Start restore."**

   Backup now starts copying files and folders *back* from the backup to your hard drive.

   If you've chosen to save files to their original locations, you may be asked what you want to happen if the original files are *still there.* Do you want the backup copies to "win," do you want to keep the originals, or do you want to keep both?

   If you choose to keep both, the restored file gets a (2) after it. So the original file would be budget.doc, for instance, and the copy would be budget (2).doc.

Complete PC Backup

Business • Enterprise • Ultimate

When your hard disk crashes, you lose more than just your personal files. You also lose your operating system and its settings—*and* all the programs you've installed. It can take you a very long time to restore your PC to that state.

Windows Complete PC Backup, a new feature in Vista, solves the problem easily. It creates a *disk image*—a perfect snapshot—of your *entire* hard drive at this moment: documents, email, pictures, and so on, *plus* Windows, *and* all your programs and settings. Someone could steal your *entire hard drive,* or your drive could die, and you'd be able to install a new, empty one and be back in business inside of an hour.

It's a good idea to make a fresh Complete PC Backup every few months, because you'll probably have installed new programs and changed your settings in the interim.

Note: For the techies scoring at home, the disk image created by Complete PC Backup is a .vhd file, the same kind that's created by Microsoft's Virtual PC software–and therefore, you can mount it using Virtual PC, if you like.

Make the Image

To make a Complete PC Backup, choose Start→Control Panel. Under the System and Maintenance heading, click "Back up your computer." On the following screen, click "Back up computer" again (instead of "back up files").

As described in the previous steps, you're now asked where you want to store the backup image. But your options aren't quite the same this time:

- You can't back up to a network folder.

- You can only back up to hard disks or removable disks that are formatted with the NTFS file system.

After you make your selection, click Next. You'll be shown your backup location as a way for you to confirm it. You'll also be told how many discs you'll need; be prepared, because if you're backing up to CDs or DVDs, you'll probably need a *lot* of them.

Click "Start backup"; the backup begins. You'll be prompted when you need to insert new DVDs or other discs.

Restore the Image

Restoring your entire system using Complete PC Restore is very easy. From the Backup and Restore Center, click Restore Computer, and follow the prompts.

Just be forewarned that this process *reformats your hard drive,* and in the process *wipes out* all your data and files. They'll be replaced with the Windows Complete PC Restore snapshot, and with the data from the most recent backup you've made.

System Restore
All Versions

As you get more proficient on a PC, pressing Ctrl+Z—the keyboard shortcut for Undo—eventually becomes an unconscious reflex. In fact, you can sometimes spot veteran Windows fans twitching their Ctrl+Z fingers even when they're not near the computer—after knocking over a cup of coffee, locking the car with the keys inside, or blurting out something inappropriate in a meeting.

Vista offers one feature in particular that you might think of as the mother of all Undo commands: System Restore. This feature alone can be worth hours of your time and hundreds of dollars in consultant fees.

The pattern of things going wrong in Windows usually works like this: the PC works fine for a while, and then suddenly—maybe for no apparent reason, but most often following an installation or configuration change—it goes on the fritz. At that point, wouldn't it be pleasant to be able to tell the computer: "Go back to the way you were yesterday, please"?

System Restore does exactly that. It "rewinds" your copy of Windows back to the condition it was in before you, or something you tried to install, messed it up.

Tip: If your PC manages to catch a virus, System Restore can even rewind it to a time before the infection—*if* the virus hasn't gotten into your documents in such a way that you reinfect yourself after the system restore. An up-to-date antivirus program is a much more effective security blanket.

In fact, if you don't like your PC after restoring it, you can always restore it to the way it was *before* you restored it. Back to the future!

Note: A new subfeature of System Restore in Vista also makes daily safety copies of your *documents*. See "Shadow Copies" on page 654.

About Restore Points

System Restore works by taking snapshots of your operating system. Your copy of Vista has been creating these memorized snapshots, called *restore points*, ever since you've been running it. When the worst comes to pass, and your PC starts acting up, you can use System Restore to rewind your machine to its configuration the last time you remember it working well.

Windows automatically creates landing points for your little PC time machine at the following times:

POWER USERS' CLINIC

System Restore vs. Your Hard Drive

Ever wonder where it stashes all these backup copies of your operating system? They're in a folder called System Volume Information, which is in your Local Disk (C:) window. Inside *that* are individual files for each restore point. (System Volume Information is generally an invisible folder, but you can make it visible following the instructions on page 84. You still won't be allowed to move, rename, or delete it, however—thank goodness. In fact, you won't even be able to look inside it.)

Now, in Windows XP, you could set a limit on how much disk space all of these restore points consumed. But no longer. What you see is what you get. You can turn off System Restore entirely, but you can't change how much space is devoted to it.

So what are you supposed to do when you're getting pressed for disk space?

In such times of crisis, you can delete all but the *most recent* system restore point. To get there, choose Start→All Programs→Accessories→System Tools→Disk Cleanup.

Click "Files from all users on this computer"; authenticate yourself (page 191). Select the hard drive you want to clean up—probably your C: drive.

After the program examines your system, it displays a list of the files you can clean. Click the More Options tab, and then click the "Clean up" button in the System Restore section.

Note, however, that this process also deletes the backups of all your *documents* (those created by the Shadow Copy feature described on page 654). In fact, it even deletes any Complete PC Backup images that you could have used to restore your PC to a pristine state in a crisis (page 647).

So be careful out there.

- After every 24 hours of real-world time (unless your PC is turned off all day; then you get a restore point the next time it's turned on).

- Every time you install a new program or install a new device driver for a piece of hardware.

- When you install a Windows Update.

- When you make a backup using Windows Backup.

- Whenever you feel like it—for instance, just before you install some new component.

To create one of these checkpoints *manually*, choose Start→Control Panel. In Classic view, open Backup and Restore Center; in the task pane at left, click "Create a restore point or change settings." Authenticate yourself (page 191).

Now the System Properties dialog box appears, already open to the System Protection tab (Figure 22-4). Click Create, type a name for the restore point, click Create again, and the restore point is created. Don't include the date and time in the name of the restore point; you'll see that when you get around to doing an actual restoration.

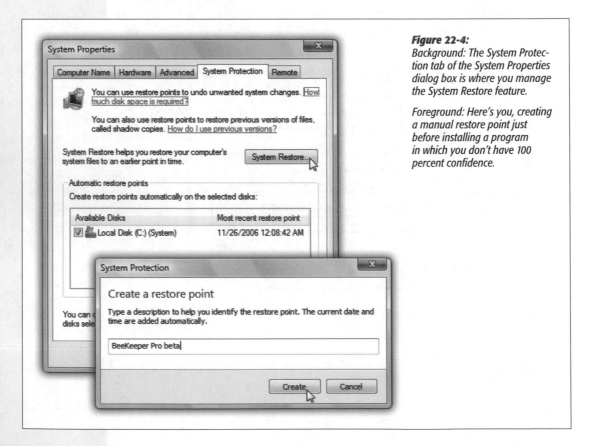

Figure 22-4:
Background: The System Protection tab of the System Properties dialog box is where you manage the System Restore feature.

Foreground: Here's you, creating a manual restore point just before installing a program in which you don't have 100 percent confidence.

Note: When your hard drive is running low on space, System Restore turns off automatically, without notice. It turns itself back on when you free up some space.

As you can well imagine, storing all these copies of your Windows configuration consumes quite a bit of disk space. Out of the box, System Restore can use up to 15 percent of every hard drive—that adds up quickly!

That's why Windows Vista automatically begins *deleting* restore points when it's running out of disk space. That's also why the System Restore feature stops working if your hard drive is very full.

And that's *also* why you should run the System Restore feature promptly when your PC acts strangely.

Performing a System Restore

If something goes wrong with your PC, here's how to roll it back to the happy, bygone days of late last week—or this morning, for that matter:

1. **Choose Start→Control Panel. In Classic view, open Backup and Restore Center. In the task pane at left, click "Repair Windows using System Restore." Authenticate yourself (page 191).**

   The "Restore system files and settings" screen appears (Figure 22-5).

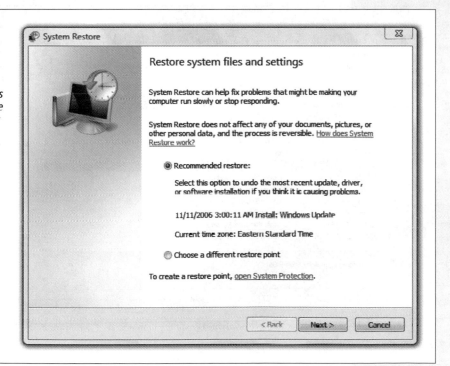

Figure 22-5:
When you use System Restore, you'll be shown the date and time of your most recent restore point, as well as why the restore point was created—for example, because you installed a new piece of software, or because you applied a Windows Update. That's a clue as to which restore point you should use.

2. **If you want to use the recommended restore point, click Next. Otherwise, skip to step 5.**

   Windows recommends that you use the most *recent* restore point. When you click Next, it asks you to confirm your decision.

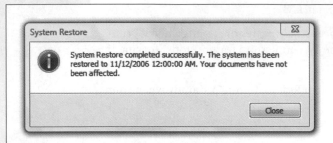

Figure 22-6:
When you've successfully restored your PC to an earlier time, you'll get this message. Click Close, and go on your merry way.

3. **Close all open files and programs. Click Finish.**

   You have one more chance to back out: Windows asks if you *really* want to continue.

4. **Click Yes.**

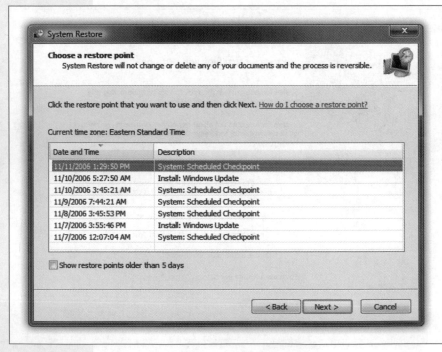

Figure 22-7:
The Description column for checkpoints shows you why the restore points were created—for example, because a Windows Update was installed. You can provide your own names for restore points only when you create them manually. (You'll see their names here.)

Windows goes to town, reinstating your operating system to reflect its condition on the date you specified. Leave your PC alone while this occurs.

When the process is complete, the computer restarts automatically. When you log back in, the message shown at the bottom of Figure 22-6 appears. Welcome back to the past.

5. **If you want a different restore point, select "Choose a different restore point," and then click Next.**

   Now you see a list of all restore points (which Windows also calls checkpoints) that have been created in the last five days (Figure 22-7). For each checkpoint, you'll see the time, date, and a description. If you want to see checkpoints from before five days ago, turn on the "Show restore points older than 5 days" checkbox.

6. **Click the checkpoint you want, and then click Next.**

   You'll be asked to confirm that you want to use that checkpoint.

7. **Close all files and programs. Click Finish.**

   Windows restores your PC to the past, as outlined in step 2.

Tip: If rewinding your system to the golden days actually makes matters worse, you can always reverse the entire Restore process. To do so, choose Start→Control Panel. In Classic view, open Backup and Restore Center. In the task pane at left, click "Repair Windows using System Restore." From the System Restore screen that appears, click Undo System Restore. Click Next, click Finish, click Yes, and wait for the process to reverse itself.

Turning System Restore Off

You really shouldn't turn off System Restore. You really, really shouldn't. It's just so incredibly useful, when you're pressed for time and things start going wacky, to be

---

Your Invisible Best Friend: Windows Resource Protection

One of Vista's best PC-health features has no control panel, no window, and no icon of its own. It's a behind-the-scenes, automatic feature that may have already saved your PC's hide a time or two without your knowledge. It's Windows Resource Protection, which replaces the System File Protection feature in Windows Me and Windows XP.

This feature solves the age-old "My-application's-installer-replaced-an-important-system-file-with-an-older-version-and-now-nothing-works!" snafu. It also protects the Windows Registry (page 787) against unauthorized changes. In fact, it protects all of your important Windows files and settings from being changed in a way that could harm your PC.

Simply put, Windows Vista doesn't let any program replace a Windows file with an older version. True, this may mean that some older programs won't run—but better to do without them than your entire PC. It also won't allow older programs, or malware—or even you—to make permanent changes to certain system files.

---

able to hit rewind and grant yourself a perfectly smooth PC, even if you never do find out what the trouble is.

But if you're an advanced power user with no hard drive space to spare—is there such a person?—here's how you shut off this feature:

1. **Open the Start menu. While it's open, right-click Computer; from the shortcut menu, choose Properties.**

   The System Properties control panel appears.

2. **In the left-hand pane, click "Advanced system settings." Authenticate yourself (page 191).**

   You arrive at the Advanced tab of the System Properties dialog box.

3. **Click the System Protection tab. Turn off the checkboxes for the hard drives in the Available Disks list.**

   Vista asks if you're sure you want to turn System Restore off.

4. **Click Turn System Restore Off. Click OK.**

   That's it. You're flying without a net now, baby.

Shadow Copies
Business • Enterprise • Ultimate Edition

System Restore is an amazing, powerful, career-saving feature—but it's awfully self-interested. It cares only about protecting *Windows*.

How can you rewind your *documents* to their earlier, healthier, or pre-edited conditions?

The Shadow knows…Shadow Copy, that is.

The new Vista feature called *Shadow Copy* is a time machine for documents in the same way System Restore is a time machine for your system software. It's an incredible safety net against damage, accidental modification, or late-night bouts of ill-advised editing.

UP TO SPEED

What Shadow Copies Aren't

The Shadow Copy feature isn't a substitute for backing up your computer. For example, this feature won't help you if you *deleted* a document, because it's designed only to give you previous versions of *existing* documents. It's also no protection against hard drive death, since shadow copies are usually stored on the same hard drive as the originals. See page 641 for details on making proper backups.

Shadow copies also aren't the same as an infinite Undo command. Copies are made only once a day, so you can't, for example, rewind a document to the state it was in three hours ago.

Making Shadow Copies

The beauty of Shadow Copy is that it's automatic and invisible. It's *part* of System Restore, actually, meaning that unless you've turned System Restore *off*, Shadow Copy is protecting your documents, too. To save time and disk space, Shadow Copy only bothers copying files that have changed since the last Restore Point was created.

Recovering Old Document Versions

If the worst should happen, and you realize that you really preferred the draft of your novel that you had three revisions ago, right-click the file or folder in question. From the shortcut menu, choose Restore Previous Version.

The Previous Versions tab of the Properties dialog box opens (Figure 22-8), complete with a list of all the shadow copies of the file. Select the file you want to restore.

Figure 22-8:
Older versions of a file are listed on the Previous Versions tab. Before restoring a file, it's a good idea to open it first and preview it, to make sure you do want to use that version instead of the current one. For absolute safety, click Copy; the screen on the right appears, letting you save a copy of the file in a different folder.

Now, you *could* just click Restore; that would certainly do the trick. Trouble is, this is a permanent maneuver, so once you restore a document to the Tuesday version, today's more recent draft is gone forever.

Therefore, it's a good idea to play it safer using one of these techniques:

- Highlight the file; click Open. The document opens on the screen so you can make sure this is the version you wanted.

• Select the file and click Copy. A dialog box appears so you can peel off a copy of the older document instead of nuking the modern one.

Note: Here's a warning to anyone who *dual-boots* between Vista and Windows XP (page 623): for some extremely technical and extremely unfortunate reasons, starting up in Windows XP *deletes* all of your shadow copies *and* restore points (*and* all Complete PC backups, described later in this chapter, except for the most recent one).

The only workaround is to turn off the hard drive that contains these files before starting up in Windows XP. Microsoft is very sorry.

Safe Mode and the Startup Menu
All Versions

If the problems you're having are caused by drivers that load just as the computer is starting up, turning them all off can be helpful. At the very least, it allows you to get into your machine to begin your troubleshooting pursuit. That's precisely the purpose of the Startup menu—a menu most people never even know exists until they're initiated into its secret world by a technically savvy guru.

Making the Startup menu appear is a matter of delicate timing. First, restart the computer. Immediately after the BIOS startup messages disappear, press the F8 key (on the top row of most keyboards).

The BIOS startup messages—the usual crude-looking text on a black screen, filled with copyright notices and technical specs—are the first things you see after turning on the computer.

If you press the F8 key after the Windows logo makes its appearance, you're too late. But if all goes well, you see the Advanced Boot Options screen (Figure 22-9). Displayed against a black DOS screen, in rough lettering, is a long list of options that includes Safe Mode, Safe Mode with Networking, Safe Mode with Command Prompt, Enable Boot Logging, and so on. Use the arrow keys to "walk through" them.

Here's what the Startup menu commands do:

• **Safe Mode.** Safe Mode starts up Windows in a special, stripped-down, generic, somewhat frightening-looking startup mode—with the software for dozens of hardware and software features *turned off*. Only the very basic components work: your mouse, keyboard, screen, and disk drives. Everything else is shut down and cut off. In short, Safe Mode is the tactic to take if your PC *won't* start up normally, thanks to some recalcitrant driver.

Once you select the Safe Mode option on the Startup menu, you see a list, filling your screen, of every driver that Windows is loading. Eventually, you're asked to log in.

Your screen now looks like it was designed by drunken cavemen, with jagged, awful graphics and text. That's because in Safe Mode, Windows doesn't load the driver for your video card. (It avoids that driver, on the assumption that it may be causing the very problem you're trying to troubleshoot.) Instead, Windows loads a crude, generic driver that works with *any* video card.

The purpose of Safe Mode is to help you troubleshoot. If you discover that the problem you've been having is now gone, you've at least established that the culprit is one of the drivers that Windows has now turned off. Safe Mode also gives you full access to the technical tools of Windows Vista, including System Restore (page 648), the Device Manager (page 567), the Registry Editor (page 788), the Backup and Restore Center, and Help. You might use the Device Manager, for example, to roll back a driver that you just updated (page 570), or System Restore to undo some other installation that seems to have thrown your PC into chaos.

If this procedure doesn't solve the problem, contact a support technician.

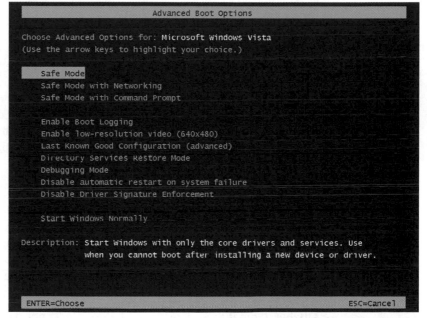

Figure 22-9:
Let's hope you never need to see this screen. It's the Advanced Boot Options screen—a graphically uninteresting, but troubleshootingly critical starting point. To make a selection, press the up or down arrow keys to walk through the list. Press Enter when you've highlighted the option you want.

- **Safe Mode with Networking.** This option is exactly the same as Safe Mode, except that it also lets you load the driver software needed to tap into a network, if you're on one, or onto the Internet—an arrangement that offers a few additional troubleshooting possibilities, like being able to access files and drivers on another PC or from the Internet. (If you have a laptop that uses a PC Card networking card, however, this option still may not help you, since the PC Card driver itself is still turned off.)

- **Safe Mode with Command Prompt.** Here's another variation of Safe Mode, this one intended for ultra–power users who are more comfortable typing out text commands at the command prompt (page 255) than using icons, menus, and the mouse.

- **Enable Boot Logging.** This startup method is the same as Normal, except that Windows records every technical event that takes place during the startup in a log file named *ntbtlog.txt* (located on the startup drive, in the Windows folder).

  Most of the time, you'll use the Boot Logging option only at the request of a support technician you've phoned for help. After confirming the operating system startup, the technician may ask you to open ntbtlog.txt in your Notepad program and search for particular words or phrases—usually the word "fail."

- **Enable VGA Mode.** In this mode, your PC uses a standard VGA video driver that works with all graphics cards, instead of the hideously ugly generic one usually seen in Safe Mode. Use this option when you're troubleshooting video-display problems—problems that you're confident have less to do with drivers than with your settings in the Display control panel (which you're now ready to fiddle with).

  (Of course, VGA means 640 x 480 pixels, which looks huge and crude on today's big monitors. Do not adjust your set.)

- **Last Known Good Configuration.** Here's yet another method of resetting the clock to a time when your PC was working correctly, in effect undoing whatever configuration change you made that triggered your PC's current problems. It reinstates whichever set of drivers, and whichever Registry configuration, was in force the last time the PC was working right. (This option, however, isn't as effective as the System Restore option, which also restores operating-system files in the process.)

- **Directory Services Restore Mode.** This extremely technical option is useful only in corporations with specialized *domain controller* computers running Windows .NET Server or Windows 2000 Server.

- **Debugging Mode.** Here's another extremely obscure option, this one intended for very technical people who've connected one PC to another via a serial cable. They can then use the second computer to analyze the first, using specialized debugger software.

- **Disable automatic restart on system failure.** Under normal conditions, Windows will automatically reboot after a system crash. Choose this option if you don't want it to reboot.

- **Disable Driver Signature Enforcement.** As a way to protect your PC, Windows uses a technique called Driver Signature Enforcement, which is designed to load only drivers that are verified to be valid. Of course, there are plenty of times when drivers aren't verified, but in fact are usable. If you suspect that to be the case, choose this option; Windows will load all your drivers.

- **Start Windows Normally.** This option starts the operating system in its usual fashion, exactly as though you never summoned the Startup menu to begin with. The Normal option lets you tell the PC, "Sorry to have interrupted you…go ahead."

Problem Reports and Solutions

All Versions

What may one day become Vista's best new troubleshooting feature is its ability to find problems with your PC *automatically*—and then offer to fix them for you. It's like a built-in tech support staff on your PC, except that you never get put on hold.

To use the feature, choose Start→Control Panel. Click "System and Maintenance," and then "Problem Reports and Solutions." The Problem Reports and Solutions window (Figure 22-10) appears.

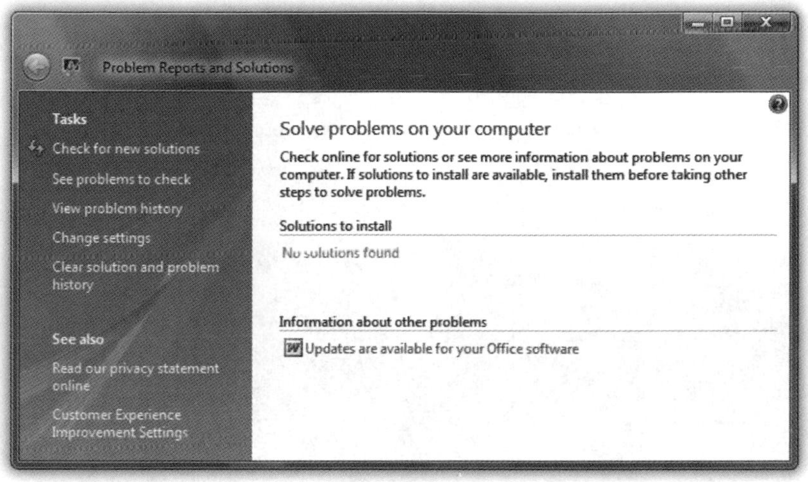

Figure 22-10:
If Windows detects crashes, freezes, or hiccups on your PC that can be solved by downloading updates or installing other fixes, it tells you here. Click the solution or update, and Windows automatically installs it.

If any fixes or updates are available, they'll be shown here. Performing the fix is simplicity itself—click it and follow the directions.

Down the left-hand side of the screen, you'll find these links that will help you with more troubleshooting:

- **Check for new solutions** checks your system to see whether there are solutions for problems you've had. During this process, your PC may send information about system crashes to Microsoft.

  The idea, of course, is that if enough thousands of people report the same problems to Microsoft's Master Glitch Database, the engineers there may be able to piece together what's going on—and to work with the software companies in question to come up with a fix.

- **See problems to check** lists all the errors and problems that Windows has detected but hasn't yet fixed or checked. These problems may not necessarily be current; for example, one could be a one-time instance of an application not responding.

When you see the results, turn on the checkboxes for any that you want to find solutions for; then let Vista see if there are solutions. If it finds any, a wizard appears to help you fix the problem.

- **View problem history** displays a list of program crashes, freezes, and other glitches that Windows has detected and fixed, or couldn't find a fix for but reported to Microsoft anyway. You'll see the product, program, or service that had a problem,

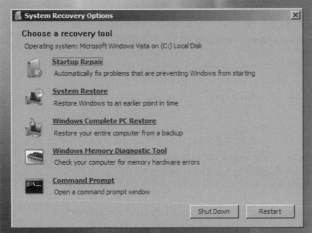

Figure 22-11:
If your hard drive won't even let you in, insert your original Vista installation DVD.

Top: At the main installation screen, click "Repair your computer." Specify which copy of Windows you want to repair (not shown).

Bottom: The new Startup Repair suite, at your disposal.

what the problem was, the occurrence date, and the status of the problem. Double-click any for more details.

Tip: If you want to send the details to tech support for additional help, click Copy to Clipboard. Once the text is in the Clipboard, you can paste it into a text file to send.

- **Change settings** lets you change how solutions are checked and solved. Ordinarily, Windows checks for solutions on its own, but if you prefer, it will ask you for permission first when an error occurs.

- **Clear solutions and problem history** clears the list of your problems. Note that this list includes problems that don't yet have solutions—and if you clear them, you may not be able to find solutions to those problems.

Startup Repair (Windows Recovery Environment)

You might play by all the rules. You might make regular backups, keep your antivirus software up to date, and floss twice a day. And then one day, you get your reward: the PC won't even start up. You can't use any of Vista's software troubleshooting tools, because you can't even get to Windows.

In those most dire situations, Microsoft is pleased to introduce Startup Repair, known to techies as WinRE (Windows Recovery Environment). As shown in Figure 22-11, it's a special recovery mode that runs from the *Windows DVD* so that it can fix whatever's damaged or missing on the hard drive's copy of Windows.

Note: Depending on who sold you your PC, you might not have a traditional Windows DVD. Your PC company might even have replaced Startup Repair with a similar tool; check its Web site or manual.

To open Startup Repair, follow these steps:

1. **Start up from your Vista installation DVD.**

   Insert the DVD. Then restart the PC—but as it's coming to life, press the F8 key. Your PC says something like, "Press a key to boot from CD or DVD." So do it—press a key.

   After a moment, the Vista installation screen appears (Figure 22-11, top). But you're not going to install Windows—not yet.

2. **Click "Repair your computer."**

   It's a link at the lower-left corner. Now you're asked which copy of Windows you want to repair. Chances are you've got only one.

3. **Click your copy of Windows.**

   Now the Recovery Environment appears (Figure 22-11, bottom).

At this point, you have some powerful tools available to help you out of your PC's mess. Because you're running off the DVD, you can perform surgeries on the hard drive that you wouldn't be able to if the hard drive itself were in control. That'd be like trying to paint the floor under your own feet.

Your options are:

- **Startup Repair.** If there is indeed a missing or damaged file in your copy of Windows, click this link to trigger an automatic repair job. You're running off the original installation DVD, for heaven's sake, so it's extremely easy for Startup Repair to reach into its bag of spare parts if necessary.

- **System Restore.** Remember System Restore, described at the beginning of this chapter? When better to rewind your Windows installation to a healthier, happier time than right now? Click this link to choose a restore point. With any luck, the rewinding job will include restoring the undamaged startup files that your PC needs right about now.

- **Windows Complete PC Restore.** If you, the proud owner of the Business, Enterprise, or Ultimate edition of Vista, have taken advantage of the Complete PC backup feature (page 647), then you're in luck. You have at your disposal a complete disk image of your hard drive, presumably made when the disk was working fine. This mirror includes everything on it: your copy of Windows, all your programs, all your documents and settings, the works. It's like super System Restore. Click this link to copy the whole schmear back onto your hard drive. (Of course, you'll lose any documents or settings you've changed since the backup was made.)

- **Windows Memory Diagnostic Tool.** Click this link if you suspect that it's your RAM (memory), not the hard drive, that's causing your problems. The software does a quick check to make sure your memory hardware is actually working right.

- **Command Prompt.** If you're lucky enough to know what you're doing at the command prompt (page 255), you're in luck. You can use it to issue commands and perform repair surgery.

Thanks to these powerful tools, there's less reason than ever to pay $35 for the privilege of talking to some technician named "Mike" who's actually in India, following a tech-support script that instructs you to first erase your hard drive and reinstall Windows from scratch.

Part Seven: The Vista Network

7

Chapter 23: Accounts (and Logging On)

Chapter 24: Setting Up a Workgroup Network

Chapter 25: Network Domains

Chapter 26: Network Sharing and Collaboration

Chapter 27: Vista by Remote Control

Accounts (and Logging On)

For years, teachers, parents, tech directors, and computer lab instructors struggled to answer two difficult questions. How do you rig one PC so that several different people can use it throughout the day, without interfering with each other's files and settings? And how do you protect a PC from getting fouled up by mischievous (or bumbling) students and employees?

Introducing User Accounts
All Versions

Windows Vista was designed from the ground up to be a multiple-user operating system. Anyone who uses the computer must *log on*—click (or type) your name and type in a password—when the computer turns on. Upon doing so, you discover the Windows universe just as you left it, including these elements:

- **Desktop.** Each person sees his own shortcut icons, folder icons, and other stuff left out on the desktop.

- **Start menu.** If you reorganize the Start menu, as described in Chapter 1, you won't confuse anybody else who uses the machine. No one else can even *see* the changes you make.

- **Documents folder.** Each person sees only her own stuff in the Documents folder.

- **Email.** Windows maintains a separate stash of email messages for each account holder—along with separate Web bookmarks, a Windows Messenger contact list, and other online details.

- **Favorites folder.** Any Web sites, folders, or other icons you've designated as Favorites appear in *your* Favorites menu, and nobody else's.

- **Internet cache.** You can read about *cached* Web pages in Chapter 11. This folder stores a copy of the Web pages you've visited recently for faster retrieval.

- **History and cookies.** Windows maintains a list of recently visited Web sites independently for each person; likewise, it stores a personal collection of *cookies* (Web site preference files).

- **Control Panel settings.** Windows memorizes the preferences each person establishes using the Control Panel (see Chapter 8), including keyboard, sound, screen saver, and mouse settings.

Note: Not all Control Panel settings are available to everyone. Really important ones that affect the entire PC, like the date and time, and network settings, can be changed only by the Lord of the PC–the *administrative* account holder, described in a moment.

- **Privileges.** Your user account also determines what you're allowed to do on the network and even on your own computer: which settings you can change in the Control Panel, and even which files and folders you can open.

Behind the scenes, Windows stores *all* these files and settings in a single folder—your Personal folder, the one that bears your name. You can open it easily enough; it's at the top right of the Start menu. (Technically, your Personal folder is in the Computer→Local Disk (C:)→Users folder.)

This feature makes sharing the PC much more convenient, because you don't have to look at everybody else's files (and endure their desktop design schemes). It also adds a layer of security, making it less likely for a marauding 6-year-old to throw away your files.

Tip: Even if you don't share your PC with anyone and don't create any other accounts, you might still appreciate this feature because it effectively password-protects the entire computer. Your PC is protected from unauthorized fiddling when you're away from your desk (or if your laptop is stolen)–especially if you tell Windows to require your logon password any time after the screen saver has kicked in (page 167).

Since the day you first installed Windows Vista or fired up a new Vista machine, you may have made a number of changes to your desktop—fiddled with your Start menu, changed the desktop wallpaper, added some favorites to your Web browser, downloaded files onto your desktop, and so on—without realizing that you were actually making these changes only to *your account*.

Accordingly, if you create an account for a second person, when she turns on the computer and signs in, she'll find the desktop exactly the way it was as factory-installed by Microsoft: basic Start menu, nature-photo desktop picture, default Web browser home page, and so on. She can make the same kinds of changes to the PC that you've made, but nothing she does will affect your environment the next time *you* log on.

You'll still find the desktop the way you left it: *your* desktop picture fills the screen, the Web browser lists *your* bookmarks, and so on.

In other words, the multiple-accounts feature has two components: first, a convenience element that hides everyone else's junk; and second, a security element that protects both the PC's system software and other people's work.

If you're content simply to *use* Windows, that's really all you need to know about accounts. If, on the other hand, you have shouldered some of the responsibility for *administering* Windows machines—if it's your job to add and remove accounts, for example—read on.

Windows Vista: The OS with Two Faces
All Versions

As you may remember from the beginning of Chapter 1, Vista is designed to handle either of two different kinds of networks: *workgroups* (small, informal home or small-business networks) and *domains* (corporate, professionally and centrally administered).

This distinction becomes particularly important when it comes to user accounts.

- **A workgroup network.** In this smaller kind of network, each computer stores its own security settings, such as user accounts, passwords, and permissions. You can't open files on another computer on the network unless its owner has created an account for you on *that* computer. Before you can access the files on the Front Desk PC and the Upstairs PC, for example, you must create an account for yourself on each of those machines.

  Clearly, setting up an account on every PC for every employee would get out of hand in a huge company.

  If you're part of a workgroup network (or no network), you'll find that Windows gives you simplified, but less secure, access to user accounts and permissions, both of which are described in this chapter.

- **A domain network.** In a corporation, your files may not be sitting right there on your hard drive. They may, in fact, sit on a network server—a separate computer dedicated to dishing out files to employees from across the network. As you can probably imagine, protecting all this information is somebody's Job Number One.

  That's why, if your PC is part of a domain, you'll find Windows Vista more reminiscent of Windows 2000, with more business-oriented features and full access to the account-maintenance and permissions-management options. (Only the Business, Enterprise, and Ultimate editions of Vista can speak to domain networks.)

This chapter tackles these two broad feature categories—the workgroup scenario and the domain scenario—one at a time.

Local Accounts

All Versions

This section is dedicated to computers in a workgroup network—or no network at all. If your computer is a member of a corporate domain, skip to "Local Accounts on a Domain Computer," later in this chapter.

To see what accounts are already on your PC, choose Start→Control Panel, and then, under User Accounts and Family Safety, click "Add or remove user accounts."

You're asked to authenticate yourself (page 191), and then you see a list of existing accounts (Figure 23-1).

Figure 23-1:
This screen lists everyone for whom you've created an account. From here, you can create new accounts or change people's passwords. (Hint: To change account settings, just click the person's name on the bottom half of the screen. Clicking the "Change an account" link at the top requires an extra click.)

If you see more than one account here—not just yours—then one of these situations probably applies:

- You created them when you installed Windows Vista, as described in Appendix A.

- You bought a new computer with Vista preinstalled, and created several accounts when asked to do so the first time you turned on the machine.

- You upgraded the machine from an earlier version of Windows. Vista gracefully imports all of your existing accounts.

If you're new at this, there's probably just one account listed here: yours. This is the account that Windows created when you first installed it.

Administrator vs. Standard Accounts

It's important to understand the phrase that appears just under each person's name. On your own personal PC, the word Administrator probably appears underneath yours.

Because you're the person who installed Vista, the PC assumes that you're one of its *administrators*—the technical wizards who will be in charge of it. You're the teacher, the parent, the resident guru. You're the one who will maintain this PC and who will be permitted to make system-wide changes to it.

You'll find settings all over Windows (and all over this book) that *only* people with Administrator accounts can change. For example, only an administrator is allowed to:

- Create or delete accounts and passwords on the PC.

- Install new programs (and certain hardware components).

- Make changes to certain Control Panel programs that are off limits to non-administrators.

- See and manipulate *any* file on the machine.

There's another kind of account, too, for people who *don't* have to make those kinds of changes: the Standard account.

Now, until Vista came along, people doled out Administrator accounts pretty freely. You know: the parents got Administrator accounts, the kids got Standard ones.

The trouble is, an Administrator account *itself* is a kind of security hole. Any time you're logged in with this kind of account, any nasty software you may have caught from the Internet is *also*, in effect, logged in—and can make changes to important underlying settings on your PC, just the way a human administrator can.

Put another way: If a Standard account holder manages to download a computer virus, its infection will be confined to his account. If an *administrator* catches a virus, on the other hand, every file on the machine is at risk.

In Vista, therefore, Microsoft recommends that *everyone* use Standard accounts—even you, the wise master and owner of the computer!

So how are you supposed to make important Control Panel changes, install new programs, and so on?

That's gotten a lot easier in Vista. Using a Standard account no longer means that you can't make important changes. In fact, you can do just about everything on the PC that an Administrator account can—*if* you know the *name and password* of a true Administrator account.

Note: Every Vista PC can (and must) keep at least one Administrator account on hand, even if you rarely log in with that account.

Whenever you try to make a big change, you're asked to authenticate yourself. As described on page 191, that means supplying an Administrator account's name and password, even though you, the currently logged-in person, are a lowly Standard account holder (Figure 23-2).

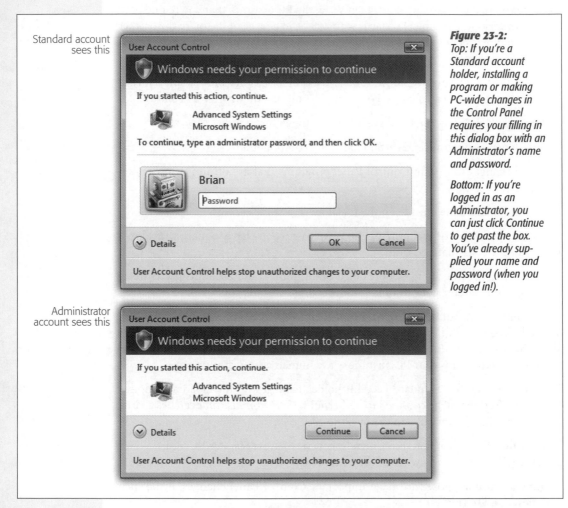

Standard account sees this

User Account Control

Windows needs your permission to continue

If you started this action, continue.

Advanced System Settings
Microsoft Windows

To continue, type an administrator password, and then click OK.

Brian

Password

Details   OK   Cancel

User Account Control helps stop unauthorized changes to your computer.

Administrator account sees this

User Account Control

Windows needs your permission to continue

If you started this action, continue.

Advanced System Settings
Microsoft Windows

Details   Continue   Cancel

User Account Control helps stop unauthorized changes to your computer.

Figure 23-2:
Top: If you're a Standard account holder, installing a program or making PC-wide changes in the Control Panel requires your filling in this dialog box with an Administrator's name and password.

Bottom: If you're logged in as an Administrator, you can just click Continue to get past the box. You've already supplied your name and password (when you logged in!).

The idea is that if you really *are* a Standard account holder, you can call over an Administrator to approve the change you're making. And if you really are the PC's owner, you know the Administrator account's password anyway, so it's no big deal.

Now, making broad changes to a PC when you're an Administrator *still* presents you with those "prove yourself worthy" authentication dialog boxes. The only difference is that you, the Administrator, can click Continue to bypass them, rather than having to type in a name and password.

You'll have to weigh this security/convenience tradeoff. But you've been warned: the least vulnerable PC is one where everyone uses Standard accounts.

Adding an Account

Once you've opened the Manage Accounts window in the Control Panel, it's easy to create a new account: click the "Create a new account" link shown in Figure 23-1. (You see this link only if you are, in fact, an administrator.)

The next screen asks you to name the account and choose an account type: Administrator or Standard (Figure 23-3).

When you're finished with the settings, click Create Account (or press Enter). After a moment, you return to the User Accounts screen (Figure 23-1), where the new person's name joins whatever names were already there. You can continue adding new accounts forever or until your hard drive is full, whichever comes first.

Tip: If you never had the opportunity to set up a user account when installing Windows Vista—if you bought a PC with Windows already on it, for example—you may see an account named Owner already in place. Nobody can use Windows at all unless there's at least *one* Administrator account on it, so Microsoft is doing you a favor here.

Just use the User Accounts program in the Control Panel to change the name Owner to one that suits you better. Make that account your own using the steps in the following paragraphs.

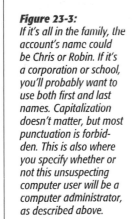

Figure 23-3:
If it's all in the family, the account's name could be Chris or Robin. If it's a corporation or school, you'll probably want to use both first and last names. Capitalization doesn't matter, but most punctuation is forbidden. This is also where you specify whether or not this unsuspecting computer user will be a computer administrator, as described above.

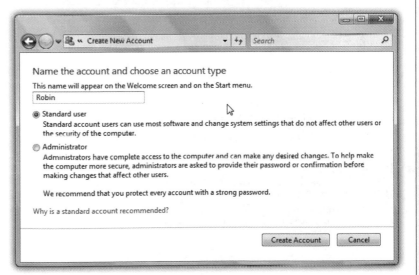

Editing an Account

Although the process of creating a new account is swift and simple, it doesn't offer you much in the way of flexibility. You don't even have a chance to specify the new person's password, let alone the tiny picture that appears next to the person's name and at the top of the Start menu (rubber ducky, flower, or whatever).

That's why the next step in creating an account is usually *editing* the one you just set up. To do so, once you've returned to the main User Accounts screen (Figure 23-1), click the name or icon of the freshly created account. You arrive at the screen shown at the top in Figure 23-4, where—if you are an administrator—you can choose from any of these options:

- **Change the name.** Click "Change the account name." You'll be offered the opportunity to type in a new name for this person and then click the Change Name button—just the ticket when one of your co-workers gets married or joins the Witness Protection Program.

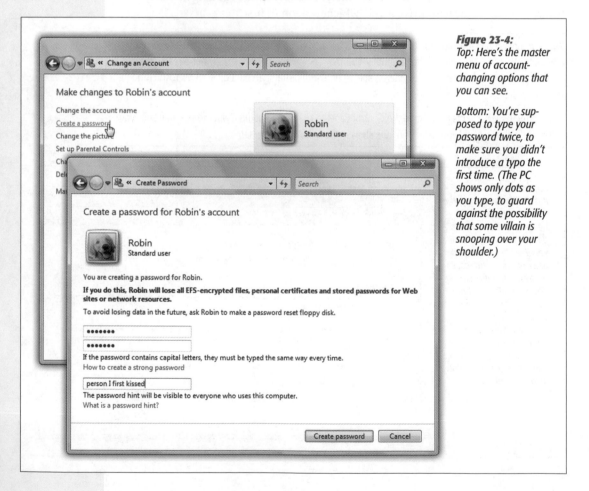

Figure 23-4:
Top: Here's the master menu of account-changing options that you can see.

Bottom: You're supposed to type your password twice, to make sure you didn't introduce a typo the first time. (The PC shows only dots as you type, to guard against the possibility that some villain is snooping over your shoulder.)

- **Create a password.** Click this link if you'd like to require a password for access to this person's account (Figure 23-4, bottom). Capitalization counts.

The usual computer book takes this opportunity to stress the importance of having a long, complex password, such as a phrase that isn't in the dictionary, something made up of mixed letters and numbers, and *not*, by the way, the word "password." This is excellent advice if you create sensitive documents and work in a corporation.

But if you share the PC only with a spouse or a few trusted colleagues in a small office, you may have nothing to hide. You may see the multiple-users feature more as a convenience (for keeping your settings and files separate) than a way of protecting secrecy and security.

In these situations, there's no particular need to dream up a convoluted password. In fact, you may want to consider setting up *no* password—leaving both password blanks empty. Later, whenever you're asked for your password, just leave the Password box blank. You'll be able to log on and authenticate yourself that much faster each day.

If you do decide to provide a password, you can also provide a *hint* (for yourself or whichever co-worker's account you're operating on). This is a hint that anybody can see (including bad guys trying to log on as you), so choose something meaningful only to you. If your password is the first person who ever kissed you plus your junior-year phone number, for example, your hint might be "first person who ever kissed me plus my junior-year phone number."

Later, when you log in and can't remember your password, leave the Password box empty and hit Enter. You'll wind up back at the login screen to try again—but this time, your hint will appear just below the Password box to jog your memory.

Tip: When you're creating accounts that other people will use to access their machines from across the network, set up the same passwords they use when logging onto their own computers. You'll save them time and hassle. Once they've logged onto another machine on the network, they'll be able to connect to their own computer without having to type in another name and password.

- **Remove the password.** By removing the password, you open up the opportunity for this person to replace it with something better.

By the way, be careful when you remove someone else's password after they've been using the computer for a while. If you do, you'll wipe out various internal security features of their accounts, including encrypted files, access to their stored Web site passwords, and stored passwords for shared folders and disks on the network (Chapter 26). See the box on page 676 for details.

- **Change the picture.** The usual sign-in screen (Figure 23-1) displays each account holder's name, accompanied by a little picture. When you first create the account, however, it assigns a picture to you at random—and not all of the pictures are necessarily appropriate for your personality. Not every extreme-sport headbanger, for example, is crazy about being represented by a dainty flower or kitten.

If you like one of the selections that Microsoft has provided, just click it to select it as the replacement graphic. If you'd rather use some other graphics file on the hard drive instead—a digital photo of your own face, for example—you can click the "Browse for more pictures" link (Figure 23-5). You'll be shown a list of the graphics files on your hard drive so you can choose one, which Windows then automatically scales down to postage-stamp size (48 pixels square).

- **Set up Parental Controls.** Whenever you edit a Standard account, this link is available, on the premise that this person is either a child or someone who acts like one. See page 361 for the Parental Controls details.

Figure 23-5:
Here's where you change your account picture. If a camera or scanner is attached, you get an extra link here, "Get a picture from a camera or scanner"—instant picture.

- **Change the account type.** Click this link to change a Standard account into an Administrator account, or vice versa.

- **Delete the account.** See page 676.

You're free to make any of these changes to any account at any time; you don't have to do it immediately after creating the account.

Tip: The Start menu offers a big, fat shortcut to the Edit Account dialog box shown in Figure 23-4: just click your picture at the top of the open Start menu.

The Forgotten Password Disk
As described above, Windows contains a handy hint mechanism for helping you recall your password if you've forgotten it.

But what if, having walked into a low-hanging branch, you've completely forgotten both your password *and* the correct interpretation of your hint? In that disastrous situation, your entire world of work and email would be locked inside the computer forever. (Yes, an administrator could issue you a new password—but as noted in the box on page 676, you'd lose all your secondary passwords in the process.)

Fortunately, Windows offers a clever solution-in-advance: the Password Reset Disk. It's a CD or USB flash drive (not a floppy, as in Windows XP) that you can use like a physical key to unlock your account, in the event of a forgotten password. The catch is, you have to make this disk *now,* while you still remember your password.

To create this disk, insert a blank CD or a USB flash drive. Then open the Start menu and click your picture (top right). The "Make changes to your account" window opens (Figure 23-4).

The first link in the task pane says, "Create a password reset disk." Click that to open the Forgotten Password Wizard shown in Figure 23-6. Click through it, supplying your current password when you're asked for it. When you click Finish, remove the CD or flash drive. Label it, and don't lose it!

Tip: Behind the scenes, Vista saves a file onto the CD or flash drive called *userkey.psw.* You can guess what that is.

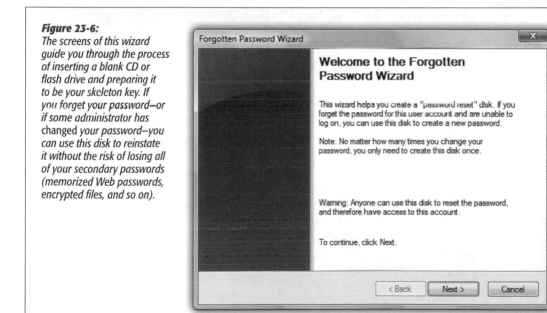

Figure 23-6:
The screens of this wizard guide you through the process of inserting a blank CD or flash drive and preparing it to be your skeleton key. If you forget your password—or if some administrator has changed your password—you can use this disk to reinstate it without the risk of losing all of your secondary passwords (memorized Web passwords, encrypted files, and so on).

Forgotten Password Wizard

Welcome to the Forgotten Password Wizard

This wizard helps you create a "password reset" disk. If you forget the password for this user account and are unable to log on, you can use this disk to create a new password.

Note: No matter how many times you change your password, you only need to create this disk once.

Warning: Anyone can use this disk to reset the password, and therefore have access to this account.

To continue, click Next.

[< Back] [Next >] [Cancel]

When the day comes that you can't remember your password, leave the Password box empty and hit Enter. You'll wind up back at the login screen; this time, in addition to your password hint, you'll see a link called "Reset password." Insert your Password Reset CD or flash drive and then click that link.

A Password Reset Wizard now helps you create a new password (and a new hint to remind you of it). You're in.

Even though you now have a new password, your existing Password Reset Disk is still good. Keep it in a drawer somewhere, for use the next time you experience a temporarily blank brain.

Deleting User Accounts

It happens—somebody graduates, somebody gets fired, somebody dumps you. Sooner or later, you may need to delete an account from your PC.

To delete a user account, open the User Accounts program, click the appropriate account name, and then click "Delete the account."

Windows now asks you if you want to preserve the contents of this person's Documents folder. If you click the Keep Files button, you'll find a new folder, named for the dearly departed, on your desktop. (As noted in the dialog box, only the documents, the contents of the desktop, and the Documents folder are preserved—but *not* programs, email, or even Web favorites.) If that person ever returns to your life, you can create a new account for him and copy these files into the appropriate folder locations.

UP TO SPEED

Passwords Within Passwords

The primary password that you or your administrator sets up in the User Accounts program has two functions. You already know that it lets you log on each day, so you can enter your Windows world of desktop clutter, Start menu tailoring, Web bookmarks, and so on.

But what you may not realize is that it's also the master key that unlocks all the *other* passwords associated with your account: the passwords that Internet Explorer memorizes for certain Web sites, the passwords that get you into shared disks and folders on the network, the password that protects your encrypted files, the password that protects your .NET Passport (and its Wallet for electronic payments, if you set one up), and so on. The simple act of logging onto your account also unlocks all of these other secure areas of your PC life.

But remember that anyone with an Administrator account can *change* your password at any time. Does that mean that whoever has an Administrator account—your teacher, boss,

or teenager, for example—has full access to your private stuff? After you leave the household, company, or school, what's to stop an administrator from changing your password, thereby gaining access to your electronic-brokerage account (courtesy of its memorized Internet Explorer password), buying stuff with your Passport Wallet, and so on?

Fortunately, Microsoft is way ahead of you on this one. The instant an administrator changes somebody else's password, Windows *wipes out* all secondary passwords associated with the account. That administrator can log onto your account and see your everyday files, but not Web sites with memorized passwords, and so on.

Note that if you change your *own* password—or if you use a Password Reset Disk, described in these pages—none of this applies. Your secondary passwords survive intact. It's only when *somebody else* changes your password that this little-known Windows security feature kicks in, sanitizing the account for your protection.

If you click the Delete Files button, on the other hand, the documents are gone forever.

A few more important points about deleting accounts:

- You can't delete the account you're logged into.

- You can't delete the last Administrator account. One account must always remain.

- You can create a new account with the same name and password as one that you deleted earlier, but in Vista's head, it's still not the same account. As described in the box on the facing page, it won't have any of the original *secondary* passwords (for Web sites, encrypted files, and so on).

- Don't manipulate accounts manually (by fooling around in the Users folder, for example). Create, delete, and rename them only using the User Accounts program in the Control Panel. Otherwise, you'll wind up with duplicate or triplicate folders in Users, with the PC name tacked onto the end of the original account name (Bob, Bob.DELL, and so on)—a sure recipe for confusion.

Tip: If you're an administrator, don't miss the Users tab of the Task Manager dialog box. (Press Ctrl+Alt+Delete to get to the Task Manager.) It offers a handy, centralized list of everybody who's logged into your machine, and buttons that let you log them off, disconnect them, or even make a little message pop up on their screens. All of this can be handy whenever you need some information, a troubleshooting session, or a power trip.

POWER USERS' CLINIC

The Other Administrator Account

In previous versions of Windows, there's another kind of Administrator account–*the* Administrator account.

This is a usually invisible, emergency, backup account with full administrator powers and *no password*. Even if you delete all of your other accounts, this one still remains, if only to give you some way to get into your machine. It's called Administrator, and it's ordinarily hidden.

Most people see it only in times of troubleshooting, when they start up their PCs in Safe Mode (page 656). It's the ideal account to use in those situations. Not only does it come with no password assigned, but also it's not limited in any way. It gives you free powers over every file, which is just what you may need to troubleshoot your computer.

The problem is, of course, that anyone who knows about it can get into Windows with full Administrator privileges–and

no need to know a password. Your kid, for example, could blow right past your carefully established Parental Controls (page 361)–and let's not even consider what a virus could do.

So in the more security-minded Vista, the secret Administrator account is still there; you can see it in the Console in Figure 23-8. But it's ordinarily disabled. It comes to life *only* if (a) you're starting your PC in Safe Mode, and (b) if there are no other, *real* Administrator accounts on the machine.

(That's on a standard home or small-office PC. On a corporate domain network, only a networking geek who's got a Domain Admins account can start up in Safe Mode. You know who you are.)

Disabling Accounts

If you *do* expect that your colleague may one day return to your life, you might consider *disabling* the account instead of deleting it. A disabled account doesn't show up on the login screen or in the User Accounts program, but it's still there on the hard drive, and you can bring it back when necessary.

There's no pretty Control Panel link for disabling an account; you'll have to get your hands greasy in the power-user underpinnings of Windows. See "Account is disabled" on page 683 for details.

NOSTALGIA CORNER

The Secret, Fully Automatic Logon Trick

You're supposed to do most of your account-editing work in the User Accounts program of the Control Panel, which is basically a wizard that offers one option per screen. That requirement may not thrill veteran Windows 2000 fans, however, who are used to the much more direct—and more powerful—User Accounts screen.

Actually, it's still in Windows Vista. To make it appear, open the Start menu; type out *control Userpasswords2,* authenticate yourself (page 191), and then press Enter. You see the program shown here.

Most of the functions here are the same as what you'd find in the User Accounts program—it's just that you don't have to slog through several wizard screens to get things done. Here you can add, remove, or edit accounts all in a single screen.

This older Control Panel program also offers a few features that you don't get at all in the new one. For example, you can turn off the checkbox called, "Users must enter a user name and password to use this computer." When you do so, you get, when you click OK, a dialog box called Automatically Log On, where you can specify a user name and password of one special person. This lucky individual won't have to specify any name and password at logon time, and can instead turn on the PC and cruise directly to the desktop. (This feature works only at *startup time.* If you choose Start→Log Off, the standard Logon dialog box appears, so that other people have the opportunity to sign in.)

This automatic-logon business is ordinarily a luxury enjoyed by solo operators whose PCs have only one account and no password. By using the secret User Accounts method, however, you can set up automatic logon even on a PC with several accounts, provided you recognize the security hole that it leaves open.

The Guest Account

Actually, Administrator and Standard aren't the only kinds of accounts you can set up on your PC.

A third kind, called the Guest account, is ideal for situations where somebody is just visiting you for the day. Rather than create an entire account for this person, complete with password, hint, little picture, and so on, you can just switch on the Guest account.

The on/off switch is a tad buried; you have to open the Microsoft Management Console—a program intended for techies (Figure 23-8). The quickest way to get there is to open the Start menu and type *comput*. Double-click Computer Management in the search results and then authenticate yourself (page 191).

In the list at the left side, expand the Local Users and Groups flippy triangle; click the Users folder inside it. Double-click Guest; in the Properties dialog box, turn *off* "Account is disabled," and click OK.

Now, when the visitor tries to log in, she can choose Guest as the account. She can use the computer, but can't see anyone else's files or make any changes to your settings.

When the visitor to your office is finally out of your hair, healthy paranoia suggests that you turn off the Guest account once again. (To do so, follow precisely the same steps, except turn *on* "Account is disabled" in the final step.)

Local Accounts on a Domain Computer

Business • Enterprise • Ultimate

When your computer is a member of a corporate domain, the controls you use to create and manage user accounts are quite a bit different.

In this case, when you choose Start→Control Panel, you see a category called "User Accounts" instead of "User Accounts and Family Safety." And the option called "Add or remove user accounts" on a workgroup PC is now called "Give other users access to this computer."

When you click that option, you see the dialog box shown in Figure 23-7. The layout is different, but the idea is the same: you can see all of the accounts on the computer.

This dialog box lets you create *local* accounts—accounts stored only on your computer, and not on the corporate domain machine—for existing citizens of the domain.

Why would you need a local account, if all of your files and settings are actually stored elsewhere on the network? Because certain tasks, like installing drivers for new hardware, require you to log on using a *local* Administrator account.

Note: This business of creating a local account that corresponds to an *existing domain account* isn't quite the same thing as creating a completely new account for a completely new person. For that purpose, see the following pages.

Creating a Local Account for a Domain Member

When you click the Add button (Figure 23-7), an Add New User Wizard appears. It lets you specify the person's name and the name of the domain that already stores his account. (You can also click the Browse button to search your domain for a specific person.)

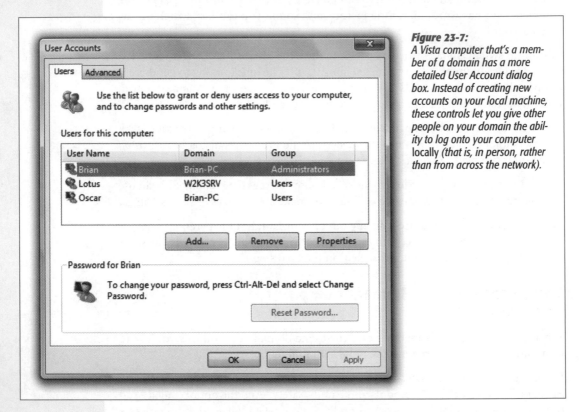

Figure 23-7:
A Vista computer that's a member of a domain has a more detailed User Account dialog box. Instead of creating new accounts on your local machine, these controls let you give other people on your domain the ability to log onto your computer locally (that is, in person, rather than from across the network).

When you click Next, the wizard prompts you to specify what level of access you want to grant this person. You have three choices:

- **Standard user.** This person will be allowed to change certain system settings and install programs that don't affect Windows settings for other users.

- **Administrator.** This person gets the same privileges as a local administrative user.

- **Other.** If you choose this option, you'll be allowed to specify what local *group* this person belongs to, as described later in this chapter.

Once the account you selected appears in the user accounts list, that person is now ready to log into your PC using the local account.

Local Users and Groups

All Versions

The control panels you've read about so far in this chapter are designed for simplicity and convenience, but not for power. Windows offers a second way to create, edit, and delete accounts: an alternative window that, depending on your taste for technical sophistication, is either intimidating and technical—or liberating and flexible.

It's called the Local Users and Groups console.

Opening the Console

You can open up the Local Users and Groups window in any of several ways:

- Choose Start→Control Panel→Classic View→Administrative Tools→Computer Management. Authenticate yourself (page 191). Click the Local Users and Groups icon in the left pane of the window.

- Choose Start→Run, type *Lusrmgr.msc*, and click OK. Authenticate yourself.

- Open the Start menu and type *comput*. The Search results list Computer Management. Double-click it, and then authenticate yourself. In the list at the left side, expand the Local Users and Groups flippy triangle; click the Users folder inside it.

- *Domain PCs only:* Choose Start→Control Panel. Click User Accounts→User Accounts→Manage User Accounts. Click the Advanced tab, then click the Advanced button.

In any case, the Local Users and Groups console appears, as shown in Figure 23-8.

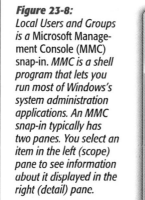

Figure 23-8:
Local Users and Groups is a Microsoft Management Console (MMC) *snap-in. MMC is a shell program that lets you run most of Windows's system administration applications. An MMC snap-in typically has two panes. You select an item in the left (scope) pane to see information about it displayed in the right (detail) pane.*

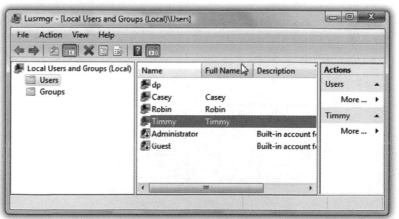

In this console, you have complete control over the local accounts (and groups, as described in a moment) on your computer. This is the real, raw, unshielded command center, intended for power users who aren't easily frightened.

The truth is, you probably won't use these controls much on a domain computer. After all, most people's accounts live on the domain computer, not the local machine. You might occasionally have to log in using the local Administrator account to perform system maintenance and upgrade tasks, but you'll rarely have to create *new* accounts.

Workgroup computers (on a small network) are another story. Remember that you'll have to create a new account for each person who might want to use this computer—or even to access its files from across the network. If you use the Local Users and Groups console to create and edit these accounts, you have much more control over the new account holder's freedom than you do with the User Accounts control panel.

Creating a New Account

To create a new account in the Local Users and Groups console, start by double-clicking the Users folder in the middle of the window. It opens to show you a list of the accounts already on the machine. It includes not only the accounts you created during the Vista installation (and thereafter), but also the Guest and secret Administrator accounts described earlier in this chapter.

To create a new account, choose Action→New User. In the New User dialog box (Figure 23-9), type a name for the account, the person's full name, and if you like, a description. (The description can be anything you like, although Microsoft no doubt has in mind "Shipping manager" rather than "Short and balding.")

Figure 23-9:
When you first create a new user, the "User must change password at next logon" checkbox is turned on. It's telling you that no matter what password you make up when creating the account, your colleague will be asked to make up a new one the first time he logs in. This way, you can assign a simple password (or no password at all) to all new accounts, but your underlings will still be free to devise passwords of their own choosing, and the accounts won't go unprotected.

In the Password and Confirm Password text boxes, specify the password that your new colleague will need to access the account. Its complexity and length are up to your innate sense of paranoia.

Tip: If you can't create a new account, it's probably because you don't have the proper privileges yourself. You must have an Administrator account (page 669) or belong to the Administrators *group* (page 685).

If you turn off the "User must change password at next logon" checkbox, you can turn on options like these:

- **User cannot change password.** This person won't be allowed to change the password that you've just made up. (Some system administrators like to maintain sole control over the account passwords on their computers.)

- **Password never expires.** Using software rules called *local security policies,* an administrator can make account passwords expire after a specific time, periodically forcing employees to make up new ones. It's a security measure designed to foil intruders who somehow get hold of the existing passwords. But if you turn on this option, the person whose account you're now creating will be able to use the same password indefinitely, no matter what the local security policy says.

- **Account is disabled.** When you turn on this box, this account holder won't be able to log on. You might use this option when, for example, somebody goes on sabbatical—it's not as drastic a step as deleting the account, because you can always reactivate the account by turning the checkbox off. You can also use this option to set up certain accounts in advance, which you then activate when the time comes by turning this checkbox off again.

Note: When an account is disabled, a circled down-arrow badge appears on its icon in the Local Users and Groups console. (You may have noticed that the Guest account appears this way when you first install Windows Vista.)

When you click the Create button, you add the new account to the console, and you make the dialog box blank again, ready for you to create another new account, if necessary. When you're finished creating accounts, click Close to return to the main console window.

Groups

As you may have guessed from its name, you can also use the Local Users and Groups window to create *groups*—named collections of account holders.

Suppose you work for a small company that uses a workgroup network. You want to be able to share various files on your computer with certain other people on the network. You'd like to be able to permit them to access some folders, but not others. Smooth network operator that you are, you solve this problem by assigning *permissions* to the appropriate files and folders (page 692).

In fact, you can specify different access permissions to *each file for each person.* But if you had to set up these access privileges manually for every file on your hard drive, for every account holder on the network, you'd go out of your mind—and never get any real work done.

That's where groups come in. You can create one group—called Trusted Comrades, for example—and fill it with the names of every account holder who should be allowed to access your files. Thereafter, it's a piece of cake to give everybody in that group access to a certain folder, in one swift step. You end up having to create only one permission assignment for each file, instead of one for each *person* for each file.

Furthermore, if a new employee joins the company, you can simply add her to the group. Instantly, she has exactly the right access to the right files and folders, without your having to do any additional work.

Creating a group

To create a new group, click the Groups folder in the left side of the Local Users and Groups console (page 681). Choose Action→New Group. Into the appropriate boxes (Figure 23-10), type a name for the group, and a description, if you like. Then click Add.

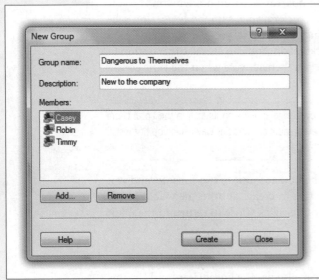

Figure 23-10:
The New Group dialog box lets you specify the members of the group you are creating. A group can have any number of members, and a person can be a member of any number of groups.

A Select Users dialog box appears. Here, you can specify who should be members of your new group. Type each account-holder's name into the text box, separated by semicolons, and then click Check Names to make sure you spelled them right. (You can always add more members to the group, or remove them later.)

Finally, click OK to close the dialog box, and then click Create to add the group to the list in the console. The box appears empty again, ready for you to create another group.

Built-in groups

You may have noticed that even the first time you opened the Users and Groups window, a few group names appeared there already. That's because Windows comes with a canned list of ready-made groups that Microsoft hopes will save you some time.

For example, when you use the User Accounts control panel program to set up a new account, Windows automatically places that person into the Standard or Administrators group, depending on whether or not you made him an administrator (page 669). In fact, that's how Windows knows what powers and freedom this person is supposed to have.

Here are some of the built-in groups on a Vista computer:

- **Administrators.** Members of the Administrators group have complete control over every aspect of the computer. They can modify any setting, create or delete accounts and groups, install or remove any software, and modify or delete any file.

  But as Spiderman's uncle might say, with great power comes great responsibility. Administrator powers make it possible to screw up your operating system in thousands of major and minor ways, either on purpose or by accident. That's why it's a good idea to keep the number of Administrator accounts to a minimum—and even to avoid using one for everyday purposes yourself.

NOSTALGIA CORNER

The Double-Thick Security Trick

If you use Windows Vista in a corporation, you may see the startup box shown here when you first turn on the machine. You don't proceed to the Classic logon box (Figure 23-12) until you first press Ctrl+Alt+Delete.

This somewhat inconvenient setup is intended as a security feature. By forcing you to press Ctrl+Alt+Delete to bypass the initial Welcome box, Windows rules out the possibility that some sneaky program (such as a Trojan-horse program),

Press CTRL + ALT + DELETE to log on

designed to *look* like the Classic logon box, is posing *as* the Classic logon box—in order to "capture" the name and password you type there.

This two-layer logon system is what you get when you add your PC to a network domain during the Windows Vista installation. If you want to use it on a workgroup machine, you can, but you have to do a little digging to find it. Press ⊞+R to open the Run dialog box; type *control Userpasswords2,* and then press Enter. Authenticate yourself (page 191). You see the program shown on page 680—the old-style User Accounts box. Click the Advanced tab.

At the bottom of the Advanced tab, turn on "Require users to press Ctrl+Alt+Delete," and then click OK. From now on, turning on the PC greets you not with a logon screen, but with the unfakeable Welcome box shown here.

- **Power Users.** Members of this group were a big deal in Windows XP—they had fewer powers than Administrators, but still more than mere mortals in the Users group. But Microsoft felt that they added complexity and represented yet another potential security hole. In Vista, this group is essentially abandoned.

- **Users.** Standard account holders (page 669) are members of this group. They can access their own Start menu and desktop settings, their own Documents folders, the Shared Documents folder, and whatever folders they create themselves—but they can't change any computer-wide settings, Windows system files, or program files.

  If you're a member of this group, you can install new programs—but you'll be the only one who can use them. That's by design; any problems introduced by that program (viruses, for example) are limited to your files and not spread to the whole system.

  If you're the administrator, it's a good idea to put most new account holders into this group.

- **Guests.** If you're in this group, you have pretty much the same privileges as members of the Users group. You lose only a few nonessential perks, like the ability to read the computer's *system event log* (a record of behind-the-scenes technical happenings).

In addition to these basic groups, there are some special-purpose groups like Backup Operators, Replicator, Cryptographic Operators, Event Log Readers, and so on. These are all groups with specialized privileges, designed for high-end network administration. You can double-click one (or widen its Description column) to read all about it.

Note: You can add an individual account to as many groups as you like. That person will have the accumulated rights and privileges of all of those groups.

Modifying Users and Groups

To edit an account or group, just double-click its name in the Local Users and Groups window. A Properties dialog box appears, as shown in Figure 23-11.

You can also change an account password by right-clicking the name and choosing Set Password from the shortcut menu. (But see page 676 earlier in this chapter for some cautions about this process.)

Fast User Switching
All Versions

Suppose you're signed in, and you've got things just the way you like them. You have eleven programs open in carefully arranged windows, your Web browser is downloading some gigantic file, and you're composing an important speech in Microsoft

Word. Now Chris, a co-worker/family member/fellow student, wants to duck in to do a quick email check.

In the old days, you might have rewarded Chris with eye-rolling and heavy sighs, or worse. If you chose to accommodate the request, you would have had to shut down your whole ecosystem—interrupting the download, closing your windows, saving your work, and exiting your programs. You would have had to log off completely.

Figure 23-11:
In the Properties dialog box for a user account, you can change the full name or description, modify the password options, and add this person to, or remove this person from, a group. The Properties dialog box for a group is simpler still, containing only a list of the group's members.

Thanks to Fast User Switching, however, none of that is necessary. All you have to do is press the magic keystroke, ⊞+L. (Or, if you've misplaced your keyboard, you can choose Start→Switch User.)

Now the Welcome screen (Figure 23-12) appears, ready for the next person to sign in. Looking at the screen now, you may *think* you've just logged off in the usual way.

But look at it closely: the word *Locked* indicates that you haven't actually logged off at all. Instead, Windows has memorized the state of affairs in your account—complete with all open windows, documents, and programs—and shoved it into the background.

By clicking Switch User, Chris (or whoever) can now sign in normally, do a little work, or look something up. When Chris logs out, the Welcome screen comes back once again, at which point *you* can log on again. Without having to wait more than a couple of seconds, you find yourself exactly where you began, with all programs and documents still open and running.

Tip: In Windows Vista, Fast User Switching can't be turned off.

This feature requires a good deal of memory, of course. However, it's an enormous timesaver.

Tip: Here's the power user's version of Fast User Switching (Administrator account required). Press Ctrl+Alt+Delete to open the Task Manager dialog box (shown on page 192), whose Users tab reveals the list of logged-on accounts. Right-click the account you want, choose Connect from the shortcut menu, and *boom!*—you're switched. You don't even have to listen to the two-note musical switching theme.

Logging On
All Versions

When it comes to the screens you encounter when you log onto a Windows Vista computer, your mileage may vary. What you see depends on how your PC has been set up. For example:

You Get the Windows Welcome Screen

This is what people on standalone or workgroup computers see most of the time (Figure 23-12).

To sign in, click your account name in the list. If no password is required for your account, you proceed to your Windows desktop with no further interruption.

Figure 23-12:
At this moment, you have several alternatives. If you click the ⏻ button (lower-right corner of the screen), you can make the computer turn off, restart, sleep, and so on—maybe because you're in a sudden panic over the amount of work you have to do. Or you can just log in.

If there *is* a password associated with your account, you'll see a place for it (Figure 23-13). Type your password and then press Enter (or click the blue arrow button).

There's no limit to the number of times you can try to type in a password. With each incorrect guess, you're told, "The user name or password is incorrect," and an OK button appears to let you try again. The second time you try, your *password hint* appears, too (page 673), as shown in Figure 23-13.

Tip: If your Caps Lock key is pressed, another balloon lets you know. Otherwise, because you can't see anything on the screen as you type except dots, you might be trying to type a lowercase password with all capital letters.

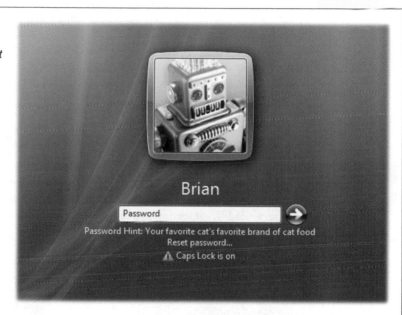

Figure 23-13:
Here's what you see after at least one unsuccessful attempt to plug in your password. If you've created a password reset disk (page 674), you'll see a note here suggesting that you go grab it.

Brian

Password

Password Hint: Your favorite cat's favorite brand of cat food
Reset password...
⚠ Caps Lock is on

You Zoom Straight to the Desktop

If you are the sole account holder, and you've set up no password at all for yourself, you can cruise all the way to the desktop without any stops. The setup steps appear in the box on page 678.

This password-free scenario, of course, is not very secure; any evildoer who walks by your machine when you're in the bathroom has complete access to all of your files (and protected Web sites). But if you work in a home office, for example, where the threat of privacy invasion isn't very great, it's by far the most convenient arrangement.

You Get the "Press Ctrl-Alt-Delete to Begin" Dialog Box

You or your friendly network geek has added your PC to a domain while installing Vista and activated the "Require Users to Press Ctrl-Alt-Delete" option mentioned earlier. This is the most secure configuration, and also the least convenient.

Tip: Even when you're looking at the standard, friendly Welcome screen (Figure 23-12), you can switch to the older, Classic logon screen: just press Ctrl+Alt+Delete. (If you're having trouble making it work, try pressing down the Alt key *before* the other ones.)

You may be used to using the Ctrl+Alt+Delete keystroke for summoning the Task Manager, as described on page 192, but at the Welcome to Windows box, it means something else entirely.

Profiles
All Versions

As you've read earlier in this chapter, every document, icon, and preference setting related to your account resides in a single folder: by default, it's the one bearing your name in the Local Disk (C:)→Users folder. This folder's friendly name is your Personal folder, but to network geeks, it's known as your *user profile*.

The Public Profile

Each account holder has a user profile. But your PC also has a couple of profiles that aren't linked to human beings' accounts.

Have you ever noticed, for example, that not everything you actually see in your Start menu and on your desktop is, in fact, in *your* user profile folder?

Part of the solution to this mystery is the Public profile, which also lurks in the Users folder (Figure 23-14). As you can probably tell by its name, this folder stores many of the same kinds of settings your profile folder does—except that anything in C:→Users→Public→Desktop appears on *everybody's* desktop.

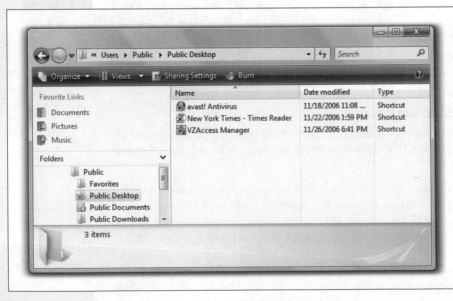

Figure 23-14:
Behind the scenes, Windows maintains another profile folder, whose subfolders closely parallel those in your own. What you see—the contents of the Desktop, Documents folder, Favorites list, and so on—is a combination of what's in your own user profile folder and what's in the Public folder.

All of this is a long-winded way of suggesting another way to make some icon available to everybody with an account on your machine. Drag it into the Desktop folder in the Public profile folder.

But if you're wondering where the common Start menu items are, you'll have to look somewhere else. If you're prowling around your hard drive, you'll find then in C:→ProgramData→Microsoft→Windows→Start Menu. But you can get to it faster by right-clicking the Start menu and choosing Open (or Explore) All Users.

Whose software is it, anyway?

These locations also offer a handy solution to the "Whose software is it, anyway?" conundrum, the burning question of whose Start menu and desktop reflects new software that you've installed using your own account.

As noted in Chapter 6, some software installers ask if you would like the new program to show up only in your Start menu, or in *everybody's* Start menu. But not every installer is this thoughtful. Some installers automatically deposit their new software into the ProgramData and Public folders, thereby making its Start menu and desktop icons available to everybody when they log on.

On the other hand, some installers may deposit a new software program only into *your* account (or that of whoever is logged in at the moment). In that case, other account holders won't be able to use the program at all, even if they know that it's been installed, because their own Start Menu and Desktop folders won't reflect the installation. Worse, some people, not seeing the program's name on their Start menus, might not realize that you've already installed it—and may well install it *again*.

One possible solution is to open the Start Menu→Programs folder in your user profile folder (right-click the Start menu and choose Explore), copy the newly installed icon, and paste it into the C: →ProgramData→Microsoft→Windows→Start Menu→Programs folder. (Repeat with the Desktop folder, if you'd like everyone to see a desktop icon for the new program.) You've just made that software available and visible to everybody who logs onto the computer.

Note: Because of Vista's tight security restrictions, this trick doesn't *always* work. If it doesn't, try to find an updated version of the program that plays well with Vista's User Account Control (page 191).

The Default User Profile

When you first create a new account, who decides what the desktop picture will be—and the Start menu configuration, assortment of desktop icons, and so on?

Well, Microsoft does, of course—but you can change all that. What a newly created account holder sees is only a reflection of the Default user profile. It's yet another folder—this one usually hidden—in your C: →Users folder, and it's the common starting point for all profiles.

If you'd like to make some changes to that starting point, turn on "Show hidden files and folders" (page 84). Then open the C:→Users→Default folder, and make whatever changes you like.

NTFS Permissions: Protecting Your Stuff
All Versions

There's one final aspect of user accounts that's worth mentioning: *NTFS permissions,* a technology that's a core part of Vista's security system. Using this feature, you can specify exactly which co-workers are allowed to open which files and folders on your machine. In fact, you can also specify *how much* access each person has. You can dictate, for example, that Gomez and Morticia aren't allowed to open your Fourth-Quarter Projections spreadsheet at all, that Fred and Ginger can open it but not make changes, and George and Gracie can both open it and make changes.

Your colleagues will encounter the permissions you've set up like this in two different situations: when tapping into your machine from across the network, or when sitting down at it and logging in using their own names and passwords. In either case, the NTFS permissions you set up protect your files and folders equally well.

Tip: In Chapter 26, you can read about a very similar form of access privileges called *share permissions.* There's a big difference between share permissions and the NTFS permissions described here, though: share permissions keep people out of your stuff only when they try to access your PC from *over the network.*

Actually, there are other differences, too. NTFS permissions offer more gradations of access, for example. And using NTFS permissions, you can declare individual *files*—not just folders—accessible or inaccessible to specific co-workers. See page 695 for details.

Using NTFS permissions is most decidedly a power-user technique because of the added complexity it introduces. Entire books have been written on the topic of NTFS permissions alone.

You've been warned.

Setting Up NTFS Permissions
To change the permissions for an NTFS file or folder, you open its Properties dialog box by right-clicking its icon, and then choosing Properties from the shortcut menu. Click the Security tab (Figure 23-15).

Step 1: Specify the person
The top of the Security tab lists the people and groups that have been granted or denied permissions to the selected file or folder. When you click a name in the list, the Permissions box at the bottom of the dialog box shows you how much access that person or group has.

The first step in assigning permissions, then, is to click Edit. You see an editable version of the dialog box shown in Figure 23-15.

If the person or group isn't listed, click the Add button to display the Select Users or Groups dialog box, where you can type them in (Figure 23-16).

Figure 23-15:
The Security tab of an NTFS folder's Properties dialog box. If you have any aspirations to be a Windows power user, get used to this dialog box. You're going to see it a lot, because almost every icon on a Windows system—files, folders, disks, printers—has a Security tab like this one.

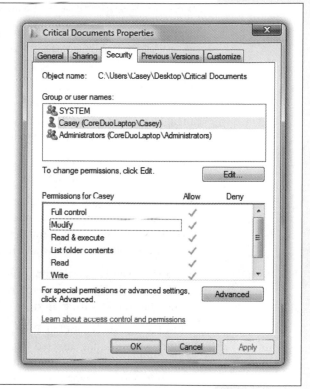

Figure 23-16:
Type the names of the people or groups in the "Enter the object names to select" box at the bottom, trying not to feel depersonalized by Microsoft's reference to you as an "object." If you're adding more than one name, separate them with semicolons. Because remembering exact spellings can be iffy, click Check Names to confirm that these are indeed legitimate account holders. Finally, click OK to insert them into the list on the Security tab.

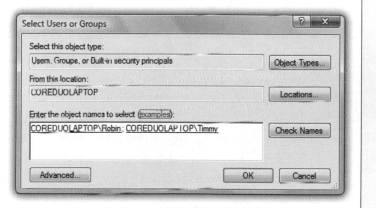

Tip: Instead of typing in names one at a time, as shown in Figure 23-16, you can also choose them from a list, which lets you avoid spelling mistakes and having to guess at the variations. To do so, click the Advanced button to display an expanded version of the dialog box, and then click Find Now to search for all of the accounts and groups on the computer. Finally, in the resulting list, click the names of the people and groups you want to add (Ctrl-click to select more than one at once). Click OK to add them to the previous dialog box, and click OK again to add the selected users and groups to the Security tab.

If you've used Windows 2000, you might wonder why this process is so much more convoluted in Vista than it was in Windows 2000. The answer is: good question!

Step 2: Specify the permissions

Once you've added the users and groups you need to the list on the Security tab, you can highlight each one and set permissions for it. You do that by turning on the Allow or Deny checkboxes at the bottom half of the dialog box.

The different degrees of freedom break down as follows (they're listed here from least to most control, even though that's not how they're listed in the dialog box):

- **List folder contents,** available only for folders, means that the selected individuals can see (but not necessarily open) the files and folders inside. That may sound obvious—but believe it or not, if you *don't* turn on this option, the affected people won't even be able to see what's in this folder. The folder will just appear empty.

- **Read** lets people examine the contents of the file or folder, but not make changes. (They can also examine the permissions settings of these files and folders—the ones that you're setting up right now.)

- **Read & execute** is a lot like Read, except that it also lets people run any programs they find inside the affected folder. When applied to a folder, furthermore, this permission adds the ability to *traverse* folders. (Traversing means directly opening inner folders even when you're not allowed to open the outer folder. You might get to an inner folder by double-clicking a shortcut icon, for example, or by typing the folder's path into the Address bar of a window.)

INFREQUENTLY ASKED QUESTION

Allow vs. Deny

Why do I see both Allow and Deny checkboxes in the Permissions dialog box? Isn't not allowing permission the same as denying it?

In this case, no. "Deny" permissions always take precedence over "Allow" permissions.

For example, if somebody has been granted access to a file or folder because he's a member of a group, you can explicitly revoke his permission by using the Deny checkboxes for his

account. You've just overridden the group permission, just for him, leaving the rest of the group's permissions intact.

You can also use the Deny checkboxes to override permissions granted by *inheritance* from a parent folder. For example, you can grant somebody access to the C: drive by sharing it and assigning her Allow permissions to it, but then prevent her from accessing the C:\Program Files folder by sharing that and *denying* her permission.

- **Write** is like Read, but adds the freedom to make and save changes to the file. When applied to a folder, this permission means that people can create new files and folders inside it.

- **Modify** includes all of the abilities of the Write and Read & Execute levels, plus the ability to *delete* the file or folder.

- **Full Control** confers complete power over the file or folder. The selected person or group can do anything they like with it, including trashing it or its contents, changing its permissions, taking ownership of it (away from you, if they like), and so on.

Of course, turning on Allow grants that level of freedom to the specified user or group, and turning it off takes away that freedom. (For details on the Deny checkbox, see the box on the facing page.)

Note: If you're not careful, it's entirely possible to "orphan" a file or folder (or even your entire drive) by revoking everyone's permission to it, even your own, making it *completely* inaccessible by anyone. That's why, before you get too deeply into working with NTFS permissions, you might consider creating an extra user account on your system and granting it Full Control for all of your drives, just in case something goes wrong.

Groups and Permissions

Once you understand the concept of permissions, and you've enjoyed a thorough shudder contemplating the complexity of a network administrator's job (six levels of permissions × thousands of files × thousands of employees = way too many permutations), one other mystery of Windows will fully snap into focus: the purpose of *groups*, introduced on page 683.

On those pages, you can read about groups as canned categories, complete with predefined powers over the PC, into which you can put different individuals to save yourself the time of adjusting their permissions and privileges individually. As it turns out, each of the ready-made Vista groups also comes with predefined permissions over the files and folders on your hard drive.

Here, for example, is how the system grants permissions to your Windows folder for the Users and Administrators groups:

	Users	Administrators
Full control		X
Modify		X
Read & execute	X	X
List folder contents	X	X
Read	X	X
Write		X

If you belong to the Users group, you have the List Folder Contents permission, which means that you can see what's in the Windows folder; the Read permission, which means that you can open up anything you find inside; and the Read & Execute permission, which means that you can run programs in that folder (which is essential for Windows Vista itself to run). But people in the Users group aren't allowed to change or delete anything in the Windows folder, or to put anything else inside. Windows Vista is protecting itself against the mischievous and clueless.

Members of the Administrators group have all of those abilities and more—they also have Modify and Write permissions, which let them add new files and folders to the Windows folder (so that, for example, they can install a new software program on the machine).

When Permissions Collide

If you successfully absorbed all this information about permissions, one thing should be clear: people in the Administrators group ought to be able to change or delete any file in your Windows folder. After all, they have the Modify permission, which ought to give them that power.

In fact, they can move or delete anything in any folder *in* the Windows folder, because the first cardinal rule of NTFS permissions is this:

NTFS permissions travel downstream, from outer folders to inner ones

In other words, if you have the Modify and Write permissions to a folder, then you ought to have the same permissions for every file and folder inside it.

But in Windows XP, there was something called the Power Users group. It's been turned off in Vista, but for the sake of illustration, let's say you're part of it. You'd find that you can't, in fact, delete any files or folders in the Windows folder. That's because each of them comes with Modify and Write permissions turned *off* for Power Users, even though the folder that encloses them has those permissions turned on.

Why would Microsoft go to this trouble? Because it wanted to prevent people in this group from inadvertently changing or deleting important Windows files—and yet it wanted these people to be able to put *new* files into the Windows folder, so they can install new programs.

This is a perfect example of the second cardinal rule of NTFS permissions:

NTFS permissions that have been explicitly applied to a file or folder always override inherited permissions

Here's another example: Suppose your sister, the technical whiz of the household, has given you Read, Write, Modify, Read & Execute, and List Folder Contents permissions to her own Documents folder. Now you can read, change, or delete every file there. But she can still protect an individual document or folder *inside* her Documents folder—the BirthdayPartyPlans.doc file, for example—by denying you all permissions to it. You'll be able to open anything else in there, but not that file.

Believe it or not, NTFS permissions get even more complicated, thanks to the third cardinal rule:

Permissions accumulate as you burrow downward through subfolders

Now suppose your sister has given you the Read and List Folder Contents permissions to her Documents folder—a "look, but don't touch" policy. Thanks to the first cardinal rule, you automatically get the same permissions to every file and folder *inside* Documents.

Suppose one of these inner folders is called Grocery Lists. If she grants you the Modify and Write permissions to the Grocery Lists folder so you can add items to the shopping list, you end up having Read, Modify, *and* Write permissions for every file in that folder. Those files have *accumulated* permissions—they got the Read permission from Documents, and the Modify and Write permissions from the Grocery Lists folder.

Because these layers of inherited permissions can get dizzyingly complex, Microsoft has prepared for you a little cheat sheet, a dialog box that tells you the bottom line, the net result—the *effective* permissions. To see it, follow these steps:

1. **Click the Advanced button on the Security tab.**

   The Advanced Security Settings dialog box appears.

2. **Click the Effective Permissions tab; click Select.**

   Now you see the same Select User or Group dialog box you saw earlier when you were creating permissions.

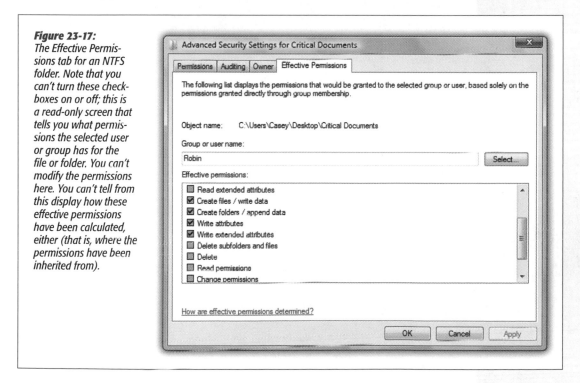

Figure 23-17:
The Effective Permissions tab for an NTFS folder. Note that you can't turn these checkboxes on or off; this is a read-only screen that tells you what permissions the selected user or group has for the file or folder. You can't modify the permissions here. You can't tell from this display how these effective permissions have been calculated, either (that is, where the permissions have been inherited from).

3. **Click the user or group whose effective permissions you want to see, and then click OK.**

You now see checkmarks next to the permissions that are in effect, taking into account folder-permission inheritance and all other factors, for the user or group of that particular file or folder (Figure 23-17).

Setting Up a Workgroup Network

It's a rare Windows Vista machine indeed that isn't connected, sooner or later, to some kind of office network (officially known as a *local area network,* or *LAN*). And no wonder: the payoff is considerable. Once you've created a network, you can copy files from one machine to another just as you'd drag files between folders on your own PC. Everyone on the network can consult the same database, phone book, or calendar. When the workday's done, you can play games over the network. You can even store your MP3 music files on one computer and listen to them on any other. Most importantly, you can share a single printer, cable modem or DSL Internet connection, fax modem, or phone line among all the PCs in the house.

If you work at a biggish company, you probably work on a *domain network,* which is described in the next chapter. You, lucky thing, won't have to fool around with building or designing a network, because your job, and your PC, presumably came with a fully functioning network (and a fully functioning geek responsible for running it).

If you work at home, or if you're responsible for setting up a network in a smaller office, this chapter is for you. It guides you through the construction of a less formal *workgroup network,* which ordinary mortals can put together.

You'll soon discover that, when it comes to simplicity, setting up a network has a long way to go before it approaches, say, setting up a desk lamp. It involves buying equipment, hooking up (or even installing) network adapter cards, and configuring software. Fortunately, Vista's Network and Sharing Center makes the software part as painless as possible.

Kinds of Networks
All Versions

You can connect your PCs using any of several different kinds of gear. Many of the world's offices are wired with *Ethernet cable,* but wireless networks are very popular for small offices and homes. Here and there, a few renegades are even installing networking systems that rely on the phone or power lines already in the walls. Here's an overview of the most popular networking systems.

Note: Be sure that whatever networking gear you buy is compatible with Windows Vista, either by checking logos on the package or checking the maker's Web site. Networking is complicated enough without having to troubleshoot some gadget that's not designed for Vista.

Ethernet

Ethernet is the world's most popular networking protocol. It gives you fast, reliable, trouble-free communication that costs very little and imposes few limitations on where you can place the PCs in a home or small office.

In addition to the computers themselves, an Ethernet network requires three components:

- **Network adapters.** A network adapter is the little chunk of circuitry that provides the Ethernet jack (Figure 24-1), where you can plug in a network wire. Your PC almost certainly came with one built in; Vista-compatible PCs without built-in Ethernet are rarer than Bigfoot sightings. (You may also hear a network adapter called a *network interface card* or NIC ["nick"].)

  In the freakish event that your desktop PC doesn't have an Ethernet jack, you can buy a network adapter either in the form of a PCI card (which you must open up your computer to install) or a USB box (which connects to the back of the computer and dangles off of it).

  If you have a laptop, you can use one of these USB adapters or a card that slips into your card slot.

- **A router.** If you have a cable modem or DSL connection to the Internet, a *router* (about $60) distributes that Internet signal to all the computers on your network. (The dialog boxes in Windows call these devices *gateways,* although almost no one else does.)

  Routers with five or eight ports (that is, Ethernet jacks where you can plug in computers) are popular in homes and small offices.

  It's worth noting that you can inexpensively expand your network by plugging a *hub* or *switch* into one of the router's jacks. Hubs and switches are similar-looking little boxes that offer *another* five or eight Ethernet jacks, connecting all of your computers together. (A *switch* is more intelligent than a hub. It's more selective when sending data to the right PCs on your network; as a result, the bits and bytes move a little faster.)

Tip: There's also such a thing as a *wireless* router, which offers both physical Ethernet jacks and wireless antennas that broadcast the signal throughout your place.

To set up a router, plug it into your cable or DSL modem using an Ethernet cable. Restart the cable modem. Now use whatever software came with the router to set up its security features. Often, the software is actually built into the *router*; you're supposed to view it by opening up a special page in your Web browser, of all things.

The router then logs onto your Internet service and stands ready to transmit Internet data to and from all the computers on your network.

Figure 24-1:
Top: The Ethernet cable is connected to a computer at one end, and the router (shown here) at the other end. The computers communicate through the router; there's no direct connection between any two computers. The front of the router has little lights for each connector port, which light up only on the ports in use. You can watch the lights flash as the computers communicate with one another.

Bottom: Here's what a typical "I've got three PCs in the house, and I'd like them to share my cable modem" setup might look like.

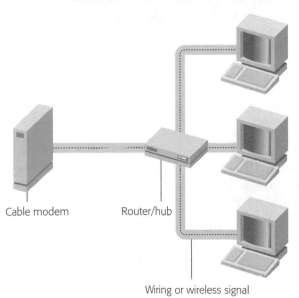

Cable modem   Router/hub

Wiring or wireless signal

As a bonus, the router provides excellent security, serving as a firewall that isolates your network computers from the Internet and keeps out hackers. (See Chapter 10 for much more on firewalls.)

- **Ethernet cables.** The cables used for most Ethernet networks look something like telephone cables, but they're not the same thing—and they're definitely not interchangeable! Both the cable itself (called *10BaseT, 100BaseT cable,* or *Cat 5* cable) and the little clips at each end (called *RJ-45* connectors) are slightly fatter than those on a phone cable (Figure 18-1). You can buy Ethernet cables in a variety of lengths and colors. Each computer must be connected to the hub, switch, or router with a cable that's no longer than about 100 yards long.

Tip: If you've got a computer that sits in one place, like a desktop PC, you should use an Ethernet cable even if you have a wireless network.

One reason is security (page 359). Another is speed. Yes, wireless technologies like 802.11g promise speeds of 54 megabits per second, which is very fast. But first of all, the real-world speed is about half of that; second, that speed is shared among all computers on the network. As a result, if you're copying a big file across the network, it will probably go twice as fast if it's going between one wireless and one wired PC than between two wireless PCs.

UP TO SPEED

Network Devices Have Speed Limits

Ethernet cards and hubs are available in different speeds. The most common are *10BaseT* (10 megabits/second, or Mbps) and *100BaseT* (100 Mbps, sometimes cleverly called *Fast Ethernet*).

Note, however, that the speed of the network has no effect on your computers' *Internet* speed—Web surfing, email downloading, and so on. The reason: even the slowest network operates far faster than your Internet connection. Remember, the top speed of a cable modem or DSL connection is between 512 and 4,096 kilobits/second (Kbps)—still 10 to 20 times slower than the *slowest* home network (10BaseT network). Even a T-1 line, a permanent leased telephone line commonly used for corporate Internet connections, costing thousands of dollars a month, runs at only 1,544 Kbps.

So why does a faster network matter? Primarily to save time when you're transferring big files between the PCs on the network. For example, you can play MP3 music files stored on another computer over a 10BaseT connection with no

problems at all. However, if you plan to install video cameras all around your palatial estate and want to watch all of the video feeds simultaneously, opt for Fast Ethernet—or even Gigabit Ethernet, the current Ethernet speed champ (1,000 Mbps).

Much of the Ethernet equipment on the market today is designed to run either at Fast Ethernet speed, or at *both* 10 and 100 Mbps. If you buy a *dual-speed* router or hub (often labeled "10/100"), each PC connected to it will run at its own maximum speed. If one computer has a 10BaseT network card and one has 100BaseT, they'll still be able to communicate. But if your hub operates *only* at 100BaseT speed, then 10BaseT cards won't work at all.

The bottom line? As you shop for gear, buy Fast Ethernet (or 10/100) hubs, which aren't much more expensive than the slower, 10 Mbps hubs. You may as well go for the higher speed, so you'll be ready for any high-bandwidth application that comes down the pike.

Ethernet gear can be shockingly inexpensive; a search at *www.buy.com,* for example, reveals five-port Ethernet hubs for $30 from no-name companies. If you're willing to pay slightly more—$20 for the card, $50 for the hub, for example—you can get brand-name gear (like D-Link, Netgear, 3Com, or LinkSys) whose support with installation, phone help, and driver updates through the years may reward you many times over. Setting up an Ethernet network generally goes very smoothly, but in the few cases where trouble arises, cheapo equipment is often the problem.

Network hookups

On paper, the hardware part of setting up the network is simple: Just connect each computer to the router or hub using an Ethernet cable.

It's that "using an Ethernet cable" part that sometimes gets sticky. Depending on where your PCs are and how concerned you are about the network's appearance, this wiring process may involve drilling holes in floors or walls, stapling cables to baseboard trim, or calling in an electrician to do the job.

When all of your computers are in the same room, you can run the cables along the walls and behind the furniture. (Buying cables that are the same color as your walls or floors can help hide the installation.) If you have to run cables between rooms, you can secure the cables to the floor or baseboards using staples—use the round kind that won't crush the cables—or plastic "raceways" with adhesive backing.

Of course, you might not be thrilled about having *any* exposed cables in your home or office. In that case, the installation process can be much more complicated. You should probably hire a professional cable installer to do the job—or don't use cables at all. Read on.

Wireless Networks (WiFi or 802.11)

So far, this discussion has focused on using wired Ethernet to hook up your computers. Millions of people, however, have embraced the flexibility of a networking system that involves no wires at all—a cordless networking technology called *WiFi* or *802.11* ("eight-oh-two dot eleven"). (Your Macintosh friends probably call the same thing *AirPort,* because that's what Apple calls it.)

To get onto a wireless network, your PC needs a WiFi transmitter. Almost every laptop sold today has WiFi built in. You can also add it to a desktop in the form of a wireless card or USB adapter; either way, you gain a little antenna. Once all of your equipment is wireless, that's it: your PCs can now communicate with one another.

The real point of all this, of course, is to get onto the *Internet* wirelessly, so you can join the ranks of people who casually move around from the TV couch to the desk with their WiFi laptops, in wireless touch with their cable modem or DSL connection the whole time.

In that case, you also need an *access point* (about $50)—a box that connects to your router or hub and broadcasts the Internet signal to the whole house or office. The usual suspects—LinkSys, Netgear, D-Link, and others—sell these access points (also called base stations).

Now, 802.11 equipment has a range of about 150 feet, even through walls. In concept, this setup works much like a cordless phone, where the base station is plugged into the wall phone jack and a wireless handset can talk to it from anywhere in the house.

Wireless networking is not without its downsides, however. You may get intermittent service interruptions from 2.4-gigahertz cordless phones and other machinery, or even the weather. Furthermore, big metal things, or walls *containing* big metal things (like pipes) can interfere with communication among the PCs, much to the disappointment of people who work in subways and meat lockers.

Wireless networking isn't as secure as a cabled network, either. If you drive around a typical middle-class American neighborhood these days with your wireless-equipped laptop turned on, you'll be surprised at how many home wireless networks you can get onto, piggybacking onto other people's cable modems because they failed to turn on the optional password feature of their wireless systems.

UP TO SPEED

802.11 Networks: Regular or Supersized?

Wireless gear comes in several flavors, each offering different degrees of speed, distance, and compatibility. They have such appetizing-sounding names as 802.11b, 802.11a, 802.11g, and 802.11n.

So what's the difference? Equipment bearing the "b" label transfers data through the air at up to 11 megabits per second; the "g" system is almost five times as fast. (Traditionally, geeks measure network speeds in megabits, not megabytes. Here's a translation: The older "b" gear has a top speed of 1.4 megabytes per second, versus more than 6 megabytes per second for the "a" and "g" stuff. Remember, though, you'll usually get around half that speed. Your wireless network uses a lot of the bandwidth for such network housekeeping chores as correcting transmission errors.)

The beauty of 802.11g gear, though, is that it's backward-compatible with the older "b" gear. If your laptop has an 802.11b card, you can hop onto an 802.11g base station simultaneously with people using "g" cards. And if you have an 802.11g card, you can hop onto older base stations. You won't get better speed, of course, but at least you won't need a separate base station.

(That's not true of "a" equipment, though. 802.11a cards require 802.11a base stations, and vice versa, and have much shorter range. Word to the wise: Don't buy "a" gear.

In fact, you should go for "g" whenever possible. However, don't be scared off by 802.11a/b/g gear, since it can talk to all three types of networks.)

There's even such a thing as 802.11n, an emerging standard due to be finalized in 2007, that offers better speed *and* better range (thanks to multiple antennas) than its predecessors. Remember, though, that you won't get the better speed unless *both* your base station *and* your networking cards speak "n."

Don't buy faster equipment thinking that you're going to speed up your email and Web activity, though. A cable modem or DSL box delivers Internet information at a fraction of the speed of your home or office network. The bottleneck is the Internet connection, not your network.

Instead, the speed boost you get with "g" gear is useful only for transferring files among computers on your own network, streaming video or audio to (and from) your home theater, and playing networked games.

Finally, the great thing about wireless networking is that it all works together, no matter what kind of computer you have. There's no such thing as an "Apple" wireless network or a "Windows" wireless network. All computers work with any kind of access point.

Still, nothing beats the freedom of wireless networking, particularly if you're a laptop lover; you can set up shop almost anywhere in the house or in the yard, slumped into any kind of rubbery posture. No matter where you go within your home, you're online at full speed, without hooking up a single wire.

Other Kinds of Networks

There are a couple of other network types that are worth looking into. Both of them are wired networks, but they use wires that you already have.

Phone line networks

Instead of going to the trouble of wiring your home with Ethernet cables, you might consider using the wiring that's already *in* your house—telephone wiring. That's the idea behind a kind of networking gear called HomePNA. With this system, you can use the network even when using the modem or talking on the phone, although you can't make a modem and voice call simultaneously.

Unfortunately, the average American household has only two or three phone jacks in the *entire house,* meaning that you don't have much flexibility in positioning your PCs. If you're trying to avoid the plaster-dust experience of installing additional wiring, consider WiFi or Powerline networking.

Power outlet networks

Here's another way to connect your computers without rewiring the building: use the electrical wiring that's already in your walls. Unlike phone jacks, electrical outlets are usually available in every room in the house.

If you buy *Powerline adapters* (also called HomePlug adapters), you get very fast speeds (from 14 up to 100 Mbps), very good range (1,000 feet, although that includes the twists and turns your wiring takes within the walls), and the ultimate in installation simplicity. You just plug the Powerline adapter from your PC's Ethernet or USB jack into any wall power outlet. Presto—all of the PCs are connected.

UP TO SPEED

PC-to-PC Micronetworks

If your network has modest ambitions—that is, if you have only two computers you want to connect—you can ignore all this business about hubs, routers, and wiring. Instead, you just need an Ethernet *crossover cable,* about $10 from a computer store or online mail-order supplier. Run it directly between the Ethernet jacks of the two computers. Everything else in this chapter works exactly as though you had purchased a hub and were using a "real" Ethernet network.

And if both computers have WiFi, you can even save yourself the price of that cable. Instead, you can create a tiny, two-computer network between them.

To bring about this arrangement, called an *ad hoc* network, choose Start→Control Panel. In Control Panel Home view, click Network and Internet→Network and Sharing Center→"Set up a connection or network."

Now click "Set up a wireless ad hoc (computer-to-computer) network." Vista walks you through the steps to set up the connection.

Powerline adapters are inexpensive (about $40 apiece) and extremely convenient.

Sharing an Internet Connection
All Versions

If you have broadband (high-speed) Internet service, like a cable modem or DSL service, you're a very lucky individual. Not only do you get spectacular speed when surfing the Web or doing email, but you also have a full-time connection. You never have to wait for a modem to dial (screeching all the way), and wait again for it to disconnect.

If your broadband company didn't supply a piece of equipment (like a wireless or Ethernet router) for sharing that connection with more than one computer, shame on them!

Fortunately, setting up such a system is fairly easy, and practically a requirement if your home or office has more than one PC. There are two ways to go about it.

Get a Broadband Router

As noted earlier, a router (a *gateway* in Microsoft lingo) is a little box, about $60, that connects directly to the cable modem or DSL box. In most cases, it doubles as a hub, providing multiple Ethernet jacks to accommodate your wired PCs. (Some, on the other hand, offer only a single jack into which you plug a hub, sold separately.) The Internet signal is automatically shared among all the PCs connected to the router.

Use Internet Connection Sharing

Internet Connection Sharing (ICS) is a built-in Vista feature that *simulates* a router. Like a hardware router, ICS distributes a single Internet connection to every computer on the network—but unlike a router, it's free. You just fire it up on the *one* PC that's connected directly to your cable modem or DSL box—or, as networking geeks would say, the *gateway* or *host* PC.

But there's a downside: if the gateway PC is turned off or goes into Sleep mode, nobody else in the house can go online.

Also, the gateway PC requires *two* network connections: one that goes to the cable modem or DSL box, and another that connects it your network.

It might be two Ethernet cards, two WiFi cards, or—most commonly of all, especially for laptops—one Ethernet and one WiFi card. One connects to the Internet (for example, via a cable modem, DSL box, or WiFi), and the other goes to the hub or the router to distribute the signal to the other computers.

Tip: If the "receiving" computers (the ones sharing the connection) are all wireless, you can skip that business about the hub or router. Plug the gateway PC into the cable modem via Ethernet. Then let each of the other wireless computers create *ad hoc* connections to it wirelessly, as described in the box on page 705.

If you decide to use Internet Connection Sharing, make sure the gateway PC can already get onto the Internet, on its own, before you attempt to enable ICS.

Choose Start→Control Panel. Open Network. At the top, click "Network and Sharing Center." At left, click "Manage network connections."

Right-click the icon of the network connection you want to share. From the shortcut menu, choose Properties. Authenticate yourself (page 191), and then click the Sharing tab. Finally, turn on "Allow other network users to connect through this computer's Internet connection," shown in Figure 24-2, and click OK.

Thereafter, other computers on the network can share the gateway PC's Internet connection, even if they're running earlier versions of Windows, or even Mac OS X and Linux. In fact, they don't need to be computers at all: you can use ICS to share your Internet connection with a video game console or palmtop!

Tip: If you've created a VPN (virtual private network) on the gateway machine (page 758), *all* of the PCs sharing the Internet connection can get onto the corporate network!

Figure 24-2:
Internet Connection Sharing lets you broadcast your cable modem/DSL's signal to all of the grateful, connectionless computers in the house. Your savings: the price of a hardware router.

And now the fine print:

- Internet Connection Sharing doesn't work with domain networks, DNS servers, gateways, or DHCP servers (you know who you are, network geeks).

- The "receiving" PCs (the ones that will share the connection) can't have static (fixed) IP addresses. To check, sit down at each one. Choose Start→Control Panel. In Classic view, open Network Connections.

Right-click the icon of the network connection; from the shortcut menu, choose Properties. Authenticate yourself (page 191). Double-click "Internet Protocol Version 4 (TCP/IPv4); turn on "Obtain an IP address automatically."

- The gateway machine is now the only thing protecting you from all the worms, Trojans, and bad guys on the Internet. If, on the advice of some cable modem technician during a spasm of troubleshooting, you momentarily plug one of the "downstream" PCs directly into the cable modem, you might forget that it has no protection at all.

The Network and Sharing Center
All Versions

Once you've set up the networking equipment, Vista does a remarkable job of determining how to configure everything. To see how well it's doing, visit the Network and Sharing Center. This, by the way, is where you set up the sharing of files, folders, printers, and multimedia files over the network.

To open the Center, choose Start→Control Panel. In Classic view, open the Network and Sharing Center (Figure 24-3). It gives you an excellent central status screen for your network.

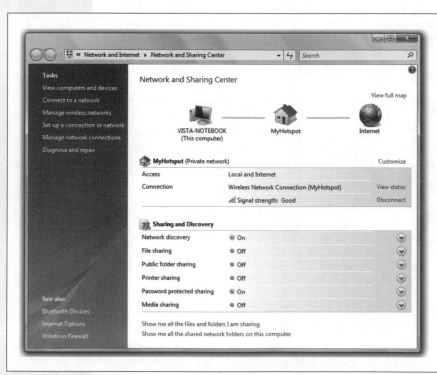

Figure 24-3:
The Network and Sharing Center is where you specify how Vista talks to the network. The network map at the top gives you, at a glance, reassurance that you're connected both to your network and to the Internet.

To *do* anything with your network, however, you generally refer to the options listed in the task pane at the left side. Here's a summary.

"View computers and devices"

Click here to view icons that represent all the computers in your workgroup or corporate domain (see Chapter 25), as shown in Figure 24-4. If one of your computers is configured to share music or video files (page 469), you'll see a separate entry for it here. You can double-click any of the icons in this view to see which shared resources are available on it (such as music, files, and printers).

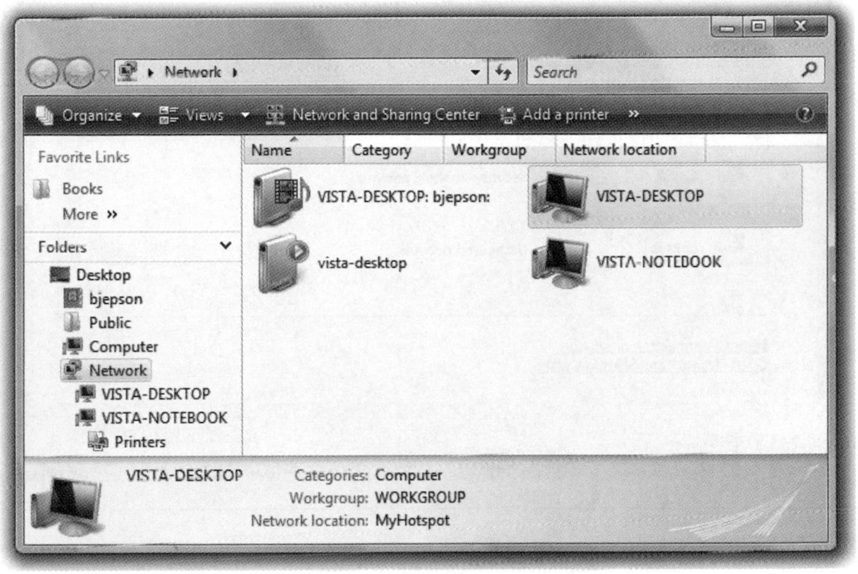

Figure 24-4:
This view shows all the computers and other networked gadgets in your vicinity. You can see that VISTA-DESKTOP has two entries for shared music and photos: the bottom-left icon lets you browse to see which users are sharing media, and the top-left icon takes you directly to bjepson's shared music library.

"Connect to a network"

This option brings up a list of available networks, including wireless networks, dial-up connections, and VPN connections (page 758). Select a network and click Connect to establish a connection to it. You can disconnect from your current network by selecting it and clicking Disconnect.

In Figure 24-5, for example, the dialog box shows The Dude Behind You (a computer-to-computer network, probably set up by another user in the same Internet café); Cox25, which seems to be a residential hot spot (and is password-protected); and linksys, which is a wide-open network. Whoever set it up didn't bother to change the default network name, "linksys." (Wireless access points usually come with their names set to match the manufacturer's.)

"Manage wireless networks"

This option lets you control how Vista connects to wireless networks. You can drag and drop them to choose the priority of each network. That is, if Vista detects *two* wireless networks where you are, it will connect to the one closer to the top of the list.

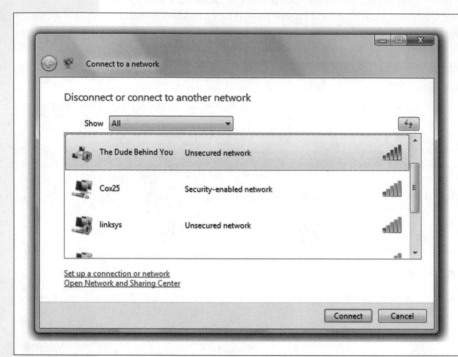

Figure 24-5:
This view of all available networks is especially useful if you're a laptopper. How do you know what WiFi networks are available in the spot where you're standing? Here, in this master list. (Hit F5 to refresh the list—for example, if a new network has just come online.)

You can double-click a network's name to open its Properties dialog box, where you can specify whether or not you want to connect to the network automatically. Actually, the factory settings are usually just fine.

"Set up a connection or network"

Most of the time, Vista does the right thing when it encounters a new network. For example, if you plug in an Ethernet cable, it assumes that you want to use the wired network and automatically hops on. If you come within range of a wireless network, Vista offers to connect to it.

Some kinds of networks, however, require special setup. They're listed here:

• **Connect to the Internet.** Use this option when Vista fails to figure out how to connect to the Internet on its own. You can set up a WiFi, PPPoE broadband connection (required by certain DSL services that require you to sign in with a user name and password), or a dial-up networking connection.

• **Set up a wireless router or access point.** You can use this option to configure a new wireless router that's not set up yet, although only some routers can "speak" to Vista in this way. You're better off using the configuration software that came in the box with the router.

- **Manually connect to a wireless network.** Some wireless networks don't announce (broadcast) their presence. That is, you won't see a message popping up on the screen, inviting you to join the network, just by wandering into it. Instead, the very name and existence of such networks are kept secret to keep the riffraff out. If you're told the name of such a network, use this option to type it in and connect.

- **Set up a wireless ad hoc (computer-to-computer) network.** Consult the box on page 705.

- **Set up a dial-up connection.** See page 323.

- **Connect to a workplace.** That is, set up a secure VPN connection to the corporation that employs you, as described on page 758.

"Manage network connections"

Click this link to view a list of all your network adapters— Ethernet cards and WiFi adapters, mainly—as well as any VPNs or dial-up connections you've set up on your computer.

Double-click a listing to see its connection status (see Figure 24-6), which leads to several other dialog boxes where you can reconfigure the connection or see more information.

Note: The Properties button presents a list of protocols that your network connection uses. Double-click "Internet Protocol Version 4" to tell Vista whether to get its IP and DNS server addresses automatically, or whether to use addresses that you've specified. Ninety-nine times out of 100, the right choice is to get those addresses automatically. Every once in a while, though, you'll come across a network that requires manually entered addresses.

"Diagnose and repair"

Very few problems are as annoying or difficult to troubleshoot as flaky network connections. You visit the Network and Sharing Center, and instead of seeing those reassuring double lines connecting your PC's icon to the network icon and the Internet icon, you see a broken line. Instead of being told you're connected to "Local and Internet" (meaning "other computers in your building and the Internet"), you see only "Local" (and sometimes not even that).

With this option, Microsoft is giving you a tiny head start. When you click "Diagnose and repair," Vista does its best to reconfigure your connection. Invisibly and automatically, it performs several geek tweaks that were once the realm of highly paid networking professionals: it renews the DHCP address, re-initializes the connection, and, if nothing else works, turns the networking card off and on again.

"View full map"

The map that appears when you first open the Network center has only three icons, representing your PC, your network, and the Internet.

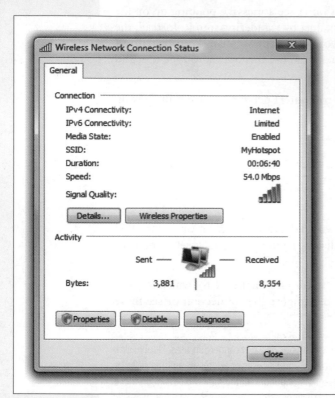

Figure 24-6:
The network connection status dialog box lets you view the details and properties of a connection, disable (or enable) the adapter, or diagnose a problem with a network connection.

But if you click "View full map," your PC sends out silent signals to all the other computers on your network. It then processes the responses so that it may draw you a far more detailed map, showing *all* the computers on the network.

All right, not *all*. The mapping feature relies on Vista's new Link-Layer Topology Discovery (LLTD) technology, which, despite its fancy name, is actually pretty simple. It provides a way for computers and other devices to describe themselves to one another, announcing their presence to the other machines on the network.

Unfortunately, computers that don't know about LLTD don't show up in the map. Windows Vista, of course, has LLTD, and Microsoft intends to write a software add-on for Windows XP that will add LLTD to it. Older Windows computers (not to mention Macs and Linux machines), however, are out of luck.

If you're on a home or office network, clicking "View full map" makes Vista query the computers and devices on your network and draw a map of the results.

Note: On networks that you've designated as public (such as wireless hot spots), no map appears, for
security reasons.

"Customize"

The first time you connect to a network, you're asked to specify whether it's a public
or private network. This choice determines how friendly your computer will be with
other devices on the network.

On a public network, like a wireless hot spot, Vista tries to be as stealthy as possible in
an effort to keep your laptop invisible to bad guys attempting to sniff the airways. On
a private (home or office) network, Vista is much more open about what it's sharing
with other computers and people.

If you click Customize, the Set Network Location dialog box appears. Here, you can
switch between public and private, select which icon you want to use to represent
the network, or give the network a new name. (This name doesn't affect the wireless
ID of the network, but it changes the name that appears in many of Vista's network
dialog boxes.)

You can also click "Merge or delete network locations" to combine two or more locations into one, or delete a location that's no longer needed.

"View status"

Click this link to bring up the network connection status.

Sharing and Discovery

This section is the master control panel of on/off switches for Vista's *network sharing*
features. For example:

- **Network discovery** makes your computer visible to others and allows your computer to see other computers on the network. (It's that LLTD feature in action.)

- **File sharing** lets you share files and printers over the network (page 729).

- **Public folder sharing** lets you share whatever files you've put in the Users→Public
  folder (page 730).

- **Printer sharing** makes a printer connected to your PC available to other people
  on the network.

- **Password protected sharing** requires other people to supply their account names
  and passwords before they can access the shared files, folders, and printers on your
  PC—including, by the way, the Public folder (page 730).

  If this feature is turned off, other people can get at your stuff *without* having to sign
  in, which makes life easier if you're on a small network among trusted colleagues.
  You can still protect your shared files and folders using *permissions,* however (page
  732). For instance, you might say that other people can see what files you've shared,
  but not view or edit them.

• **Media sharing** lets you share your music, pictures, and videos with other people on the network. Even if you turn on this switch, you still have to open Windows Media Player and tell it what to share there (Chapter 14).

"Show me..."

These options let you see all of the shared files and folders (these are accessible to other users on your computer), as well as folders that you've shared with other people on your network.

Testing the Network

After all of this setup, here's how you can find out whether or not the gods are smiling on your new network. Start by choosing Start→Network.

The network window opens, revealing the folders and disks that your machine can "see" on other computers in the network. You should see the names and icons of the other computers you've set up, as shown in Figure 24-7. In Chapter 25, you can find out how to burrow into these icons, using the files and folders of other networked PCs exactly as though they were on your own computer.

Tip: All recent generations of Windows can "see" each other and work joyously side-by-side on the same network. On older machines, you would open the equivalent window by double-clicking the My Network Places or Network Neighborhood icon on the desktop instead of using the Start menu.

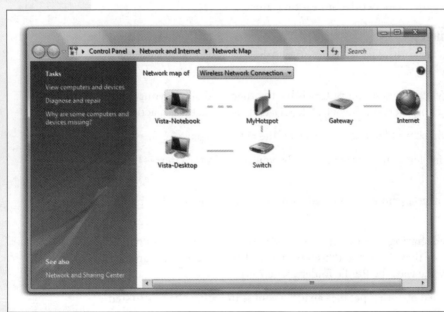

Figure 24-7:
Vista maps out your network as best it can, and even shows wireless access points and wired routers.

If you don't see the icons for your other computers, something has gone wrong. Check to see that:

- Your cables are properly seated in the network adapter card and hub jacks.

- Your router, Ethernet hub, or wireless access point is plugged into a working power outlet.

- Your networking card is working. To check, open the System program in Control Panel→System and Maintenance. Click Device Manager. Look for an error icon next to your networking card's name. See Chapter 18 for more on the Device Manager.

If you don't find a problem, visit the Network and Sharing Center and click Diagnose and Repair. If it has no suggestions that solve the problem, you'll have to call Microsoft or your PC company for help.

Network Domains

Windows Vista was designed to thrive in two very different kinds of network worlds: the *workgroup* (an informal, home or small-office network) and the *domain* (a hard-core, security-conscious corporate network of dozens or thousands of PCs). Depending on which kind of network your PC belongs to, the procedures and even dialog boxes you experience are quite a bit different.

Chapter 24 guides you through the process of setting up a workgroup network, but no single chapter could describe setting up a corporate domain. That's a job for Super Geek, otherwise known as the network administrator—somebody who has studied the complexities of corporate networking for years.

This chapter is designed to help you learn how to *use* a corporate domain. If your PC is connected to a workgroup network or no network at all, on the other hand, feel free to use these pages as scratch paper.

Note: In the context of this chapter, the term *domain* refers to a group of Windows computers on the same network. It's not the same as an *Internet* domain, which you may occasionally see mentioned. An Internet domain is still a group of computers, but they don't have to be connected to the same network, and they don't have to be running Windows. In addition, the domain name (like *amazon.com*) must be registered to ensure that there's no duplication on the Internet. Because Windows domains are private, they can be named any way the administrator chooses.

The Domain

Business • Enterprise • Ultimate

As you may remember from Chapter 24, nobody else on a workgroup network can access the files on your PC unless you've created an account for them on your machine. Whenever somebody new joins the department, you have to create another new account; when people leave, you have to delete or disable their accounts. If something goes wrong with your hard drive, you have to recreate all of the accounts.

What's Wrong with Workgroups

You must have an account on each shared PC, too. If you're lucky, you have the same name and password on each machine—but that isn't always the case. You might have to remember that you're *pjenkins* on the front-desk computer, but *JenkinsP* on the administrative machine.

Similarly, suppose there's a network printer on one of the computers in your workgroup. If you want to use it, you have to find out whose computer the printer is connected to, call him to ask if he'll create an account for you, and hope that he knows how to do it. You either have to tell him your user name and password, or find out what user name and password he's assigned to you. In that case, every time you want to use that printer, you might have to log on by typing that user name and password.

If you multiply all of this hassle by the number of PCs on your small network, it's easy to see how you might suddenly find yourself spending more time managing accounts and permissions than getting any work done.

The Domain Concept

The solution to all of these problems is the network domain. In a domain, you only have a single name and password, which gets you into every shared PC and printer on the network. Everyone's account information resides on a central computer called a *domain controller*—a computer so important, it's usually locked away in a closet or a data-center room.

A domain controller keeps track of who is allowed to log on, who *is* logged on, and what each person is allowed to do on the network. When you log onto the domain with your PC, the domain controller verifies your credentials and permits (or denies) you access.

Most domain networks have at least two domain controllers with identical information, so if one computer dies, the other one can take over. (Some networks have many more than two.) This redundancy is a critical safety net, because without a happy, healthy domain controller, the entire network is dead.

Without budging from their chairs, network administrators can use a domain controller to create new accounts, manage existing ones, and assign permissions. The domain takes the equipment-management and security concerns of the network out of the hands of individuals and puts them into the hands of trained professionals. You may sometimes hear this kind of networking called *client/server networking*.

Each *workstation*—that is, each mere mortal PC like yours—relies on a central server machine for its network access.

If you use Windows in a medium- to large-sized company, you probably use a domain every day. You may not even have been aware of it, but that's no big deal; knowing what's been going on right under your nose isn't especially important to your ability to get work done. After all, it's not your job—it's the network administrator's. But understanding the domain system can help you take better advantage of a domain's features.

Active Directory

As you know, Microsoft sells several versions of Windows Vista: Home Basic, Home Premium, Business, Enterprise, and Ultimate. One key difference is that computers running the two Home editions can't join a domain.

There are other versions of Windows, however: the specialized ones that run on those domain controller computers. To create a domain, at least one computer must be running either Windows .NET Server 2003 or Windows 2000 Server. These are far more expensive operating systems (the price depends on the number of machines that they serve) and they run only on high-octane PCs. They also require high-octane expertise to install and maintain.

One key offering of these specialized Windows versions is an elaborate application called *Active Directory.* It's a single, centralized database that stores every scrap of information about the hardware, software, and people on the network. (The older operating system called Windows NT Server can create domains, but it doesn't include Active Directory.)

After creating a domain by installing Active Directory on a server computer, network administrators can set about filling the directory (database) with information about the network's resources. Every computer, printer, and person is represented by an *object* in the database and *attributes* (properties) that describe it. For example, a *user object's* attributes specify that person's name, location, telephone number, email address, and other, more technical, elements.

Active Directory lets network administrators maintain an enormous hierarchy of computers. A multinational corporation with tens of thousands of employees in offices worldwide can all be part of one Active Directory domain, with servers distributed in hundreds of locations, all connected by wide-area networking links. (A group of domains is known as a *tree.* Huge networks might even have more than one tree; if so, they're called—yes, you guessed it—a *forest.*)

The objects in an Active Directory domain are arranged in a hierarchy, something like the hierarchy of folders within folders on your hard drive. Some companies base their directory-tree designs on the organization of the company, using departments and divisions as the building blocks. Others use geographic locations as the basis for the design, or use a combination of both.

Unless you've decided to take up the rewarding career of network administration, you'll never have to install an Active Directory domain controller, design a directory tree, or create domain objects. However, you very well may encounter the Active Directory at your company. You can use it to search for the mailing address of somebody else on the network, for example, or locate a printer that can print on both sides of the page at once. Having some idea of the directory's structure can help in these cases.

Domain Security

Security is one of the primary reasons for Active Directory's existence. First off, all of the account names and passwords reside on a single machine (the domain controller), which can easily be locked away, protected, and backed up. The multiple domain controllers automatically *replicate* the changes to one another, so that each one has up-to-date information.

Active Directory is also a vital part of the network's other security mechanisms. When your computer is a member of a domain, the first thing you do is log on, just as in a workgroup. But when you log into a domain, Windows Vista transmits your name and password (in encrypted form) to the domain controller, which checks your credentials and grants or denies you access.

Joining a Domain

Business • Enterprise • Ultimate

If you work in a corporation, the computer supplied to you generally has Windows Vista already installed and joined to the domain, ready to go.

But if you ever have occasion to add a PC to a domain yourself, here's how you go about it. (You can make your PC join a domain either during the installation of Windows Vista, or at any time afterward.)

1. **Log on using the local Administrator account.**

   See page 669 for details.

2. **Choose Start→Control Panel→System and Maintenance→System. In the page that comes up, click the Change Settings button under "Computer name, domain, and workgroup settings."**

   Authenticate yourself (page 191). You should now see the names of your computer and any workgroup or domain it belongs to (see Figure 25-1).

3. **Click the Network ID button.**

   The Join a Domain or a Workgroup Wizard appears.

4. **Click "This computer is part of a business network," and then click Next.**

   Now the wizard wants to know: "Is your company network on a domain?"

5. **Click "My company uses a network with a domain," and then click Next.**

An information screen appears. It lets you know that, before you can join a domain, you need a domain user account, user name, and password. Your network administrator should create and give these to you in advance.

6. **Click Next.**

The next page asks you to "Type your user name, password, and domain name."

Figure 25-1:
The Computer Name tab of the System Properties dialog box displays the name of your computer and the workgroup or domain of which it is currently a member. From here, you can change the computer or workgroup name or join a new domain. The Network ID button launches a Network Identification Wizard, while the Change button displays a dialog box in which a more experienced person can perform the same tasks.

7. **Enter the user account name and password supplied by your administrator, plus the name of the domain in which your account has been created.**

Remember this domain name; you'll need it again later to log on.

8. **Click Next again.**

If the wizard asks you whether you want to use the existing domain account for your computer, say Yes. Otherwise, you'll be prompted to specify the name of your computer and the domain the *computer object* is in. If you see this page, it means that your computer isn't listed in the Active Directory domain you specified on the previous wizard screen. Flag down your network administrator and point out the problem. Then click Next to proceed.

In any case, you should now arrive at a page where you're asked whether you want to enable the domain user account as a local account for your computer. Of course, if you're going to be logging onto a domain, you don't really need a local account on your PC.

9. Click "Do not add a domain user account." Click Next, and finally click Finish to complete the wizard.

You wind up back at the System Properties dialog box.

10. Click OK to dismiss the System Properties dialog box.

Restart the computer for your changes to take effect.

Four Ways Life Is Different on a Domain

Business • Enterprise • Ultimate

The domain and workgroup personalities of Windows Vista are quite different. Here are some of the most important differences.

Logging On

What you see when you log onto your PC is very different when you're part of a domain. Instead of the standard Welcome screen (which shows a list of people with accounts on your PC), you generally encounter a two-step sign-in process:

- First, you see a startup screen that instructs you to press Ctrl+Alt+Delete to log on. (As noted on page 685, this step is a security precaution.)

- When you select Switch User from the Logon screen, you'll have the opportunity to click "Other User" and then log into the domain you joined (see Figure 25-2).

Tip: You can turn off the requirement to press Ctrl+Alt+Delete at each log on, if you like. Choose Start→Control Panel; then click User Accounts→User Accounts. Next, click Manage User Accounts. (You may be prompted for a local administrator's password.) Now select the Advanced tab and turn off the "Require users to press Ctrl-Alt-Delete" checkbox.

UP TO SPEED

Knowing What You're Logging Onto

You may remember from Chapter 23 that there are two kinds of accounts: *domain* accounts, maintained by a highly paid professional in your company, and *local* accounts—accounts that exist only on the PC itself. It's actually possible to find domain accounts and local accounts that have the same name—a perennial source of confusion for beginners (and occasionally experts).

For example, you know that every Vista computer has an Administrator account, which the Vista installer creates automatically. The trouble is, so does the domain controller.

In other words, typing *Administrator* into the User Name text box might log you onto either the local machine or the domain, depending on what password you supply. (With luck, the two accounts won't have the same password, but you never know.)

To avoid this kind of confusion, Windows Vista lets you specify which domain to log onto. Just prefix the account name with the domain name, like this: *2K3DOMAIN\Administrator.*

And if you forget this secret code, you can always click the link marked "How do I log onto another domain?" at the logon screen, as shown in Figure 25-2.

As you see in Figure 25-2, the Log onto Windows dialog box provides a place for you to type your user name and password. To save you time, Windows fills in the User Name box with whatever name was used the last time somebody logged in.

Browsing the Domain

When your PC is part of the domain, all of its resources—printers, shared files, and so on—magically appear in your desktop windows, the Start→Network window, and so on (Figure 25-3).

Tip: If you open the Network window (Start→Network), a message might appear that says, "Network discovery and file sharing are turned off," which means you're cut off from the network. To rejoin the game, click this message (or click Network and Sharing Center in the toolbar) to turn on Network Discovery.

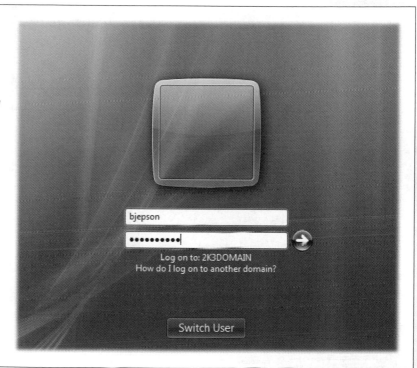

Figure 25-2:
Joining a domain lets you keep using the Windows Vista Welcome screen, but you can click Switch User and choose Other User to have the opportunity to log in as a domain user.

bjepson

••••••••••

Log on to: 2K3DOMAIN
How do I log on to another domain?

Switch User

Searching the Domain

You can read all about the Vista Search command in Chapter 3. But when you're on a domain, this tool becomes far more powerful—and more interesting.

When you choose Start→Network, the toolbar changes to include an option to Search Active Directory. Click it to open the dialog box shown at top left in Figure 25-4.

The name of this dialog box depends on what you're looking for. Your choices are:

• **Users, Contacts, and Groups.** Use this option to search the network for a particular person or network group (Figure 25-4). If your search is successful, you can, for

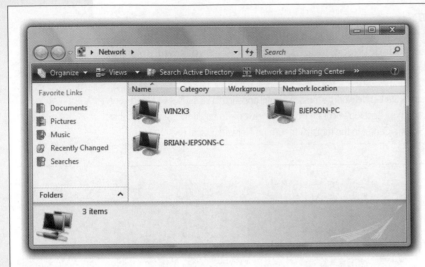

Figure 25-3:
When you choose Start→Network, you see an icon for each computer on the network. You can browse through the computers in a domain and access their shared folders (if you have the appropriate permissions) just as you would those of a workgroup. On a large network, you'll just see a lot more computers.

Figure 25-4:
Top left: Searching for people in your network's Active Directory is like using a phone book. You supply the information you know about the person.

Lower right: When you find that person (technically, her user object), you can view the information stored in the user object's attributes. Of course, the usefulness of this feature depends on how much information your network administrators enter when creating the user objects.

example, find out someone's telephone number, email address, or mailing address, or see what users belong to a particular group.

- **Computers.** This option helps you find a certain PC in the domain. It's of interest primarily to network administrators, because it lets them open a Computer Management window for the computer they find. It also lets them manage many of the PC's functions by remote control.

- **Printers.** In a large office, it's entirely possible that you might not know where you can find a printer with certain features—tabloid-size paper, for example, or double-sided printing. That's where this option comes in handy (see Figure 25-5).

- **Shared Folders.** In theory, this option lets you search for shared folders on the domain's computers—but you'll quickly discover that searches for a certain shared folder generally come up empty-handed.

That's because just sharing a folder on your computer doesn't "publish" it to Active Directory, which would make it available to this kind of search. Only network administrators can publish a shared folder in Active Directory.

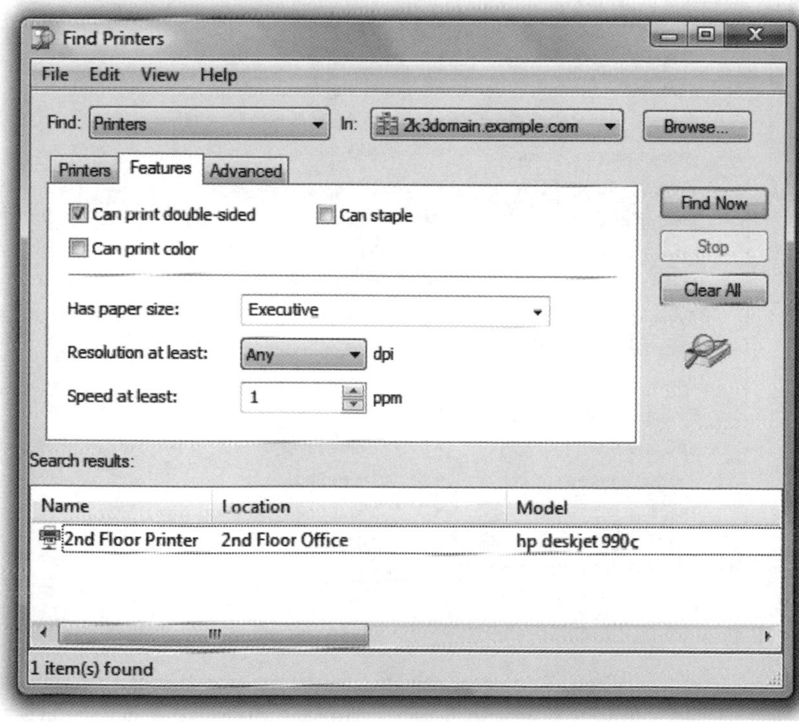

Figure 25-5:
Searching for a printer in Active Directory lets you find the printing features you need. Network administrators may also record the physical locations of the network printers. This way, when your search uncovers a printer that can handle executive paper and also print double-sided, you can simply look at its attributes to find out that it's located on the second floor of the building.

• **Organizational Units.** You may not have heard of organizational units, but your network administrator lives and breathes them. (They're the building blocks of an Active Directory hierarchy.) You, the mere mortal, can safely ignore this search option.

Custom Searches

In addition to these predefined searches, you can also create a custom search of your own by looking for information in specific fields (that is, attributes) of Active Directory, as shown in Figure 25-6.

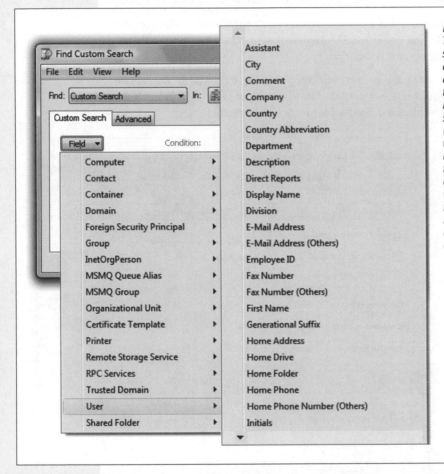

Figure 25-6:
To perform a custom search, use the drop-down menus to select an object type and then a particular field in that object. You then specify a condition (such as whether you want to search for an exact value or just the beginning or end of the value) and the value you want to look for. When you click Find Now, a list of the objects matching your criteria appears.

When used creatively, these custom searches can be powerful indeed, in ways you might not expect. For example, suppose your car won't start, and you need a ride home from the office. You can open this dialog box, click the Field button, and choose User→Home Phone. Change the Condition drop-down menu to Starts With, then type your own area code and telephone exchange into the Value text box. When you click the Find Now button, you'll get a list of co-workers who live in your neighborhood (as indicated by the first three digits of their phone numbers).

Assigning Permissions to Domain Members

Chapter 26 describes the process of assigning permissions to certain files and folders, so that only designated people and groups can open them from across the network. When you're a member of a domain, the process is the same, except that you can select people and groups from the domain as well.

When you open the Properties dialog box for a file or folder, click the Security tab, then click Edit and then Add, you don't get the same dialog box that you'd see on a workgroup network. On a domain, it's called the Select Users, Computers, or Groups dialog box (Figure 25-7). You'll also see this dialog box if you right-click on a folder, click Share, and then select Find from the drop-down menu to the left of the Add button.

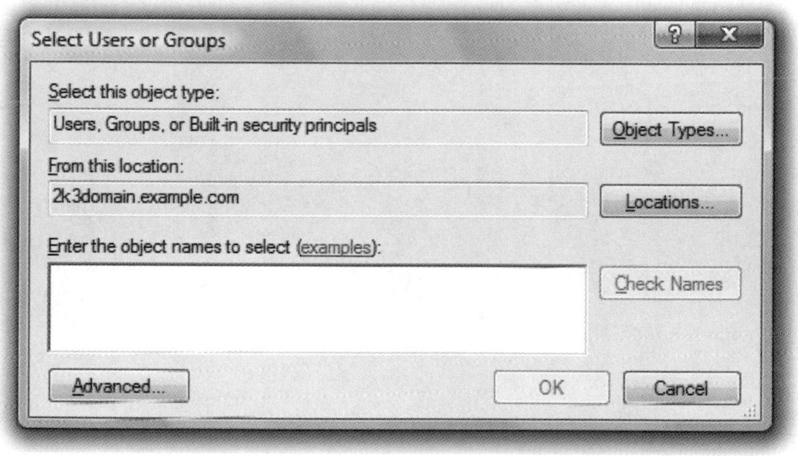

Figure 25-7:
Note that the standard location for the objects is your current domain. You can still click the Locations button and select your computer's name (to specify local user and group accounts), or even choose another domain on the network, if others are available.

Network Sharing and Collaboration

Whether you built the network yourself (Chapter 24) or work in an office where somebody has done that work for you (Chapter 25), all kinds of fun can come from having a network. You're now ready to share the following components among the various PCs on the network:

- **Printers.** You don't need a printer for every PC; all of the PCs can share a much smaller number of printers. If several printers are on your network—say, a high-speed laser printer for one computer and a color printer on another—everyone on the network can use whichever printer is appropriate to a particular document. You'll find step-by-step instructions starting on page 544.

- **Your Internet connection.** Having a network means that all the PCs in your home or office can share a single connection (Chapter 24).

- **Files, folders, and disks.** No matter what PC you're using on the network, you can open the files and folders on any *other* networked PC, as long as the other PCs' owners have made these files available for public inspection. That's where *file sharing* comes in, and that's what this chapter is all about. (File sharing also lets you access your files and folders on the road, using a laptop. See Chapter 27 for more information on this road-warrior trick.)

The uses for file sharing are almost endless. At its simplest, you can use file sharing to finish writing a letter in the bedroom that you started downstairs at the kitchen table—without having to carry a flash drive around. But you can also store your library of MP3 music files on one computer and play them from any other computer on the network.

Getting a slick file-sharing system going involves two steps:

- Sharing the files on one computer on the network; and

- Knowing how to reach them from the other computers.

That's the structure of this chapter.

Sharing Files
All Versions

It's not easy being Microsoft. You have to write *one* operating system that's supposed to please *everyone,* from the self-employed first-time PC owner to the network administrator for General Motors. Clearly, the two might have slightly different attitudes toward the need for security and flexibility.

That's why Windows Vista offers two ways to share files:

- **The Public folder.** It's a folder on every Vista PC that's free for anyone on the network to access, like a grocery store bulletin board. Super-convenient, super-easy.

  There are only two downsides, and you may not care about them. First, you have to move or copy files *into* the Public folder before anyone else can see them. Depending on how many files you wish to share, this can get tedious.

  Second, this method isn't especially secure. If you worry about people rummaging through the files and deleting or vandalizing them, or if bad things could happen if the wrong person in your building gets a look at them, well, then, don't use this method. But if it's just you and your spouse—and you trust your spouse—the Public-folder method makes a lot of sense. (Besides, you can still give the Public folder a password.)

- **Any folder.** You can also make any ordinary folder available for inspection by other people on the network. This method means that you don't have to move files into the Public folder, for starters. It also gives you elaborate control over who is allowed to do what to your files. You might want to permit your company's executives to see and edit your documents, but allow the peons in accounting only to see them. And Andy, that unreliable goofball in sales? You don't want him even seeing what's in your shared folder.

The Public Folder Method
Behind the scenes, the Public folder (there's one per PC) sits in the Local Disk (C:)→Users folder.

To find it faster, open any Explorer window, and then click Public in the Navigation pane (Figure 26-1).

Within the Public folder, Microsoft has thoughtfully suggested an internal folder structure: Public Documents, Public Music, Public Pictures, and so on. (They start out empty, except for some sample files in the music, pictures, and videos folders.) You can use these folders, if you like, or replace them with whatever folders you prefer.

Figure 26-1:
The Public folder is a central public square, a shared meeting point for all PCs on the network. Anything in one of these folders is available to anyone on the network—free and clear. You can find the Public folder listed either among the links (top left) or in the Folder list (bottom left).

Job One is to drag into them any files and folders you want to share with all comers on the network.

Before you go live with your Public folder, though, you have a few more administrative details to take care of, all of which are designed to let you fiddle with the convenience/security balance:

- **Set up accounts.** Ordinarily, each person who wants to get into your PC from the network requires an account (Chapter 23). They already have accounts on their own machines, of course, but you need to create corresponding ones on your machine.

Tip: If the names and passwords you create for them on your machine are *exactly* the same as the accounts on their own machines, you'll make life simpler for them. They won't see the "Connect to" login box shown in Figure 26-7 every time they connect—they'll go straight to your stuff.

- **Turn off the password requirement (optional).** Anyone who doesn't have an account can see what's in the Public folder, open it, and make their own copies of it—but can't make changes to it. Such people can't add files, delete anything, or edit anything. (Technically, they'll be using the Guest account feature of every Windows PC.)

To set up password-free access, choose Start→Control Panel. Under the Network and Sharing heading, click "Set up file sharing." You arrive at the Network and Sharing Center.

As shown in Figure 26-2, "Public folder sharing" comes turned on. Out of the box, it requires your guests to type their names and passwords when connecting (page 730). But if you expand the "Password protected sharing" panel as shown in Figure 26-2, you'll see that you can turn *off* the requirement for a password. Now anyone will be able to see what's in your Public folder, even without an account on your machine.

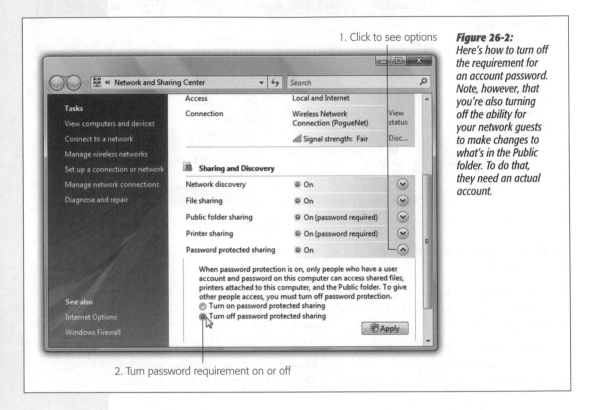

1. Click to see options

Figure 26-2:
Here's how to turn off the requirement for an account password. Note, however, that you're also turning off the ability for your network guests to make changes to what's in the Public folder. To do that, they need an actual account.

2. Turn password requirement on or off

To make your changes stick click Apply, and then authenticate yourself (page 191).

- **Make the Public folder "read-only."** You can institute a "look, but don't touch" policy for your Public folder. Network guests can see and open what's there, but can't add, delete, or edit anything there.

(Yes, this is exactly the same situation described above—but this time, you're laying down the read-only policy on *everyone,* even legitimate account holders.)

To set this up, open the Network and Sharing Center as described above. This time, though, expand the "Public folder sharing" panel, and proceed as shown in Figure 26-3.

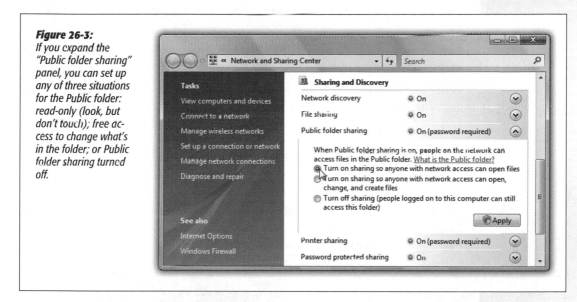

Figure 26-3:
If you expand the "Public folder sharing" panel, you can set up any of three situations for the Public folder: read-only (look, but don't touch); free access to change what's in the folder; or Public folder sharing turned off.

After making your changes, click Apply. Authenticate yourself (page 191).

- **Turn off Public folder sharing altogether.** Proceed as described above, but click "Turn off sharing" (shown in Figure 26-3). Now your Public folder is completely invisible on the network.

So now that you've set up Public folder sharing, how are other people supposed to access your Public folder? See page 739.

GEM IN THE ROUGH

Sharing Disks

You can share files and folders, of course, but also *disks.*

Sharing an entire disk means that every folder on it, and therefore every file, is available to everyone on the network. If security isn't a big deal at your place (because it's just you and a couple of family members, for example), this feature can be a timesaving convenience that spares you the trouble of sharing every new folder you create.

On the other hand, people with privacy concerns generally prefer to share individual *folders.* By sharing only a folder or two, you can keep *most* of the stuff on your hard drive private, out of view of curious network comrades. For that matter, sharing only a folder or two does *them* a favor, too, by making it easier for them to find files you've made available. This way, they don't have to root through your entire drive looking for the folder they actually need.

The "Share Any Folder" Method

If the Public folder method seems too simple, restrictive, and insecure to you, then you can graduate to what Microsoft cleverly calls the "share any folder" method. In this scheme, you can make *any* folder available to other people on the network.

This time, you don't have to move your files anywhere; they sit right where you have them. And this time, you can set up elaborate *sharing permissions* that grant individuals different amount of access over your files.

Better yet, files you share this way are available *both* to other people on the network *and* other account holders on the *same computer*.

Here's how to share a file or folder disk on your PC:

1. **In an Explorer window, highlight the file or folder you want to share. On the toolbar, click Share.**

   The "Choose people to share with" dialog box appears (Figure 26-4). You wanted individual control over each account holder's access? You got it.

Note: The steps for sharing a *disk* are different. See page 736.

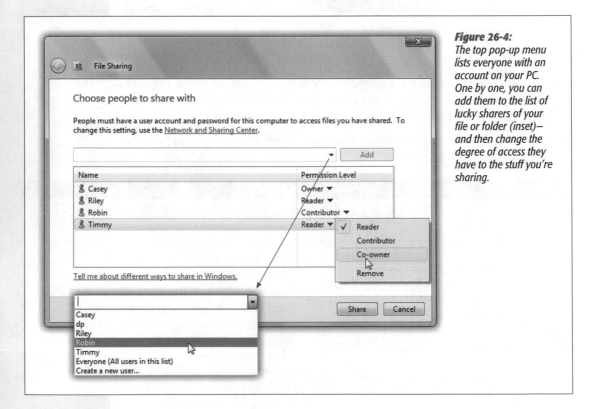

Figure 26-4:
The top pop-up menu lists everyone with an account on your PC. One by one, you can add them to the list of lucky sharers of your file or folder (inset)—and then change the degree of access they have to the stuff you're sharing.

2. **Choose a person's name from the upper pop-up menu (Figure 26-4), and then click Add.**

This is the list of account holders (Chapter 23)—or account-holder *groups,* if someone has created them (page 683).

If the person who'll be connecting across the network doesn't yet have an account on your machine, choose "Create a new user" from this pop-up menu. (This isn't some kind of sci-fi breakthrough. You are not, in fact, going to create a human being—only an account for an *existing* person.)

The name appears in the list.

Now your job is to work through this list of people, specify *how much* control each person has over the file or folder you're sharing.

3. **Click a name in the list. Click the ▾ in the Permission Level column and choose Reader, Contributor, or Co-owner.**

A *Reader* is that "look, but don't touch" business. This person can see what's in the folder (or file) and can copy it, but can't delete or change the original.

Contributors (available for folders only—not files) have much broader access. These people can add, change, or delete files in the shared folder—but only files *that they put there.* Stuff placed there by other people (Owners or Co-owners) appears as "look, but don't touch" to a Contributor.

A *Co-owner* has the most access of all. This person, like you, can add, change, or delete any file in the shared folder.

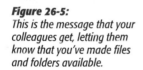

Figure 26-5:
This is the message that your colleagues get, letting them know that you've made files and folders available.

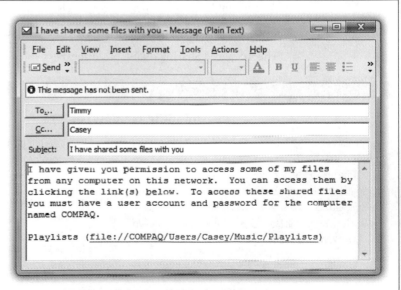

This stuff may sound technical and confusing, but you have no idea how much simpler it is than it was before Vista came along.

4. **Click Share.**

The "Your folder is shared" dialog box appears. This is more than a simple message, however; it contains the *network address* of the files or folders you shared. Without this address, your colleagues won't know that you've shared stuff, and will have a tough time finding it.

5. **Click e-mail or copy (Figure 26-5).**

The e-mail link opens a new, outgoing message in Windows Mail, letting the gang know that you've shared something and offering them a link to it. The copy link copies the address to the Clipboard, so you can paste it into another program—which is your best bet if Mail isn't your email program of choice.

Advanced Folder Sharing—and Disk Sharing

Microsoft made a noble step forward in simplicity with the "share any folder" wizard described in the previous pages. But the older, more complicated—yet more flexible—method is still available. Here's a quick review of this alternate route (which is, by the way, the *only* route for sharing entire *disks):*

1. **Right-click the folder or disk you want to share. If it's a folder, choose Properties from the shortcut menu; if it's disk, choose Share. In the dialog box, click the Sharing tab.**

   At this point, you *could* click the Share button (if you're operating on a folder, anyway). You'd arrive at the dialog box shown in Figure 26-4, where you could specify the account holders and permission levels, just as described earlier. But don't.

2. **Click Advanced Sharing. Authenticate yourself (page 191).**

   The Advanced Sharing dialog box appears.

POWER USERS' CLINIC

Unhiding Hidden Folders

As sneaky and delightful as the hidden-folder trick is, it has a distinct drawback—*you* can't see your hidden folder from across the network, either. Suppose you want to use another computer on the network—the one in the upstairs office, for example—to open something in your hidden My Novel folder (which is downstairs in the kitchen). Fortunately, you can do so—if you know the secret.

On the office computer, choose Start→Run. In the Run dialog box, type the path of the hidden folder, using the format *Computer Name\Folder Name.*

For example, enter *kitchen\my novel$* to get to the hidden folder called My Novel$ on the PC called Kitchen. (Capitalization doesn't matter, but don't forget the $ sign.) Then click OK to open a window showing the contents of your hidden folder. (See page 742 for more on the Universal Naming Convention system.)

---

3. **Click "Share this folder." (See Figure 26-6, top.) Next, set up the power-user sharing options.**

For example, you can limit the number of people who are browsing this folder at once. You can click Permissions to fine-tune who can do what (Figure 26-6, bottom). And you can edit the "Share name"—in fact, you can create *more than one* name for the same shared folder—to make it more recognizable on the network when people are browsing your PC.

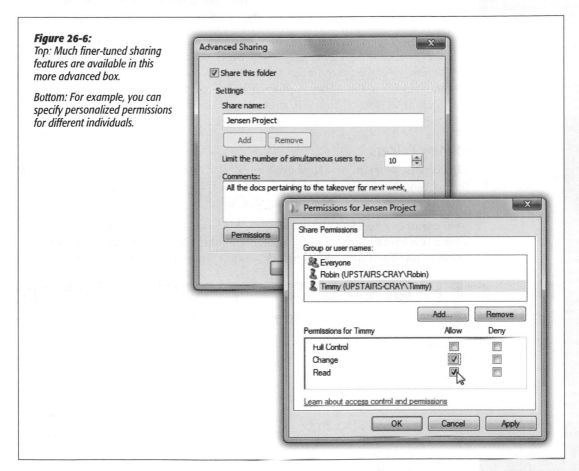

Figure 26-6:
Top: Much finer-tuned sharing features are available in this more advanced box.

Bottom: For example, you can specify personalized permissions for different individuals.

Notes on File Sharing

And now, the fine print on sharing files:

- Sharing a folder also shares all of the folders inside it, including new ones you create later.

On the other hand, it's OK to *change* the sharing settings of a subfolder. For example, if you've shared a folder called America, you can make the Minnesota folder inside it off-limits by making it private. Similarly, if you've turned *off* "Allow network users to change my files" for the America folder, you can turn it back *on* for the Minnesota folder inside it.

To do this, right-click the inner folder, choose Properties→Sharing, click Advanced Sharing, and use the dialog box shown in Figure 26-6.

- Be careful with nested folders. Suppose, for example, that you share your Documents folder, and you permit other people to change the files inside it. Now suppose that you share a folder that's *inside* Documents—called Spreadsheets, for example—but you turn *off* the ability for other people to change its files.

  You wind up with a strange situation. Both folders—Documents and Spreadsheets—show up in other people's Network windows, as described below. If they double-click the Spreadsheets folder directly, they won't be able to change anything inside it. But if they double-click the Documents folder, and then open the Spreadsheets folder inside *it*, they *can* modify the files. (See the more complete discussion of permissions on page 692.)

Hiding Folders

If a certain folder on your hard drive is really private, you can hide the folder so that other people on the network can't even *see* it. The secret is to type a $ symbol at the end of the *share name* (see step 3 on page 737).

For example, if you name a certain folder My Novel, anyone else on the network can see it (even if they can't read the contents). But if you name the share *My Novel$*, it won't show up in anybody's Network window. They won't even know that it exists.

GEM IN THE ROUGH

Accessing Macs Across the Network

When it comes to networking, Macs are people, too.

Windows Vista is perfectly capable of letting you rifle through a Mac's contents from across the network. Here's how to set that up.

On the Mac, choose →System Preferences. Click Sharing, and then turn on Windows Sharing. Click Accounts to specify *which* Mac user accounts you want to be able to access. Before you close System Preferences, study the line at the bottom of the dialog box, where it says:

"Windows users can access your computer at \\192.168.1.203\casey"

Those numbers are the Mac's IP address, which you'll need shortly. (You will *not* need the initial pair of backslashes.)

Now, on the PC, proceed exactly as though you were trying to connect to another Windows PC. But when you see the dialog box shown in Figure 26-7, type the Mac's IP address, a backslash, and then your Mac account name, like this:

192.168.1.203\casey

Put in your Mac's account password, too. And if you turn on "Remember my password," you won't be bothered for a name or password the next time you perform this amazing act of détente.

Accessing Shared Files
All Versions

Now suppose you're not you. You're your co-worker, spouse, or employee. You're using your laptop downstairs, and you want access to the stuff that's in a shared folder on the Beefy Main Dell computer upstairs. Here's what to do; the steps are the same whether the Public folder or *any* folder was shared.

1. **Choose Start→Network.**

   The Network window appears, showing icons for all the computers on the network.

Tip: Alternatively, you can click the Network icon in the Folders list at the left side of every Explorer window. The same Navigation pane is available in the Save and Open dialog boxes of your programs, too, making the entire network available to you for opening and saving files.

   If you *don't* see a certain computer's icon here, it might be turned off, or off the network. It also might have *network discovery* turned off; that's the feature that lets a PC announce its presence to the network. (Its on/off switch is one of the buttons shown in Figure 26-2.)

   And if you don't see any computers at *all* in the Network window, then network discovery might be turned off on *your* computer.

2. **Double-click the computer whose files you want to open.**

   If you're on a corporate domain, you may first have to double-click your way through some other icons, representing the networks in other buildings or floors, before you get to the actual PC icons.

   In any case, the Connect To box may now appear (Figure 26-7, top).

3. **Fill in your name and password.**

   This, of course, is a real drag, especially if you access other people's files frequently.

   Fortunately, you have three time-saving tricks available to you here.

   First, if your name and password are the same on both machines, you get to skip the "Connect to" dialog box.

   Second, if you turn on "Remember my password," then you'll never see this box again. The next time you want to visit the other PC, you'll be able to double-click its icon for instant access.

   Finally, if you're trying to get to someone's Public folder, and you don't need to modify the files, just read or copy them, you don't need a password, ever. Just type *guest* into the "User name" box and click OK. You'll have full read-only access (page 735). And here again, next time, you won't be bothered for a name or password.

CHAPTER 26: NETWORK SHARING AND COLLABORATION

Tip: In the unlikely event that you want Vista to *stop* memorizing your password, choose Start→Control Panel. Click User Accounts and Family Safety, then "Change your account," and finally "Manage your network passwords." You'll find a list of every password Vista has memorized for you; use the Add, Remove, Edit, or "Back up" buttons as suits your fancy.

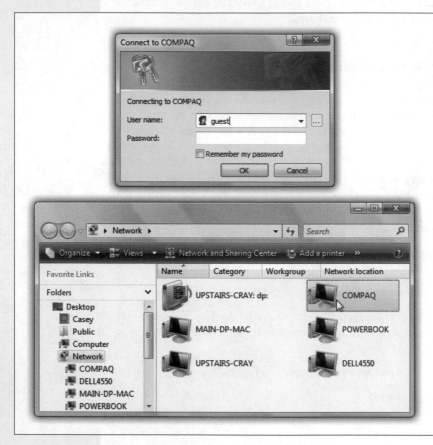

Figure 26-7:
Top: Supply your account name and password as it exists on the distant PC, the one you're trying to access.

Bottom: The computers on your network are arrayed before you! Double-click the one you want to visit.

4. **Click OK.**

   If all went well, the other computer's window opens, presenting you with the icons of its shared folders and disks.

Tip: Working with the same shared folders often? Save yourself a lot of time and burrowing—make a desktop shortcut of it right now!

Once you've opened the window that contains the shared folder, grab your mouse. Right-click the shared item and drag it to the desktop. When you release the mouse, choose "Create Shortcuts Here" from the shortcut menu. From now on, you can double-click that shortcut to open the shared item directly.

Once you've brought a networked folder onto your screen, you can double-click icons to open them, drag them to the Recycle Bin, make copies of them, and otherwise manipulate them exactly as though they were icons on your own hard drive. (Of course, if you weren't given permission to change the contents of the shared folder, you have less freedom.)

Tip: There's one significant difference between working with "local" icons and working with those that sit elsewhere on the network. When you delete a file from another computer on the network (if you're allowed to do so), either by pressing the Delete key or by dragging it to the Recycle Bin, it disappears instantly and permanently, without ever appearing in the Recycle Bin.

You can even use Vista's Search feature to find files elsewhere on the network. This kind of searching can be very slow, however; see page 113 for details on how Search handles networked disks.

FREQUENTLY ASKED QUESTION

Accessing Other Computers from Non-Vista Machines

How do I access my Vista machines from my non-Vista machines?

Piece of cake. Turns out all versions of Windows use the same networking scheme, so you can share files freely among PCs using different Windows versions.

Once some files are shared (on any PC), here's how to find them:

In Windows Vista: Choose Start→Network.

In Windows XP or Windows Me: Choose Start→My Network Places.

In earlier versions: Double-click the desktop icon called Network Neighborhood or My Network Places.

Now you see icons that correspond to the computers of your network (including your own machine), much as shown in Figure 26-4.

If you don't see the Vista computers, it may because all the machines don't have the same *workgroup* name. (A workgroup is a cluster of networked machines. See Chapter 24 for details.) To change your Windows XP computer's workgroup name to match, choose Start→Control Panel; click "Performance and Maintenance," and then open System. Click the Computer Name tab, and then select Change.

Or, to change your *Vista* PC's workgroup name, choose Start→Control Panel; click System and Maintenance; open System. Under the "Computer Name, Domain, and Workgroup Settings" heading, click Change Settings.

Truth is, you can even open Windows machines' icons if you're using Mac OS X. Click the Network icon in your Sidebar, as shown here. Then click the Workgroup folder—that's the standard name for Windows network clusters, although someone may have changed it. Inside, you find your Windows PCs listed, ready to open (assuming you have an account on them).

Extra Credit: Universal Naming Convention (UNC)

For hard-core nerds, that business of double-clicking icons in the Network folder is for sissies. When they want to call up a shared folder from the network, or even a particular document *in* a shared folder, they just type a special address into the Address bar of any folder window, or even Internet Explorer—and then press the Enter key. You can also type such addresses into the Start→Run dialog box.

It might look like this: *laptop\shared documents\salaries 2007.doc*.

Tip: Actually, you don't have to type nearly that much. The AutoComplete feature proposes that full expression as soon as you type just a few letters of it.

This path format (including the double-backslash before the PC name and a single backslash before a folder name) is called the *Universal Naming Convention (UNC)*. It was devised to create a method of denoting the exact location of a particular file or folder on a network. It also lets network geeks open various folders and files on networked machines without having to use the Network window.

You can use this system in all kinds of interesting ways:

- Open a particular folder like this: *computer name\folder name*.

- You can also substitute the IP address for the computer instead of using its name, like this: *192.1681.44\my documents*.

- You can even substitute the name of a shared *printer* for the folder name.

- As described later in this chapter, Windows can even access shared folders that sit elsewhere on the Internet (offline backup services, for example). You can call these items onto your screen (once you're online) just by adding *http:* before the UNC code and using regular forward slashes instead of backwards slashes, like this: *http://Computer Name/Folder Name*.

WORKAROUND WORKSHOP

Automatic Reconnections Can Be Tricky

If you select "Reconnect at logon" when mapping a shared disk or folder to a letter, the order in which you start your computers becomes important. The PC containing the shared disk or folder should start up before the computer that refers to it as, say, drive K:. That way, when the second computer searches for "drive K:" on the network, its quest will be successful.

On the other hand, this guideline presents a seemingly insurmountable problem if you have two computers on the network, and each of them maps drive letters to folders or disks on the other.

In that situation, you get an error message to the effect that the permanent connection is not available. It asks if you want to reconnect the next time you start the computer. Click Yes.

Then, after all the computers have started up, open your Computer window or an Explorer window. You can see the mapped drive, but there's a red X under the icon. Ignore the X. Just double-click the icon. The shared folder or disk opens normally (because the other machine is now available), and the red X goes away.

Tip: A great place to type UNC addresses is in the Address bar at the top of any desktop window.

**Accessing
Shared Files**

Mapping Shares to Drive Letters
All Versions

If you access network shares on a regular basis, you may want to consider another access technique, called *mapping shares*. Using this trick, you can assign a *letter* to a particular shared disk or folder on the network. Just as your hard drive is called C: and your floppy drive is A:, you can give your Family Stuff folder the letter F: and the backup drive in the kitchen the letter J:.

Doing so confers several benefits. First, these disks and folders now appear directly in the Computer window. Getting to them this way can be faster than navigating to the Network window. Second, when you choose File→Open from within one of your applications, you'll be able to jump directly to a particular shared folder instead of having to double-click, ever deeper, through the icons in the Open File dialog box. You can also use the mapped drive letter in pathnames anywhere you would use a path on a local drive, such as the Run dialog box, a File→Save As dialog box, or the command line.

To map a drive letter to a disk or folder, open any folder or disk window. Then:

1. **In any Explorer window, press Alt (or F10) to make the old menu bar appear. Choose Tools→Map Network Drive.**

   The Map Network Drive dialog box appears, as shown in Figure 26-8.

2. **Using the drop-down list, choose a drive letter.**

   You can select any unused letter you like (except B, which is still reserved for the second floppy disk drive that PCs don't have anymore).

3. **Indicate which folder or disk you want this letter to represent.**

   You can type its UNC code into the Folder box, choose from the drop-down list of recently accessed folders, or click Browse.

Tip: Most people use the mapping function for disks and drives elsewhere on the network, but there's nothing to stop you from mapping a folder that's sitting right there on your own PC.

---

4. **To make this letter assignment stick, turn on "Reconnect at logon."**

   If you don't use this option, Windows forgets this assignment the next time you turn on the computer. (Use the "Connect using a different user name" option if your account name on the shared folder's machine isn't the same as it is on this one.)

5. **Click Finish.**

   A window opens to display the contents of the folder or disk. If you don't want to work with any files at the moment, just close the window.

From now on (depending on your setting in step 4), that shared disk or folder shows up in your Navigation pane along with the disks that are actually in your PC, as shown at bottom in Figure 26-8.

Tip: If you see a red X on one of these mapped icons, it means that the PC on which one of the shared folders or disks resides is either off the network or turned off completely.

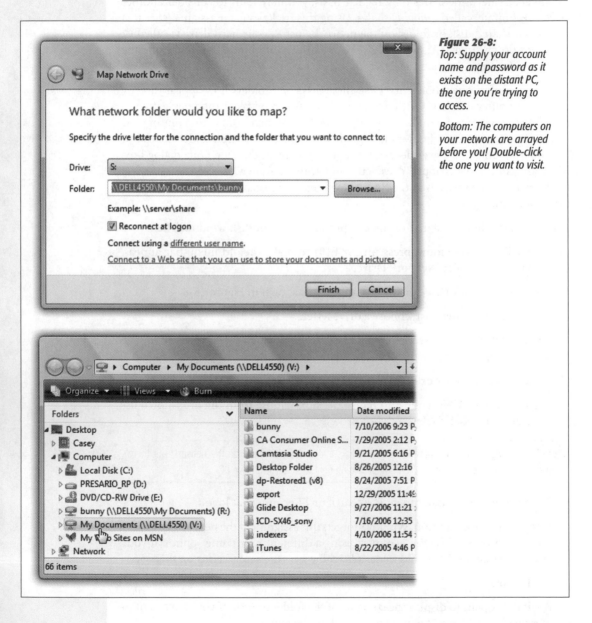

Figure 26-8:
Top: Supply your account name and password as it exists on the distant PC, the one you're trying to access.

Bottom: The computers on your network are arrayed before you! Double-click the one you want to visit.

Windows Meeting Space

Home Premium • Business • Premium • Ultimate

Once you've got a nice home or office network humming along, files aren't the only things you can share. You can also share time and ideas.

That's the idea behind Windows Meeting Space, a new program for collaborating with up to 10 other people, over your office network or even across the Internet. It's a worthy successor to programs like NetMeeting.

Note: All participants must have Windows Vista. If you're using the Home Basic edition, you can join other people's meetings in Meeting Space, but you can't host or start one. That'll teach you to be a cheapskate.

Calling a Meeting to Order

The first time you choose Start→All Programs→Windows Meeting Space, you go through a little setup wizard. Along the way, you need to:

- Click "Yes, continue setting up Windows Meeting Space."

- Authenticate yourself (page 191).

- Set up People Near Me, a feature that autodetects other computers nearby. Here, you'll type in the name by which you wish to be known in the Meeting Space world.

At last you arrive at the shaded blue happy world of Windows Meeting Space. If your intent is to join a meeting in progress, double-click its name, as shown in Figure 26-9 at bottom.

If *you* want to begin the meeting, though, do the following:

1. **Click "Start a new meeting."**

   You're asked to name the meeting and provide a long password for it. You certainly wouldn't want unauthorized strangers to find out what you're talking about!

2. **Make up a name and password for your meeting.**

   Another note to the paranoid: if you click the Options link, you can designate this meeting as invisible, so that it won't show up in other people's Meeting Space lists, ready for clicking; they'll have to know the meeting's name.

Tip: If, in the Options dialog box, you turn on "Create a private ad hoc wireless network," you can use Meeting Space without even having a network. You and a fellow wireless laptopper can connect through the air with each other, even in the absence of an existing office network.

---

3. **Press Enter (or click the green arrow button).**

   You've just entered the meeting, as made clear by the picture of a projector screen.

Inviting Participants

At this point, the lucky meeting members can join you in any of four ways:

- Anyone in the vicinity who fires up Meeting Space sees your meeting listed. People can double-click its name to "enter the room" (after supplying the password).

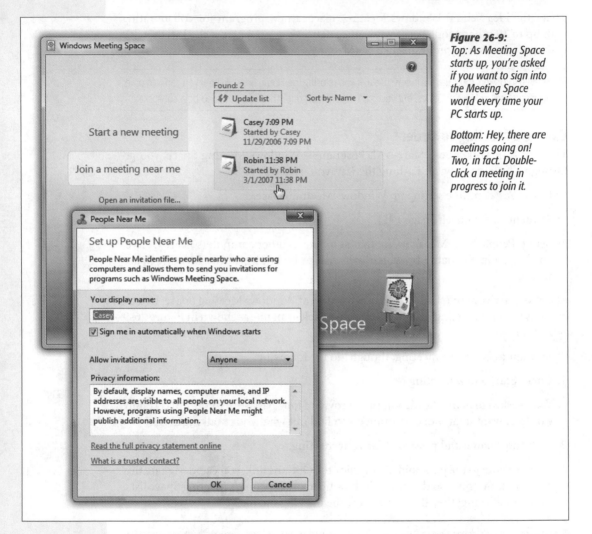

Figure 26-9:
Top: As Meeting Space starts up, you're asked if you want to sign into the Meeting Space world every time your PC starts up.

Bottom: Hey, there are meetings going on! Two, in fact. Double-click a meeting in progress to join it.

- You can invite someone electronically by clicking the "Invite people" link. A list of people who've been through the Meeting Space setup process appears; turn on the checkboxes of the people you want to meet in cyber-meeting space, and then click "Send invitations."

Note: Recipients won't get your invite unless they're either (a) running Meeting Space; or (b) they've signed into People Near Me. They can do that by choosing Start→Control Panel, clicking "Network and Internet," and then clicking the "Sign in or out of People Near Me" link. If they also click "Change People Near Me settings," they'll find a checkbox called "Sign me in automatically when Windows starts," so they won't miss any more invitations in the future.

- You can invite someone by email, which is just the ticket if you want to conduct a collaboration session across the Internet. To do that, after clicking "Invite people," click "Invite others." You'll see the "Send an invitation in e-mail" option. The recipient gets an email message with an attachment—one that, when double-clicked, asks for the password and sends the person into your meeting.

- You can create an invitation file that you distribute in some other form—on a flash drive or CD, for example. The recipient can double-click this file to join your meeting. (OK, this scenario is far-fetched, but you never know.)

  Use the "Invite others" option described above, but in the resulting dialog box, click "Create an invitation file."

Tip: After a while, it dawns on you that there are now *three* remote-access programs in Vista: Remote Assistance (Chapter 5), Remote Desktop (Chapter 27), and Meeting Space, all fairly similar. Read up and decide.

Fun in Meetings

Once your meeting gets started, each participant shows up with an icon (Figure 26-10).

Here's the kind of collaboration fun you can have:

- **Share your desktop.** Other people in the meeting can actually see your PC screen image. They see what you're doing, in other words.

  When you click "Share a program or your desktop" (and then dismiss the warning box), the "Start a shared session" dialog box appears. Double-click the name of the program or window you want other people to see.

Tip: Alternatively, you can drag a document icon from your desktop directly into the main Meeting Space window, whereupon it opens. Everyone else can see it, too.

The screen may blink, things may get fritzy, but sure enough, other people now see your screen. In fact, they can even request *control* of your computer—to point out an error in your work, for example. To do that, someone can click the ▾ next to "Casey is in control" just above the shared window and, from the pop-up menu, choose Request Control. (Or you can choose Give Control from *your* menu bar.)

If you grant control to someone, the keyboard and mouse are no longer yours to operate.

Tip: If you don't like the way things are going when someone else is manipulating your screen, you can seize control back again—just hit ⊞+Esc.

- **Pass a note.** Double-click a participant's icon to open a note window. Type your note and then hit Send. Your correspondent can reply to you, and you can continue chatting behind everyone else's backs as the meeting proceeds. (The window holds only one response at a time, so it's not really like a chat program.)

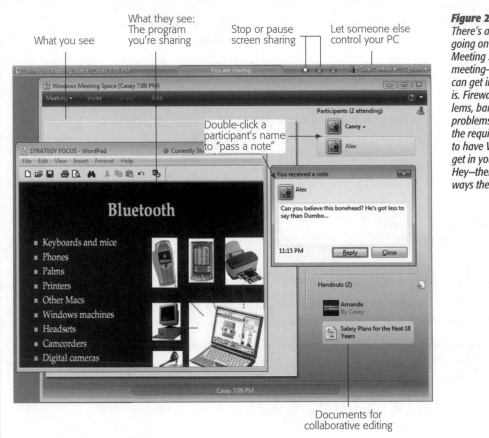

Figure 26-10:
There's a lot going on in a Meeting Space meeting—if you can get in, that is. Firewall problems, bandwidth problems, and the requirement to have Vista may get in your way. Hey—there's always the phone.

What you see

What they see:
The program
you're sharing

Stop or pause
screen sharing

Let someone else
control your PC

Double-click a
participant's name
to "pass a note"

Documents for
collaborative editing

- **Distribute a handout.** Click "Add a handout" to select a document that you want to pass to everyone else in the meeting. They'll be able to edit the copy one person at a time; the changes they make appear magically in everyone else's copies. (Your original remains untouched.)

Meeting Space Weirdness

Windows Meeting Space is ambitious, but also fairly fraught with technical obstacles. A firewall—the built-in Windows one or one you've added—can stop Meeting Space in its tracks. The Meeting Space Help screens, in fact, offer pages and pages of trouble-shooting tactics, some of which are best handled by a networking pro.

It's worth noting, too, that Meeting Space requires you to be on what Microsoft, in Vista, calls a *private* network; see the box on page 359 for details.

You may also notice that when somebody's sharing his desktop or a program window, weird black areas appear on your screen. That's because Meeting Space shows you *only* the parts of the presenter's screen that are actually occupied by the program he's sharing. All other areas appear black to you—including areas where another program is covering up the shared program.

Handout sharing can get tricky, too. Whoever makes changes (and saves them) most recently "wins." If you and Riley both make changes at the same time, but you save the document and *then* Riley does, Riley's changes wipe out yours. (You've been warned.)

FREQUENTLY ASKED QUESTION

FTP Sites and Other Online Disks

How do I bring an FTP server, or one of those Web-based backup drives, onto my PC?

The trick to bringing these servers online is the "Add a network place" link—but you won't find it in the task pane of the Network window, as it did in Windows XP.

The trick is to right-click a blank spot in the *Computer* window. From the shortcut menu, choose "Add a Network Location."

When the wizard appears, click Next. Then, on the second screen, click "Choose a custom network location." Click Next.

Finally you arrive at the critical screen, where you can type in the address of the Web site, FTP site, or other network location that you want your new shortcut to open.

Into the first text box, you can type any of these network addresses:

The UNC code. As described earlier in this chapter, a UNC code pinpoints a particular shared folder on the network. For example, if you want to open the shared folder named Fami-lyBiz on the computer named Dad, enter *dad\familybiz*. Capitalization doesn't matter. Or, to open a specific file, you could enter something like *dad\finances\budget.xls*.

http://website/folder. To see what's in a folder called Customers on a company Web site called BigBiz.com, enter *http://bigbiz.com/customers*. (You can't just type in any old Web address. It has to be a Web site that's been specifically designed to serve as a "folder" containing files.)

ftp://ftp.website/folder. This is the address format for FTP sites. For example, if you want to use a file in a folder named Bids on a company site named WeBuyStuff.com, enter *ftp://ftp.webuystuff.com/bids*.

What happens when you click Next depends on the kind of address you specified. If it was an FTP site, you're offered the chance to specify your user name. (Access to every FTP site requires a user name and password. You won't be asked for the password until you actually try to open the newly created folder shortcut.)

Click Finish to complete the creation of your network shortcut, which now appears in the Network Location area in the Computer window. To save you a step, the wizard also offers to connect to and open the corresponding folder.

You can work with these remote folders exactly as though they were sitting on your own hard drive. The only difference is that because you're actually communicating with a hard drive via the Internet, the slower speed may make it feel as if your PC has been drugged.

Vista by Remote Control

Windows Vista provides many avenues for accessing one PC from another across the Internet. If you're a road warrior armed with a laptop, you may be delighted by these features. If you're a corporate employee who used to think that you could escape the office by going home, you may not.

In any case, each of these *remote access* features requires a good deal of setup and some scavenging through the technical underbrush, and each offers slightly different benefits and drawbacks. But when you're in Tulsa and a spreadsheet you need is on your PC in Tallahassee, you may be grateful to have at least one of these systems in place.

And besides—if you're connecting to PCs at your corporate office, your corporate IT people have probably already done all the hard work of getting the computers at work set up for you to connect to them from home or the road.

Remote Access Basics
All Versions

The two most common scenarios for using these remote access features are: (a) controlling your home PC remotely using a laptop, and (b) connecting to your office network from your PC at home. To help you keep the roles of these various computers straight, the computer industry has done you the favor of introducing specialized terminology:

- The *host computer* is the home-base computer—the unattended one that's waiting for you to connect.

• The *remote computer* is the one you'll be using: your laptop on the road, for example, or your home machine (or laptop) when you tap into the office network.

The remaining pages of this chapter cover three systems of connecting:

• **Dialing direct.** The remote computer can dial the host PC directly, modem to modem, becoming part of the network at the host location. At that point, you can access shared folders exactly as described in the previous chapter.

The downside? The host PC must have its own phone line that only it answers. Otherwise, its modem answers every incoming phone call, occasionally blasting the ears of hapless human callers. No wonder this is becoming a less common connection method.

• **Virtual private networking (VPN).** Using this system, you don't have to make a direct connection from the remote PC to the host. Instead, you use the Internet as an intermediary. You avoid long-distance charges, and the host PC doesn't have to have its own phone line. Once again, the remote computer behaves exactly as though it has joined the network of the system you're dialing into.

• **Remote Desktop.** This feature doesn't just make the remote PC join the network of the host; it actually turns your computer *into* the faraway host PC, filling your screen with its screen image. When you touch the trackpad on your laptop, you're actually moving the cursor on the home-base PC's screen, and so forth.

Tip: For added protection against snoopers, you should use Remote Desktop *with* a VPN connection.

To make Remote Desktop work, you have to connect *to* a computer running Windows Vista, XP Pro, or Windows Server. But the machine you're connecting *from* can be any relatively recent Windows PC, a Macintosh (to get a free copy of Remote Desktop Connection for Mac, visit *www.microsoft.com/mac/*), or even a computer running Linux (you'll need the free rdesktop client, available from *www.rdesktop.org*).

Tip: The world is filled with more powerful, more flexible products that let you accomplish the same things as these Windows Vista features, from software programs like LapLink, Carbon Copy, and PC Anywhere to Web sites like *www.gotomypc.com*.

On the other hand, Remote Desktop is free.

Note, by the way, that these are all methods of connecting to an *unattended* machine. If somebody is sitting at the PC back home, you might find it far more convenient to connect using Windows Meeting Space, described in Chapter 26. It's easier to set up and works even with Windows Vista Home Basic on either end, yet offers the same kind of "screen sharing" as Remote Desktop.

Dialing Direct

All Versions

Here, then, is Method 1, dialing in from the road, modem to modem. To set up the host to make it ready for access from afar, you first must prepare it to answer calls. Then you need to set up the remote computer to dial in.

Setting Up the Host PC

If your host PC has its own private phone line—the lucky thing—here's how to prepare it for remote access:

1. **Choose Start→Control Panel→Network and Internet→Network and Sharing Center.**

   The Network and Sharing Center appears.

2. **Click the "Manage network connections" link on the left side.**

   The Network Connections window appears. Icons now appear, representing your various network connections. (See Chapter 9.)

3. **Press the Alt or F10 key to make the menu bar appear. Choose File→New Incoming Connection.**

UP TO SPEED

Remote Networking vs. Remote Control

When you connect to a PC using direct dial or virtual private networking (VPN), you're simply joining the host's network from far away. When you try to open a Word document that's actually sitting on the distant PC, your *laptop's* copy of Word opens and loads the file. Your laptop is doing the actual word processing; the host just sends and receives files as needed.

Vista's Remote Desktop feature is a different animal. In this case, you're using your laptop to *control* the host computer. If you double-click that Word file on the host computer, you open the copy of Word *on the host computer.* All of the word processing takes place on the distant machine; all that passes over the connection between the two computers is a series of keystrokes, mouse movements, and screen displays. The host is doing all the work. Your laptop is just peeking at the results.

Once you understand the differences between these technologies, you can make a more informed decision about which to use when. For example, suppose your PC at the office has a folder containing 100 megabytes of images you need to incorporate into a PowerPoint document. Using a remote networking connection means that you'll have to wait for the files to be transmitted to your laptop before you can begin working—and if you've connected to the office machine using a dial-up modem, you'll be waiting, literally, for several *days.*

If you use a Remote Desktop connection, on the other hand, the files remain right where they are: on the host computer, which does all the processing. You see on your screen exactly what you would see if you were sitting at the office. When you drag and drop one of those images into your PowerPoint document, all the action is taking place on the PC at the other end.

Of course, if the computer doing the dialing is a brand-new Pentium 7 zillion-megahertz screamer, and the host system is a 5-year-old rustbucket on its last legs, you might actually *prefer* a remote network connection, so the faster machine can do most of the heavy work.

The Allow Connections to this Computer wizard appears (Figure 27-1, top). You're now looking at a list of every account holder on your PC (Chapter 23).

4. **Choose the names of the users who are allowed to dial in.**

If you highlight a name and then click Account Properties, you can turn on the *callback* feature—a security feature that, after you've dialed in, makes your host PC hang up and call you back at a specific number. You can either (a) specify a callback number at the host machine in advance, so that outsiders won't be able to connect, or (b) let the remote user *specify* the callback number, which puts most of the telephone charges on the host computer's bill (so that you can bypass obscene hotel long-distance surcharges). Click OK to close the dialog box.

5. **Click Next.**

Now you can choose how remote users will connect (Figure 27-1, bottom).

6. **Select "Through a dial-up modem." Select your modem in the list, and then click Next.**

Now you're prompted to choose which networking capabilities to offer over the dial-up connection. Ensure that the "Internet Protocol Version 4" and "File and Printer Sharing for Microsoft Networks" options are selected.

7. **Click "Allow access."**

The final screen says, "The people you chose can now connect to this computer. To connect, they will need the following information:"—and then you see your computer's official name.

Truth is, though, if you plan to dial in, you don't even need to know that; all you need is your phone number!

A new icon in your Network Connections window, called Incoming Connections, is born.

Your home-base PC is ready for connections. When the phone rings, the modem answers it. (Of course, you shouldn't use this feature with the same phone line as your answering machine or your fax machine.)

You might want to make a few changes to the configuration now. Right-click on the incoming connection's icon; from the shortcut menu, choose Properties.

In the Incoming Connections Properties dialog box, you can open your *modem's* Properties to turn on "Disconnect a call if idle for more than __ minutes." Doing so makes sure that your home-base PC won't tie up the line after your laptop in the hotel room is finished going about its business.

Setting Up the Remote PC

Next, go to the remote computer and get it ready to phone home. Here's what to do:

1. Choose Start→Network. In the toolbar, click Network and Sharing Center. In the Tasks on the left, click "Set up a connection or network."

   The "Set up a connection or network" wizard appears.

2. Scroll down, if necessary, and double-click "Connect to a workplace."

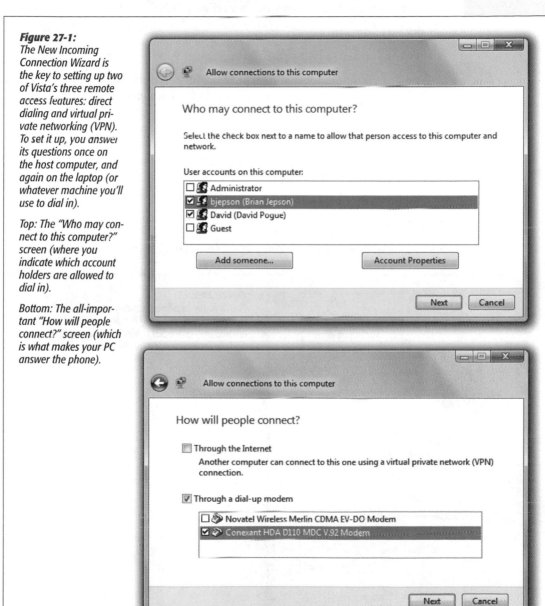

Figure 27-1:
The New Incoming Connection Wizard is the key to setting up two of Vista's three remote access features: direct dialing and virtual private networking (VPN). To set it up, you answer its questions once on the host computer, and again on the laptop (or whatever machine you'll use to dial in).

Top: The "Who may connect to this computer?" screen (where you indicate which account holders are allowed to dial in).

Bottom: The all-important "How will people connect?" screen (which is what makes your PC answer the phone).

If you already have a dial-up connection, Windows asks you if you want to use a connection you already have. "No, create a new connection" is already selected.

3. **Click Next.**

Now Windows wants to know if you'll be connecting via modem ("Dial directly") or via Internet ("Use my Internet connection (VPN)").

4. **Click "Dial directly."**

Now you're asked to type in the phone number you'll want your laptop to call.

5. **Type in the phone number and a name for your connection (like "Phone home"). Click "Don't connect now; just set it up so I can connect later" and then click Next.**

Another screen, another form to fill out.

6. **Type in your user name and password, and if a network administrator so dictates, specify a domain name. Then click Create.**

Windows tells you, "The connection is ready to use."

7. **Click Close.**

You're now ready to establish a connection between the two computers.

Figure 27-2:
You're ready to phone home. If you click the Properties button, you can invoke a dialing rule, if you created one (page 331), which can save you a bit of fiddling with area codes and access numbers.

Making the Call

Once you've configured both computers, make sure both the host and remote systems are running. To connect from the remote system to the host, follow these steps on your laptop:

1. **Choose Start→Connect To.**

   A list of connections appears.

2. **Double-click the connection you created.**

   The Connect dialog box shown in Figure 27-2 appears.

Note: If you're using a laptop while traveling, you might have to tell Vista where you are before you attempt to connect. If you're in a different area code, for example, open Control Panel→Hardware and Sound →Phone and Modem Options. Make sure that you've specified your current location, complete with whatever fancy dialing numbers it requires. (See page 331 for instructions on establishing these locations.) Click the current location and then click OK. Now Windows knows what area code and prefixes to use.

---

3. **Check your name, password, and phone number.**

   This is the same name and password you'd use to log in at the Welcome screen if you were sitting in front of the host PC (Chapter 23).

   Don't blow off this step. Typing the wrong name and password is the number-one source of problems.

4. **Click Dial.**

Figure 27-3:
Top: Congratulations—you're in.

Bottom: Disconnect by clicking the notification area icon and choosing "Connect or disconnect."

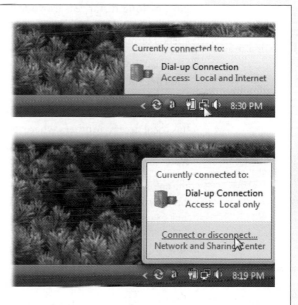

Windows dials into your home or office PC, makes the connection, and—if the phone number, name, and password are all correct—puts an icon for this connection into the notification area (Figure 27-3, top).

You're free to open up any shared folders, even use shared printers, on your network back home. And although it may make your brain hurt to contemplate it, you can even surf the Internet if your home PC has, say, a cable modem.

Note: Don't try to run any *programs* that reside on your host PC, however; you'll be old and gray by the time they even finish opening. (See the box on page 753.)

When you're finished with your email check, address lookup, document transfer, or whatever, click the little network icon in your notification area, choose "Connect or disconnect" and choose Disconnect from the dialog that appears (Figure 27-3, bottom).

Virtual Private Networking
All Versions

If you're a frequent traveler who regularly connects to a distant home or office by dialing direct, you must be the toast of your long-distance phone company.

Fortunately, there's a more economical solution. Virtual private networking (VPN) is a fancy way of saying, "Your remote computer can become part of your host network by using the Internet instead of a long-distance phone connection."

It's a lot like the direct-dialing feature described above—except this time, you don't pay any long-distance bills, your host PC doesn't require its own phone line, and (if the computers on both ends have fast connections) you're not limited to the sluglike speeds of dial-up modems.

With a VPN connection, both the host and the remote computers connect to the Internet the usual way: WiFi, DSL, cable modem, *or* good old dial-up. If you travel with a laptop, that's a good argument for signing up with a cellular data plan (see "Cellular Wireless" in Chapter 9) or using a national or international dial-up ISP that has local access numbers wherever you plan to be.

Note: To make VPN work, both computers require Internet connections; that much is obvious.

The one at home (or at the office) is probably all set. You should, however, put some thought into getting the *laptop* online. You'll have to find wireless hot spots, for example, or, if you do this a lot, you can sign up for a cellular modem plan (page 322) or even a dial-up account.

Not only can VPN save the frequent traveler quite a bit of money in phone calls, but it's also extremely secure. When you connect using VPN, the information traveling between the two connected computers is encoded (encrypted) using a technology called *tunneling*. Your connection is like a reinforced steel pipe wending its way through the Internet to connect the two computers.

To create a VPN connection, the host computer has two important requirements. If you're VPNing into a corporation or school, it's probably all set already. Otherwise:

- It must be on the Internet at the moment you try to connect. Usually, that means it needs a full-time Internet connection, like cable modem or DSL. But in a pinch—if it has only a dial-up modem, for example—you could phone a family member or co-worker just before you need to connect, and beg her to go online with your home PC.

- It needs a fixed *IP address*. (See the note below.)

On the other hand, the remote computer—your laptop—doesn't have any such requirements. It just needs an Internet connection.

Note: Several of the remote-connection methods described in this chapter require that your home-base PC have a *fixed, public* IP address. (An IP address is a unique number that identifies a particular computer on the Internet. It's made up of four numbers separated by periods.)

If you're not immediately nodding in understanding, murmuring, "Aaaaah, right," then download the bonus document available on this book's "Missing CD" at *www.missingmanuals.com*. The free PDF supplement you'll find there is called "Getting a Fixed, Public IP Address."

Setting Up the Host Machine

To set up the host PC for the VPN connection, do exactly as you would for direct-dial connections (page 754)—but in step 5, choose "Through the Internet" instead of "Through a dial-up modem." When the wizard finishes its work, the host machine is ready for action. Instead of setting up the modem to answer incoming calls, Vista now listens for incoming VPN connection requests from the Internet.

Making the Connection

Now move to the laptop, or whatever machine you'll be using when you're away from the main office. These steps, too, should seem familiar—they start out just like those that began on page 755. But in step 4, instead of clicking "Dial directly," you should choose "Use my Internet connection (VPN)."

Now you arrive at screen that says, "Type the Internet address to connect to." Proceed like this:

1. **Type the host name or registered IP address of the VPN host—that is, the computer you'll be tunneling into. Click "Don't connect now; just set it up so I can connect later," and then click Next.**

   If you're connecting to a server at work or school, your system administrator can tell you what to type here. If you're connecting to a computer you set up yourself, specify its public IP address. (See the Note above.)

This is *not* the private IP address on your home network, and definitely not its computer name (despite the fact that the New Incoming Connection Wizard told you that you would need to use that name); neither of these work when you're logged into another network.

2. **Type your user name, password, and, if required by the network administrator, the domain name. Then click Create.**

Windows tells you, "The connection is ready to use."

3. **Click Connect Now, or, if you plan to connect later, Close.**

The result is a new entry in the "Connect to a network" dialog box shown in Figure 27-3; choose Start→Connect To to see it.

When you make the VPN connection, you've once again joined your home or office network. Exactly as with the direct-dial connection described earlier, you should feel free to transfer files, make printouts, and so on. Unless both computers are using high-speed Internet connections, avoid actually running programs on the distant PC.

When you want to disconnect, click the connection icon in your notification area, choose Connect or Disconnect from the box that pops up, and then click Disconnect in the dialog box that appears.

(You can also disconnect using the Network and Sharing Center.)

Remote Desktop
Business • Enterprise • Ultimate (Home editions are limited)

The third remote-access option, Remote Desktop, offers some spectacular advantages. When you use Remote Desktop, you're not just tapping into your home computer's network—you're actually bringing its screen onto your screen. You can run its programs, print on its printers, "type" on its keyboard, move its cursor, manage its files, and so on, all by remote control.

Remote Desktop isn't useful only when you're trying to connect to the office or reach your home computer from the road; it even works over an office network. You can actually take control of another computer in the office—to troubleshoot a novice's PC without having to run up or down a flight of stairs, perhaps, or just to run a program that isn't on your own machine.

If you do decide to use Remote Desktop over the Internet, consider setting up a VPN connection first; using Remote Desktop *over* a VPN connection adds a nice layer of security to the connection. It also means that you become part of your home or office network—and you can therefore connect to the distant computer using its private network address or even its computer name.

Tip: The computers on the *receiving* end of the connections require the Business, Enterprise, or Ultimate editions of Vista. The laptop you're using can be running any Vista edition.

In fact, it can be running any version of Windows all the way back to 95, and even Mac OS X or Linux. To install the Remote Desktop Connection client on Mac OS X or an older version of Windows, visit the Microsoft Download Center (*www.microsoft.com/downloads/*) and search for Remote Desktop Connection. For Linux, get the free rdesktop program at *www.rdesktop.org*.

Setting Up the Host Machine

To get a PC ready for invasion—that is, to turn it into a host—proceed like this:

1. **Choose Start→Control Panel. In Classic view, double-click System, and then click the "Remote settings" link.**

   Authenticate yourself (page 191). The System Properties dialog opens to the Remote tab, as shown in Figure 27-4.

Figure 27-4:
Turning on the "Allow connections" checkbox makes Windows Vista listen to the network for Remote Desktop connections. Now you can specify who, exactly, is allowed to log in.

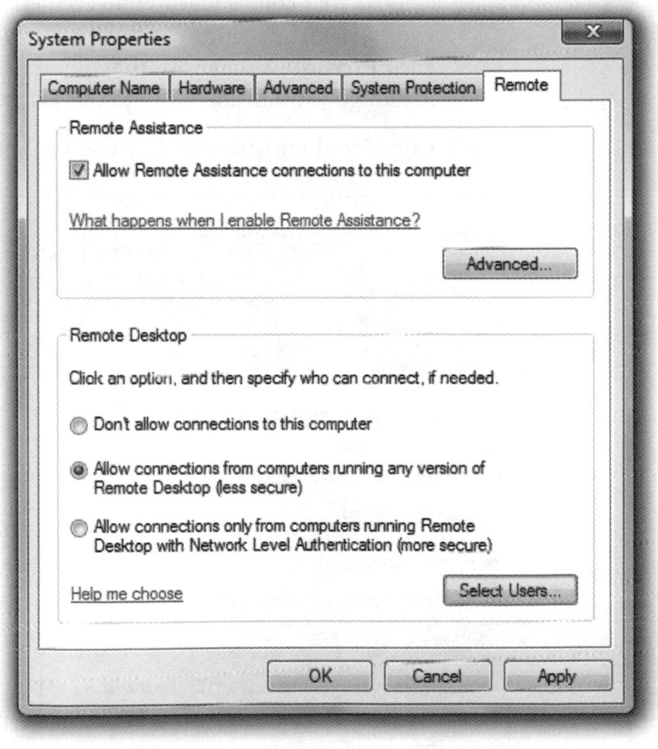

2. Turn on "Allow connections from computers running any version of Remote Desktop (less secure)."

You've just turned on the master switch that lets outsiders dial into your machine and take it over.

Tip: If this "less secure" option works, you can return later and try the "more secure" option. It's less likely to work, but at least you can go back to the "less secure" method.

3. **Click Select Users.**

   The Remote Desktop Users dialog box appears. You certainly don't want casual teenage hackers to visit your precious PC from across the Internet, playing your games and reading your personal info. Fortunately, the Remote Desktop feature requires you to specify precisely who is allowed to connect.

4. **Click Add. In the resulting dialog box, type the names of the people who are allowed to access your PC using Remote Desktop.**

   This dialog box might seem familiar—it's exactly the same idea as the Select Users, Computers, or Groups dialog box shown on page 693.

   Choose your comrades carefully; remember that they'll be able to do anything to your system, by remote control, that you could do while sitting in front of it. (To ensure security, Vista insists that the accounts you're selecting here have passwords. Although you can add them to this list, password-free accounts can't connect.)

5. **Click OK three times to close the dialog boxes you opened.**

Figure 27-5:
Type in the IP address, registered DNS name, or local computer name of your host computer. When prompted, fill in your name and password (and domain, if necessary), exactly the way you would if you were logging onto it in person.

The host computer is now ready for invasion. It's listening to the network for incoming connections from Remote Desktop clients.

Making the Connection

When you're ready to try Remote Desktop, fire up your laptop, or whatever computer will be doing the remote connecting. Then:

1. **Connect to the VPN of the distant host computer (page 759).**

   If the host computer is elsewhere on your local network—in the same building, that is—you can skip this step.

2. **Choose Start→All Programs→Accessories→Remote Desktop Connection.**

   The Remote Desktop Connection dialog box appears.

3. **Click Options to expand the dialog box (if necessary). Fill it out as shown in Figure 27-5.**

   The idea is to specify the IP address or DNS name of the computer you're trying to reach. If it's on the same network, or if you're connected via a VPN, you can use its computer name instead.

4. **Click Connect.**

   Now a freaky thing happens: after a moment of pitch-blackness, the host computer's screen fills your own (Figure 27-6). Don't be confused by the fact that all of the open windows on the computer you're using have now *disappeared*. (In fact, they

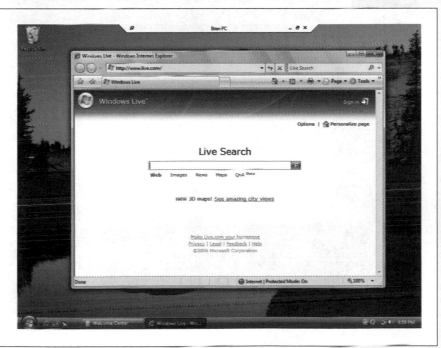

Figure 27-6:
The strange little bar at the top of your screen lets you minimize the distant computer's screen or turn it into a floating window. To hide this title bar, click the pushpin icon so that it turns completely horizontal. After a moment, it slides into the top of the screen, out of your way, until you move the cursor to the top edge of the screen.

won't if you click the Display tab and choose a smaller-than-full-screen remote desktop size before you connect.)

You can now operate the distant PC as though you were there in the flesh, using your own keyboard (or trackpad) and mouse. You can answer your email, make long-distance printouts, and so on. All the action—running programs, changing settings, and so on—is actually taking place on the faraway host computer.

Tip: You can even shut down or restart the faraway machine by remote control. Open a command prompt and run the command *shutdown /s*. The computer will shut down in less than a minute.

Keep in mind a few other points:

- You don't need to feel completely blocked out of your own machine. The little title bar at the top of the screen offers you the chance to put the remote computer's screen into a floating window of its own, permitting you to see both your own screen and the home-base computer's screen simultaneously (Figure 27-7).

- You can copy and paste highlighted text or graphics between the two machines (using regular Copy and Paste), and even transfer entire documents back and forth (using Copy and Paste on the desktop icons). Of course, if you've made both desktops visible simultaneously (Figure 27-7), you can move more quickly between local and remote.

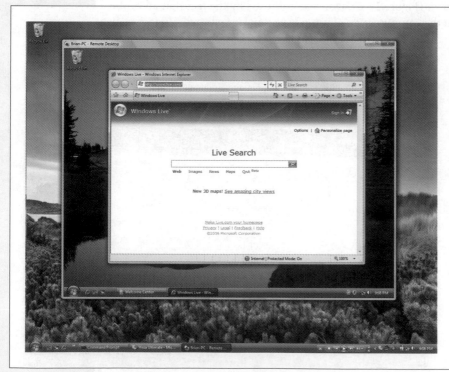

Figure 27-7:
By putting the other computer's screen into a window of its own, you save yourself a little bit of confusion. You can even minimize the remote computer's screen entirely, reducing it to a tab on your taskbar until you need it again.

- Even Windows Vista can't keep its mind focused on two people at once. If somebody is trying to use the host machine in person, you'll see a message to the effect that you're about to bump that person off the PC.

  Similarly, if somebody tries to log on at the host computer while you're connected from the remote, *you* get unceremoniously dumped off. (You just get a message that tells you "Another user connected to the remote computer.") Fortunately, you don't lose work this way—your account remains logged on behind the scenes, just as in Fast User Switching. When you connect again later (after the interloper has signed off), you'll find all your programs and documents open exactly as you left them.

- Back at the host computer, nobody can see what you're doing. The standard Welcome screen appears on the remote PC, masking your activities.

Keyboard Shortcuts for the Hopelessly Confused

When the Remote Desktop Connection window is maximized (that is, it fills your entire screen), all of the standard Windows keyboard shortcuts operate on the *host* computer, not the one you're actually using. When you press the ⊞ key, for example, you see the host computer's Start menu.

Note: There's one exception. When you press Ctrl+Alt+Delete, *your* computer processes the keystroke.

But when you turn the Remote Desktop Connection into a floating window that doesn't fill your entire screen, it's a different story. Now your current computer "hears" your keystrokes. Now, pressing ⊞ opens *your* Start menu. So how, with the remote PC's screen in a window, are you supposed to operate it by remote control?

Microsoft has thought of everything. It's even given you alternatives for the key combinations you're accustomed to using. For example, suppose you've connected to your office PC using your laptop. When the Remote Desktop window isn't full-screen, pressing Alt+Tab switches to the next open program on the laptop—but pressing *Alt+Page Up* switches to the next program on the host computer.

Here's a summary of the special keys that operate the distant host computer—a table that can be useful if you are either an extreme power user or somebody who likes to win bar bets:

Standard Windows Key Combination	Remote Desktop Key Combination	Function
Alt+Tab	Alt+Page Up	Switches to the next open program
Alt+Shift+Tab	Alt+Page Down	Switches to the previous open program
Alt+Esc	Alt+Insert	Cycles through programs in the order in which you open them
Ctrl+Esc (or ⊞)	Alt+Home	Opens the Start menu
Ctrl+Alt+Delete	Ctrl+Alt+End	Displays the Windows Security dialog box.

(Actually, you should use the alternative key combination for the Security dialog box whether the Remote Desktop window is maximized or not, because Ctrl+Alt+Delete is always interpreted by the computer you're currently using.)

Disconnecting

To get out of Remote Desktop mode, click the Close box in the strange little title bar at the top of your screen, as shown in Figure 27-6. Or, from the Start menu, choose X. (Yes, X. This special button means "Disconnect," and when you're using Remote Desktop, it replaces the ☺ symbol at the bottom of the Start menu.)

Figure 27-8:
Click the Options button if you don't see these tabs. Once you've made them appear, a few useful (and a lot of rarely useful) settings become available. On the Display tab (left), for example, you can effectively reduce the size of the other computer's screen so that it fits within your laptop's. On the Experience tab (right), you can turn off special-effect animations to speed up the connection.

Note, however, that this method leaves all your programs running and your documents open on the distant machine, exactly as though you had used Fast User Switching. If you log on again, either from the road or in person, you'll find all of those programs and documents still on the screen, just as you left them.

If you'd rather log off in a more permanent way, closing all your distant documents and programs, choose Start→Log Off (from the other computer's Start menu, not yours).

Fine-tuning Remote Desktop Connections

Windows offers all kinds of settings for tailoring the way this bizarre, schizophrenic connection method works. The trick is, however, that you have to change them *before* you connect, using the tabs on the dialog box shown in Figure 27-8.

Here's what you'll find:

- **General tab.** Here's where you can tell Windows to edit or delete credentials (user name and password) from your last login, or to save all of the current settings as a shortcut icon, which makes it faster to reconnect later. (If you connect to a number of different distant computers, saving a setup for each one in this way can be a huge timesaver.)

- **Display tab.** Use these options to specify the *size* (resolution) of the host computer's display (see Figure 27-8).

- **Local Resources tab.** Using these controls, you can set up local peripherals and add-ons so that they behave as though they were connected to the computer you're using. This is also where you tell Windows which PC should "hear" keystrokes like Alt+Tab, and whether or not you want to hear sound effects played by the distant machine.

- **Programs tab.** You can set up a certain program to run automatically as soon as you connect to the host machine.

- **Experience tab.** Tell Windows the speed of your connection, so it can limit fancy visual effects like menu animation, the desktop wallpaper, and so on, to avoid slowing down the connection. The Desktop Composition option controls whether Remote Desktop uses Vista's Aero glass effects (if, in fact, your computer has the horsepower).

Part Eight: Appendixes

Appendix A: Installing Windows Vista

Appendix B: Fun with the Registry

Appendix C: Where'd It Go?

Appendix D: The Master Keyboard Shortcut List

8

Installing Windows Vista

If your computer came with Windows Vista already installed on it, you can skip this appendix—for now. But if you're running an earlier version of Windows and want to savor the Vista experience, this appendix describes how to install the new operating system on your computer.

Before You Begin

Believe it or not, most of the work involved in installing Windows Vista takes place well before the installation DVD so much as approaches your computer. You have a lot of research and planning to do, especially if you want to avoid spending a five-day weekend in Upgrade Hell.

For example, you must ensure that your PC is beefy enough to handle Vista—not a sure thing at all. You also have to decide which of two types of installation you want to perform: an *upgrade* or a *clean install*. (More on this in a moment.)

If you opt for the clean install (a process that begins with *erasing your hard drive completely*), you must back up your data. Finally, you have to gather all of the software bits and pieces you'll need in order to perform the installation.

Hardware Requirements

Before you even buy a copy of Vista, your first order of business should be to check your computer against the list of hardware requirements for Windows Vista, as published by Microsoft. Vista, as it turns out, is a serious hog—for memory, speed, disk space, and, above all, graphics-card horsepower. 2004-era computers (and earlier ones) probably aren't up to the challenge.

Turns out there are two degrees of Vista-readiness: the lame one and the real one.

"Vista ready"

A lower-powered computer can *run* Vista. It may feel slow, and you don't see the Aero Glass look (transparent window edges, taskbar thumbnails, and so on; see Chapter 1). It does, however, offer all the other Vista security and feature enhancements.

Here's what such a computer requires:

- **Processor:** 800 megahertz or faster
- **Memory:** 512 megabytes or more
- **Hard-disk space:** At least 15 gigabytes free
- **Monitor:** Super VGA (800 x 600) or higher-resolution
- **Graphics card:** DirectX 9 support (check the packaging or, for laptops, the manufacturer's Web site)
- **DVD drive**

"Vista Premium"

You need a beefier machine if you want the full Vista experience:

- **Processor:** 1 gigahertz or faster
- **Memory:** 1 gigabyte or more
- **Hard-disk space:** At least 15 gigabytes free
- **Graphics card:** Works with DirectX 9, WDDM (Windows Vista Display Driver Model), 128 MB of graphics memory, Pixel Shader 2.0, and 32 bits per pixel. (Again, this may be tough to figure out. A sticker that says "Vista Premium-Ready" is a good sign.)
- **DVD-ROM drive, audio output, Internet access**

If your computer doesn't meet these requirements, then consider a hardware upgrade—especially a memory upgrade—before you even attempt to install Windows Vista. With memory prices what they are today (read: dirt cheap), you'll thank yourself later for adding as much RAM as you can afford.

Adding more hard disk space is also a reasonably easy and inexpensive upgrade, and there are inexpensive graphics adapters that will handle Vista's visual effects (the Aero business described in Chapter 1).

The one place where you may be stuck, though, is on the processor issue. The state of the art in processor speeds seems to advance almost weekly, but it's safe to say that a PC running at 800 MHz or less is certifiably geriatric. It may be time to think about passing the old girl on to the kids or donating it to a worthy cause and getting yourself a newer, faster computer. As a bonus, it will come with Windows Vista preinstalled.

The Compatibility Issue

Once you've had a conversation with yourself about your equipment, it's time to investigate the suitability of your existing software and add-on gear for use with Vista.

- **Hardware.** In general, products released since October 2006 are Vista–compatible, but you should still proceed with caution before using them with Windows Vista. You should by all means check the Web sites of these components' manufacturers in hopes of finding updated driver software.

- **Software.** *Most* programs and drivers that work with Windows XP work fine in Windows Vista, but not all. And programs designed for Windows 95, 98, and Me may well cause you problems.

Unless you're that lucky individual who's starting fresh with a brand new PC and software suite, you'd be wise to run the Windows Vista Upgrade Advisor program *before* you move into Vista World.

If you haven't yet bought Vista, you can download this important program from Microsoft's Web site at *http://go.microsoft.com/fwlink/?linkid=60497*. It runs only on Windows XP (and, pointlessly, Vista), and it scans your system to produce a report on the Vista compatibility of your hardware and software.

If you do have Vista, insert the Windows Vista DVD. On its welcome screen (Figure A-2, top), click "Check compatibility online," and then download the Windows Vista Upgrade Advisor.

Tip: A compatibility checker also runs automatically during the installation process itself.

The Upgrade Advisor first offers to download updates from Microsoft's Web site. If you can get online, it's an excellent idea to take it up on this offer. You'll get all the patches, updates, and bug fixes Microsoft has released since the debut of Windows Vista.

Next, the advisor shows you a report that identifies potential problems. Almost everybody finds some incompatibilities reported here, because Microsoft is particularly conservative about which programs will work with Vista.

But if the report lists a serious incompatibility, it's not worth proceeding with the Vista installation until you've updated or uninstalled the offending program.

Note: Utilities like hard-drive formatting software, virus checkers, firewall programs, and so on are especially troublesome. Do not use them in Vista unless they're specifically advertised for Windows Vista compatibility.

Upgrade vs. Clean Install

If your PC currently runs Windows XP, the next big question is whether or not you should *upgrade* it to Windows Vista.

Upgrading the operating system retains all of your existing settings and data files. Your desktop colors and wallpaper all remain the same, as do some more important elements, including your Favorites list and the files in your Documents folder.

Sounds great, right? Who wouldn't want to avoid having to and redo all those preferred settings?

Unfortunately, in past version of Windows, upgrading from an older copy of Windows often brought along unwelcome baggage. Windows preserved outdated drivers, fragmented disk drives, and a clutter of unneeded registry settings when you upgraded. If all this artery-clogging gunk had already begun to slow down your computer, upgrading to a newer version of Windows only made things worse.

Microsoft says that it's drastically improved the upgrade process. "Upgrades to Windows Vista are no longer a merge with the old OS," writes the author of the setup software on his blog. "First, Windows Vista's setup gathers old OS settings, user settings, and data, and stores them. Then it wipes away the old OS and applies the new operating system image. Next, Setup applies stored settings and data to this clean install, which magically brings back your applications and data in a brand new OS. Your registry and file system are free of goo that is no longer needed by Windows Vista."

Even so, some caution is still justified. The upgrade of the operating system itself may go smoothly, but there's no telling what glitches this procedure may introduce in all your non-Microsoft programs. In general, such programs prefer to be installed fresh on the new operating system.

Actually, the decision may not be yours to make. If you're running any version of Windows besides XP, you'll have to backup everything and perform a *clean install*, as described in the following pages.

And even if you *are* running Windows XP, your Vista upgrade options depend on which *version* of XP you have now:

- **Windows XP Home.** You can upgrade to the Home Basic, Home Premium, Business, or Ultimate versions of Vista.

- **Windows XP Professional, Windows XP Tablet PC.** You can upgrade only to Business or Ultimate.

- **Windows XP Media Center.** You can upgrade to either Home Premium or Ultimate.

Note: The Enterprise edition of Windows Vista isn't for sale to mere mortals. It's available only to corporations, whose system administrators will handle all the upgrading hassles without your involvement.

Buying Windows Vista

If you do decide to upgrade from Windows XP, you'll save some money, because the Upgrade version of Vista is less expensive than a Full version.

If you're not sure whether the Upgrade version will work on your machine, check this Web page: *www.microsoft.com/windowsvista/getready/upgradeinfo.mspx.*

And remember: If your computer is currently running anything but Windows XP, you have to buy the Full version of Vista and perform a clean install.

Tip: As you shop, remember, too, that you can start now with one of the less expensive editions—and later, if you find your style cramped, upgrade your installed copy to a more powerful edition quickly and easily. For a price, every Vista DVD can be unlocked to unleash the full power of higher-priced Vista versions... all the way up to the Ultimate edition.

To start this upgrade, choose Start→Control Panel. Click "System and Maintenance," and then click Windows Anytime Upgrade.

About the Clean Install

The alternative to an upgrade is the *clean install* of Windows Vista. During a clean install, you repartition and reformat your hard disk, wiping out everything on it. The overwhelming advantage of a clean install is that you wind up with a fresh system, 100 percent free of all of those creepy little glitches and inconsistencies that have been building up over the years. Ask any Windows veteran: the best way to boost the speed of a system that has grown sluggish is to perform a clean install of the operating system and start afresh.

Backing up

The drawback of a clean install, however, is the work it will take you to back up all of your files and settings before you begin. If your computer has a tape drive, DVD burner, or external hard drive, that's not much of a problem. Just perform a full backup (or simply drag and drop every last file that's important to you), test it to make sure that everything you need has been copied and is restorable, and you're ready to install Windows Vista.

Tip: One of the most convenient solutions is to install a new hard drive before you upgrade, and put your current hard drive in an external enclosure that you've bought off the Web. You can put it on a shelf for safe keeping, and plug it in every time you need to grab a file from your old installation.

You can even do this with some laptops whose hard drives is user-replaceable: inexpensive USB or FireWire enclosures are available in both 2.5" (laptop hard drive) and 3.5" (desktop hard drive) size, and installation only takes a few minutes. Just be sure you know what kind of hard drive you have (Serial ATA or Parallel ATA, and in some cases, SCSI) before you choose either your new internal hard drive or your enclosure, because both of these must be compatible with whatever you're currently using.

If you have a second computer, you can also consider backing up your stuff on to it, via a network (Chapter 26). In any of these cases, you'll probably want to use the new Windows Easy Transfer for this purpose (page 783).

Even having a full backup, however, doesn't mean that a clean install will be a walk in the park. After the installation, you still have to reinstall all of your programs, reconfigure all your personalized settings, re-create your network connections, and so on.

Tip: It's a good idea to spend a few days writing down the information you need as you're working on your computer. For example, if you're using dial-up Internet, copy down the phone number, user name, and password that you use to connect to your Internet service provider (ISP), and the user names and passwords you need for various Web sites you frequent.

Performing a clean install also means buying the Full Edition of Windows Vista. It's more expensive than the Upgrade Edition, but at least you can install it on a blank hard disk without having to install an old Windows version first or have your original installation CDs available.

Overall, a clean install is preferable to an upgrade. But if you don't have the time or the heart to back up your hard drive, wipe it clean and re-establish all of your settings, the upgrade option is always there for you.

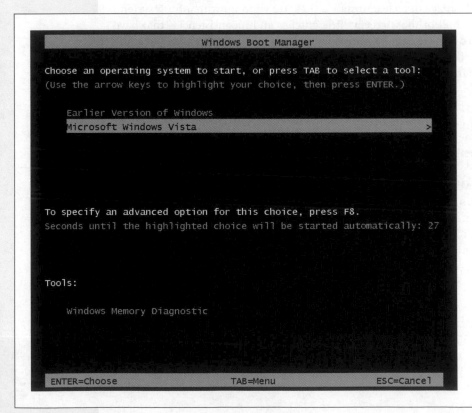

Figure A-1:
When you dual boot, this menu appears each time you turn on your PC, offering you a choice of OS. (If you don't choose in 30 seconds, the PC chooses for you.)

Dual Booting

Here's yet another decision you have to make before you install Windows Vista: whether or not you'll want to be able to *dual boot*.

In this advanced scenario, you install Vista onto the same PC that contains an older version of Windows, maintaining both of them side by side. Then, each time you turn on the PC, it *asks you* which operating system you want to run for this computing session (see Figure A-1).

Dual booting comes in handy when you have some program or hardware gadget that works with one operating system but not the other. For example, if you have a scanner with software that runs on Windows XP but not Vista, you can start up the PC in XP only when you want to use the scanner.

If you intend to dual boot, here's some important advice: *Don't install both operating systems onto the same hard drive partition*. Your programs will become horribly confused.

Instead, keep your two Windows versions separate using one of these avenues:

- Buy a second hard drive. Use it for one of the two operating systems.

- Back up your hard drive, erase it completely, and then *partition* it, which means dividing it so that each chunk shows up in the Disk Management window (Chapter 21) with its own icon, name, and drive letter. Then install each operating system on a separate disk partition.

- If you're less technically inclined, you might prefer to buy a program like Partition-Magic (*www.partitionmagic.com*). Not only does it let you create a new partition on your hard drive without erasing it first, but it's flexible and easy.

There's just one wrinkle with dual-booting. If you install Vista onto a separate partition (or a different drive), as you must, you won't find any of your existing programs listed in the Start menu, and your desktop won't be configured the way it is in your original operating system. You'll generally wind up having to reinstall every program into your new Vista world, and re-establish all of your settings, exactly as though the Vista "side" were a brand-new PC.

Installing Windows Vista

Once you've decided to take the plunge and install Windows Vista, you can begin the countdown.

Preparing for the Installation

If you've made all the plans and done all the thinking described so far in this chapter, you have only a short checklist left to follow:

- Update your virus program and scan for viruses. Then, if you're updating an existing copy of Windows, *turn off* your virus checker, along with other auto-loading programs like non-Microsoft firewall software and Web ad blockers.

- Confirm that your computer's BIOS—its basic startup circuitry—is compatible with Windows Vista. To find out, contact the manufacturer of the computer or the BIOS.

  Don't skip this step. You may well need to upgrade your BIOS if the computer was made before mid-2006.

- Gather updated, Vista–compatible drivers for all of your computer's components. Graphics and audio cards are particularly likely to need updates, so be sure to check the manufacturers' Web sites—and driver-information sites like *www.windrivers. com* and *www.driverguide.com*—and download any new drivers you find there.

- Disconnect any gear that's not absolutely necessary for using your computer. You'll have better luck if you reconnect them *after* Vista is in place. This includes scanners, game controllers, printers, and even that USB-powered lava lamp you like so much.

If you've gone to all this trouble and preparation, the Windows Vista installation process can be surprisingly smooth. The Vista installer is much less painful than the ones for previous versions of Windows. You won't see the old DOS-style startup screens, the installation requires fewer restarts, and if you're doing a clean install, it's amazingly fast (often 15 minutes or less).

Performing an Update Installation

Here's how you upgrade your existing version of Windows to full Vista status. (If you prefer to perform a clean install, skip these instructions.)

1. **Start your computer. Insert the Windows Vista DVD into the drive.**

   The Setup program generally opens automatically (Figure A-2, top). If it doesn't, open My Computer, double-click the DVD-ROM icon, and double-click the Setup. exe program in the DVD's root folder.

2. **Click Install Now.**

   The "Get important updates for installation" screen appears. Clearly, Microsoft thinks it's a good idea to download any software updates that have appeared since you bought your copy of Vista.

3. **Click "Go online to get the latest updates for installation."**

   The installer searches the Web for updates and then downloads them for you. Then the "Type your product key" screen presents itself.

4. **Type in your 25-character Vista serial number (product key).**

   The product key comes in the Vista box or on the DVD case.

If you turn on "Automatically activate Windows when I'm online," Vista will try to activate itself after three days.

Note: If you leave the product key blank, you'll be offered the chance to enter it after Vista's installed. If you do leave it blank, you'll see a screen where you have to choose the version of Vista you purchased. If you don't pick the right one, your product key won't work with it, and you'll have to perform a clean install at some point.

Figure A-2:
Top: The Vista Setup program is ready for action. Close the doors, take the phone off the hook, and cancel your appointments. The installer will take at least an hour to go about its business—not including the time it will take you to iron out any post-installation glitches.

Bottom: Use the button on the top of this screen to indicate whether you want a clean installation or an upgrade installation.

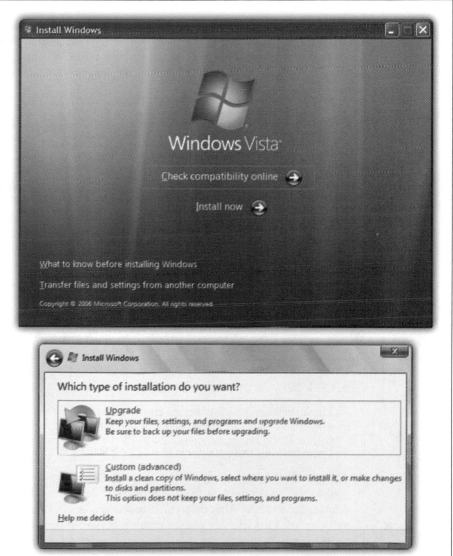

5. **Click Next.**

A screen full of legalese appears.

6. **Review the work of Microsoft's lawyers, and then click "I accept the license terms."
Click Next.**

Now you're asked to choose between an upgrade and clean install (Figure A-2, bottom).

7. **Click Upgrade.**

Now the installer checks to see if any of your PC's components are incompatible with Vista. If so, the Compatibility Report screen appears, shown in Figure A-3. There's not much you can do about it at this point, of course, other than to make a note of it and vow to investigate Vista-compatible updates later.

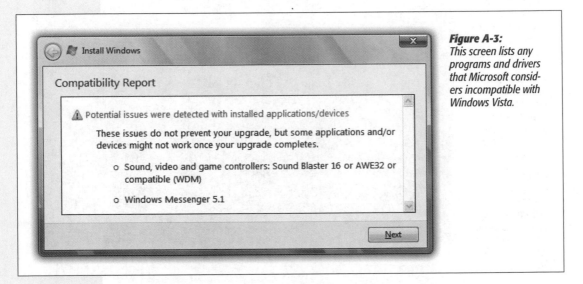

Figure A-3:
This screen lists any programs and drivers that Microsoft considers incompatible with Windows Vista.

8. **Click Next.**

The installation program begins copying files and restarting the computer several times.

Unfortunately, this part can take a *lot* longer than 15 minutes.

After the final restart, you're almost there. Before you can log in for the first time, you're asked to choose how to configure Vista's protection features. Select "Use recommended settings." After that, you're asked to confirm your date and time settings, and then tell Vista whether your network is at home, work, or a public location (for more information on the implications of these choices, see page 359).

Finally, Vista pops up a polite screen that says "Thank you". Click Start to begin your Vista experience. After you log in (page 688), the Welcome Center appears, described later in this appendix.

Performing a Clean Install (or Dual-Boot Install)

To perform a clean installation of Windows Vista, or to install it onto an empty partition for the purpose of dual booting, the steps are slightly different:

1. **Start up your PC from your Windows Vista DVD.**

   Every Vista–compatible computer can start up from a DVD instead of from its hard drive. Sometimes, if you start up the computer with a DVD in the drive, instructions for booting from it appear right on the screen (you may be directed to hold down a certain key, or any key at all). If you don't see such an instruction, you might have to check with the computer's maker for instructions on this point.

   At the beginning of the setup process, you'll wait for a moment while the installer loads ups.

2. **When the Install Windows screen appears, click Next to bypass the Regional and Language Options screen.**

   Bypass it, that is, unless you don't speak English or don't live in the United States.

3. **At the next screen, click Install Now. On the "Type your product key" screen, enter the 25-character product key and click Next.**

   Again, the product key is the serial number that came with your Windows Vista DVD. If you turn on "Automatically activate Windows when I'm online," Vista will try to activate itself in the next three days.

   Now the usual legal notice pops up.

4. **Review the licensing agreement, if you like, click "I accept the license terms," and then click Next to continue.**

   Since you booted from the DVD, you don't have the option of performing an upgrade installation.

5. **Click "Custom (advanced)" to proceed with a clean install.**

   Now Windows shows you a list of the *partitions* on your hard drive. Unless you've set up your hard drive for *dual booting* as described on page 623, you probably have only one.

6. **By pressing the up and down arrow keys, highlight the name of the partition (or choose some unallocated space) on which you want to install Vista, and then click Next.**

   Use the Drive Options at the bottom of this window to delete, create, or format partitions.

   After the formatting process is complete, the Setup program begins copying files to the partition you selected, and eventually restarts the computer a time or two.

7. **Choose a name for your main account, a password, and a picture.**

You can read more about *accounts* in Chapter 23. This very first account, the one you're creating here, is very important; it's going to be an Administrative account (page 669). Once you log in using *this* account, you can create accounts for other people.

Tip: *If it's just you and your laptop, you can leave the password blank; you'll be able to log in, wake the computer from sleep, and otherwise get to your stuff that much faster. Note, however, that if your account password is blank, some Vista features won't work (including Remote Desktop, described in Chapter 27).*

8. **Click Next.**

Vista asks you to type a computer name and choose a desktop background.

9. **Either accept the proposed computer name (your name followed by "-PC"), or type one that's short and punctuation-free (hyphens are OK).**

You can always change the computer name later; see page 312.)

10. **Click Next.**

Now you can choose how to configure Vista's protection features.

11. **Select "Use recommended settings."**

The date and time settings screen appears.

12. **Set the date, time, and time zone, and then click Next.**

Now Vista tries to connect to your network, if you have one. If it succeeds, it asks whether your network is at home, work, or a public location (for more information on the implications of these choices, see page 359).

Finally, Vista thanks you.

13. **Click Start to begin your Vista experience!**

When it's all over, the Welcome Center appears, described next.

Welcome Center

The first time you log into Vista (and every time thereafter until you turn off "Run at startup"), the Welcome Center appears. From this program, you can perform a number of post-installation tasks, including:

- Connecting to the Internet (using a dial-up modem, cable modem/DSL connection, or wireless network).
- Transfer files from your old computer (see "Windows Easy Transfer").
- Register Windows Vista. That is, submit your name and address to Microsoft in hopes of getting sent valuable junk mail.

Note: Registering is not the same as *activation* (page 781). Registering is optional; activation is not (and does not entail surrendering your contact information).

- Find out what's new, learn about the basics of Vista, and see some demos.

- Add users to Vista. That means adding *accounts* to a PC that will be used by more than one person, as described in Chapter 23.

- View computer details (this leads to a screen where you can join a *domain* network, as described in Chapter 25).

If you ever want to visit the Welcome Center when you *haven't* just started up, you can find it in Start→All Programs→Accessories.

Activation

After 30 days, Vista will insist that you *activate* it, as shown in Figure A-4. You'll see several reminders that grow increasingly stern before Vista forces you to activate.

Activation is copy protection. In some countries, a huge percentage of all copies of Windows are illegal duplicates; activation, introduced in Windows XP, is designed to stop such piracy in its tracks. Unfortunately, it also prevents you from installing one copy of Vista on even *two* computers. That's right: If you have a desktop PC as well as a laptop, you have to buy Windows twice.

How does it know that you're being naughty? When you first install Windows, the operating system inspects ten crucial components inside your PC: the hard drive, motherboard, video card, memory, and so on. All this information is transmitted, along with the 25-character serial number on the back of your Windows DVD (the

---

WORKAROUND WORKSHOP

When No Vista DVD Comes With Your PC

It's becoming increasingly common for computer manufacturers to sell you a new PC without including an operating system CD-ROM. (Every 11 cents counts, right?) The machine has Windows installed on it—but if there's no Vista installation CD or DVD, what are you supposed to do in case of emergency?

Instead of a physical Windows disc, the manufacturer provides something called a *restore image*—a CD-ROM or DVD (or more than one) containing a complete copy of the operating system *and* other software that was installed on the computer at the factory. If the contents of the computer's hard disk are ever lost or damaged, you can, in theory, restore the computer to its factory configuration by running a program on the restore image.

Of course, this image is a bit-by-bit facsimile of the computer's hard disk drive, and therefore, restoring it to your computer *completely erases* whatever files are already on the drive. You can't restore your computer from an image disk without losing all of the data you saved since you got the computer from the manufacturer. (Talk about a good argument for keeping regular backups!)

Furthermore, some manufacturers install a copy of these installation files right on the hard drive, so that you won't even have to hunt for your CDs.

Product Key), to Microsoft's database via your Internet account. The process takes about two seconds, and involves little more than clicking an OK button. You have just *activated* Windows Vista.

Note: If you don't have an Internet connection, activation is a much more grueling procedure. You have to call a toll-free number, read a 50-digit identification number to the Microsoft agent, and then type a 42-digit confirmation number into your software. Do whatever it takes to avoid having to endure this fingertip-numbing ritual.

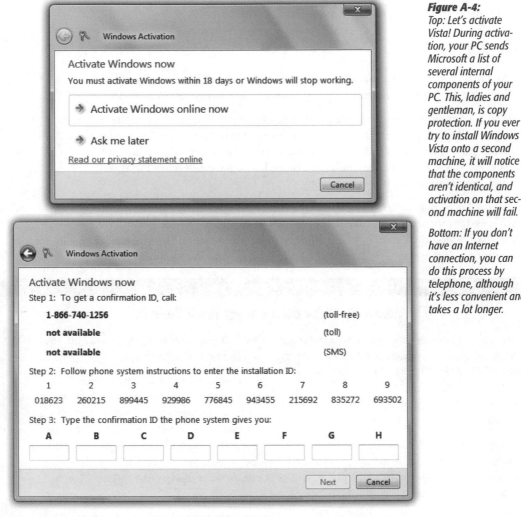

Figure A-4:
Top: Let's activate Vista! During activation, your PC sends Microsoft a list of several internal components of your PC. This, ladies and gentleman, is copy protection. If you ever try to install Windows Vista onto a second machine, it will notice that the components aren't identical, and activation on that second machine will fail.

Bottom: If you don't have an Internet connection, you can do this process by telephone, although it's less convenient and takes a lot longer.

Later, if you try to install the same copy of Windows onto a different computer, it will check in with Microsoft and discover that the new machine's components aren't the same. It will conclude that you have tried to install the same copy of the operating system onto a different machine—and it will lock you out.

This aspect of Windows Vista has frightened or enraged many a computer fan. In truth, though, it isn't quite as bad as it seems. Here's why:

- If you buy a new PC with Windows Vista already installed, you don't have to activate anything; it's already been done.

- Copies of Vista that are distributed within corporations don't require this activation business, either.

- No information about *you* is transferred to Microsoft during this activation process—only a list of the components in your PC make the trip. (Later in the installation process, you're also asked to *register* your copy of Windows—a completely different affair. This time, personal information *is* transmitted to Microsoft—but this part is optional.)

- Don't believe the Internet Chicken Littles who claim that activation will shut down your PC if you try to upgrade the memory or another component. In fact, you would have to replace four of the ten key components within a period of four months—your basic hardware-upgrade frenzy—before Windows stopped recognizing your computer. And even then, you can just call Microsoft and explain what happened; in most cases, the company will cheerfully provide a new activation number.

If, during installation, you turned on "Automatically activate Windows when I'm online" (on the same screen where you enter your product key), Vista tries to activate itself for the first three days of installation by sending signals back to Microsoft.

If you don't activate it in time, Vista switches into what's tactfully called Reduced Functionality Mode, in which many features become time-limited or stop working. For more information on Reduced Functionality Mode, see *http://support.microsoft. com/kb/925582*.

Windows Easy Transfer

Windows Easy Transfer is a new tool included with Windows Vista. It's designed to round up the files and preference settings from one computer—and copy them into the proper places on a new one. For millions of upgrading Windows fans, this little piece of software is worth its weight in gold.

You can use Windows Easy Transfer in several ways:

- If you have two computers, you can run Windows Easy Transfer on the old computer, package its files and settings, and then transfer them to the new computer.

  You can make the transfer over a network connection, a direct cable connection, or via flash drive, hard drive, or recordable CD/DVD. The Vista DVD includes a version of the wizard that you can run directly from the DVD on another Windows computer, even one that's not running Windows Vista.

- If you have only one computer, you can run the wizard from the Vista DVD before you install, saving the files and settings to a disk or a second hard drive. Then, after performing a clean install of Windows Vista, you can run the wizard again, neatly importing and reinstating your saved files and settings.

Note: Easy Transfer doesn't bring over your programs—just your files and settings.

Phase 1: Backing up the Files

To save the files and settings on your old computer (or your old operating system), proceed like this:

1. **Insert the Windows Vista DVD into the drive.**

   The Setup program opens automatically.

2. **Select Transfer Files and Settings.**

   Windows Easy Transfer opens up (Figure A-5, top).

3. **Click Next. On the Choose How to Transfer screen, specify how you want to transfer the files and settings (Figure A-5, middle).**

   You can choose from a link to another computer using a direct cable or network connection, or to a flash drive, external hard disk, CD, or DVD.

4. **Click Next.**

   If you selected CD, DVD, or other removable media, you'll need to choose between a CD, USB flash drive, or external hard disk. The last option also lets you use a network location, which could be a file server or another computer on your network.

5. **Click the option you want to use, and provide a location and password if necessary. Click Next.**

   The "What do you want to transfer?" screen appears.

6. **Specify which information you want to transfer to the other computer.**

   You can elect to transfer all the user accounts on the computer, complete with their files and settings, or just *your* account, files, and settings. (See Chapter 23 for details on accounts.)

   You can also use Advanced Options button (on the "What do you want to transfer?" screen) to build a customized list of the *specific* files and settings you want to transfer.

7. **Click Next.**

   The "Review selected files and settings" screen appears.

8. Click the option you want to use and review your choice.

If you click "Customize," a screen appears that lets you add folders, files, or drives to your list of items that the wizard stores. You can also remove items from the list.

9. Click Next.

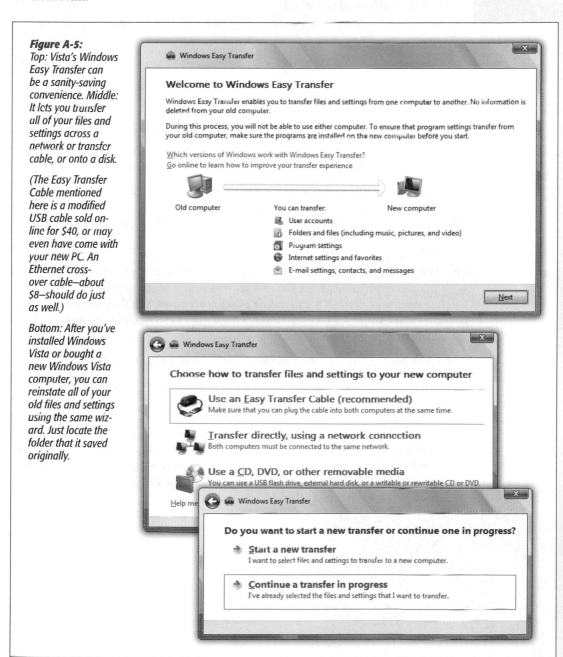

Figure A-5:
Top: Vista's Windows Easy Transfer can be a sanity-saving convenience. Middle: It lets you transfer all of your files and settings across a network or transfer cable, or onto a disk.

(The Easy Transfer Cable mentioned here is a modified USB cable sold online for $40, or may even have come with your new PC. An Ethernet cross-over cable—about $8—should do just as well.)

Bottom: After you've installed Windows Vista or bought a new Windows Vista computer, you can reinstate all of your old files and settings using the same wizard. Just locate the folder that it saved originally.

The progress screen appears. The wizard proceeds to search your drives for the necessary information, compress it, and send it to the location you specified.

10. **Click Close.**

Phase 2: Restoring the Files

To transfer the settings and files you've saved to your new Vista computer, use the following procedure.

1. **Choose Start→All Programs→Accessories→System Tools→Windows Easy Transfer.**

   Windows Easy Transfer appears.

   The "Where did you copy the files and settings you want to transfer?" screen appears.

2. **Specify the location of the files and settings you saved on the other computer.**

   The location you specify could be a path to a hard drive folder, network location, a floppy or CD-ROM drive, or a direct cable/network connection to another computer running the wizard. (See page 41 for details on paths.)

3. **Click Next.**

   Now verify the names of the accounts you're transferring to the new computer. You can either transfer the files and settings into to existing people's accounts, or create new accounts. (If you choose existing accounts, you'll *replace* their current files and settings. Of course, if this is a fresh install of Vista, those people probably don't have many settings or files yet.)

4. **Click Next and review the settings. If everything looks OK, click Next again.**

   The wizard proceeds to copy the files and apply the saved settings on the new computer.

5. **Click Finish to close the wizard.**

   Windows Easy Transfer now reports how the transfer went. If Vista couldn't restore some of your settings, you'll have to re-create these settings manually. Depending on the settings you saved, you may have to log off and log on again before the transferred settings take effect.

Fun with the Registry

Occasionally, in books, articles, and conversations, you'll hear hushed references to something called the Windows Registry—usually accompanied by either knowing or bewildered glances.

The Registry is your PC's master database of preference settings. For example, most of the programs in the Control Panel are nothing more than graphic front ends that, behind the scenes, modify settings in the Registry.

The Registry also keeps track of almost every program you install, every peripheral device you add, every account you create (Chapter 23), your networking configuration, and much more. If you've noticed that shortcut menus and Properties dialog boxes look different depending on what you're clicking, you have the Registry to thank. It knows what you're clicking and what options should appear as a result. In all, there are thousands and thousands of individual settings in your Registry.

As you can well imagine, therefore, the Registry is an extremely important cog in the Windows machine. That's why Windows marks your Registry files as invisible and non-deletable, and why it makes a Registry backup every single time you shut down the PC. If the Registry gets damaged or randomly edited, a grisly plague of problems may descend upon your machine. Granted, the System Restore feature (described in this chapter) can extract you from such a mess, but now you know why the Registry is rarely even mentioned to novices.

In fact, Microsoft would just as soon you not even know about the Registry. There's not a word about it in the basic user guides, and about the only information you'll find about it in the Help and Support center is a page that says, "Ordinarily, you do not need to make changes to the registry. The registry contains complex system information that is vital to your computer, and an incorrect change to your registry could render your computer inoperable."

Still, the Registry is worth learning about. You shouldn't edit it arbitrarily, but if you follow a step-by-step "recipe" from a book, magazine, Web site, or technical-help agent, you shouldn't fear opening the Registry to make a few changes.

Why would you want to? Because there are lots of Windows settings that you can't change in any other way, as you'll see in the following pages.

Meet Regedit

Windows comes with a built-in program for editing Registry entries, a little something called (what else?) the Registry editor. (There are dozens of other Registry-editing, Registry-fixing, and Registry-maintenance programs, too—both commercial and shareware—but this one is already on your PC.)

As an advanced tool that Microsoft doesn't want falling into the wrong hands, the Registry editor has no Start-menu icon. You must fire it up by typing its name into the Start menu's search box. Type *regedit* to find the program; select it in the results list.

Authenticate yourself (page 191). After a moment, you see a window like Figure

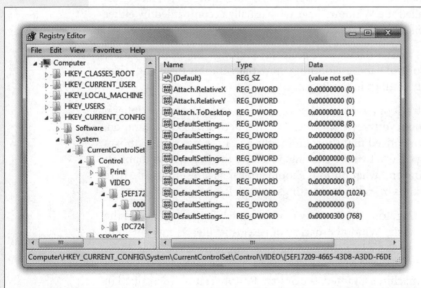

Figure B-1:
The Registry's settings are organized hierarchically; in fact, the Registry editor looks a lot like Windows Explorer. But there's no easy way to figure out which part of the Registry holds a particular setting or performs a particular function. It's like flying a plane that has no windows.

B-1.

The Big Five Hives

It turns out that Microsoft has arranged all of those software settings into five broad categories. Microsoft calls them *hives* or *root keys,* but they look and act like folders in a Windows Explorer window. You expand one of these folders (keys) just as you would in Explorer, too, by clicking the little flippy triangle button beside its name.

The names of these five hives are, frankly, just as weird as the term hives itself:

- **HKEY_CLASSES_ROOT.** This root key stores all kinds of information about files: filename extensions, file types, shortcut menus, and so on.

Note: A number of Registry entries appear in more than one place, live mirrors of each other, for convenience and clarity. Edit one, and you make a change in "both" places.

This root key, for example, is a pointer to the key at HKEY_LOCAL_MACHINE\SOFTWARE\Classes. (More on this slash notation below.)

- **HKEY_CURRENT_USER.** As you'd guess, here's where you'll find the settings pertaining to your account: your desktop arrangement, your wallpaper setting, and so on, plus information about connections to printers, cameras, and so on. (This key, too, is a live duplicate—of the identical one in HKEY_USERS, described below.)

- **HKEY_LOCAL_MACHINE.** All about your PC and its copy of Windows. Drivers, security settings, hardware info, the works.

- **HKEY_USERS.** Here's where Windows stores the information about all of the account holders (user profiles) on your PC, including the "Current_User's." You'll rarely be asked to edit this root key, since the good stuff—what applies to your own account—is in the CURRENT_USER key.

- **HKEY_CURRENT_CONFIG.** Most of this root key is made up of pointers to other places in the Registry. You'll rarely be asked to edit this one.

Keys and Values

If you expand one of these hives by clicking its flippy triangle, you'll see long list of inner "folders," called *keys*. These are the actual settings that the Registry tracks, and that you can edit.

Some keys contain other keys, in fact. Keep clicking the + buttons until you find the key you're looking for.

In books, magazines, and tutorials on the Web, you'll often encounter references to particular Registry subkeys written out as a Registry path, like this:

```
HKEY_CURRENT_USER→Control Panel→Mouse
```

(You may see backslashes used instead of the arrows.) That instruction tells you to expand the HKEY_CURRENT_USER root key, then expand Control Panel within it, and finally click the Mouse "folder." It works just like a folder path, like C:→Users→Chris→Desktop.

If you actually try this maneuver, you'll find, in the right half of the window, a bunch of keys named DoubleClickSpeed, MouseSpeed, MouseTrails, and so on. These should sound familiar, as they correspond to the options in the Mouse program of your Control Panel. (Figure B-2 clarifies this relationship.)

Each value usually contains either a number or a block of text. DoubleClickSpeed, for example, comes set at 500. In this case, that means 500 milliseconds between clicks, but each Registry value may refer to a different kind of unit.

Tip: Many of the Windows Explorer keyboard shortcuts also work in regedit. For example, once you've clicked a key, you can press the right or left arrow to reveal and hide its subkeys. You can also type the first letter of a subkey's name to highlight it in the left pane—same with a value's name in the right pane. And you can press the Backspace key to jump to the "parent" key, the one that contains the subkey.

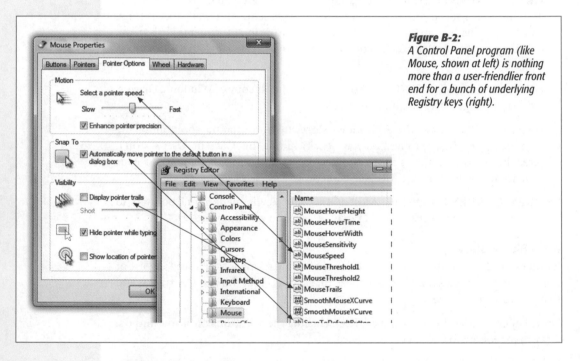

Figure B-2:
A Control Panel program (like Mouse, shown at left) is nothing more than a user-friendlier front end for a bunch of underlying Registry keys (right).

Backing Up Key Values

In general, you won't go into the Registry unless you truly want to make a change. That's why the program is called regedit, not regviewer.

As you know, though, making the wrong change can botch up your copy of Windows—and regedit has no Undo command and no "Save change before closing?" message.

That's why it's essential to *back up* a Registry key—or even its entire root key—before you change it. Later, if the change you made doesn't work the way you'd hoped, you can restore the original.

To back up a key (including and all its values and subkeys), just select it and then choose File→Export. Save the resulting key somewhere safe, like your desktop. Later, you can reinstate the key by double-clicking the .reg file you exported. (Or, if you're paid by the hour, open regedit, choose File→Import, and manually open the .reg file.)

Note: Importing a .reg file merges it with the data already in the Registry. Any values you edited will go back to their original versions, provided you haven't renamed them.

This means, for instance, that if you export a key, rename one of the values in that key, and then re-import the .reg file, the value you renamed will still be there, along with the value by its original name. In other words, a .reg file is a very good idea, but it's not a "get out of jail free card" that undoes all types of changes.

The only way to get a true Registry backup is to back up the Registry hive files themselves. Only the Complete PC Backup program described on page 647 can do this for you.

Regedit Examples

Here are three typical regedit tweaks, spelled out for you step by step.

Encrypt/Decrypt from the Shortcut Menu

As you know from page 633, one of the perks of using Vista (Business, Enterprise, or Ultimate) is that you can encrypt files and folders, protecting them from people who try to open them from across the network or using a different account.

If you use this feature quite a bit, however, you'll quickly grow tired of opening the Properties box every time you want to encrypt something. Wouldn't it be much more convenient if the Encrypt and Decrypt commands were right there in the shortcut menu that appears when you right-click an icon?

Of course it would. To make it so, do this:

- **Navigate to:** HKEY_CURRENT_USER→Software→Microsoft→Windows→ CurrentVersion→Explorer→Advanced.

   Now, for this trick, you're going to need a key that doesn't actually exist yet. Fortunately, it's very easy to create a new key. In this case, just right-click the Advanced "folder," and then, from the shortcut menu, choose New→DWORD (32-bit) Value. You'll see "New Value #1" appear in the right side of the window, ready to be renamed; type *EncryptionContextMenu*, and then press Enter.

Tip: The birth of a new Registry entry is a good opportunity to name it, but you can rename any value or key at any time, just the way you'd rename a file icon. That is, you can open the renaming rectangle by right-clicking or by pressing F2

• **Double-click this value on the right side:** EncryptionContextMenu.

• **Make this change:** in the "Value data" box, type 1.

• **Wrap up:** click OK and quit regedit. When you right-click any file or folder icon, you'll see the new Encrypt command in the shortcut menu. (Or, if it's already encrypted, you'll see a Decrypt command.)

A Really, Really Clean Desktop

Windows XP used to nag you every now and then to get unused icons off your desktop. (Mercifully, the Desktop Cleanup Wizard isn't part of Vista.)

But why stop there? If you've got the world's most beautiful desktop wallpaper set up, you might not want any icons marring its majesty.

If you think about it, you can get by just fine without a single icon on the desktop. The Computer and similar icons are waiting in your Start menu. You can put things into the Recycle Bin without dragging them to its icon. (Just highlight icons and then press the Delete key, for instance.)

The following regedit hack doesn't actually remove anything from your desktop. It just hides them. You can still work with the icons on your desktop by using Windows Explorer to view the contents of your Desktop folder, for example.

• **Navigate to:** HKEY_CURRENT_USER→Software→Microsoft→Windows→ CurrentVersion→Policies→Explorer.

• **Double-click this value on the right side:** NoDesktop. (If you don't see this value, create it. Right-click the Explorer folder, choose New→Binary Value, and name the new value NoDesktop.)

• **Make this change:** In the "Value data" box, type *01 00 00 00*. (Regedit puts the spaces in automatically.) Click OK.

• **Wrap up:** click OK, quit regedit, and then restart the PC. (To reverse the procedure, just delete the NoDesktop value you created.)

Tip: If you find your pulse racing with the illicit thrill of making tweaks to your system, why stop here? You can find hundreds more regedit "recipes" in books, computer magazines, and Web sites. A quick search of *regedit hacks* on Google will unearth plenty of them.

Slow Down the Animations

Vista's window animations and other eye candy are very cool. But they happen fast; Microsoft didn't want them to get in your way. That's a shame if you want to study the visual-FX majesty of these animations in more detail.

If you make this regedit tweak, though, you can make the window animation slow down on command—specifically, whenever you're pressing the Shift key.

• **Navigate to:** HKEY_CURRENT_USER→Software→Microsoft→Windows→ DWM.

- **Right-click** the DWM folder. From the shortcut menu, choose New→DWORD (32-bit) Value. Name the new value AnimationsShiftKey.

- **Double-click this value on the right side:** The AnimationsShiftKey entry you just made. In the "Value data" box, type 1. Click OK.

- **Wrap up:** Quit regedit and then restart the PC. (To reverse the procedure, just delete the AnimationsShiftKey value you created.)

To see the effects in slow motion, press the Shift key just before they start to occur. For example, Shift-click a window's Close box—and watch in amazement as it *slowwwwly* fades into total transparency, like a ghost returning to the world beyond.

Or summon the Flip3D effect (page 90) by pressing ⊞+Tab. Then, once the "deck of cards" window effect appears, hold down Shift as you tap your arrow keys, or click windows, to shuffle through them.

Where'd It Go?

A s the saying goes, you can't make an omelette without breaking a few eggs. And on the road to Windows Vista, Microsoft broke enough eggs to make a Texan soufflé. Features got moved, renamed, and ripped out completely.

If you're fresh from Windows XP or another version of Windows, you might spend your first few weeks with Vista wondering where things went. Here's a handy cheat sheet: features that aren't in Vista (or aren't where you think they should be).

- **"Add or Remove Programs" control panel.** The Control Panel applet called Programs and Features performs the software-removal function (Start→Control Panel→Programs→Programs and Features). No Control Panel applet remains to *add* software, because all software these days comes with its *own* installer.

- **Backgammon.** All of Windows XP's "play across the Internet" games are gone from Vista.

- **CDF protocol.** Gone.

- **Checkers.** All of Windows XP's "play across the Internet" games are gone from Vista.

- **Clipbook Viewer.** This handy multi-Clipboard feature is no longer in Vista.

- **.doc file support in WordPad.** Gone. WordPad can no longer read Microsoft Word documents. (Microsoft must *really* want you to buy Microsoft Office.)

Tip: So how are you supposed to open and create Word files if you don't actually have Microsoft Word?

One free, easy way is to use Google's own online word processor, Docs (*http://docs.google.com*). It can both create Word documents and open other people's.

- **DirectAnimation.** This technology has been removed from Vista.

- **Discuss pane.** This Windows XP panel did nothing unless some technically proficient administrator set up something called a SharePoint Portal Server—a corporate software kit that permits chat sessions among employees. Anyway, it's no longer in Windows.

- **Documents & Settings folder.** Now called Users.

- **Explorer bar.** Gone.

- **Favorites folder.** Favorites are still around, in the sense of bookmarks from Internet Explorer. But the one that can also list folder windows, documents, and other icons is gone. Microsoft suggest that you use the new Favorite Links list in its place (page 66).

- **File types.** In Windows XP, you could define new file types and associate them with programs yourself, using the File Types tab in the Folder Options dialog box. In Vista, the File Types tab is gone. There's a similar dialog box now (page 223), but it doesn't let you make up your own file types and associations. It doesn't let you define custom secondary actions, either, or ask Explorer to reveal filename extensions only for specific file types.

- **Files & Settings Transfer Wizard.** Renamed Windows Easy Transfer (Appendix A).

- **Filmstrip view (Explorer windows).** Replaced by the any-size-you-like icon view feature.

- **Gopher.** Removed.

- **Hardware profiles.** Removed.

- **Hearts (Internet Hearts).** All of Windows XP's "play across the Internet" games are gone from Vista.

- **Hotmail accounts in Outlook Express.** Gone. Windows Mail can't check Web-based email accounts.

- **HyperTerminal.** This old-time, text-only terminal program is gone, along with the BBS systems that were once its *raison d'être.*

- **Image toolbar (Internet Explorer).** Removed. Most of the commands that were on this auto-appearing IE 6 toolbar, though—Save Picture, E-mail Picture, Set as Background, and so on—are now in the shortcut menu that appears when you right-click any picture on the Web.

- **Indexing Service.** This technical, generally ignored search option has been reborn in the glorious form of Windows Search (Chapter 3).

- **Internet games.** Those old Windows XP games that you could play against other people online—Backgammon, Hearts, Reversi, Spades, and Checkers—have been removed.

- **IP over FireWire.** Removed.

- **Macintosh services.** The software that offered file and print sharing via the Apple-Talk protocol (which even Apple has abandoned) is gone.

- **Media toolbar.** The Windows Media Player toolbar is the same idea: it lets you control your music playback right from the taskbar.

- **My Network Places.** To see the other computers on your network in Windows Vista, choose Start→Network.

- **NetMeeting.** Removed. Microsoft says that Windows Meeting Space (Chapter 26) is its successor—but Meeting Space lacks NetMeeting's voice- and video-chat features. Well, there's always Skype.

- **Offline browsing (Internet Explorer).** In Windows XP, you could right-click a Web page's name in your Favorites menu and store it for later perusal when you were no longer online—complete with whatever pages were linked to it. Internet Explorer would even update such pages automatically each time you got back online. This feature is gone from Internet Explorer 7.

- **"Parent folder" button.** In Windows XP, you could click this button to go up one folder (that is, to see the folder that enclosed the current one). It's gone in Vista, although you can perform the same function by pressing Alt+up arrow key (or by clicking one of the folder names in the Address bar's "breadcrumb trail").

- **Password protecting a .zip archive.** Removed. In the window of any open .zip file, there's still a column that indicates whether or not each file is password-protected—but in Vista, there's no way to add such a password yourself.

- **Pinball.** Gone, although there are several good new games that come with Vista.

- **PowerToys.** Not available at Vista's release in January 2007, although Microsoft reserves the right to come up with these freebie software goody bag later.

- **Reversi.** All of Windows XP's "play across the Internet" games are gone.

- **Run command.** It may seem to be missing from the Start menu, but you can put it right back (page 46). Or you can just press ⊞+R to call it up.

- **Search assistant (Internet Explorer).** Replaced by the new Search bar at the upper-right corner of the Internet Explorer window.

- **Search pane.** By choosing View→Explorer Bar→Search, you could open Windows XP's Search program. But the new Start menu Search box (Chapter 3) is infinitely superior.

- **SerialKeys.** This feature for specialized gadgets for the disabled is no longer supported.

- **Spades.** All of Windows XP's "play across the Internet" games are gone from Vista.

- **Startup Hardware Profiles.** Removed.

- **Taskbar dragging.** You can no longer drag the taskbar's top edge off the screen to hide it manually. You can't drag the taskbar to the middle of screen anymore, either. And you can't drag a folder to edge of screen to turn it into a toolbar. (One guess: Too many people were doing this stuff *accidentally* and then getting frustrated.)

- **Telnet.** Removed—or so it seems. Fortunately, you can restore it using the "Turn Windows Features on and Off" feature described on page 232; select Telnet Client.

- **The prefix "My."** Gone, thank heaven. Now your folder names are Computer, Music, Pictures, Documents, and so on—not My Computer, My Music, and so on. (Was there really any doubt *whose* those folders were?)

- **Tip of the Day.** No longer part of Windows. Microsoft must expect you to get your tips from computer books now.

- **TweakUI.** Not available for Vista, at least at its release. Microsoft may well come up with a similar super-tweaking program later.

- **Wallpaper.** Now called Desktop Background. (Right-click the desktop; from the shortcut menu, choose Personalize.)

- **Web Publishing Wizard.** Gone.

- **What's This? button in dialog boxes.** This little link is gone from Windows dialog boxes, probably because it didn't work in most of them. Now, if help is available in a dialog box, it lurks behind the ? button.

- **Windows Address Book.** Replaced by Windows Contacts—a folder more than a program. Page 250.

- **Windows Components Wizard.** Now called the Windows Features dialog box (page 232).

- **Windows Messenger.** Microsoft's chat program no longer comes preinstalled in Windows, thanks to antitrust legal trouble the company encountered. There is, however, a link on the Welcome screen that lets you download it.

- **Windows Picture and Fax Viewer.** This old program's functions have been split. Now you view pictures in Windows Photo Gallery Viewer, and faxes in Windows Fax and Scan (available in the Business, Enterprise, and Ultimate editions of Vista).

- **XBM images.** Gone.

- **Yahoo accounts in Outlook Express.** Gone. Windows Mail can't check Web-based email accounts.

The Master Keyboard Shortcut List

H ere it is, by popular, frustrated demand: The master list of every secret (or not-so-secret) keystroke in Windows Vista. Clip and post to your monitor (unless, of course, you got this book from the library).

Explorer windows

Highlight the Address bar	Alt+D
Open Previous Locations list (Address bar)	F4
Refresh the window	F5
Open this folder's parent window	Alt+Up arrow
Back (previous window)	Alt+Left arrow or Backspace
Forward	Alt+Right arrow
Cancel the current task or search	Esc
Make menu bar visible	F10 or Alt
Close window	Alt+F4 or Ctrl+W
Open Search window	F3, Ctrl+F, or ⊞+F
Open another window for this folder	Ctrl+N
Full Screen Mode on/off	F11
Open this window's Control menu	Alt+Space
Cycle through open windows	Alt+Tab
Cycle through open windows without closing the menu	Ctrl+Alt+Tab
Open Start menu	⊞ or Ctrl+Esc

Open Task Manager   Ctrl+Shift+Esc

Resize columns to fit their contents   Ctrl+Plus sign (+) on numeric
                                                         keypad

Instant Search box (top of each Explorer window)

Select the Instant Search box (next to Address bar)   Ctrl+E

Search and open Search Pane   Alt+Enter

Search in Internet Explorer   Shift+Enter

Open a selected program elevated
(Start Menu searches)   Ctrl+Shift+Enter

Working with icons

Select all icons in a document or window   Ctrl+A

Select last icon in the window   End

Select first item in the window   Home

Move to last item in the window without
selecting it   Ctrl+End

Move to first item in the window without
selecting it   Ctrl+Home

Select non-adjacent icons   Ctrl+Arrow keys to move,
                                                        Space bar to select

Select adjacent icons   Shift+arrow keys
                                                        Shift with any arrow key

Open a selected icon's shortcut menu   Shift+F10

Rename the selected icon   F2

Open Properties dialog box for the selected icon   Alt+Enter

Move selected icon to the Recycle Bin   Delete or Ctrl+D

Delete selected icon without moving it to the
Recycle Bin first   Shift+Delete

Navigation pane

Open all subfolders of selected folder   Num Lock+Asterisk (*) on
                                                        numeric keypad

Display contents of the selected folder   Num Lock+Plus sign (+) on
                                                        numeric keypad

Collapse the selected folder   Num Lock+Minus sign (-) on
                                                        numeric keypad

Collapse folder (if expanded), or select
parent folder (if not)   Left arrow

Display folder's contents (if collapsed), or select first subfolder (if not)	Right arrow
View previous folder	Alt+Left arrow
View next folder	Alt+Right arrow

Windows-key shortcuts

Open or close the Start menu	⊞
Open icon in Quick Launch toolbar	⊞+1 (first item), ⊞ +2 (second item), etc.
Open System Properties dialog box	⊞+Break key
Display the desktop, hide all windows	⊞+D
Minimize all Explorer windows	⊞+M
Restore minimized windows to the desktop	⊞+Shift+M
Open Computer window	⊞+E
Search for a file or folder	⊞+F
Search for computers (on a network domain)	Ctrl+⊞+F
Lock your computer or switch users	⊞+L
Run dialog box	⊞+R
Cycle through programs on the taskbar	⊞+T
Open Windows Flip 3-D	⊞+Tab
Bring Windows Sidebar to the front	⊞+Space
Cycle through Sidebar gadgets	⊞+G
Open Ease of Access Center	⊞+U
Open Windows Mobility Center	⊞+X

Login screen

Open Restart/Sleep/Hibernate/Shut Down menu	Alt+S
Highlight other account-holder tiles	Arrow keys

Security screen

Change password	Alt+C
Lock machine	Alt+K
Log off	Alt+L
Open Task Manager	Alt+T
Switch user	Alt+W

Miscellaneous/Editing

Copy	Ctrl+C
Cut	Ctrl+X or Shift+Delete
Paste	Ctrl+V
Undo	Ctrl+Z
Redo	Ctrl+Y
Help	F1
Cycle through parts of a window or dialog box	F6
Create shortcut	Ctrl+Shift-drag an icon
Highlight a block of text	Ctrl+Shift with arrow keys
Move insertion point to next word	Ctrl+Right arrow
Move insertion point beginning of previous word	Ctrl+Left arrow

Index

Index

32-bit vs. 64-bit versions, 7
802.11 *see* **WiFi**
⊞ **key**
  keyboard shortcut list, 235, 799-802
  reveal desktop, 89

A

Accelerated Graphics Port (AGP), 564
accessibility *see* **Ease of Access Center**
Accessories folder, 253-273
  System Tools folder, 271-273
accounts, 665-698 *see also* **passwords**
  administrator vs. standard, 669-671, 680
  Administrator account (emergencies only),
    677
  creating during Vista install, 780-781
  creating on a domain, 680
  creating using Control Panel, 671
  creating using Users & Groups console, 682-
    683
  defined, 665-667
  deleting, 676-678
  disabling, 678, 683
  domain computers, 679-680
  editing, 672-674
  fully automated login, 678
  Fast User Switching, 686-688
  Guest account, 679
  groups, 683-685, 695
  installing programs, 229
  in workgroups vs. domains, 667
  local accounts, 668-679
  Local Users and Groups console, 681-686
  locking, 32-33, 687
  passwords for, 673
  parental controls, 3, 361-365, 674

  pictures, 673-674
  Standard accounts, 669-671
  Switch User command, 33
Acrobat (PDF) format, 541
activation, 312, 781-783
Active Directory, 719-722
  searching, 723-726
ActiveX controls, 349
  add-ons (Internet Explorer), 349
ad hoc networks, 705
  wireless, 745
Add Hardware
  Control Panel, 286
  wizard, 566
Add or Remove Programs, 795 *see also* **Pro-**
    grams and Features
Add a Network Location, 749
Address bar, 5, 60-63
  back and forward buttons, 61
  Internet Explorer, 369-370
  navigating from, 62
  recent pages and folders lists, 61
  Refresh button, 61
  searching from, 62
  slash notation, 61
  things to click, 61
  triangle notation, 61
  Web addresses, 62
address book *see* **Contacts**
Address Space Layout Randomization (ASLR),
    33, 34
Address toolbar, 99
administrative mode, 191
Administrative Tools
  Control Panel, 286
Administrator accounts, 669-672
  secret emergency account, 677

Adobe PDF format, 541
Advanced Boot Options, 656-658
adware, 341
Aero, 3, 22-24
    color schemes, 160-163
    customizing appearance, 157-174
    Remote Assistance, 184
    speed tweaks, 162
    taskbar thumbnails, 94
    themes, 170-171
    turning off, 159, 613
    windows Experience Index, 20
    Windows Flip 3D, 90-91
All Programs menu, 28-30
    auto-sorting, 48
    colored highlighting on new items, 47
    editing, 51
    Games, 274-280
    installing programs, 229
    program groups, 29
    source folders, 51
    Startup folder, 29
alphabetical order *see* **sorting**
Alt-clicking, 14
Alt-tab, 89-90
AND searches, 110
antivirus software, 336
Anytime Upgrade, 273-274
appearance, 157-174
    screen savers, 165-167
    turning off eye candy, 612-613
    wallpaper, 163-165
applets, 282
arrow notation, 9
authentication, 191
authors
    editing author names, 69
    grouping by, 77
    searching by, 108, 123
    stacking by, 78
autocomplete, 370
autofill, 369
AutoPlay, 286-287
    cameras, 426-427
    flash drives, 611

B

Back button, 370
    address bar, 61
Backgammon, 795
Backup and Restore Center, 288
backups, 3, 641-648
    automatic, 641-647
    backup disks, 642

Complete PC Backup, 647-648
    file based, 641-647
    getting started, 643-644
    image-based, 647-648
    limitations of, 642
    previous versions, 134
    restoring files, 645-647
    Shadow Copy, 654-656
    System Restore, 648-654
basic disks, 622
batteries
    power settings, 298-301
    status, 573
battery meter, 572
BIOS startup messages, 656
bit rates, 472
BitLocker Drive Encryption, 3, 637-640
    Control Panel, 288
    flash drive workaround, 640
Blu-Ray movies, 479-481
Bluetooth adaptors, 562
BMP format, 429
bookmarks *see* **favorites**
Boolean searches, 110
boot logging, 658
"breadcrumbs"
    address bar, 60-63
Briefcase, 587
broadband connections, 319-320
    dialup connections, 321-325
    sharing an Internet connection, 706-708
burning CDs and DVDs, 151-156
    blank disc formats, 476
    compatibility issues, 154-156
    format options, 151
    from Movie Maker, 493-494
    from Media Player, 475-476
    Mastered vs. Live File System, 151-152
    of photos in Media Center, 526-527
    saving TV shows, 515-516
Business edition, 5-8

C

C:> prompt, 255
cable modems, 319-320
    sharing an Internet connection, 706-708
cache files
    erasing, 353
Calculator, 253-255
calendar *see also* **Windows Calendar**
    filtering icons, 81
    in Sidebar, 214
camcorders *see* **Movie Maker**

cameras *see* digital cameras; Photo Gallery; photos
captions, 441
catalog of gadgets, 214-221
CD-RW discs, 476
CDF Protocol, 795
CDs *see also* burning CDs and DVDs
    AutoPlay, 286-287
    filling in track names, 470
    playing music CDs, 466-471
    ripping CDs, 471-472
cellphones
    Sync Center, 587 592
Character Map, 272
chats, searching, 48
Check Disk, 599-601
checkbox selection, 85, 136-137
Checkers, 795
Chess Titans, 274-275
clean install, 773, 779-780
    vs. upgrade install, 772-774
ClickLock, 296
Clipbook Viewer, 254, 795
clocks *see* date and time
Close button, 59
closing windows, 59, 88
CMS profiles, 547
Code Integrity Checking, 334
color depth, 172
color management, 547
colors
    of Windows look, 160-163
    themes, 170-171
columns
    adding or removing, 74
    column widths, 74
    rearranging, 74
Command prompt, 237, 255-256
    at startup, 662
command-line interface, 255
compatibility
    CDs and DVDs, 154-156
    software programs, 236-238
compatibility mode, 236-238
Complete PC Backup, 647-648
    restore from startup screen, 662
component video connectors, 508
compressing files and folders, 147-151, 629-633
    defined, 629
    NTFS compression, 147-148, 630-631
    zip folders, 149-151, 631-633
Computer Management console, 679
computer name, 312, 780
    changing, 741

Computer window, 36-37
    display on desktop, 22
    display as menu, 45
Connect to, 35
    adding to Start menu, 46
Connect to a Network Projector, 256
contacts
    Sidebar gadget, 215, 397
    Windows Contacts, 250-252
Contacts folder, 128
Content Advisor, 363
Control menu, 59
cookies, 349-352
    adjusting threshold, 351-352
    backing up, 352
    blocking, 351
    defined, 349
    erasing, 353
    examining one by one, 350
    terminology, 350
copy and paste
    moving icons, 140-141
    within documents, 199-200
cover pages (fax), 553
Control Panel, 35, 281-316
    Accounts, 668-669
    Add Hardware, 286
    Administrative Tools, 286
    AutoPlay, 286-287
    Backup and Restore Center, 288
    BitLocker Drive Encryption, 288, 640
    catalog of applets, 286-316
    categories, 282-285
    date and time, 288-289
    Default Programs, 290
    Defender, 340-346
    desktop background, 163-165
    Device Manager, 290
    display as menu, 45
    Ease of Access Center, 266-271, 291
    Environment Variables, 312
    Folder Options, 291
    Fonts, 291
    Game Controllers, 291
    Home vs. Classic view, 281-285
    Indexing Options, 292
    Internet Options, 292
    iSCSI Initiator, 292-293
    Java, 293
    Keyboard, 293-294
    mobile PC, 575
    Mobility Center, 315, 572-574
    Mouse, 295-297
    Network and Sharing Center, 297

Offline Files, 297
Parental Controls, 297, 361-365
Pen and Input Devices, 298
Performance Information and Tools, 298
Personalization, 298
Phone and Modem Options, 298
Power Options, 298-301
Printers, 301, 537-538
problem reports and solutions, 193, 301-303, 659-661
Program Access and Defaults, 226
Programs and Features, 232-233, 304
restoring desktop icon, 22
Regional and Language Options, 304-307
Scanners and Cameras, 307
screen savers, 165-167
Search, 284
Security Center, 307, 335-336
Sounds, 307-310
Speech Recognition Options, 310
Startup and Recovery, 312
Sync Center, 310, 587-588
System, 311-313
System Protection, 312
Tablet PC Settings, 313
Taskbar and Start menu, 313
Text to Speech, 313
User Profiles, 312
Welcome Center, 313, 781
Windows CardSpace, 313-315
Windows Defender, 315
Windows Firewall, 315
Windows Mobility Center, 315, 572-574
Windows Sidebar Properties, 315
Windows Sideshow, 316
Windows Update, 286, 316, 614-619
cropping photos, 449-450
in Media Center, 526
crossover cables, 705
Ctrl+Alt+Delete
login method, 689-690
task manager, 192-194
Ctrl-clicking, 14
Currency gadget, 216
cursors
adjusting behavior of, 169-171
blinking rate, 294
enlarging or changing, 269
pointer speed, 296
snap to OK button, 296
cut and paste
moving icons, 140-141
within documents, 199-200

D

Data Execution Prevention, 345
date and time
Control Panel, 288-289
formats, 304
in Sidebar, 215
Internet time, 289
of photos, 433-434
searching by, 121
Debugging Mode, 658
Default Programs, 34-35, 290
adding to Start menu, 46
Defender, 2, 315, 340-346
alert levels, 342
history, 343
quarantined items, 344
scanning your PC, 342
Software Explorer, 344-345
SpyNet, 345-346
deleting *see also* **Recycle bin**
accounts, 676-678
calendar events, 247
email messages, 403-404
files and folders, 141-145
metadata, 72
photos, 438
shortcut icons, 146
songs or playlists, 474
Desktop, 22-24
color schemes, 160-163
background *see* wallpaper
keyboard shortcut, 89
restoring desktop icons, 22
themes, 170-171
toolbar, 100-101
wallpaper, 163-165
Desktop folder, 128
Details pane, 64-65
Device Manager, 290, 312, 567-570
dial tones, 332
dialing rules, 331
dialog boxes
adjusting type size, 161
basics of, 197
help, 180
Narrator, 269-271
dialup connections, 321-325
automatic connections, 328-331
connecting and disconnecting, 328-331
dial tones, 332
disconnecting, 330
for remote access, 753-758
modem settings, 331-332
setting up, 323-324

digital cameras *see also* **Photo Gallery; photos**
movies, 429
AutoPlay, 286-287, 426-427
Photo Gallery, 423-461
DirectAnimation, 796
directories *see* **folders**
Directory Services Restore Mode, 658
Discuss pane, 796
Disk Cleanup, 595-596
Disk Defragmenter, 596-599
Disk Management, 601-605
changing drive letters, 602
drive formatting, 604
drive paths, 604
dual booting, 603
dynamic disks, 621-629
junction points, 604
mounted drives, 604
partitioning a drive, 603
disks *see also* **drive letters**
basic disks, 622
hard drives, 621-640
properties, 132
sharing, 733, 736-737
quotas, 634
spanned volumes, 623
tags and metadata, 69-71
Display Control Panel *see* **Personalization**
displays *see* **monitors**
DNS addresses, 325-327
document preview, 5
Documents, 39
backups, 641-648
closing, 198
display as menu, 45
exporting and importing, 201
file formats, 197
filename extensions, 221-229
previous versions, 134
printing, 533-551
scanning, 557-558
searching, 106-129
Shadow Copy, 654-656
Documents and Settings, 796
Documents folder, 128, 194-198
documents tab
saving, 194-198
domains, 717-727
Active Directory, 719-722
advantages of, 718-719
assigning permissions, 727
browsing, 723
defined, 667, 717
domain controller, 718

joining, 720-722
searching, 723-726
security, 720
DOS *see also* **command prompt**
del and *erase* commands, 142
filenames, 129
programs, 237
secret Dell partition, 623
double-click speed, 295
Downloads folder, 128
drag and drop, 200-201
drive letters
changing, 602
history of, 126
hiding/showing, 85
mapping shares to, 743
drive paths, 604-605
drivers, 15, 559-560
Device Manager, 567-570
Microsoft vs. manufacturer, 564
notification area, 562-563
rollback, 570
Safe Mode, 656-658
signing, 566-567, 658
updating, 569-570
DSL, 319-320
sharing an Internet connection, 706-708
dual booting, 623, 775
restore points, 656
Shadow Copy, 656
DVD Maker, 4, 494-499
burning a DVD, 499
designing scene menus, 496-499
importing videos and pictures, 494-495
slideshows, 499
DVD-R discs, 476
DVDs *see also* **burning CDs and DVDs; DVD Maker**
AutoPlay, 286-287
burning, 151-156
burning a slideshow, 499
movies, 479-481
photo slideshows, 460-461
saving TV shows, 515-516
DVI connectors, 508, 562
Dvorak keyboard, 102, 304-305
dynamic disks, 621-629
spanned volumes, 623

E

Ease of Access Center, 266-271
Control Panel, 291
cursor enlargement, 269
high contrast mode, 268

Magnifier, 269
Mouse Keys, Sticky Keys, Toggle Keys, 267
Narrator, 269-271
On-Screen keyboard, 271
visual "beeps", 269
email *see* **Mail**
emailing photos, 458-460
emptying the Recycle Bin, 143
Encrypting File System (EFS), 633-637
encrypting files and folders, 633-637
  backdoor, 636
  including in search, 118
  show in color, 85
  troubleshooting, 636
  using the shortcut menu, 791
energy savings
  power settings, 298-301
Enterprise edition, 5-8
Environment Variables, 312
error reporting, 193
  Problem Reports and Solutions, 301-303
Esc key, 111, 799
  cancel loading Web page, 371, 389
  cancel dragging, 138
  cancel playback, 264
Ethernet, 700-702
  crossover cables, 705
  equipment, 702
  speed variations, 702
EXIF data, 439-441
exiting programs, 190
expansion cards, 563-564
Explorer Bar, 796
Explorer windows, 60-87 *see also* **columns;
    icons; windows**
  address bar, 5, 60-63
  applying changes to all folders, 81-82
  color schemes, 160-163
  column headings, 63
  Details pane, 64-66
  Details view, 71-74
  document preview, 5
  Favorite Links pane, 66-67
  filtering, 5
  filtering, 78-79
  Folder Options, 82-86
  folders list, 67-69
  grouping, 5, 77-78
  hiding and showing columns, 71-74
  icon views, 71-74
  keyboard shortcuts, 68, 799-802
  list views, 71-74
  making menu bar appear, 65
  metadata, 69-71

navigation pane, 66-69
new panes, 5
preview pane, 65-66
properties, 69-71
search pane, 64, 120-123
searching in, 119-126
show window contents, 162
sorting, 75-77
stacking, 5
stacking, 77-78
tags, 69-71
themes, 170-171
tiles view, 71-74
toolbars, 63
uni-window vs. multi-window, 80-81
Views menu, 73
exporting and importing, 201
ExpressCards, 562
extensions *see* **filename extensions**
Extras and Upgrades folder, 273-274

F

Fast User Switching, 686-688
favorite links, 66-67
Favorites, 376-378
  adding to Start menu, 46
  creating and organizing, 377
  Links toolbar, 378
Favorites folder, 129, 796
Fax and Scan, 4, 553-557
  scanning, 557-558
faxing, 551-557
  auto-printing, 556
  cover pages, 553
  receiving faxes, 555-557
  saving as graphics, 556
  sending faxes, 551-555
file associations *see* **filename extensions**
file sharing *see* **sharing files and folders**
file sizes
  searching by, 123
filename extensions, 130, 221-229
  can't create new associations, 796
  defined, 221
  hidden by default, 130
  hiding/showing, 84, 222-223
  hooking up to different programs, 223-229
  Open With command, 224-227
  unknown file types, 223
filenames
  eight dot three, 129
  forbidden characters, 130
  maximum length, 130
  renaming files, 130
  searching by, 122

files, 130-151
  changing icons of, 135
  checkbox selection, 85, 136-137
  compressing, 629-633
  compressing files and folders, 147-151
  copying and moving, 138-141
  deleting, 141-145
  encrypting, 633-637
  file formats, 197
  filename extensions, 221-229
  hidden, 84
  previous versions, 134
  printing, 541-542
  properties, 132-134
  searching, 106-129
  shortcut icons, 145-147
  tags and metadata, 69-71
  views, 71-74
Files & Settings Transfer Wizard *see* **Windows Easy Transfer**
Filmstrip view, 796
Filter Keys, 267
filtering (icons), 5, 78-79
Firewall, 336-339
  customizing outbound connections, 340
  defined, 337
  exceptions, 338
  fine tuning, 338
  logging attacks, 340
FireWire ports, 562
flash drives
  AutoPlay, 286-287, 611
  BitLocker Drive Encryption, 640
  ReadyBoost, 610-612
flicks, 583-584
Folder Options, 82-86
  Control Panel, 291
  customzing Search, 115-119
folder paths, 41, 130
  in tooltips, 112
  showing in title bar, 83-84
  Universal Naming Convention (UNC), 742
folders *see also* **sharing files and folders**
  Address bar, 60-63
  Apply to All Folders, 81
  changing icons of, 135
  checkbox selection, 85, 136-137
  compressing, 629-633
  compressing files and folders, 147-151
  copying and moving, 138-141
  defined, 105
  deleting, 141-145
  encrypting, 633-637
  exclude from search, 116-119

  file size info, 83
  folder templates, 134
  hidden, 84, 736
  jumbo icons, 73
  of Windows Vista, 126-129
  opening with Run command, 43
  properties, 134
  remember view settings, 84
  searching, 106-129
  searching by, 120-121
  shortcut icons, 145-147
  tags and metadata, 69-71
  Universal Naming Convention (UNC), 742
Folders list, 67-69
folders templates, 134
fonts, 550-551
  Control Panel, 291
  Internet Explorer text size, 385
  smooth edges, 162
Forward button, 370
  address bar, 61
Freecell, 275
frozen programs, 192-194
FTP servers, 749

G

gadgets *see also* **Sidebar**
  calendar, 214
  clock, 215
  contacts, 215, 397
  CPU meter, 216
  currency, 216
  Feed Headlines, 217
  Notes, 217
  Picture Puzzle, 218
  Slide Show, 219
  Stocks, 218
  Weather, 219
Game Controllers, 291
game port, 562
Games, 38, 274-280
  display as menu, 45
  parental controls, 364
  ratings, 364
Games Explorer, 276
gestures, 578-580
  Input panel, 577
getting help, 175-186
GIF format, 428
Google
  in IE search bar, 371-372
Gopher, 796
group policies, 6
grouping icons, 5, 77

groups (users), 683-685, 695
    Administrators, 685
    creating, 684
    default groups, 685
    Guests, 686
    modifying, 6868
    NTFS permissions,   695-696
    Power Users, 686
    Users, 686
Guest account, 679

H

handwriting recognition, 575-582
    correcting errors, 580-582
    flicks, 583-584
    scratching out writing, 579
hard drives, 621-640 *see also* **backups; drive letters**
    BitLocker Drive Encryption, 637-640
    changing drive letter, 602
    checkups, 599-601
    Disk Cleanup, 595-596
    Disk Defragmenter, 596-599
    Disk Management, 601-605
    disk quotas, 634
    dynamic disks, 621-629
    formatting, 604
    mounted drives (junction points), 604
    partitioning, 603
    power setting, 298-301
    sharing, 733, 736-737
    spanned volumes, 623
    System Restore, 648-654
    Windows ReadyDrive, 613
hardware, 559-570
    Add Hardware wizard, 566
    compatibility issues, 771
    Device Manager, 567-570
    driver signing, 566-567
    drivers, 15
    expansion cards, 563-564
    hard drives, 621-640
    installing printers, 533-538
    maintenance, 595-619
    printing, 533-551
    speeding up Windows, 609-613
    Task Scheduler, 606-609
    troubleshooting, 564-565
    USB devices, 560-562
    Windows Experience Index, 20
Hardware Compatibility List (HCL), 559
Hardware Profiles, 796
HD-DVD movies, 479-481
HDMI connectors, 508

Hearts, 276
Help and Support, 34, 175-186
    adding to Start menu, 46
    dialog boxes, 180
    how to use, 175-178
    Microsoft support, 185-186
    Remote Assistance, 178-184
hibernate, 32, 34
    vs. Sleep mode, 32
hidden files and folders, 84, 736
hidden icons, 78-79
High Contrast mode, 268
History list, 379-380
    configuring, 380
    erasing, 352-353
    revisiting, 380
    searching, 48
Home Basic edition, 5-8
    Aero not available, 24
home page
    blank, 384
    Internet Explorer, 371
    multiple, 384
    setting, 383
Home Premium edition, 5-8
Hotmail accounts, 393
hotspots *see* **WiFi**
HyperTerminal, 796

I

icons, 130-151
    adjusting type size, 161
    changing, 135
    checkbox selection, 85, 136-137
    compressing files and folders, 147-151
    copying and moving, 138-141
    copying and pasting, 140-141
    deleting, 141-145
    filename extensions, 221-229
    filtering, 78-79
    folders, 73
    grouping, 77
    hiding, 78-79
    master keyboard shortcut list, 799-802
    opening with single clicks, 137
    printing, 541-542
    properties, 131-135
    renaming, 130
    restoring desktop icons, 22
    searching, 106-129
    selecting, 136-138
    Send To command, 140
    shortcut icons, 145-147
    sorting, 75-77

stacking, 77
thumbnails on/off, 83
views, 71-74
Image toolbar, 796
IMAP accounts, 393
index files (Search), 112-113
including encrypted files, 118
including or excluding folders, 116-119
moving, 118
rebuilding, 119
what's indexed, 113
Indexing Options, 292
Indexing Service, 797
Information bar, 354-356
highlighting, 389
infrared printers, 534-536
InkBall, 276
Input Panel, 100, 575-582
gestures, 577
insertion point
disappears while typing, 297
enlarging for better vision, 269
installing new hardware, 559-570
Add Hardware wizard, 566
printers, 533-538
installing software, 229-233
installing Windows Vista, 769-786
account creation, 780-781
activation, 781-783
clean install, 779-780
Disk Management, 601-605
restore image, 781
upgrade vs. clean install, 772-774
upgrading to Vista, 775-778
Welcome Center, 781
Windows Easy Transfer, 783-786
international
Regional and Language Options, 304-307
Internet
cellular wireless, 322
Defender, 2, 315, 340-346
dialup connections, 321-325
getting connected, 319-332
Internet Explorer, 367-390
Mail, 391-420
managing connections, 325-327
newsgroups, 418-420
security, 333-365
security zones, 357-359
sharing an Internet connection, 706-708
time limits, 364
Internet Connection Sharing, 706-708
Internet Explorer 7, 4, 367-390
activeX controls, 349

address bar, 369-370
autocomplete, 370
autofill, 369
Back button, 370
basics of, 368-372
Content Advisor, 363
cookies, 349-352
desktop icon, 22
emailing Web pages, 386
erasing history, 352-353
favorites, 376-378
forward button, 370
full-screen, 383
history, 379-380
home page, 371, 383
how it recognizes phishing, 347
information bar, 354-356
Internet Options, 292
keyboard shortcuts, 387-390
Links toolbar, 378
managing add-ons, 349
menu bar, restoring, 369
no add-ons, 272
parental controls, 361-365
phishing filter, 346-349
photos online, 385
pop-up blocker, 353-356
printing Web pages, 386-387
privacy, 352-353
Program Access and Defaults, 226
refresh button, 370
RSS news feeds, 380-382
saving Web pages to disk, 385-386
search, 371
security zones, 357-359
status bar, 372
stop button, 371
tabbed browsing, 373-376
text size, 385
tips and tricks, 382-390
turning off animations, 387
without graphics, 384
zooming in and out, 385
Internet Options, 292
Internet radio, 479
Internet time, 289
IP addresses, 325-328
IP over FireWire, 797
ipconfig **command**, 256
ISA slots, 564
iSCSI Initiator, 292-293
ISO format, 151-152
ISP (Internet service providers), 323-324
iTunes, 463

J

Java, 293
JPEG format, 428
junction points, 604-605
junk email *see* **spam**

K

keyboard shortcuts, 13-14
    address bar, 369-370
    Alt+Tab, 89-90
    by voice, 204
    closing windows, 88
    DVD playback, 481
    effect in list view, 86
    explorer folder list, 68
    files and folders, 146
    help, 46
    hiding the taskbar, 98
    Internet Explorer, 387-390
    master keyboard shortcut list, 799-802
    minimize, maximize, restore, 86
    Narrator, 269-271
    navigating folders, 124
    Remote Desktop, 765
    results menu, 110-112
    reveal desktop, 89
    save dialog box, 196-197
    Search, 107
    selecting icons, 136
    selecting text, 263
    Sidebar, 211
    Start menu, 26-28
    switching keyboard layouts, 307
    tabbed browsing, 373-376
    taskbar, 92-104
    Windows Flip 3D, 90-91
    w-key shortcuts, 235
keyboards, 293-294
    adjusting repeat rate, 293-294
    assistance for the disabled, 267
    layouts, 102, 304-305

L

Language bar, 102, 307
language kits, 102, 304-305
laptops
    battery meter, 572
    Briefcase, 587
    brightness, 573
    dialup connections, 321-325
    Mobility Center, 4, 315, 572-574
    offline files, 589-592
    power settings, 298-301
    Presentation Settings, 574

    projectors, 574
    remote access, 751-767
    scrolling tricks, 13
    speaker volume, 573
    special features for, 571-575
    Sync Center, 587-592
    Tablet PCs, 575-585
    Virtual Private Networking (VPN), 758-760
Last Known Good Configuration, 658
left-handed mouse, 12, 294
line conditioners, 600
Links folder, 129
links toolbar, 100, 378
Live File System (UDF) format, 151-152
Local Disk (C:), 127
local intranet zone, 357
local security policies, 683
Local Users and Groups console, 681-688
    creating accounts, 682-683
    creating groups, 683-684
    managing groups, 684-686
Lock command, 32-33, 687
log files, 257-258
Log Off command, 32-33
logging in, 688-690
    bypassing Welcome screen, 679
    Classic login screen, 690
    Ctrl-Alt-Delete message, 689
    password hint, 689
    to a domain, 722
    Welcome screen, 688-689

M

MAC address filtering, 361
Macintosh
    accessing on the network, 738
    Macintosh services, 797
    Remote Desktop, 761
    sharing files and folders, 741
Magnifier, 269
Mahjong Titans, 277
Mail, 391-420
    attaching files, 401
    CC, BCC lines, 398-400
    checking one account, 394
    composing and sending, 393-402
    contacts, 397, 401
    deleting messages, 403-404
    filing, 405
    flagging messages, 406
    forwarding, 405
    junk filter options, 412
    mail folders, 396, 405
    mailing lists, 404

message rules, 407-411
newsgroups, 418-420
opening attachments, 407
pictures in messages, 402-403
POP, IMAP, and Web-based, 393
printing, 405
Program Access and Defaults, 226
reading messages, 402-411
replying, 404-405
selecting messages, 403
searching, 48
Send To command, 140
setting up, 392-393
settings, 414-418
signatures, 399-401
spam filters, 411-414
Windows Contacts, 250-252
mailing lists, 404
maintenance, 595-619
backups, 641-648
Disk Cleanup, 595-596
Disk Defragmenter, 596-599
Disk Management, 601-605
disk quotas, 634
hard drive check, 599-601
hard drives, 621-640
System Restore, 648-654
Task Scheduler, 606-609
Windows Update, 614-619
Maintenance folder, 280
mapping folders to drive letters, 743-744
Master Boot Record, 624
Mastered (ISO) format, 151-152
Maximize button, 59, 86
taskbar, 95
Media Center, 501-529
advanced settings, 527-529
burning photos or videos to disc, 526-527
buying and renting movies, 516
editing photos, 525-527
hardware requirements, 501-502
moving your media libraries, 509
music, 517-523
music queue, 522
online music stores, 520-521
pausing/rewinding TV, 512
photos and videos, 523-527
playing back TV, 514
playing music, 519-520
playlists, 521-522
recording TV, 509-514
ripping CDs, 517-518
saving TV shows to DVD, 515-516
searching the library, 521
set-up, 502-509
shares library with Media Player, 509
slideshows, 524-525
speaker setup, 508
Media Center extenders, 502
Media Player *see* **Windows Media Player**
Meeting Space, 4, 745-749
beginning the meeting, 745
inviting participants, 746
sharing your desktop, 747-748
troubleshooting, 748-749
memory (RAM)
how much you have, 311
SuperFetch, 610
virtual memory, 615
Windows Memory Diagnostic Tool, 662
memory cards
auto-erase, 426
AutoPlay, 286-287
ReadyBoost, 610-612
USB card readers, 428
menu bar
bringing back, 65
show/hide, 83
turning off menu shadows, 162
message rules, 407-411
metadata, 69-71
deleting, 72
editing, 70
Photo Gallery, 439-441
Microsoft Support, 185-186
Microsoft Word
selecting text, 263
Microsoft XPS format, 541
Mimesweeper, 277
Minesweeper, 277-278
Minimize button, 59, 86
taskbar, 95
missingmanuals.com, 10
Mobility Center, 4, 315, 572-574
modems, 331-332
monitors
brightness, 573
color depth, 172
multiple, 172-174, 574
power setting, 298-301
refresh rate, 174
resolution, 171
screen rotation, 574
screen savers, 165-167
settings, 171-174
mounted drives, 604-605
mouse
adjusting behavior of, 167-171
ClickLock, 296

Control Panel, 295-297
double click speed, 295
left-handed mouse, 294
pointer trails, 297
right-clicking, 11-12
scroll wheel, 13
snap to OK button, 169
speed, 296
swapping right and left buttons, 12
wheel settings, 297
Windows Flip 3D, 90-91
Mouse Keys, 267
mousegrid, 208
Movie Maker, 483-494
adding music, 492-493
AutoMovie, 492
exporting finished movie, 493-494
importing video and music, 483-487
organizing clips, 487
recording narration, 493
splitting clips, 488
titles and credits, 490
transitions and effects, 48 9
movies, 429 *see also* **DVD Maker; Movie Maker**
buying and renting online, 51 6
in Media Center, 523-527
in Media Player, 482
Media Center, 501-529
moving windows, 87-88
MP3 CDs, 476
Multiple Document Interface, 88
multiple monitors, 172-174
Music, 38 *see also* **Windows Media Player**
display as menu, 45
Media Center, 517-523
Media Center, 501-529
online music stores, 477-479
playing in Media Center, 519-520
playing music CDs, 466-471
ripping CDs, 471-472
sharing on the network, 469
tags and metadata, 69-71
Windows Media Player, 463-482
Music folder, 129
music players, 476-477
My Computer, My Documents, etc.
restoring desktop icons, 22
My Network Places, 797
restoring desktop icons, 22
"My" prefix on folders, 26

N

Narrator, 269-271
navigation *see* **Address bar; Explorer windows**

Navigation pane, 66-69
moving icons, 139
simple folder view, 83
NetMeeting, 797
Network
adding to Start menu, 46
Network Access Protection, 334
network adapters, 700
Network and Sharing Center, 708-715
choosing a network, 320
Control Panel, 297
network map, 708-715
network connections
notification area, 327-328
network printers, 534
network projectors, 256
networking, 35 *see also* **domains; workgroups**
accessing shared files and folders, 739-743
ad hoc networks, 705
domains, 717-727
Ethernet, 700-702
hidden folders, 736
Home vs. Work vs. Public, 324, 359-360, 778
Internet connection sharing, 706-708
joining a domain, 720-722
kinds of networks, 700-706
MAC address filtering, 361
managing connections, 325-327, 711
mapping folders to drive letters, 743-744
Meeting Space, 745-749
Network and Sharing Center, 708-715
network discovery on/off, 713
network map, 712
offline files, 590-592
phone line networks, 705
power outlet networks, 705
Public vs. Private, 324, 359-360, 778
remote access, 751-767
Remote Desktop, 760-767
routers, 700-702
security, 333-365
setting up a network, 699-715
sharing a printer, 544-545
sharing an Internet connection, 706-708
sharing files and folders, 729-744
sharing music, 469
testing the network, 714-715
troubleshooting, 711
Universal Naming Convention (UNC), 742
Virtual Private Networking (VPN), 758-760
WiFi, 703-705
wireless, 320-321
newsgroups, 418-420
defined, 418
downloading, 420

downloading master list, 420
replying and composing, 419
subscribing, 418
nkdir **command**, 256
NOT searches, 110
Notepad, 257-258
notification area, 92-93
   auto hiding, 93
   battery meter, 572
   hiding individual icons, 93
   installing drivers, 562-563
   network connections, 327-328
NTFS compression, 147-148, 630-631
NTFS formatting, 621
NTFS permissions, 692-698
   changing, 692-694
   conflicts, 696-698
   defined, 692
   for groups, 695-696
   inheritance, 696-698
   on a domain, 727
   read, modify, write, etc., 694-695
   rules of, 696-698
number formats, 304

O

offline browsing, 797
Offline Files, 589-592
   Control Panel, 297
On-Screen keyboard
   Narrator, 271
online music stores
   in Media Center, 520-521
Open dialog box, 198
Open With command, 224-227
opening programs
   by voice, 204
optical character recognition (OCR), 556
OR searches, 110
Outlook Express *see* **Mail**

P

Page Up and Page Down keys, 13
Paint, 258-259
palmtops, 586
   Sync Center, 587-592
parallel printers, 534-536
Parental Controls, 3, 361-365, 674
   activity reports, 364
   Control Panel, 297
   games, 364
   time limits, 364
partitions
   Disk Management, 601-605

passwords
   account passwords, 672-673, 683
   editing in Local Users & Groups console, 686
   forcing password changes, 683
   Forgotten Password disk, 674-676
   editing in Local Users & Groups console, 686
   hints, 673, 689
   login, 689
   making Internet Explorer forget, 353
   on network sharing, 713
   on Public folder, 731
   on screen savers, 167
   no-password accounts, 673, 678, 780
   removing from accounts, 673
   required on wake up, 300
   Password Reset wizard, 675-676
   removing, 673
   resetting, 674
   secondary passwords, 673, 676
PatchGuard, 334
path names
   address bar, 63
PC cards, 562
PCI cards, 564
   power setting, 298-301
PCs
   backups, 641-648
   hardware, 559-570
   maintenance, 595-619
   properties, 131
   sleep mode, 30-32
   speeding up Windows, 609-613
   system properties, 311-313
   System Restore, 648-654
   Windows Easy Transfer, 783-786
   your computer's name, 312
   your processor details, 311
PDF format, 541
Pen and Input Devices
   Control Panel, 298
People Near Me, 298, 745
   signing in our out, 747
Performance Information and Tools, 298
peripherals, 559-570
permissions
   NTFS permissions, 692-698
   Public folder, 732-733
   share permissions, 692
   sharing folders, 735-737
Personal folder, 38-39, 128-130
   display as menu, 45
   indexed, 113
   restoring desktop icons, 22
Personalization
   Control Panel, 298

personalized menus

personalized menus, 47
Photo Gallery, 423–461
  adjusting exposure and color, 452
  auto adjust photos, 448
  auto-erase cards, 426
  captions, 441
  cropping photos, 449-450
  deleting photos, 438
  duplicating photos, 438
  editing photos, 446-455
  enlarging photos, 446
  file formats, 428-430
  importing photos, 424-430
  info panel, 439-441
  movies, 429
  navigation tree, 432-434
  ordering prints, 455-457
  organizing photos, 432-436
  photo screen saver, 460-461
  printing photos, 455-457
  ratings, 434, 442-446
  red eye, 451
  renaming photos, 440
  reverting to original, 454
  rotating photos, 452
  search, 444-446
  selecting photos, 436-438
  sending photos by email, 458-460
  slideshow movies, 460-461
  slideshows, 430-432
  slideshows on DVD, 460-461
  sorting, 435
  table of contents, 441
  tags, 442-446
  undo command, 447
  USB card readers, 428
  "watched" picture folders, 424-425
phishing, 346-349
  adjusting filter settings, 347-349
  defined, 346
  filter, 2
  reporting Web sites, 348
Phone and Modem Options
  Control Panel, 298
pictures *see* **photos; screenshots**
photos *see also* **Photo Gallery**
  account pictures, 673-674
  as desktop backgrounds, 163-165
  burning to CD or DVD, 460-461
  editing, 446-455
  editing in Media Center, 525-527
  in Internet Explorer, 385
  in Media Center, 523-527
  in Media Player, 482

  in Sidebar, 219
  Media Center, 501-529
  Photo Gallery, 423-461
  red eye, 451
  scanning, 427
  slideshows, 430-432
  tags and metadata, 69-71
Photoshop format, 429
Picture and Fax Viewer, 798
Picture Puzzle gadget, 218
Pictures, 38 *see also* **photos; Photo Gallery**
  folder, 129
Pinball, 797
ping **command**, 256
PKZip, 632
playlists, 473-474
  in Media Center, 521-522
  in Media Player, 473-474
  of photos and movies, 482
PNG format, 429
pointer trails, 297
pointers *see* **cursors**
POP accounts, 393
pop-up blocker, 353-356
  overriding, 355
Post-it Notes gadget, 217
Power Options, 298-301
power plans, 298-301
PowerToys, 797
Presentation Settings, 574
Preview pane, 65
Previous Versions, 134, 655
  Shadow Copy, 654-656
Print dialog box, 538-540
Print Screen key, 262
Printers
  adding to Start menu, 46
  Control Panel, 301
  finding on the domain, 725
Printers window, 537-538
printing, 533-551
  color management, 547
  fake printers, 537
  fonts, 550-551
  from Internet Explorer, 386-387
  from programs, 538-540
  from the desktop, 541-542
  installing printers, 533-538
  limiting hours of access, 547
  pausing or rearranging printouts, 542-543
  photos, 455-457
  printer icons, 537-538
  printing queue, 541-542
  separator pages, 548

sharing a printer, 544-545
to a file, 545-546
troubleshooting, 549-550
privacy
erasing tracks, 352-353
Problem Reports and Solutions, 193, 301-303,
659-661
changing settings, 661
problem history, 660
processor
power setting, 298-301
product key, 312
Profiles (user profiles), see **user profiles**
Program Access and Defaults, 226
Program files folder, 127, 135
programs *see also names of individual programs*
16-bit programs, 236-237
Accessories folder, 253-273
button groups, 94-97
closing, 190
DOS programs, 237
DVD Maker, 494-499
Ease of Access Center, 266-271
Fax and Scan, 553-557
freezing, 192-194
Games, 274-280
Internet Explorer, 367-390
included with Vista, 239-280
installing, 229-233
Mail, 391-420
Media Center, 501-529
Meeting Space, 745-749
Movie Maker, 483-494
Open and Save dialog boxes, 194-198
opening, 189-190
opening with Run command, 40-44
Photo Gallery, 423-461
printing, 533-551
Problem Reports and Solutions, 301-303
Program Access and Defaults, 226
run as Administrator, 238
searching, 106-129
Sidebar, 211-221
speech recognition, 202-211
taskbar, 92-104
uninstalling, 233-236
Windows Flip 3D, 90-91
Windows Journal, 582-583
Windows Media Player, 463-482
written for earlier Windows versions, 237-238
Windows Vista compatibility, 236-238
Programs and Features, 304
Programs Menu
Accessories folder, 253-273

projectors, 574
Presentation Settings, 574
Properties, 14-15, 69-71
computer, 20
icons, 131-135
Protected Mode, 2, 334
Public folder sharing, 730
permissions, 732-733
sharing, 730-733
Public vs. Private networks, 324, 359-360, 778
Purble Place, 278-279

Q

Quick Launch toolbar, 97, 101-102
Quicktabs (Internet Explorer), 374

R

radio, 479
RAM *see* **memory (RAM)**
ratings
filtering or stacking by, 79
music files, 65, 69-70
Photo Gallery, 434
photos, 442-446
RAW format, 429-430
ReadyBoost, 5, 610-612
requirements, 611
ReadyDrive, 613
Recent Folders list
Address bar, 61
Recent Items, 37
number to display, 48
turning off, 37
Recent Pages list
Address bar, 61
reconnect at logon, 742
Recycle Bin, 141-145
auto-emptying, 144
customizing, 143-144
emptying, 143
keyboard shortcuts, 141
restoring files and folders, 142
red-eye
fixing in Media Center, 525-527
fixing in Photo Gallery, 451
Refresh button, 370
Address bar, 61
refresh rate, 174
regedit, 788
slideshow themes, 430
Regional and Language Options, 304-307
Registry, 787-793
defined, 787
examples, 791-793

hives, keys, values, 788-791
regedit, 788
remote access, 751-767
  basics of, 751-752
  dialup connections, 753-758
  Remote Desktop, 753, 760-767
  three methods, 752
  Virtual Private Networking (VPN), 758-760
Remote Assistance, 178-184
Remote Desktop, 753, 760-767
  adjusting settings, 767
  disconnecting, 766
  keyboard shortcuts, 765
  making the connection, 763
  setting up the host, 761
renaming
  icons, 130
  photos, 440
  Start menu items, 52
resolution, 171
restart, 32
restore button, 59, 86
restore points
  dual booting, 656
restoring files *see* **backups**
restricted sites, 357
Reversi, 797
right-clicking, 11-12
  Properties, 14
ripping CDs, 471-472
  in Media Center, 517-518
routers, 700-702
  broadband, 706
RSS news feeds, 380-382
  defined, 380
  in Sidebar, 217
  recognizing, 381
  subscribing, 381
run as Administrator, 238
"Run as" mode, 236-238
Run command, 40-44, 797
  adding to Start menu, 46

S

S-video connectors, 508
Safe Mode, 656-658
Save dialog box, 194-198
  file formats, 197
Saved Games folder, 129
saved searches, 123-126
saving documents, 194-198
ScanDisk, 599-601
scanners
  documents, 557-558
  photos, 427

text for editing, 556
Scanners and Cameras, 307
screen savers, 165-167, 460-461
  password protecting, 167
screens *see* **monitors**
screenshots, 260-262
scroll bars, 13, 59
scrolling tricks, 13
Search (Instant Search), 37, 106-129
  adding to Start menu, 46
  address book, 111
  Boolean, 110
  by size, 123
  by authors, 123
  by date, 121-122
  by file type, 109-111, 120-121
  by location, 120-121
  by name, 122
  by tags, 123, 109-111
  Calendar events, 247
  canceling, 111
  communications, 48
  Control Panel, 284
  customizing, 115-119
  diacritical marks, 119
  disabling, 112
  encrypted files, 118
  excluding file types, 118
  Explorer windows, 119-126
  favorites, 48
  help system, 177
  history, 48
  how it works, 112-113
  Internet Explorer, 371
  in Media Center, 521
  include compressed files, 116
  include encrypted files, 118
  include non-indexed files, 123
  include subfolders option, 116
  index file, 112-113
  Indexing Options, 292
  limiting by criteria, 108
  moving the index file, 118
  natural language, 108
  network domains, 723-726
  partial matches, 116
  photos, 444-446
  programs, 48
  results menu, 110-112
  results window, 114
  saved searches, 123-126
  search Internet, 112
  Search pane, 120-123
  Search window, 123

special codes, 109-111
Start menu, 106-119
tags, 111-112
tooltips, 112
turning off result categories, 118
troubleshooting, 119
what to index, 116-119
where Vista looks, 113
Windows Contacts, 250-252
Search box
Start menu, 27-28
Search folders, 123-126
Search pane, 64, 120-123
Search window, 123
Searches folder, 129
security, 2-3, 333-365
address layout randomization (ASLR), 334
Address-Space Randomization, 3
application isolation, 334
BitLocker Drive Encryption, 637-640
blocking downloads, 363
blocking Web sites, 362
Code Integrity Checking, 334
common sense, 335
Content Advisor, 363
cookies, 349-352
Data Execution Prevention, 345
Defender, 2, 315, 340-346
domains, 720
Encrypting File System (EFS), 633-637
Firewall, 336-339
MAC address filtering, 361
Network Access Protection, 334
parental controls, 361-365
PatchGuard, 334
phishing filter, 2
pictures in messages, 402-403
pop-up blocker, 353-356
protected mode, 334
security zones, 357-359
service hardening, 2, 334
UAC, 2, 191
Virtual Private Network (VPN), 360
Windows Defender, 2, 315, 340-346
Windows Resource Protection, 653
Windows Update, 614-619
wireless security, 359-361
Security Center, 2, 335-336
antivirus software, 336
Control Panel, 307
selecting
email messages, 403
icons, 85, 136-138
photos, 436-438
text, 263

Send To, 140
serial printers, 534-536
SerialKeys, 798
Service Hardening, 2, 334
Shadow Copy, 654-656
dual booting, 656
sharing disks, 733, 736-737
sharing files and folders, 729-744
accessing shared files and folders, 739-743
advantages of, 729
file sharing with Macs, 738, 741
hiding folders, 738
mapping folders to drive letters, 743-744
nested folders, 738
Public folder method, 730-733
Share Any Folder Method, 734-737
sharing wizard, 85
sharing printers, 544-545
shield icon, 191
Shift-clicking, 14
shortcut icons, 145-147
creating and deleting, 146
keyboard shortcuts, 146
revealing original icon, 146
shortcut menus, 11-12
compressing files and folders, 147-151
Send To command, 140
shut down, 32, 34
Sidebar, 5, 211-221 *see also* **gadgets**
adding gadgets, 212
configuring gadgets, 213
defined, 211
floating on top, 213
hiding or quiting, 213
installing more gadgets, 221
keyboard shortcuts, 211
moving or closing gadgets, 211-212
opening a gadget twice, 213
removing gadgets, 221
searching gadgets, 213
SideShow, 590
Signatures (email), 399-401
Sleep mode, 30-32
power setting, 298-301
vs. hibernate, 32
Slideshow gadget, 219
slideshows, 430-432
burned to DVD, 499
in Media Center, 524-525
in Photo Gallery, 430-432
SnagIt, 262
snap to OK button, 169
Snipping Tool, 4, 260-262

software *see* **programs; documents; Windows Vista**
Software Explorer, 344-345
Solitaire, 279
sorting, 52
    All Programs menu, 48
    icons, 75-77
    Start menu, 50
Sound Recorder, 262-264
sounds
    changing system events, 23, 308
    configuring hardware, 308
    Control Panel, 307-310
    modem volume, 332
    Sound Recorder, 262-264
    sound schemes, 310
    speech recognition, 202-211
    text to speech, 209
    visual "beeps", 269
Spades, 798
spam, 411-414
    ways to avoid, 412
spanned volumes, 623, 625-627
speakers
    configuring, 308-309
    in Media Center, 508
    modem volume, 332
    volume, 93, 573
speech
    Narrator, 269-271
    text to speech, 209
Speech Recognition, 4, 202-211
    Control Panel, 310
    controlling by voice, 203
    correcting errors, 206-208
    mousegrid, 208
    show numbers, 205
    spaces after a period, 211
    tutorial, 202
speed tips, 162, 609-613
    ReadyBoost, 610-612
    SuperFetch, 610-612
    turning off Aero, 161, 613
    turning off eye candy, 612-613
    turning off visual effects, 162
Spider Solitaire, 280
SpyNet, 345-346
spyware
    Defender, 2, 315, 340-346
    defined, 341
spyware *see also* **security**
stacking, 5
stacking icons, 77
Standard accounts, 669-672

standard mode, 191
Start menu, 24-55
    Add Listing wizard, 51
    adding subfolders, 53-56
    all programs, 28-30
    anatomy of, 24-26
    alphabetizing, 51
    colored highlighting on new items, 47
    Computer window, 36
    Connect To, 35
    Control Panel, 35
    customizing Classic Start menu, 47
    customizing, 44-55
    Default Programs, 34-35
    display browser, 48
    display email program, 48
    documents, 39
    dragging icons onto, 49-50, 47
    games, 38
    Help and Support, 34
    hibernate, 32-34
    icon size, 48
    lock, 32
    Log Off, 32-34
    most frequently used items, 25
    music, 38
    Network, 35
    Personal folder, 38-39
    pictures, 38
    pinned items, 25
    recent items, 37
    removing items from, 52
    renaming items, 52
    reorganizing, 52-55
    restart, 32-34
    restoring Classic look, 26
    restoring traditional listings, 36
    run command, 40-44
    Search box, 27-28
    search, 37-38, 106-119
    shut down, 32-34
    sleep, 30-32
    sorting, 50
    source folders, 51
    startup folder, 29-30
startup
    folder, 29-30, 280
    hard drive check, 599-601
    menu, 656-658
    programs that open at startup, 29
    Safe Mode, 656-658
    Windows Memory Diagnostic Tool, 662
    Windows Recovery Environment, 660-662
Startup and Recovery, 312

Startup Hardware profiles, 798
Startup Repair, 660-662
Sticky Keys, 267
Stocks gadget, 218
Stop button, 371
striped volumes, 628-629
subscribing to RSS news feeds, 381
suffixes *see* filename extensions
SuperFetch, 5, 610
Switch User command, 33
Sync Center, 574, 587-592
    Control Panel, 310
    creating a partnership, 587-588
    offline files, 589-592
syncing with Media Player, 476-477
System, 311-313
system files
    hiding/showing, 84
System properties, 20
System Protection, 312
System Restore, 648-654
    from startup screen, 662
    limiting disk space, 649
    recovering a restore point, 651-653
    restore points, 649-651
    Shadow Copy, 654-656
    turning off, 653-654
System Tools folder, 271-273
system tray *see* notification area

T

tabbed browsing, 373-376
    Quicktabs (thumbnails), 374
    settings for, 375-376
Tablet PCs, 575-585
    correcting errors, 580-582
    flicks, 583-584
    gestures, 578-580
    handwriting recognition, 575-582
    Input panel gesture, 577
    Input Panel, 100, 575-582
    Mobile PC control panel, 575
    scratching out writing, 579
    screen rotation, 574
    Settings, 313
    Windows Journal, 582-583
tabs (word processing), 265
tags, 69-71
    editing, 69-70
    photos, 442-446
    search, 111-112
    searching by, 123
task manager, 192-194
Task Scheduler, 606-609
    adding a task, 607

editing tasks, 608
taskbar, 92-104
    button groups, 94-97
    can't drag anymore, 798
    customizing, 97-98
    defined, 92
    hiding, 98
    moving, 97-98
    multiple clocks, 288-289
    notifcation area, 92
    resizing, 98
    restoring classic look, 96
    thumbnails, 94
    toolbars, 98-102
Taskbar and Start menu, 313
Telnet, 798
text size
    adjusting, 161
    in Internet Explorer, 385
text to speech, 209
    Control Panel, 313
    Narrator, 269-271
themes, 170-171
thumbnails *see also* **Photo Gallery**
    on icons, 83
    Quicktabs (Internet Explorer), 374
    taskbar, 94
TIFF format, 428
Tip of the Day, 798
title bar, 58
    folder path in, 83
to do lists, 250
Toggle Keys, 267
toolbars
    address toolbar, 99
    building your own, 103-104
    desktop toolbar, 100
    explorer windows, 63
    language bar, 102, 307
    Language toolbar , 102
    links toolbar, 100
    Links toolbar, 378
    Quick Launch toolbar, 101-102
    redesigning, 103
    Tablet PC Input Panel, 100
    taskbar, 98-102
    windows media player toolbar, 99
tooltips
    file size info, 83
    hiding/showing, 85
    search, 112
touch screens *see* **Tablet PCs**
Trojans *see* security
troubleshooting
    Device Manager, 567-570

driver signing, 566-567
frozen programs, 192-194
Meeting Space, 748-749
networking, 711
newly installed gear, 564-565
printing, 549-550
Problem Reports and Solutions, 301-303, 659-661
recovering encrypted data, 636
registry, 787-793
Safe Mode, 656-658
Search command, 119
startup menu, 656-658
System Restore, 648-654
task manager, 192-194
testing the network, 714-715
uninstalling programs, 234-236
Windows Memory Diagnostic Tool, 662
Windows Recovery Environment, 660-662
Trusted Platform Module (TPM), 638-639
trusted sites, 357
Turn Windows Features On or Off, 232, 283
TV
Media Center, 501-529
pausing/rewinding, 512
recording in Media Center, 509-514
saving shows to DVD, 515-516
TweakUI, 798

U

UAC (User Account Control), 2, 191, 670-671
turning off, 191
UDF format, 151-152
Ultimate edition, 5-8, 274
uninstalling programs, 233-236
troubleshooting, 234-236
uninterruptible power supplies, 600
universal access *see* **Ease of Access Center**
Universal Naming Convention (UNC), 742
Upgrade Advisor *see* **Vista Upgrade Advisor**
upgrading to Vista, 775-778
clean install, 773
compatibility issues, 771
vs. clean install, 772-774
usability assistance *see* **Ease of Access Center**
USB, 560-562
1.0 vs. 2.0, 562
hubs, 560
card readers, 428
printers, 533
user accounts, *see* **accounts**
User Profiles, 312, 690-692
default user profile, 691-692
Public profile, 690-691
Users folder, 127

V

VGA connectors, 508, 562
VGA mode, 658
videos *see* **movies**
Videos folder, 129
Views menu, 73
virtual memory, 615
Virtual Private Networking (VPN), 360, 758-760
making the connection, 759-760
setting up the host, 759
viruses *see also* **security**
admin vs. standard accounts, 669
Windows Update, 614-619
Vista Upgrade Advisor, 559, 771
voices
text to speech, 209
volume (sound), 573
of DVD playback, 480-481
of laptop speaker, 573
of modem speaker, 332
of music in Media Center, 519
of soundtrack in Movie Maker, 492-493
of speakers (notification area), 93
volumes *see also* **disks; drive letters; hard drives**
basic disks, 622
defined, 622
extending, 625
sharing, 733, 736-737
spanned volumes, 623
spanning, 625-627
striping, 628-629

W

wallpaper, 163-165, 798
Web graphics, 165
WAV files
Sound Recorder, 262-264
Weather gadget, 219
Web *see* **Internet; Internet Explorer; security**
Web pages
opening with Run command, 44
parental controls, 361-365
Web Publishing wizard, 798
Web-based accounts, 393
Welcome Center, 19-21, 313, 780-781
Welcome (login) screen, 687-690
WEP encryption, 361
what's new in Vista, 2-8
WiFi (wireless networks), 320-321, 703-705
antennae on/off, 573
cellular wireless, 322
choosing a network, 320, 710
dialup connections, 321-325

MAC address filtering, 361
power setting, 298-301
setting up, 703-705
WEP encryption, 361
wireless security, 359-361
WPA encryption, 361
windows
Address bar, 60-63
Alt-tab, 89-90
button groups, 94-97
cascading and stacking, 96
closing, 59, 88
control menu, 59
edges, 58
elements of, 57-59
layering, 88-89
minimize and maximize, 59, 86
moving, 87-88
multiple document interface, 88
resizing and moving, 58, 86-89
restoring, 86
scroll bars, 59
taskbar, 92-104
title bar, 58
Windows Flip 3D, 90-91
Windows Aero *see* **Aero**
Windows Anytime Upgrade *see* **Anytime Upgrade**
Windows basics, 11-16
selecting text, 263
Windows Calendar, 4, 240-250
day/week/month views, 241
deleting events, 247
editing events, 245-247
event categories, 247-248
making appointments, 242-245
publishing to the Web, 248-250
recurring events, 244
reminders, 245
to do lists, 250
Windows CardSpace, 313-315
Windows Contacts *see* **Contacts**
Windows Defender *see* **Defender**
Windows DVD Maker *see* **DVD Maker**
Windows Easy Transfer, 20, 783-786
windows Experience Index, 20, 311
Windows Explorer *see* **Explorer windows**
Windows Fax and Scan *see* **Fax and Scan**
Windows Firewall, *see* **Firewall**
Windows Flip, 89-90
Windows Flip 3D, 90-91
Windows folder, 127
Windows Journal, 582-583
Windows Live Messenger, 252

Windows Mail *see* **Mail**
Windows Marketplace, 273
Windows Media Center *see* **Media Center**
Windows Media Player 11, 4, 463-482
bit rates, 472
burning your own CDs, 475-476
Classic menus, 465
columns, 74
deleting songs or playlists, 474
DVD movies, 479-481
filling in track names, 470
graphic equalizer, 470-471
Internet radio, 479
online music stores, 477-479
pictures and videos, 482
playing music CDs, 466-471
playlists, 473-474
portable music players, 476-477
restoring Classic menu bar, 465
ripping CDs, 471-472
shares library with Media Center, 509
sharing music on the network, 469
skins, 467-468
toolbar, 99-100
tour of, 464-466
visualizations, 466
Windows Meeting Space *see* **Meeting Space**
Windows Memory Diagnostic Tool, 662
Windows Messenger, 798
Windows Mobile devices, 586
Windows Mobility Center, 315, 572-574
Windows Movie Maker *see* **Movie Maker**
Windows Photo Gallery *see* **Photo Gallery**
Windows ReadyDrive, 613
Windows Recovery Environment, 660-662
Windows Resource Protection, 653
Windows Sidebar *see* **Sidebar**
Windows Sidebar Properties, 315
Windows SideShow, 316
Windows Ultimate Extras, 273
Windows Update, 316, 614-619
changing settings, 616-619
removing and hiding updates, 618
Windows Vista
32-bit vs. 64-bit, 7
Accessories folder, 253-273
accounts, 665-698
activation, 781-783
adding/removing features, 232, 283
Anytime Upgrade, 273-274
backups, 641-648
basics of, 11-16
BitLocker Drive Encryption, 637-640
burning CDs and DVDs, 151-156

color schemes, 160-163
compatibility issues, 771
Complete PC Backup, 647-648
Control Panel, 281-316
cosmetic overhaul, 3
customizing appearance, 157-174
Defender, 2, 315, 340-346
differences in version, 5-8
DVD Maker, 494-499
Ease of Access Center, 266-271
Explorer windows, 60-87
faxing, 551-557
features, moved or removed, 795-798
Folder Options, 82-86
Games, 274-280
getting help, 175-186
getting online, 319-332
hard drives, 621-640
hardware requirements, 769-770
hardware, 559-570
history, -16
icons, 130-151
included programs, 239-280
installing components of, 232-233
installing, 769-786
Internet Explorer, 367-390
laptop features, 571-575
Mail, 391-420
maintenance, 595-619
major folders of, 126-129
master keyboard shortcut list, 799-802
Media Center, 501-529
Meeting Space, 745-749
Movie Maker, 483-494
Network and Sharing Center, 708-715
Photo Gallery, 423-461
printing, 533-551
Problem Reports and Solutions, 659-661
product key, 312
Programs and Features, 304
registry, 787-793
remote access, 751-767
Remote Assistance, 178-184
RSS news feeds, 380-382
Safe Mode, 656-658
screen savers, 165-167
search, 106-129
Security Center, 335-336
Security, 2-3
security, 333-365
setting up a network, 699-715
sharing files and folders, 729-744
Sidebar, 211-221
similarity to Mac OS X, 5
speech recognition, 202-211

speed tweaks, 162, 609-613
Start menu, 24-55
Sync Center, 587-592
System Restore, 648-654
Tablet PCs, 575-585
Task Scheduler, 606-609
taskbar thumbnails, 94
taskbar, 92-104
UAC (User Access Control), 191
Upgrade Advisor, 559, 771
versions of, 773
wallpaper, 163-165
what version you have, 311
what's new, 2-8
Windows Easy Transfer, 783-786
Windows Flip 3D, 90-91
windows in, 57-59
Windows Media Player, 463-482
Windows Recovery Environment, 660-662
Windows Update, 614-619
Windows Vista Upgrade Advisor, 559, 771
wireless networks *see* **WiFi**
wireless security, 359-361
wizards, 13
WMA CDs, 476
WMA files
    Sound Recorder, 262-264
word processing
    cut and paste, 199-200
    drag and drop, 200-201
    lost formatting, 201
    selecting text, 263
    speech recognition, 202-211
    WordPad, 264-266
WordPad, 264-266, 795
    selecting text, 263
workgroups
    defined, 667, 699
    kinds of networks, 700-706
    Local Users and Groups console, 681-688
    Meeting Space, 745-749
    Network and Sharing Center, 708-715
    setting up a network, 699-715
    sharing files and folders, 729-744
    testing the network, 714-715
    WiFi, 703-705
WPA encryption, 361
WPD format, 429

X

XBM images, 798
XBox 360, 502
XMP data, 439-441
XPS format, 541

Y

Yahoo accounts, 798

Z

.zip files, 149-151, 631-633
    Send To command, 140
Zune, 463

Colophon

Due to an annoying and permanent wrist ailment, the author wrote this book by voice, using Dragon Naturally Speaking on an assortment of old and new PCs. The book was created in Microsoft Word XP, whose revision-tracking feature made life far easier as drafts were circulated from author to technical and copy editors. SnagIt (*www.techsmith.com*) was used to capture illustrations; Adobe Photoshop CS2 and Macromedia Freehand MX were called in as required for touching them up.

The book was designed and laid out in Adobe InDesign CS2 on a PowerBook G4, and Power Mac G5. The fonts used include Formata (as the sans-serif family) and Minion (as the serif body face). To provide the ⊞ and ⏻ symbols, custom fonts were created using Macromedia Fontographer.

The book was generated as an Adobe Acrobat PDF file for proofreading and indexing, and final transmission to the printing plant.

Better than e-books

Buy *Windows Vista: The Missing Manual* and access
the digital edition FREE on Safari for 45 days.

Go to www.oreilly.com/go/safarienabled
and type in coupon code MWLASBI

Search
thousands of
top tech books

Download
whole chapters

Cut and Paste
code examples

Find
answers fast

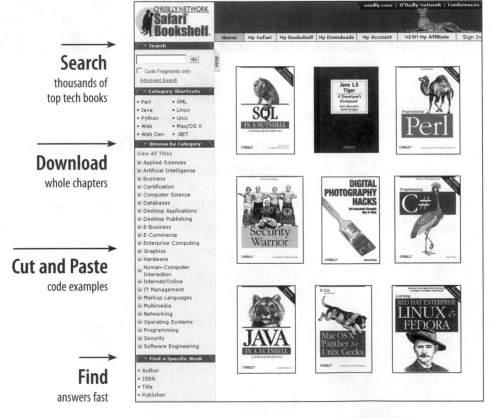

Search Safari! The premier electronic reference
library for programmers and IT professionals.